Nutrition Almanac

Nutrition Almanac

SIXTH EDITION

JOHN D. KIRSCHMANN

AND

NUTRITION SEARCH, INC.

New York   Chicago   San Francisco   Lisbon   London   Madrid   Mexico City
Milan   New Delhi   San Juan   Seoul   Singapore   Sydney   Toronto

Library of Congress Cataloging-in-Publication Data

    Nutrition almanac.—6th ed. / John Kirschmann and Nutrition Search, Inc.
       p.   cm.
      Includes bibliographical references and index.
    ISBN 0-07-143658-8
    1. Nutrition.   2. Health.   3. Food—Composition—Tables.   I. Kirschmann,
John D.   II. Nutrition Search, Inc.

  RA784.N837   2007
  613.2—dc22   2006031909

 2 3 4 5 6 7 8 9 10 11 12 13 14 15 WCK/WCK 0 9 8 7

ISBN-13: 978-0-07-143658-8
ISBN-10:   0-07-143658-8

McGraw-Hill books are available at special quantity discounts to use as premiums and sales promotions, or for use in corporate training programs. For more information, please write to the Director of Special Sales, Professional Publishing, McGraw-Hill, Two Penn Plaza, New York, NY 10121-2298. Or contact your local bookstore.

The publisher acknowledges the invaluable contributions of Molly Siple, M.S., R.D., nutrition editor at *Natural Health* and author of several acclaimed cookbooks, including *Low-Cholesterol Cookbook for Dummies* (John Wiley & Sons, 2004), *Healing Foods for Dummies* (IDG, 1999), and *Recipes for Change: Nutrition/Cookbook on Foods for Menopause* (Dutton, 1996).

The material in this book is not intended to serve as a replacement for professional medical advice. Any attempt to diagnose and treat your specific situation should come under the direction of a physician who is familiar with nutritional therapy. It is possible that some individuals may suffer allergic reactions from the use of various dietary supplement preparations or the medium in which they are contained; if such reactions occur, consult your physician. Nutrition Search, Inc., and the publisher specifically disclaim any and all liability arising directly or indirectly from the use or application of any information contained in this book.

This book is printed on acid-free paper.

Contents

SECTION 5

Food Lists

SECTION 6

Tables of Food Measurements and Composition

Preface

John D. Kirschmann began his mission in his early fifties. It was then that he started to have discomforting health issues that made him pause from his busy life to think of why these things were happening to him and at such an early age.

So began his commitment to a research project that would ultimately lead to the first health book that addressed "nutrition in practice."

In 1971 in Minneapolis, Minnesota, John D. put together a staff of a dozen professionals from the medical and health fields. After two years of research and study and compiling a library of thousands of books in related fields, *Nutrition Almanac* was independently printed and published. The *Almanac* was defined by the health food stores as the "bible of nutrition."

John D. knew the book needed to be published by a company with international appeal and it must be available in other languages so it could reach as many people as possible. He wanted everyone to benefit from his labor of love. So began the partnership with Nutrition Search, Inc., and McGraw-Hill. After all these years the partnership remains strong with close to 4 million copies in print, and now the 6th edition in your hands.

John D. remained active as director of the *Nutrition Almanac* for more than twenty-eight years until his death in 1999. John's daughters, LaVon and Gayla, have been instrumental in the research and publication as authors. The family looks forward to continuing their work on future *Nutrition Almanac* editions.

We end with a foreword written for the 4th edition by Gayla. It still about says it all . . .

Nature is a true miracle and there are few people who can grasp and report effectively on its wonder. I believe that my father is one such person. The way that natural nutrition happens in life is what laid the ground work for the objective and simple approach that he used to put together the very first Nutrition Almanac *more than twenty [thirty] years ago. Over these many years, he has continued to help those who wish to help themselves research their own state of well-being. . . .*

Across time, across countries, and across many different cultures, the Almanac *has prevailed as one of the leading alternative health publications of this century. As the field of nutrition blossoms even further, we hope to report the most up-to-date information to you in a manner that is in the true spirit of the creation we call the* Nutrition Almanac.

Weston and Jiselle Kirschmann
Nutrition Search, Inc.
Board of Directors

Nutrition Almanac

Nutrition and Health

that happens along the entire gastrointestinal tract. When the food passes into the stomach's entrance, a bank of muscle called the cardiac sphincter contracts and closes so that the bolus cannot slip back.

Active chemical digestion begins in the middle portion of the stomach where food is mixed with gastric juices containing hydrochloric acid (HCl), water, and more enzymes that break up protein and other substances. It is here that the stomach acid kills bacteria that can enter the body along with food; the cells of the stomach wall protect themselves from this same acid by secreting a mucus (a white polysaccharide) that coats the stomach's lining. Also, salivary amylase will not function in this acidic environment and it is at this time that the digestion of starches gradually diminishes. The amino acids in the amylase are then absorbed into other body proteins.

The major digestive accomplishment of the stomach is initiating the breakdown of proteins. This is achieved by the enzyme pepsin and the stomach acid itself, both of which act as catalysts. Lesser actions are the digestion of some fat and, to a small extent, sucrose by stomach acid as well as the secretion of intrinsic factor, necessary for the absorption of vitamin B_{12}. Intrinsic factor is a glycoprotein made in the stomach.

After one to four hours, depending on the combination of foods eaten, peristalsis pushes the bolus, which is now in the liquid form of chyme, out of the stomach by means of the pyloric sphincter and into the small intestine. By this time the digestion of all three of the energy-yielding nutrients has begun. They leave the stomach in the following order: carbohydrates, proteins, and fats, which take the longest to break down.

When chyme enters the small intestine, the pancreas secretes its digestive juices. Bile, produced by the liver and stored in the gallbladder, is secreted if fats are present. This digestive aid is an emulsifier, not an enzyme, that separates the fat into small droplets so pancreatic enzymes can break it down for absorption. The pancreatic juice that enters through the common bile duct contains enzymes that continue the breakdown of proteins and carbohydrates; it also contains the substance sodium bicarbonate, which neutralizes the acidic chyme.

After the absorption of the available nutrients, the remaining undigested products enter the large intestine by means of the ileocecal valve, another sphincter. No digestive enzymes are secreted here, but the bacteria present in the large intestine produce vitamin K, which is also absorbed in this section of the gut.

Other bacteria in the large intestine guard against certain diseases.

The leftover residue that enters the large intestine includes some fibers that are not absorbed but continue through the colon, providing a semisolid mass that helps stimulate the muscles of the gastrointestinal tract to perform peristalsis efficiently. This fiber incorporates bile acids, sterols (including cholesterol), and fat, and it also holds water, keeping the stool soft. The strong muscles of the rectum hold back this semisolid waste until it is time to defecate. The muscles then relax and the last sphincter, the anus, allows the waste to pass.

Some of the Many Components of the Digestive Process and Their Functions

The ending *-ase* indicates an enzyme; the root of the word tells what it digests.

- **Amylase**   An enzyme that breaks down amylose, a form of starch
- **Bicarbonate**   Occurs widely in all cell fluids; secreted by the pancreas and passed into the intestine through the common bile duct
- **Bile**   An exocrine secretion of the liver stored in the gallbladder made from cholesterol that emulsifies fats
- **Carbohydrase**   An enzyme that breaks down carbohydrates
- **Gastric glands**   Exocrine glands in the stomach wall that secrete gastric juice into the stomach
- **Gastric juice**   Rennin (curdles milk protein, which readies it for pepsin action), pepsin (for protein), and lipase (for emulsified fats) secreted by the gastric glands out of the stomach wall
- **Intestinal juice**   Secretion of the intestinal glands; contains the enzyme for the digestion of carbohydrate and protein and a minor enzyme for fat digestion
- **Lipase**   An enzyme that breaks down lipids (fats)
- **Mucus**   A relative of carbohydrate that is secreted outward by the cells in the stomach wall (mucous membrane)
- **Pancreatic juice**   Contains enzymes for the digestion of carbohydrate, fat, and protein, which is secreted into the small intestine (The production of insulin, a hormone that facilitates the uptake and use of blood sugar and other hormones, is also a function of the pancreas.)
- **Pepsin**   A protein-digesting enzyme that secretes out of the stomach wall
- **Protease**   An enzyme that breaks down protein

Absorption

Absorption is the process by which nutrients are taken up by the intestines and passed into the bloodstream to facilitate cell metabolism. Within three to four hours after a meal has been eaten, the body must find a way to absorb millions of nutrient molecules including amino acids (proteins), monosaccharides (carbohydrates), fatty acids, glycerol and monoglycerides (fats), vitamins, and minerals.

Absorption takes place primarily in the small intestine, which has a surface area comparable to a quarter of a football field and a length of twenty feet. The surface is wrinkled into hundreds of folds that are covered with small fingerlike projections called villi. A single villus magnified is composed of several hundred cells, each covered with microscopic hairs called microvilli. These villi are in constant motion. Any nutrient molecules small enough to be absorbed are trapped in the microvilli and are drawn into the cells underneath and absorbed. Some partially digested nutrients from the stomach are also caught in the microvilli, digested further by enzymes, and absorbed into the cells.

The cells of the three portions of the small intestine (duodenum, jejunum, and ileum) are specialized to absorb different nutrients. Nutrients that are readily available (broken down or water soluble) are absorbed near the top of the tract while those that take longer to be digested are absorbed farther down. The duodenum is specialized to absorb calcium, vitamin A, and the B vitamins thiamin and riboflavin. Fats are mostly absorbed by the jejunum, and vitamin B_{12} is absorbed by the ileum. The process of chelation combines minerals and amino acids for increased absorption.

Once a molecule has entered a cell in a villus, it may enter either the vascular or the lymphatic system of transport. The water-soluble nutrients (including the smaller products of fat digestion) move into the vascular system from the cells under the villi by way of capillaries. Blood, pumped in a figure-eight pattern throughout the body, directly picks up the nutrients through a portal vein that goes straight to the liver. Blood leaving the liver transports some of these nutrients to the heart by way of the hepatic vein while other nutrients are stored or used within the liver. The heart then pumps the nutrients in the blood to wherever the body needs them. The liver is strategically located within this system of circulation so that it will have the first chance to screen all products absorbed from the intestinal tract and guard against any harmful agents that may try to invade the body.

Unlike those entering the vascular system, the larger fats and fat-soluble vitamins that are transported by the lymphatic system do not go to the liver first; they go to the heart. For these nutrients, direct access into the blood is impossible because they are both too big and insoluble in water, which is the main component of blood. Their eventual entrance into the bloodstream is by a one-way route through the liquid spaces between the cells; the nutrients move from one section to another as muscles contract and push them into a large duct (thoracic) behind the heart. This duct ends in a vein (subclavian) that can accept the nutrients and moves them into the bloodstream and the heart for distribution. The body's cells remove the parts they can use. The final stop is the liver, where whatever is left is reassembled to again enter the bloodstream. (See Section 2 for more information on fats.)

In the liver, many different enzymes help change the nutrient molecules into new substances for specific purposes. Unlike digestion, which prepares nutrients for absorption and transport, the reactions in the liver produce the end products needed by individual cells to give us healthy bodies.

Delivery of Nutrients into the Blood

Food broken down into its component parts during digestion is absorbed via the bloodstream. Water-soluble vitamins also take this route. Fat-soluble nutrients enter via the lymphatic system. The following shows the pathways of specific nutrients.

Vascular System

- **Carbohydrates** Monosaccharides
- **Lipids** Glycerol, short-chained fatty acids, medium-chained fatty acids
- **Proteins** Amino acids
- **Water-soluble nutrients** Vitamin C, B-complex vitamins, non-B nutrients

Lymphatic System

- **Fat-soluble nutrients (in lipids)** Monoglycerides, triglycerides, cholesterol, phospholipids
- **Fat-soluble vitamins** Vitamin A, vitamin D, vitamin E, vitamin K

The Unique Process of Digestion and Absorption for the Six Basic Nutrients and Fiber

The basic nutrients—carbohydrates, fats, proteins, vitamins, minerals, and water—are each digested in a specific way depending on what is required for absorption and elimination of the substance.

Fiber, Dietary

Dietary fiber is that which remains after food is digested and is not a nutrient.

- **Mouth**   Teeth crush fiber to mix with saliva, readying it for swallowing.
- **Stomach**   Fiber adds bulk to food.
- **Small intestine**   Fiber binds minerals such as bile salts used by the body to prepare fat for absorption.
- **Large intestine**   Most fiber passes untouched through the digestive tract and goes to the large intestine, where bacterial enzymes digest hemicellulose into glucose, which is absorbed. However, energy contribution is very small. Dietary fibers exercise intestinal muscles so they retain their health and tone. Cholesterol and some minerals are bound and excreted with fiber.

Carbohydrates

Starch and sugar are carbohydrates.

- **Mouth**   Salivary gland excretes the enzyme salivary amylase, beginning the digestion of starch to polysaccharides and maltose.
- **Stomach**   Acid and enzymes start to digest salivary enzymes, stopping the digestion of starch. Maltose and sucrose are partially broken down by the stomach acid.
- **Small intestine**   Carbohydrase is released by the pancreas, which breaks polysaccharides into maltose. Enzymes on the surface cells of the small intestine break down the polysaccharides into disaccharides and then to monosaccharides, which are absorbed through the cells and into the bloodstream.
- **Large intestine**   No absorption of carbohydrates takes place.

Fats

Fats include triglycerides (fats and oils), phospholipids (lecithins), and sterols (cholesterol, vitamin D, and the sex hormones).

- **Mouth**   Lingual lipase is secreted, and fats melt as they reach body temperature.
- **Stomach**   Triglycerides are split into diglycerides. Breakdown is minimal for all fats except milk fats. Acids are mixed with fats and water. Gastric lipase finds and hydrolyzes a small amount of fat.
- **Small intestine**   Bile from the liver flows through the common bile duct to emulsify the fat.

Pancreatic lipase breaks down the emulsified fat into monoglycerides, glycerol, and fatty acids for absorption.

- **Large intestine**   Some fat and cholesterol remain in the feces.

Proteins

Proteins are amino acids linked into chains.

- **Mouth**   Protein foods are chewed and made ready to swallow.
- **Stomach**   Acid undoes protein strands, and enzymes are activated. Proteins become smaller polypeptides.
- **Small intestine**   Polypeptides are split by pancreatic and small intestine (protease) enzymes. More enzymes on the surface of the intestinal cells hydrolyze the peptide and then absorb the amino acids.
- **Large intestine**   No absorption of protein takes place.

Vitamins

Vitamins are organic, essential nutrients that are required in minute amounts and yield no energy.

- **Mouth**   No action takes place on vitamins in the mouth or esophagus.
- **Stomach**   Intrinsic factor (a necessary compound for absorption) attaches to vitamin B_{12}.
- **Small intestine**   Fat-soluble vitamins are emulsified by bile and are absorbed with other fats as well as the water-soluble vitamins.
- **Large intestine**   Vitamin K, produced by bacteria, is absorbed.

Minerals and Water

Minerals are small inorganic molecules that yield no energy, and water is inorganic and yields no energy.

- **Mouth**   Water is secreted with saliva to integrate and bind food.
- **Stomach**   Acid (HCl) reduces iron for absorption. The stomach secretes watery fluid to turn moist, chewed food into watery chyme.
- **Small intestine**   The pancreas, liver, and small intestine add enough fluid that the total secreted into the intestine in a day is approximately 2 gallons. Minerals are absorbed. Calcium is provided with vitamin D to be properly absorbed.
- **Large intestine**   The remainder of the minerals and more water are absorbed.

Metabolism

Once absorbed, the handling of food within the body has reached its final stage. The process of metabolism involves all the chemical changes that nutrients undergo from the time they are absorbed until they become a part of the body or are excreted. Metabolism is the conversion of the digested nutrients into components for energy or for building material for living tissue.

The basic units of metabolism are
- **Glucose**   From carbohydrates
- **Glycerol**   From fats
- **Fatty acids**   From fats
- **Amino acids**   From proteins

Metabolism happens in two general phases that occur simultaneously, anabolism and catabolism. Anabolism (uses energy) involves all the chemical reactions that the nutrients undergo in constructing body chemicals and tissues such as the skin, cartilage, muscles, and nerves. Catabolism (usually releases energy) involves the reactions in which various compounds are used to do the body's work, to produce heat, or to be stored for later use.

Energy from carbohydrates, fats, and proteins for the body's cells comes from their conversion to glucose, which combines with oxygen in a series of chemical reactions that form carbon dioxide, water, and cellular energy. The energy is used for body functions, and the carbon dioxide and water are waste products carried out of the body by the bloodstream.

Carbohydrate is the ideal source of glucose because it is composed mostly of that substance. The starches and sugars are readily convertible to glucose. Complex carbohydrates are more slowly processed, making them valuable for maintaining constant energy levels. (See Section 2 for more information on carbohydrates.)

When the body metabolizes fats, the glycerol component donates only 5 percent of its structure to glucose. Fat lends itself more readily to storage than energy. Since the brain and the nervous system both thrive on glucose for their nutrition, fat becomes an inefficient source. And when there is too much fat for the liver to handle, the remainder is stored throughout the body in the kind of fat that we often try to lose by dieting. Fats play a vital role in the functioning of a healthy body and sufficient amounts are essential; however, too much fat can put one at risk for many degenerative diseases. (See Section 2 for more information on fats.)

When the body needs to grow or needs to be regenerated, it turns to the metabolism of protein to provide the material. Protein is a fairly good source of glucose when carbohydrate is not available, but providing for the body's energy needs should be secondary to its major building function. Sufficient carbohydrates need to be taken along with protein to achieve a maximum operating level. (See Section 2 for more information on proteins.)

The process of metabolism requires that extensive systems of enzymes be maintained to facilitate the thousands of different chemical reactions that must be performed, and also to regulate the rate at which these reactions proceed. The presence of protein, vitamins, and minerals is essential for these enzymes to perform their functions at their very best.

Factors Inhibiting Digestion/Absorption

The gastrointestinal tract is sensitive and responsive to conditions within the environment. The movements of the stomach are interfered with by nervousness and anxiety. Eating while agitated, fatigued, or worried may give rise to gastrointestinal disturbances. In a person under stress, digestive secretions are reduced and the blood is routed to the muscles more than to the digestive tract. This action impairs efficient absorption of nutrients. To digest and absorb food best, one should be relaxed and tranquil at mealtimes. Hurried meals under tense conditions are not beneficial to normal digestion. Weather variations and physical disorders also may inhibit normal digestion.

foods can also be helpful for weight loss since they tend to contain fewer calories and because they slowly release sugar into the blood, abating hunger for longer periods of time. Individuals lacking sustained energy throughout the day can also benefit by the gradual and sustained release of energy produced from low glycemic index foods.

The glycemic index of a food is calculated from an approximate average of a group of individuals tested and often from an average of tests that have been conducted in a number of different countries. Most studies use pure glucose and its glycemic index of 100 as the reference item. All foods are measured in equivalent amounts of 50 grams of carbohydrate. This should be kept in mind when reading glycemic index values because 50 grams of carbohydrate is far above the normal amount eaten at one time. Researchers have come up with a way to address this discrepancy—the glycemic load, a reference number, referring to a particular food, indicating the effect a typical serving size has on blood sugar. For example, while 50 grams of raw carrots has a relatively high glycemic index of 47, 1 medium raw carrot, which amounts to only 11 grams, has a glycemic load of 3.

Table 2.1 gives the glycemic index and the glycemic load of various common foods based on research conducted at the University of Sydney in Australia. In several cases, the glycemic load may actually be significantly higher because the serving size indicated is smaller than the amount typically consumed. For instance, this is true of the entries for white bread. While 1 ounce has a glycemic load of 10, 2 ounces has a glycemic load of 20. Following a low-carbohydrate diet for weight loss, a recommended maximum glycemic load per day is about 50.

Low Glycemic Index:	Low Glycemic Load:
below 55	10 or less
Intermediate Glycemic Index: 56–69	**Intermediate Glycemic Load:** 11–19
High Glycemic Index: 70 or more	**High Glycemic Load:** 20 or more

Fiber

Natural carbohydrate foods are the only source of nonnutritive fiber, which is a polysaccharide and therefore part of the carbohydrate family. The walls of plant foods are made up of fibers found in the skins of fruits and vegetables and are largely indigestible by humans. They contribute very little energy to the diet; however, on a high-fiber diet as much as 15 percent of one's energy allowance can be achieved.

Caution should be used because nutrient deficiencies can be created if too much fiber is consumed. Excess fiber causes vitamins and minerals to be bound and excreted before the body can use them.

Dietary fibers are characterized by their chemical structure, their digestibility by bacterial enzymes, and their solubility in water. Human enzymes cannot break down fibers, except for hemicellulose, which is digested by bacteria in the large intestine.

The major impact of dietary fiber is on the colon, the last part of the gastrointestinal tract where cancer and diverticular disease can arise. Dietary fiber exercises the intestinal muscles so they retain their health and tone and helps this area of the digestive tract move smoothly and thus maintain regular elimination. Wheat bran seems to be one of the most effective stool-softening fibers, provided the larger particles are consumed. Fibrous foods help satisfy the appetite and increase the bulk of food along the intestine. Soluble fibers such as pectin and guar, which form gels in water, prolong the time of transit of materials through the intestine, while insoluble fibers such as cellulose tend to reduce transit time.

Fiber may play a role in the management of medical problems such as excess weight and obesity, constipation and diarrhea, hemorrhoids, appendicitis, diverticulosis, colon cancer, elevated blood lipids and cardiovascular disease, and diabetes.

Consuming purified fiber such as cellulose may not give the same benefits as consuming the same substance from a food source such as whole grains. Wheat bran, which is mostly cellulose, does not lower cholesterol, whereas soluble fiber in oat bran and in apples, which contain pectin, does.

Fats

Fats—or lipids, the chemical name—are the most concentrated source of energy in the diet. There are three classes of lipids: triglycerides, phospholipids, and sterols. When oxidized, fats furnish more than twice the number of calories per gram than carbohydrates or proteins. One gram of fat yields approximately 9 calories to the body. Fats provide about 60 percent of the body's energy requirement during rest. Fats perform vital functions in the body, but consuming too much fat can be a problem. The diet must be designed to include optimal amounts but avoid any excess that may lead to future health problems.

Over the course of time, nature has ensured that a constant reserve of energy is made available for our needs. One of these provisions is the glucose that is

Table 2.1
Glycemic Index and Glycemic Load of Common Foods

Foods	Glycemic Index	Serving Size	Glycemic Load	Foods	Glycemic Index	Serving Size	Glycemic Load
Breads				Potato, baked	85	5 ounces	26
White bread	70	1 ounce	10	Yam, peeled, cooked	37	5 ounces	13
Whole wheat bread	77	1 ounce	9	Pumpkin	75	3 ounces	3
Bagel, white	72	½ bagel	25	**Fruit**			
Bran muffin, small	60	3.5 ounces	25	Apple, fresh, medium	38	4 ounces	6
Blueberry muffin, small	59	3.5 ounces	28	Apricots, canned in			
Breton wheat crackers	67	6 crackers	10	light syrup	64	4 halves	12
Grains				Apricots, dried	30	17 halves	8
Rice, parboiled	72	1 cup	26	Apricots, fresh	57	3 medium	5
White rice, instant,				Banana, fresh, medium	52	4 ounces	12
cooked 6 minutes	87	1 cup	36	Orange, fresh, medium	42	4 ounces	5
Jasmine rice, white,				Orange juice, unsweet-			
cooked	109	1 cup	46	ened, reconstituted	53	8 ounces	9
Brown rice, cooked	50	1 cup	16	Avocado	0	¼	0
Oatmeal, cooked				**Protein Foods**			
1 minute	66	1 cup	17	Beef	0	4 ounces	0
Fettuccine, egg, cooked	32	1½ cups	15	Pork	0	4 ounces	0
Spaghetti, white,				Lamb	0	4 ounces	0
cooked 5 minutes	38	1½ cups	18	Eggs, large	0	2	0
Spaghetti, durum wheat				Fish	0	4 ounces	0
cooked 20 minutes	64	1½ cups	27	Fish sticks	38	3.5 ounces	7
Legumes				**Nuts**			
Green peas	48	⅓ cup	3	Almonds	0	1.75 ounces	0
Kidney beans, cooked	23	⅔ cup	9	Peanuts	14	1.75 ounces	1
Lentils, brown, cooked	29	¾ cup	5	Walnuts	0	1.75 ounces	0
Vegetables				**Beverages**			
Carrots, peeled, cooked	49	½ cup	2	Whole milk	27	250 mL	3
Carrot juice, fresh	43	8 ounces	10	Soy milk, reduced fat	44	250 g	8
Celery, raw	0	2 stalks	0	Red wine	0	3.5 ounces	0
Broccoli, raw	0	1 cup	0	Gin	0	1 ounce	0
Beets, canned	64	½ cup	5				

stored in the liver and muscles in a form called glycogen. When needed, enzymes will break down the glycogen to glucose, which is then ready to work for the body. Liver stores of glycogen can support the body's activities for only about four hours. Another provision is fat that is stored under the layers of the skin and throughout the body, metabolized to produce energy when the liver's stores are depleted. Unlike the fat in the liver, the dispersed body fat is able to accumulate in unlimited amounts, serving as a source of energy to all the body's cells for as long as the reserve allows.

Triglycerides, one class of fats, consist of a backbone of glycerol (an alcohol) and three carbon chains. The carbon chains are called fatty acids and because they vary in structure, fatty acids give fats their different flavors, textures, and melting points. Fats are easy to identify in foods. They are the skin on poultry and the creamy-white marbling in red meat, the cheese on bodies become swollen with edema and a fatty liver. Kwashiorkor is not particular to any society or culture; it is worldwide.

Marasmus is basically starvation because not only is protein not available, there is little or no food at all. Marasmus victims (six to eighteen months) look weathered far beyond their age and are most likely sick and very thin. These children have no fat accumulations in the body to protect against cold. Marasmus is found across the world in overpopulated poor areas and in rural populations where infant formulas are not adequate.

Stunted growth, which often goes unnoticed, may be the most common indication of protein malnutrition among children in developed countries. Loss of hair and hair pigment, swelling of the joints, and weakening of muscles, including the heart muscle, are symptoms.

In adults, protein deficiency may result in lack of vigor and stamina, mental depression, weakness, and poor resistance to infection. Antibodies may not function as well as they could—a condition that impairs the healing of wounds and recovery from disease. The RDA for protein, published by the Food and Nutrition Board of the Institute of Medicine, National Academy of Sciences, is the dietary intake level considered sufficient to meet the nutrient requirements of nearly all individuals in a group. According to these RDAs, in adults, the minimum daily protein requirement—the smallest amino acid intake that can maintain optimum growth and good health—is 0.8 grams of high-quality protein per kilogram of ideal body weight. The minimum daily requirement for pregnant and lactating women is 1.1 grams per kilogram, using prepregnancy weight. In infants, the minimum daily requirement is 1.5 grams per kilogram. Ideal body weight is used to estimate protein needs rather than actual weight because amino acids are needed by lean body mass, not fat cells. To calculate individual protein requirements for an individual, start with his or her appropriate weight in pounds, divide that number by 2, and the result will indicate the approximate number of grams of protein required each day. For example, a person whose ideal body weight is 120 pounds requires approximately 60 grams of protein daily.

A general rule of thumb used in standard nutrition practice is that protein should contribute 15 percent of calories. However, protein requirements can differ according to the nutritional status and activity of the individual. Protein needs may increase during illness, after surgery, and during healing. Eating more protein, while reducing carbohydrate intake, has also been shown to promote weight loss, fueling the enormous recent popularity of high-protein diets. However, high-protein eating has its detractors. In the Western world, individuals consume far more protein-rich foods, often high in fat, than people living in the Third World.

While those in the West have far less deficiency diseases, they do suffer more from degenerative and chronic diseases such as heart disease, diabetes, and cancer. Some studies have linked high-meat diets with colon cancer. And likely, the higher the diet is in protein, the fewer fruits, grains, and vegetables consumed. Diets high in protein may also promote calcium excretion, which depletes the bones of minerals. Excessive intake of protein may also cause fluid imbalance.

One or another of the basic nutrients predominate in the various categories of food. For example, meat is an excellent source of protein while grains are high in carbohydrates. Table 2.3 gives an overview of the rich food sources of nutrients for carbohydrates, fats, proteins, and water.

Table 2.3
Rich Food Sources of Nutrients

Carbohydrates	Fats	Proteins	Water
Whole grains	Butter and margarine	Meat, fish, and poultry	Fruits
Sugar, syrup, and honey	Vegetable oils	Soybean products	Vegetables
Fruits	Fats in meats	Eggs	Beverages
Vegetables	Whole milk and milk products	Milk and milk products	
	Nuts and seeds	Whole grains	

Micronutrients: Vitamins, Minerals, and Water

The RDAs for vitamins and minerals provided in this book are based on the standards published by the Food and Nutrition Board, Institute of Medicine, National Academies of Science in 2004. The RDAs are the desirable levels for those vitamins whose requirements are known to be essential to healthy humans. They are based upon available scientific knowledge and are considered adequate to meet the known nutritional needs of practically all healthy people. These levels are intended to apply to people whose physical activity is considered "light" and who live in temperate climates. They also are intended to provide a safety margin for each vitamin above the minimum level that will maintain health. RDA values are for the expected absorption by the body of nutrients when they are found in food only. For example, because the body absorbs only 10 percent of the iron eaten in food, the RDA is set at 10 to 18 milligrams to make up for the lost iron. The same principle applies for the minerals. Since each individual is different, precise needs are impossible to predict.

The RDA is no longer the only reference value for nutrients. In 1997, the Food and Nutrition Board, in partnership with Health Canada, created the Dietary Reference Intakes, or DRIs. These include the earlier RDAs, plus three new categories. First is Adequate Intake (AI), in cases when no RDA has been established. Second is the Estimated Average Requirement (EAR), the intake value estimated to meet the needs of 50 percent of an age-specific and gender-specific group. Third is the Tolerable Upper Intake Level (UL), to caution against excessive intakes of nutrients such as vitamin D. It is the maximum level of daily intake unlikely to cause harm to almost all of the individuals in the group for whom it is designed.

Vitamins

All natural vitamins are organic food substances found only in living things, that is, plants and animals. Fewer than twenty substances have been discovered so far that are believed to be active as vitamins in human nutrition; however, more and more new substances that work side by side with vitamins are being found. These are the phytonutrients (discussed later in this section), along with the vitamins and minerals that are present in varying quantities in specific foods,

and they are absolutely necessary for proper growth, maintenance of health, and prevention of disease.

With a few exceptions, the body cannot make its own vitamins. They must be supplied in the diet or by supplements, but eating wholesome foods cannot be stressed highly enough. Science searches to isolate the substances from foods that heal, maintain health, and prevent disease, but the true source of these substances is found in special combinations in the foods that we eat. For instance, studies on beta-carotene supplements have shown that other carotenoids in combination with beta-carotene may be responsible for the antioxidant action associated with carotenoids. Eating the carotenoid-rich food in its whole and natural form eliminates the guesswork.

Taking vitamin and mineral supplements may be desirable because, although awareness is growing, many people still do not eat adequately balanced meals on a consistent basis. The elderly are especially vulnerable, since they not only lose some ability to taste—which changes their eating habits—but also lose some of the bodily processes necessary to digest, absorb, and assimilate food. Where there is doubt that the requirements for certain nutrients are being met through diet alone, supplementing is beneficial.

The nutrient content of the soil that our food is grown in affects the quality and the quantity of the vitamins that are in the food we eat. Insufficient nutrient levels result in nutrient-deficient foods—another reason to supplement. Vitamins are also lost in the foods we eat today because of processing and storage of foods for convenience. In addition, nutrients are lost through cooking.

Supplements, whether vitamins or minerals, should be taken with meals unless stated otherwise on the packaging. Vitamin therapy does not produce results overnight. Regeneration or the alteration in body chemistry necessary for repair takes weeks and sometimes months before the full benefits are felt. When a nutrient is ingested in an amount above that which the body needs, especially over a prolonged period of time, it may cause toxicity and stress in the body. It may cause urinary loss of another nutrient, or it may impair, suppress, or interfere with normal physiological processes. Studies have shown that once the intake of a certain nutrient, such as a fat-soluble vitamin or mineral, has produced a balance, an excess can accumulate in the body and remain unmetabolized. An exception may be vitamin C. Its use is beneficial at higher than normal amounts because of its effects as an antioxidant and any excess is rapidly excreted only a few hours after ingestion.

vitamin A. While the RDA for women who are lactating is higher than the standard RDA for women, the RDA for pregnant women remains at 800 RE/mcg. Higher doses of vitamin A can lead to abnormal development of the embryo. Caution also needs to be used by persons with liver disease and those who abuse alcohol. Taking oral contraceptives can also increase blood levels of vitamin A.

Fat-soluble vitamin A, the kind derived from animal sources, can be toxic if excessive amounts are consumed. Overdoses of vitamin A damage the same body systems that exhibit symptoms in a vitamin A deficiency. Toxicity from carotenes, plant-derived vitamin A, is far less likely because the body cannot convert beta-carotene quickly enough to create a toxic condition. However, when large amounts of carotene supplements or carotene-rich foods such as tomato and carrot juice are consumed, accumulation may occur in the fat cells under the skin, causing the skin to become slightly orange. Even at low doses, a tint may be visible, possibly indicating the presence of hypothyroidism (reduced thyroid activity) or diabetes.

Symptoms of toxicity can develop over time from taking therapeutic dosages of vitamin A that range from 10,000 RE to 20,000 RE. These symptoms may include loss of appetite, nausea, weight loss, skin that is dry and flaking, fatigue, bone and joint pain, headache, hair loss, irritability, cessation of menstruation, and a feeling of pressure inside the skull. Excessive daily use of vitamin A may also lead to abnormalities in the mucous membranes. Growth retardation, enlargement of the liver and spleen, and red blood cell breakage may occur.

If symptoms of toxicity occur, dosage should be reduced to 3,000 RE or discontinued. Symptoms of toxicity will disappear in a few days if the vitamin is withdrawn. Vitamin C can help prevent the harmful effects of vitamin A toxicity.

Certain disease states make vitamin A toxicity more likely. Overdose of vitamin A may cause bone disease (excessive serum calcium) among those with chronic kidney failure. Kidney patients who are undergoing dialysis may be at risk for reabsorption of the bone, which leads to high levels of calcium in the blood. This condition is rare in normal individuals, but people with kidney conditions should consult their physician before taking vitamin A.

Because children need less vitamin A than adults, they are most vulnerable to vitamin A toxicity. They may experience toxicity symptoms at doses as low as 5,000 RE. Many forms of fortified foods such as milk and some breakfast cereals as well as chewable supplements—all of which contain 100 percent of the daily minimum requirement—are found on the market.

Two vitamin A derivatives prescribed for skin problems, accutane and etretinate, must not be used under any circumstances by pregnant women or by those who are of childbearing age and not using contraception. These substances cause birth defects. While accutane remains in the body for about a week, etretinate remains in the body for a period of two years or more.

Beta-carotene, which doesn't require a prescription, has the same results of vitamin A with none of the side effects. Recommendations are 1,000 RE to 5,000 RE daily in supplemental form. This dosage, along with some carotenoid-rich foods daily, will protect against deficiencies and promote normal cell functioning. These doses of beta-carotene are equally safe for children. An average-size carrot contains 1,000 RE of beta-carotene. Given the properties of beta-carotene in comparison with preformed vitamin A, it is unnecessary to take the preformed type unless advised to do so by a physician.

DEFICIENCY EFFECTS AND SYMPTOMS. Vitamin A deficiency may occur when an inadequate dietary supply exists, when the body is unable to absorb or store the vitamin (as in ulcerative colitis, cirrhosis of the liver, and cystic fibrosis, which obstructs the bile ducts), when an ailment interferes with the conversion of carotene to vitamin A (as in diabetes mellitus and hypothyroidism), and when any rapid bodily loss of the vitamin occurs (as in pneumonia, hyperthyroidism, chronic nephritis, scarlet fever, and some respiratory infections).

The eyes are well-known indicators of vitamin A deficiency. One of the first symptoms is night blindness, an inability of the eye to adjust to darkness. Another eye-related disorder, xerophthalmia, is the collective name of all eye deficiency symptoms. In xerosis the cornea (outer covering of the eye) loses luster and becomes dry, hard, and inflamed, reducing visual acuity. Another serious symptom is keratomalacia, which is the softening or weakening of the tissues leading to total blindness.

Other signs of deficiency include rough, dry, or prematurely aged skin; skin blemishes in which the cells of the skin harden and flatten; loss of sense of smell; drying and hardening of the salivary glands in the mouth allowing for a susceptibility to infection; loss of appetite; sties in the eyes; fatigue; and a weakened immune system leading to frequent respiratory, digestive, bladder, vaginal, and other infections. Kidney stones, impaired growth, cessation of bone growth, anemia (small-cell type), and painful joints are all indications of deficiency. Vitamin A may be lacking when hair loses its sheen and luster and fingernails become brittle. Studies of animals have shown that cancer-causing carcinogens remain much more active when there is a vitamin A deficiency.

Deficiency of vitamin A leads to the rapid loss of vitamin C. Since vitamin A needs zinc to get it out of storage, a zinc deficiency can mimic a vitamin A deficiency. A drastic drop in serum A has been found in severely injured patients.

BENEFICIAL EFFECTS ON AILMENTS.
Vitamin A is a powerful ally in fighting infections. Researchers find that 180 milligrams of beta-carotene per day stimulates production of immune T-helper (lymphocyte) cells, vital functionaries that guard against all infections. In addition, by giving strength to cell walls, vitamin A helps protect mucous membranes against invading bacteria. Some people who do not respond to vitamin C for fighting a cold may respond to vitamin A. Higher doses may be required to fight colds for people who breathe polluted air, which increases their susceptibility to infection. If infection has already occurred, therapeutic doses of vitamin A will help keep it from spreading.

Well known for its benefit to the eyes, vitamin A is crucial in maintaining good eyesight and has been successful in treating such disorders as night blindness, blurred vision, and cataracts as well as crossed eyes, nearsightedness, xerophthalmia, and Bitot's spots (white, elevated, sharply outlined patches on the white of the eye). Therapeutic dosages of vitamin A are necessary for treatment of glaucoma and conjunctivitis, an inflammation of the mucous membrane that lines the eyelids. Vitamin A, zinc, and vitamin B_6 will help with disturbances of smell and taste during colds and pregnancy, when zinc is depleted, often as a result of taking antibiotics.

Administration of vitamin A has helped shorten the duration of communicable diseases (including measles, scarlet fever, and the common cold) and infections of the middle ear, intestines, ovaries, uterus, and vagina. Vitamin A has proved successful in treating cases of bronchial asthma, chronic rhinitis, and dermatitis. It also has been effective in reducing high cholesterol levels and atheroma, fatty degeneration or thickening of the walls of the large arteries. A high intake of carotenes is associated with reduced risk of heart disease. Vitamin A has also been helpful in treating patients suffering from tuberculosis, cirrhosis of the liver, emphysema, gastritis, and hyperthyroidism. Patients with nephritis (inflammation of the kidney),

migraine headaches, and tinnitus (ringing in the ear) have benefited from vitamin A therapy. A deficiency of vitamin A has been linked to increased mortality in AIDS patients.

Much research has focused on the relation of vitamin A and the risk of cancer. Vitamin A protects the epithelial tissues of the inner and outer linings of the skin, throat, and lungs from becoming cancerous. These effects are likely due to vitamin A's ability to support proper cell differentiation, maintain cell integrity and the healthy functioning of the mucous lining, and improve the immune response. Epidemiological studies show a much more significant association of low rates of cancer with carotene than preformed vitamin A. This may be due to carotene's function as an antioxidant, immune booster, and anticarcinogen. The results of many studies suggest that cancers of the bladder, larynx, esophagus, stomach, colon/rectum, uterus, cervix, and prostate benefit from beta-carotene.

There recently has been controversy about beta-carotene's ability to prevent lung cancer. Supporters of the use of beta-carotene to prevent lung cancer suggest that beta-carotene must be coupled with various antioxidant nutrients such as vitamin C, vitamin E, and selenium to be effective. Beta-carotene oxidizes easily and may increase damage to the liver, especially in persons who consume alcohol, resulting in the formation of cancer-causing compounds. While several recent studies have cast doubt on the benefits of taking beta-carotene supplements, hundreds of studies have yielded good evidence for the ability of a diet rich in carotenes and other plant antioxidants to prevent cancer.

Vitamin A can significantly reduce the immune-depressive effects of radiation treatment and cancer chemotherapy. The addition of beta-carotene enabled researchers to increase dosages of radiation and chemotherapy in laboratory animals sufficiently to get complete regression of tumors in most cases.

Vitamin A is related to sexual development and reproduction. It is essential in the chemical process whereby cholesterol is converted into female estrogens and male androgens. Insufficient supply of these sex hormones results in degeneration of the sex organs. Animals in this condition that were given vitamin A resumed normal hormonal activity. Studies conducted on men having varying levels of sperm deficiency showed that when vitamin A was administered along with vitamin E, the sperm level returned to normal.

When applied topically and locally, vitamin A may clear up a variety of skin problems, such as impetigo, boils, carbuncles, and open ulcers. A derivative and anemia. Schizophrenia and diabetic neuropathies are aided by the B complex.

Thiamin (Vitamin B₁)

DESCRIPTION. Thiamin, or vitamin B_1, is a water-soluble vitamin. Its prime role is as a coenzyme in reactions associated with energy production. Thiamin participates in the complex process of converting carbohydrates, proteins, and fats into energy. This nutrient is also vital for normal functioning of the nervous system, which depends on glucose for energy. In addition, vitamin B_1 plays a role in the release of acetylcholine, the chemical that regulates memory. Thiamin is linked with improving individual learning capacity, and it supports immune function. Maintenance of the heart and red blood cells are jobs of thiamin. It is necessary for consistent growth in children and for the improvement of muscle tone in the stomach, intestines, and heart. Thiamin is essential for stabilizing the appetite by improving food assimilation and digestion, particularly of starches, sugars, and alcohol.

Pork, organ meats, and oysters are rich in thiamin. Legumes, collard greens, and blackstrap molasses are also reliable sources. Bread should be whole grain or enriched, since thiamin is a component of the germ and bran of wheat, the husk of rice, and that portion of all grains that is commercially milled away to give the grain a lighter color and finer texture.

ABSORPTION AND STORAGE. Thiamin is rapidly absorbed in the upper and lower small intestine. It is then carried by the circulatory system to the liver, kidneys, and heart. Thiamin is not stored in the body in any great quantity and, therefore, must be supplied daily. Body tissues deplete rapidly when a deficiency occurs. It is excreted in the urine in amounts that reflect the intake and the quantity stored.

Thiamin is destroyed by alcohol, which interferes with the absorption of all nutrients, but especially B_1 and B_2. Eating excessive amounts of sugar will cause thiamin depletion as will smoking.

DOSAGE AND TOXICITY. The daily RDA for thiamin is 1.2 milligrams for men and 1.1 milligrams for women. Thiamin needs are proportional to the energy a person expends, not just to energy intake. People who are fasting or on a low-calorie diet must maintain their thiamin intake as if they weren't cutting calories. In addition, as calorie intake increases, especially of carbohydrates, the amount of thiamin needed increases.

When taken orally, there are no known toxic levels of thiamin. A typical daily dosage is 50 to 100 milligrams but can be as high as 8 grams for treating patients with Alzheimer's disease.

DEFICIENCY EFFECTS AND SYMPTOMS. A severe deficiency of thiamin leads to beriberi, a condition that plagued nineteenth-century sailors who lived on foods lacking adequate amounts of thiamin. Classic signs of beriberi include fatigue, anorexia, weight loss, gastrointestinal disorders, and weakness. Patients may experience mental confusion, difficulty walking, high blood pressure, heart disorders (cardiomegaly and tachycardia), fluid retention (in wet beriberi), and muscle wasting (in dry beriberi). There may also be emotional instability with irritability and depression. In the Western world today, instances of beriberi are rare, except in alcoholics.

Mild thiamin deficiency also affects the nervous system, digestive function, and circulatory system. Early signs are loss of appetite, gastrointestinal upset, nausea, headache, weight loss, pins-and-needles sensations, numbness of the legs, muscle weakness, and fatigue. A thiamin deficiency can also lead to inflammation of the optic nerve. During alcohol withdrawal, paralysis sets in when thiamin is missing.

Sulfites, a common food additive, destroy thiamin. Thiamin is vulnerable to moist heat and alkalies such as baking soda. A deficiency is also more likely with a high-fat diet and one high in sugars, which require thiamin for their conversion to energy but which do not supply thiamin. Dieting and fasting can also lead to thiamin deficiency. People who drink alcohol excessively need 10 to 100 milligrams of thiamin per day.

There is evidence suggesting that older people use thiamin less efficiently; therefore, a higher intake, along with other B vitamins, may be advantageous. The need for additional B_1 increases during severe diarrhea, fever, stress, and surgery. There are no known toxic effects with thiamin, although large doses may cause a B-complex imbalance.

BENEFICIAL EFFECTS ON AILMENTS. Thiamin is used in the treatment of beriberi to improve the excretion of fluid stored in the body, decrease rapid heart rate, reduce the size of enlarged hearts, and normalize electrocardiograms. Thiamin is also given to improve mental function. It is useful in treating patients with Alzheimer's disease, older persons with impaired mental function, and psychiatric patients.

Alcoholism has been successfully treated with thiamin. Acute alcohol toxicity should be treated with injections of 100 to 250 milligrams of thiamin before any glucose is given. Giving glucose without thiamin may lead to Wernicke-Korsakoff syndrome or worsen preexisting conditions.

Many other ailments, including diabetes, have been aided by administering thiamin. It is essential in the manufacture of hydrochloric acid, which aids digestion. It helps in eliminating nausea, especially that caused by air or sea sickness. Thiamin helps improve muscle tone in the stomach and intestines, which in turn relieves constipation. Thiamin also can protect against lead poisoning and sudden infant death syndrome (SIDS). Thiamin will help energize neutrophils, which aid the immune system in fighting bacteria. Mental ability and IQ have improved with the use of thiamin.

Dental postoperative pain is promptly and completely relieved in many patients by the administration of thiamin. Pain can often be prevented by administration of B_1 to the patient before the operation. Thiamin therapy has reduced the healing time of dry tooth sockets. Evidence shows that replacement of thiamin to injured and diseased nerves not only restores proper functioning but also relieves pain.

Riboflavin (Vitamin B₂)

DESCRIPTION. Vitamin B_2, also known as riboflavin, is a water-soluble vitamin that occurs naturally in combination with other B vitamins in various foods. Riboflavin is a unique B vitamin in that it both functions within the cell and protects the cell from damage. Like thiamin (vitamin B_1), riboflavin plays a role in the production of energy from carbohydrates, fats, and proteins, converting to the coenzyme flavin adenine dinucleotide (FAD) in the respiratory transport chain. Because of its involvement with energy production, riboflavin is the exerciser's best friend as it is stored in the muscles and used in times of physical exertion.

Riboflavin also helps regulate glutathione, a powerful antioxidant that protects against free radicals. In this capacity, riboflavin may protect against certain cancers. It supports the detoxification function of the liver and fat metabolism as well. And riboflavin plays a role in the metabolism of such nutrients as niacin, vitamin B_6, vitamin K, and folic acid, thus affecting a wide range of body functions.

Small amounts of riboflavin are found in various foods. Good sources of riboflavin are liver, tongue, and other organ meats; milk; yogurt; dark leafy greens; almonds; and brewer's yeast. While bread is enriched with vitamin B_2, a person eating the standard American diet who does not include dairy products in meals may not take in sufficient amounts of this nutrient.

Riboflavin is not destroyed by heat, oxidation, or acid. Only a small amount is lost in cooking. However, this vitamin disintegrates in the presence of alkali or light, especially ultraviolet light. Milk, which contains riboflavin, should not be stored in clear bottles, since sunlight can destroy the vitamin in milk within a few hours. A significant amount of riboflavin is lost also in grains stored in glass containers and when fruits and vegetables are sun-dried.

ABSORPTION AND STORAGE. Riboflavin is easily absorbed through the walls of the small intestine, especially when taken with food and when there is an increase in bile salts. However, certain substances such as alcohol and antacids may slow absorption. In addition, caffeine, saccharin, vitamins such as vitamin C, zinc, and other substances may chelate riboflavin, reducing its bioavailability.

Once absorbed, riboflavin is carried by the bloodstream to body tissues, and it is excreted in the urine and released through sweat. The amount excreted depends on the intake and relative need of the tissues and may be accompanied by a loss of protein from the body. Small amounts of riboflavin are found in the liver and kidneys, but it is not stored to any great degree in the muscles. Because riboflavin is water soluble, it is not stored in the body and must be added to the diet daily through food sources or supplementation.

DOSAGE AND TOXICITY. The RDA for riboflavin is 1.3 milligrams daily for adult males and 1.1 milligrams per day for adult females. For those who exercise, recommended intake is 2 to 2.5 milligrams daily. A typical therapeutic range is 50 to 200 milligrams per day.

There is no known toxicity of riboflavin. However, prolonged ingestion of large doses of any one of the B-complex vitamins, including riboflavin, may result in high urinary losses of other B vitamins. Therefore, it is important to take a complete B complex with any single B vitamin.

DEFICIENCY EFFECTS AND SYMPTOMS. Unlike thiamin, riboflavin is not available in a wide variety of foods, so the most common cause of a deficiency is an unbalanced diet. This may be due to long-established faulty dietary habits, food likes or dislikes, restriction of foods to relieve symptoms of digestive problems, or a restricted therapeutic diet to treat such diseases as peptic ulcer or diabetes. Deficiency is also common among the elderly who often have poor eating habits, in patients postsurgery, and for individuals who drink excessive amounts of alcohol and consequently have a loss of appetite. Some vegans and people on raw food diets also show riboflavin deficiencies.

Women, in particular those who exercise, may need more riboflavin as do others who participate in rigorous daily activities. Tranquilizer use, hypothyroidism, and borate toxicity are also related to a riboflavin deficiency. People who consume foods containing bisulfite preservatives or who use Lasix (furosemide), digoxin, and antacids are likely to experience a B_2 deficiency. Heavy coffee and tea drinkers are also at risk.

The elderly often exhibit low levels of riboflavin. Signs may include burning and soreness of the mouth, lips, and eyes; itching and burning of the eyes; sensitivity to light and a loss of vision; and cracks in the corners of the mouth. There may be fatigue or muscle weakness. Severe deficiency of vitamin B_2 is rare. Symptoms of a severe lack include inflammation of mucous membranes of the mouth and a reddening of the eyes, dry skin and scaling skin, and possibly hysteria or depression. A lack of vitamin B_2 can also result in anemia.

BENEFICIAL EFFECTS ON AILMENTS. Used for prevention, riboflavin protects against free-radical damage that is the result of exercise. This nutrient also boosts athletic performance. Riboflavin is also necessary for the maintenance of skin, nails, and hair. Increased dosages of riboflavin are needed for hyperthyroidism, fever, stress, injury or surgery, acne, eczema, seborrheic dermatitis, somatitis, arthritis, diabetes, and malabsorption. Riboflavin is of value in treating recovering alcoholics and individuals with impaired ability to detoxify drugs and toxins. This nutrient also may protect against esophageal and prostate cancers. Patients with sickle cell anemia have benefited from riboflavin supplementation. And preliminary research suggests that vitamin B_2 can help prevent migraine headaches.

Undernourished women during the end of pregnancy often suffer from conditions such as visual disturbances, burning sensations in the eyes, excessive watering of eyes, and failing vision. These conditions can be helped by supplementing the diet with large doses of B_2.

There is some evidence that low levels of riboflavin are linked to the development of cataracts. While supplementation may be necessary to restore amounts to normal, excessive dosages are not recommended, since research has shown that the interaction of riboflavin, light, and oxygen can promote cataracts. Limiting daily supplementation to 10 milligrams is warranted.

Niacin (Vitamin B₃)

DESCRIPTION. Niacin, also referred to as vitamin B_3, is a member of the vitamin B complex nutrients, all of which are water soluble. It is more stable than thiamin or riboflavin because of its remarkable resistance to heat, light, air, acids, and alkaline compounds.

Vitamin B_3 in nutritional supplements is in one of three forms: nicotinic acid and nicotinate, both referred to as niacin, and nicotinamide, called niacinamide. Niacin can also be made by the body from protein, specifically from the amino acid tryptophan. The niacin "equivalent" listed in dietary tables refers to either pure niacin or an adequate supply of tryptophan, which the body can convert into niacin. Foods such as liver and other organ meats, eggs, poultry, fish, and peanuts are rich sources of both niacin and tryptophan, as are dietary supplements such as brewer's yeast, wheat germ, and desiccated liver. Good sources of niacin alone are whole grains (except corn), legumes, and avocados. Milk is a poor source of niacin but a good source of tryptophan.

Niacin plays an important role in many body processes. As a coenzyme, niacin, similar to riboflavin and thiamin, assists enzymes in the breakdown and utilization of proteins, fats, and carbohydrates. It is vital for the proper activity of the nervous system and for formation and maintenance of healthy skin, tongue, and digestive system tissues. Niacin is necessary for the synthesis of sex hormones. And it supports detoxification processes, even for such substances as narcotics and alcohol. Niacin is also important therapeutically, with the various forms of this nutrient each having their own specific beneficial effect. Nicotinic acid is known for its cholesterol-lowering properties. Type I diabetes and arthritis are helped by niacinamide.

ABSORPTION AND STORAGE. Niacin is absorbed in the stomach and small intestine and is stored primarily in the liver. The vitamin is water soluble and any excess is eliminated via the urine. Excessive consumption of sugar and starches will deplete the body's supply of niacin, as will certain antibiotics.

DOSAGE AND TOXICITY. The 1997–98 RDA for niacin is 16 milligrams for adult males and 14 milligrams for adult females. However, during illness, tissue trauma, and general growth periods, and after physical exercise the daily requirement increases.

Tryptophan may provide part, or all, of the daily niacin requirement; 60 milligrams of tryptophan yield 1 milligram of niacin. Three and a half ounces of light-meat chicken contain about 325 milligrams of tryptophan and 8 ounces of milk about 120 milligrams.

Doses of 1,000 milligrams nicotinic acid—and in some cases higher—appear safe. However, even doses as small as 25 milligrams can produce uncomfortable side effects. The most well known is an intense flushing of the skin that occurs within fifteen minutes of taking a niacin supplement. There may also be tingling and itching sensations and a throbbing in the head owing to a dilation of the blood vessels. A sudden release of histamine causes this flush. For this reason, individuals with peptic ulcers or asthma are not advised to take supplemental niacin without the advice of a physician. Starting with a low dosage and carefully increasing the dose is often recommended. Other toxic symptoms may include nausea and cramps.

Niacinamide does not produce these side effects. Another alternative is inositol hexaniacinate, which is considered the safest form, producing no side effects other than occasionally mild stomach upset or skin irritation in certain individuals. Time-released niacin also reduces symptoms, but this supplement form is more toxic and can cause liver damage.

Large doses of nicotinic acid, more than 2 grams, have been reported to produce skin discoloration and dryness, decreased glucose tolerance, high uric acid levels (a concern for patients with gout), abnormal liver function tests, and even symptoms that resemble some of those that accompany hepatitis. Other toxic effects of taking too much niacin are nausea, cramps, diarrhea, a feeling of faintness, and accelerated or irregular heartbeat (a concern for people with significant heart rhythm disturbances). Medical supervision when taking such amounts is essential. Since niacin is involved in the release of stomach acid, patients using large doses should take the vitamin on a full stomach.

DEFICIENCY EFFECTS AND SYMPTOMS. The classic signs of niacin deficiency are dermatitis, dementia, diarrhea, and death in the condition known as pellagra. In the early stages, a niacin insufficiency can cause muscular weakness, general fatigue, loss of appetite, indigestion, and various skin eruptions. Severe niacin deficiency also results in rough and inflamed skin, tremors, and nervous disorders such as depression. Lack of niacin may also lead to many digestive abnormalities causing irritation; inflammation of mucous membranes in the mouth and gastrointestinal tract also develop from a niacin deficiency. An individual may develop bad breath, tender gums, canker sores, burning mouth and tongue, small ulcers, nausea, and vomiting as well as recurring headaches, irritability, and insomnia.

BENEFICIAL EFFECTS ON AILMENTS. Niacin in the form of nicotinic acid slows the process of atherosclerosis and may even reverse the progression, demonstrating better overall results than other lipid-lowering agents. Large doses of nicotinic acid have the ability to lower undesirable LDL cholesterol while raising desirable HDL cholesterol, and also to reduce levels of lipoprotein (a), triglycerides, and fibrinogen. It has been shown that taking 2 grams of niacin per day increases HDL cholesterol. Niacin is often used to increase circulation in cramped, painful legs of the elderly. Smokers can benefit from niacin because this nutrient widens blood vessels and removes lipids from arterial walls—opposite of the actions of nicotine. Niacin may also reduce blood pressure.

Initial studies suggest that niacinamide can prevent type I diabetes from progressing if given soon enough at the onset of this form of diabetes. Various mechanisms appear to be at work, including enhancing insulin secretion and increasing insulin sensitivity.

Niacin has also been very effective in the treatment of joint disease. Arthritics have experienced increased joint mobility and decreased joint stiffness and pain, as well as greater muscle strength and lessened fatigue with the administration of niacin. In most cases, long-term treatment is needed for optimum results. Niacin has also been used very successfully in cases of rheumatoid arthritis and osteoarthritis.

Very important for brain metabolism, niacin is sometimes used for the treatment of depression and impaired memory. In cases of pellagra, high doses of niacin have brought complete relief from delirium within twenty-four to forty-eight hours. For this reason, it is thought that people with schizophrenia could benefit from increased amounts of niacin. In studies, along with other vitamins, schizophrenic symptoms such as paranoia and hallucinations were relieved. Large doses have helped elderly patients who were mentally confused. Because of its calming effects, niacin can reduce the amount of tranquilizers needed or may even be able to replace them. Many insomniacs respond well to the sleep-inducing effects of this nutrient.

Niacin has helped stimulate production of hydrochloric acid to aid impaired digestion. Acne has been successfully treated with niacin. Fluid loss from severe burns can be lessened with niacin. Niacin can aid in the control of alcoholism. Crohn's disease is helped with niacinamide; vitamins C, E, B_6; magnesium; and pyridoxine. Niacin may help prevent the extreme pain of migraine headaches when taken at the first sign of attack.

Vitamin B$_5$ (Pantothenic Acid, Pantethine)

DESCRIPTION. Pantothenic acid, a part of the vitamin B complex, is water soluble. It takes its name from the Greek word, *pantos*, meaning "all" or "entire," because this nutrient is found in all living cells, being widely distributed in yeasts, molds, bacteria, and individual cells of all animals and plants. It is also synthesized in the body by the bacterial flora of the intestines. Organ meats, brewer's yeast, egg yolks, peanuts, pecans, perch, and whole grain cereal such as oatmeal are the richest sources.

Pantothenic acid, in food and inside the cells of the body, is in the form of coenzyme A (CoA), a crucial component of Krebs cycle energy production. Like the three B vitamins, thiamin, riboflavin, and niacin, pantothenic acid participates in the release of energy from carbohydrates, fats, and proteins. In addition, there is a close correlation between pantothenic acid tissue levels and functioning of the adrenal cortex. This B vitamin stimulates the adrenal glands and increases production of cortisone and other adrenal hormones important for healthy nerves and skin. Consequently, pantothenic acid can improve the body's ability to withstand stressful conditions.

Pantothenic acid is also involved in the synthesis of cholesterol, several amino acids, steroid hormones, vitamin D, fatty acids, and red blood cells. It aids in the utilization of other vitamins, especially riboflavin. This B vitamin also works with coenzyme Q10 and carnitine in the transport and use of fatty acids.

ABSORPTION AND STORAGE.   Coenzyme A in food is converted to pantothenic acid during digestion. It is found in the blood, particularly in the plasma, and is excreted daily in the urine. It is presumed that folic acid aids in its assimilation. The vitamin along with royal jelly has proved more effective than pantothenic acid alone.

Approximately 33 percent of the pantothenic acid content of meat is lost during cooking; about 50 percent is lost by the milling of flour. Pantothenic acid is stable in moist heat but destroyed by dry heat. It is also easily destroyed by heating in acids such as vinegar or alkalies such as baking soda.

DOSAGE AND TOXICITY.   According to the 1997–98 DRIs, the adequate intake for pantothenic acid is 5 milligrams for adult males and females. But needs are higher during pregnancy, lactation, and periods of stress, such as after injury, severe illness, or antibiotic therapy. Also, the needed amount can vary according to daily food intake and urinary excretion levels. An average American diet will provide between 6 and 16 milligrams daily.

A common therapeutic dosage range is 50 to 250 milligrams daily, although dosages can be as high as 1,000 milligrams. To treat allergies and provide adre-

nal support, the dosage is 250 milligrams twice daily. No toxicity has been reported even with higher doses than this, with no serious side effects other than diarrhea. People with rheumatoid arthritis should consult their physicians before taking larger doses, but 2 grams daily has been used successfully.

DEFICIENCY EFFECTS AND SYMPTOMS. Pantothenic acid is widely distributed in foods, so a true deficiency is rare. However, when the body lacks the intestinal flora needed to synthesize pantothenic acid, this can contribute to a possible deficiency. The means of detecting deficiency is limited, although low intakes may slow metabolic processes.

The list of deficiency symptoms reflects impaired health of cells in many tissues. Signs of reduced immunity to some infections have been noted in a pantothenate deficiency. Symptoms of a deficiency may include upper respiratory infections and reduced antibody formation as well as vomiting, abdominal pains, restlessness, burning feet, muscle cramps, and sensitivity to insulin. A deficiency may lead to skin disorders, adrenal exhaustion, and low blood sugar (hypoglycemia). A lack of pantothenic acid may result in duodenal ulcers.

When a deficiency exists, the function of the adrenal gland is diminished, a condition that may lead to physical and mental depression, insufficient secretions of hydrochloric acid in the stomach, and disturbances of the motor nerves. Because the brain contains one of the highest concentrations of pantothenic acid, mental symptoms such as insomnia, fatigue, and depression can be the result of a deficiency.

BENEFICIAL EFFECTS ON AILMENTS. Pantothenic acid supports adrenal function. It is probably the greatest defense against stress and fatigue and is used to improve athletic ability. Its role in defending against stress will aid the heart patient. It also helps build antibodies for fighting infection and boosts immunity when teamed with the rest of the B vitamins. Adequate intake of pantothenic acid reduces the toxicity effects of many antibiotics.

A decrease in blood levels of pantothenic acid is characteristic of rheumatoid arthritis; the more severe the symptoms, such as morning stiffness and severity of pain, the lower the pantothenic acid level. Daily injections may lead to a rise in blood levels of this nutrient. It is also helpful in preventing and alleviating arthritis and treating bone disorders.

The most active, stable form of pantothenic acid is pantethine, a metabolite of the vitamin. The standard dosage is 300 milligrams three times a day. Clinical trials show that 600 to 1,200 milligrams of pantethine daily lowers cholesterol after a few weeks, and also improves the ratio of LDL cholesterol to HDL cholesterol, and reduces triglyceride levels to help prevent cardiovascular disease. These benefits are particularly noteworthy, in that pantethine appears to have no side effects or toxicity. Research shows that pantethine also lowers blood fats in diabetics without any harmful effects on control of blood sugar.

Research also supports many other applications of pantothenic acid supplementation. Pantothenic acid has been used successfully to treat paralysis of the gastrointestinal tract after surgery, appearing to stimulate gastrointestinal movement. It also aids in the prevention of nerve degeneration (due to a deficiency), including peripheral neuritis, nerve disorders, and epilepsy. Pantothenic acid is also thought to speed wound healing, offer protection against cellular damage caused by excessive radiation, and slow the aging process by removing age spots and preventing wrinkles. In animal studies, this nutrient slowed graying.

Vitamin B$_6$ (Pyridoxine, Pyridoxal, and Pyridoxamine)

DESCRIPTION.   Vitamin B$_6$ is a water-soluble vitamin consisting of three related compounds: pyridoxine, pyridoxal, and pyridoxamine. All three forms can be readily utilized by the body. Because this vitamin is involved in the assembly and breakdown of carbohydrates, proteins, and fats, it is one of the most valued and recommended nutrients, and one of the most well researched. Vitamin B$_6$ is necessary for the conversion of one amino acid into another and the conversion of protein into fats and carbohydrates for energy or storage. In particular, vitamin B$_6$ plays a vital role in the production of protein compounds, including hemoglobin, cells of the immune system, hormones, brain chemicals such as serotonin, RNA and DNA, and many enzymes. It is also involved in the manufacture of prostaglandins, hormonelike substances that regulate body processes such as muscle contraction and blood pressure. It is required for the proper functioning of more than sixty enzymes.

Vitamin B$_6$ is involved in the energy cycle by activating the release of glycogen from the liver and muscles. For this reason it is essential to physical activity. This nutrient helps maintain the balance of sodium and potassium, which regulates body fluids and promotes the normal functioning of the nervous and musculoskeletal systems. It also aids in the conversion of the amino acid tryptophan to niacin and helps linoleic acid, an essential fatty acid, function better in the body.

The most stable form of vitamin B$_6$ is pyridoxine, found almost exclusively in plant foods. Good sources are bananas, navy beans, sunflower seeds, walnuts, and wheat germ. Other forms are present in salmon, the white meat of chicken, beef, and liver.

ABSORPTION AND STORAGE.   This nutrient is readily absorbed and transported in plasma and red blood cells. A daily supply of vitamin B$_6$, together with the other B-complex vitamins, is necessary because it is excreted within eight hours of ingestion. Most of the body's store of this nutrient is in the muscles. Fasting and reducing diets can deplete the body's supply if proper supplements are not taken.

DOSAGE AND TOXICITY.   The 1997–98 RDA of vitamin B$_6$ for adult males and females is 1.3 milligrams. However, several factors can increase the need for vitamin B$_6$: pregnancy, lactation, exposure to radiation, cardiac failure, and the use of oral contraceptives. The need can also increase with age: the RDA for adult men fifty-one years of age and older is 1.7 milligrams a day; and for older women, 1.5 milligrams a day. And vitamin B$_6$ requirements are dependent on protein metabolism, so the more protein consumed, the more B$_6$ is needed.

No more than 50 milligrams a day of vitamin B$_6$ should be taken without the advice of a physician. Typically therapeutic dosages range between 50 and 100 milligrams per day, taken in divided dosages of no more than 50 milligrams at one time. Excessive amounts can be toxic and cause neurological damage. Toxicity symptoms are numbness in the feet and an unstable gait. This effect has been demonstrated in daily intakes of greater than 2 grams a day. But doses as low as 200 milligrams a day may become toxic and cause nerve damage. Reducing the dosage and adding brewer's yeast and zinc or a multiple vitamin (without copper) can eliminate the symptoms. Because B$_6$ is involved in the production of hydrochloric acid, people with stomach ulcers should seek a doctor's advice before taking the vitamin in large doses.

DEFICIENCY EFFECTS AND SYMPTOMS.   A true vitamin B$_6$ deficiency is quite rare, but when this does occur, symptoms include depression, glucose intolerance, impaired nerve function, cracking of the lips and tongue, loss of hair, dermatitis, eczema, arthritis, slow learning, and convulsions, especially in children. A deficiency can also cause disturbances in the bone marrow, which then causes anemia.

Water retention during pregnancy, morning sickness, and carpal tunnel syndrome are symptoms of deficiency. If a vitamin B$_6$ deficiency is allowed to continue through late pregnancy, stillbirths or postdelivery infant mortality may result. Infants born to deficient mothers may have convulsions. Studies have shown that pregnant women retain more B_6 than non-pregnant women; therefore, supplemental doses may be needed to make sure the fetus is adequately supplied. Some people may have an unbalanced metabolism caused by a genetic dependency on B_6.

Symptoms are similar to those seen in niacin and riboflavin deficiencies and may include muscular weakness, nervousness, irritability, depression, inability to concentrate, and loss of short-term memory, as well as a distorted reality for the autistic. A deficiency can have a profound effect on cognition and general brain function. Arthritis may also be present.

Insufficiency of this nutrient is sometimes associated with nervous system problems, mood disorders, pregnancy, cigarette smoking, and the use of amphetamines, oral contraceptives, or estrogen replacement therapy. A deficiency is also associated with low levels of B_{12}, as B_6 is required for its proper absorption.

BENEFICIAL EFFECTS ON AILMENTS.   If a deficiency is already there, taking the vitamin can aid in the improvement of acne and dry and itchy skin. Vitamin B_6 helps control diabetes in those whose bodies are receptive. Since the vitamin is a diuretic, B_6 benefits hypertensive individuals and those with edema, thus helping promote weight loss. A certain type of anemia characterized by red blood cells that are too small, apparently the result of a defective hereditary factor, responds very well to vitamin B_6. The vitamin boosts immunity and increases hormone response. It has been used in the treatment of nervous disorders and in the control of nausea and vomiting during pregnancy.

Vitamin B_6 has been used successfully to help treat male sexual disorders, eczema, thinning and loss of hair, elevated cholesterol levels, diarrhea, hemorrhoids, pancreatitis, ulcers, muscular weakness, some types of heart disturbances, burning feet, some types of kidney stones, acne, and tooth decay. Individuals who are especially sensitive to sunlight and quickly sunburn have been treated successfully with B_6. The lessening of the cloudiness of the eyes that is characteristic of cataracts may be aided. Vitamin B_6 causes a spectrum of biochemical actions in the brain that affect the bundles of symptoms of schizophrenia in a positive manner.

Various studies have shown a significant benefit of B_6 on premenstrual syndrome (PMS). Because vitamin B_6 helps regulate estrogen and progesterone, it has helped women who suffer from temporary premenstrual symptoms, such as tension, and protects against metabolic changes caused by oral contraceptives. It may also be useful in treating infertility.

A low level of vitamin B_6 in the blood is associated with an increased risk of cardiovascular disease. A lack of pyridoxine leads to a buildup of homocysteine in the blood, a substance that damages the walls of the arteries. Vitamin B_6 also helps prevent atherosclerosis by inhibiting platelet aggregation.

Vitamin B_{12}

DESCRIPTION.   Vitamin B_{12}, a water-soluble vitamin, contains cobalt, giving the crystalline structure of this nutrient a bright red color. Vitamin B_{12}, working with folic acid, is required for the synthesis of DNA. It is involved in protein, fat, and carbohydrate metabolism and is responsible for normal metabolism of nerve tissue. This vitamin is required for the formation of the myelin sheath that surrounds nerve cells, and it also speeds the transmission of signals along nerve cells. Vitamin B_{12} helps ensure formation of normal red blood cells. It also helps iron function better in the body, promotes the absorption of carotene and the conversion of vitamin A, and aids folic acid in the synthesis of choline. Vitamin B_{12} has been known as the energizer if a person is vitamin deficient, under stress, fatigued, or recovering from illness.

B_{12} is the product of bacterial metabolism. Animal protein is the only source of vitamin B_{12} in significant quantities. Excellent sources are liver, clams, oysters, and sardines. Eggs and dairy products also contain some. Foods containing folic acid in balanced proportions are essential here too.

There is a misconception that fermented foods, such as tempeh and miso, and seaweed, like wakame or nori, are reliable sources of vitamin B_{12}. However, research shows that content amount varies greatly and the form of B_{12} in such items does not appear to be biologically active in humans. Vegans, who eat neither animal foods nor dairy, include such foods in their diet in part for this reason. If they do not supplement with vitamin B_{12}, vegans may risk vitamin B_{12} deficiency in the future.

ABSORPTION AND STORAGE.   The proper absorption of vitamin B_{12} requires two gastric secretions, hydrochloric acid and intrinsic factor, a mucoprotein enzyme in digestive juices that binds with the nutrient and assists in its absorption in the lower intestine. B_{12} also needs to be combined with calcium during absorption to benefit the body, and taking it with meals increases absorption. After absorption, B_{12}

is bound to serum protein (globulins) and is transported in the bloodstream to various tissues. Unlike other water-soluble B vitamins, B_{12} is stored in various body tissues. The highest concentrations are found in the liver, kidneys, heart, pancreas, testes, brain, blood, and bone marrow—all play a role in the formation of red blood cells.

To help ensure adequate stores of vitamin B_{12}, the absorption rate adjusts to nutrient intake and need. When intake of vitamin B_{12} is low, 60 percent to 80 percent of the vitamin is absorbed. When high amounts are taken, the absorption decreases from 50 percent to 10 percent of the vitamin. Absorption also increases during pregnancy.

In addition, the body reabsorbs some vitamin B_{12}. Of the 5 to 10 micrograms that are excreted each day from the liver into the intestines, normally 3 to 5 micrograms are reabsorbed. Consequently, the healthy adult vegan, who consumes only very small amounts of vitamin B_{12}, with no gastric, pancreatic, or small bowel dysfunction, is protected from developing vitamin B_{12} deficiency disease for twenty to thirty years. As body reserves fall, the absorption rate can rise to nearly 100 percent. However, infants of macrobiotic mothers can rapidly develop deficiency because they receive almost no vitamin B_{12} from their mothers, so little of this nutrient is present to be reabsorbed.

Various medical conditions can interfere with absorption, including pancreatic and small bowel dysfunction. In autoimmune disease, compounds can bind with intrinsic factor, preventing B_{12} absorption, and the body may be unable to produce intrinsic factor. Many AIDS patients may be lacking B_{12}, due to reduced intake and absorption of the vitamin being blocked by the drug AZT. Decreased gastric function, usually due to a lack of intrinsic factor and more likely after the age of fifty, can also reduce absorption. Hydrochloric acid aids in absorption (and is given orally) as does a properly functioning thyroid gland. The use of laxatives also depletes B_{12}, as can a deficiency of iron, calcium, and vitamin B_6. Stomach surgery will also impair absorption, making the use of injections and lozenges necessary. Problems with gastric secretion, pancreatic secretion, or malabsorption can lead to vitamin B_{12} deficiency in one to three years.

DOSAGE AND TOXICITY. The 1997–98 RDA for vitamin B_{12} is 2.4 micrograms for adult males and females. The normal daily intake of vitamin B_{12} of nonvegetarians is 3 to 7 micrograms.

A vegetarian or macrobiotic diet frequently is low in vitamin B_{12} and high in folic acid, which may mask a vitamin B_{12} deficiency. Vegetarians who regularly eat eggs and foods made with eggs should be fine; others must supplement. Some clinicians suggest at least 100 micrograms per day. Methylcobalamin, rather than cyanocobalamin, is the preferred form, taken as a sublingual tablet.

Vitamin B_{12} has no known toxicity.

DEFICIENCY EFFECTS AND SYMPTOMS. Symptoms of a vitamin B_{12} deficiency often take three to five years to manifest but may occur sooner, after the body's supply from natural sources has been restricted. The brain and nervous system are first affected by vitamin B_{12} deficiency, which results in faulty formation of nerve cells. There may be soreness and weakness in the legs and arms, diminished reflex response and sensory perception, difficulty walking and speaking (stammering), jerking of limbs, memory loss, weakness and fatigue, disorientation, neuritis, and impaired touch or pain perception, occurring in various degrees and combinations. Burning of the mouth has been traced to B_{12} deficiency. In the elderly, who commonly are deficient in B_{12}, symptoms of impaired mental function can mimic Alzheimer's disease. Deficiency of B_{12} is also a major cause of depression in this older population group. In addition, a lack of B_{12} has been found to cause a type of brain damage resembling schizophrenia.

The classic symptom of vitamin B_{12} deficiency is pernicious anemia. Because of its role in supporting normal cell replication of the DNA, a deficiency of B_{12} will impair the development of the rapidly growing blood cells in bone marrow, a condition that produces a type of anemia characterized by large, immature red blood cells. A blood sample alone cannot be used to assess vitamin B_{12} status, because high amounts of folic acid can mask a deficiency of B_{12}. Folic acid is able to prevent the indicative changes in red blood cells that are a sign of anemia. However, folic acid does not prevent damage to the brain that is associated with a lack of B_{12}. When folic acid masks a B_{12} deficiency, the attention of a skilled physician is needed. If folic acid is given when B_{12} is needed, neurological paralysis and permanent nerve damage can result.

BENEFICIAL EFFECTS ON AILMENTS. The primary form of synthetic vitamin B_{12} is cyanocobalamin, which the body must first convert to an active form. However, an active form of B_{12} is available commercially in tablet form, methylcobalamin. Taking vitamin B_{12} orally is reliable and effective in the appropriate dosage, even in the absence of intrinsic factor; taking injections of the vitamin is not necessary. Pernicious anemia is treated with 2,000 micrograms a day for at least one month and then 1,000 micrograms daily.

Vitamin B$_{12}$ is known for its beneficial effect on disturbances of the nervous system and on brain deficiencies. Vitamin B$_{12}$ alleviates neuropsychiatric disorders and prevents mental deterioration. It has provided relief of the following symptoms: increased nervous irritability, mild impairment in memory, inability to concentrate, mental depression, insomnia, and lack of balance. Correcting deficiency of B$_{12}$ is also helpful in the treatment of tinnitus.

Chronic fatigue syndrome is helped with B$_{12}$, which stimulates metabolism. A dose of 1,000 micrograms in lozenge form has been used effectively. Vitamin B$_{12}$ seems to accelerate and restore appetite and vigor. Diabetic neuropathy is aided. In addition, B$_{12}$ can help cold sores and shingles. Similar to folic acid, vitamin B$_{12}$ has been effective in the treatment of the intestinal syndrome sprue. It can help patients recover faster from viral and bacterial diseases and sometimes from surgical procedures. Vitamin B$_{12}$ has been shown to be especially helpful in treating childhood asthma and can also be used to block the effects of sulfites in sulfite-sensitive persons. Sulfite food additives can cause headaches, runny nose, congestion, and bronchial spasms. Research also shows that treatment with B$_{12}$ can raise sperm count. Low blood levels of B$_{12}$ and disturbed B$_{12}$ metabolism are sometimes associated with multiple sclerosis, and research suggests that a deficiency of this nutrient plays a role in the pathogenesis of this condition. Oral doses have been shown to improve both visual and auditory potentials.

The secretion of melatonin, a hormone that influences sleep-waking cycles, is influenced by vitamin B$_{12}$. A low level of melatonin in the elderly is treated with B$_{12}$ to correct sleep disorders.

Vitamin B$_{12}$ plays a role in the prevention of atherosclerosis by helping maintain lower blood levels of homocysteine, associated with a higher risk of heart disease. Adequate folic acid and vitamin B$_6$ are also necessary in this context as they assist in lowering the elevated levels of homocysteine associated with this disease.

Folate

DESCRIPTION.   Folate, also called folic acid and folicin, is a family of water-soluble compounds with a common molecular structure. These terms have their origin in the Latin word *folium*, which means "leaf," because folic acid was first extracted from spinach. Green leafy plants such as spinach, kale, beet greens, and mustard greens are a good source of this nutrient as are brewer's yeast, legumes, liver, brown rice, and oranges. Folic acid has also been added to the list of fortifiers in products such as breakfast cereals and commercial breads.

Folic acid is a carbon carrier, able to donate or receive a one-carbon group, also called a methyl group. Folate also participates in the synthesis of the amino acid methionine and certain nucleic acids. In these capacities, folic acid is central to the manufacture of neurotransmitters and DNA. Folate is a key element in the enzyme that makes DNA replication possible. This nutrient plays a role particularly in rapidly dividing cells, including cells of the gastrointestinal tract, germinal cells, and blood cells. Folate is essential for the formation of heme, the iron-containing protein found in hemoglobin, necessary for the formation of red blood cells.

Folic acid is also involved in the formation of myelin, making it necessary for proper brain function. It is concentrated in the spinal fluid and extracellular fluids and is essential for mental and emotional health. Folate also increases appetite and stimulates production of hydrochloric acid. In addition, it supports liver function. The formation of glutathione, a powerful antioxidant, is also indirectly dependent on this nutrient.

Folic acid is easily destroyed by exposure to light or heat.

ABSORPTION AND STORAGE.   Folic acid is absorbed from the small intestine by active transport and diffusion through the vascular system. Small amounts are stored in the liver and other tissues, while excess is excreted in the urine.

Various substances may interfere with the absorption or function of folic acid, including estrogens prescribed for contraception and hormone replacement therapy, chemotherapy medications such as methotrexate, anticonvulsant drugs, and barbiturates. Conditions of the digestive tract that interfere with absorption of food can impair absorption. These include sprue, celiac disease, and any illness accompanied by vomiting or diarrhea. Sulfa drugs, such as sulfasalazine used to treat ulcerative colitis and Crohn's disease, may interfere with bacteria in the intestines, which manufacture folic acid. Alcohol impedes the absorption of folate as well as increasing its excretion. Smoking also has a negative effect.

DOSAGE AND TOXICITY.   The RDA for folate is 400 micrograms daily for adult men and women. However, requirements can vary with individual metabolic rates. Hemolytic anemia and hyperthyroidism need higher quantities. Stress and disease increase the body's need for folic acid, as does the consumption of alcohol and the use of medications such as dilantin, phenobarbital, primidone, triamterene, oral contraceptives, and sulfasalazine. Folic acid increases sensitivities to estrogen. Always consult a physician before starting any new therapy.

There is no known toxicity of this vitamin. However, high doses—up to 15 milligrams a day in sensitive persons—may result in nausea, loss of appetite, flatulance, insomnia, and irritability. In addition, large doses given to epileptics may trigger seizures. Another problem with excessive intake of folic acid is that it can mask a vitamin B_{12} deficiency. Either folate or vitamin B_{12} deficiency can lead to macrocytic anemia. Supplementing with folate will correct this condition, but if there is also an underlying deficiency of B_{12} that is not detected, permanent damage to the nervous system due to the lack of B_{12} can occur. Because of their close relationship, vitamin B_{12}, in almost every case, should accompany any folic acid therapy, especially when taking folic acid in high doses. The most active form of folic acid is folinic acid, which is most efficient at increasing the amount stored in the body.

DEFICIENCY EFFECTS AND SYMPTOMS. Deficiency of folic acid is quite common. A folic acid deficiency results mostly from an unbalanced diet but can also be the result of taking certain medications, estrogen, and other substances. Excessive intake of beverages that act as a diuretic, such as coffee, can contribute to lower stores of this nutrient. A deficiency of B_{12} can also cause a folic acid deficiency.

A lack of folate has the greatest impact on cells that are rapidly dividing, such as in the digestive system, the genital tract, and red blood cells. Consequently, symptoms of folic acid deficiency may manifest as gastrointestinal disturbances such as diarrhea, lesions and impaired absorption, gingivitis and glossitis (tongue inflammation), and lesions at the corner of the mouth (cheilosis). Other signs include anemia, an abnormal Pap smear for women, and poor growth. There may also be shortness of breath and fatigue accompanying anemia, loss of appetite, and adverse effects on cognition and mood, such as forgetfulness, depression, and irritability.

Pregnancy can put women at risk for a deficiency. The fetus, meeting its needs for rapid growth, easily depletes the mother's reserves. The World Health Organization (WHO) reports that one-third to one-half of pregnant women are folic acid–deficient in the last three months of pregnancy. Almost any interference with the metabolism, or neural tube defects of folic acid in the fetus, encourages deformities such as cleft palate, brain damage, spina bifida, slow development, and poor learning ability in the child. A deficiency has been found in mentally retarded children. In addition, a deficiency may lead to toxemia, premature birth, afterbirth hemorrhaging, and megaloblastic anemia in both the mother and the child. Deficiency, whether or not during pregnancy, increases the chance of cervical cancer and of dysplasia, which often leads to cancer.

A deficiency has been found in people with ailments such as Hodgkin's disease and leukemia, in which the requirement for folic acid is above normal. Alcoholics are prone to be deficient in folic acid. The elderly, because of poor diet, malabsorption, and drug interactions, are at risk.

BENEFICIAL EFFECTS ON AILMENTS. Folic acid prevents spina bifida and other neural tube defects, potentially reducing the incidence of these conditions by up to 80 percent. Conversely, having an insufficient amount of this nutrient can lead to abnormal development of the spinal cord and brain in the embryonic stage of fetal development. Because the damage can occur at this early stage, the recommendation is that all women of childbearing age, even before becoming pregnant, consume 400 micrograms of folic acid daily. During pregnancy 600 micrograms daily are recommended and during lactation, 500 micrograms daily. In addition, abortion and miscarriage have been averted when folate was supplemented.

Folate is used to improve or normalize Pap smears of women diagnosed with cervical dysplasia. This condition is considered precancerous. Folic acid also protects against melanoma and cancer of squamous cells due to smoking. This nutrient also acts as a mild antidepressant.

Folic acid plays a role in the prevention of cardiovascular disease by facilitating the conversion of homocysteine into methionine. An increased concentration of homocysteine in the blood can potentially damage arteries. In addition, because homocysteine plays a role in the development of osteoporosis, having sufficient levels of folate may reduce the risk of this disease as well. The conversion of homocysteine to methionine requires vitamin B_{12}. In patients suffering from atherosclerosis, folate may also improve circulation, visual acuity, and skin temperature.

Folic acid prevents and treats megaloblastic anemia. Gargling with a high-folate mouthwash helps reduce gum inflammation. And folate taken with B_{12} benefits arthritis.

Biotin

DESCRIPTION. Biotin is a water-soluble B-complex vitamin and one of the most stable of this group of nutrients. Biotin plays a role in the metabolism of fats, sugar, and protein. As a coenzyme, it assists in the making of fatty acids and nucleic acids, and in the oxidation of fatty acids and carbohydrates. Without biotin, the body's fat production is impaired. It also aids in the utilization of protein, folic acid, pantothenic acid, and vitamin B_{12}.

Biotin is in all animal and plant tissue. The primary source of biotin is the biotin produced by intestinal bacteria in the gut. While many foods contain biotin, the vitamin is often present only in trace amounts. Rich food sources include egg yolks, pork and lamb liver, sardines, peanuts, cauliflower, mushrooms, milk, soybeans, lentils, unpolished rice, whole wheat, and brewer's yeast.

ABSORPTION AND STORAGE. Some biotin is absorbed in the intestines but much is excreted readily via the kidneys. Biotin is stored mainly in the liver, kidney, brain, and adrenal glands. A vegetarian diet enhances the synthesis and promotes the absorption of biotin due to changes in the gut bacteria resulting from this way of eating. However, antibiotics interfere with the production of the intestinal bacteria from which biotin is produced. Alcohol also interferes with the absorption and utilization of biotin.

DOSAGE AND TOXICITY. The 1997–98 DRI suggested intake of biotin for adult males and females is 30 micrograms per day. The average American diet supplies approximately 30 to 40 micrograms a day. Biotin is not toxic, even in high amounts.

DEFICIENCY EFFECTS AND SYMPTOMS. A deficiency of biotin is uncommon. However, deficiency can arise when an individual is taking antibiotics such as sulfonamides or oxytetracycline, which diminish the growth of biotin-producing bacteria in the gut. A deficiency can also develop by consuming large amounts of raw egg white over an extended period of time, because egg white contains the protein avidin, which binds with biotin and prevents its absorption. Cooked egg whites do not present this problem, because cooking deactivates avidin.

Deficiencies of biotin have occurred in infants and in hospitalized patients being fed by tube or intravenously. People who are on low-calorie diets are also at risk.

Biotin deficiency mainly affects the skin and hair. Symptoms include dry skin, dermatitis, grayish skin, a rash around the nose and mouth, and progressive loss of hair and hair color. Other symptoms include muscular pain, poor appetite, lack of energy, sleeplessness, a disturbed nervous system, and depression. In severe deficiency, there may be impairment of fat metabolism. A lowered hemoglobin level, a raised cholesterol level, and a decrease in biotin excretion are signs of biotin deficiency. Male genitalia, bone marrow, and the liver and kidneys are also targets of biotin deficiency.

BENEFICIAL EFFECTS ON AILMENTS. Because of biotin's participation in the metabolism of fats, carbohydrates, and protein, it is used for the treatment of skin conditions, graying hair or baldness, and diabetes. Dermatitis has shown improvement when treated with biotin. Riboflavin, niacin, vitamin B_6, vitamin A, and vitamin D work together with biotin for healthy skin.

Biotin has been used to treat baldness, but supplementation will only reverse this condition if baldness is caused by biotin deficiency. Many hair treatments contain biotin for healthy hair. Biotin also promotes strong nails by increasing their thickness.

Research indicates that biotin enhances the sensitivity of cells to insulin and increases the activity of an enzyme that enables the liver to make use of glucose. Both type I and type II diabetics taking supplemental biotin experienced an improvement in their control of blood glucose. In addition, large doses of biotin have been useful in the treatment of diabetic neuropathy.

Bioflavonoids

DESCRIPTION. Bioflavonoids are one component of a group of plant pigments known as flavonoids. Bioflavonoids, which are not strictly considered vitamins, include nutrients such as rutin, hesperidin, quercetin, and naringin. They are water soluble and are usually found with vitamin C in many fruits and vegetables. Citrus fruits are a primary source, especially oranges, grapefruit, and lemon. There is ten times the concentration of bioflavonoids in the edible pith and membranes of the fruit than in the strained juices. Garlic and onion are sources of quercetin. Other foods that contain bioflavonoids are grapes, plums, black currants, apricots, buckwheat, cherries, blackberries, and rose hips.

Bioflavonoids aid in the absorption of vitamin C and protect it from oxidation, thereby enhancing its effectiveness. The primary role of bioflavonoids in the body is to strengthen capillary walls and regulate their permeability. Bioflavonoids may assist vitamin C in keeping collagen, the intracellular cement, in healthy condition. These actions help prevent hemorrhages and ruptures in the capillaries and connective tissues and build a protective barrier against infection.

ABSORPTION AND STORAGE. The absorption and storage properties of bioflavonoids are very similar to those of vitamin C. They are readily absorbed from the gastrointestinal tract into the bloodstream. Excessive amounts are excreted through urination and perspiration.

DOSAGE AND TOXICITY. There is no RDA for bioflavonoids. A typical therapeutic dosage is 500 milligrams bioflavonoids taken one to three times a day. Supplements also are available in 125- and 250-milligram dosages. In clinical research, a standardized mixture of rutin compounds, equivalent to 2,000 to 6,000 milligrams of bioflavonoids, is used to treat venous insufficiency and hemorrhoids. Citrus bioflavonoids are considered extremely safe and do not cause side effects even during pregnancy.

DEFICIENCY EFFECTS AND SYMPTOMS. Symptoms of a bioflavonoid deficiency are closely related to those of a vitamin C deficiency. Especially of note is the increased tendency to bleed or hemorrhage and bruise easily. A deficiency may also make inflammation such as that associated with arthritis more likely.

BENEFICIAL EFFECTS ON AILMENTS. Because bioflavonoids have beneficial effects on capillary permeability and blood flow, they have proved to be beneficial in treating various degrees of capillary fragility and have been found to minimize bruising that occurs in contact sports and in those who bruise easily. Rutin is especially helpful in the prevention of recurrent bleeding arising from weakened blood vessels and in the treatment for varicose veins, hemorrhoids, night cramps, and other circulatory problems. Bioflavonoids have also been used successfully to treat weakness of the capillaries associated with ulcers. And the blood vessel disorder of the eye that affects diabetics seems to respond to bioflavonoid/vitamin C treatment. Bleeding gums can also be helped with bioflavonoids.

In France, bioflavonoids have been used successfully for a number of gynecological problems. Physicians have found that these compounds effectively replace hormone therapy in cases of irregular or painful menstrual flow not caused by anatomical damage. Some of the compounds have prevented bleeding and regulated menstrual flow after insertion of intrauterine contraceptive devices. Bioflavonoids and vitamin C, taken together, may help prevent repeated miscarriages.

Dr. Carl Pfeiffer has used rutin, at an oral dose of 50 milligrams, for depressed patients. His studies have shown that rutin has a sedative-stimulant effect on the brain. There are also indications that rutin, in oral doses of 60 milligrams, raises blood histamine and lowers serum copper in the body, helpful for certain schizophrenics.

Similar to quercetin, bioflavonoids also possess some anti-inflammatory action and are antiallergy. Asthma has been successfully treated by the administration of bioflavonoids.

Vitamin C (Ascorbic Acid)

DESCRIPTION. Vitamin C is a water-soluble compound that most mammals are able to synthesize from glucose. However, humans, because of a missing enzyme, do not produce endogenous vitamin C and must rely on diet or supplements as their source. Although fairly stable in acid solution, vitamin C is normally the least stable of vitamins and is very sensitive to oxygen. Its potency can be lost through exposure to light, heat, and air, which stimulate the activity of oxidative enzymes.

The adrenal glands use the most vitamin C, with the brain the next biggest user. While citrus is well known as a good source of vitamin C, many fruits and vegetables can have even higher amounts. Sweet red peppers, kale and other dark leafy greens, broccoli, cauliflower, and brussels sprouts are all excellent sources. Fruit high in vitamin C include guava, persimmons, strawberries, and papaya.

The primary function of vitamin C is the manufacture of collagen, a protein necessary for the formation of connective tissue, tendons, and cartilage. Consequently, vitamin C plays a role in healing wounds and burns, facilitating the formation of connective tissue in the scar. Vitamin C also helps maintain healthy gums. Vitamin C is needed to form the collagen in blood vessel walls that helps them expand and contract and also helps maintain capillary walls, which tend to be fragile. In this way, vitamin C helps prevent easy bruising.

Another major role of vitamin C is as an antioxidant. In this capacity, it helps prevent aging of body tissues and cancer. Vitamin C fights bacterial infections, is frequently used in preventing and treating the common cold, and reduces the effects on the body of some allergy-producing substances, acting as an antihistamine and reducing the use of antihistamine medication. Vitamin C also aids in the formation of red blood cells and prevents hemorrhaging.

Vitamin C interacts with several nutrients. It is necessary for the conversion of the inactive form of folic acid into its biologically active form, folinic acid. In its antioxidant role, it protects thiamin, riboflavin, folic acid, pantothenic acid, and vitamins A and E from oxidation. Vitamin C is necessary for the conversion of tryptophan into serotonin, the hormone that regulates sleep. It promotes the absorption of iron, calcium, and possibly manganese, and taking a large amount of vitamin C may reduce serum levels of selenium and copper. Vitamin C protects against the toxic effects of heavy metals such as cadmium and mercury.

ABSORPTION AND STORAGE.   Vitamin C is absorbed through the mucous membranes of the mouth, stomach, and upper part of the small intestine. The larger the dose, the less is absorbed. For example, when taking 250 milligrams or less, 80 percent is absorbed while a dose of up to 2 grams results in about 50 percent absorption. If large doses of vitamin C are required for therapeutic treatment, injection of the vitamin into the bloodstream is more effective than when the same amount is taken orally.

The vitamin C that is not retained is excreted in the urine and in perspiration. Of note, increased urinary output due to ingesting a large dose is not an indication that body tissues are saturated. When a moderate amount of vitamin C is taken, blood levels peak two to three hours after ingestion. Most of the vitamin has been excreted from the body in three to four hours, which is why it must be supplied several times throughout the day. To maintain adequate serum level, the vitamin should be taken at three- to four-hour intervals. The blood level of vitamin C will return to its average level in twelve to thirteen hours after ingestion regardless of the amount taken.

The normal human body, when fully saturated with vitamin C, contains about 5,000 milligrams of the nutrient, of which 30 milligrams are found in the adrenal glands, 200 milligrams in the extracellular fluids, and the rest distributed in varying concentrations through the cells of the body. However, the amount of vitamin C absorbed or retained can be affected by various factors. The body's ability to absorb vitamin C is reduced by smoking, stress, high fever, and gasoline fumes. Sulfa drugs increase urinary output by two to three times the normal amount. In addition, drinking excessive amounts of water will deplete the vitamin.

How much vitamin C is present in food so that it can be absorbed into the system is also variable, depending upon how the food was handled before it reaches the dinner plate. Because vitamin C is vulnerable to light, air, and heat, the amount of the vitamin in foods can deteriorate rapidly during transport, processing, storage, and such food preparation procedures as cutting and cooking. In addition, baking soda added to vegetables to retain their green color creates an alkaline medium that destroys vitamin C. Cooking in copper utensils will destroy a food's vitamin C content.

Preferable ways of preparing foods to preserve vitamin C are microwaving, steaming, and stir-frying. The fresher and less cooked foods are, the better. Orange juice, if covered when stored in the refrigerator, will retain its vitamin C content for several days. The stalks of broccoli retain their stores much better than the florets. While spinach loses 105 milligrams of its vitamin C within ten days, sweet peppers can be stored for three weeks with little loss.

DOSAGE AND TOXICITY.   The National Research Council offers a RDA of 60 milligrams of vitamin C for adults. However, the ongoing debate over the actual amount a given individual may require continues. Research by Dr. Mark Levine conducted at the National Institutes of Health (NIH) found that seven healthy males needed 200 milligrams per day. In addition, it is known that animals normally produce amounts of vitamin C relatively much higher than the doses suggested for humans. Dogs and cats produce five to eight times the amount of vitamin C suggested in the current RDA for humans, and goats produce 30 to 190 times the amount.

Vitamin C requirements in humans may vary with weight, amount of activity, rate of metabolism, ailments, and age. Periods of stress such as anxiety, infection, injury, surgery, burns, or fatigue increase the body's need for this vitamin. Estrogen therapy increases the need for vitamin C as well as B$_6$. In addition, individuals who are hypoglycemic or are on a high-protein diet need more vitamin C because these conditions interfere with vitamin C metabolism. Elevated blood levels of iron require more vitamin C. More vitamin C may also be needed when copper serum levels are high, which may be the case for smokers and women who take contraceptive pills, are menstruating, or are in the last months of pregnancy. In the latter case, consulting with a physician is recommended before increasing vitamin C.

When vitamin C is given for therapeutic reasons, taking a sufficiently high dose is very important to ensure effectiveness. Higher doses are required for treating extremely high or low temperatures; toxic levels of lead, mercury, or cadmium; and chronic use of medications such as aspirin and barbiturates. When megavitamin doses are given, it is important that calcium intake also be increased.

Large doses of vitamin C may cause side effects in some people. Symptoms can include a slight burning sensation during urination, loose bowels or diarrhea, intestinal gas or abdominal pain, skin rashes, and nausea. When symptoms occur, dosage should be reduced. It can also be helpful to take the vitamin after a meal for better assimilation of the vitamin C and to experiment with various forms of supplemental vitamin C to find the one that is best tolerated.

There have been worries that taking high-dosage vitamin C therapy can lead to the formation of kidney stones in the general population. But recent research indicates that only in certain cases is this potentially a problem—in persons with recurrent kidney stones, with severe kidney disease, with gout, or on hemodialysis. For susceptible individuals, vitamin C in the form of sodium ascorbate is recommended. Megadoses of vitamin C may also cause hemolytic anemia, the breakdown of red blood cells, in certain ethnic groups, including African Americans, Africans, Sephardic Jews, and Asians. Those with sickle cell anemia are especially vulnerable.

Another concern is that vitamin C can alter laboratory test results, specifically a false reading for the glucose oxidase test (except the hexokinase test) and the test for blood in the feces. Taking too much of the vitamin may increase iron absorption, leading to an overdose of this mineral.

Lowering the dosage of vitamin C after ingestion of high doses can result in symptoms of scurvy. This is especially true for newborns. Slow reduction of the vitamin over time is important to allow the body to adjust.

DEFICIENCY EFFECTS AND SYMPTOMS.

The condition of classic vitamin C deficiency is known as scurvy, which occurs when the total body stores of the vitamin decline to about 300 milligrams. Some of the first signs of vitamin C deficiency are fatigue, weakness, and lethargy. Other symptoms are loss of appetite, swollen legs and arms, depression, and shortness of breath. Even minimal vitamin C deficiency can cause gum disorders that allow bacteria and toxic substances into the tissues, causing periodontal disease and associated bleeding gums. Other symptoms of vitamin C insufficiency can include impaired wound healing, easy bruising, frequent infections, dry and scaly skin, swollen and tender joints, muscle cramps, loose teeth, and cardiovascular disease.

Smoking lowers the level of vitamin C, and alcoholics typically have very low blood levels of the vitamin because the body uses so much of the vitamin to counteract the toxic effects of alcohol. The elderly and chronically ill can develop scurvy. Dental and orthopedic patients, cancer patients, and those undergoing dialysis are subject to deficiencies.

BENEFICIAL EFFECTS ON AILMENTS.

Because of the antioxidant and immune-enhancing abilities of vitamin C, this multifunctional nutrient is useful in the prevention and treatment of a wide variety of conditions. Vitamin C combats heart disease by strengthening the arteries, raising desirable HDL cholesterol while lowering total cholesterol, reducing blood pressure, acting as an antioxidant, and helping prevent blood clots by inhibiting platelet aggregation. Research shows that high doses of vitamin C help lower histamine levels in asthmatics.

Vitamin C fights infection by increasing white blood cell function and activity and raising the level of interferon, the body's natural anticancer and antiviral compound. Taken at the first sign of infection, vitamin C may reduce the severity and duration of the common cold. It is also useful in the treatment of herpes, vaccinia, hepatitis, polio, encephalitis, measles, pneumonia, and AIDS. Vitamin C, once it is catalyzed by copper ions, reduces oxygen molecules to molecules that in turn attack the nucleic acid of the virus. Vitamin C works against bacteria in the same way for the treatment of tuberculosis, diphtheria, tetanus, staphylococcus, and typhoid fever.

As an antioxidant, vitamin C is useful in the treatment of alcoholic liver disease due to its ability to raise tissue glutathione levels. In addition, massive doses of vitamin C have been used to cure drug addicts, including users of heroin, methadone, and barbiturates. New research also suggests that vitamin C, working as an antioxidant, can slow down the progression of Parkinson's disease in patients not yet taking medication for treatment.

Acting as an antioxidant and protecting DNA from damage, vitamin C may lower the risk of many forms of cancer. In various studies, vitamin C offered protection against cancers of the digestive tract, lung cancer, cervical and breast cancer, and pancreatic cancer. Vitamin C also lowers cancer risk by preventing the formation of carcinogenic nitrosamines from nitrites and nitrates found in some foods such as cured meats. And vitamin C minimizes the effects of environmental airborne pollution, including carbon monoxide and cigarette smoke. In the treatment of cancer, at a minimum, vitamin C enhances immune function. Several studies also have shown that in some instances, vitamin C increases length of survival of cancer patients. Vitamin C protects against the harmful effects of toxins such as cadmium, mercury, lead, iron, copper, arsenic, benzene, and some pesticides.

And the long list of benefits of vitamin C continues. Arthritis sufferers benefit from vitamin C. The lubricating fluid of joints (synovial fluid) becomes thinner (allowing freer movement) when the serum levels of ascorbic acid are high, thereby giving pain relief. Physicians in Scotland report that vitamin C counteracts bleeding in the gastrointestinal tract caused by aspirin or alcohol. It has been used successfully to treat snake and spider bites, insect stings, and rabies. A combination of vitamin C, vitamin E, and bioflavonoids has been used in the treatment of varicose veins. Vitamin C helps overcome male infertility. The vitamin enhances the use of zinc, magnesium, copper, and potassium, all vital to normal sperm function. The risk of cataracts and macular degeneration is lower when vitamin C intake is high, and vitamin C is used in the treatment of these conditions. And as a builder of collagen, vitamin C speeds the healing of tissues due to wounds, burns, or frostbite.

More than average intake of vitamin C helps preserve the integrity of intervertebral disks and helps prevent back problems. For diabetics with bleeding gums, slow wound healing, and rapidly aging skin, vitamin C may be helpful. Russian athletes use the vitamin to build muscle tissue.

Vitamin C can reduce the amount needed of some drugs, including L-dopa and painkillers given to cancer patients, as the vitamin prevents certain enzymes from breaking down the natural painkilling compounds of the brain. Vitamin C enhances the effectiveness of antipsychotic drugs such as haloperidol, requiring less of the drug, potentially decreasing side effects. Vitamin C alone has been shown to decrease psychoticlike behavior. And large doses of vitamin C help reduce levels of vanadium, which has been associated with manic-depressive disorder. Defects in water and electrolyte metabolism are involved.

Vitamin C helps victims of shock from injury, electric voltage, and lightning. It prevents prickly heat and heat stroke. Leukemia, pancreatitis, asthma, and rheumatic heart disease respond well to vitamin C therapy. Powdered vitamin C mixed with water to form a paste and then applied on the skin will clear up poison ivy or poison oak in twenty-four hours if adequate oral doses of the vitamin are taken at the same time.

The most economical and commonly used form of vitamin C is ascorbic acid. Vitamin C is also available buffered, combined with a mineral to reduce its acidity. This form is useful for people whose stomachs are bothered by vitamin C and for people needing to restore acid-alkaline balance. Combining vitamin C with bioflavonoids can increase absorption if the amount of bioflavonoids is equal to or greater than the amount of vitamin C.

Choline

DESCRIPTION.   Choline has only recently been recognized as essential for human health. Choline exists in the diet in two forms, as free choline and as lecithin or phosphatidylcholine, a fatty substance consisting of a phosphate group, two fatty acids, and choline. The human body is also able to manufacture lecithin, a process that occurs in the liver where this substance is especially needed. Lecithin prevents fats from accumulating in this organ and is also important for bile metabolism and kidney health. It is also an emulsifying agent, acting as a bridge that joins water to fat. It keeps fats in solution in the blood and in other body fluids. Lecithin also facilitates the movement of fats into the cells.

Choline, which is referred to as one of the lipotropic B vitamins, is necessary for the metabolism of fats and plays an important role in the transmission of nerve impulses. For this reason, choline is referred to as the "memory vitamin." It is also essential for the health of the myelin sheaths of the nerves, which are the principal components of nerve fibers. Choline's principal uses are in the treatment of elevated cholesterol levels, liver disorders, Alzheimer's disease, and bipolar disorder.

Free choline is found in foods such as whole grains, vegetables like lettuce and cauliflower, peanuts, grape juice, soybeans, and beef liver. However, during food preparation, choline may leach into water or be destroyed by cooking or storage. The choline-containing compound lecithin is present in especially high amounts in egg yolk and beef liver but is also present in much smaller amounts in such foods as potatoes, oranges, and apples. Certain commercial food products also contain lecithin, added as an emulsifier to fatty foods such as ice cream, chocolate, margarine, and mayonnaise.

ABSORPTION AND STORAGE.   Choline is readily absorbed from the intestines. It also is one of the few vitamins able to cross the blood-brain barrier where it participates in brain chemistry. The body absorbs free choline and choline as a component of lecithin. Once ingested, lecithin breaks down into its component parts, including choline. Any lecithin the body requires is manufactured by the liver. The liver can also manufacture choline, from either of two amino acids, methionine or serine, plus vitamin B_{12} and folic acid. Choline is present in all living cells.

DOSAGE AND TOXICITY.   The 1997–98 DRI for choline is 550 milligrams for adult males and 425 milligrams for adult females. Lower values are set for children, ranging from 200 to 250 milligrams, while higher levels are set for pregnant or lactating women, 450 milligrams and 550 milligrams respectively. The average diet has been estimated to contain 400 to 900 milligrams of choline per day. Usual therapeutic doses range from 500 to 1,000 milligrams.

While choline has no known toxic effects, prolonged ingestion of massive doses of isolated choline may induce a deficiency of vitamin B_6 and could aggravate symptoms of epilepsy. Large doses of supplemental lecithin can cause digestive upset, sweating, salivation, and loss of appetite. It is important to remember that B-complex vitamins, including choline, function better when all are taken together.

Choline in rare instances will cause the body to have a fish odor, which indicates that intake should be lowered or discontinued since there may be an enzyme disorder. Also rare is depression caused by large doses of choline.

DEFICIENCY EFFECTS AND SYMPTOMS. A choline deficiency is associated with fatty deposits in the liver and cirrhosis, bleeding stomach ulcers, high blood pressure, hardening of the arteries and atherosclerosis, and blockage of the tubes of the kidneys. Insufficient supplies of choline may cause hemorrhaging of the kidneys. It has also been suggested that choline deficiency contributes to the development of Alzheimer's disease, due in part to a relative deficiency of acetylcholine in the brain. One origin of choline deficiency can be a diet containing too little protein.

BENEFICIAL EFFECTS ON AILMENTS. Disorders of the liver are treated with choline. It can be used to treat fatty liver, liver damage, cirrhosis of the liver, and hepatitis as it improves the emulsification of fat as well as its transport and use. By decongesting the liver, choline may also be helpful in detoxification therapies. It is also used for kidney damage, hemorrhaging of the kidneys, and nephritis. Dietary phosphatidylcholine has been helpful in the treatment of gallstones.

Choline is used to treat atherosclerosis and hardening of the arteries. It has been successful in reducing high blood pressure because it strengthens weak capillary walls. Symptoms such as heart palpitation as well as dizziness, headaches, and constipation have been relieved or removed entirely within five to ten days after administration of choline treatments. Insomnia, visual disturbances, and blood flow to the eyes have also benefited from choline therapy. And AL 721, a phosphatidylcholine-containing lipid aggregate prevents the replication of the HIV virus, has antiviral activity, and is useful in the treatment of AIDS.

Choline is called the memory vitamin because of the role it plays in brain function, improving memory as well as aiding the brain's ability to reason and learn. However, studies show mixed results for the use of choline to treat Alzheimer's disease. While the brain tissues of these patients have decreased levels of the choline compound and neurotransmitter acetylcholine, diminished memory may actually be due to impaired activity of an enzyme. While supplemental phosphatidylcholine may be useful to treat mild to moderate dementia, using 15 to 25 grams a day as a two-week trial, further research is needed to determine choline's value in treating Alzheimer's.

In some patients, supplementing with phosphatidylcholine is effective in treating manic depression, also called bipolar disorder, significantly improving this condition or lessening symptoms of the manic phase.

Choline and inositol are useful in the treatment of diabetes. A dose of 1,000 milligrams of choline and 500 milligrams of inositol aids in hypoglycemia. This vitamin also offers nutrition support for women and along with pantothenic acid, aids glaucoma. Because of choline's ability to increase acetylcholine levels, it is also useful in the treatment of myasthenia gravis (weakening of the muscles).

Supplemental choline and phosphatidylcholine have been found to be helpful in the treatment of tardive dyskenesia, Parkinson's disease, Huntington's disease, Tourette's syndrome, and familial spinocerebellar degeneration (Frederick's ataxia). Lecithin can prevent morphine dependence and facilitate withdrawal using the AL 721 source. Lecithin has also been found to reduce levels of LDL cholesterol.

Vitamin D

DESCRIPTION. Vitamin D is not one nutrient but a group of related vitamins that are fat soluble and belong to the class of substances known as sterols. Vitamin D_2 is the form of vitamin D known as ergocalciferol, the kind added to food products to fortify them with the vitamin and the form most often used in supplements. Fortified orange juice is a new dietary source of vitamin D. Vitamin D_3, known as cholecalciferol, is the natural form and is present in foods such as cold-water fish, egg yolks, and butter.

Vitamin D is also produced in the body in a process that begins when the skin is exposed to ultraviolet light. For this reason vitamin D is referred to as the "sunshine vitamin." The sun's rays activate a form of cholesterol (one of many beneficial functions of cholesterol), converting it to cholecalciferol. This compound then travels to the liver and kidneys and is converted to two active forms of circulating vitamin D, 25-hydroxycholecalciferol and 1,25-dihydroxycholecalciferol.

A unique aspect of vitamin D is that it functions very much like a hormone and has been referred to as one, as it targets organs such as the kidneys and intestines. Other target tissues are the brain, pancreas, skin, bones, reproductive organs, and some cancer cells. Vitamin D may also enhance immune function when coupled with vitamin A.

Vitamin D is one of a growing list of nutrients now recognized for their ability to maintain bone growth and health. Specifically, vitamin D promotes bone mineralization by helping synthesize those enzymes in the mucous membranes that are involved in the active transport of calcium. Vitamin D is necessary for normal growth in children, for without this nutrient bones and teeth do not calcify properly.

Vitamin D supports bone health in adults as well because of its interaction with calcium and phosphorus. Vitamin D maintains calcium and phosphorus in the blood by stimulating the absorption of these minerals from the gastrointestinal tract, mobilizes calcium and phosphorus out of the bones and into the blood, and stimulates retention of these minerals by the kidneys. Without vitamin D, only 10 percent to 15 percent of dietary calcium is absorbed. By contrast, when there is sufficient vitamin D, 30 percent is absorbed. Vitamin D is also valuable in maintaining a stable nervous system, normal heart action, and normal blood clotting because all these functions are related to the body's supply and utilization of calcium and phosphorus. New research shows that vitamin D may also help prevent certain cancers. Vitamin D is best utilized when taken with vitamin A. Fish-liver oils are the best natural source of both vitamins A and D.

ABSORPTION AND STORAGE.   Vitamin D consumed in food, along with fats, is first emulsified by bile and then absorbed through the intestinal wall and into the circulatory system. In contrast, the vitamin D the body produces is directly absorbed. Next, vitamin D from either source is transported to the liver for storage; other deposits are found in the skin, brain, spleen, and bones.

The amount of vitamin D that reaches target cells can be altered by various factors. Dark-skinned individuals produce less vitamin D than fair-complexioned persons because skin pigment blocks the rays of the sun that initiate manufacture. In the same way, sunscreen rated eight or above prohibits synthesis of the vitamin. The sun's action on the skin can also be inhib-

ited by such factors as smoke, window glass, and clothing. Mineral oil can destroy dietary vitamin D that is already stored in the intestinal tract.

Significant improvement in the absorption of vitamin D has been observed in patients receiving 100 IU of supplemental vitamin D. Cow's milk as well as breast milk does not contain sufficient amounts of vitamin D; both need to be supplemented or fortified.

DOSAGE AND TOXICITY.   The 1997–98 DRI for vitamin D is 5 micrograms of cholecalciferol per day for adult males and females to the age of fifty, 10 micrograms from age fifty-one to seventy, and 15 micrograms above age seventy. (Amounts of vitamin D were formerly expressed in IU. The conversion formula is 100 IU = 2.5 micrograms and 400 IU = 10 micrograms.) The body's needs for vitamin D can be met by exposure to sunlight, which does not pose a toxic threat. Exposure to sunlight for ten to fifteen minutes a day, two to three times a week, is sufficient to maintain good vitamin D nutrition. However, while light-skinned people will synthesize sufficient vitamin D in thirty minutes, to reach the same plateau, dark-skinned people will require three hours of sunshine, so times need to be adjusted according to skin pigmentation.

For those living in cloudy, sunless, or smoggy areas, sufficient vitamin D can be alternatively supplied by diet. Those who live where there is limited sunshine or those who are restricted from obtaining sunlight need about 2 cups of fortified milk a day or adequate egg yolks, fatty fish, and liver, depending on sunshine exposure. Since some of these foods (eggs and liver) are high in cholesterol, personal histories and cholesterol levels should be carefully considered before adding these foods to the diet. Supplements are available either alone or with other nutrients.

Taking extra vitamin D to prevent osteoporosis will be of no benefit if calcium and phosphorus requirements are not met. No extra benefit is obtained from taking more than the RDA except for therapeutic reasons. In excess, vitamin D is the most toxic vitamin of all. Supplements should be used with caution. Dosages greater than 25 micrograms are certainly not recommended. Supplements should be kept out of reach of children. Drops for infants should be carefully monitored. Consult a responsible physician for therapeutic doses.

Excess vitamin D enhances calcium absorption, which can lead to an increase in amounts of calcium in the blood, a potentially dangerous condition known as hypercalcemia. High doses can also lead to calcification of soft tissues and the walls of the blood vessels and kidney tubules as well as formation of kidney stones. Symptoms of acute overdose are increased frequency of urination, loss of appetite, nausea, vomiting, diarrhea, constipation, tiredness, drowsiness, muscular weakness, and dizziness. In more severe cases, symptoms include confusion, high blood pressure, kidney failure, and coma.

Some infants react hyperactively to the amount of vitamin D found in fortified milk that contains 10 micrograms per quart. This reaction could result in further medical complications. Hypercalcemia that has developed in children ingesting average supplementation may be an indication of hyperreactivity to the vitamin. A physician should be consulted for the kind of vitamin D for those who have Down syndrome, since vitamin B$_6$ may be needed.

Absorption problems in some arthritic people may cause an abnormal accumulation of D$_3$. Calcitrol should never be taken without the advice of a physician. Animal sources vary in strength because of differing exposures of the animals to sunlight.

DEFICIENCY EFFECTS AND SYMPTOMS. A deficiency of vitamin D leads to inadequate absorption of calcium from the intestinal tract and retention of phosphorus in the kidney, leading to faulty mineralization of bone structures. Consequently, a vitamin D deficiency in children can lead to rickets and osteomalacia in adults, both involving a softening of the bones. This is mostly likely to occur in women who have continual pregnancies and periods of lactations, and in the elderly who do not receive an adequate amount of sunshine or dietary vitamin D or who cannot absorb this nutrient. There may also be faulty development of tooth structure.

Low calcium related to vitamin D deficiency may also cause tetany, a condition characterized by muscle numbness, tingling, and spasm. Inadequate vitamin D may cause slow, progressive hearing loss and nearsightedness because of loss of calcium from the cochlea, a bone in the middle ear, and changes in eye muscles.

Diseases that affect either the kidneys or the liver may produce the symptoms of deficiency. Alcoholics, those who do not drink milk or have malabsorption problems, and those who take drugs that interfere with absorption (cholestyramine, mineral oil, diphenylhydantoin, and phenobarbital) are at risk for a deficiency. Celiac disease is indirectly related to a vitamin D deficiency resulting from structural damage and unabsorbed fats, calcium salts, and vitamin D that are eliminated in the stool.

Obesity is associated with vitamin D deficiency. The vitamin, whether dietary or manufactured by the body, is stored in body fat and is not bioavailable. With increased fat stores, more of the vitamin is removed from circulation away from tissue that may need it.

All vitamin D deficiency diseases are helped or arrested with vitamin D therapy. However, some damage cannot be rectified.

BENEFICIAL EFFECTS ON AILMENTS. Vitamin D helps prevent and cure rickets, a disease resulting from insufficient calcium, phosphorus, or vitamin D. It also aids in repairing osteomalacia in adults. In addition, both vitamin D and calcium help keep bones strong during menopause. It may be helpful in preventing hip fractures in the elderly. The vitamin also plays an important role in dentition. Besides being necessary for proper tooth eruption and linear growth, it continually strengthens the teeth.

Vitamin D is thought to be an immunomodulator that slows or stops bacteria that cause disease. Vitamins D and A, along with vitamin C, have been beneficial in reducing the incidence of colds. In animal research, vitamin D has also prevented the development of common autoimmune diseases such as type I diabetes, rheumatoid arthritis, and multiple sclerosis in mice prone to these conditions. Vitamin D may also participate in the production of insulin, helping to manage blood glucose levels. Researchers have also reported that acidity of gastric juices is affected by the amount of vitamin D in the diet, increasing the risk of stomach ulcers. Ulcer patients should be checked to see whether their diet supplies a sufficient amount of vitamin D.

According to a recent review paper on vitamin D by Michael F. Holick, one of the most unappreciated functions of 1,25-dihydroxycholecalciferol is its ability to downregulate hyperproliferative cell growth. Both normal and cancer cells often respond to this form of vitamin D. This may be one reason that vitamin D is helpful in treating psoriasis.

Vitamin E

DESCRIPTION. Vitamin E, a fat-soluble compound, is a general term referring to a family of eight related compounds. Knowing the various names for these and what they mean is important in selecting vitamin supplements and making sure to take a variety of these compounds, since in combination they are considered more beneficial than when taken alone.

Vitamin E compounds include the tocopherols (alpha, beta, gamma, and delta) and the tocotrienols (alpha, beta, gamma, and delta). There is also a newly discovered vitamin E, alpha-tocomonoenol, found in fish eggs. Alpha-tocopherol is the most potent form of vitamin E and has the greatest nutritional and biological value. Vitamin E is usually available as the d-isomer of alpha-tocopherol, that is, d-alpha tocopherol, d-alpha tocopheryl acetate, and d-alpha tocopheryl succinate. Vitamin E supplements ideally contain alpha-tocopherols as well as gamma, beta, and delta. The tocotrienols are also ideally taken as a mixture. The natural forms of vitamin E are designated *d-*, while the synthetic forms are designated *l-*. And a dl-alpha-tocopherol contains both forms. In clinical practice, the d-forms are most often used.

The predominant forms of vitamin E in the diet are alpha and gamma tocopherols. Vitamin E occurs in highest concentrations in cold-pressed vegetable oils, all whole raw seeds and nuts, and soybeans. Some vitamin E is also in vegetables such as asparagus and leafy greens like spinach, in grains such as brown rice and rye, and in fish like salmon. Eggs also contain some. Wheat germ oil is the source from which vitamin E was first obtained. Animal fats have very little of this vitamin.

Vitamin E's prime role is as an antioxidant, which means it opposes oxidation of substances in the body. Oxidation involves a compound called an oxidizer that attacks another compound, removing an electron (called a free radical). Free radicals readily react with other molecules they come in contact with, altering cellular structure. They can be highly destructive, causing extensive damage to the body, from blood clots to cancer when they react with DNA. Vitamin E protects other substances by being oxidized itself, taking the brunt of any free-radical attack. One theory of aging is that changes in the body are primarily due to this process of oxidation, making vitamin E the primary anti-aging nutrient.

A highly important function of vitamin E as an antioxidant is to prevent the oxidation of unsaturated fatty acids in cell membranes and the formation of toxic peroxides. This leaves the red blood cells more fully supplied with pure oxygen, which the blood then carries to the heart and other organs. This nutrient strengthens capillary walls and protects red blood cells from destruction. Vitamin E prevents both the pituitary and adrenal hormones from being oxidized and promotes proper functioning of linoleic acid, an unsaturated fatty acid.

Vitamin E protects against the damaging effects of many environmental poisons in the air, water, and food, and it protects the lungs and other tissues from damage by air pollution. The vitamin prevents ozone from oxidizing lung lipids. In this process, vitamin E itself is used up and needs to be replaced in order for it to continue its protection.

Vitamin E also helps prevent the oxidation of other nutrients, protecting vitamin A from breaking down. A sufficient amount of vitamin E allows greater storage of vitamin A and reduces the requirements for vitamin A. Vitamin B complex and vitamin C (ascorbic acid) are also protected from oxidation when vitamin E is present in the digestive tract.

Besides its function as an antioxidant, vitamin E is also of great importance in energy production, playing an essential role in cellular respiration of all muscles, especially cardiac and skeletal. The vitamin makes it possible for these muscles and their nerves to function with less oxygen, thereby increasing their endurance and stamina. It also causes dilation of the blood vessels, permitting increased flow of blood to the heart. The vitamin is a diuretic, of benefit to heart patients with edema (excessive fluid in body tissues). Vitamin E is a highly effective antithrombin in the bloodstream, preventing clots from forming by inhibiting coagulation of the blood.

ABSORPTION AND STORAGE. Vitamin E, like other fat-soluble vitamins, is absorbed in the presence of bile salts and fat. From the intestines, it is absorbed into the lymphatic system and is transported in the bloodstream to the liver where high concentrations of it are stored. Vitamin E is found primarily in the lipid membrane of cells but is also stored in fatty tissues, the heart, muscles, the testes, the uterus, blood, and the adrenal and pituitary glands. In ointment form, vitamin E can also be absorbed through the skin and mucous membranes.

Excessive amounts of vitamin E are excreted in the urine, and all effects disappear within three days. People who eat a regular diet should get about 15 IU daily from whole grains, vegetable oils, enriched flour, leafy greens, and other vegetables.

There are several substances that interfere with, or even cause a depletion of, vitamin E in the body. For example, when the inorganic form of iron and vitamin E are administered together, the absorption of both substances is impaired. In *Vitamin E for Ailing and Healthy Hearts,* Dr. Wilfred Shute suggests that for proper absorption of this nutrient, vitamin E should be taken in one dose and all iron taken eight to twelve hours later. However, there are multivitamins that have compatible formulas of iron and include iron compounds such as ferrous fumarate. Improper absorption may be partly responsible for muscular problems, poor performance in athletes, digestive problems such as peptic ulcers, and cancer of the colon. Poor absorption can impair survival of red blood cells.

The amount of vitamin E taken into the body also depends upon how the foods in the diet are prepared. Vitamin E is destroyed by heating foods, for instance deep-frying, stir-frying, or processing with heat. And the vitamin E in food that is old and stale can become oxidized. Fresh and lightly processed foods are the most desirable. Vitamin E is destroyed by ultraviolet light, alkaline environments (as in baking soda), oxygen, and ferric salts. Copper and iron utensils can also diminish vitamin E.

DOSAGE AND TOXICITY. The 1989 RDA for vitamin E is 10 milligrams or 15 IU for men, and 8 milligrams or 12 IU for women. However, many nutritionists consider these RDAs exceedingly low. Several factors can alter the amount of vitamin E actually needed. The more unsaturated fats or oils consumed, the more vitamin E required to protect these fats from damaging oxidation. People who use fish oils or eat a lot of foods rich in polyunsaturated fats should take at least 30 IU daily to combat the rancidification of the oils. In addition, the female hormone estrogen is a vitamin E antagonist. Intake of this hormone makes it difficult to estimate the amount of alpha-tocopherol the individual is lacking. And chlorine in drinking water, ferric chloride, rancid oil or fat, the contraceptive pill, and inorganic iron compounds destroy vitamin E in the body. Mineral oil used as a laxative depletes the vitamin. Air pollution also increases the need for vitamin E.

Vitamin E is generally thought to be one of the safest vitamins. Supplemental vitamin E, in dosages as high as 3,200 IU daily in clinical trials, did not result in any unfavorable side effects, and dosages of 2,000 IU have been used therapeutically with excellent results. Common supplemental dosages for therapeutic and general purposes are 400 IU to 800 IU per day. Selenium has been found to increase the beneficial effects of vitamin E, and, therefore, it is suggested that they be taken together.

While vitamin E is considered nontoxic, supplementing with vitamin E may cause problems in certain individuals. People who take anticoagulation drugs such as warfarin, or who have reduced coagulation factors such as those with vitamin K deficiencies, may be predisposed to potentially dangerous bleeding if vitamin E is taken in doses greater than 400 IU daily. Vitamin E may also enhance the blood-thinning action of aspirin. Individuals with high blood pressure or a predisposition to high blood pressure who take

supplemental vitamin E may experience an increase in blood pressure. Starting a patient with chronic rheumatoid heart disease on high doses of vitamin E can lead to rapid deterioration or death. And diabetics should avoid high doses. As a general rule, when supplementing with vitamin E, it is best to begin with small doses, gradually increasing the amount. Consult a physician for dosages before starting any therapy.

Toxicity symptoms are fatigue, nausea, stomach upset, skin disorders, cuts and burns that don't heal, or unexplained bleeding. People who experience blood clots should alert the physician as to vitamin E intake. Megadoses may reduce thyroid hormones, resulting in muscle weakness. The effect of taking synthetic vitamin E, the l-form, over the long term is unknown.

DEFICIENCY EFFECTS AND SYMPTOMS. A lack of vitamin E increases the susceptibility of cell membranes to oxidative damage. Nerve cells in particular are vulnerable. While severe deficiency of vitamin E is rare, there are certain conditions in which low levels of this nutrient are common. Ailments involving fat malabsorption, such as post-gastrectomy syndrome, cystic fibrosis, and celiac disease, are associated with vitamin E deficiency. Hereditary disorders of red blood cells such as sickle cell disease and thalassemia are also associated with deficiency. And premature infants and patients on hemodialysis may suffer from a lack of vitamin E.

In adults, symptoms can include nerve damage, breaking of red blood cells leading to hemolytic anemia, muscle weakness, poor coordination, and involuntary eye movement. Premature infants deficient in vitamin E may have hemolytic anemia and retrolental fibroplasia, a severe eye disorder.

According to Dr. Shute, the lack of vitamin E in the American diet is partially due to the milling process, which eliminates the highly perishable wheat germ, a significant source of vitamin E. About 90 percent of the vitamin E is lost in the milling process.

BENEFICIAL EFFECTS ON AILMENTS. As the foremost antioxidant that is active in the fatty portions of cells, vitamin E helps prevent a long list of common ailments and health conditions. Because it protects the thymus gland from damage as well as circulating white blood cells, vitamin E boosts immune function. It is especially important for fighting chronic viral illnesses such as chronic viral hepatitis and AIDS. Stomach or duodenal ulcers are helped with vitamin E, B complex, pantothenic acid, and licorice.

Vitamin E helps prevent diseases of the circulatory system, protecting against heart disease and stroke, especially when coupled with other natural therapies. Clinical practice and several large studies give evidence of its effectiveness. It protects LDL cholesterol from damage by free radicals and has been shown to slow the progression of coronary artery lesions. Under normal conditions, vitamin E reduces the formation of thrombin, a clotting agent that tends to reduce the risk of the formation of a blood clot. It may also reduce tissue damage resulting from ischemia or heart surgery.

Vitamin E aids rheumatic heart disease and early stages of cardiac complications by returning abnormal capillaries to normal and reducing fluid accumulation with and between cells. This promotes normal gas interchange across the cell membranes, which seems to arrest the disease. Vitamin E is also useful in patients with congenital heart disease. The nutrient cannot alter the defective structure of the heart that is characteristic of the disease, but its oxygen-saving effects and its antithrombin activity are vital for patients who are not treated surgically. Many congenital heart disease patients have cyanosis, an insufficient supply of oxygen in the blood, and with adequate dosage of vitamin E, this condition has disappeared.

Vitamin E can also bring relief to intermittent claudication, a severe pain in calf muscles that results from inadequate blood supply caused by arterial spasms, also called "restless leg." It relieves pain in the extremities, speeds up blood flow, and reduces clotting tendencies. A combination of vitamin E, vitamin C, and bioflavonoids, along with exercise, have been used to help treat varicose veins as an alternative to surgery. The vitamin also relieves the pain of varicose veins by decreasing the amount of oxygen needed by the tissues involved.

Vitamin E therapy has been able to help diabetics. After administration of the vitamin, some patients found that their blood sugar levels became normal or near normal, and the amount of insulin required was reduced. Because of its ability to protect tissues from damage, it has also been used to prevent and treat gangrene in diabetics. Neurovascular disease of the eyes and a type of cataract common in diabetics is also helped with vitamin E.

Many studies have shown that having low levels of vitamin E, particularly when coupled with low levels of selenium, increases the risk of cancer, especially cancers of the lungs and gastrointestinal tract. Vitamin E's antioxidant effect in the lungs guards against environmental pollutants. People with high levels of vitamin E in the blood were 2.5 times less likely to develop lung cancer. Supplementation is required as diet alone cannot deliver effective amounts.

A dose of 400 IU of vitamin E daily has been used successfully to treat all symptoms of PMS. It may reduce symptoms such as breast tenderness. Vitamin E has also been successful in regulating excessive or scant flow during menstruation. To treat symptoms of menopause, vitamin E, in combination with other nutrients, may be a replacement for estrogen therapy if supplements are taken with an adequate diet. Vitamin E is recognized as a treatment for hot flashes. It is known to relieve itching and inflammation of the vagina when applied in ointment form or taken orally.

Vitamin E is important for eye health, sparing the vitamin A in the eye from oxidative damage and also acting directly as an antioxidant, protecting tissues of the retina. The nutrient is used to ease headaches and migraine attacks because it preserves the oxygen in the blood for an extended period of time. Bursitis, gout, and arthritis are improved with vitamin E therapy. Skeletal muscular myopathy present in chronic use of alcohol may be helped. It may also be useful in the treatment of nephritis. And people with blood disorders such as sickle cell anemia will benefit from supplementation. There is also some evidence that vitamin E can help memory loss in Alzheimer's patients and slow the progression of the disease. Vitamin E has also been touted as a treatment to help wounds heal better and to boost libido, but these claims have been proven false.

Inositol

DESCRIPTION. While not a B vitamin, inositol is usually grouped with these nutrients as it is closely associated with choline and biotin. In addition, animal studies have shown that vitamin B_6, folic acid, pantothenic acid, and PABA have a close working association with inositol. In cell membranes, inositol is in the form of phosphatidylinositol. Lecithin contains both inositol and choline.

Both animal and plant tissues contain inositol. In animal tissues it occurs as a component of phospholipids, substances containing phosphorus, fatty acids, and nitrogenous bases. In plant cells it is found in phytic acid, an organic acid that binds calcium and iron in an insoluble complex and interferes with absorption.

The primary function of inositol, in the form of phosphatidylinositol, is to contribute to the structure and integrity of cell membranes. Inositol is lipotropic, promoting the transport of fat from the liver. Large quantities are found in the spinal cord nerves, cerebral spinal fluid, and brain. It is needed for the growth and survival of cells in bone marrow, eye membranes, and the intestines. Inositol is also important for muscle function.

Inositol is found in unprocessed whole grains, citrus fruit (except lemons), brewer's yeast, crude unrefined molasses, cantaloupe, lima beans, cabbage, raisins, some nuts, and liver. Americans are estimated to consume about 1,000 milligrams of inositol a day from diet. Fresh fruits and vegetables have more inositol than frozen, canned, or salt-free products.

ABSORPTION AND STORAGE. Inositol is readily obtained from food, and the body also makes some. About 7 percent of ingested inositol is converted to glucose. Of the B vitamins, body stores of inositol are second only to niacin. It is found in many body tissues, including skeletal, heart, reproductive, and nerve tissue. The amount the body excretes daily in the urine is small, averaging 37 milligrams. The diabetic excretes more inositol than individuals who are not diabetic. Large amounts of coffee may deplete the body's storage of inositol.

DOSAGE AND TOXICITY. The RDA has not been established for inositol. The body can manufacture inositol and it is easily available in food, but most authorities recommend consuming the same amount of inositol and choline. One tablespoon of yeast provides approximately 40 milligrams each of choline and inositol. The standard therapeutic dosage is about 500 milligrams. This dosage, given twice a day for two weeks, resulted in considerable improvement to patients with diabetic peripheral neuropathy. Some practitioners recommend taking inositol as lecithin, along with choline and other B vitamins, rather than as inositol alone. Three grams have been given by mouth with no side effects.

DEFICIENCY EFFECTS AND SYMPTOMS. Inositol deficiency is uncommon, but caffeine (drinking more than two cups of coffee a day) and sulfonamides may lead to low levels of the nutrient. Diuresis, as in diabetes insipidus and an excess intake of water, can cause a loss of inositol. Low levels may cause constipation, eczema, hair loss, eye problems, and elevated cholesterol, increasing the risk of plaque in arteries. A lack of inositol may have adverse effects in the nerves of diabetics who have diabetic peripheral neuropathy.

BENEFICIAL EFFECTS ON AILMENTS. Inositol can help with liver problems such as fatty liver because of its ability to promote the elimination of fat from this organ. Diabetic peripheral neuropathy is helped by the use of inositol along with choline, reducing pain and numbness. A dose of 500 milligrams inositol and 1,000 milligrams choline aids hypoglycemia. Inositol relieves mild hypertension by gradually lowering blood pressure. It helps maintain healthy hair and skin and is used to treat skin disease such as eczema. Significant proof of the benefits of taking inositol to reduce cholesterol and heart disease is lacking.

Nerve transmission may be helped with the B complex and inositol. Dr. Carl Pfeiffer, at his Brain Bio Center, has studied the effect of inositol on brain waves. Results have shown that the vitamin has an antianxiety effect similar to Librium. Librium is a drug that acts as a sedative, and it carries the risk that a person taking it may develop a dependency on it. Because of this sedative effect, inositol is a useful treatment for insomnia. Inositol is also used to treat depression. Patients with multiple sclerosis are also helped by inositol as they are more likely to have a deficiency.

As a supplement, inositol is available as inositol monophosphate. Commercial lecithin contains only small amounts.

Vitamin K

DESCRIPTION. Vitamin K is present in foods but is also made in the body. There are three forms of vitamin K: phylloquinone (K_1), the almost exclusive form found in the food supply; menaquinone (K_2), a highly bioavailable form produced in the intestinal tract in the presence of certain intestinal bacteria and found in some foods; and menadione (K_3), a synthetic compound with a similar chemical structure. K_1 and K_2 are fat soluble, while K_3 is water soluble and twice as potent as the other forms.

Vitamin K has appropriately been called the bandaid vitamin for its major role in blood clotting. It is necessary for the formation of four of the thirteen components that allow the blood to clot, one of which is prothrombin. Vitamin K plays a role in bone mineralization by converting a protein, osteocalcin, from its inactive to its active form. Osteocalcin joins with calcium to hold this mineral within the bone. Researchers from Brigham and Women's Hospital in Boston found that women with a lower dietary intake of vitamin K have many more hip fractures than women who consume high amounts of about 100 to 250 micrograms a day. Vitamin K is also involved in the storing of blood sugar in cells for later use as a source of energy. It is also necessary for normal liver function.

Vitamin K can be safely used as a preservative to control fermentation in foods. It has no bleaching effect, unlike sulfur compounds used to preserve dried fruit, and has no unpleasant odor.

Excellent sources of vitamin K are the dark leafy greens such as kale and turnip greens, cabbage, romaine lettuce, spinach, broccoli, green tea, and natto, a form of fermented soybeans. Other good sources are green peas, asparagus, whole wheat, and oats. Egg yolks, cheese, and liver also contain small amounts. The average diet provides about 75 to 150 micrograms per day. It is estimated that half of the daily need is supplied by the diet and the other half is manufactured in the intestine.

The body's production of vitamin K can be enhanced by eating fermented dairy products such as yogurt, kefir, and acidophilus milk. In addition, unsaturated fatty acids and a low-carbohydrate diet increase the amounts produced by intestinal flora. Vitamin K is absorbed in the upper intestinal tract with the aid of fat-emulsifying bile or bile salts. It is transported to the liver where it is essential for the synthesis of several proteins, including prothrombin, involved in blood clotting.

The absorption rate of vitamin K can vary dramatically. In one instance, researchers discovered that from a large serving of spinach, providing 1,000 micrograms of the vitamin, less than 1 percent was absorbed if eaten raw and without fat. When the same portion was consumed with butter, 25 percent was absorbed. And the absorption rate of the supplemental form of vitamin K may be as high as 50 percent. The absorption rate also varies in each individual by an estimated 10 percent to 70 percent.

Various factors can interfere with the absorption of vitamin K, including any obstruction of the bile duct that limits the secretion of bile salts, failure of the liver to secrete bile, and dicumarol, an anticoagulant medication that reduces the activity of prothrombin in the blood. Calcium, vitamin A, and vitamin E are vitamin K antagonists.

The forms of vitamin K, in food and made in the body, are readily excreted, while the synthetic form, which is more potent, can accumulate in body tissues.

Vitamin K is heat stable. Cooking does not reduce the amount of vitamin K in foods.

DOSAGE AND TOXICITY.   The 1989 RDAs for vitamin K are 80 micrograms for adult males and 65 micrograms for adult females. A typical supplemental dosage is 100 to 500 micrograms per day.

Natural vitamin K, stored in the body, produces no toxicity signs. However, when the synthetic form, which is more potent, accumulates in body tissues, toxicity can result. Toxicity brings about a form of anemia that results in an increase in the breakdown of red blood cells (hemolytic anemia), jaundice, and brain damage. Toxicity has occurred when large dosages of synthetic vitamin K were injected into pregnant women. Flushing, sweating, itching, and chest constrictions are symptoms of synthetic vitamin K toxicity.

Newborns are typically given a one-time dose of 1 milligram of vitamin K to prevent hemorrhagic disease, or abnormal bleeding, because of a sterile intestinal tract and poor fat transmission through the placenta. Toxicity in infants manifests as kernicterus, a condition in which yellow pigment infiltrates the spinal cord and brain areas. It usually develops during the second to eighth day of life. Heinz bodies, or granules in the red blood cells, resulting from damage to the hemoglobin molecules, are seen in infants suffering from an overdose of vitamin K.

DEFICIENCY EFFECTS AND SYMPTOMS.   A true deficiency of vitamin K is rare except in newborn infants. The intestinal tract in newborns is not yet developed and lacks the bacteria that produce vitamin K. However, a marginal, subclinical deficiency that does not affect blood-clotting ability can be due to various factors.

The diet may be low in foods such as dark leafy greens that are high in vitamin K. Deficiency of vitamin K can also be the result of poor digestive function. A deficiency is common in diseases that affect the absorbing mucosa of the small intestine and cause a rapid loss of intestinal contents, such as celiac disease (intestinal malabsorption), sprue (malabsorption in adulthood), ileitis, colitis, and after surgery. In such cases, intravenous administration is needed. A deficiency should be treated by a physician.

Deficiency can also arise when the amount of vitamin K produced in the gut is diminished by certain ailments such as a yeast infection and parasites, as well as long-term use of antibiotics and sulfa drugs, which kill off the bacteria that make this nutrient.

The anticoagulant medication Coumadin (warfarin) counteracts the coagulant action of vitamin K as does aspirin. As a result, individuals taking blood thinners need to keep the servings of vitamin K–rich foods fairly consistent since a sudden large amount of such foods can change the required dosage of the medication. And dosages of vitamin E greater than 600 IU possibly block the blood-clotting action of vitamin K.

In addition, rancid fats, radiation, x-rays, and industrial air pollution all destroy the vitamin, and ingestion of mineral oil will cause rapid excretion. Signs of subclinical deficiency of vitamin K are bruising easily and visible ruptured capillaries.

The elderly are susceptible to vitamin K deficiency due to poor diet and impaired digestion. Others who may be deficient are persons on low-calorie diets, those on prolonged antibiotic therapy, and individuals taking drugs such as cholestyramine, anticonvulsants, and some cephalosporin antibiotics.

BENEFICIAL EFFECTS ON AILMENTS.
Vitamin K is necessary to promote blood clotting, especially when jaundice is present. As noted, it is administered to heart patients who are using anticoagulant drugs. Carefully measured doses of vitamin K are given to these patients to raise the prothrombin level slightly while not allowing the vitamin to completely counteract the effect of the anticoagulant.

Therapeutic dosages of vitamin K are sometimes given before and after operations to reduce blood losses and to pregnant women prior to labor to protect against hemorrhaging. An injection of vitamin K is given to newborns to prevent hemorrhagic disease, or sometimes the mother during pregnancy and the child after birth are given vitamin K orally. And vitamin K is frequently used with vitamin C in the prevention and improvement of hemorrhages in various parts of the eye. Patients with liver disease or jaundice receive vitamin K to promote normal blood clotting.

Vitamin K has proved beneficial in treating menorrhagia, excessive menstrual flow, and it often has lessened or relieved menstrual cramps. This nutrient helps prevent and treat osteoporosis. In research, the lower the blood level of vitamin K, the more severe the bone fracture. Supplemental vitamin K is given when there is decreased bile secretion to reduce joint irritation in cases of rheumatoid arthritis. It has also been used to prevent cerebral palsy.

Preliminary laboratory research indicates that the synthetic form of vitamin K may be useful in inhibiting the growth of various cancers, including that of the ovary, breast, stomach, colon, bladder, kidney, and liver.

Pangamic Acid

Pangamic acid, also referred to as vitamin B_{15}, is still a fairly controversial nutrient. It may not qualify for its designation as a vitamin, as vitamins by definition must be supplied by external sources and be essential in the diet. There are also no clear signs of deficiency. Consequently there is no RDA for pangamic acid.

This substance, which is water soluble, was originally isolated from apricot kernels, and later obtained in crystalline form from rice bran, rice polish, whole grain cereals, brewer's yeast, steer blood, and horse liver. Most of the studies of pangamic acid were conducted in the former Soviet Union; this research is now dated and more is needed. While many of pangamic acid's therapeutic uses are unproven, there are many reports of its benefits. In Russia, this substance is used to increase athletic endurance and to treat such varied conditions as alcoholism and drug abuse, heart disease, senility, and autism. In Europe, pangamic acid is used as an anti-aging nutrient, providing protection from damaging air pollution.

In the United States, the Food and Drug Administration (FDA) has banned the distribution of all pangamic acid products with accompanying labeling making disease claims, including products containing dimethyl glycine mixed with other compounds such as calcium gluconate. However, dimethyl glycine alone, thought to increase pangamic acid production in the body, is available. Benefits may include increased energy and enhanced immunity. A standard dosage is 50 to 100 milligrams taken twice daily with meals.

Para-Aminobenzoic Acid (PABA)

DESCRIPTION. Para-aminobenzoic acid (PABA) is a member of the B family of vitamins. It is water soluble and considered unique as a "vitamin within a vitamin," as it appears to be a component of folic acid. Para-aminobenzoic acid is made by bacteria in the intestines and is also readily available in food, including liver, yeast, wheat germ, whole grains, eggs, and molasses. It is also manufactured in the intestines by friendly bacteria if conditions are favorable.

As a coenzyme, para-aminobenzoic acid functions in the breakdown and utilization of proteins and in the formation of blood cells, especially red blood cells. PABA plays an important role in determining skin health and hair pigmentation. It is important to the health of the intestines where it stimulates intestinal bacteria to produce folic acid, which in turn aids in the production of pantothenic acid. PABA also acts as a sunscreen, blocking damaging ultraviolet rays, and is incorporated into some skin lotions.

ABSORPTION AND STORAGE. PABA is stored in the tissues. It is also manufactured in the intestines by friendly bacteria if conditions are favorable.

DOSAGE AND TOXICITY. The need for para-aminobenzoic acid in human nutrition has not yet been established. Routine supplementation is no higher than 30 milligrams a day. However, therapeutic nutritional protocols may include 50- to 100-milligram amounts, given three times a day. A maximum therapeutic dosage is 1,000 milligrams per day.

Continued ingestion of high doses of PABA is not recommended and can be toxic to the liver, heart, and kidneys. Symptoms of toxicity are nausea, vomiting, and diarrhea. Excessive amounts could produce fever, anorexia, skin rash, and even vitiligo (a disorder that causes discoloration of the skin).

DEFICIENCY EFFECTS AND SYMPTOMS.
Medications that interfere with the normal func-

tioning of friendly bacteria in the intestinal tract, such as sulfa drugs or antibiotics, may result in PABA deficiency. The sulfa compounds in drugs kill the intestinal bacteria because they resemble PABA in structure and are able to substitute for the PABA nutrient that the bacteria need. While deficiency of PABA is unlikely, should an inadequacy develop, the signs are fatigue, depression, irritability, digestive problems such as constipation, headache, and graying hair.

BENEFICIAL EFFECTS ON AILMENTS. Para-aminobenzoic acid is used therapeutically to treat skin conditions and acts as a sunscreen. People normally susceptible to sunburn have been able to remain many hours in the sun after applying an ointment containing PABA. The pain of sunburn and other burns is alleviated immediately. However, PABA in such products has been found to cause allergic reactions and irritation of the skin, and its use has declined in popularity. This nutrient often soothes the pain of accidental burns even more effectively than vitamin E. With mixed results, PABA has been used to treat pemphigus, a severe blistering of the skin; scleroderma, an autoimmune disease; and vitiligo.

Combined with other nutrients such as folic acid, PABA may be useful in restoring graying or white hair to its natural color, but only if a person is deficient in B vitamins. A daily intake of PABA and folic acid should be continued to prevent the hair from turning gray once again. In addition, PABA has also been used to treat Rocky Mountain spotted fever and other parasitic diseases.

Dr. Carl Pfeiffer reports that large doses, 2 grams per day, have been used with good results in treating schizophrenia. He speculates that PABA may prevent certain amines from forming hallucinogens. Hypoglycemia is aided by the use of PABA, vitamin C, and pantothenic acid, along with glandular therapy. Along with folic acid, PABA increases estrogen levels. A dose of 200 milligrams daily has greatly improved the ability of women who have a history of infertility to conceive. Supplements for both potential parents before conception are 100 milligrams per day for the man and 200 milligrams per day for the woman. Potaba, the potassium salt of PABA, is used for the treatment of Peyronie's disease, a disorder of the penis involving excess fibrosis that affects erections.

Minerals

Minerals are nutrients that exist in the body and in food in organic and inorganic combinations. Approximately seventeen minerals have been found to be essential in human nutrition. Although only 4 percent or 5 percent of the human body weight is mineral matter, minerals are vital to overall mental and physical well-being. All tissues and internal fluids of living things contain varying quantities of minerals. Minerals are constituents of the bones, teeth, soft tissue, muscle, blood, and nerve cells. They are important factors in maintaining physiological processes, strengthening skeletal structures, and preserving the vigor of the heart and brain as well as all muscle and nerve systems.

Minerals help maintain the delicate water balance essential to the proper functioning of mental and physical processes. They keep blood and tissue fluids from becoming either too acid or too alkaline and permit other nutrients to pass into the bloodstream. They also help draw chemical substances in and out of the cells and aid in the creation of antibodies.

Calcium, chlorine, phosphorus, potassium, magnesium, sodium, and sulfur are known as the macrominerals, because they are present in relatively high amounts in body tissues. They are measured in milligrams. Other minerals, termed "trace minerals," are present in the body only in the most minute quantities but are essential for proper body functioning. Trace minerals are measured in micrograms.

Minerals, just like vitamins, act as catalysts for many biological reactions within the human body, including muscle response, transmission of messages through the nervous system, digestion, and metabolism or utilization of nutrients in foods. They are important in the production of hormones.

Minerals coexist with vitamins, and their work is interrelated. For example, some B-complex vitamins are absorbed only when combined with phosphorus. Vitamin C greatly increases the absorption of iron, and calcium absorption would not occur without vitamin D. Zinc helps vitamin A to be released from the liver. Some minerals are even part of vitamins: vitamin B_1 contains sulfur and B_{12} contains cobalt.

Most vitamins absorb into the body quite easily; however, minerals do not. One of the most effectively absorbed forms of minerals is that which has been chelated with amino acids. Studies show that when a mineral becomes attached to an amino acid during digestion, the amino acid effortlessly carries the mineral across the intestinal wall and into the bloodstream. However, minerals that do not become attached to amino acids can become bound to phytic acids (from cereal grains), which prohibit their absorption. For this reason, it is essential to consume complete proteins with each meal.

Amino acids are also found naturally along the intestinal wall and act as receptors for the minerals. Mutual attraction draws the two elements together; but even if a mineral is in the right position, it may not have the opportunity to become attached, because chemically similar minerals compete for the same amino acid carriers. If there are not enough carriers or sites available, the weaker minerals lose out. If the minerals are moving along within a mass of food, they may pass through the intestinal tract without having a chance to attach.

Although the minerals are discussed separately, it is important to note that their actions within the body are interrelated; no one mineral can function without affecting others. Physical and emotional stress causes a strain on the body's supply of minerals. A mineral deficiency often results in illness, which may be checked by the addition of the missing mineral to the diet.

Aluminum

DESCRIPTION. Aluminum is found throughout nature, in the earth and the sea. Small amounts are present in both animals and plants. Currently there is no known nutritional requirement for aluminum, and the degree of its toxicity is still under investigation. But in certain instances it is clearly harmful and can undermine health. Theories of the ways in which this may occur include reducing levels of vitamins, interacting with magnesium, binding to DNA, and weakening the tissues of the gastrointestinal tract.

Possibilities of exposure to aluminum abound. It can be found in tap water because aluminum sulfate that is used in water purification is not completely filtered out. It is also a common food additive. Processed cheese contains the emulsifier sodium aluminum phosphate, table salt contains sodium silicoaluminate and/or aluminum calcium silicate to prevent caking, and flour is whitened with potassium alum. Aluminum foil used to wrap foods such as potatoes for baking, aluminum cookware (and acid foods such as tomatoes cooked in aluminum pots), soft drinks and colas in aluminum cans, and deodorants made with aluminum salts are other common sources. And aluminum is a major ingredient in certain stomach antacids.

ABSORPTION AND STORAGE. Aluminum is easily absorbed. Most of the aluminum taken into the system is ultimately excreted via the feces and urine and to a lesser degree, through sweat. When stored in the body, highest accumulations are found in the tissues of the lungs, brain, kidneys, liver, and thyroid. The body adjusts to higher intakes over time, but in young people with hypophosphatemia (a low level of phosphate in the blood, as with rickets) or individuals with abnormal bone metabolism, this adjustment may not easily occur. And more aluminum is retained, especially in the bones, when there is decreased kidney function.

DOSAGE AND TOXICITY. The average amount of aluminum in the human body is 65 milligrams but can range from 50 to 150 milligrams. Daily intake may be 10 to 110 milligrams. Symptoms of aluminum poisoning include constipation, colic, loss of appetite, nausea, skin ailments, twitching of leg muscles, excessive perspiration, and loss of energy. Patients with chronic kidney problems have an increased risk of suffering from aluminum toxicity as the ability to eliminate aluminum via the kidneys becomes compromised. Small quantities of soluble salts of aluminum in the blood cause a slow form of poisoning characterized by motor paralysis and areas of local numbness, with fatty degeneration of the kidney and liver. There are also anatomical changes in the nerve centers and symptoms of gastrointestinal inflammation. These symptoms result from the body's effort to eliminate the poison.

In particular, dialysis patients, exposed to large doses of aluminum, are at risk for osteomalacia and dialysis encephalopathy, an Alzheimer's-like disease. During the 1970s, aluminum-containing tap water was sometimes used to dialyze patients, impairing brain function, before physicians became aware of the risks of using such water. A switch to aluminum-free solutions greatly reduced the incidence of related disease.

Antacids that contain aluminum hydroxide can become a major source of aluminum if taken regularly, preventing the absorption of phosphate and leading to the development of osteomalacia, softening of the bones. In the intestine, aluminum binds with phosphorus, an essential component of bone crystals, and aluminum also reduces bone formation and increases resorption, resulting in bone loss. Alcoholics who use antacids are at extra risk. In addition, Lou Gehrig's disease has been traced to high levels of aluminum coupled with exposure to manganese.

Recent research has found correlations between aluminum toxicity and brain aging disorders, including Alzheimer's disease and senility syndromes. The accumulation of aluminum may be a consequence of Alzheimer's disease rather than a cause. However, studies in which animals were fed aluminum in their diet showed development of neurofibrillary tangles, the same abnormality found in the brain tissue of Alzheimer's patients.

Strategies for preventing aluminum toxicity include choosing colas in bottles rather than cans, using cookware with a stainless steel surface, and installing a home water filter. Avoid taking an antacid with citrus juice such as orange juice, a source of citric acid that tightly binds to aluminum, increasing its absorption and toxicity. Some supplements also contain citric acid, such as calcium citrate, a popular form in supplements.

DEFICIENCY EFFECTS AND SYMPTOMS. Currently there is no known nutritional requirement for aluminum.

BENEFICIAL EFFECTS ON AILMENTS. There are no known therapeutic uses for aluminum.

Beryllium

Beryllium is a hard, gray metal that is lightweight, heat resistant, and strong. It is an ideal choice for making a range of products from airplanes to fishing rods. It is also found in many common household products as well as in neon signs, electronic devices, some alloys (including steel), and bicycle wheels. It is a toxic mineral that can undermine health by depleting the body's stores of magnesium and lodging in organ tissue where it impairs function by interfering with a number of the body's enzyme systems.

Smoke and exhaust from industrial use of beryllium exposes humans to the airborne mineral dust. Inhaling the contaminated air can result in respiratory problems that include coughing, phlegm, shortness of breath, and lung inflammation. This may lead to injury of the lungs, causing scarring or fibrosis and even complete disability as the lungs become seriously damaged. There may even be an increased risk of cancer.

Bismuth

Bismuth is a brittle, reddish metal. This mineral is a by-product of the smelting of tin, lead, or copper, the usual source, but bismuth is also sometimes found as a metal deposit in the earth. Bismuth is present in some medications, especially stomach remedies such as Pepto-Bismol, and is a component of certain rectal suppositories and antidiarrhea products.

The body contains about 3 milligrams of the metal. However, daily intake can be higher if bismuth is present in food, water, and airborne contaminants. In ordinary amounts, bismuth is nontoxic, but high doses or prolonged exposure may result in toxicity. Bismuth may interfere with absorption of zinc. Most is excreted in the urine and feces.

Symptoms of toxicity can resemble mental illness, resulting in a staggering gait, poor memory, body tremors, visual and hearing disturbances, difficulty in judging time and distance, and, in some cases, occurrences of auditory and visual hallucinations. Symptoms disappear when use of the mineral is discontinued.

Boron

DESCRIPTION. Boron is a trace mineral essential for healthy bones and joints. The major function of boron is its role in calcium and magnesium metabolism. It is found in vegetables such as leafy greens and winter squash, many fruits, grains, legumes, and a variety of nuts.

ABSORPTION AND STORAGE. Absorption of boron is rapid. Excess is excreted in urine.

DOSAGE AND TOXICITY. While there is no RDA for boron, a suggested standard intake is 1.5 to 3 milligrams per day. However, individuals at risk for osteoporosis may require 3 to 9 milligrams per day. While relatively safe, very high doses of more than 300 milligrams per day can result in nausea, vomiting, diarrhea, and dermatitis.

DEFICIENCY EFFECTS AND SYMPTOMS. Individuals eating the standard American diet are likely to be deficient in boron, given that typical foods are poor sources of boron and very few Americans eat the recommended servings of fruits and vegetables. Due to an impairment of calcium metabolism, deficiency increases the risk of postmenopausal bone loss and central nervous system dysfunction.

BENEFICIAL EFFECTS ON AILMENTS. Boron is thought to be beneficial for those suffering from postmenopausal osteoporosis. The USDA determined that postmenopausal women lost 40 percent less calcium, one-third less magnesium, and slightly less phosphorus in their urine when supplementing with 3 milligrams of boron for eight days. These women were also found to have significant increases in the production of an active form of estrogen and testosterone. Boron enhances estrogen's beneficial effect on bone health. Boron is also useful in the treatment of arthritis and may be helpful in cases of ischemic heart disease and other forms of cardiovascular disease. In addition, for individuals taking diuretics or digitalis, boron may hinder the excretion of magnesium associated with these medications.

Cadmium

DESCRIPTION. Cadmium is a toxic trace mineral that is similar to zinc in structure and function.

It has no biological function in the human body. Cadmium's toxic effects are kept under control when balanced by adequate body stores of zinc.

Whole foods have a more desirable ratio of cadmium to zinc than refined foods such as white flour, white rice, and sugar. In refining, much of the zinc is removed and cadmium predominates. Coffee, tea, and shellfish are other dietary sources of cadmium. The metal is also present in cigarette smoke. One pack of cigarettes deposits 2 to 4 micrograms into the lungs of a smoker, while some of the smoke passes into the air to be inhaled by smokers and nonsmokers alike. Cadmium is also present in air pollution found around zinc factories and especially in industrial cities. In addition, soft water usually contains higher levels of cadmium than hard water. Soft water, especially if it is acidic, leaches cadmium from metal water pipes.

ABSORPTION AND STORAGE. The liver and kidneys are storage areas for cadmium as well as zinc. Both are also stored in the testes. The total body concentration of cadmium increases with age, usually peaking around age 50, and varies in different areas of the world. It is not very well absorbed, but cadmium is also not well eliminated. If the daily intake of zinc is high, zinc will be stored and cadmium excreted. Cadmium also interferes with the absorption of copper.

DOSAGE AND TOXICITY. Daily intakes of cadmium have been estimated at 25 to 60 micrograms per day, with considerable variation according to sources and types of food. The toxicity of cadmium is likely to be due to its similarity with zinc, displacing zinc when the cadmium-zinc ratio favors cadmium and, consequently, interfering with zinc's important enzymatic and organ functions.

Cadmium poisoning is a very subtle process and can accumulate over a lifetime. Cadmium deposits in the kidneys, causing kidney tissue damage and high blood pressure or hypertension as well as calcium kidney stones. It also settles into arteries, resulting in atherosclerosis.

Dr. Henry A. Schroeder, a trace mineral researcher, developed a theory about cadmium as a major cause of hypertension or high blood pressure as well as related heart ailments. In animal studies, Dr. Schroeder found that regular high doses of cadmium caused increased blood pressure, with pressure returning to normal when the cadmium treatment ceased. Studies also found elevated cadmium levels associated with atherosclerosis, an increase in heart size, and reduced kidney function. In humans, the urine of hypertensive patients contains up to 40 percent more cadmium than the urine of normotensive persons. These findings suggest that cadmium is involved in, or at least contributes to, high blood pressure.

Airborne cadmium can lead to pulmonary emphysema. Anemia proteinuria and amino aciduria are associated with high levels in the liver and kidneys. And when zinc and cadmium are at odds with each other, there may be problems with sperm formation and enlarged prostate. Cadmium also appears to weaken immune function, and it may increase the risk of prostate and lung cancer. Bone and joint health is also vulnerable to cadmium toxicity. Itai-itai ("ouch-ouch") disease, first documented in Japan, identified this syndrome caused by cadmium pollution, characterized by bone aches and pains and weak and deformed bones.

Good first steps to take to prevent cadmium toxicity are (1) avoidance of sources of cadmium, such as coffee, tea, and shellfish in the diet, (2) avoidance of cadmium in the environment in soft water and air pollution, and (3) an increased intake of zinc. Cadmium can also be detoxified with selenium. And alginates (found in seaweed) bind to cadmium and remove it from the body.

DEFICIENCY EFFECTS AND SYMPTOMS. No available information.

BENEFICIAL EFFECTS ON AILMENTS. When zinc antagonizes cadmium, protection from cancer may occur.

Calcium

DESCRIPTION. Calcium is the most abundant mineral in the body and contributes 1.5 percent to 2 percent body weight. Most of this calcium, 98 percent, is found in the bones and teeth. The remaining calcium is in soft tissues, intracellular fluids, and the blood. One of the most important minerals, calcium is vital for the development and maintenance of bone structure and rigidity as well as the performance of numerous vital tasks throughout the body. These functions include release of neurotransmitters, muscle stimulation, regulation of heartbeat, parathyroid hormone function, the clotting of blood, and metabolism of vitamin D. Calcium is present in significant amounts in a very limited number of foods. Dairy products are an excellent source of calcium, except for cottage cheese, which has very little. Canned sardines and salmon, which include the softened and edible bones of the fish; tofu; and leafy vegetables are also good sources. Kale and mustard, turnip, and collard greens are rich sources of absorbable calcium. However, the calcium in spinach is poorly absorbed.

While natural sources of calcium are best, taking supplemental calcium, which has become increasingly common in recent years to prevent osteoporosis, can help in reaching daily adequate intake. There are many forms of calcium supplements to choose from. Both dolomite and bonemeal are good sources of absorbable calcium but may contain heavy metals including lead. Other forms of calcium may also contain lead, such as unrefined calcium carbonate and organic chelates bound to citrate, gluconate, or lactate. In contrast, refined calcium carbonate has been found to have only minimal amounts of lead. However, calcium citrate and other forms such as lactate and aspartate are the best choices for optimal absorption. A supplement that can be readily absorbed should dissolve at room temperature in vinegar in half an hour.

The major function of calcium is to act in cooperation with phosphorus to build and maintain bones and teeth. The bones also store calcium for use by other systems of the body. The amount of calcium in the bones is constantly fluctuating, influenced by diet and the body's demands for the mineral. Calcium, as well as magnesium, is needed to maintain the cardiovascular system. It assists in the process of blood clotting and helps maintain normal pH of the blood. The mineral's delicate messenger ions help regulate heartbeat.

Calcium affects neurotransmitters (serotonin, acetylcholine, and norepinephrine), nerve transmission, muscle growth, and muscle contraction. It acts as a messenger from the cell surface to the inside of the cell and helps regulate the passage of nutrients in and out of the cell walls. Calcium aids in the body's utilization of iron, helps activate several digestive enzymes (catalysts important for metabolism), and eases insomnia.

ABSORPTION AND STORAGE.   On average, adults absorb only about 30 percent to 50 percent of ingested calcium. And average daily losses of calcium are estimated to be 320 milligrams. About 100 to 200 milligrams are filtered through the blood and excreted in the urine. Another 125 to 180 milligrams are excreted in the feces. Some is lost in sweat but only when there is illness or extreme physical activity in dry, hot environments.

Calcium is best absorbed in an acid environment, hence the recommendation to take calcium supplements in smaller doses several times a day—between meals, when the stomach is more acid, and at night before bedtime, which also promotes sleep. Absorption takes place in the duodenum and ceases in the lower part of the intestinal tract when food content becomes alkaline. Many other factors also influence the actual amount of calcium absorbed. When in need, the body absorbs calcium more effectively; therefore, the greater the need and the smaller the dietary supply, the more efficient the absorption. Absorption is also increased during rapid periods of growth.

The absorption of calcium also depends on the presence of adequate amounts of vitamin D, which works with the parathyroid hormone to regulate the amount of calcium in the blood. Vitamins A and C are also necessary for absorption, helping support normal membrane transfer of the mineral. Fat content in moderate amounts, moving slowly through the digestive tract, helps facilitate absorption as do bile and bile salts. Even moderate exercise encourages absorption. Neither zinc nor magnesium interferes with absorption.

There are also various substances that can interfere with the absorption of calcium. When excessive amounts of fat, protein, or sugar combine with calcium, an insoluble compound is formed that cannot be absorbed. Insufficient vitamin C intake or excess phosphorus and magnesium hinder the absorption of calcium. Oxalic acid, found in chocolate, spinach, beet greens, Swiss chard, soybeans, almonds, cashews, kale, and rhubarb, when combined with calcium, makes another insoluble compound that may form stones in the kidney or gallbladder. However, a typical diet should not cause this condition. Large amounts of phytic acid present in unleavened grains may also inhibit absorption. Other interfering factors include lack of exercise, physical and emotional stress, excitement, depression, and too rapid a flow of food through the intestinal tract.

Once calcium is absorbed, the parathyroid gland located in the neck helps adjust the body's storage of the mineral, making sure that when calcium levels in the blood are too high (calcium rigor), calcium is deposited in its storage place in the bones. If these glands are not functioning properly, accumulation may occur. The remedy is to renew the proper function of the parathyroid glands rather than to cut down on calcium intake. Calcium can also accumulate in soft tissues and joints. This occurs if there is not sufficient acid present in the body so that the mineral does not dissolve and cannot be used as needed by the body or when taking excessive amounts of calcium supplements.

DOSAGE AND TOXICITY.   The RDA for calcium is 1,000 milligrams a day for adults and 1,200 milligrams a day for preadolescent, growing children and women during pregnancy and lactation. It is recommended that postmenopausal women have 1,500 milligrams per day because of decreased absorption and higher elimination. Supplementation of up to 2,500 milligrams daily is considered safe. A cup of milk has 300 milligrams of calcium.

Too much calcium can interfere with the functions of the nervous and muscular systems. An excess amount in the blood causes calcium rigor, which is characterized by muscles that contract and cannot relax. When an excess is added to plasma, coagulation does not take place. Too much calcium will decrease the body's absorption of zinc and iron. There is only inconclusive evidence that calcium leads to kidney stones; however, those who have them should not take supplements and a physician should be consulted.

People with high blood levels of calcium (from overactive parathyroid gland and cancer) should not take supplements. Those who are taking high doses of vitamin D for medical problems should consult a physician before taking supplements. Calcium may interfere with the effects of verapamil, a calcium channel blocker for the heart.

If calcium intake is high, magnesium levels also need to be high. Too little magnesium results in calcium accumulation in the muscles, heart, and kidneys. Sufficient magnesium in relation to calcium, at least 50 percent of calcium intake, is also necessary for strong bones. In addition, phosphorus is needed in an amount equal to that of calcium but should not exceed this. The body uses these together to give firmness to bones. If excessive amounts of either mineral are taken, that excess cannot be used efficiently.

DEFICIENCY EFFECTS AND SYMPTOMS. Calcium deficiencies are widespread in human societies, with only one-third to one-half of the necessary RDA being consumed. One of the first signs of a deficiency is a nervous affliction called tetany, which is characterized by muscle cramps, numbness, and tingling in the arms and legs. Other signs of a moderate deficiency are heart palpitations, increased cholesterol levels, slow pulse rates, insomnia, impaired growth, excessive irritability of nerves, brittle nails, and eczema. A deficiency can also result in bone malformation due to a softening of the bones, a condition known as *rickets* when in children and *osteomalacia* in adults.

Another deficiency disease is osteoporosis, in which the bones become porous and fragile because calcium is withdrawn from the bones faster than it is deposited in them. The disease is also characterized by a decrease in the nonmineral framework (organic matrix) of bone that contributes significantly to bone structure. Osteoporosis affects more than twenty million people in the United States. Both men and women typically start losing bone density starting at about age forty, but women are at a greater risk for the disease. A good accumulation of calcium in the bones during early stages in life is the best prevention of age-related bone loss and fractures. Low calcium can also affect children during tooth formation when a deficiency may be irreversible for tooth structure and resistance to decay.

Adequate calcium alone cannot prevent osteoporosis, with many minerals and vitamins playing a role in bone health. Magnesium also plays an important role, and vitamin C, the B vitamins, vitamin D, zinc, copper, manganese, strontium, and boron also exert beneficial effects on the skeletal system. In addition, phosphorus is needed in the same amount as calcium but should not exceed this specific quantity, to make sure the body can use these two minerals efficiently. Unfortunately, the typical American diet is low in calcium and high in phosphorus due to such foods as soda pop, diet soda, and processed foods (lunch meats, cheese, and other convenience items). However, calcium deficiency can be due to factors other than diet. Deficiency may result from a lack of vitamin D or abnormal concentrations of hormones that affect the availability of bone calcium to the blood, as in hyperthyroidism.

Low levels of calcium increase the risk of hypertension as calcium may counteract the effects of sodium in the development of hypertension. Severe deficiency can also lead to abnormal heartbeat, dementia, convulsions, slow blood clotting, or hemorrhaging. The elderly are at risk for deficiency as the ability to absorb the mineral declines with age. Taking antacids that contain aluminum also increases the risk of calcium deficiency, as does drinking alcohol; being lactose intolerant; consuming a low-calorie, high-protein, or high-fiber diet; taking cortisone; rarely exercising; and being pregnant. Confinement, most commonly experienced in bed rest following an illness, depletes calcium from the bones and nitrogen from muscle tissue. To prevent this condition from becoming serious, gradual exercise should be undertaken as soon as possible.

BENEFICIAL EFFECTS ON AILMENTS. Calcium is a natural tranquilizer and tends to calm the nerves; when taken twenty to forty minutes before bedtime, calcium promotes deep sleep. Its role in the skeletal system is well known. Calcium significantly prevents bone loss, even without the addition of estrogen. Supplements may help prevent bone fractures in postmenopausal women who already have osteoporosis. Calcium is used to treat rickets, osteomalacia, and tooth and gum disorders; supplementation when deficient protects bones and teeth from developing lead deposits. Arthritis, structural rigidity often caused by depletion of bone calcium, may be helped with regular supplements of calcium, although this has not been proved scientifically; early consumption of calcium may help prevent the disease. Rheumatism may also be treated successfully with calcium therapy.

Symptoms of menopause can also be treated with calcium. Problems such as nervousness, irritability, insomnia, and headaches have been overcome with administration of calcium, magnesium, and vitamin D. Prevention of premenstrual tension and menstrual cramps has been shown.

The mineral is thought to be good for the heart, lowering cholesterol and blood pressure due to its effect on the smooth muscles that surround the blood vessels. Calcium is a recognized aid for muscle cramps in the feet and legs. It helps patients suffering from "growing pains." Calcium can be used to treat sunburn. Because an antioxidant enzyme in the skin is calcium-sensitive, supplementation may help slow the signs of aging of the skin, especially when coupled with vitamin A. This combination also can be used as a neutralizing agent against the poison of a black widow spider or bee sting. Calcium participates in the structuring of DNA and RNA and activates the digestive enzyme lipase. Nephritis has been cleared up with the administration of calcium and other nutrients.

Because of calcium's dietary association with vitamin D, it reduces the occurrence of cancer of the large intestine. Calcium appears to bind to the cancer-promoting fats and inhibits their ability to start the cancer process. A high dietary intake of calcium may protect against harmful effects of radioactive strontium 90. Supplements along with vitamin D may also have a strong preventive effect on colorectal cancer. Calcium also protects against sun-caused skin cancers as well as sunburn.

Chloride

DESCRIPTION.   Chloride exists in nature and in the body as a negatively charged ion. This ion is regularly encountered as a component of common table salt, sodium chloride. Chloride is not to be confused with chlorine, a poisonous gas soluble in water. Chloride constitutes 0.15 percent of total body weight and is widely distributed throughout the body.

Chloride helps regulate the balance of acid and alkali in the blood, with the kidneys retaining chloride to shift pH. It helps in the distribution of body fluids by maintaining the osmotic pressure that causes fluid to pass in and out of cell membranes. The concentration of dissolved particles eventually equalizes on both sides. Chloride is a component of stomach hydrochloric acid, an enzymatic juice needed in the stomach for digestion of protein and rough fibrous foods. The mineral may help the liver to function as a filter for toxins and help clean waste products out of the system. It aids in keeping joints and tendons in youthful shape, and it helps distribute hormones.

While the most common dietary source of chloride is table salt, chloride compounds are also in most foods. Especially good sources are sea vegetables such as kelp and dulse, rye flour, ripe olives, lettuce, tomatoes, and celery. Water-treatment plants sometimes add chlorine gas to water for purification purposes because it destroys waterborne diseases such as hepatitis and typhoid.

There has been much controversy over the relative merits of adding chlorine to drinking water supplies, because it is a highly reactive chemical that may join with inorganic minerals and other chemicals to form harmful compounds and carcinogens. It is known that chlorine in drinking water destroys vitamin E. It also destroys many of the intestinal flora that help in the digestion of food.

ABSORPTION AND STORAGE.   Chloride is easily absorbed in the intestine. There are 600 milligrams of chloride for every 100 milliliters of blood. Excess chloride is excreted via the kidneys and in perspiration, and some can be lost with vomiting and diarrhea.

The highest body concentrations of chloride are stored in the cerebrospinal fluid and in the secretions of the gastrointestinal tract. Muscle and nerve tissue have low amounts. Chloride compounds such as sodium chloride are found primarily within the blood and in the extracellular fluid along with sodium. Some chloride is found within cells, less than 15 percent of the body's total chloride, with red blood cells having the highest concentration. Lesser amounts are found in the skin, gonads, gastric mucosa, muscle, and nerve tissue. Small amounts are present in bone and connective tissue.

DOSAGE AND TOXICITY.   There is no RDA for chloride since it is so abundant in the American food supply. However, it's estimated that infants probably need about 0.5 to 1 gram per day. Needs increase with age, with a range of 1.7 to 5 grams daily for adults, easily met with the standard modern diet.

DEFICIENCY EFFECTS AND SYMPTOMS. Vomiting, diarrhea, and sweating are all deficiency symptoms. A deficiency of chloride can cause hair and tooth loss, poor muscular contraction, adrenal insufficiency, and impaired digestion. Chloride losses usually mean that there is also a sodium loss. Disturbances in acid-base balance result. If chlorine is left out of baby formulas, infants may develop metabolic alkalosis, hypovolemia, and significant urinary potassium loss. Psychomotor defects and memory loss may also occur. In animal studies, a deficiency resulted in growth retardation. All symptoms will disappear if chloride is replaced in the diet.

BENEFICIAL EFFECTS ON AILMENTS. Chloride is beneficial in treating diarrhea and vomiting.

Chromium

DESCRIPTION. Once considered a toxic mineral, chromium is now recognized as a major component of glucose tolerance factor (GTF), essential for regulating carbohydrate metabolism. Niacin and the amino acids glycine, glutamic acid, and cysteine are the other components of GTF. The body requires chromium only in extremely small amounts, found in the blood in concentrations of 20 parts of chromium per 1 billion parts of blood. Chromium as a free metal is not found in nature.

Chromium-containing GTF enhances the activity of insulin. Insulin facilitates the storage of glucose in cells, and GTF improves the uptake of this glucose. One theory is that GTF may bind insulin to its receptors in the cellular membrane. In this way chromium helps prevent hypoglycemia and diabetes and secondarily cardiovascular disease that can develop from diabetes. Chromium may play a role in the metabolism of fats and lower cholesterol levels while mildly increasing beneficial HDL cholesterol. The mineral may also be involved in the synthesis of protein through its binding action with RNA molecules. In the blood it competes with iron in the transport of protein.

Measuring chromium content of food can be misleading because the chromium is in different forms with varying absorption rates. For instance, the form of chromium in eggs cannot be completely utilized. The most biologically active form is organic trivalent chromium (a +3 charge). Primary sources of the most biologically available chromium are meats and whole grains rather than fruits, vegetables, or dairy products. Calf's liver is an excellent source as is whole wheat and brewer's yeast. Other sources are beef, ham, chicken, processed meats such as ham, shellfish, wheat germ, rye, potatoes with their skins, green pepper, apples, bananas, grape juice, black pepper,

and butter. However, food sources of chromium vary widely. Mushrooms and beets possibly are a source. Hard water can supply from 1 percent to 70 percent of the daily intake.

According to a report sponsored by the USDA, the intake of dietary chromium in the United States and other developed countries is suboptimal based on the minimum U.S. suggested safe and adequate daily intake of 50 micrograms. Even well-balanced diets may supply suboptimal levels of chromium. A major cause for this deficiency is the consumption of a diet high in refined foods, because chromium is removed in the manufacturing process. Americans also tend to be deficient because the loss of topsoil, due to poor agricultural practices, reduces the amount of chromium that can eventually be absorbed by some crops or reach the water supply.

ABSORPTION AND STORAGE. Chromium is difficult to absorb. Only about 0.5 percent to 3 percent of chromium consumed in the diet is retained in the body. Chromium status will affect absorption. Preliminary findings showed that chromium-containing GTF is better absorbed than inorganic trivalent chromium, but other evidence suggests that organic chromium may be readily absorbed but quickly eliminated and unused. The absorption of chromium is increased by ascorbic acid, amino acids, and starch and is decreased by zinc. In addition, aspirin may increase absorption and antacids reduce it. Chromium is excreted primarily through the kidneys with minor amounts lost in the feces.

Chromium appears to be widely distributed throughout the body, including the muscles, fat, skin, heart, pancreas, brain, kidneys, spleen, and testes. It has been found in some enzymes and in RNA. It is present in low concentrations with no tissue or organ having especially high amounts.

DOSAGE AND TOXICITY. The Food and Nutrition Board of the National Academy of Sciences gives an Adequate Intake of chromium of 35 micrograms a day for adult males and 25 micrograms a day for adult females. But because of poor absorption, health practitioners usually recommend a target of 50 to 200 micrograms a day. Dietary trivalent chromium, the form in all chromium supplements, is very safe. It can be tolerated in quantities larger than the estimated safe amounts for short-term regimens. In extremely high amounts, trivalent chromium may cause gastric irritation but not act as a toxic element interfering with essential biochemistry. However, exposure to high amounts of chromium, usually airborne in an industrial setting, can cause more severe effects such as allergic dermatitis, skin ulcers, and bronchogenic carcinoma.

DEFICIENCY EFFECTS AND SYMPTOMS. Chromium deficiency can lead to elevated insulin levels and impaired glucose tolerance, or hyperglycemia with glycosuria. While debate continues over whether a chromium-deficient diet is linked to the current epidemic of type II diabetes in the United States, and to what degree, many controlled studies have demonstrated the positive effects of treating problems of glucose tolerance with chromium. Deficiency associated with diabetes may also increase the progression of cardiovascular disease and atherosclerosis.

Deficiency is more likely in the elderly; in active people such as runners who enjoy regular, strenuous exercise; and in pregnant women, because the fetus requires so much chromium. Postoperative patients receiving glucose intravenously for nourishment also need extra chromium. Studies have shown that when patients are given 60 grams of glucose intravenously, the blood level of chromium drops significantly. If the patient also has a virus infection, the blood chromium level drops even more. Anyone consuming a diet high in refined foods is also likely to have a deficiency of chromium. This way of eating is a significant risk factor, since refined foods are low in chromium, and such foods, which are absorbed and enter the bloodstream quickly, increase production of insulin, which leads to increased need for chromium to help the body deal with them.

BENEFICIAL EFFECTS ON AILMENTS. Chromium helps regulate sugar levels in the blood for the treatment of diabetes and hypoglycemia. The mineral may have an effect on lipid metabolism. It has been shown to lower elevated cholesterol levels and triglycerides in diabetic patients and has also been effective in lowering blood lipids in nondiabetic subjects. Benefits are greater if body chromium levels are very low. Typical changes are small but can be significant for circulatory health. Diabetic weight loss and nerve disorders may also be helped with chromium.

Preliminary studies suggest supplemental chromium picolinate can enhance weight loss by leading to a gain in muscle, which has greater fat-burning potential. A 400-microgram dose was shown to be most effective. The immune system may also benefit from chromium, increasing immunoglobulins and decreasing serum cortisol. Infants suffering from kwashiorkor (a disease caused by protein deficiency) have benefited from oral administration of chromium. Schizophrenics need extra niacin and have an impaired glucose tolerance; therefore, it is possible that they may greatly benefit from chromium supplementation, creating the formation of more GTF.

Cobalt

DESCRIPTION. Cobalt is considered an essential mineral and is an integral part of vitamin B_{12}. It is needed in very small amounts. The normal concentration of cobalt in the blood is 80 to 300 micrograms per milliliter. As a component of vitamin B_{12}, it is essential for red blood cell formation and is also helpful for the normal functioning and maintenance of other cells. Cobalt also plays a role in enzyme function, substituting for manganese in activating a number of enzymes such as dipeptidase and glycylglycine, replacing zinc in some enzymes and activating others.

Best sources of cobalt are animal foods such as meats, liver, and kidney as well as clams and oysters. Ocean fish, sea vegetables, and milk are also sources. Some cobalt can be found in plant foods such as figs, cabbage, spinach, beet greens, buckwheat, lettuce, and watercress, but in very small amounts. For this reason strict vegetarians are more susceptible to a deficiency than are meat eaters.

ABSORPTION AND STORAGE. Cobalt is not easily absorbed into the bloodstream from the gastrointestinal tract and must be absorbed as a component of vitamin B_{12}. It is stored in red blood cells and plasma, the liver, kidneys, pancreas, and spleen. Most is excreted in the feces after being used by the body.

DOSAGE AND TOXICITY. There is no RDA for cobalt because the dietary need for it is low and it can be supplied in protein foods. The average daily intake of cobalt is 5 to 8 micrograms.

Cobalt added to beer as part of the manufacturing process has led to beer drinker's cardiomyopathy, or enlarged heart, and congestive heart failure. In addition, high cobalt intake may possibly result in an enlarged thyroid gland, a condition that should reverse if intake is reduced. Excessive cobalt can affect the thyroid and cause overproduction of red blood cells or polycythemia, thickened blood, and normoblastic hyperplasia in the bone marrow. Less-severe symptoms include paleness, fatigue, diarrhea, heart palpitations, and numbness in fingers and toes. A hidden source of cobalt is food contaminated with the mineral. It has been found that high-quality protein in the diet helps protect against the toxic effects of cobalt.

DEFICIENCY EFFECTS AND SYMPTOMS. A deficiency of cobalt may be responsible for the symptoms of pernicious anemia and a slow growth rate. If a deficiency is not treated, permanent nerve damage may result.

BENEFICIAL EFFECTS FOR AILMENTS. Therapeutic doses of cobalt have been used in the treatment of pernicious anemia. This action is attributed to cobalt's importance as a builder of red blood cells.

Copper

DESCRIPTION. Copper is a trace mineral found in all body tissues, with the total amount being 75 to 100 milligrams. This mineral plays a role in respiration since it is involved in the synthesis of hemoglobin, the portion of the blood that carries oxygen. In addition, it is involved in the production of collagen and the neurotransmitter noradrenalin. It is also one of the most important blood antioxidants and prevents the rancidity of polyunsaturated fatty acids and helps the cell membranes remain healthy.

Copper is present in many enzymes that break down or build up body tissue. It aids in the conversion of the amino acid tyrosine into a dark pigment (melanin) that colors the hair and skin. It is also involved in protein metabolism and in healing processes. Copper is required for the synthesis of phospholipids, substances essential in the formation of the protective myelin sheaths surrounding nerve fibers.

Copper helps the body oxidize vitamin C and works with this vitamin in the formation of elastin, a chief component of the elastic connective tissue throughout the body. It is necessary for proper bone formation and maintenance and also necessary for the production of RNA.

Oysters and nuts, especially Brazil nuts, are the richest sources. Other foods that are good sources are whole grains such as buckwheat and whole wheat, most dried peas and beans, beef liver, lamb chops, shellfish, dark leafy greens, and dried fruit. Copper is also found in thyme, paprika, bay leaves, and black pepper. The amounts vary in plant sources according to the mineral content in the soil in which the plants are grown. Drinking water may be a major source of copper. Water leaches the mineral from copper piping (soft water leaches the most). Copper is also present in copper cookware, insecticides, and both city and well water.

ABSORPTION AND STORAGE. Approximately 35 percent to 70 percent of ingested copper is used by the body, which contains about 100 milligrams. The absorption takes place in the upper intestine. Copper moves from the intestine into the bloodstream fifteen minutes after ingestion. Most of the dietary copper is excreted in the feces and bile, with very little lost in urine. Iron needs copper to be absorbed, and copper is usually found in the foods that contain iron. Nutrients that interfere with copper absorption are zinc, calcium, and iron when in excess.

Copper is stored in the tissues, with the highest concentrations in the liver, kidneys, heart, and brain. Bones and muscles have lower concentrations of copper, but because of their mass they contain more than 50 percent of the total amount in the body.

DOSAGE AND TOXICITY. The DRI for copper is 900 micrograms daily for both adult men and adult women. Copper intake needs to be balanced with zinc. An imbalance of these two minerals can cause thyroid problems. Copper is nontoxic to humans in small amounts, with an upper limit of 10 milligrams. However, there are worries of toxicity because of the small difference between therapeutic and toxic amounts. Very high doses can be lethal. Supplemental copper is indicated when copper is deficient, but plasma and red blood cell levels of copper must be monitored by a qualified physician.

Toxicity symptoms are nausea, vomiting, epigastric pain, headache, dizziness, weakness, diarrhea, and a metallic taste in the mouth. In severe toxic cases tachycardia, hypertension, jaundice, uremia, coma, and death can result.

The biochemical makeup of some people makes them prone to copper accumulation. One instance is patients with Wilson's disease, a rare genetic disorder that results from abnormal copper metabolism, bringing about excess retention in the liver, brain, kidneys, and cornea of the eyes. This condition leads to irreversible disease in the central nervous system, cirrhosis of the liver, and corneal degradation; it allows kidney and brain damage. There should be no supplementation for individuals with this condition coupled with a low copper diet and use of chelating agents.

Copper may be a factor in a certain kind of schizophrenic who has low histamine levels and abnormally high levels of copper in the blood. Testing by a qualified physician is necessary. High and low levels of copper have been found in those with emotional problems; however, hypoglycemia and neurotransmitter imbalance may be involved. It may be that copper accumulates to help fight the problem.

Many conditions are associated with high copper levels: hypertension (due to the use of oral contraceptives or smoking), stuttering, autism, childhood hyperactivity, toxemia of pregnancy, premenstrual tension (hormone activity raises blood levels), insomnia, premature baldness, tinnitus (ringing in the ears), nephritis, eczema, hemochromatosis (characterized by an accumulation of iron under the skin), painful joints, functional hypoglycemia, cirrhosis of the liver, hypoproteinemia, niacin deficiency, infections, heart attack, leukemia, mood swings, depression, senility, and mental illness. Certain kinds of anemia not helped by iron, such as hemolytic anemia and sickle cell anemia, may be an indication of elevated levels. Hemolytic anemia as well as hemoglobinuria and jaundice result from a sudden release of copper into the bloodstream. And elevated levels associated with many cancers have been found to be not the cause but the consequence of the disease.

Serum copper, elevated by estrogens, rises progressively during pregnancy. After delivery, it takes two to three months before the copper level lowers to an acceptable amount. This high level may cause the postpartum depression and psychosis that women often experience after giving birth. In addition, studies of pregnant women indicate that high copper levels can cause a decrease in body iron and a deficiency of molybdenum. Serum levels may also increase with the long-term use of birth control pills.

DEFICIENCY EFFECTS AND SYMPTOMS. Although copper deficiencies are relatively unknown, low blood levels have been noted in children with copper- or iron-deficiency anemia, edema, and kwashiorkor. People whose diets are high in fructose or zinc are at risk for deficiency. Taking megadoses of vitamin C or zinc and regularly using antacids are also risk factors. Patients receiving intravenous feeding and premature infants have also shown a deficiency. And particularly noteworthy, babies who are fed soy milk, which, unlike cow's milk, is not a significant source of copper, are at risk for copper deficiency; the development of the structure of the bone and nerve and lung tissue may be altered.

Symptoms include general weakness, impaired respiration, and skin sores. In a deficiency there is faulty collagen formation, which results in connective tissue that is easily damaged. Lack of this mineral can lead to disintegration of neurotransmitter concentrations, diminished skin pigmentation, and the demineralization of bone with consequent bone and joint problems.

Inadequate amounts can result in inefficient use of iron and protein, diarrhea, and stunted growth. Red blood cells have a shortened life span and white blood cell counts are low. Menkes syndrome, a copper-deficiency disease, leads to kinky hair, aneurisms, impaired growth, cerebral deterioration, and even death. Kidney disease and sprue are also associated with low body levels of copper.

BENEFICIAL EFFECTS ON AILMENTS. Copper works with iron to form hemoglobin, thereby helping in the treatment of anemia. Animal studies have shown that copper may protect against chemically induced cancers and some RNA viruses that may have a role in human cancers. In addition, the mineral may protect against the harmful effects of cigarette smoke and air pollution and enhance immunity.

Copper compounds protect against free radicals by preserving the structural strength of the membranes where the reactions take place. Copper plays a role in oxidase systems such as superoxide dismutase (SOD), cytochrome oxidase, and lysyl oxidase. The antioxidant SOD in liposomes has helped those with rheumatoid arthritis, scleroderma, dermatomyositis, and severe radiation-induced necrosis (wasting of tissue). Copper-zinc superoxide works as an antioxidant and anti-inflammatory. Possibly because of these actions, patients with rheumatoid arthritis wear copper bracelets. With perspiration, the copper absorbs into the skin.

Fluoride

DESCRIPTION. Fluoride is found in the earth in combination with other minerals and it is also naturally present in seawater. Tap water often contains fluoride in the form of sodium fluoride that has been added by municipalities to prevent dental caries. The richest food sources of fluoride are sea vegetables, such as laver and dulse, and seafood, including salmon, haddock, and shrimp. The fluoride content of crops varies according to environmental conditions, prevailing winds, and use of fertilizers and sprays that contain fluorine. Kidney beans, lettuce, spinach, and corn may contain small amounts. Foods made with water such as tea and gelatin can also be sources. Fluorine, not to be confused with fluoride, is a poisonous gas.

It is estimated that the body contains only about 2 to 3 grams of fluoride, mostly in the bones and teeth. The skeletal system benefits from this mineral because fluoride stimulates the formation of bone and helps prevent tooth decay. Bones and teeth have a crystalline structure that is strengthened by fluoride. Fluoride combines with calcium to produce a compound that is less soluble than other calcium salts so that calcium tends to remain in the bone rather than being reabsorbed into the circulation, and teeth are better able to withstand the wearing effect of acids present in the mouth.

ABSORPTION AND STORAGE. Fluoride is absorbed primarily in the intestines, although some may be taken up by the stomach. About 90 percent of ingested fluoride is found in the bloodstream, which normally contains about 2.8 milligrams per 100 milliliters. Half of ingested fluoride is readily absorbed by the skeletal system with the other half excreted through urine and sweat. Substances interfering with absorption include aluminum salts of fluoride and insoluble calcium.

DOSAGE AND TOXICITY. Intake of fluoride can range widely from 0.2 to 3.4 milligrams daily. The average adult may ingest from 0.24 to 0.35 milligrams of the mineral in food plus 1.0 to 1.5 milligrams from drinking water and water used in cooking. Fluoride is added to tap water at a concentration of one part per million. It is not mandated that fluoride be added to drinking water.

The Adequate Intake for fluoride, established by the Food and Nutrition Board of the National Academy of Sciences, is 4 milligrams per day for adult males and 3 milligrams for adult females. Although trace amounts are beneficial to the body, excessive amounts are definitely harmful. The mineral can destroy the enzyme phosphatase, which is vital to many body processes including the metabolism of vitamins. It also inhibits the activities of other important enzymes and appears to be especially antagonistic to brain tissues.

While fluoride in drinking water at one part per million has proven to be safe, even a small increase to two parts per million can cause problems. Dental fluorosis (mottled, dull, or pitted teeth) may occur at fluoride concentrations of two to eight parts per million, although the teeth are usually strong and cavity free; fluorosis of the bones that results in arthritis-like symptoms in the bones and joints occurs with intakes of greater than eight parts per million. And intake of greater than twenty parts per million over many years can depress growth, cause calcification of the ligaments and tendons, and bring about degenerative changes in the kidneys, liver, adrenal glands, heart, central nervous system, and reproductive organs. Fatal poisoning can occur at fifty parts per million, or 2,500 times the recommended level.

There have been reports that fluoride may be a carcinogen, but this has not been proven conclusively. Diseases such as Down syndrome have been linked to fluoridated water, and some research suggests that drinking fluoridated drinking water is possibly linked to mongolism. Calcium is an antidote for fluoride.

DEFICIENCY EFFECTS AND SYMPTOMS. A diet deficient in fluoride may lead to poor tooth development and subsequent dental caries. Fluoride deficiencies are unusual in persons consuming the American diet.

BENEFICIAL EFFECTS ON AILMENTS. Fluoride reduces tooth decay, the greatest benefit experienced when consuming the mineral from birth through tooth development. Research has shown that drinking fluoridated water rather than using toothpaste that contains fluoride is most effective. However, fluoridation of drinking water to prevent cavities may result in mottled teeth. While in some areas of the United States, nonfluoridated water has resulted in a high rate of dental caries, where fluoride levels in the water were high, tooth enamel discoloration occurred.

The mineral has also been used in the treatment and prevention of osteoporosis. Fluoride is the only nonhormonal agent known to be able to stimulate new bone growth and work with calcium to accomplish this. Bones are more stable and resistant to degeneration; however, supplementing with large doses of fluoride, 30 milligrams a day, to treat existing osteoporosis, may cause problems. Some studies indicate that the bone formed is not of high quality and the risk of hairline fractures increases. Taking high doses can also have serious side effects such as vomiting, anemia, gastrointestinal problems, and arthritis.

Preliminary research also shows that another medical use of fluoride may be to improve hearing in the elderly. Fluoride promotes recalcification of the inner bone structure of the ear, thus relieving otosclerosis, or spongy bone in the ear. Fluoride also plays a role in protecting against cardiovascular disease, including hardening of the arteries, and degenerative diseases of the musculoskeletal system.

Iodine

DESCRIPTION. Iodine is a trace mineral, most of which is converted into iodide in the body. The body contains 20 to 50 milligrams of iodine. It supports the development and functioning of the thyroid gland as an integral part of thyroxine, the principal hormone produced by this gland. Iodine is used for the production of the other thyroid hormones as well.

Because iodine is a component of thyroid hormones, iodine plays a role in the many functions of the thyroid. These include regulating the body's production of energy (cellular oxidation), influencing growth and differentiation, stimulating the rate of metabolism (or the basal metabolic rate), and helping the body burn excess fat. Cognition, speech, and the condition of the hair, nails, skin, and teeth are dependent upon a well-functioning thyroid gland. The conversion of carotene to vitamin A, the synthesis of protein by ribosomes, and the absorption of carbohydrates from the intestine all proceed more efficiently when thyroxine production is normal. Iodine is also part of thyroxin, essential for stimulating the synthesis of cholesterol.

Abundant sources of iodine are seafood such as haddock, perch, salmon, tuna, shrimp, and oysters as well as sea vegetables. Dulse contains four and a half times the RDA for iodine and kelp 397 times the RDA. Spinach, broccoli, mushrooms, potatoes, and asparagus also contain small amounts, if grown in soil rich in iodine. Bakeries may add iodine to dough as a stabilizing agent. The most abundant source of iodine in the typical American diet is iodized salt, used in home cooking and the manufacture of food products. Table salt contains 70 micrograms of iodine per gram of salt. Sea salt also contains iodine but in far smaller quantities.

ABSORPTION AND STORAGE.   Iodine can be quickly absorbed through the skin or from the gastrointestinal tract. Iodine substances are degraded in the gut to iodide that is quickly and efficiently absorbed. This free form of iodine is rapidly picked up by the thyroid and kidneys. Normally about 30 percent is picked up by the thyroid, but if deficiency exists, the thyroid will absorb as much as 80 percent of the iodide. The kidneys excrete most of the remaining iodine with some lost in sweat, tears, saliva, and bile.

Only about 20 percent of iodide in the body is found in the thyroid, but the concentration in this gland is very high. The rest is in the skin and bones, with a small amount in muscle. The body does not store iodine as it does other minerals, making regular dietary intake essential.

DOSAGE AND TOXICITY.   The RDA for iodine in adults is 150 micrograms per day. It is estimated that the average intake of iodine in the United States is more than 600 micrograms per day. A good portion of this is contributed by the 3 grams of table salt that the average person consumes daily, providing more than 200 micrograms of iodine.

There have been no reported cases of toxicity resulting from intake of too much iodine when sources are limited to the naturally occurring iodine present in food and water. However, iodine supplements are sometimes recommended, for instance, for persons on therapeutic low-salt (iodized) diets. High doses of iodine may encourage acne, and excess amounts can cause sores in the mouth, a metallic taste, diarrhea, and vomiting. Iodide mumps, or sialadentitis (inflammation of the salivary glands), is a side effect of too much iodine but is easily taken care of by stopping intake. Iodide dyes in x-rays may be allergens to some

individuals. Sudden large doses of iodine administered to individuals with normal thyroids may impair the synthesis of thyroid hormones, causing temporary hyperthyroidism.

DEFICIENCY EFFECTS AND SYMPTOMS. The most prominent symptoms of iodine deficiency are goiter, an enlargement of the thyroid gland, and hypothyroidism, an abnormally low rate of secretion of thyroid hormones, including thyroxine. Iodine deficiency can also contribute to sluggish metabolism, weight gain associated with the slow metabolic rate, fatigue, cold intolerance, rapid pulse, heart palpitations, hardening of the arteries, dry hair and skin, tremor, nervousness, restlessness, irritability, and slowed mental reactions. Iodine deficiency is currently rare in the United States, but at one time it was epidemic. In the early 1920s, before iodine was added to table salt, the rate of goiter in Michigan was 47 percent of the population.

A deficiency of iodine may also result in cretinism, a congenital disease characterized by physical and mental retardation in children born to mothers who had a limited iodine intake during adolescence and pregnancy. Polio also has been associated with deficiency. The higher rate of occurrences of this disease in the summer may be caused in part by higher losses of iodine through perspiration. A deficiency may also increase the likelihood of certain cancers such as uterine, ovarian, and breast cancer.

Various foods are considered goitrogens because they block iodine utilization in thyroid hormone production, contributing to iodine deficiency. Goitrogens include such foods as cabbage, mustard, turnip, soybean, millet, cassava root, peanuts, and pine nuts. Goitrogens are usually inactivated by cooking these foods, rather than eating them raw. However, there is no reason to completely eliminate such items from the diet because of this consideration. These foods will not impair thyroid function unless excess amounts are eaten raw and the intake of iodine is low to begin with.

BENEFICIAL EFFECTS ON AILMENTS. Iodine therapy has been used successfully in the prevention and treatment of endemic goiter with the amount necessary estimated at 1 microgram per kilogram of body weight, or about 50 to 75 micrograms for an adult. Iodine helps metabolize fat. Hardening of the arteries occurs when a disturbance in normal fat metabolism allows cholesterol to collect in the arteries instead of being used or expelled. Iodine is needed to prevent this metabolic malfunction. Researchers have suggested that fibrocystic breast disease may result from iodine deficiency and that replenishing iodine may relieve symptoms.

Iodine is beneficial to children suffering from cretinism, if treatment is started soon after birth. Many of the symptoms are reversible, but if conditions persist beyond childbirth or possibly early infancy, the mental and physical retardation will be permanent. Having sufficient iodine in body tissues also protects against exposure to radioactive iodine used in medical tests and possibly in the environment. The radioactive iodine would pass through the body more quickly if the thyroid is already saturated with normal iodine.

Backcountry water can be made pure with iodine in the form of tetraglycine hydroperiodide for campers, hikers, and hunters. Topical antiseptic for the skin comes in the form of povidone-iodine known as Betadine, but may cause reactions in certain persons.

Iron

DESCRIPTION. Iron is one of the trace minerals and critical to human life because of the role it plays in helping in the transport of oxygen from the lungs to body tissues and the return of carbon dioxide from tissues to lungs. Iron also functions in cellular energy production and metabolism as a cofactor for enzymes. Iron is the most plentiful mineral in the blood.

All iron in the body is found as a component of protein compounds. Iron makes up the central core of the hemoglobin molecule, a protein that gives color to red blood cells and transports oxygen in the blood. Hemoglobin forms in the bone marrow where iron combines with protein and copper. About 70 percent of the iron in the body is in hemoglobin. Iron is also necessary for the formation of myoglobin, which holds oxygen and transports it into the skeletal muscles and heart. In this way the muscle cells receive oxygen for use in the chemical reaction that results in muscle contraction. Iron can hold and release oxygen because it can alternate between its ferrous and ferric forms. Calcium and copper must be present for iron to function properly. Iron in transit in the blood is in the form of transferrin, one of the transport and storage compounds. The main storage forms of iron are ferritin and hemosiderin.

Iron is also necessary for collagen synthesis. It is essential in the oxidation of fatty acids. Iron is found in the brain as a cofactor in neurotransmitter synthesis for serotonin, dopamine, and noradrenaline, which modulate mood and behavior.

Iron in foods comes in two forms, heme iron found in meats and nonheme iron found in plant foods. The richest source of dietary iron is the sea vegetable kelp, with clams, liver, and oysters next. Red meats such as beef and other organ meats are also excellent sources. Beans, lentils, and peas contain good amounts of iron as well as sesame, squash, pumpkin seeds, and dried fruit such as dried apricots, raisins, and prunes. Almonds, Brazil nuts, pine nuts (pignoli), green-leaf lettuce, dandelion greens, spinach, and kale, mineral-rich unsulfured molasses, salmon, and egg yolks also provide significant amounts of this mineral. Higher amounts are also in less commonly eaten foods such as octopus, goose eggs, wild duck, and squab.

Whole grains naturally contain iron, present in the outer bran and germ. During processing to produce refined flour, the great majority of this iron is removed. Enriched and fortified grain products such as breads and cereals provide some iron but in the nonheme form, which is poorly absorbed.

ABSORPTION AND STORAGE. Iron is absorbed across the intestinal wall and into the bloodstream via active transport. This occurs primarily in the upper part of the small intestine. Iron is usually absorbed slowly over two to four hours after ingestion.

Iron is absorbed from food in regulated amounts. Of at least equal importance to the amount of iron consumed is the bioavailability of the type of iron in the diet. Diets with approximately the same content of iron can vary five- to tenfold in the amount of iron that is absorbed and retained by the body. The absorption rate of heme iron found in animal foods such as meat, poultry, and fish is about 15 percent to 45 percent. In contrast, only about 1 percent to 15 percent of nonheme iron found in plant foods is absorbed. Of the iron ingested, 90 percent is never absorbed.

These percentages also depend upon other factors. When iron is deficient, absorption increases. And absorption declines when the formation of red blood cells is reduced. The degree of gastric acidity regulates the solubility and absorbability of the iron in food. Infancy, childhood, and adolescence when growth spurts occur increase needs for protein, which will also raise the rate of iron absorption.

The other foods consumed at the same time also determine absorption. Vitamin C (ascorbic acid) and foods that contain vitamin C enhance absorption of iron by helping reduce ferric iron to ferrous iron. Consuming foods rich in vitamin C along with foods rich in iron will increase the available iron in food by 30 percent. Good sources of vitamin C are citrus fruits and sweet peppers. Vitamin A, the B-complex vitamins, copper, calcium, cobalt, manganese, and molybdenum as well as the foods that provide these are needed for complete absorption of iron. Protein foods that stimulate hydrochloric acid production in the stomach also enhance absorption. And cooking acidic foods in cast-iron pots will increase available iron thirtyfold.

Conversely, many factors may contribute to diminished absorption of this mineral, with daily losses averaging 1 milligram a day. Taking antacids and low stomach acid production reduce absorption. Oxalates in spinach and other greens, phytates in whole grains, and phosphates in sodas and meats can lead to the formation of insoluble iron compounds that prevent absorption. Cellulose, tannic acid in tea, and caffeine in coffee can limit absorption; soy protein may do the same.

Certain ailments also impair iron absorption. Alcoholism interferes with absorption of iron, as does chronic liver disease and pancreatitis. Achylia and malabsorption syndrome as well as increased intestinal mobility can play a role in reduced absorption. Iron absorption is diminished by rheumatoid arthritis, and studies have shown that arthritic patients insufficiently metabolize iron, possibly resulting in deposition of the mineral in the joints. Poor iron absorption is also associated with cancer.

Various nutrients also interfere with absorption. High intake of calcium, zinc, or vitamin E and low intake of copper block absorption. Conversely, inorganic iron will inactivate vitamin E, but this can be remedied with the addition of more vitamin E. The balance of calcium, phosphorus, and iron is very important. Excess phosphorus hinders iron absorption, although if calcium is present in sufficient amounts, it will combine with the phosphates and free the iron for use.

The iron in the body is normally used efficiently. It is neither used up nor destroyed but is conserved to be used repeatedly. Of the iron that reaches the bloodstream, most is stored in the liver, spleen, bone marrow, and blood with 1 percent used to form iron enzymes involved in energy production and protein metabolism. A relatively new method of testing iron stores is to measure the amount of ferritin levels in the blood. A normal reading is 15 to 200 micrograms.

Excess iron, rather than being excreted, is stored. Only small amounts are excreted in the urine and feces and through perspiration and exfoliation of the skin. Pregnancy, menstruation, and blood loss due to injury will remove the stores of iron at the rate of 10 to 40 milligrams a day.

DOSAGE AND TOXICITY. The RDA for adult women of childbearing age and teenagers is 15 mil-

ligrams a day; for adult men and postmenopausal women the recommendation is 10 milligrams a day. On average, the daily intake of iron is approximately 6 milligrams per 1,000 calories consumed. A person consuming a 2,000-calorie daily diet would receive 12 milligrams of iron. The need for iron increases during menstruation, hemorrhage, periods of rapid growth, or whenever there is a loss of blood. Additional iron is required during pregnancy, when the developing fetus builds up its own reserve of iron in the liver.

A toxic level of iron is unlikely due to dietary sources but may occur as a result of blood transfusion, prolonged oral intake of iron, consumption of large amounts of red wine containing iron, or addiction to certain iron tonics. Too much iron, accumulating over the years, occurs often in older men. Iron overload can result in a condition called hemosiderosis, a term for excess iron storage in the body. Iron toxicity is the result of the inability of the digestive tract to eliminate excess iron. Symptoms of iron toxicity include fatigue, headaches, weight loss, nausea, vomiting, dizziness, shortness of breath, and a grayish color to the skin.

There is also a genetic condition, hemochromatosis, characterized by deposits of excess iron into soft tissues such as the liver and spleen, impairing the function of these organs. Cirrhosis, diabetes, and heart disorders can develop, and there can be a yellowing of the skin. Excessive deposits may also result from such conditions as pancreatic insufficiency, the presence of other diseases, hemolytic or aplastic anemia, early hepatitis, or a vegetarian diet. It is thought that excessive iron in soft tissues leads to production of free radicals (cancer and disease-causing agents), which increases the need for vitamin E (a free-radical scavenger). Taking too much iron when one has an infection will encourage the growth of more bacteria.

In recent years there has also been much publicity on research conducted in Finland indicating that high levels of stored iron are associated with an excess risk of heart attack in Finnish men. Yet, the strongest dietary link was the high intake of meat, increased LDL-cholesterol levels and saturated fat, factors already associated with an increased risk of heart disease. However, additional research does suggest that elevated iron levels may play a role in the development of atherosclerosis by spinning off free radicals, which may damage cholesterol or artery walls.

DEFICIENCY EFFECTS AND SYMPTOMS. Because iron is involved in energy production, an early sign of iron deficiency is decreased energy levels. However, iron deficiency can eventually lead to iron-deficiency anemia (hypochromic anemia). In this condition, the amount of hemoglobin in red blood cells declines and the cells consequently become smaller and pale. As in other forms of anemia, iron-deficiency anemia reduces the oxygen-carrying capacity of the blood.

Symptoms of anemia may include constipation, pallor, headache, changes to fingernails (lusterless, brittle, spoon-shaped, ridges that run lengthwise), extreme fatigue, difficulty breathing, learning disabilities, apathy, decreased physical performance, impaired immune function, enlarged heart, and excessive menstrual flow. Because iron is involved in energy production, an early sign of iron deficiency is decreased energy levels. Children who are deficient have a tendency to display hyperactivity, decreased attention span, and lower IQs. These conditions can be helped if iron amounts are restored.

Anemia is a worldwide concern, since it may affect as much as 50 percent of certain populations. The most common nutrient deficiency in the United States is iron. Those at highest risk are women in their childbearing years, older infants, children, the elderly, low-income people, and minorities, although the male population is also vulnerable. As much as 30 percent to 50 percent of likely populations are iron deficient. For women who are pregnant, the figures are even higher. Children in periods of growth are also especially vulnerable.

This type of anemia can be associated with infections, candidiasis, and chronic herpes. It can also occur when individuals donate blood more frequently than they can tolerate. Anemia due to internal bleeding may not be detected for some time, especially when associated with peptic ulcers. Those with a diet high in phosphorus are susceptible to iron deficiency, as are those who have experienced long-term illnesses.

Iron deficiency anemia can be masked by vitamin B_6 or B_{12} deficiency. Consult a physician for proper care. A deficiency of B_6 and zinc can cause blood disorders that mimic an iron deficiency. Measuring serum iron, not the hemoglobin, is the most efficient way to diagnose iron deficiency. A reading of less than 40 micrograms of plasma iron per 100 milliliters of plasma indicates anemia.

Unusual food cravings are associated with an iron deficiency. Cravings for ice, starch, clay, and other non-food items have also been attributed to a deficiency.

BENEFICIAL EFFECTS ON AILMENTS.
When iron-deficiency anemia is diagnosed, a diet high in iron-rich foods with a concurrent intake of vitamin C will speed up the restoration of hemoglobin levels to normal. Iron is the most important mineral for the prevention of anemia during menstruation.

The mineral may also be beneficial in the treatment of leukemia and colitis. Plummer-Vinson syndrome is cured with iron. This disease can lead to esophageal and stomach cancer. Candidiasis and herpes simplex symptoms are helped with sufficient levels of iron if a deficiency exists. Iron-requiring proteins generate oxygen radicals that kill bacteria such as those in a mother's first milk. Muscle weakness and exercise endurance are improved with iron, which enhances both cardiac and muscular performance. Iron is also used to treat psychiatric patients suffering from akathisia, a drug-induced state of agitation, and elderly patients with restless legs syndrome.

Lead

DESCRIPTION. Lead is the most common toxic mineral and the most widespread in our environment. Humans began to be exposed to lead as a by-product of silver smelting four or five thousand years ago, but our ancient ancestors had virtually no exposure. Today the human body contains about 125 to 200 milligrams of lead and can tolerate taking in only 1 to 2 milligrams of lead daily without suffering toxic effects. Lead toxicity primarily impairs the function of the brain and kidneys and the manufacture of red blood cells.

ABSORPTION AND STORAGE. Lead contained in food is poorly absorbed, normally less than 5 percent. However, children absorb higher levels of lead. The mineral is excreted mainly in the feces. Lead enters the body via the gastrointestinal tract and the skin. It is stored in the bones and soft tissues, including the liver. Absorption can be blocked by several minerals including calcium, magnesium, iron, copper, and zinc. Lead excretion keeps pace with consumption up to a certain level of intake so that retention is negligible. The lead that does accumulate in the body is retained in the central nervous system, bones, brain, glands, and hair.

DOSAGE AND TOXICITY. Critical levels of intake, above which significant lead retention occurs, are likely to depend on the individual and are difficult to define. But whatever the exact amount, there are numerous ways to exceed this. In the modern world and in industrialized countries, potential for exposure is great because this heavy metal has been used to manufacture many products. And health problems can multiply when an individual is exposed to more than one toxin, such as lead from drinking water and mercury in fish.

Water pipes built into homes before 1930 were made of lead, which could be eroded by soft and acidic water passing through them, resulting in lead in drinking water. And when copper pipes replaced these, until 1986 lead solder was used to connect the plumbing. Some earthenware pottery is made with glazes that contain lead, which can leach out into food, especially acidic items such as orange juice and coffee. Regulations have now lowered the acceptable amount of lead in pottery, but foreign products are not covered by these restrictions. There may be lead in some cosmetics and in certain calcium supplements, in particular dolomite or bonemeal, calcium carbonate, and various calcium chelates. Peeling lead-based paint and plaster are other sources. The government has now limited the use of lead in paints, but walls in older homes may still be contaminated. Eating some of this paint is a possibility for persons, especially children, with the condition called pica. Possibly due to iron deficiency, they turn to paint and other nonfoods such as paper and dirt as a source. And some insecticides contain lead. For this reason, cigarettes made with tobacco grown with these insecticides can be a source.

The burning of coal puts lead in the environment as does motor vehicle exhaust. While cars in recent years have begun to use unleaded gas, older vehicles still use leaded. This lead is inhaled and also deposits in the soil and plants along highways and in urban areas. Even though the level of lead pollution in the air has been lowered, there remains the four to five million metric tons accumulated in soil before the 1970s. Individuals living near roads or highways who grow food might want to test the soil.

Some degree of chronic lead toxicity is common, but symptoms are not always obvious, such as subtle changes in body chemistry. And early symptoms—headaches, nausea, vomiting, constipation, fatigue, anemia, muscle pains, and pallor—may be misdiagnosed. More advanced signs are irritability, impaired memory and inability to concentrate, delayed mental development and learning, hyperactivity, hallucinations, gums that turn blue, paralysis of the extremities, vertigo, depression, and blindness. Impotence in men has been found along with infertility and anemia. Consumption of alcohol allows higher levels of lead to settle in soft tissues, including the brain. Damage is most prevalent in the heart, liver, kidneys, and nervous system. Lead is able to cause abnormal brain function by competing with and replacing other vital minerals such as zinc, iron, and copper, which regulate mental processes. High levels can cause a protein deficiency, and if vitamin E is also deficient, toxicity is more likely.

Acute lead toxicity is manifested in abdominal colic, anemia, and pathological conditions of the brain and spinal cord (encephalopathy and myelopathy).

The usual treatment for lead poisoning is the use of EDTA, a powerful chelating agent that attaches itself to the lead and promotes excretion. Injections of calcium chloride solution and administration of vitamin D can enhance detoxification. And a diet rich in minerals, especially calcium, helps prevent accumulation. Calcium reduces its absorption from the intestinal tract. Too little calcium in the body results in higher levels of lead in the blood, bone, and soft tissues. Vitamin C at doses up to 6 grams per day can help lead excretion. Foods that provide zinc, chromium, and copper are also important, as well as fiber-rich foods. And the sulfur-containing amino acids cysteine and methionine are protective. Sources are legumes and eggs.

DEFICIENCY EFFECTS AND SYMPTOMS. No available information.

BENEFICIAL EFFECTS ON AILMENTS. No available information.

Magnesium

DESCRIPTION. Magnesium is an essential mineral. Of the approximate 26 grams found in the human body, nearly 70 percent is located in the bones together with calcium, phosphorus, and various other minerals, while 30 percent is found in cellular fluids and some soft tissue.

This major mineral is involved in many essential metabolic processes, including the conversion of glucose into energy, protein and nucleic acid synthesis, and the metabolism of fat. Magnesium also plays a role in the formation of urea, allowing the removal of excess ammonia from the body. It also is involved with vascular tone, muscle impulse transmission, the electrical stability of the cells, and neurotransmission and activity. Most is found inside the cell where magnesium activates more than 300 enzymatic reactions necessary for metabolism. Magnesium is necessary for the proper functioning of the muscles, including those of the heart. Magnesium relaxes muscles, countering the stimulative effect of calcium.

Magnesium helps promote the absorption and metabolism of other minerals such as calcium, phosphorus, sodium, and potassium. It also helps utilize B-complex vitamins and vitamins C and E. Consequently, it aids during bone growth. Evidence suggests that magnesium is associated with the regulation of body temperature.

Prime sources of magnesium in the diet are whole grains, beans, seeds, nuts, and fresh green vegetables where magnesium is an essential element of chlorophyll, the compound that gives these vegetables their color. Other excellent sources include raw, unmilled wheat germ, soybeans, seafood, almonds, cashews, lima beans, figs, dates, and garlic.

ABSORPTION AND STORAGE. Between 30 percent to 40 percent of the average daily intake of magnesium is absorbed. However, when the intake of magnesium is low, the rate of absorption may be as high as 75 percent; conversely, when the intake is high, the rate of absorption may be as low as 25 percent. Absorption takes place in the small intestine and colon. The amount absorbed depends on the needs of the body, how much is consumed, intestinal transit time, and water absorption in the colon. Absorption and regulation of magnesium does not seem to be affected by calcitriol. Magnesium absorption may be enhanced by lactose and other carbohydrates. Vitamin D is necessary for the proper utilization of magnesium.

Absorption may be inhibited by calcium, which competes with magnesium for the same absorption sites. Phytates in grains, legumes, and seeds as well as oxalic acid found in plant foods such as sorrel, spinach, and rhubarb interfere with absorption as do cod liver oil and an excess of fats in the diet.

Magnesium is excreted via the kidneys. How much is lost depends upon the response of the kidneys to changing plasma levels. Aldosterone, a hormone secreted by the adrenal glands, helps regulate the rate of magnesium excretion. Losses tend to increase with the use of diuretics. Caffeine and alcohol also lead to magnesium loss but seem not to affect the body's magnesium status unless intake of these beverages is excessive.

DOSAGE AND TOXICITY. The 1997–98 RDA for magnesium for females ages 19 to 30 is 310 milligrams per day; for males of the same age, 400 milligrams. The RDA for females 31 years of age and older is 320 milligrams per day; for males of the same age, 420 milligrams. However, the diets of many individuals don't provide even this amount. It is estimated that the typical American diet provides 120 milligrams per 1,000 kilocalories, a level that will barely provide the recommended daily intake.

The balance between calcium and magnesium is especially important. If calcium consumption is high, magnesium intake needs to be high also. The amounts of protein, phosphorus, and vitamin D in the diet also influence the magnesium requirement. An elevated blood cholesterol level increases the need for this mineral.

Magnesium is generally very well tolerated. However, supplementation may in some cases cause a looser stool. Hypermagnesemia, or magnesium toxicity, is rare, owing to the kidney's ability to excrete excess magnesium (up to 60 grams per day) but can occur in some circumstances: when there is a considerable increase in absorption of this mineral, sometimes after intramuscular injection, and in instances of certain bone tumors and cancers. In addition, antacids and laxatives that contain magnesium can cause a surplus, especially in the elderly.

Symptoms of excess magnesium are drowsiness, weakness, and lethargy. Hypermagnesemia can also affect the central nervous system. If levels are very high, skeletal paralysis, respiratory depression, coma, and death can result. Intravenous feeding of calcium can counteract the toxic effect. Individuals with severe heart disease or kidney disease, as well as those with any of the conditions just discussed, should not take supplemental magnesium unless under physician's orders.

DEFICIENCY EFFECTS AND SYMPTOMS. The modern diet is often lacking in magnesium and is a common underlying cause of deficiency. Magnesium is refined out of many foods such as white flour during processing, and produce may be low in the mineral because commercial fertilizers often do not replace magnesium in soil. And excessive intake of white sugar, which supplies no minerals of any sort, replaces other magnesium-rich foods. In addition, the oxalic acid in foods like spinach and phytic acid in cereals bind magnesium, preventing absorption. The intake of other minerals such as calcium, in proportion to magnesium, interferes with absorption. And cooking foods removes minerals.

The elderly and women during pregnancy are at risk for deficiency. Low magnesium can occur in people with diabetes; those who use diuretics or digitalis preparations; those with pancreatitis, chronic alcoholism, cirrhosis of the liver, arteriosclerosis, kidney malfunction, lupus, or kwashiorkor; and those on low-calorie or high-carbohydrate diets or with severe malabsorption such as that caused by chronic diarrhea or vomiting. Some hormones when used as drugs can upset metabolism and cause local deficiencies. Fluoride, high zinc levels, high levels of vitamin D, and diuretics will cause a deficiency of magnesium.

Magnesium deficiency is thought to be closely related to coronary heart disease, including myocardial necrosis. An inadequate supply of this mineral may result in the formation of clots in the heart and brain and may contribute to calcium deposits in the kidneys, blood vessels, and heart. Heart failure resulting from fibrillation and lesions in the small arteries is linked to a deficiency of magnesium, as is vasodilation, which is followed by hyperkinetic behavior and fatal convulsions. When there is a deficiency of magnesium, stress increases the risk of cardiovascular damage, including hypertension, constriction and occlusion of blood vessels, arrhythmias, and sudden cardiac death.

Deficiency of magnesium is as important a factor in the development of osteoporosis as calcium. Research shows that patients with osteoporosis and magnesium deficiency also have low serum levels of vitamin D in its most active form. The reason for this possibly is that the enzyme that converts this vitamin to its active form requires magnesium. Another explanation is that magnesium plays a role in calcium metabolism.

The symptoms of magnesium deficiency are specific to the organ system affected. In terms of skeletal muscle, signs include backache, neck pain, tension headaches, tightness in the chest, cramps, muscle twitch, and jaw joint dysfunction. When smooth muscle function is affected, signs are constipation, menstrual cramps, urinary spasms, difficulty swallowing, and sensitivity to loud noise. Magnesium deficiency impairs functioning of the central nervous system, leading to symptoms such as hyperactivity, depression, premenstrual irritability, apprehensiveness, panic attacks, agoraphobia, disorientation, confusion, and personality changes. When the cardiovascular system is impacted by magnesium deficiency, the result can be palpitations, angina caused by spasms of the coronary arteries, high blood pressure, arrhythmias, and mitral valve prolapse.

BENEFICIAL EFFECTS ON AILMENTS. Magnesium protects against disorders and diseases associated with aging. The mineral is vital in helping prevent heart attacks and severe coronary thrombosis. Supplementation of magnesium may protect against ischemic heart disease in which the heart muscle is starved of oxygen due to spasms or narrowing and clogging of the arteries leading to the heart. It has been found that after a heart attack supplementation provided a much higher survival rate and showed far less life-threatening dysrhythmias. Magnesium will control the manner in which electrical charges are utilized by the body to induce the passage of nutrients in and out of the cells. Supplemental magnesium has proven to raise low HDL-cholesterol levels. Magnesium sulfate has been used conventionally to treat high blood pressure and preeclampsia and eclampsia of pregnancy.

Magnesium supplementation is used to treat fibromyalgia, glaucoma, kidney stones, migraines, hypoglycemia, insulin resistance, and diabetes. Magnesium is essential to glucose metabolism, and diabetes sufferers are commonly deficient in magnesium. The mineral may also help prevent some of the complications of diabetes, such as heart disease and retinopathy. Magnesium has also proven beneficial in the treatment of neuromuscular disorders, nervousness, tantrums, depression, sensitivity to noise, and hand tremor. Magnesium aids in PMS by lessening uterine contractions. The mineral is also prescribed for asthma, chronic fatigue syndrome, epilepsy, and all types of musculoskeletal disorders.

People with oxalate stones are aided with 200 milligrams daily of magnesium along with 10 milligrams of vitamin B_6; 300 milligrams alone may be beneficial. With vitamin B_6, kidney stones may be reduced. Magnesium helps protect against the accumulation of calcium deposits in the urinary tract. It makes the calcium and phosphorus soluble in the urine and prevents them from turning into hard stones.

In alcoholics, magnesium levels in the blood and muscles are low. Treatment with the mineral helps the body retain magnesium and often helps control delirium tremens, dizziness, muscle weakness, and twitching as well as bring about proper pH.

Magnesium is essential for the prevention and treatment of osteoporosis, in combination with calcium and other minerals. Magnesium, not calcium, helps form the kind of hard tooth enamel that resists decay. No matter how much calcium is ingested, only a soft enamel will be formed unless magnesium is present.

Magnesium therapy has been effective in treating diarrhea, vomiting, and kwashiorkor. Taking magnesium gluconate can prevent diarrhea. Because magnesium is very alkaline, it acts as an antacid and can be used in place of over-the-counter antacid compounds. Since magnesium works to preserve the health of the nervous system, it has been successfully used in controlling convulsions in pregnant women and for premature labor and epileptic seizures.

In supplementing magnesium, intake needs to be balanced with the other essential minerals, calcium, potassium, and zinc. A typical therapeutic dose ranges between 400 and 1,000 milligrams in divided doses.

Manganese

DESCRIPTION. Manganese is a trace mineral that takes part in a wide range of metabolic functions. While more needs to be learned about the activities of this mineral, research shows that having sufficient manganese is essential for health. It plays a part in protein, carbohydrate, and fat metabolism and helps regulate blood sugar. Manganese contributes to bone development, the formation of blood, collagen formation, protein digestion, the production of mother's milk, and the formation of urea, purine metabolism, and the immune system. It is a catalyst in the synthesis of fatty acids, cholesterol, and mucopolysaccharides. Manganese is essential for the formation of thyroxine, the hormone produced by the thyroid gland that regulates metabolism. Healthy nerves and brain and the maintenance of sex hormone production are functions of manganese. Prothrombin and vitamin K are formed with the help of manganese, and this mineral is important for the body's utilization of vitamin E and the treatment of iron-deficiency anemia.

This mineral plays a role in activating numerous enzymes involved in energy production and inactivating free radicals. Some allow for the utilization of choline, biotin, thiamin, and vitamin C. Manganese also functions in the special antioxidant enzyme superoxide dismutase (SOD), which helps protect cells from damage and inflammation.

The richest dietary sources of manganese are nuts, whole grains, dried fruits, and green leafy vegetables. Pecans, Brazil nuts, and almonds contain plentiful manganese. Rye, brown rice, lentils, pineapple, blackberries, sweet potato, chickpeas, and persimmon are also relatively high sources of manganese. However, the amount of manganese in a particular food can vary greatly depending upon the content of the soil in which the crop was grown. Ammonia fertilizers cause essential minerals, including manganese, to be leached from the soil. Relatively poor manganese sources are animal foods including meat, poultry, fish, and dairy products. The average diet contains 3 to 9 milligrams of manganese.

ABSORPTION AND STORAGE. The adult body contains only 15 to 20 milligrams of manganese. The absorption rate of manganese varies widely from 1 percent to 25 percent. It is thought that absorption takes place along the entire length of the small intestine. The amount of manganese in the body is likely controlled by excretion rather than absorption, as this amount does not appear to change when more or less is consumed. Phytates inhibit absorption as well as certain minerals. While large rates of consumption of calcium and phosphorus in the form of dairy foods, colas, and meat, and magnesium in antacids, have some effect on absorption, only iron significantly interferes with this process. In addition, aluminum reduces the body's reserves of the mineral.

Manganese is found in the highest concentration in the bones with the remaining concentration in the kidneys, liver, pancreas, pituitary gland, and adrenal glands. Small amounts are also in the intestinal mucosa and other tissues. Little is stored, with the most being 12 to 20 milligrams at one time. The body does not store this mineral well. Normally, people excrete about 4 milligrams each day, which must be replaced. Excretion occurs via the feces, much of it in the form of choline complex in the bile.

DOSAGE AND TOXICITY. There is no RDA for manganese. However, the estimated safe and adequate intake for adults is 2.5 to 5 milligrams per day. An individual consuming the standard American diet is likely to have low blood levels of manganese. Need is increased by a high intake of calcium and phosphorus. Very high dosages of manganese result in reduced storage and utilization of iron and may produce iron-deficiency anemia, especially if iron stores are low. This condition is reversible with the addition of iron to the diet.

Manganese in the amounts present in food and from normal supplemental amounts is one of the least toxic of minerals. However, when excessive intake occurs, manganese toxicity can produce symptoms similar to those typical of Parkinson's disease, which may be due to a loss of dopamine in the brain cells. L-dopa has been used in treating manganese toxicity. Manganese given to older schizophrenic patients to lower copper levels sometimes results in a rise in blood pressure. Giving zinc alone will normalize the blood pressure. "Manganese madness" is the name given to an unusual form of manganese toxicity. Miners in Chile, exposed to manganese dust that they inhaled, developed severe psychiatric symptoms including manic and violent behavior and hallucinations, followed by a shift to depression and excessive sleeping.

DEFICIENCY EFFECTS AND SYMPTOMS. A deficiency of manganese may interfere with the body's ability to remove excess sugar from the blood by oxidation or storage and lead to glucose intolerance and diabetes. Low manganese levels are linked to atherosclerosis and are a factor in triggering epileptic seizures. Tardive dyskinesia, a neuromuscular disease, requires additional manganese along with B vitamins. Ataxia, the failure of muscular coordination, has been linked to inadequate intake of manganese. Deficiencies may lead to paralysis, convulsion, blindness, and deafness in infants. Dizziness, ear noises, and loss of hearing may occur in adults. There is also a possible link between magnesium deficiency in its antioxidant role in SOD and cancer. In addition, animal studies have shown that magnesium deficiency can lead to sterility and is associated in offspring with poor survival rates, impaired growth and sense of balance, and seizures. Further research is needed to assess the relevance of these findings to human health.

BENEFICIAL EFFECTS ON AILMENTS. Manganese supplementation for several conditions warrants consideration. Because manganese may raise the level of activity of SOD, the injectable form of manganese, available in Europe, is used for the treatment of sprains, strains, and inflammation such as that associated with rheumatoid arthritis. Manganese supplements help control seizures in patients with epilepsy, as it is needed for optimal function of the central nervous system. And diabetics low in manganese may enjoy improved glucose metabolism when the deficiency is corrected.

Manganese is one of the several minerals required for the prevention of osteoporosis. This mineral promotes calcification of bone by stimulating the production of mucopolysaccharides that provide a structure on which calcification can occur. In animal studies, manganese deficiency was associated with bones that were thinner or more likely to break. Manganese may also be helpful in the treatment of osteoarthritis.

Other conditions that benefit from manganese are multiple sclerosis and myasthenia gravis (failure of muscular coordination and loss of muscle strength). When combined with the B-complex vitamins, manganese has helped children and adults who are suffering from devastating muscle weakness by stimulating the transmission of impulses between nerve and muscle. Also noted with the same combination is an overall feeling of well-being.

Many schizophrenics have high copper levels. Manganese, similar to zinc, is effective in increasing copper excretion from the body. Reproductive function also depends on manganese because of its role in the synthesis of cholesterol, a precursor of sex steroids.

Mercury

DESCRIPTION. Mercury occurs widely in the biosphere and is a natural part of the environment. It is also released into the air in industrial pollution. When mercury falls from the air and accumulates in streams and oceans, it becomes methylmercury. Mercury is toxic, presenting hazards associated with both ingestion and inhalation.

Humans can be exposed to mercury in various ways. One major source is seafood. According to the FDA, nearly all fish and shellfish contain traces of mercury. Mercury enters lakes, rivers, and oceans from industrial discharges. It settles into bacteria that are then eaten by algae; fish eat the algae and in this way mercury moves up the food chain. In particular, large fish contain the highest levels of methylmercury. The FDA and the Environmental Protection Agency (EPA) advise women who might become pregnant, women who are pregnant, nursing mothers, and young children to avoid eating shark, swordfish, king mackerel, and tilefish.

Some pesticides contain mercury that can make its way into crops. Mercurous chloride preparations can be purchased over the counter, including some laxative preparations containing calomel (mercurous chloride). Continued use of these products can result in mercury accumulations in body tissues, including the brain. Mercury compounds are also added to some cosmetics to kill bacteria. These preparations can be absorbed through the skin and into the body. Contaminated grain seeds consumed by wild game can affect people eating these animals. Industrial workers are exposed to mercury-containing products they manufacture.

Amalgam dental fillings are another source of mercury. For individuals with amalgam fillings, mercury vapor released from amalgam is the single largest source of systemic mercury. The average amalgam is 50 percent mercury and weighs 1 gram. After five years, as much as 50 percent of the mercury in an amalgam has been found to vaporize, potentially entering the bloodstream and accumulating in tissues. This release of mercury vapor remains fairly constant. Many developed countries have mandated health warnings about mercury fillings or issued limited bans. Once mercury amalgam is removed from dental patients, the EPA considers the amalgam to be hazardous waste and requires that it be disposed of appropriately in sealed, air-tight containers.

ABSORPTION AND STORAGE. The average intake of mercury from food is estimated to be only 0.5 milligrams daily. Mercury primarily accumulates in the kidneys and in the brain where about 10 percent of ingested mercury is found.

DOSAGE AND TOXICITY. Oral ingestion of mercury of as little as 100 milligrams of mercury chloride produces toxic symptoms, and 500 milligrams is almost always fatal unless immediately treated. Mercury poisoning in humans has been treated with penicillamine, a chelating agent. According to the World Health Organization, there are no safe levels of mercury exposure.

Mercury is a potent neurotoxin. Research also implicates mercury with Alzheimer's disease and other conditions associated with impaired central nervous system function such as depression, schizophrenia, memory problems, and Parkinson's disease. Some studies have found mercury to cause learning disabilities and lower IQ. Mercury-containing amalgams can promote periodontal disease and gingivitis. In turn, these conditions are known to increase the risk of cardiovascular disease and pre-term, low-birthweight babies.

Symptoms of subacute mercury poisoning may manifest in the digestive tract as excessive salivation, stomatitis, and diarrhea; or they may be neurological, such as Parkinsonian tremors, vertigo, irritability, moodiness, and depression. Mercury can also cause allergic and immunotoxic reactions as well as psychosis, loss of teeth, insomnia, fatigue, headache, loss of memory, and numbness of lips, hands, and feet.

Two forms of mercury, methylmercury and phenylmercury, deplete the brain tissues of zinc. Methylmercury, found in fish, can produce nerve, birth, and genetic defects. Studies of methylmercury poisoning include loss of coordination, intellectual ability, vision, and hearing. Organic mercury can produce redness, irritation, and blistering of skin. Chest pain, fever, coughing, and chills result from inhalation of mercury vapor.

DEFICIENCY EFFECTS AND SYMPTOMS. Mercury has no essential function in the body.

BENEFICIAL EFFECTS ON AILMENTS. Mercury does not benefit human health.

Molybdenum

DESCRIPTION. Molybdenum is a hard, heavy metallic element. Traces of this mineral are present in practically all plant and animal tissues but found very scarcely in the earth itself. The body contains only a minute quantity, about 9 milligrams.

It is a cofactor in three important enzyme systems—xanthine oxidase, aldehyde oxidase, and sulfite oxidase—which perform many vital functions. Xanthine oxidase aids in the production of uric acid and the metabolism of iron from liver reserves. Aldehyde oxidase is necessary for oxidation of carbohydrates and acetaldehyde, the toxic by-product of alcohol metabolism. Sulfite oxidase helps detoxify sulfites used as food preservatives and added to dried fruit, beer, and wine. Sulfites can cause allergic reactions in sensitive persons.

Molybdenum is found in meats, legumes, cereal grains, and some of the dark green leafy vegetables. Lentils, calf's liver, split peas, soybeans, oatmeal, green beans, and cauliflower are especially ample sources. However, the content in food completely depends on the amount in the soil.

ABSORPTION AND STORAGE. Molybdenum is readily absorbed with a very high percentage of total intake entering the system. Absorption occurs in the stomach and small intestine. The amount in the body is primarily regulated by excretion, which occurs via the urine and bile. At high levels of intake, excess molybdenum is rapidly excreted, and at low levels the mineral is conserved. Most molybdenum is stored in the liver (3.2 ppm), with the remainder in the kidneys (1.6 ppm) and the brain, lungs, spleen, and bones (0.4 to 0.2 ppm).

DOSAGE AND TOXICITY. The recommended DRI for molybdenum, established by the National Academy of Sciences, is 45 micrograms. However in the field of nutritional medicine, dosages of supplemental molybdenum can range from 150 to 500 micrograms. There is no RDA for this mineral. In addition, taking 2 to 3 milligrams of copper is suggested as there is possible loss of copper associated with molybdenum supplementation.

In animal studies, large amounts of molybdenum resulted in diarrhea, anemia, and depressed growth rate. High intake also can lead to copper deficiency. Doses of 10 to 15 milligrams of molybdenum daily may lead to gout. Heat and moisture change the action of molybdenum.

DEFICIENCY EFFECTS AND SYMPTOMS. At risk for molybdenum deficiency are individuals consuming a diet high in refined and processed foods, which are low in molybdenum, removed in the manufacturing process. High intakes of sulfur will also lead to reduced body stores. Symptoms of molybdenum deficiency are linked to how much sulfite has accumulated in the body. As noted previously, molybdenum helps detoxify sulfites, but a deficiency of molybdenum limits this process. Excess amounts of sulfites are toxic to the nervous system, and consequently signs of molybdenum deficiency caused by this are headache, rapid breathing and heart rate, nausea and vomiting, acute asthma attacks, visual problems, disorientation, and, finally, coma.

BENEFICIAL EFFECTS ON AILMENTS. Molybdenum helps prevent sulfite sensitivity. Molybdenum in soil in which crops are grown may play a role in lowering the risk of esophageal cancer by reducing the amount of carcinogenic nitrosamines in the soil. Consuming foods that contain molybdenum may block the formation of these same compounds in the body. Vitamin C also helps detoxify nitrosamines. There is evidence, although preliminary, that molybdenum may reduce the incidence of cavities in teeth, possibly by enhancing the effect of fluoride.

Wilson's disease is a rare, inherited disorder in which copper accumulates in the liver and is slowly released, leading to brain damage. While supplementation with zinc is the treatment of choice, increasing molybdenum intake may also be warranted because of its ability to block copper absorption.

Nickel

DESCRIPTION.   Research into the biological importance of nickel in humans is in its early stages, but results so far, based on plant and animal studies, strongly suggest that nickel is likely an essential trace mineral. Nickel enzymes in plants and the deleterious effects of nickel deficiency in animals point to an important role in human function as well. Legumes and cereal grains require nickel to complete their life cycle, and in animals, nickel participates in hydrolysis and redox reactions and the regulation of gene expression. It has an essential function closely related to vitamin B_{12} metabolism.

In humans, nickel is probably involved in hormone, lipid, and cell membrane metabolism and integrity. It appears to be an activator of some enzymes—arginase in the liver, trypsin, and carbosylase—and may also be involved in glucose metabolism. Highest concentrations of nickel are found in DNA and RNA where the mineral may act as a stabilizer of these nucleic acids. The production of prolactin, a hormone that stimulates milk production during pregnancy, may require nickel.

In the human diet, nickel is widely available. Oatmeal is the richest source among grains. Nickel is found in legumes, nuts (especially almonds), cherries, bananas, pears, and asparagus. Shellfish, lamb, and eggs also contain some. Chocolate is a plentiful source.

ABSORPTION AND STORAGE.   Nickel was once thought to be poorly absorbed. It is true that the absorption rate is less than 10 percent when the mineral is ingested in normal amounts with the typical Western refined-foods diet. In addition, common foods such as orange juice, milk, coffee, and tea, as well as vitamin C, inhibit absorption. However, nickel absorption can greatly increase with pregnancy, lactation, and iron deficiency. And nickel ingested in water, in very small amounts, or after an overnight fast, has a very high absorption rate of up to 50 percent, with a usual uptake of 20 percent to 25 percent.

Average intake is 60 to 162 micrograms per day, depending on the diet, since plant foods are relatively high in nickel and animal foods low. Nickel is absorbed in the small intestine. Unabsorbed nickel is mostly eliminated in the feces. Absorbed nickel is rapidly and efficiently excreted via the kidneys and does not accumulate in the body. Some nickel is also lost in sweat and bile.

DOSAGE AND TOXICITY.   While there is no RDA for nickel, an estimated safe and adequate intake is likely to be between 100 and 300 micrograms a day. An oral dose as low as 600 micrograms has proven to produce a reaction in individuals sensitive to nickel.

Toxicity from oral sources of nickel is very unlikely, because of the efficient homeostatic regulation and elimination of nickel via the kidneys. However, persons allergic to nickel can develop nickel dermatitis when nickel-containing items such as jewelry and dental materials come in contact with the skin. Allergic reactions to pierced ears because of nickel alloys in the posts of some earrings are common. Heart valves and prosthetic joints may also contain nickel.

Elevated levels of nickel can occur in people who have experienced myocardial infarction, stroke, uterine cancer, burns, and toxemia of pregnancy. It is not clear whether elevated levels contribute to health problems or are the result of some cellular malfunction.

Nickel is a by-product of many industries. It is found in heating fuel, cigarette smoke, superphosphate fertilizers, and car exhaust. Nickel can combine with carbon monoxide, producing nickel carbonyl. This compound is a carcinogen, increasing the risk of cancer in the air passageways and lungs. Symptoms of nickel poisoning are headache, nausea, vomiting, vertigo, coughing, respiratory problems, interference with enzymes in the Krebs cycle, skin rashes, and chest pain.

DEFICIENCY EFFECTS AND SYMPTOMS. Some nickel is found in most foods, making deficiency not likely to be a source of health problems in humans. However, a deficiency may develop due to excessive sweating, malabsorption, stress, chronic kidney failure, and cirrhosis of the liver. A nickel deficiency may affect zinc and iron metabolism, aggravating iron-deficiency anemia. Symptoms of deficiency in animals are impaired liver function, retarded growth, changes in skin color, and impaired reproductive function.

BENEFICIAL EFFECTS ON AILMENTS. There appears to be no need for supplementing with nickel to treat any disease conditions in humans.

Potassium

DESCRIPTION.   Potassium is one of the major minerals essential for health. Potassium constitutes 5 percent of the total mineral content of the body. More than 95 percent of that potassium is found in the fluid inside cells where it is the primary positive ion force. A small amount of potassium is present in the extra-cellular fluid as well.

Potassium plays a vital role in many body functions, including muscle contraction, nerve transmission, and normal growth enzymatic reactions. It is necessary for the conversion of blood sugar into glycogen, the form in which blood sugar is stored in the liver and muscles. Potassium unites with phosphorus to send oxygen to the brain and also functions with calcium in the regulation of neuromuscular activity. The synthesis of muscle protein and protein compounds in the blood requires potassium, as does the synthesis of nucleic acids. Potassium also helps keep skin healthy, protects against bone loss because of potassium's alkalizing effect in the body, and helps prevent kidney stones.

Having sufficient potassium in relation to sodium is very important for good health. Potassium and sodium help regulate water balance within the body, controlling the distribution of fluids on either side of cell walls. The two minerals also help preserve proper alkalinity of body fluids and together help normalize heartbeat. Potassium also regulates the transfer of nutrients to cells and functions in the chemical reactions that take place intracellularly. Research strongly links low-potassium and high-sodium levels with an increased risk of cancer and cardiovascular disease, including high blood pressure, heart disease, and stroke.

A wide range of plant and animal foods contain potassium. However, a diet that emphasizes processed and junk foods is a poor source. While natural ingredients are not only high in potassium, they are very low in sodium, with a potassium-to-sodium ratio of at least 50:1. Processed foods and foods cooked with salt and flavored with salty sauces can deliver twice as much sodium as potassium. Some of the vegetables highest in potassium are potatoes, spinach, mushrooms, and broccoli. Other rich sources are fruits such as dates, bananas, avocado, and many nuts, including almonds, Brazil nuts, and pecans. Orange juice is one of the most plentiful and easily obtained sources.

ABSORPTION AND STORAGE. Potassium is rapidly absorbed from the small intestine, with the body taking in almost 90 percent. An adequate supply of magnesium is needed to retain the storage of potassium in the cells. The mineral is eliminated via the kidneys. Potassium is also lost in perspiration (less than half that of sodium), and a small amount is excreted in the feces. The kidneys are able to maintain normal serum levels through their ability to filter, secrete,

and excrete potassium. Aldosterone, an adrenal hormone, stimulates potassium excretion. Consequently, there is little fluctuation within the body regardless of dietary intake.

DOSAGE AND TOXICITY. The Food and Nutrition Board of the National Academy of Sciences has established the Adequate Intake of potassium for adults as 4.7 grams per day. It is estimated that women consume about 2,500 milligrams of potassium and men about 3,000 milligrams per day. The optimal target for health is 4,700 milligrams a day.

Supplementation may also be necessary if the diet does not supply sufficient amounts, especially for athletes, individuals with high blood pressure, and the elderly. However, significant amounts are difficult to obtain from the standard potassium supplement because the FDA limits the amount to 99 milligrams per tablet, quite a low dosage, due to potential danger of excessive potassium intake. But "lite-salts," table salt substitutes that contain potassium chloride, offer an easy-to-obtain alternative and a much higher dose of potassium.

Potassium is considered safe in excess except for patients with kidney disease or for individuals with advanced diabetes. The most serious side effect of a toxic level of potassium is a dangerously irregular heartbeat. Kidney failure or the inability to urinate causes toxicity, and when these conditions are present, potassium supplements should never be taken. Elevated levels of potassium can also result from taking potassium-sparing diuretics or ACE inhibitor medications. Consult a physician.

DEFICIENCY EFFECTS AND SYMPTOMS. A lack of potassium first affects the muscles and nerves. There is muscle weakness, irritability, mental confusion, and rapid heartbeat. A deficiency may even lead to shock and death. Potassium deficiency over time is also associated with fragile bones. Sweating associated with regular or extended periods of exercise can lead to potassium deficiency. Because potassium helps the body convert glucose into energy, early signs of potassium deficiency in athletes are muscle weakness and great fatigue.

Potassium deficiency can occur for many reasons: diarrhea, excessive vomiting, dehydration, a deficiency of magnesium, kidney disease, early stage of diabetes when urinary flow increases, aging because the elderly are prone to a deficiency, burns, prolonged intravenous administration of saline, fasting, severe malnutrition and starvation, mental and physical stress, the use of some diuretics, and the use of laxatives, diuretics, or aspirin. Sweating due to extensive physical exertion for three hours a day can lead to a daily loss of 700 to 800 milligrams of potassium. Diet can also affect potassium status. A diet low in fruits and vegetables can cause a deficiency. Alcohol and coffee increase the urinary excretion of potassium. Alcohol is a double antagonist because it also depletes magnesium reserves. This mineral is required to retain potassium. Because sodium and potassium must be in balance, the excessive use of table salt that triggers excessive urinary loss of potassium depletes the body's conservation of its often scarce supplies.

A low blood sugar level is a stressful condition that strains the adrenal glands, causing an increase in potassium excreted in the urine while water and salt are held in the kidneys. An especially severe condition, hypokalemia, which leads to the paralysis of the respiratory muscles, can result. Hypokalemia can be triggered by major infection, acute dehydration, chronic renal failure, adrenal insufficiency, Addison's disease, diabetic acidosis, hemorrhaging in the gastrointestinal tract, and a too rapid breakdown of protein for energy purposes. In addition, insulin can trigger a flow of potassium that causes the condition. Infants suffering from diarrhea may have a potassium deficiency because the passage of the intestinal contents is so rapid that there is decreased absorption of the mineral. Severe potassium depletion is a serious condition requiring medical attention; a physician should be consulted.

BENEFICIAL EFFECTS ON AILMENTS. Potassium helps lower high blood pressure. A vegetarian diet high in potassium is helpful for the prevention of factors that cause hypertension. In addition, according to research, dosages of 2.5 grams to 5 grams of potassium per day have been effective in lowering blood pressure. High potassium intake dampens the effect of sodium because potassium promotes more excretion of sodium by the kidneys. Potassium is useful in the prevention of strokes. Giving potassium to patients with *mild* diabetes can reduce blood pressure and blood sugar levels. Since potassium is essential for the transmission of nerve impulses to the brain, it has been effective in treating headache-causing allergies. Therapeutic doses of potassium are sometimes used to slow the heartbeat in cases of severe injury, such as burns.

Potassium may also be useful for prevention of such problems as kidney stones by lowering the amount of calcium in the urine and increasing the amount of citrate because the citrate binds with calcium and makes the urine less acidic. Potassium may also help slow bone loss. And it may lower the risk of cancer when potassium-rich foods are coupled with sources of other cancer-fighting substances such as beta-carotene, vitamins E and C, selenium, and zinc.

Selenium

DESCRIPTION. Once thought to be toxic and nonessential, selenium in recent years has been recognized as essential for human function, and the list of its possible benefits keeps growing. It closely resembles sulfur in its physical properties. Among minerals, selenium is especially related to optimal health and a longer-than-average life span.

Selenium's prime function is as an antioxidant. It works as a component of glutathione peroxidase, an enzyme that protects cell membranes and red blood cells from damage by free radicals. As selenocysteine, it blocks the oxidation of polyunsaturated fatty acids. In this capacity, selenium maintains the elasticity of the skin for a youthful appearance, prevents hardening of the arteries, and deals with changes in hormone production and hormone receptors. As an antioxidant, selenium may also help prevent cancer due to its role in DNA repair. And selenium may help prevent cerebral palsy.

Selenium is necessary for the production of prostaglandins, substances that affect blood pressure. A prostaglandin deficiency also results in a deficiency of other compounds necessary for keeping the arteries free from platelet aggregation. Pancreatic function depends upon selenium, and during pregnancy it is important for the normal development of the fetus. Selenium boosts immune function. It may decrease signs of inflammation such as those associated with rheumatoid arthritis. The enzyme needed to produce thyroid hormone contains selenium, and this trace mineral may also enhance male fertility by increasing sperm production and motility.

By far the top food source of selenium is Brazil nuts, which provide 829 micrograms of selenium compared with many fish, considered a good source, which contain about 40 to 50 micrograms. Liver, beef, grains, and vegetables such as mushrooms are also sources of this mineral. However, soil content is a factor, whether directly, as in plant foods, or indirectly, as in animal products in which selenium levels are derived from feed. And even if selenium levels are adequate in the soil, the sulfur contained in widely used fertilizers and sulfuric compounds found in acid rain inhibit plant absorption of the mineral. Higher levels of selenium are typically found more in the western part of the United States than in eastern areas. In addition, selenium compounds are easily reduced by heat, processing, and cooking. Refining of grains reduces selenium content by 50 percent to 75 percent and boiling by 45 percent.

ABSORPTION AND STORAGE. Selenium is readily absorbed at a rate as high as 90 percent. The blood level is 0.22 micrograms per 100 milliliters. Selenium is in nonfat tissue. The liver, heart, spleen, and kidneys contain four to five times as much selenium as do the muscles and other tissues. In males, some selenium is present in the seminal vesicles and testes. Organic selenium is better absorbed than the inorganic forms of selenium.

DOSAGE AND TOXICITY. The RDA for selenium is 70 micrograms per day for adult men and 55 micrograms for adult women. Male sperm cells contain high amounts of selenium, and substantial amounts of sperm are lost during sexual intercourse. For this reason, requirements are higher for men than for women.

The average "good" diet may contain only 35 to 60 micrograms per day. A standard therapeutic supplemental dosage is 50 to 200 micrograms of selenium per day with greater amounts given only if monitored by a physician. Of note is that the difference between what is considered an adequate dosage of selenium and a toxic dose is relatively small. A dosage of more than 900 micrograms a day can be toxic.

Supplemental selenium comes in the organic forms selenium yeast and selenomethionine and the inorganic forms sodium selenite and sodium selenate. The organic type that is a specially enriched form of brewer's yeast and the synthetic L-Se-Met are safest and best. Inorganic selenium is not as well absorbed. In addition, sodium selenite reacts with vitamin C and inhibits absorption.

Selenium toxicity is rare. Signs of toxicity may include a garlic odor in sweat and breath, a metallic taste in the mouth, nausea and vomiting, nervousness, depression, mood changes, an increase in tooth decay, and inflammation of the skin. There is also speculation that overdoses of selenium can increase tooth decay. In extreme instances of toxicity, there may also be fever, increased respiratory and capillary rate, gastrointestinal distress, myelitis, liver and kidney problems, loss of hair and fingernails, and even death.

DEFICIENCY EFFECTS AND SYMPTOMS. A deficiency of selenium can lead to premature aging. Studies show that low levels of selenium are associated with a range of diseases such as heart disease, skin problems, various infections, cataracts, growth retardation, liver necrosis, muscular dystrophy, and inflammatory conditions such as eczema, psoriasis, and arthritis.

The link between low levels of selenium and cancer is particularly strong. Low levels are related to cancer of the bladder, colon, breast, ovary, prostate, skin, and lungs as well as to leukemia. In South America, which has the highest selenium levels in the soil, the rate of cancer of the large intestine is one-quarter that in the United States. A deficiency of both vitamin E and selenium is linked with fatal cancer. A deficiency of vitamin A and selenium is associated with skin cancers.

Selenium deficiency impairs reproductive function. Animal tests reveal that deficient rats produced immobile sperm and most of the sperm were broken near the tail. Other studies show that a deficiency results in infertility. Deficiencies are similar to those due to diminished vitamin E. Studies in Australia show that a selenium deficiency may relate to crib death (SIDS). A deficiency caused by defective selenium absorption mechanisms can result in neuronal ceroid lipofuscinosis, a disease that causes accumulation of pigment in nerve cells and is characterized by mental retardation, diminished vision, nerve disorders, and eventually death.

BENEFICIAL EFFECTS ON AILMENTS. Supplementation of selenium, above the amounts typically in the diet, enhances the immune system by increasing the production of white blood cells. It is useful in the treatment of infections and autoimmune diseases and appears to be of great importance to those who suffer from AIDS. Selenium is even more effective when taken with vitamin E. Arthritis and other autoimmune diseases such as osteoarthritis and rheumatoid arthritis are helped with both injected and oral types of selenium and vitamin E.

There is much evidence that selenium helps prevent cancer. In areas of the United States with high levels of selenium in the soil, males show significantly lower overall cancer death rates. Also, in these areas, there are fewer cancers in both men and women in those organ systems involved in the assimilation, metabolism, and excretion of selenium.

Selenium coupled with vitamin E is related to increased strength and vigor as well as lower rates of cardiomyopathy and myocardial deaths in heart patients. Keshan disease, found mainly in China, is a type of heart disease characterized by an enlarged heart and congestive heart failure. The disease is prevalent in children who may experience retarded growth, skeletal deformity, and muscular atrophy. This condition is due to low levels of selenium in the soil and is prevented with supplementation. Because selenium has anticlotting effects in blood, a combination of this mineral along with vitamin E may help prevent restricted blood flow, heart attack, and stroke. It is also useful for high blood pressure and has been used successfully in reducing or eliminating recurrent angina attacks.

Selenium may improve energy levels and mood. It helps prevent cataracts and a range of inflammatory conditions, including those of the skin and joints. Dandruff and seborrhea are also helped. When combined with protein, it is beneficial in treating kwashiorkor. It protects against hypertensive kidney damage. Selenium has been successful in improving patients with cystic fibrosis and those with muscular dystrophy when combined with vitamin E.

Research in the early 1970s demonstrated that selenium protects against radiation. It detoxifies metals such as mercury, cadmium, silver, and thallium, preventing their absorption and aiding in their excretion. In animal studies, selenium detoxified the cancer-fighting drug Adriamycin without preventing the medication's actions. Selenium may protect against alcoholic liver disease and also against the damage from cigarette smoking.

Silicon

DESCRIPTION.   Evidence is accumulating that silicon is essential for human health although it has not been formally designated as one of the essential minerals at this time. Research has shown that the mineral is essential in animals. Silicon is abundant in nature, second only to oxygen. The most plentiful mineral in the earth's crust is crystalline silicon or quartz. In the human body the mineral is found in the skin, bones, fingernails, hair, lungs, trachea, lymph nodes, cartilage, tendons, blood vessels, and aorta.

A prime function of silicon is to give strength and durability to tissues thanks to its ability to form long molecules. Animal studies indicate that silicon is involved in the initiation of calcification in bone and cartilage calcification. Silicon also affects cartilage composition in association with chondroitin sulfate. The mineral may also perform a vital function in the brain as it is needed to prevent detrimental changes in these tissues, particularly when intake of calcium is low, thyroid function is impaired, or levels of dietary aluminum are high. Research also provides some evidence that silicon may be important for maintaining cardiovascular health. Blood vessels contain collagen and glycosaminoglycans, which are affected by silicon deprivation.

Plant foods are richer sources of silicon than animal foods. Unrefined grains that are high in fiber, such as brown rice and oatmeal where silicon is part of the plant fiber, are an excellent source. In contrast, nearly all of the original silicon in grain is removed when grain is milled and refined. Another excellent source is root vegetables. Common vegetables such as lettuce, tomatoes, cucumbers, onions, and beets contain the mineral, as well as citrus such as oranges. Legumes and seafood also are sources. Hard drinking water may also provide silicon.

ABSORPTION AND STORAGE.   The silicon content of the standard diet has been estimated at about 20 to 45 milligrams a day. Depending upon the form of dietary silicon, absorption can range from 1 percent to 70 percent. However, it is thought that some forms of silicon are well absorbed given that the body excretes about half of the intake, indicating an excess. In addition, absorption of silicon is increased when calcium, potassium, magnesium, manganese, and boron are present. Excretion is likely to occur primarily via the kidneys. Silicon contributes about 0.05 percent of body weight.

DOSAGE AND TOXICITY.   Although there is no RDA for silicon, the basic requirement for silicon is estimated to be between 5 and 20 milligrams. A safe and adequate daily intake of silicon is about 20 to 40 milligrams. The safe upper limit is thought to be 50 milligrams a day, although toxicity due to silicon from dietary sources awaits further research. The calculated silicon content of the FDA Total Diet is 40 milligrams per day for men and 19 milligrams for women. Proper levels during growth periods are essential. Silicon levels decrease with age, and amounts should therefore be increased for the elderly.

In contrast with dietary silicon, toxicity to inhaled silicon is clearly defined, the condition known as silicosis. This is a respiratory disease characterized by an overproduction of collagen in the lungs. It is contracted by miners who inhale silicon fibers and can result in malignant tumor formation.

Although rare, there is also evidence that long-term use of antacids known as magnesium trisilicate contributes to the formation of kidney stones.

DEFICIENCY EFFECTS AND SYMPTOMS. In animal studies, silicon deficiency results in abnormal skeletal development and impaired integrity of ligaments and tendons. Based on this research, silicon deficiency in humans may be a factor in some joint disorders such as osteoarthritis and may play a role in osteoporosis. Silicon deficiency may increase the risk of heart disease, although further study is required. Research has shown that the silicon in arteries begins to decline as atherosclerosis starts to develop.

BENEFICIAL EFFECTS ON AILMENTS. In the early 1900s, studies were beginning to find evidence of the therapeutic effects of silicon, but by 1930, these results were in question. Then in 1972 silicon was reported to be essential for bone formation and reports of other benefits followed. Possible uses for silicon in treating conditions are based on its ability to strengthen tissues. Silicon may be helpful in helping prevent joint disease such as arthritis, atherosclerosis, and gastric ulcers, and it may help repair fractures and treat osteoporosis. Silicon plays a role in maintaining the firmness and elasticity of the skin, as a component of collagen.

Sodium

DESCRIPTION. Sodium is an essential mineral that is found in every cell in the body. It is present in all body fluids, predominantly in the fluid in between cells but also in the blood. About 50 percent of the body's sodium is in these fluids and the remaining is found within the bones.

Acting with potassium, this major mineral regulates the balance and distribution of fluids throughout the body and inside and outside the cells. These two minerals also help maintain the body's normal pH. Sodium and potassium are also involved in muscle contraction and expansion and in nerve stimulation.

Sodium is involved in oxygen transport and keeps other minerals in the blood soluble, preventing them from accumulating in the bloodstream. Another important function of sodium is the transport of amino acids and carbon dioxide, aiding in its elimination from the body. Sodium acts with chlorine to improve blood and lymph health. It is necessary for the production of hydrochloric acid in the stomach, thereby supporting digestive function.

This vitally important mineral is found in virtually all foods, especially sodium chloride, or table salt. Plant foods have less sodium than animal foods. Processed foods such as canned soups, cured and luncheon meats, salted crackers, and processed cheeses are high in sodium and may present a problem for those who use them regularly in their diets. It is important to read packaged food labels for sodium content of products. Less obvious sources of sodium are the many substances added to foods, such as monosodium glutamate (MSG), sodium nitrate, sodium nitrite, propionate, alginate, citrate and sulfite, baking soda, and baking powder. Soy sauce and some seasoning mixtures are also very high in sodium.

ABSORPTION AND STORAGE. Sodium is readily absorbed in the small intestine and stomach and is carried by the blood to the kidneys where it is filtered and returned to the blood in amounts needed to maintain the levels required by the body. The absorption of sodium requires energy. The adrenal hormone, aldosterone, is an important regulator of sodium levels in the body along with the autonomic nervous system and renal mechanisms. Absorption and excretion of sodium directly correlates with the amount of water taken.

Excess sodium, which usually amounts to 90 percent to 95 percent of ingested sodium, is excreted in the urine. Urinary levels reflect the dietary intake. When intake is high, the rate of excretion is high; when intake is low, the rate of excretion is low. Blood levels are maintained at 310 to 333 milligrams per 100 milliliters. Small amounts of sodium are also present in perspiration. Sweat contains only 1 gram sodium per liter. Physical exertion and humidity will extract about 46 to 92 milligrams of sodium per day. Vomiting and diarrhea can also lead to depletion of sodium. Sodium supplements may be needed in such cases.

DOSAGE AND TOXICITY. There is no established RDA for sodium, but guidelines do exist for intake. The amount of sodium considered sufficient to maintain sodium balance in the body is 500 milligrams a day (569 milligrams per day for pregnant women), and the amount of sodium considered adequate to maintain health in adults is 2,000 milligrams a day. However, the usual intake far exceeds needs. The average American ingests 2.3 to 6 grams of sodium a day, but 15 grams per day is quite common. (A teaspoon of salt contains more than 2,000 milligrams of sodium and a pinch of salt contains 267 milligrams.)

An excess of sodium in the diet may lead to loss of potassium in the urine, causing a potassium deficiency. Abnormal fluid retention (edema) accompanied by dizziness and swelling of legs, face, and other areas can also occur. For individuals who are sensitive to salt (30 percent of the population), sodium intake can cause hypertension or high blood pressure. Restricting intake can reduce blood pressure in 20 percent to 30 percent with hypertension. Controlling high blood pressure may also prevent stroke. However, potassium levels are also an important factor in these conditions no matter what the amount of sodium ingested. Lite-salt contains both sodium and potassium.

Diets containing excess amounts of salt contribute to the increasing incidences of liver, heart, and kidney disease. The most effective way to reduce sodium intake is to avoid processed foods. Salt sprinkled on foods at the table typically contributes a relatively small amount of sodium.

DEFICIENCY EFFECTS AND SYMPTOMS.
Deficiencies of sodium are rare because nearly all foods contain some. Only in exceptional cases will a deficiency occur, for instance when there is significant vomiting or diarrhea, severe fasting, or starvation. The loss of a large amount of fluid plus sodium from the body can lead to hypotension, with accompanying muscle cramps and the collapse of veins. And if fluids are replaced but not sodium, water intoxication can result. Symptoms are headache, loss of appetite, apathy, and muscle twitches.

A sodium deficiency can cause intestinal gas, weight loss, poor memory, short attention span, inability to concentrate, vomiting, low blood sugar, heart palpitations, and muscle weakness and shrinkage. The conversion of carbohydrates into fat for digestion is impaired when sodium is absent. Arthritis, rheumatism, and neuralgia (sharp pain along a nerve) may be caused by acids that accumulate in the absence of sodium.

BENEFICIAL EFFECTS ON AILMENTS. An individual suffering from high blood pressure is advised to maintain a low-sodium diet, since sodium may aggravate this ailment. Resistance to heat cramps and heat stroke may be increased by moderate sodium intake. Sodium helps keep calcium in a solution that is necessary for nerve strength. Clinical studies indicate that low-sodium diets are effective in preventing or relieving the symptoms of toxemia (bacteria poisoning), edema (swelling), proteinuria (albumin in the urine), and blurred vision. Sodium is also needed to correct hypotension. Fluids need to be replaced before sodium because without liquids sodium cannot be absorbed. A slight increase of dietary sodium throughout the day may be all that is required. Kelp is an excellent source of sodium.

Strontium

DESCRIPTION. The trace mineral strontium, not to be confused with radioactive strontium-90, a component of nuclear fallout, is widespread in the environment. It is one of the most abundant minerals in seawater and comprises about 0.04 percent of the earth's crust. Strontium is chemically similar to calcium, able to replace calcium in certain biochemical processes. Most of the strontium in the human body, 300 to 350 milligrams, is found in connective tissue and bone where it is a component of hydroxyapatite crystals.

Strontium research lost followers in the 1950s, but one researcher, Dr. Stanley Skoryna, director of medical research at St. Mary's Hospital in Montreal, persisted in searching for therapeutic uses. He found that osteoporosis patients given supplements of strontium had less bone pain. In addition, supplements promoted remineralization of fragile bone in patients with metastatic bone cancer. He also found that strontium may be protective of certain energy-producing structures within cells.

Strontium is present in most foods, in small amounts that vary depending on soil content. The amount of strontium in water also varies dramatically. Consequently, daily intake can range from 2 milligrams to more than 10 milligrams.

DOSAGE AND TOXICITY. Strontium is stable and one of the least toxic of trace minerals, even in large doses such as 400 milligrams a day, over a number of years. If taken as a supplement, a suggested dosage range is 0.5 to 3 milligrams per day. There is no RDA for strontium.

ABSORPTION AND STORAGE. The rate of absorption of strontium ranges from 20 percent to 40 percent. Most is stored in the bones and teeth. Strontium is excreted in the feces.

DEFICIENCY EFFECTS AND SYMPTOMS. Dr. Skoryna believes that the human diet probably contains insufficient quantities of strontium and may need to be supplemented. Strontium deficiency in animals results in poor calcification of teeth and bones, a decrease in growth, and an increase in tooth decay.

BENEFICIAL EFFECTS ON AILMENTS. Research indicates that strontium makes bones and teeth thicker and stronger. Strontium may participate in bone remodeling processes, helping to prevent osteoporosis. Epidemiological studies of populations consuming water with a concentration of 6 to 10 milligrams of strontium per liter had fewer cavities. It also possibly plays an important role in metastatic bone cancer. Strontium may afford protection from radioactive strontium that has accumulated in the body, able to replace strontium-90 in tissues so that this toxic form can be excreted in the urine.

Sulfur

DESCRIPTION. Sulfur is a nonmetallic element that occurs widely in nature, being present in every cell of animals and plants. Sulfur makes up 0.25 percent of the total weight of the human body. Sulfur's prime role is as a component of protein molecules. The majority of protein in the body is present in the sulfur-containing amino acids methionine, cystine, and cysteine. Sulfur is also found in thiamin and biotin, both B vitamins. Small amounts are also present in organic sulfates and sulfides.

Because of sulfur's important relationship with protein, it appears to be necessary for synthesis of collagen, the substance in the skin that keeps it firm and elastic. Sulfur is prevalent in keratin, a tough protein substance necessary for healthy maintenance of the skin, nails, and hair. Sulfur is called nature's "beauty mineral" because it keeps the complexion clear and youthful and the hair glossy and smooth. Sulfur proteins contribute to the permanent wave in hair. The smell when hair is burned is due to its sulfur content.

Sulfur is found in insulin, the hormone that regulates carbohydrate metabolism. Sulfur supports detoxification processes. Bile contains the sulfur-containing amino acid taurine. Sulfur is also a component of glutathione, the primary antioxidant in cells that helps maintain a healthy liver, the organ that cleanses the blood. Sulfur detoxifies sulfuric acid and other toxic substances, including compounds caused by pollution and radiation. This element also resists bacteria. It also occurs in carbohydrates such as heparin, an anticoagulant found in the liver and other tissues.

Sulfur works with thiamin, pantothenic acid, biotin, and lipoic acid, which are needed for metabolism and good nerve health. In addition, sulfur plays a part in tissue respiration, the process whereby oxygen and other substances are used to build cells and release energy.

The soil in many areas is deficient in sulfur; therefore, plant foods vary in content. The best source of sulfur is eggs. Other protein foods, including legumes, meat, fish, cheese, and milk, are also good sources.

ABSORPTION AND STORAGE. Supplemental sulfur is taken in the amino acid form. This element is stored in every cell of the body. The highest concentrations are found in the joints, hair, skin, and nails. Sulfolipids are found in the liver, brain, and kidneys. Excess sulfur is excreted in the urine and feces.

DOSAGE AND TOXICITY. There is no RDA for sulfur, because it is assumed that a person's sulfur requirement is met when the protein intake is adequate. Sulfur used for therapeutic purposes comes in several forms, including ointments, creams, lotions, and dusting powder.

DEFICIENCY EFFECTS AND SYMPTOMS. Vegetarians may become deficient in sulfur if they don't eat adequate sulfur-rich protein, for instance if they have eliminated eggs from their meals. There are no clearly defined signs of sulfur deficiency.

BENEFICIAL EFFECTS ON AILMENTS. Sulfur is important in the treatment of arthritis. The level of cysteine, a sulfur-containing amino acid, in arthritic patients is usually much below normal levels. Sulfur baths have long been recommended to ease joint disease, and chondroitin sulfate is a common contemporary treatment. Magnesium sulfate is a laxative. And the sulfur-containing compound methylsulfonyl methane (MSM) is sometimes suggested to treat allergies.

When used topically in the form of an ointment, sulfur is helpful in treating skin disorders, such as psoriasis, eczema, and dermatitis. It also may be beneficial in treating ringworm.

Tin

DESCRIPTION. In 1950, tin was discovered to be an essential trace element. Tin's importance for some mammals has been established, however, its specific functions in the human body are unknown. The tin that is found in the body is likely a contaminant.

Tin is present in the soil and in foods in very small quantities. Food storage containers, such as cans containing tin, are another source, leaking the metal into food, and a tin salt, stannous fluoride, is used as a preservative in foods and added to some toothpaste.

ABSORPTION AND STORAGE. The estimated daily intake of tin ranges from 1.5 to 3.5 milligrams; however, the amount can be much higher if tinned foods are consumed. It is not known how much is absorbed but the amount is thought to be minimal. Because appreciable amounts are part of air pollution, lung tissues have the highest concentration of tin. Most tin is excreted in the feces with some in sweat and urine.

DOSAGE AND TOXICITY. There is no RDA for tin and no reason to supplement. Rather, concern is focused on avoiding it. Although tin is considered only mildly toxic to humans, animal studies have identified toxicity symptoms that include impaired immune function, retarded growth, anemia, and changes in liver cells. These effects were reduced with copper and iron supplementation. In humans, tin may interfere with absorption of minerals such as zinc and may replace calcium in bone, contributing to the risk of osteoporosis.

Excessive intake can occur when the mineral leaches out of tin containers into foods and beverages. A food product can acquire as much as 35 milligrams of the metal, and even more if the container is opened and the contents stored in this for a period of time.

Acidic foods such as orange juice are particularly susceptible. The exception is lacquered tin containers, identifiable by their yellow interior surfaces, which leach out only small amounts of tin.

DEFICIENCY EFFECTS AND SYMPTOMS. Animal experiments have shown that a deficiency results in poor growth and diminished hemoglobin synthesis. Tin deficiency is thought not to be a concern in humans.

BENEFICIAL EFFECTS ON AILMENTS. There are no therapeutic uses of tin known at this time.

Vanadium

DESCRIPTION. Although vanadium began to be considered essential in humans more than a decade ago, much more needs to be learned about its functions. It is present in most body tissues. Most research is focusing on its role in glucose metabolism. Laboratory and animal studies have shown that vanadium possibly mimics the actions of insulin, suggesting that vanadium may be useful in managing diabetes in humans. There is also the beginning of some promising human research indicating the benefits for type II diabetics.

In addition, vanadium appears to be involved in lipid and catecholamine metabolism, cholesterol production, thyroid function, growth, reproduction, calcium metabolism, red blood cell production, and bone and tooth formation.

Small amounts of vanadium are also present in all foods. The most plentiful sources are grains such as buckwheat, oats, rice, and corn; vegetables, including green beans, carrots, cabbage, mushrooms, spinach; seasonings such as parsley, dill seed, and black pepper; beverages such as beer and wine; oysters and other shellfish; and soybeans. Other excellent sources are unsaturated vegetable oils such as safflower, sunflower, corn, soy, and olive.

In addition, processed and refined foods are likely to be higher in vanadium, which can leach from the stainless steel equipment used in processing the food, although this form of vanadium may not be bioavailable.

ABSORPTION AND STORAGE. The average diet provides about 15 micrograms of vanadium, but intake can range from 10 to 70 micrograms. The majority of research indicates that only 1 percent to 5 percent of ingested vanadium is absorbed, but this rate can be higher depending on such factors as the form of vanadium and composition of the diet. Absorption takes place in the upper gastrointestinal tract.

The body contains about 100 micrograms of vanadium, stored in the kidneys, liver, testes, bone, and spleen. Vanadium is rapidly used by the body but not readily absorbed, with most rapidly excreted in the urine.

DOSAGE AND TOXICITY. The body needs about 10 micrograms of vanadium per day. However, higher amounts up to about 60 micrograms are thought to be safe, as vanadium is considered fairly nontoxic, with excess not associated with any particular disease. One exception is the elevated levels of vanadium associated with bipolar disorder. In this case, toxicity may start at dosages of 10 to 20 micrograms a day. Large doses of vitamin C appear to help detoxify the excess.

In animal studies, symptoms of toxicity were loss of appetite, diarrhea, and stunted growth. There may be negative effects if vanadium and chromium are taken at the same time. The most common form of vanadium supplement is vanadyl sulfate (VS). One concern is that VS might interact with diabetic medications and have an additive effect by causing a drop in blood sugar since it increases insulin sensitivity. There is also preliminary evidence that supplemental vanadium might cause kidney damage.

DEFICIENCY EFFECTS AND SYMPTOMS. Animal studies show that vanadium deficiency results in decreased reproduction rates, increased mortality of the young, altered thyroid function, and skeletal malformation. In humans no specific signs of vanadium deficiency have been reported. However, some researchers have proposed that signs of vanadium deficiency are possibly impaired blood sugar control and cancer as well as higher cholesterol and triglyceride levels and the consequent heart disease.

BENEFICIAL EFFECTS ON AILMENTS. Vanadium may help prevent cancer and diabetes. It may also be useful in reducing cholesterol and improving bone and teeth mineralization. There is a lack of data supporting claims that vanadium increases muscle mass or blood flow in bodybuilders.

Zinc

DESCRIPTION. Zinc is an essential trace mineral. The human body contains approximately 2 to 3 grams of zinc, making this mineral second only to the trace mineral iron in quantity in the body. Zinc is present in all body tissues. The blood contains approximately 900 micrograms of zinc per 100 milliliters.

This vital trace mineral participates in body chemistry in diverse ways. It is a constituent of more than two hundred enzymes involved in such varied functions as protein digestion, aerobic and anaerobic energy production, electron transport, RNA synthesis, bone metabolism, alcohol detoxification, and the normal absorption and action of vitamins, in particular, the B vitamins.

Zinc fights disease and protects the immune system, thereby aiding in the healing of wounds and burns. This mineral also assists in the activities of various hormones, including insulin, growth hormone, and hormones produced by the thymus. Zinc is essential for the taste buds and the skin's oil gland function. And it helps regulate testosterone in the prostate.

The best source of zinc and all trace elements are natural, unprocessed foods. Diets high in protein, whole grain products, brewer's yeast, wheat bran, wheat germ, herring, and pumpkin seeds are usually high in zinc. However, soil exhaustion and the refining of food adversely affect the zinc levels.

ABSORPTION AND STORAGE. Zinc is readily absorbed in the upper small intestine at a rate of 40 percent to 50 percent depending upon body needs. However, absorption may be limited by various factors. Taking large amounts of calcium or iron can lessen absorption. Zinc absorption can also be blocked by cadmium, silver, and copper, which compete for the same absorption sites in the small intestine. Fiber in the diet—as found in grains, fruits, and vegetables—will bind with zinc in the intestine before the mineral can be absorbed. And phytic acid in certain grains may prevent absorption. It is best to take supplemental zinc apart from eating such foods. There is also a rare genetic disease in which zinc absorption is diminished, acrodermatitis enteropathica.

In the special case of giving infants sufficient zinc, breast milk is preferred to formula. The zinc in prepared formulas is not as easily absorbed.

The largest stores of zinc are found in the liver, pancreas, kidney, bones, and voluntary muscles. It is also present in certain parts of the eye, prostate gland and spermatozoa, skin, hair, nails, and white blood cells. Some zinc held in the body may be released when zinc intake is inadequate but reserves are not easily removed so the diet must be sufficient to meet body needs.

The major route of excretion is through the gastrointestinal tract in feces; little is lost in the urine. About 6 milligrams is lost daily.

DOSAGE AND TOXICITY. The National Research Council has established an RDA of 12 milligrams a day of zinc for adult women and 15 milligrams a day for adult men. The average American consumes about 10 milligrams of zinc per day.

Zinc is likely the least toxic trace mineral; however, dosages higher than, for instance, 150 or 200 milligrams a day, can produced side effects. Short-term toxic reactions include nausea, vomiting, dizziness, loss of muscle coordination, sleepiness, gastrointestinal discomfort, lethargy, renal failure, and anemia. When these signs occur, a reduction in dosage is necessary. Large dosages of zinc over extended periods of time have led to decreased levels of the desirable HDL cholesterol. High doses can also cause a copper deficiency, which is involved in an increase of LDL cholesterol, leading to higher risk of heart disease and incomplete iron metabolism. Megadoses of zinc may impair the immune system.

Increasing copper intake along with zinc is recommended, even when taking lower dosages of zinc such as 30 to 50 milligrams a day. An exception is in the case of Wilson's disease in which there are excess levels of copper in the blood. When zinc is added to the diet, vitamin A is also needed in larger amounts. Zinc also needs to be balanced with selenium, a trace mineral that protects against cancer. Zinc is a selenium antagonist and can reduce selenium's effectiveness. Conversely, when zinc antagonizes cadmium, a toxic metal that can increase the risk of cancer, zinc is protective against the disease.

DEFICIENCY EFFECTS AND SYMPTOMS. The most common cause of zinc deficiency is an unbalanced or poor diet (high in grains and cereals and low in animal protein), although other factors may also be responsible. For instance, alcohol flushes stored zinc out of the liver and into the urine. At-risk groups are preschool children, low-income populations, hospital patients, vegetarians, athletes with low zinc intake, and the elderly, who are also subject to all the other deficiencies that occur with the aging process. Pregnant women and women taking oral contraceptives may have low levels of zinc in their blood plasma. And zinc deficiency can occur in individuals who have pica, a disease in which the person eats dirt or clay (geophagia).

People living in the Middle East are more likely to be deficient in zinc. Their diet contains more kinds of cereal grains than in Western diets and very little protein. In addition, the high temperatures of the region induce sweating, which carries zinc away from the body and compounds the deficiency.

Low zinc levels are associated with various conditions such as chronic infections, renal disease, cardiovascular disease, and protein malnutrition. Low levels also may occur when receiving intravenous feeding. And low levels have been found in patients with esophageal and bronchogenic cancer, AIDS patients, and persons with intestinal parasites that interfere with absorption. Excessive zinc excretion occurs in leukemia and Hodgkin's disease. Lack of zinc may also contribute to the development of osteoporosis.

Consequences of zinc deficiency are varied, reflecting the many roles this mineral plays in body chemistry. The brain, skeleton, eyes, heart, gastrointestinal tract, and lung tissues are affected. The consequences of a deficiency are greater during growth periods. Signs of a mild deficiency can be a greater susceptibility to infection, slow wound healing, skin problems such as psoriasis and acne, and a decreased sense of taste and smell. Other physical indications often associated with low levels of zinc include mouth ulcers, bad breath, a white coating on the tongue, abnormal fatigue and mental lethargy, decreased ability to see at night, and growth retardation. There may also be impaired glucose tolerance, reduced appetite or anorexia, malabsorption syndromes, abnormal menstruation in women, rheumatoid arthritis, and connective tissue disease. Mood and behavior can also be affected, leading to alcohol abuse, sleep and behavioral disturbances, and psychiatric illness. Nausea associated with pregnancy may be a result of diminished levels of zinc and vitamin B_6.

The zinc-deficient patient has poor circulation and a tendency to faint; therefore, care must be taken in anesthetic and operative situations as these people can be prone to shock and excessive bleeding.

Zinc deficiency can affect sexual function in men. Zinc deficiency leads to delayed sexual maturation and unhealthy changes in the size and structure of the prostate gland, which contains more zinc than any other part of the human anatomy. In prostate problems, particularly prostate cancer, the levels of zinc decline. Certain deficiency symptoms are reversible, such as degeneration of the prostate gland, seminal vesicle, or sperm; however, testicular degeneration is not. Even marginal deficiency of zinc will promote decreased sexual interest, low sperm count, and impotence.

Cadmium, a toxic mineral, also plays an important role in zinc deficiencies. High intakes of cadmium will accentuate signs of zinc deficiency, and cadmium will be stored in the body in the absence of zinc. Increasing zinc intake can reverse this condition. Chelating compounds used to remove excess copper from the body also leach out zinc, which then must be replaced.

White spots on nails, marks caused by injury to the nail that are slow in healing, are commonly assumed to be signs of zinc deficiency. However, a more reliable means of assessment is a laboratory test measuring the amount of zinc in white blood cells.

BENEFICIAL EFFECTS ON AILMENTS. Zinc helps maintain a healthy immune system and when given as a supplement can restore the immune response when depressed because of zinc deficiency. T-helper lymphocytes, which fight infection, are increased with zinc and are of particular interest to those with AIDS. Research shows that low dosages of zinc are effective and do not cause an adverse effect on cholesterol levels, which can be the case when high dosages of zinc are given. Zinc may contribute to the rapid healing of internal wounds, including gastric ulcers, and external wounds or any injury to the arteries. Zinc may be helpful in preventing and shortening colds if taken at the first sign of infection. Like vitamin C, zinc also demonstrates antiviral activity.

Zinc is beneficial in the prevention and treatment of infertility. Supplements are effective in improving sperm counts and motility. It also helps in the proper growth and maturity of the sex organs. Large amounts of zinc have been recommended for the prevention and treatment of enlargement of the prostate.

This trace mineral has the ability to arrest a disease of the eye called macular degeneration. Loss of vision was significantly less, according to one study, in patients receiving 100 milligrams of zinc, compared with those taking placebo. Zinc may play a role in cancer protection. Acne vulgaris, which occurs in teenagers, coupled with zinc deficiency, has been successfully treated with supplemental zinc. This mineral may replace body hair for those who have alopecia areata totalis (total lack of body hair). Taste may also be restored to the elderly with the aid of zinc. Wilson's disease is best treated with zinc, as it is nontoxic compared with penicillamine. And zinc helps relieve the symptoms associated with rheumatoid arthritis and may be useful for other inflammatory diseases.

The administration of zinc may benefit patients suffering from Hodgkin's disease and leukemia. It also is used in the treatment of cirrhosis of the liver and alcoholism. Zinc is beneficial to the diabetic because of its regulatory effect on insulin in the blood. It has been found that the addition of zinc to insulin prolongs its effect on blood sugar. The pancreas of a diabetic contains only about half as much zinc as a healthy pancreas.

Researchers have noted that the brain and cerebrospinal fluid in Alzheimer's disease patients have significantly decreased levels of zinc. Zinc deficiency may lead to the formation of plaque and the destruction of nerve cells in brain tissue seen in this disease. When Alzheimer's disease patients in two small studies were given additional zinc, improvements in cognition were dramatic.

Water

Emerging from the warm and watery solution of the womb, the body of a newborn baby is 77 percent water. Children are 59 percent water, and adults are between 45 percent and 65 percent water. The blood is 83 percent; kidneys, 82 percent; muscles, 75 percent; brain, 74 percent; liver, 69 percent; and bones, 22 percent. Water is the principal constituent of the fluids that surround and are within all living cells.

Respiration, digestion, assimilation, metabolism, elimination, water removal, and temperature regulation are bodily functions that can be accomplished only in the presence of water. Water is essential in dissolving and transporting nutrients such as oxygen and mineral salts via the blood, lymph, and other bodily fluids. Water also keeps the pressure, acidity, and composition of all chemical reactions in equilibrium.

Only oxygen is more essential than water in sustaining the life of all organisms. Human beings can live about five weeks without protein, carbohydrates, and fats, but just five days without water (in a moderate climate). Water's circulation between the blood and bodily organs is perpetual and always maintained in a proper balance. Some health practitioners find an association between dehydration and such conditions as chronic joint pain, asthma, allergies, headaches, and heartburn. According to Dr. F. Batmanghelidj in his book *Your Body's Many Cries for Water*, these can all be the result of a lack of fluids. Having a dry mouth is simply the very last sign of dehydration.

Most water is removed by the kidneys through which the entire blood supply passes and is filtered fifteen times each hour. A certain amount is eliminated daily through evaporation or excretion and must then be replaced. Whenever the body becomes overheated, two million sweat glands excrete perspiration, which is 99 percent water. This sweat, evaporating from the surface of the skin, is cooling because the liquid sweat is converted into water vapor, the process requires a certain amount of heat, and this needed heat is drawn from the body.

A minimal but consistent loss of water occurs during the processes of breathing and tearing. Moisture is breathed out from the water-lined nasal passages and lungs. Dry climates draw more water than humid air. Tiny tear ducts carry a liquid solution to the upper eyelids, which lubricate the eyes twenty-five times every minute. The tears then pass down to the nose, where they evaporate.

To replace lost water, approximately three quarts is needed by the body each day under normal circumstances. Most strenuous activity, a high climate temperature, or a diet too high in salt may increase this requirement. The sense of thirst (as well as sleep, appetite, satiety, and sexual responses) is controlled by a part of the forebrain called the hypothalamus. Metabolic water is produced as a by-product of the food combustion process, yielding as much as a pint per day. Foods can provide up to one-half quart. For example, fruits and vegetables are more than 90 percent distilled water. Even dry foods like crackers and bread are 5 percent to 35 percent water, respectively. Drinking water is the other source of replenishment.

Unfortunately, bacteria, viruses, synthetic compounds, metals, and radionuclides may become incorporated into our drinking water. The health effects can range from low-grade illnesses, such as colds and flu, to cancer.

Most species of bacteria in water are harmless, but a few may cause disease. Among them are *Pseudomonas, Flavobacterium, Achromobacter, Proteus, Klebsiella, Bacillus, Serratia, Corynebacterium, Spirillum, Clostridium, Arthrobacter, Gallionella,* and *Leptothrix. Flavobacterium* can be harmful to those who have just undergone surgery. *Pseudomonas* can invade postoperative infections, burn-wound infections, and intestinal-urinary tract infections. *Klebsiella pneumoniae* produces infection of the nose, throat, and respiratory and genitourinary systems and has been reported as the cause of meningitis and septicemia.

Coliform organisms are generally found in the intestinal tract of humans and other warm-blooded animals and are, among other sources, a good indicator of water supply that has been contaminated by fecal matter. *Escherichia coli* (*E. coli*) causes severe inflammation of abdominal organs and membranes. *Salmonella* (also found in ice cubes) induces typhoid and intestinal fevers, and *Shigella* produces various forms of dysentery and enteritis. The coliform density limit is regulated by the Safe Drinking Water Act but is high in some surveys.

Fluoride is added to drinking water to kill bacteria but recently the National Academy of Sciences announced that the maximum amount of fluoride allowed in the nation's drinking water could cause health problems and should be lowered. Four milligrams of fluoride per liter, the highest allowable level, could cause severe dental fluorosis in children. Intake of this high level during a lifetime also increases the risk of bone fractures because fluoride can weaken bones. In addition, even half this amount can cause mild to moderate dental fluorosis. Most of the high levels of fluoride in drinking water are found in South Carolina, but exposure to excessive fluoride also has been identified in Texas, Oklahoma, and Virginia.

Harmful toxins are found in drinking water. Cumulative toxins are substances that have been taken in small doses and are stored by the body. The human system has evolved processes that can effectively expel toxins that are ingested; however, when continual exposure occurs or when new substances are encountered, adverse reactions may manifest. Chromium, compounds containing arsenic, radioactive substances, pesticides, and many other industrial contaminants are retained in the body. They accumulate in organs such as the liver, skin, bones, and fat tissue from which they may gradually be released, causing diseases such as cancer.

In laboratory tests, the purification processes of distillation and reverse osmosis were the most efficient and successful in removing contaminants. Other methods, including those that make use of charcoal, remove some forms of contaminants, but not all.

Special Functions of Nutrients

Nutrients as Antioxidants

In recent years, a new theory of aging has emerged that proposes the body deteriorates via a process similar to rusting in which free radicals react with and destroy body tissues. In fact, some oxidation action is necessary for life. These oxidants are simply the waste products of normal functions such as breathing and immune reactions. But other free radicals come from the environment and are present in cigarette smoke, toxic industrial chemicals, ionizing radiation, ultraviolet light like that from the sun, contaminants in food, and pesticides. Free radicals can also be caused by stress and "distress" type exercising (high-intensity, short-period activity). Excess free radicals are damaging and destructive to the body.

Free radicals come in many chemical forms, but the most studied are the so-called oxygen free radicals. Four destructive forms of oxygen have been identified: hydroxyl radical and superoxide radical (the two real free radicals) and the "nonradical reactive species," oxygen singlet and hydrogen peroxide.

These molecules have lost one electron, keeping them chemically unstable. To restore stability, the oxygen molecules try to grab an electron from anywhere, destroying healthy cells in the process. This creates yet another molecule missing an electron and almost instantaneously, a chain reaction begins.

Free radicals attack fat molecules in cell membranes, causing peroxidation. These fats become in effect rancid and set the stage for deterioration of the cell membrane structure and consequently disease. When these free radicals attack DNA molecules, this can cause DNA to mutate and lead to cancer. Besides cancer, destructive oxygen reactions have been linked to at least fifty diseases, including heart disease, premature aging, cataracts, peptic ulcers, diverticulosis, sickle cell disease, rheumatoid arthritis, Parkinson's disease, leukemia, pancreatitis, asthma, stroke, ulcerative colitis, bleeding in the cavity of the brain, and AIDS.

Antioxidants come to the rescue when they react with these free radicals first, before the radicals do their damage, preventing them from participating in further chemical reactions. In this case, free radicals find their missing electron in the molecule of the antioxidant. And fortunately the sources of antioxidants are many. Some the body produces. One such endogenous antioxidant is SOD, which destroys the free radical superoxide. It is thought that superoxide may be the most dangerous of the four oxygen free radicals. In addition, coenzyme Q10 (CoQ10), a vitamin-like compound that occurs naturally in the body, works with vitamin E to scavenge free radicals.

Another endogenous antioxidant is glutathione, the primary antioxidant in cells. Glutathione is vitally important, protecting and repairing DNA, detoxifying carcinogens and pollutants, reducing inflammation and enhancing immune function. Diet also supplies a small amount. Glutathione is present in produce such as asparagus, spinach, potatoes, okra, avocados, white grapefruit, melon, and strawberries. The enzyme glutathione peroxidase, as well as catalase, prevents the accumulation of peroxide and resulting oxidative tissues damage.

The body also produces alpha-lipoic acid, another powerful antioxidant. Alpha-lipoic acid is especially beneficial because it is both water and fat soluble, allowing it to do its job in watery areas of the body such as inside cells and in fat tissues, making it a more universal antioxidant than glutathione, which is only water soluble. Alpha-lipoic acid benefits heart health, deactivates genes that speed aging, and lowers the risk of cataracts. In addition, certain staple foods such as tomatoes, potatoes, peas, and broccoli contain alpha-lipoic acid, with spinach the richest source.

The vitamins that function as antioxidants and that come from outside the body are vitamin C, vitamin E, and beta-carotene, the water-soluble form of vitamin A. The mineral selenium is also considered an antioxidant. Many phytonutrients also display antioxidant activity, such as ellagic acid, lutein, lycopene, quercitin, and glutathione. (See "Phytonutrients.")

The antioxidant activity of a food is expressed in ORAC units, which stands for *oxygen radical absorbance capacity*. Blueberries top the list for fruits and watercress for vegetables. See Table 2.4 for a list of antioxidants and foods rich in antioxidants.

Because recommended therapeutic dosages of antioxidants are higher than the normal intake of food can supply, antioxidant supplements are often part of nutritional regimens. A standard dosage of vitamin C for adults is 1,000 milligrams per day and that of vitamin E is 400 IU. Natural vitamin E is more beneficial than synthetic. Natural forms include d-alpha tocopherol, d-alpha-tocopheryl acetate, and d-alpha-tocopherol succinate. Of these, d-alpha tocopherol has the most antioxidant activity. A typical daily dose for carotene is 25,000 IU. A selenium supplement is also thought to be beneficial, as it potentiates the effects of vitamin E. Other minerals that support detoxification processes include manganese, copper, and zinc. (A physician should be consulted before any vitamin therapy is begun.)

Antioxidant vitamin supplements should be taken with meals, and the water-soluble ones like vitamin C should be taken several times during the day. Fresh, fresh-packaged, or frozen foods will have more antioxidants than the canned, processed, or heated kinds. The more colorful the fruit or vegetable, the more antioxidants will be present. Raw or microwaved foods are better than boiled or steamed; whole foods are better than juices; and extra-virgin cold-pressed oils rather than heat-extracted oils are best. Foods should be

Table 2.4
Antioxidants and Antioxidant Foods

Antioxidants	Antioxidant Foods
Vitamin E	Sweet potatoes
Vitamin C	Butternut and winter squash
Selenium	Pumpkin
Coenzyme Q10	Carrots
L-carnosine	Spinach
L-methionine	Broccoli
L-taurine	Endive
Polyphenols-p-coumaric, chlorogenic acid	Tomatoes
Glutathione	Cantaloupe
Alpha-lipoic acid	Apricots
Lutein	Mangoes
Zeaxanthin	Papaya
Lycopene	Watercress
Ascorbyl palmitate	Kale
Vitamin B_{12}	Asparagus
Pantothenic acid	Blackberries
Thiamin	Cranberries
Riboflavin	Strawberries
Niacin	
Folic acid	
Zinc citrate	
Inositol	
Copper	
Beta-carotene	

eaten as soon after purchase as possible. Washing with a biodegradable soap to remove chemical residues is advised.

Phytonutrients

Research into phytonutrients began in the 1970s. By the 1990s, it was clear that their discovery was issuing in a new era in nutritional medicine. Now thousands of formerly unknown or overlooked substances are being studied for their effects on human health. *Phytonutrient* refers to a wide variety of compounds in plants, other than the usual vitamins, minerals, or starches, that protect the plant from various threats such as weather, sun damage, and hungry bugs. Some function as an immune system, battling viruses, bacteria, and fungi. Others give scent or flavor to a plant to attract bees but repel harmful insects. Strong taste and pungent smell are signs that a food is a good source of phytochemicals. Because many phytonutrients are pigments, saturated color in a fruit or vegetable also indicates that it harbors these healing compounds.

Nutritionists and health professionals have become intrigued with these substances because of the many ways in which they can potentially prevent various illnesses. Among their numerous functions, phytonutrients act as antioxidants, fight inflammation, and support the body's processes of detoxification. Because of these actions and others, phytonutrients can cut the risk of heart disease by lowering blood pressure, reducing cholesterol levels, and preventing the oxidation of cholesterol. And these substances play an important role in preventing cancer, interfering in virtually every stage of development. Some appear to stop cancer at its inception by preventing the formation of carcinogens or blocking enzymes that activate cancer genes. They prevent carcinogens from damaging tissues or help destroy cancer-causing compounds. Others help stop the spread of cancer. Animal studies offer broad proof of the link between phytonutrients and cancer prevention, and human evidence is highly suggestive.

Numbering in the hundreds of thousands, phytonutrients work in concert. They are synergistic, one bolstering and complementing the function of another. A few are available as supplements, such as lutein and zeaxanthin, but food is a far more beneficial source. Only food, such as fruits and vegetables, contains a wide range of these nutrients—those that have been discovered and those that have not—in a complementary assortment. Whole foods are the best source rather than refined and processed foods that have been stripped of nutrients or had their nutrients destroyed during manufacture.

Table 2.5 and the following text offer a brief overview of some of the phytonutrients currently being studied.

Carotenoids

One of the first discoveries that lay outside the known nutrients was the carotenoids. While more than six hundred carotenoids exist in nature, only about fifty are found in foods that humans eat and only about half of these are absorbed into the system. Examples include beta-carotene, alpha-carotene, lutein, and lycopene. These nutrients function as antioxidants. A variety of carotenoids, rather than any one carotenoid alone, are responsible for their amazing antioxidant achievements. Carotenoids are also pigments, their sunny hues falling somewhere in the yellow-orange-red range. They are also present in leafy greens such as kale and spinach, but the green of the chlorophyll in these dominates so the carotenoid colors are not seen. Carrots, sweet potatoes, mangoes, cantaloupe, pumpkins, squash, apricots, and dark leafy greens all contain beta- or alpha-carotene.

Lutein

The carotenoid lutein is a component of the macula of the eye and shields it from damaging ultraviolet light. Lutein has also been shown to help prevent cataracts. Kale, in particular, but also collard greens, spinach, watercress, parsley, red seedless grapes, zucchini, and pumpkin are excellent sources of lutein.

Zeaxanthin

This carotenoid works in tandem with lutein to protect the macula of the eye from oxidative damage. These nutrients accumulate in the retina and macula of the eye and filter out damaging blue light. The highest source of both lutein and zeaxanthin is egg yolks, with corn also a good source of both. However, several foods conventionally recommended as a good source of both, although they contain lutein, in fact, contain little to no zeaxanthin. These include spinach, celery, brussels sprouts, scallions, broccoli, and green lettuce. One reliable source is orange peppers, a vegetable in which zeaxanthin is the major carotenoid.

Lycopene

The carotenoid lycopene is one of the most potent free-radical scavengers in nature. In the American diet, tomatoes supply most of the lycopene. It's also found in rosy foods such as pink grapefruit and watermelon. Regular consumption of tomato products of a serving or more a day was found to significantly reduce the

Table 2.5

Phytonutrients

Phytochemical Class	Types of Compounds	Food Sources
Carotenoids	Alpha-beta carotene, lycopene, lutein	Richly colored fruits/vegetables
Isothiocyanates, indoles	Sulphorophane, indole-3-carbinol	Cruciferous vegetables, horseradish
Inositol phosphates	Phytate, inositol	Whole grains, soybeans
Phenolics	Chlorogenic acid, ellagic acid	Citrus fruit, vegetables, coumarins, limonene
Phytoestrogens	Isoflavones (diadzein, genistein)	Lignins—Flax, rye, lignans
Phytosterols	Campesterol, beta-sitosterol	Nuts, seeds, whole grains, legumes
Polyphenols	Flavonoids	Fruits, vegetables, tea, red wine
Saponins	Soyasaponins	Soy, legumes, nuts
Sulfides, thiols	Diallyl sulfides, etc.	Onions, garlic, cruciferous vegetables

Source: *Nutrition Reviews* 1999; 57:S3

risk of prostate cancer in men. And in a study conducted at Erasmus University in the Netherlands, participants who had the highest blood levels of lycopene had a 45 percent reduced risk for atherosclerosis. To maximize the amount of lycopene that is absorbed, tomatoes need to be eaten cooked, not raw, along with some fat because lycopene is fat soluble.

Phenolics

Tomatoes also contain many other protective compounds such as p-coumaric acid and chlorogenic acid. These are the so-called phenolic acids. They are antioxidants, similar to lycopene, but they also fight cancer by inhibiting the formation of nitrosamines in the body. Nitrosamines are powerful carcinogens, present in processed meat but also produced by the body when nitrogen reacts with elements of proteins called amines.

Ellagic Acid

Another phenolic is ellagic acid, found abundantly in fruits and vegetables. This compound detoxifies carcinogens such as benzopyrene and aflatoxin found in moldy peanuts. Ellagic supports both phase I and phase II processes of detoxification in the liver, preventing the formation of carcinogens and facilitating the removal from the body of those that form. It also functions as an antioxidant. In animal studies, it has been shown to prevent cancer of the esophagus and colon. Good food sources include berries, apples, grapes, and nuts, especially walnuts.

Sulforaphane

Sulforaphane supports the liver in detoxifying carcinogens. Detoxification by the liver involves a two-step enzymatic process. While phase I enzymes directly neutralize some chemicals, many others are converted to intermediate forms that are chemically more active. It is the job of phase II enzymes to neutralize these or make them more easily excreted. Sulforaphane fights cancer by boosting the level of the phase II enzymes. Research also shows that sulforaphane can stop the cell cycle of cancer cells and trigger their death. Cruciferous vegetables such as broccoli, bok choy, brussels sprouts, cabbage, cauliflower, collards, kale, kohlrabi, mustard greens, radishes, rutabaga, turnip greens, and turnips contain sulforaphane. Sulforaphane is very stable and cannot be destroyed by either microwaving or cooking.

Indoles

Indoles, found in cruciferous vegetables, fight cancer two ways. They block estrogen receptor sites in breast cancer cells. Indoles also affect estrogen balance. They stimulate production of a form of estrogen that does not stimulate breast cancer, while reducing production of a more potent form that can be harmful. In broccoli, the most important indole is indole-3-carbinol.

Phytoestrogens

Phytoestrogens have an estrogen-like effect on the system. They mimic and modulate the hormone in various ways, for instance, by binding with estrogen receptor sites in breast tissue and thereby blocking the activity of cancer-promoting estrogen.

Studies have shown that women with high levels of phytochemicals in the blood have lower levels of potent forms of estrogens in their bodies. Women in Japan who eat the traditional diet, high in soy foods that are rich in phytohormones, are four times less likely to develop breast cancer than American women. They also have fewer fractures of the hip and have an easier time through menopause.

Genestein

This compound is a powerful phytoestrogen. It is present in peanuts, mung beans, and alfalfa sprouts but the best source is soybeans. Fresh soybeans contain the highest amounts, followed by tempeh, miso, soy milk, and textured soy flour. Soy sauce and soybean oil do not exhibit estrogenic activity. Research shows that genestein blocks enzymes that activate cancer genes and inhibits the growth of new blood vessels that feed cancer cells. It may prevent breast cancer by blocking the entry of estrogen into cells and also may protect against prostate cancer.

Polyphenols

Polyphenols are present in onions, apples, strawberries, nuts, yams, wine, coffee, and both black and green tea. They give tea its texture and body, which distinguish it from the feel of coffee. Catechin flavonoid, a polyphenol in tea, is an antioxidant and prevents blood platelets from sticking together. Tea may protect against cancer of the stomach, liver, and lung, and it lowers cholesterol. Research shows that green tea has several benefits. It burns body fat, promotes high antioxidant free-radical activity, works with vitamins C and E for optimal benefit, guards smokers from free radicals, protects the skin from ultraviolet light, prevents clotting, lowers LDL and raises HDL cholesterol, lowers blood pressure, protects against cavities and gingivitis, protects against food poisoning, and inhibits the flu virus. Pregnant women should not drink more than 5 cups per day. Polyphenols also act as antioxidants, helping prevent stomach and lung cancer as well as heart disease.

Quercetin

This phytonutrient is a flavonoid and one of the most biologically active. Onions are an exceptionally rich source. Quercetin is abundant in yellow and red onions (but not white) as well as shallots, red grapes, Italian yellow squash, and broccoli. It inhibits tumor-stimulating enzymes, protects DNA from damage, and inactivates several cancer-causing substances.

Anthocyanins

These are reddish-blue pigments found in berries, red grape skins, citrus, and yams. They function as antioxidants, preventing eye tissue from free radical damage. They inhibit prostaglandin production that can lead to abnormal blood clotting. Anthocyanins protect DNA from damage and rid the body of carcinogens. These compounds may help lower the risk of macular degeneration, circulatory disease, and some cancers.

Allicin

These compounds, also called allylic or allyl sulfides, give onions and garlic their characteristic odor and flavor. Allicin compounds thin blood, lower LDL cholesterol, and help prevent heart attack and stroke. They also fight bacterial, virus, and fungal infection. Epidemiological studies have shown that regularly consuming garlic and onions is associated with a lower risk of cancers of the stomach and digestive tract.

Capsaicin

This fiery phytonutrient is found in chili peppers, the hotter the better. Capsaicin inhibits carcinogens from nitrates and cigarette smoke from triggering the formation of cancerous cells. This compound may also be able to kill the bacteria responsible for causing ulcers. It is a stimulant, increasing circulation, and may be of benefit in cancer prevention.

Foods, Beverages, and Supplementary Foods

M any factors influence eating patterns and, therefore, affect nutrition. For example, taste preferences, states of health, and various social and cultural customs all determine what foods a person eats. Poor nutrition may be the result of consuming too little, too much, or the wrong kinds of food for any number of reasons.

The foods and beverages we consume should provide our bodies with the nutrients necessary for good health. Protein builds and maintains body cells, and carbohydrates, fats, and some proteins provide calories for energy. Vitamins and minerals help regulate the many chemical reactions within the body.

Fresh, raw fruits and vegetables are generally more nutritious than prepared ones, although many kinds of foods are more palatable when cooked. Studies indicate that considerable losses of nutrients, especially B-complex vitamins, vitamin C, and the bioflavonoid complex occur during storage and cooking. As a result, it is essential to select, store, and prepare foods wisely in order to retain these nutrients and benefit from them. Precautions should also be taken to avoid foodborne illnesses caused by the growth of harmful bacteria. This list provides some basic rules for food storage and preparation to retain nutrient content and to prevent food poisoning.

- Cook meats, especially hamburger, pork, and poultry, thoroughly in order to kill harmful bacteria. Beef reaches medium doneness at 135–140°F. In pork, trichinosis is killed at 137°F and the meat is slightly pink but moist at 150°F. Chicken breast is done at 160°F, and the thigh is done at 165°F.
- Guard against the growth of harmful bacteria by immediately refrigerating leftovers or foods cooked for later use. Do not allow them to cool to room temperature first. If necessary, split portions to speed cooling and refrigerate each portion separately.
- Keep perishable foods, especially chopped and processed meats, mashed potatoes, custards, pastries, and dairy products, in the refrigerator to avoid bacterial contamination.
- When buying fish, transport it directly from the store to home without delay. Refrigerate immediately and preferably cook the same day.
- Destroy cans that bulge or canned contents that bubble out when the can is opened, in order to avoid food poisoning. Botulism is the only foodborne bacterial toxin that is deadly and cannot be killed by heat.
- Ensure thorough cooking of frozen foods by allowing them to thaw completely before cooking, unless otherwise stated on the package.
- Store fresh foods as soon as possible to minimize nutrient loss.
- To protect against the loss of water-soluble vitamins, avoid soaking fruits, vegetables, or meats in water.
- Supplementary foods may be useful for further increasing the nutritional value of meals and must also be stored and prepared properly in order to prevent nutrient loss.

In the following sections, types of foods, beverages, and supplementary foods are discussed alphabetically with respect to their nutrient content and special features. This information is intended for use with the Tables of Food Composition in Section 6.

Any reference to a body disorder or disease in connection with a food or beverage is not meant to be prescriptive but merely represents research findings.

Foods

Nature provides an abundance of foods from plant and animal sources that can sustain life and prevent disease. The following present the many health benefits of dozens of common foods and some specialty items. To maximize nutrient intake and variety, it is important to include a range of such foods in the diet and to eat these foods in their most natural and unprocessed forms. Choosing organic and residue-free over nonorganic and conventionally raised is also a mainstay of healthy eating to avoid pesticides used on produce and chemicals and added hormones present in meats and fish.

Eggs

Eggs are an excellent source of complete protein, since they contain the right proportions for all essential amino acids. (One large egg contains 6 or 7 grams of high-quality protein.) Also found in eggs are vitamins A, B$_2$, D, and E; niacin; the minerals copper, iron, sulfur, and phosphorus; and unsaturated fatty acids. The egg yolk contains the richest known source of choline, found in lecithin, which is necessary for keeping the cholesterol within the egg emulsified and keeping cholesterol moving in the bloodstream. The yolk contains approximately 214 grams of cholesterol, 65 milligrams of sodium, 5 grams of fat (of which 1.6 grams are saturated), 1 gram of carbohydrates, and 75 calories. The yolk also contains biotin, one of the B-complex vitamins.

People with high blood cholesterol (low-density lipoprotein, or LDL, levels) and those with coronary artery disease should avoid eggs. However, those individuals who do not have high levels of LDL and have increased levels of high-density lipoprotein, or HDL (the good kind), need not worry. One or two eggs per day has been shown to be safe. The kind of cholesterol contained in eggs is not as harmful as that found in the visible fat of animals. Eggs are easy to digest, inexpensive, versatile, and readily available. They are a very nutritious food for the elderly.

Eggs should be kept refrigerated at all times (45°F–55°F) because temperature variations will cause the whites to become thin. A soiled egg should be wiped clean with a dry cloth rather than washed, to preserve the natural protective film on the porous eggshell. This film prevents odors, flavors, molds, and bacteria from entering the egg. Eggs retain their freshness and quality better if stored large end up in their original carton.

Raw eggs should not be consumed in great quantity because the whites contain a protein called avidin, which may be harmful to the body if consumed over a long period of time. Avidin interferes with the use of biotin but is also inactivated by heat. Salmonella bacteria have been found inside eggs, and thorough cooking is recommended to avoid any illness.

Fiber

Fiber is the part of food that is not digested by the human body, such as the skin of an apple and the husk of a wheat kernel. The normal functioning of the intestinal tract depends upon the presence of adequate fiber. A low-fiber diet has been associated with heart disease, poor control of blood sugar, cancer of the colon and rectum, diverticulosis, varicose veins, phlebitis, obesity, and many other conditions. Water-soluble fibers include pectin, mucilages, and gum. In transit, they absorb water and cholesterol and form a gel-like or viscous substance. This type of fiber is found especially in some fruits and vegetables, legumes, barley, oats, and oat bran. Insoluble fibers remain essentially unchanged during digestion. Examples include cellulose, lignin, and some hemicellulose. Fruits and vegetables contain this type of fiber as well, and it is also present in cereal grains and whole wheat products. The recommended daily intake of fiber is 20 to 35 grams with sufficient water intake.

Fish and Fish Oils

Fish is an excellent source of high-grade protein, polyunsaturated fatty acids (omega-3s), and minerals, especially iodine and potassium.

Seafood is categorized as freshwater or saltwater fish and shellfish. These types differ slightly in nutritive value. Magnesium, phosphorus, iron, and copper are provided by freshwater fish. Saltwater fish and shellfish are rich in iodine, fluoride, and cobalt. The unsaturated fat content of fish and shellfish varies with the species and season of year. Fatty fish, such as halibut, mackerel, and salmon, are good sources of vitamins A and D, and herring, oysters, and sardines contain vanadium and zinc. All of these fish contain the omega-3 fatty acids, essential for disease prevention and optimal health. The concern about eating shellfish is that it is high in cholesterol. While shrimp does contain a significant amount (the least harmful kind), crab and scallops have levels like those found in chicken.

Both fish and fish oils prevent heart attack deaths (an ounce a day or two servings a week), guard against glucose intolerance in type II diabetes, raise HDL cholesterol, and are anti-inflammatory agents that aid in rheumatoid arthritis symptoms. They also help psoriasis, high blood pressure, osteoarthritis, Raynaud's disease, ulcerative colitis, and migraines, and they hold promise for aiding multiple sclerosis. Some fish are high in the antioxidant nutrients coenzyme Q10 and selenium, which are especially useful in the prevention of colon cancer and the spread of breast cancer. Fish that are the highest in the omega-3 fatty acids are dark fleshed, such as salmon and mackerel. Sardines are rich sources of the nucleic acids RNA/DNA.

Fish and shellfish may be purchased fresh, frozen, canned, salted, dried, or smoked. Because of the possibility of bacterial infection, fresh fish and shellfish should be immediately refrigerated upon returning home from the store. Pat the fish dry and wrap it tightly in foil or plastic. Seal the fish in an airtight bag. At normal refrigerator temperatures (35°F–40°F), store no more than a few hours. If the coldest part of the refrigerator is 31°F, the fish can be stored overnight if set in a pan of crushed ice. There should be a layer of waxed paper between the ice and the fish. Fish and shellfish are best cooked at low temperature (300°F to 325°F) and should not be overcooked, in order to preserve flavor, juices, and nutrients.

Fruits

Fresh fruits are good sources of vitamins and minerals, especially vitamins A and C, carbohydrates in the form of cellulose, and natural sugars and water. They are good substitutes for fat-laden candy, cookies, and cakes, which contain few nutrients.

Yellow fruits such as apricots, cantaloupe, and persimmons are good sources of carotene, which is converted to vitamin A in the body. Aside from acerola cherries and rose hips, the best natural sources of vitamin C are red and green peppers and citrus fruits such as oranges, grapefruit, lemons, and tangerines. Other sources of vitamin C are cantaloupe, strawberries, and tomatoes.

- **Pineapples** are antiviral, antibacterial, and, because of their manganese content, help prevent both osteoporosis and bone fractures. They contain bromelain, a natural enzyme that aids in the digestion of the fruit. Bromelain is available as a supplement. Taken between meals, it acts as a powerful anti-inflammatory agent. It is also known to help dissolve blood clots.

- **Apples** reduce cholesterol, are anti-inflammatory, fight bacteria and viruses (including colds), stabilize blood sugar, prevent cancer, aid the cardiovascular system, and contain boron, which boosts the action of estrogen. Apples also may be eaten before meals to suppress the appetite. They contain valuable bulk fiber, both pectin and cellulose, which is needed for regular bowel movement. Two or three apples a day are beneficial—just one apple a day doesn't do it anymore.

- **Bananas** and **plantains** are high in magnesium and may be useful in treating diarrhea, colitis, ulcers, dyspepsia, and protein allergies. They also have antibiotic capabilities. Bananas strengthen the stomach lining and lower blood cholesterol. Plantains give protection from ulcers, and their fiber is good for the heart. The fiber in bananas and plantains are also good for regularity.

- **Pears** and **bananas** have the highest amount of natural sugars of any fruits.

- **Apricots** are best known for laetrile, a substance taken from the kernel of the apricot. Laetrile helps fight cancers that are related to cigarette smoking as well as cancers of the pancreas. Apricots are highly concentrated in beta-carotene, especially in the dried form.

- **Figs** are an excellent source of minerals, including potassium, calcium, magnesium, iron, and zinc. Supplying significant amounts of fiber, figs are a home remedy for constipation. Because of their mix of minerals, they also build bones. And they have been shown to shrink tumors. The juice fights parasites such as roundworms and bacteria. Digestion and ulcers are aided. Figs may trigger headaches in sensitive persons.

- **Dates** contain calcium and boron and are high in a natural form of aspirin. They act as a laxative and also supply potassium, which is lost due to diarrhea. Dates and other dried fruit are linked to lower pancreatic cancer rates. However, they may trigger headaches in some people.

- **Prunes** are high in fiber. Because they act as a highly effective laxative, prunes should be eaten slowly over time. One-half cup a day is beneficial. They also contain natural aspirin.

- **Oranges** are high in vitamin C, which protects against respiratory infection, viruses, and gum disease. They also contain many cancer-fighting compounds—antioxidants, beta-carotene, vitamin C, terpenes, and flavonoids. They are associated with a reduced risk of pancreatic cancer. The membranes and pith contain flavonoids that strengthen capillary walls, helping prevent varicose veins and heart and circulatory disease. These compounds also have an estrogen-like effect. In animal studies, oranges protected sperm from damage by radiation and they may help boost fertility.

- **Grapefruit** lowers blood cholesterol and reverses clogged arteries due to a unique form of soluble fiber that the fruit contains. Grapefruit juice alone does not provide this benefit. Like other citrus, grapefruit is high in vitamin C and is antiviral. The fruit also contains the phytonutrient naringenin, which inhibits an aspect of detoxification processes that generate carcinogens out of harmless substances. Grapefruit retards tumor growth, fighting stomach and pancreatic cancer. Pink and red grapefruit also contain lycopene, another cancer-fighting compound. However, eating grapefruit or drinking the juice is not recommended when taking drugs or exposed to high levels of toxins, as naringenin slows their elimination and the medications can consequently accumulate in the system. Grapefruit may cause heartburn in some people.

- **Lemon** and **lime** contain antioxidants and other chemicals that block cancer. The compound limonene, found especially in the rind but also in the juice, inactivates a range of carcinogens, in particular, a nitrosamine in cigarette smoke. Limonene is present in other citrus fruits as well. And the fuzzy core of lemons is exceptionally high in capillary-strengthening flavonoids. Because of their vitamin C content, lemon and lime also prevent scurvy. Lemon is an astringent, diuretic, and diaphoretic, good for sore throats, sunburn, and hiccoughs.

- **Kiwi fruit** is used in the treatment of stomach and breast cancer in Chinese traditional medicine and is high in vitamin C.

- **Grapes**, only the red variety, have great cancer-fighting properties; they are high in the antioxidant quercetin. The skins inhibit blood clotting and also raise the good HDL cholesterol level, as does grape seed oil. In test tubes, grapes act as antiviral and antibiotic agents. A delay in tooth decay has been noted in animal studies.

- **Plums** are antiviral, antibacterial, and a natural laxative.

- **Cherries**, the tart red variety, contain anthocyanins, reddish-blue pigments that have anti-inflammatory properties. Anecdotal evidence exists for the benefits of drinking the juice for reducing the pain of arthritis and gout. Cherries, both sweet and tart, may also be good for the heart, protecting the arterial walls from damage. In addition, they may be protective against cancer as part of a general anticancer diet. The juice of the **black cherry** possesses enzyme activity that guards against plaque, which causes tooth decay.

- **Black currants** contain anthocyanosides that kill bacteria such as *Escherichia coli* (*E. coli*). Consequently, an extract of black currant is sold as a treatment for diarrhea. Blueberries also contain anthocyanins. Currants are also a source of phytoestrogens that help reduce symptoms of menopause by promoting hormone balance. As a source of iron, currants are a useful part of a regimen to treat anemia.

- **Blueberries** are ranked at the top of the list of fresh fruits that demonstrate antioxidant activity. This is due to the large amount and wide range of anthocyanin purple-blue pigments, as well as the chlorogenic acid they deliver. Blueberries also contain powerful anti-inflammatory compounds. These phytonutrients block damage to blood vessels, including those in the brain, thereby helping prevent strokes and aging of the brain. Because blueberries prevent bacteria from clinging to the walls of the bladder, this fruit fights urinary tract infections and is used to control diarrhea. They are also antiviral and contain natural aspirin. Raw berries are much more beneficial than cooked as heat damages anthocyanins.

- **Cranberries** prevent bladder and kidney infection by preventing bacteria from clinging to tissue. The same action can prevent bacteria in the mouth from sticking to the teeth and causing the formation of plaque. Cranberry juice is used in the treatment of cystitis. And the anthocyanin pigments protect cholesterol from oxidation and thin the blood. Cranberries also may prevent kidney stones. Two glasses of the juice per day may be beneficial.

- **Raspberries** are antiviral and anticancer and contain natural aspirin.

- **Strawberries** are antiviral and block cancer-forming substances. They also benefit the cardiovascular system and are high in the fiber pectin. They may cause allergies in certain people.

- **Melons** in general are one of the most alkaline fruits, a useful antidote for the typically acidic

Western diet. Melons contain potassium, calcium, magnesium, iron, and some copper and manganese. Potassium helps regulate blood pressure. Cantaloupe is a source of the antioxidants beta-carotene, glutathione, and vitamin C, which protect the heart and help prevent cancer.

- **Watermelon** provides ample amounts of the two powerful antioxidants lycopene and glutathione. It also fights bacteria and helps prevent blood clots.
- **Rhubarb** stimulates uterine contractions and has been used to encourage menstruation. Pregnant women should not use this food in any other than culinary amounts. Rhubarb is also very high in oxalates and should be carefully chosen by those who are prone to kidney stones.
- **Mangosteen** is a fruit native to Southeast Asia and Cambodia that is drawing attention for its medicinal properties. The fruit is used traditionally to treat infection and ailments of the skin and digestive tract. Its antioxidant content suggests a use in fighting cancer. The rind, pulp, and seeds contain active compounds including xanthones and polysaccharides. Sold as a fruit in a few Asian markets, mangosteen is currently more widely available as a juice.

Fresh fruits offer a rich source of vitamins and minerals as well as appetite appeal in color, flavor, and texture. Fresh, ripe fruits purchased in season will be higher in nutrient quality and more economical in price than frozen, dried, or canned fruits. However, with the improved packaging methods used today, many precut and flash-frozen forms also retain their nutrient values. But once purchased and brought home, if fruits are not properly stored or if they are refrigerated for extended periods of time, their nutrient value will deteriorate.

It is preferable to obtain ripe rather than green fruits, since ripe fruits contain the highest levels of nutrients and simple sugars, which are very easily assimilated by the digestive system. Fruits that are not fully ripe should be allowed to ripen at room temperature and then stored in a cool, dark place or in the refrigerator. Fresh fruits should always be washed prior to eating so that any possible chemical residue is removed, and they should be eaten whole or peeled thinly so that nutrients found in the skin are conserved. If fruits are to be cooked, they should be cooked quickly. The processes of drying and canning fruit will lose valuable nutrients if done improperly.

Dried fruits that are rich in thiamin and iron should be softened and then cooked in the same water and stored in a cool, dry place. Home-canned fruits should be stored in a dark place to preserve their vitamin C content. Water-packed fruits are preferable to those packed in heavy syrups that contain large amounts of added sugar.

Grains

Grains are often referred to as cereals; they are the seeds of various grasses such as wheat, rye, oats, rice, and barley. Often called the "staff of life," grains provide the bulk of the world's food supply. Common foods made from these grains are flours, breads, breakfast cereals, and pasta.

A single grain of whole wheat has three different parts. (See Figure 3.1.) The germ is the heart of the grain, which sprouts when the seed is planted. It is especially rich in the B vitamins, vitamin E, protein, unsaturated fat, minerals (particularly iron), and carbohydrates. The endosperm constitutes the largest part of the grain. It is composed chiefly of carbohydrates in the form of starch, with some incomplete protein and traces of vitamins and minerals. The bran portion of the grain is the covering. It is composed chiefly of the carbohydrate cellulose, with traces of B vitamins, minerals (especially iron), and incomplete proteins.

When grain is refined, the bran and germ are removed during milling in order to reduce the chance of rancidity and to improve the storage quality of the grain. At the same time, important nutrients such as the B vitamins, vitamin E, chromium, magnesium, manganese, copper, molybdenum, selenium, zinc, silicon, iron, numerous enzymes, and fiber are lost. In order to enrich flour, bread, and cereal products, only a few select nutrients are added during processing. Refined grains are nutritionally inferior to whole grains.

Many whole grains have demonstrated a variety of health benefits. In epidemiological studies they are closely linked to a reduced risk of heart disease. And a recent Danish study found that replacing refined grain products with whole grains helped maintain a constant blood sugar level and lower the risk of diabetes. Insulin levels were also reduced.

- **High-fiber whole wheat** and **wheat bran** help eliminate constipation. Bran is one of the best fighters of cancer of the colon. For women, bran is good for breast cancer. Wheat bran also has antiparasitic capabilities. Wheat is known to be one of the foods most likely to trigger allergies, rheumatoid arthritis, neurological illnesses, and irritable bowel syndrome.
- **Oats**, eaten daily, are well known for lowering cholesterol because of the soluble fiber they contain.

FIGURE 3.1: TOTAL NUTRIENTS IN THE KERNEL OF WHEAT

Germ is 2½% of kernel	Bran is 14% of kernel	Endosperm is 83% of kernel
Of the whole kernel, the germ contains:	Of the whole kernel, the bran contains:	Of the whole kernel, the endosperm contains:
64% Thiamin	73% Pyridoxine	70–75% Protein
26% Riboflavin	50% Pantothenic acid	43% Pantothenic acid
21% Pyridoxine	42% Riboflavin	32% Riboflavin
8% Protein	33% Thiamin	12% Niacin
7% Pantothenic acid	19% Protein	6% Pyridoxine
2% Niacin		3% Thiamin

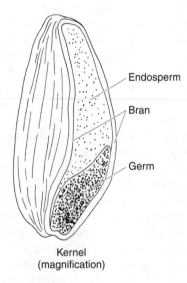

Endosperm

Bran

Germ

Kernel
(magnification)

Other nutrients found in the whole wheat grain are:

Calcium	Chlorine
Iron	Sodium
Phosphorous	Silicon
Magnesium	Boron
Potassium	Barium
Manganese	Silver
Copper	Inositol
Sulfur	Folic Acid
Iodine	Choline
Fluorine	Vitamin E

And other trace materials

Psychoactive compounds may help depression and aid in nicotine craving. Oats are estrogenic and have antioxidant activity. Oats in the whole form, such as whole rolled oats, help stabilize blood sugar while instant oatmeal is rapidly digested and absorbed and quickly enters the bloodstream. This cereal may cause bowel troubles in some people. Oat bran, one cup cooked (or one-half cup dry) consumed in various meals throughout the day, is beneficial as are commercial cereals made with whole oat flour.

• **Barley** reduces cholesterol, is an antioxidant, is antiviral, improves bowel function and constipation, and is an anticancer food. In the Middle East, barley has been traditionally eaten to benefit the heart. Hulled barley is the most nutritious form with only the outer husk removed; however, it has a lengthy cooking time and is very chewy. Pearl barley, the form commonly sold in markets, has had the bran removed and contains fewer nutrients. However, barley, in whatever form, is a healthy addition to the diet. It is low in gluten, supports the liver in detoxification, and also supports the lymphatic system. Denuded pearl barley also works. Beer made from barley contains no helpful cholesterol-suppressing compounds.

Breads, Cereals, and Pastas

The main constituent of breads is flour. Flour is the product resulting from the milling process, which involves grinding and sifting of cleaned grains. The type of flour or grain from which it originates often determines the color, texture, flavor, and nutritive value of the bread. Cereals can be made from a variety of grains, such as corn, barley, oats, wheat, rice, and rye.

• **Whole grain flour** must be refrigerated and ideally kept in the freezer compartment because it still retains the germ of the grain, which is rich in oils that can become rancid. Whole wheat flour is best for baking breads and other yeast-containing baked goods. Whole wheat pastry flour is lighter and good for cookies, cakes, pie crusts, and other desserts. The breads should be stored at room temperature or frozen until used. Refrigerated bread loses moisture and thus becomes stale faster than if frozen or kept at room temperature.

- **All-purpose flour** is a blend of different refined wheat grains. Bleached flour has been whitened to create a more uniform texture. Self-rising flour contains added salt and leavening in proper proportions.
- **Enriched flour** has the nutrients thiamin, riboflavin, and niacin of the vitamin B complex, and sometimes iron returned to it. This enrichment process also applies to other "enriched" products, such as breakfast cereals and pasta. Folic acid has recently been added to the list of enrichment nutrients. A deficiency of folic acid is associated with birth defects.
- **Pastas** can be made from a variety of whole grain flours, including whole wheat, rice, corn, and spelt. Cook whole grain pasta twelve to fifteen minutes to eliminate the raw flour taste. The pasta will remain firm.

Rice

Of all grains, rice is the most easily digested and the least likely to cause allergic reactions. Its fiber content helps guard against constipation. Rice clears up psoriasis and is anticancer and antidiarrheal; rice bran lowers cholesterol and prevents kidney stones.

- **Whole brown rice** contains a generous supply of B vitamins, plus calcium, magnesium, phosphorus, and iron.
- **Wild rice** contains twice as much protein, four times as much phosphorus, eight times as much thiamin, and twenty times as much riboflavin as white rice.
- **White rice**, or dehulled polished rice, has no significant amount of B vitamins but may also be enriched, similar to flour and cereals.
- **Converted rice** has undergone a process similar to milling and has a somewhat higher vitamin content than white rice.

Legumes

Legumes are plants that have edible seeds within a pod. They include peas, beans, lentils, and peanuts. Legumes are a rich source of incomplete protein, iron, and the B vitamins thiamin, riboflavin, and niacin. When sprouted, they provide an excellent source of vitamin C. Legumes are a hearty and versatile food. Because of their high but incomplete protein content, legumes can be used as a meat substitute to accompany other protein foods when coupled with a grain to supply additional amino acid. This coupling creates a complete protein like that found in meat.

- **Beans** are helpful in lowering cholesterol if consumed daily. They are good for diabetics because they regulate blood sugar. They also lower cancer rates. Beans are high in fiber, which makes them good for the colon, constipation, hemorrhoids, and other bowel problems. They also help lower cholesterol. Many people have difficulty digesting beans due to a missing enzyme, alpha-galactosidase, necessary to digest bean sugars such as raffinose. Friendly bacteria in the gut feed on these sugars. Gas may be a result.
- **Peas** contain antifertility agents. They are a natural contraceptive. When rats were fed 20 percent of their diet in peas, litter size was reduced—and 30 percent had no offspring. Dried beans and peas should be stored in tightly covered containers in a cool, dry place. They should be cooked in liquid to soften their cellulose fiber and to restore flavor and moisture that is lost in the drying process. Adding baking soda to the water in which legumes are cooked retains their color and freshness but destroys their thiamin content.
- **Soybeans** are high in protein, calcium, iron, and zinc, and they are low in fat and calories. Soy also contains isoflavones, estrogenic phytonutrients that are a standard part of diets designed to balance hormones, recommended for instance during menopause or because of problems with premenstrual syndrome (PMS). These hormonelike compounds may also protect against estrogen-related cancers such as breast cancer because they replace more potent estrogens in key tissues. Soybeans also fight prostate cancer and may inhibit fertility. In addition, they relieve constipation, regulate blood sugar, promote contraception, regulate bowels, reduce triglycerides, prevent or dissolve gallstones, and lower cholesterol. Soybeans have been shown to dissolve kidney stones in animals. Eating soy products six times a month will yield a benefit. In addition, soybeans contain vitamins and minerals in a natural relationship that is similar to the human body's needs. Generous supplies of soybean products may serve as the major protein source in a meatless diet. However, the balance of essential amino acids in soybeans is not the same as that in meats; therefore, more grams of this protein

are required to supply the essential amino acids adequately.

- **Soy flour**, soybean oil, and soy milk are used in a variety of home-cooked and commercial products. Soy flour has a creamy yellow color and a slightly nutty taste. It is a rich source of the vitamin B complex, calcium, phosphorus, potassium, magnesium, and iron. **Texturized soy protein** is made from soy flour and is compressed until the protein fibers change in structure. Soy protein must be rehydrated before use and can replace (as a meat extender) all or part of the meat portion in meatloaf, hamburgers, chili, and other such dishes. Soy products of this nature can be made to imitate bacon, hot dogs, sausage, and cold cuts. These foods can be found in health food stores and increasingly in regular supermarkets.
- **Soybean oil** contains large amounts of linoleic acid, an omega-6 fatty acid that is essential to the human body. Soybean oil is stable against oxidation and flavor deterioration because of its lecithin and vitamin E content.
- **Soy milk** is often recommended for those who are allergic to cow's milk. It is low in fat, carbohydrates, calcium, phosphorus, and riboflavin but rich in iron, thiamin, niacin, protein, minerals, and isoflavones. Some brands enrich the milk with the nutrients that are lacking—vitamin D, calcium, and vitamin B_{12}.
- **Pressed soybean cakes**, or **tofu**, the product resulting from grinding the soybean residue after the soybeans have been processed for soy oil, can be added to a variety of cooked dishes.
- **Natto** is made from whole cooked soybeans that are fermented by adding a culture of *Bacillus natto* until the mixture develops a sticky coating. It has a cheeselike texture and a pungent smell, can be used for soups and spreads, and is a good source of isoflavones.
- **Miso** is fermented bean paste that is packed with protein and isoflavones. It is used as a condiment in soups or as a flavoring in many dishes.
- A fermented soybean patty made from whole soybeans that has a nutty, slightly smoky flavor, **tempeh** is similar to mushrooms even in texture.
- **Soy sauce** is an Asian seasoning that is used all over the world. Spores are added to roasted soybeans and wheat and are grown for three days, mixed with salt water, and brewed for up to one year. Low-sodium types can be found in the market. Naturally brewed kinds are superior in taste compared with the synthetic types. There are no isoflavones in soy sauce; however, scientists believe that other anticarcinogenic compounds are present.
- **Sprouted soybeans** contain increased amounts of vitamins. Other products are soy powder, soy grits, soy nuts, and textured vegetable protein (TVP).

Meats

Meat commonly refers to the flesh of animals and is the most important source of complete protein in the modern diet. In addition to protein, beef, lamb, and pork are good sources of the B-complex vitamins (especially thiamin and riboflavin), phosphorus, iron, sulfur, potassium, and copper. Poultry is another type of meat that is a good source of protein and contains the B-complex vitamins (especially niacin), iron, and phosphorus.

The quality of **beef**, **lamb**, and **pork** is designated by the cut—prime, choice, or good—when purchased over the counter. The meat's flavor, tenderness, and ease of cooking vary with the grade and do not affect its nutritional value. Prime and choice cuts are often not the highest in protein content because the animals were "fattened" before slaughter. In general, lean cuts with less fat are preferable. The fat they do contain, visible as marbling, increases tenderness. Lean cuts contain more protein per pound and less LDL, the artery-clogging form of cholesterol. **Luncheon meats**, **frankfurters**, and **sausages** are usually high in fats and often contain nitrites, which can be converted to cancer-causing nitrosamines in the stomach. **Turkey meat** versions of these products are healthy alternatives, typically lower in saturated fats.

Variety meats, or **organ meats**, are usually richer in vitamins and minerals than muscle meats. Variety meats include liver, tongue, kidneys, heart, brains, and sweetbreads (glands of calves or lambs). Liver is a very rich source of complete protein and B vitamins, especially riboflavin, niacin, and B_{12}. It is also a good source of vitamins A, C, and D as well as iron, phosphorus, and copper. Because of the high iron and vitamin B_{12} content, liver can aid the body in combating iron-deficiency and pernicious anemia.

Meats should not be soaked in water, because this leads to loss of water-soluble nutrients. It is preferable that meats be cooked without adding fats. Broiling and baking meats at moderate temperatures gives a higher nutrient content. Juices obtained during cooking contain valuable nutrients and should be served with the meat. Hamburger needs to be cooked thoroughly to avoid severe illness and possibly death from

E. coli bacteria. Pork, or any raw product containing pork, should be cooked thoroughly to kill any trichinosis organisms that may be present. Cooking to an internal temperature of 137°F will kill trichinae but to provide a safety margin for inaccurate thermometers, cooking to an internal temperature of 150°F to 165°F is ideal, still retaining the juiciness and tenderness of the meat.

Both raw and cooked meat should be refrigerated at a temperature of 30°F to 32°F. In order to be at their best flavor and nutritive value, meats should be used within two or three days after purchase. Ground meats and variety meats should be used within twenty-four hours to prevent spoilage. Meats should be frozen quickly and kept at temperatures of 10°F or lower to retard deterioration. Nearly all meats freeze well and maintain their quality if wrapped and stored properly, although meat that is frozen for more than six months may show freezer burn (drying) and changes in texture.

Poultry that is inspected for quality is graded A, B, or C, with A being the top quality. White poultry meat is especially rich in niacin and is easier to digest than dark meat, which is higher in fat and connective tissue. Dark meat, however, is superior to white meat as a source of thiamin and riboflavin. Chicken soup is good for colds and flu because the cysteine in the meat contains an agent that breaks down mucus. In addition, inhaling the steam from a hot soup or broth helps kill bacteria in nasal passageways.

Chilled raw poultry may be kept one to two days in the coldest part of the refrigerator. Stuffing from cooked poultry should be removed and stored separately in a covered container. It is also recommended that poultry be frozen without stuffing and stuffed immediately prior to cooking. Thaw completely to enable thorough cooking. The body cavity or skin of chickens and turkeys may contain a bacterium that causes food poisoning. In order to prevent a large bacterial growth from moisture, whole birds should be stored with loose wrapping so that the surface of the bird will be slightly dry.

Raw meats should be handled separately from cooked foods. Wash all areas that come in contact with a raw product before moving on to another type of preparation. This includes washing plates, cooking utensils, preparation surfaces, and, especially, hands. Raw meat should never be left out, and thawing should be done in the refrigerator. Bacterial growth is the highest at temperatures that range from 45° to 145°F. Meats are safe for short periods of time at 32° to 45°F (refrigerated), and bacteria do not grow but are not killed below 32°F (freezer storage).

Most types of cooking produce toxic compounds. When high temperatures are reached in baking, roasting, broiling, and frying, carcinogenic compounds called heterocyclic amines (HAAs) and polycyclic aromatic hydrocarbons (PAHs) are formed. Fat from the meat drips onto the coals during grilling, undergoes chemical changes, and the resulting toxic airborne compounds rise in the smoke from the coals to contaminate the meat above. These compounds concentrate on the charred spots and have been shown to cause cancer. In moderation there is no risk, but those who have cancer or who have family histories may want to be cautious. To make grilling a little safer, cook meat to medium rather than well done. Cook as far away from the coals as possible, trim fat, and use lean cuts of meat. Using smaller portions and adding lots of fresh vegetables, salads, and other side dishes to a grilled-meat meal are also good choices.

Milk and Milk Products

Milk and milk products are excellent sources of calcium, complete protein, and riboflavin. Milk also contains phosphorus, thiamin, and vitamin B_6 and B_{12}, but it contains little iron, magnesium, or vitamin C. A cup of milk contains about 300 milligrams of calcium, and two cups per day supply the needed amount of calcium for adults. Three cups daily for teenagers are recommended and two cups daily for children. Pregnant, lactating, and older women should consume three cups daily.

Milk is available in several forms. Most milk is pasteurized to kill bacteria and thereby prevent the spread of milkborne diseases. The pasteurization process involves heating the milk to a high temperature and cooling it rapidly. Homogenized milk has its fat content finely dispersed throughout and, therefore, is more easily digested than nonhomogenized milk.

- **Whole milk** usually contains about 3.5 percent fat by weight.
- **Skim milk** is whole milk from which virtually all the fat is removed; **2 percent milk** contains 2 percent fat, which gives it more body and flavor than skim milk; **1 percent milk**, which contains 1 percent fat, has less body than 2 percent.
- **Dried milk** results from the removal of 95 percent to 98 percent of the water from whole milk; nonfat dry milk is skim milk with the water removed. Nonfat dry milk and fluid skim milk, unless fortified, contain no significant amounts of vitamins

A and D because these fat-soluble vitamins are removed with the fat. However, they are rich in protein, calcium, and vitamin B_2.

- **Fortified milk** has one or more nutrients (commonly vitamins A and D) added.
- **Acidophilus milk** is liquid yogurt fermented by helpful bacteria that aid in digestion and stop the conversion of cancer-causing agents in the colon.
- **Evaporated milk** is whole milk with half of its water content removed.
- **Condensed milk** has water removed and sugar added.
- **Buttermilk** may be obtained from the residue of the butter-making process or it may be cultured. Most commercial buttermilk is made by the latter process, in which a harmless bacteria is added to skim milk or churned buttermilk.

Milk, as well as other dairy products such as cheese, helps prevent osteoporosis, cavities, and chronic bronchitis from smoking. It helps fight infection, increases mental energy (low-fat kinds), and protects the stomach by combining with harsh foods and drugs. Milk (especially low-fat milk) has cancer-fighting capabilities for the colon (if two to three cups daily are consumed), lung, stomach, and cervix. Acidophilus milk may prevent colon cancer. Skim milk helps lower cholesterol and may help prevent high blood pressure. However, daily fat in cheese and high-fat milk is linked to breast cancer and heart disease.

Fat globules may kill bacterial toxins such as *E. coli*, which stick to the walls of the small bowel. While whole milk may aid in drowsiness because of the fat, skim or low-fat kinds actually increase brain activity (as little as one-half cup to revitalize) by delivering tyrosine to the brain and triggering production of norepinephrine and dopamine. These neurotransmitters stimulate the brain to think alertly and sharply.

Plain cow's milk should never be fed to infants, since it may cause or contribute to colic, sleeplessness, rashes, epileptic seizures, diabetes, respiratory problems, migraines, and ear infections. Infant formula should be used. Milk brings on more stomach acid and does not aid in the healing of ulcers; however, it may help ease the pain. The fat in whole milk may contribute to gastrointestinal diseases as well as childhood diarrhea.

Allergic reactions that cause asthma, irritable bowel syndrome, rheumatoid arthritis, and diarrhea can result from drinking milk. People who are allergic to milk may substitute buttermilk, goat's milk, yogurt, and possibly soy milk, although soy milk lacks much of the value of cow's milk because it is low in calcium

and phosphorus. Those with lactose intolerance or irritable bowel syndrome may experience distress. Pill form aids are available for these conditions. Persons who are lactose intolerant and want or need to eat dairy products have several options—types of milk that contain lactose, the enzyme required for digestion of lactose, and lactose intolerance remedies that come in pill form and supply lactose as well as other digestive aids such as acidophilus.

Butter

Butter is made from milk products, contains vitamins A and D, and is high in fat. It is a concentrated saturated fat that can cause the development of cholesterol in the arteries. Spreads made from unsaturated oils are a preferable substitute unless the omega-6s need to be restricted for rheumatoid arthritis, psoriasis, or other inflammatory diseases. When selecting a spread of a margarine product, read the label to check that it does not contain partially hydrogenated oil or trans fats. Other saturated fats to avoid are cream, lard (the large, easily visible areas of fat in meats), and the saturated vegetable oils of palm and coconut.

Cheese

Cheese is made by separating most of the curd, or milk solids, from the whey or water part of the milk. Its texture and flavor vary with ripening (aging). Most cheeses contain protein, milk, fat, calcium, phosphorus, vitamin A, and riboflavin. The best way to store cheese is by leaving it in its original wrapper in the refrigerator. If the wrapper is torn, protect the surface from drying out by covering the exposed surface with plastic. Cheeses with a strong odor should be kept in a container with a tight cover. Low-fat cheese products are preferable since the fat in cheese has been linked with heart disease and breast cancer.

Yogurt

Milk that has been fermented by a mixture of bacteria and yeasts forms a custardlike product called yogurt. The milk is defatted and soured with *Lactobacillus acidophilus* and other bacteria that are necessary for health of the intestine. Yogurt aids digestion and controls the action of the intestine by favorably stimulating the kidneys.

Yogurt contains the B-complex vitamins and has a higher percentage of vitamins A and D than does the milk it was made from; it is also high in protein. Its calcium content benefits women.

The beneficial bacteria in yogurt make it a natural antibiotic and anticancer agent. A cup or two a day will boost the immune system. Yogurt has been found to be beneficial in treating colds and upper respiratory infections, high cholesterol levels, arthritis, constipation, diarrhea, gallstones, halitosis, hepatitis, vaginitis, osteoporosis, kidney disorders, cancer-causing bacteria in the colon, and skin diseases. When taking antibiotics, adding yogurt to the diet helps prevent gastrointestinal distress caused by the medications.

Both live and dead cultures in plain yogurt, with *Lactobacillus bulgaricus* and *Streptococcus thermophilus* cultures, blocked lung cancers in animals. Live cultures in yogurt are safe for those with lactose intolerance. The sugar in commercial yogurt tends to nullify its therapeutic effects. Sugar is antagonistic to the B vitamins that are made from the bacteria found in yogurt.

Nuts

Nuts are the dry fruits or seeds of some kinds of plants, usually trees. They contain anticancer and heart-protective properties. The soft inside part of the nut is the meat, or kernel, and the outer covering is the shell. Nuts are a concentrated food source of proteins, unsaturated fats, B-complex vitamins, vitamin E, calcium, iron, potassium, magnesium, phosphorus, and copper.

Some readily available nuts are **pecans**, **filberts**, **peanuts** (regulate insulin and are estrogenic, but of any food, are the most likely to trigger an allergic reaction), **Brazil nuts** (rich in the antioxidant selenium), **walnuts** (cancer fighter, omega-3 source, and cholesterol reducer), **almonds** (help reduce cholesterol), and **cashews**. Patients with Parkinson's disease have been found to have a lack of nuts in the diet prior to contracting the disease. According to the large epidemiological Nurses' Health Study conducted by Harvard University School of Public Health and Brigham and Women's Hospital, Boston, women who ate more than 5 ounces of nuts a week had a significantly lower risk of heart disease. Replacing saturated fat with the mono- and polyunsaturated fats in nuts is likely a factor in these positive results.

Nuts may be eaten fresh, roasted, or boiled, or in the form of flour or butter. Nuts may interfere with digestion unless they are chewed well or chopped into fine particles. When nuts are purchased in the shell, attention should be paid to the firmness of the seal since partially cracked nuts soon become dry and rancid. Nuts that are shelled should be stored in airtight containers, preferably in the refrigerator, to preserve their freshness and to prevent oxidation and rancidity of their fat content. Shopping for nuts in a store with a high turnover of these products helps guarantee freshness.

Oils

Oil refers to fats in a liquid state. Oils are removed from seeds or from beans (like soybeans) by heat extraction or by pressing. Oils removed by pressing are referred to as cold-pressed and retain their contents of vitamins A and E better than those extracted by heat.

All vegetable oils contain some portions of all the forms of fat—saturated, monounsaturated, and polyunsaturated—and all contain omega-6 fatty acids; some also contain the omega-3 fatty acids.

Polyunsaturated oil, which predominates in polyunsaturated fatty acids (PUFAs), is important in the diet because of its content of **linoleic acid (omega-6s)** and **linolenic acid (omega-3s)**, which are necessary for growth and maintenance of the cells. However, too much of those oils that are high in the omega-6s will incorporate their ingredients into LDL cholesterol particles and become harmful. Large amounts of PUFA in the diet may lower the good cholesterol (HDL) and increase the formation of bile acids in the intestine, which make cancer-causing agents. Antioxidant compounds such as vitamins C and E and beta-carotene may counter these adverse effects.

A balance of both is vital, with the **omega-3s** being most often lacking. Good sources of the omega-3s are flax oil (linseed oil), fish-oil supplements, or fatty fish, including chinook, sockeye, king and pink salmon, and albacore and bluefin tuna. Norwegian sardines; Atlantic, Pacific, and jack mackerel; halibut; and Pacific and Atlantic herring are other sources. Canola has the best ratio of both omega fats, and soy and walnut oils also contain the omega-3s along with the omega-6s in varying amounts.

Vegetable oils, such as corn, cottonseed, safflower, peanut (high in monounsaturates), soybean, sesame (high in monounsaturates), and sunflower, are all high in omega-6s with no omega-3s. Mixing flax oil with these oils will make them much healthier. **Flax oil** contains 50 percent to 60 percent omega-3s, almost twice as much as fish oil. Flax oil has been found to be beneficial in the treatment of heart disease, cancer, diabetes, arthritis, asthma, PMS, allergies, inflammatory conditions, water retention, and skin conditions. It also improves overall vitality. **Canola oil** (lowest in saturated fats and high in monounsaturates) and **olive oil** (highest in monounsaturated fat) are highly recommended. The oil from the first pressing is called extra-virgin olive oil; it is the least treated form and highest in nutrients.

Tropical oils include coconut, palm (extracted from the flesh of the palm fruit), palm kernel, cocoa, and shea nut. These fats are staples of the food supply in tropical regions of the world. Here they are consumed fresh and in their natural state, high in such nutrients as vitamin E, tocotrienols, and carotenes. For thousands of years, these fats have been regularly consumed in countries with a lower incidence of degenerative disease than in the Western world.

In the 1980s, worries about saturated fat and heart disease led to warnings about consuming tropical oils since they are relatively very high in saturated fats compared to vegetable oils such as olive and corn. However, the type of saturated fat in, for instance, coconut and palm oil is the medium-chain fatty acids that have no negative effect on cholesterol. (Butter contains short-chain fatty acids that do raise cholesterol.) In addition, research shows that unrefined coconut oil has antibacterial and antiviral properties and palm oil is rich in antioxidants. With greater appreciation for the nuances of their chemistry, these tropical oils are coming back into favor. While tropical oils that have been refined, deodorized, and possibly hydrogenated for use in the manufacture of such items as margarine should still be avoided, minimally processed versions, consumed in small amounts, can have a place in a healthy diet. These products can be found in natural food stores.

Margarine is a butter substitute made by converting liquid vegetable oils into a fat that is solid at room temperature. Margarine contains some salt and flavoring compounds to make it resemble butter in taste. Manufacturers use hydrogenated oils such as corn, soybean, and cottonseed in baked goods to enhance taste and texture and to lengthen shelf life. The process of hydrogenation involves adding hydrogen atoms to a polyunsaturated fat, which puts an unnatural twist in the structure of many of the fat molecules in the oil. These twisted molecules are called **trans fatty acids**. Trans fats are known to have a more significant effect on the ratio of LDL to HDL cholesterol, a marker for heart disease, than saturated fat. The Seven Countries Study, conducted by Dutch researchers in association with the University of Minnesota, followed more than twelve thousand middle-aged men and found a strong positive association between heart disease deaths during a twenty-five-year period and the men's intake of trans fatty acids. Trans fats are also thought to make it easier for cancer-causing agents to enter the cells, and research indicates that trans fats increase the risk of type II diabetes. Beginning in January 2006, the FDA required the number of grams of trans fats per serving to be listed on the nutrition facts panel of food labels, appearing on a separate line under saturated fat. Multiplying the number of grams of trans fats listed

per serving by the number of servings eaten gives the total grams of trans fat consumed. Several brands of spread now state "no trans fats" on their labels.

Large amounts of total fat, including both PUFAs (tumor-promoting) and animal sources, have increased cancer risks. Another study finding was that animals with excessive amounts of PUFAs showed an increase in gallstones. Also, the oxidation of polyunsaturated oils creates free radicals, agents that travel throughout the body damaging cells and protein. Fortunately, polyunsaturates themselves are often sources of the antioxidant vitamin E, which helps counter the negative effects.

Heating PUFAs to very high temperatures in laboratory tests resulted in toxic and cancer-promoting agents. The results of ingesting these oils, in animal studies, were diarrhea, kidney and liver damage, loss of appetite, and even death. Lower temperatures used in commercial kitchens and in homes showed no significant ill effects. However, reheating and using rancid oils may cause toxins to be made.

Oil, margarine, and all other fats should be kept refrigerated. They should also be well covered to prevent the absorption of odors from other foods.

Seasonings, Culinary Herbs and Spices, and Extracts

Seasonings, herbs, spices, and extracts derived from foods, because they are consumed in minute amounts, normally supply small amounts of nutrients and non-nutrient substances. Added to meals, they perform many useful functions, including giving variety to the flavor of foods, stimulating the appetite, and encouraging the flow of digestive juices. Many culinary herbs and spices also have healing or soothing properties. Herbs are the fragrant leaves of various plants, while spices are derived from the bark, buds, roots, fruits, seeds, and stems of various plants and trees.

Dried herbs and spices lose their true bouquet and flavor after six months of shelf life. They should be stored in tightly covered containers away from heat and light so that they will not become stale.

Liquid extracts, including vanilla, almond, and fruit extracts (such as lemon and orange), should be stored in a cool, dry place so as not to develop off-flavors or aromas. They must be tightly capped to prevent evaporation.

- **Salt**, or sodium chloride, is the most commonly used seasoning as well as an essential body mineral. Most people, however, consume many times too much salt. The body needs only a small amount, about 2 to 3 grams per day. An excess of table salt may cause mineral imbalances in the body because sodium upsets the potassium and calcium levels. Salt that is used in the home should be iodized, or be sea salt that is evaporated from seawater, which contains many trace minerals (including iodine).

- **Pepper** ranks next to salt as a common seasoning and is available in two forms: black (for flavor) and white (for certain foods). Both are obtained from the dried berries of the same tropical vine, but they differ in the manner of processing. Red pepper, known for its heat, is a third kind and is described later in this list.
- **Allspice** is a digestive aid that promotes digestive enzymes. It relieves pain in muscles and joints. It is also a local anesthetic and first-aid agent for tooth and gum pain.
- **Anise** is a cough remedy and digestive aid, promotes milk production in nursing mothers, and may relieve the pain of menstruation. Along with other therapies, anise may aid in prostate cancer. Hepatitis and cirrhosis may be helped.
- **Basil** is good for intestinal parasites and acne, and also is an immune system stimulant that aids in fighting infection.
- **Bay leaf** is good for stress, and infection (bacteria and fungi), and may be an antidote for the poison strychnine. Crushed bay leaves around the kitchen will repel cockroaches.
- **Caraway** is a digestive aid and is an antispasmodic that soothes the digestive tract and aids in menstrual cramps.
- **Cayenne** or chili pepper has valuable properties (see "Vegetables").
- **Celery seed** is a diuretic that is good for weight loss, PMS, high blood pressure, and congestive heart failure. Celery seed contains a substance that acts as a sedative. Blood sugar is reduced, and menstruation is promoted. Chemicals in celery seed have been used to treat psoriasis and T-cell lymphoma.
- **Cinnamon** helps those with type II diabetes and has mild anticoagulant activity.
- **Cloves** are an anti-inflammatory (contain eugenol) and help rheumatoid arthritis. Cloves have long been known to help kill toothache and other mouth pain when oil of clove is applied topically.
- **Coriander** is a digestive aid, prevents infection from minor cuts; kills bacteria, fungi, and insect larvae that attack meat; is an anti-inflammatory that may help arthritis; and may help reduce blood sugar levels.

- **Dill** is good for digestion and urinary tract infections (in bathwater), and may reduce blood pressure.
- **Fennel** is a digestive aid, may be used for infant colic, promotes menstruation, promotes milk production, aids in menopause, and aids in prostate cancer when used along with other therapies.
- **Fenugreek** is a Middle Eastern spice that has antidiabetic powers. It also curbs or prevents intestinal gas; is antiulcer, antidiarrheal, and anticancer; and helps lower blood pressure.
- **Ginger** is used for nausea and motion sickness. Ginger also prevents headaches, helps rheumatoid arthritis, is an antibiotic and an anti-inflammatory, boosts HDL cholesterol (the good kind), lowers LDL cholesterol (the bad kind), kills salmonella and staph infections in the test tube, is anticlotting, fights ulcers in animal studies, and contains an antidepressant ingredient. It functions as an antidiarrheal and ranks high in anticancer activity. Asians have long used ginger for chest congestion, colds, headache, cholera, diarrhea, rheumatism, nervous diseases, stomachache, and vomiting.
- **Marjoram** is a digestive aid and an antispasmodic for menstrual cramps, and it inhibits growth of herpes and cold sores.
- **Mint** is one of the best-known herbs around the world with more than thirty species. The two most widely available species are peppermint and spearmint. Peppermint is pungent with a peppery flavor while spearmint is milder. Mint is used medicinally as a digestive aid, an anesthetic for the skin, and a decongestant; it also fights infection in herpes, cold sores, and wounds. Mint allays pain and spasms of both the stomach and bowel and is an effective treatment for motion sickness. It is good for cramps and menstrual promotion and should not be used by those who are pregnant.
- **Mustard** made from mustard seeds aids digestion and has also been used to treat chronic constipation. A plaster made of black mustard seed is a classic remedy for such ailments as asthma and backache and can bring relief of congestion associated with colds and flu. It is antibacterial and a metabolism booster, which burns calories. Three-fifths of a teaspoon will boost metabolic rate by 25 percent, which burns about 45 extra calories per hour.
- **Oregano** is a cough remedy, expectorant, and digestive aid. It may also expel intestinal worms.
- **Parsley** is a diuretic that helps such conditions as high blood pressure, congestive heart failure, and PMS. It is high in antioxidants so it is good for

treating cancer. Parsley neutralizes the carcinogens in cigarette smoke and may help T-cell lymphoma. Parsley is a breath freshener, stimulates the uterus to promote menstruation, inhibits allergies, and lowers fevers. Pregnant women should eat only culinary or cooking amounts.

- **Saffron** lowers cholesterol, increases oxygen in the blood, reduces blood pressure, and stimulates the uterus. Pregnant women should avoid large amounts. Saffron may also promote menstruation.
- **Sage** is an antiperspirant, helps heal wounds and stop infections, and is used as a preservative. Since it fights salmonella, it is a good choice to add to foods that will be consumed away from home and outside. It is a digestive aid, reduces blood sugar (on an empty stomach), soothes sore throats, and aids bleeding gums and canker sores. Sage is a menstrual promoter.
- **Tarragon** is an anesthetic used for toothache and infections in cuts and wounds (fresh), and may prevent narrowing of the artery wall, fighting heart disease.
- **Thyme** is an antiseptic and digestive aid and may relieve menstrual cramps. Large amounts are a stimulant, and pregnant women should not use this herb in any other than culinary amounts. Thyme is also an expectorant that helps with coughs and colds.
- **Turmeric** is a spice that contains curcumin, the ingredient that gives it its yellow color. Curcumin is an anti-inflammatory agent and thus is useful for many diseases, including rheumatoid arthritis. It also eases stomach acid, prevents blood clotting, arrests poisonous toxins before they reach the liver, lowers blood sugar and cholesterol, and prevents and treats cancer.

Seeds

Seeds are the ripened ovules of plants. Edible seeds such as pumpkin, sesame, and sunflower are rich in protein, phosphorus, calcium, iron, fluoride, iodine, potassium, magnesium, and zinc as well as the B complex and vitamins A, D, and E. Unsaturated fatty acids are also included. Sesame seeds are high in calcium content. Sunflower seeds contain up to 50 percent protein.

Seeds have a variety of uses and may be eaten raw, dried, roasted, or cooked. Pumpkin, sesame, and sunflower seeds are popular snack foods, and others, such as caraway, dill, celery, poppy, and anise, are used as seasonings. Seeds can be especially nutritious additions to soups, salads, casseroles, and baked goods.

Unhulled seeds have a long shelf life, provided they are kept in a cool, dry place in a tightly sealed container. Hulled seeds should be refrigerated immediately and used within several weeks, because oxidation of their fat content may make them rancid.

Sweeteners

Sugars and other concentrated sweets furnish needed quick energy to the body in a readily digestible form. Sugar is a sedative, painkiller, tranquilizer, sleep inducer, antidepressant, wound healer (if applied externally), and antibacterial agent. Cane and beet sugars (from which table sugar is produced), jellies, jams, candy, syrups, molasses, and honey are concentrated sources of sugar. Fruits are natural sweeteners that also furnish bulk, vitamins, and minerals in the diet.

White table sugar is a major carbohydrate source but does not contain the proteins, vitamins, and minerals that are necessary for its own metabolism. B vitamins are robbed from other parts of the body to do the job. Excessive consumption of sugar also leads to an imbalance in the calcium-phosphorus relationship and may be a contributing factor in excess weight and obesity, diabetes, Crohn's disease, arthritis, tooth decay, pyorrhea, asthma, mental illness, nervous disorders, and low blood sugar.

Natural sources of sugar, such as fruits, usually contain adequate supplies of vitamins essential for digestion and metabolism. Brown sugar (made from cane or sugar beets) has only a slightly higher nutritive value than white sugar. Honey, maple syrup, barley malt, date sugar, unrefined granulated sugar cane juice, and concentrated fruit juices are preferable sweeteners, more nutritious than table sugar.

Artificial sweeteners, including aspartame or its trade name NutraSweet, have been found in clinical studies to have numerous undesirable side effects, especially if consumed in large amounts or when heated, such as when aspartame is added to hot coffee. Saccharin, also an artificial sweetener, has been shown to cause cancer in laboratory animals. A new artificial sweetener on the market, sucralose with the trade name of Splenda, is produced by chlorinating white table sugar. Far fewer studies exist on the safety of Splenda in comparison with other artificial sweeteners, but so far animal studies indicate that sucralose in animals can lead to such problems as shrunken thymus glands, enlarged liver and kidneys, reduced growth rate, and abnormal pregnancy. And in a small human study, results showed a lessening of blood sugar control in diabetic patients.

Another noncaloric sweetener is stevia, a leafy plant grown primarily in South America where it has been used for more than six hundred years. In Japan, stevia is used to sweeten beverages, pickles, and tea. Stevia is 250 to 300 times sweeter than sugar and sold in natural food stores.

Carob

Carob is a natural sweetener rich in B vitamins and minerals with a flavor similar to that of chocolate. It is often used as a substitute for chocolate or cocoa, especially by people who are allergic to chocolate or who wish to avoid the caffeine it contains. Carob also contains a fair amount of protein and carbohydrate and some calcium and phosphorus. It is available in tablet, powder, syrup, and wafer forms.

Chocolate and Cocoa

Chocolate contains more than three hundred naturally occurring chemicals. It contains two stimulants, caffeine and theobromine, that speed up the heartbeat and stimulate the central nervous system. Theobromine stimulates the release of endorphins, triggering a sense of well-being. Chocolate in particular delivers abundant antioxidants such as phenols and flavonoids, which can be as high as 10 percent by weight in dark chocolate. Cocoa flavonoids can lower blood pressure, decrease LDL cholesterol, and reduce harmful blood-clotting properties of blood. Contrary to popular belief, chocolate does not cause acne and it does not raise cholesterol. About 30 percent of fatty acids in chocolate are stearic acid, a saturated fat that when ingested is converted to a monounsaturated fat. When chocolate is added to milk, lactose intolerance is helped.

The downside of chocolate bars, cocoa mixes for hot chocolate, and chocolate baked goods is that these products usually contain lots of sugar and should be consumed with care. Chocolate also contains oxalic acid, an excess of which could interfere with calcium absorption and thereby promote kidney stones. Indigestion and heartburn may be caused by chocolate. Cocoa is lower in fat than chocolate and therefore will keep for longer periods of time. It also has a slightly higher nutritive value. White chocolate lacks cocoa and consists of basically only fat, milk, and sugar.

Honey

Honey is one of nature's finest energy-giving foods, consisting of carbohydrates in the most easily digestible form. It has strong antibiotic, sleep-inducing, and tranquilizing properties. Honey varies in texture, flavor, and color, depending upon its place of origin and the flowers from which the nectar was gathered. Because honey is almost twice as sweet as cane or beet sugar, smaller amounts of it are needed for sweetening purposes. Honey contains large amounts of carbohydrates in the form of sugars, small amounts of minerals, and traces of the B-complex vitamins and vitamins C, D, and E. Never feed honey to infants, since there is a chance of botulism, a deadly bacteria.

Molasses

Molasses is a thick, sticky syrup, light to dark brown in color, with a strong, distinctive flavor. Ordinary molasses is a good mineral and vitamin source, rich in iron, calcium, copper, magnesium, phosphorus, pantothenic acid, inositol, vitamin E, and the B vitamins. Blackstrap molasses is the residue left after the last possible extraction of sugar from the cane or beet. (See more on blackstrap molasses later in this section.)

Vegetables

Vegetables are composed primarily of complex and simple carbohydrates, water, and very little protein. Vegetables provide vitamins, minerals, nonnutrients like polyphenols and phytochemicals, and add bulk to the diet. They also contribute appetite appeal to a meal through color, texture, and flavor. In general, light green vegetables provide vitamins, minerals, and a large amount of the carbohydrate cellulose, which provides necessary bulk. Yellow and dark green vegetables are excellent sources of vitamin A and its precursor form, beta-carotene. Cruciferous vegetables like broccoli and cauliflower are rich in phytonutrients. Dark leafy greens are usually rich in calcium, iron, magnesium, vitamin C, and many of the B vitamins. The greener the leaf, the richer it is in nutrients. Vegetables are commonly available fresh, frozen, or canned. Fresh, raw vegetables generally contain more vitamins and minerals than the processed products, although quick-freezing causes almost no nutrient loss. Properly canned vegetables usually contain as many vitamins and minerals as home-cooked fresh vegetables, but commercially canned vegetables are usually cooked too long, depleting nutrient value.

Before being eaten or cooked, fresh vegetables should be thoroughly washed so that chemical sprays and dirt are removed. The vegetable skins should be left on or pared as thinly as possible so that the vitamins and minerals are preserved. Cooking time should be kept to a minimum to preserve nutrients and retain flavor. Baked and steamed vegetables will have a higher concentration of nutrients than boiled vegetables.

- **Potatoes** are relatively high in protein and are excellent sources of vitamin A, vitamin C, niacin, thiamin, and riboflavin as well as iron and calcium. The potassium in the potato may help prevent high blood pressure and stroke. Potatoes contain cancer inhibitors. A medium-size potato contains about 90 calories.
- **Sweet potatoes**, not yams, which are rarely sold in U.S. markets, are full of antioxidants like beta-carotene that help prevent heart disease, cancer, strokes, and cataracts. The wild Mexican yam, which is not considered an edible food, contains diosgenin, an estrogenic substance that tastes bitter and soapy. Diosgenin, a hormonelike compound, is used in the manufacture of supplemental progesterone.
- **Onions**, including shallots, chives, scallions, and leeks, are antioxidants with lots of cancer-fighting agents. They are thought to thin blood, inhibit stomach cancer, lower LDL cholesterol, raise HDL cholesterol, discourage blood clots, and fight atherosclerosis, chronic bronchitis, asthma, hay fever, and infections. Onions are antibiotic, anti-inflammatory, and antiviral and act as a sedative. Heartburn may be irritated and gas is a consequence.
- **Garlic** is a member of the onion family. Raw garlic works best as a powerful antibiotic that fights bacteria, parasites, and viruses. Encephalitis has been cured with high doses. Garlic is good for heart disease (two or three cloves a day lessen the chance of heart attacks) and stroke, and it contains many preventive, anticancer compounds and antioxidants (raw, cooked, or aged are best). Garlic is good for colds (decongestant and expectorant) and works as an antidiarrheal. It is good for boosting immunity, is an antispasmotic, lowers cholesterol and blood pressure, and works as an anti-inflammatory. It helps relieve gas, is estrogenic, and works as an antidepressant. Eating both raw and cooked garlic will give the most general protection.
- **Eggplant** is used as a topical skin cream that aids in basal cell carcinoma. It may lower blood cholesterol, counteract detrimental effects of fatty foods on the blood, and act as an antibacterial and diuretic agent.
- **Parsnips** contain six types of anticancer agents. This sweet root vegetable has an especially high glycemic index.

- **Pumpkin** is high in beta-carotene and other carotenoids and has antioxidant capabilities. Cancer, heart attacks, and cataracts are all helped.
- **Horseradish** is a decongestant and expectorant. The root vegetable is also an antibacterial and increases metabolism, which burns calories.
- **Mushrooms** like shiitake help prevent and treat cancer, high blood cholesterol, high blood pressure, viral diseases such as flu and polio, and sticky blood platelets. The shiitake mushroom has been claimed to produce an extract that is stronger than AZT in fighting AIDS. Tei-shi mushrooms also treat and prevent cancer. Tree ear mushrooms thin the blood. The kombucha mushroom has healing properties.
- **Avocado** lowers blood cholesterol, is a vasodilator, and contains an antioxidant called glutathione that blocks thirty different carcinogens. In the test tube, avocado also prevents agents in the AIDS virus from forming.
- **Kale** is rich in cancer-fighting antioxidants and has more beta-carotene and lutein (another carotenoid) than any other vegetable. Kale helps regulate estrogen and fights colon cancer.
- **Corn** has anticancer and antiviral agents and estrogen-boosting capabilities. Corn is also an allergen and may contribute to migraine-induced epilepsy, rheumatoid arthritis, and irritable bowel syndrome.
- **Collard greens** are full of anticancer agents and may block the spread of breast cancer. Collards contain oxalates and are not recommended for those with kidney stones.
- **Carrots** are a beta-carotene food that has powerful antioxidant capabilities. Beta-carotene fights cancer, protects arteries, fights infections, and boosts immunity. Chest pain, eye problems such as cataracts, macular degeneration and other eye diseases are also helped. Cooking does not destroy the carotene.
- **Spinach** is a dark leafy green, first among types of vegetables that fight cancer. It is rich in the antioxidants beta-carotene and lutein and also high in fiber. Raw or lightly cooked spinach is recommended.
- **Cauliflower** is a member of the cruciferous family, fights cancer, and regulates hormones. Colon cancer and breast cancer are helped. Raw or lightly cooked cauliflower is best.
- **Broccoli** is another member of the cruciferous family and is loaded with antioxidants. It helps breast, colon, and lung cancer; speeds estrogen removal; is antiviral and antiulcer; and regulates insulin and

blood sugar. Eat it raw or lightly cooked, since some agents are destroyed by heat.

- **Cabbage** and **bok choy** are cancer fighters and speed estrogen metabolism. Polyps leading to colon cancer are discouraged (several servings per week), and breast cancer is prevented. Two tablespoons per day may protect against stomach cancer. Cabbage is also antiulcer (the juice), antibacterial, and antiviral. It may cause gas and trigger migraines if eaten in the sauerkraut form. The most rewards are gained by eating cabbage raw, as in salads.
- **Brussels sprouts**, also from the cruciferous family, contain antioxidants as well as phytochemicals that fight cancer and are estrogenic.
- **Chili peppers** contain capsaicin, a phytonutrient that dissolves blood clots, opens air passages, acts as an expectorant and decongestant, and helps prevent emphysema, bronchitis, and stomach ulcers. Capsaicin may alleviate headaches when inhaled and joint pain when injected. Hot paprika is a natural aspirin. Hot peppers in foods speed up metabolism, which burns calories. They also contain antibacterial and antioxidant capabilities. A pinch of cayenne, sipped in warm water, helps relieve symptoms of chest congestion.
- **Bell peppers** are rich in vitamin C and also antioxidants. Macular degeneration, bronchitis, colds, asthma, respiratory infections, cataracts, atherosclerosis, cancer, and angina are aided. Orange bell peppers are a source of zeaxanthin, an antioxidant that helps prevent macular degeneration.
- **Asparagus** is a strong anticancer food with antioxidant capabilities. It is an excellent dietary source of the potent antioxidant glutathione.
- **Celery** is good for high blood pressure and as a mild diuretic. It contains eight anticancer compounds that detoxify pollutants and cigarette smoke.
- **Tomatoes** are great anticancer fighting vegetables with the antioxidant agents that fight free radicals. They are linked to low rates of pancreatic and cervical cancers.

Beverages

Beverages such as alcohol, cola, and coffee add little nutritive value to the diet. However, milk drinks and fruit and vegetable juices contribute fair amounts of protein, fat, nonnutrients, vitamins, and minerals to the diet. Tea contains polyphenols, which aid in preventing cancer.

Alcoholic Beverages, Wine, and Beer

Alcoholic beverages may be those produced by fermentation, such as ale, beer, and most wines, and those that are distilled, such as whiskey and vodka. Alcoholic beverages are pure carbohydrates and supply minimal nutrients and lots of calories.

Wine, in moderation, may benefit the cardiovascular system (two glasses per day). Good cholesterol, HDL, is raised by both red and white wine, with red being especially effective. The skins of the red grape contain substances (polyphenols) that fight cancer, bacteria, and heart disease, and thin the blood and prevent blood clots, lowering the risk of stroke. White wine does not use the skins of the grape and, therefore, does not produce the same benefits. Wine boosts estrogen levels, kills bacteria, inhibits viruses, and discourages gallstones. Red wine is a migraine trigger, and in excess any kind of wine will cause heart, liver, and brain damage.

One or two **beers** per day may prevent the blockage of the arteries in the heart and may raise the good HDL cholesterol levels in the body. Beer also contains magnesium, which is not easily found in common foods (six cans contain half the daily requirement). However, beer may also cause gout, elevated blood pressure, and cancer of the urinary tract, rectum, lung, and breast. Risks increase with amount consumed. Moderate amounts increase the risk of heart attack. The potbellies of those who love to indulge in this alcoholic beverage are due to the decreased intake and absorption of protein-rich foods that keep the stomach structure firm. Instead, the digestive system expands. The risk of using alcohol for any benefit must be weighed against the many ailments and disorders that too much consumption can cause. If there is a problem, help should be sought.

Carbonated Beverages

Carbonated beverages such as colas are high in sugar content and have no nutritional value whatsoever. In order to hold the sugar in suspension and keep it from crystallizing, all soft drinks contain acid, usually orthophosphoric or citric, that eats away tooth enamel and can impair the appetite and the stomach. The high consumption of colas among Americans significantly contributes to the acidifying effects of the typical Western diet. Colas and some soft drinks contain large amounts of caffeine, which stimulates the metabolism. Diet sodas contain artificial sweeteners known to cause either cancer (saccharin) or other undesirable side effects (aspartame). Research shows that consumption of regular and diet colas is associated with an increased risk of developing high blood pressure.

Coffee

Coffee is produced from the coffee bean. It contains, among other substances, caffeine—a psychoactive drug that is very strong. Because of the norepinephrine released in the brain, coffee quickens the respiration process, strengthens the pulse, raises the blood pressure, stimulates the kidneys, temporarily relieves fatigue or depression, and excites the functions of the brain, improving mental performance. Caffeine is an emergency remedy for an asthma attack, and regular consumption has been shown to produce less asthma and less wheezing because bronchial tubes are dilated. Coffee may have a calming effect on most people because of several opiate-related compounds that have a mild heroinelike reaction in the brain. These substances are found in decaf as well.

If consumed in excess, coffee can be mildly addictive and may trigger headaches. It may cause increased nervous symptoms, including panic attacks, anxiety, insomnia, and psychiatric disturbances. Coffee consumption is also associated with aggravated heart and artery disorders. Drinking more than two cups of coffee a day can cause a rise in both triglyceride levels and cholesterol in the blood. **Boiled coffee** seems to have a greater effect than filtered coffee. The source of the harm is thought to be the oils and bits of beans in sediment-rich coffee such as **espresso**, **cappuccino**, and **French-press prepared coffee**. Decreased sensitivity to insulin, depression, irritated lining of the stomach, diarrhea, and heartburn are other possible side effects of drinking coffee. Coffee may encourage fibrocystic breast disease in women. And a recent study found that drinking four or five cups of coffee daily raised estrogen levels in women age thirty-six to forty-five. It may also create inositol and biotin deficiencies, prevent iron from being properly utilized, and cause other vitamins to be pumped out of the body before they can be properly absorbed.

Research indicates that healthy people can consume up to 200 milligrams of caffeine per day. A standard cup of coffee contains 90 to 150 milligrams of caffeine; however, **gourmet** versions sold in trendy coffee emporiums may have double and triple these amounts. An alternative is **caffeine-free coffee substitutes**, powdered vegetable preparations usually made with a barley or chicory-root base. Various satisfying and tasty versions are available in natural food stores.

Fruit and Vegetable Juices

Juices could be known as the world's fastest food. They can be made in minutes from fresh produce right in one's own kitchen, and although the nutritive value of the whole fruit is slightly higher and also includes fiber, juice is an excellent source of the vitamins and minerals necessary for the maintenance of good health. Within weeks, the skin, hair, and overall vitality may improve. Juicing enables the body to skip a step in the digestive process, which allows for instant absorption. The only element that interferes with the quality of the nutrients is the air that the juice comes in contact with. Nutrients enter the system as pure and perfect as nature made them.

Fresh **fruit juices** usually have a pleasing flavor and are easily digested. Juice should be extracted from chilled fruit immediately prior to serving. It should not be allowed to stand, because vitamin C and other water-soluble nutrients begin to lose their potency very quickly. If storing for a special purpose, juices should be refrigerated in covered containers to ensure that they will lose as few of their nutrients through oxidation as possible.

A common guideline for consumption is 16 ounces of juice per week. Fruit juice in excess may cause problems for those who are overweight or diabetic or those who have candidiasis or gout. A physician should be consulted before starting any treatment plan.

Green juices, or "green drinks," are highly recommended for building blood cells but need to be made more palatable with a sweet juice such as carrot or apple. Others that are good mixers are cantaloupe, pineapple, and pear. Holding the juice in the mouth and moving it around will incorporate enzymes that are secreted in saliva. In preparing juice, to keep the softer substances moving through the machine, juice harder vegetables first and then fold sprouts and herbs in cabbage or lettuce leaves and press these into the feeding tube of the juicer. Then follow with more hard items and juice these last.

Fresh **vegetable juices** are an excellent source of minerals and vitamins. Juices from dark green, yellow, and orange vegetables are especially high in carotenoids. Phytochemicals and polyphenols are also abundant in fruits and vegetables. People who want a change from raw or cooked vegetables may find juices appealing and easy to digest. Vegetable juices may also be the preferred form for people suffering from digestive system disorders.

Fruits and vegetables should be washed thoroughly. If the produce is not organic, using one of the natural citrus-based fruit and vegetable washes sold in food markets is also necessary to remove any chemical residues. If produce is organic (the best), just a rinse to remove any dirt is sufficient.

These are just a few of the many combinations recommended by the "Juiceman," Jay Kordich:

- *Antivirus cocktail*   Two apples and one orange
- *"The arouser"*   4 ounces of black grapes and ½ cup of black, pitted cherries
- *Aches and pains*   Two thick pineapple rounds
- *After a meal or workout*   One orange, ¼ grapefruit, and ¼ lemon with the skin
- *Regulation at night*   Two apples and one pear
- *Eye openers*   One orange and one grapefruit
- *Motion sickness*   Two apples, one pear, and 1 inch of gingerroot
- *Immune stimulator*   Three carrots, one stalk of celery, one apple, ½ beet, ½ handful of wheatgrass, and ½ handful of parsley
- *Ulcers*   ½ tomato, one wedge of green cabbage, and two stalks of celery
- *Blemishes of the skin*   Six carrots and ½ bell pepper
- *Cleanse the body*   Two to three carrots, ½ cucumber, and ½ beet with greens

Tea

Tea is similar to coffee in that it contains caffeine, but it also has tannin, or tannic acid, and essential oils as well. The caffeine is the stimulating element; the tannin gives it its color and body, and the oils give it flavor and aroma.

Tannin in its concentrated form has had harmful effects on the mucous membrane of the mouth and the digestive tract, but it is generally believed that tannin does not occur in significant enough amounts in tea to be harmful. Tannin in regular tea as well as in peppermint tea has been linked to high rates of cancer of the esophagus and the stomach. Adding small amounts of milk will bind the tannin and minimize its effects. Two cups per day are safe. Tea actually has strong nutritive value with its polyphenol and fluoride content.

Chinese teas, like **green** or **oolong**, or **American black teas** have pharmacological activity because of the presence of catechins (disease-fighting agents). These teas are antibiotic, antidiarrheal, antiviral, analgesic, diuretic, sedative, antiulcer, anticoagulant, and antibiotic. They also protect the arteries. **Green tea** is most potent, followed by oolong and then black (found anywhere in the United States in bags or loose). Excessive consumption of tea may be harmful to the body because of the caffeine content. Symptoms of overconsumption include PMS, anxiety, and insomnia. Tea also contains oxalates, which encourage the formation of kidney stones.

Herbal teas contain active chemicals that can heal and prevent disease; however, they can also disturb normal body functions. The elements in the herbs are where many prescription drugs are sourced. Herbal teas contain impurities and active components and should be used with care. Reading the labels (including side effects) and not taking anything that is not described, or acquiring the help of an herbalist or other professional, is strongly advised. Teas that may be allergens are chamomile, marigold, yarrow, and goldenrod. Fatal allergic shock may be experienced by those who are vulnerable to asters, ragweed, and chrysanthemums. St. John's wort may cause delayed reactions to sunlight. Teas that can cause diarrhea are from dock roots, senna leaves, buckthorn bark, aloe leaves, flowers, and bark. Teas that may produce adverse effects on the nervous system are catnip, juniper, nutmeg, jimsonweed, hydrangea, and wormwood. Poisonous teas are shavegrass or horsetail, mistletoe leaves, and Indian tobacco.

Supplementary Foods

Supplementary foods may be useful for individuals who wish to increase the nutritional value of their meals. Supplements may be in the form of tablets, liquids, powders, syrups, capsules, granules, or bars; various forms may have differing nutrient characteristics. *Any information concerning ailments is not meant to be prescriptive but merely represents research findings.*

Acidophilus

The colon should contain about 85 percent lactobacillus bacteria and about 15 percent coliform bacteria, but these percentages are usually reversed. For this reason, excessive gas, bloating, toxicity, constipation, malabsorption problems, and excessive growth of candida result. Acidophilus may help neutralize these conditions. Acidophilus can be found in buttermilk, yogurt, kefir, cheese, and acidophilus milk, in which much of the lactose has been predigested. Supplements are also available, to be taken on an empty stomach one hour before meals; never take with antibiotics. Maxidophilus and megadophilus are other forms that are equally effective.

Blackstrap Molasses

Blackstrap molasses is a truly rich source of minerals and vitamins. As the last possible extraction of the cane in refining sugar, it is the richest in nutrients of the sugar-related products. It contains more calcium than milk, more iron than many eggs, and more potassium than any food, and it is an excellent source of B vitamins. It is also rich in copper, magnesium, phosphorus, pantothenic acid, inositol, and vitamin E. One tablespoon of blackstrap molasses contains 3 milligrams of iron and more than 100 milligrams of calcium. It is also a good source of natural sugar. Recommended daily dosage is 1 tablespoon dissolved in 1 cup of lukewarm water or milk; half that amount is recommended for children. Molasses may be used as a sugar substitute in cereals and may be eaten instead of jam or jelly. Varicose veins, arthritis, ulcers, dermatitis, hair damage, eczema, psoriasis, angina pectoris, constipation, colitis, anemia, and nervous conditions may respond to supplementing the diet with this mineral-rich molasses.

Brewer's Yeast

Brewer's yeast is a nonleavening yeast that can be added to all foods to increase their nutritional value. Brewer's yeast is one of the best sources of B vitamins and minerals. It contains sixteen amino acids, fourteen minerals, and seventeen vitamins. Brewer's yeast is high in phosphorus in relation to calcium; therefore, 8 ounces of skim milk or 4 tablespoons of dry powdered milk should be taken with every tablespoon of yeast. The recommended supplemental allowance of brewer's yeast is 1 tablespoon daily.

Brewer's yeast and wheat germ taken daily may be helpful in preventing heart trouble. Brewer's yeast may protect against toxicity of large doses of vitamin D. It is used to prevent constipation and is a good source of enzyme-producing agents. Brewer's yeast is one of the best sources of RNA, a nucleic acid that is important in keeping the body immune to degenerative diseases. Brewer's yeast is available in powder, flake, and tablet forms.

Kombucha Mushroom

The kombucha mushroom is a living organism thought to have many curative properties. It may be purchased but should not be used without first consulting a qualified physician. According to anecdotal evidence, kombucha strengthens the immune system, increases energy levels, improves the digestive system, aids the skin, works as an antitoxin, and promotes overall well-being.

Lecithin

Lecithin is a natural constituent of every human cell and helps emulsify cholesterol in the body. Lecithin is available both naturally in egg yolk, liver, nuts, whole wheat, unrefined vegetable oils, soybeans, and corn and as a supplement in capsule, liquid, and granule forms. Lecithin is high in phosphorus and unites with iron, iodine, and calcium to give power and vigor to the brain and aid in the digestion and absorption of fats. Lecithin also consists of unsaturated fatty acids and choline.

Lecithin may break up cholesterol and allow it to pass through arterial walls, helping prevent atherosclerosis. It has also been found to increase immunity against virus infections and to prevent the formation of gallstones. Even distribution of body weight is also aided by lecithin. Lecithin plays an important part in maintaining a healthy nervous system and is found naturally in the myelin sheath, a fatty protective covering for the nerves. Lecithin also helps cleanse the liver and purify the kidneys. Two tablespoons daily are recommended.

Seaweed and Kelp

Seaweed is a vegetable from the ocean that is rich in minerals. Sea plants have an advantage over land crops because they grow in seawater, in which the minerals are constantly being renewed. Seaweed is rich in all necessary minerals. There are several varieties, including brown kelp (laminaria), nori, dulse wakame, and Irish moss, all of which have a salty flavor.

Kelp is one of the best natural sources of iodine; it is also rich in the B-complex vitamins; vitamins D, E, and K; calcium; and magnesium. It is often used as a salt substitute and is available in dried, powdered, and tablet forms. Kelp is antibacterial and antiviral. It kills the herpes virus and lowers blood and cholesterol levels. Dulse is dark red in color and rich in iodine. It can be used fresh in salads, but it should be soaked several times in water first. Wakame boosts immunity, and nori helps heal ulcers, disperses blood clots, and kills bacteria.

Seaweed is beneficial in maintaining the health of the mucous membranes and in treating arthritis, constipation, nervous disorders, rheumatism, colds, and skin irritations. Since seaweed is high in iodine, acne may be irritated when there are flareups. However, all seaweeds have cancer-fighting properties. Seaweed such as kelp, because of its iodine content, has been used traditionally as an antidote for exposure to radiation.

Wheat Germ

Wheat germ is the heart of the kernel of wheat. It is an excellent source of protein (24 grams per half cup), B-complex vitamins, vitamin E, and iron. It also contains copper, magnesium, manganese, calcium, and phosphorus. It is high in phosphorus in relation to calcium, so 8 ounces of skim milk or 4 tablespoons of dry milk powder should be taken with every tablespoon of wheat germ. Since wheat germ contains a vegetable oil, which easily becomes rancid if improperly stored, jars of wheat germ should be tightly sealed and refrigerated. Wheat germ oil is extracted from wheat germ. It is a supplemental food high in unsaturated fatty acids and is one of the richest known sources of vitamin E.

Ailments and Other Stressful Conditions

Good health is an inner level of being that sets the groundwork for physical, emotional, and spiritual well-being. It is the end result of a combination of heredity, environment, and nutrition. A well-balanced diet that is rich in all essential nutrients and nonnutrients is necessary to maintain one's well-being.

A deficiency of one or more nutrients impairs body function and can result in an unhealthy immune system, which in turn allows for disease. Despite adequate food supplies, nutritional deficiencies exist in our society. Most diseases caused by such deficiencies can be corrected when all essential nutrients are eventually supplied; however, in some cases when a severe deficiency occurs, irreparable damage occurs.

This section lists common ailments and stressful conditions that many authorities believe are related to nutrition. These ailments and conditions are listed alphabetically with explanations, including nutritional information regarding the nature of the ailments. The part of the body affected by each ailment is also identified.

Individual tolerances to the nutrients may differ significantly. Along with a physician or another qualified professional, each person needs to determine the quantity of a nutrient that will be beneficial in the treatment of a disorder. Factors influencing individual tolerances include a person's normal eating habits, previous amounts of vitamins ingested, height, weight, metabolic rate, reaction to stress, and environmental variances. Increase the dosages slowly; it took a long time for your body to become ill, so take your time in trying to heal it. If you wish to take large amounts of a nutrient, consult a physician.

The value of alternative treatments for ailments is being appreciated as we begin to realize that there is more than just one manner in which to approach an illness. The power of healing may very well benefit the most from combination therapies. In particular, combination therapies may be most useful for the degenerative diseases because it is in this area that medical cures have met with the most disappointment. Holistic medicine is an approach that is used to treat all aspects of the mind, body, and spirit with the focus on the organism or root of the problem, not the symptoms. Anodyne imagery, massage therapy, biofeedback, tai chi chuan, eye movement desensitization and reprocessing (EMDR) for posttraumatic stress disorder, acupuncture, animal-assisted therapy, group therapies, pain management involving cognitive behavioral therapy (CBT), and an overall feeling of bringing the environment of the treatment of ailments down to a natural and "homey" kind of level are alternatives that are accepted in varying degrees by traditional medicine. Chelation (an intravenous solution that improves metabolic and circulatory function by removing toxic chemicals), herbs, aromatherapy, and homeopathy are other alternative therapies. Research continues to substantiate their viability.

We strongly suggest that a qualified physician, preferably one who has some training in nutrition or an alternative health professional such as an herbalist, homeopath, or aromatherapist be consulted before taking on any responsibility for self-treatment. How to apply each method's principles and practices should be left to those who are the experts in their fields.

Herbs, the earth's bounty of medicinal plants, have been used for thousands of years for the treatment of ailments. Their ingredients are now being properly credited for many prescription as well as over-the-counter drugs that are used by millions of people every day. Scientific research continues as the evidence of the effectiveness of herbs becomes substantiated.

Homeopathy, based on the Law of Similars, is the practice of treating the symptoms of an illness with a substance that will produce the same symptoms in a well person, thereby stimulating the body's own immune system and eliciting speedier and more intense healing. Homeopathic remedies come in tablet or liquid form and are made from natural substances such as plants and herbs and from biological sources such as minerals. They are diluted in a complex manufacturing process under controlled conditions until they are ready for the body to use. There is no waiting period between the time of ingestion and time of absorption; they work immediately. Homeopathy has been used for the past two hundred years, and scientific studies have proved that these remedies have remarkable, valuable preventive as well as healing properties. Most remedies are available over the counter; however, there are some that must be obtained by licensed physicians.

Aromatherapy came about as our ancient ancestors began to place substances and plant life in their surrounding environment into such categories as medicines, foods, poisons, and those that altered the consciousness. Burning certain types of incense (frankincense, for instance) would make people feel relaxed, drowsy, euphoric, or ecstatic. The oils of sandalwood, camphor, and rosewater warded off infection, and mixtures of the oils of certain herbs and spices guarded against the plague. Aromatic plants were placed on the floors of Norman homes to act as insecticides to ward off lice and fleas.

Today, some believe that these oils can heal many conditions, even mental depression and anxiety. By using a method of application that involves massage, the healing essence of the oils is directly inhaled as the prescription is gently circulated over the pathways of the nerve centers of the spine; the oils are also absorbed into the body through the skin. This method is thought to work more intensely than if the oils were taken in pill form. To allow for each person's needs

to be met, individual prescriptions are given. Consult a professional aromatherapist. Massage should not be used when any of the following conditions are present: fever, inflammation (of skin or joints), phlebitis, skin ulcers, rashes or eruptions, bruises, torn muscles and ligaments, sprains, swellings, advanced heart disease, varicose veins, thrombosis, broken bones, or burns. Gentle aromatherapy massage for cancer patients may lift spirits. A few people may be allergic to peppermint oil, basil, ylang-ylang, bergamot, geranium, lemongrass, melissa, and ginger in high concentrations; vegetable oil may be substituted. Asthma sufferers should be aware that steam inhalations may trigger an asthma attack.

For pregnant women, nursing mothers, or children under the age of twelve, one-half the regular strength of oils is recommended. A qualified aromatherapist must be consulted before using any oils for babies or small children. In such cases, it is important to research each oil. If no information can be found on its appropriate use in young persons, do not use it. Never take essential oils internally.

Abscess

An abscess is a localized infection with a collection of pus in any part of the body. The pustule can be located externally or internally and may be initiated by lowered resistance to infection, bacterial contamination, or injury. Symptoms of abscess include tenderness and swelling in the infected area, fever, and chills. A sluggish digestive tract and poor elimination may be a cause.

Antibiotics may be used to treat the infection, although in the case of a severe abscess, surgery may be necessary. Nutrients may be helpful. Zinc and vitamin A are recommended. Because the antibiotics used in treatment may interfere with the absorption of the B vitamins, supplementary B-complex vitamins may be required. Fever increases the body's need for calories, extra fluids, and vitamins A, C, and E. Diet may be beneficial in recovery. Increasing fresh fruits and vegetables is recommended while fatty foods, eggs, dairy products, meat, refined carbohydrates, and sweet foods should be avoided.

Herbs that may be helpful are echinacea, dandelion, violet, wild chrysanthemum, and Chinese golden thread. Aromatherapy is oil of tea tree. Homeopathic remedies are Belladonna 6c and Hepar sulphuris 6c.

Accidents, Shock, and Surgery

Following injury, the body's need for all nutrients increases dramatically. The pituitary and adrenal glands release large quantities of hormones that result in the loss of body protein and prevent the formation of new proteins needed for healing. (This can continue for a month or longer.) Soon the adrenals become exhausted from lack of pantothenic acid and riboflavin. Salt and potassium are depleted, causing partial intestinal and urinary paralysis. Bacteria in the intestine feed on stagnant food, and gas begins to form. Vitamin C is rapidly depleted. A temporary deficiency of digestive enzymes and hydrochloric acid occurs.

Nutrients may help. Sufficient amounts of protein are vital for healing. Protein can be synthesized only when adequate amounts of vitamins and minerals are present. A lack of a single nutrient can delay healing. Vitamin C is vital for re-forming connective tissue. The speed of healing is directly proportional to the amount of vitamin C the body has available for its use. The vitamin is also involved in forming new blood vessels at the damaged area and in preventing hemorrhaging. In addition, it detoxifies the body of medications and harmful substances that may form.

Exhausted adrenals can be greatly helped by pantothenic acid. Vitamins B_{12} and C and pantothenic acid can relieve patients who are unable to urinate. After any injury, 500 milligrams of vitamin C every two hours for several days aids in healing and reinforces the body's defense against the stress that occurs from pain, x-rays, medications, intravenous feedings, and catheterizations.

Vitamin E, used both internally and externally, helps the scarring process and relieves the itching and pain as scar tissue contracts. It also protects the cells from destruction by decreasing their need for oxygen. Vitamin E helps form new blood vessels at the site of injury and prevents the formation of blood clots. Proper blood clotting is a complex process and, in addition to vitamin E, requires many nutrients, including calcium and vitamins C and K. Vitamin A is also recommended for the treatment of tissue damage.

An injured person who is unconscious benefits substantially from an intravenous formula containing all nutrients. Adequate feeding given to unconscious patients results in healthy skin and hair and, later, to a quicker recovery. When poison has been swallowed, vitamin B_2, pantothenic acid, and large doses of vitamin C are recommended. Vitamin E and sufficient protein taken during the following days will also help the liver detoxify the poison.

Shock that is not treated quickly can result in irreversible damage and sometimes death. Undernourished people are particularly vulnerable to shock. Vitamin C and most of the B vitamins are rapidly lost. Investigators studying shock report that when the cells of the body are damaged, their enzymes chemically change from being constructive to being destructive. These cells then release histamine, a primary shock-producing substance. Adequate vitamin C will prevent this transition. The vitamin will reverse shock occurring in many areas of medicine. Intravenous dosages of up to 120 grams of sodium ascorbate during a three-hour period keep the body tissues saturated and successfully aid recovery. When shock has been brought on by severe hemorrhage, 3,000 milligrams of vitamin C and 300 International Units (IU) of vitamin E given as soon as possible can reduce the damage caused by an inadequate supply of oxygen to the tissues.

Preparation for surgery should begin at least a month in advance. Often, if the body has been adequately supplied, intravenous feeding may be unnecessary following surgery. Sufficient protein, all vitamins and minerals, digestive enzymes, and acidophilus should be taken. Adelle Davis, author of *Let's Get Well*, recommends that on the eve of surgery, the following be taken: 1,000 milligrams of vitamin C, 500 milligrams of pantothenic acid, 20 milligrams of vitamins B_2 and B_6, 1,000 IU of vitamin D, 300 IU of vitamin E, and 500 milligrams of calcium. Physicians have found that after surgery and in the following twenty-four hours, vitamin C is dramatically lost from the body. They recommend 10 grams of vitamin C before surgery, 10 grams in each tube-feeding bottle after surgery, and 10 grams orally after fluids are discontinued.

Convalescence requires a greater than normal amount of all nutrients. If supplements cannot be taken because of vomiting, vitamins stirred into creams can be absorbed through the skin. (Injections or surface application of vitamin B_6 may relieve the vomiting.) Homeopathic remedies are Hypericum for deep cuts, Calendula for incised wounds, Ledum palustre for puncture wounds, Hepar sulphuris calcareum for any injury that forms a pus, gunpowder for blood poisoning, and echinacea and staphysagria. For burns, use Arnica 200x or, if there is fright, Aconite 200x. Other remedies for burns are Hypericum, Urtica urens, Causticum, Cantharis, and Calendula officinalis. Aromatherapy also has applications for treating skin damage. Use geranium and lavender for burns and scalds. To heal wounds, cuts, and scrapes, use cedarwood, eucalyptus, frankincense, geranium, lavender, lemon, patchouli, tea tree, and vetiver.

Acne

Acne is the most common skin disorder. Testosterone stimulates the manufacture of sebum, a mixture of oils and waxes, and of keratin, a fibrous protein. These substances block skin pores, setting the stage for the development of acne. When there is partial blockage of skin pores, blackheads form; when blockage is complete, whiteheads form. Blocked pores also allow bacteria to overgrow, promoting inflammation. Acne occurs primarily on the face and sometimes on the back, shoulders, chest, and arms. Acne occurs mostly in males, during puberty, when hormones influencing the secretion of the oil glands are at their peak level of activity. Premenstrual syndrome (PMS) worsens acne.

Psychological stress may be a significant cause of acne; therefore, all nutrients needed to meet stress should be emphasized. Proper nutrition and skin cleanliness (twice daily washings with unperfumed soaps) together with adequate rest, exercise, fresh air, and sunlight, are helpful in the treatment of acne. Because the ultraviolet light of the sun contains actinic rays that sterilize the skin, use of a sunlamp when sunlight is unavailable, three times a week, may prevent bacterial infection and the resultant acne pimples.

Diet also plays a role in the development of acne. Although careful studies have shown that chocolate, potato chips, nuts, cola, shellfish, pizza, and foods with high fat content do not cause acne (hormones do), avoidance of fried foods, milk, sugar, and trans fatty acids can be helpful. Oily cosmetics and face creams also need to be avoided.

For individuals sensitive to iodine, ingestion of too much iodized salt has been shown to cause problems. Fast foods have been found to contain thirty times the Recommended Daily Allowance (RDA) of iodine. Milk is also high in iodine. Improvement in two weeks and complete recovery in two months has been observed in patients given a low-salt diet.

Calcium helps maintain the acid-alkali balance of the blood necessary for a clear complexion. An excess of oxalic acid found in chocolate, cocoa, spinach, and rhubarb may inhibit the body's absorption of calcium.

Nutrients may help relieve acne. Vitamin A is especially beneficial for clear, healthy skin (5,000 to 10,000 IU daily); however, large doses are extremely toxic. Taking vitamin A in the form of beta-carotene is highly recommended. Vitamin A in its derivative form of Accutane is successful against cystic acne. Tretinoin, another derivative of vitamin A that contains the ingredient Retin-A, is effective against acne vulgaris (the teenage kind) when applied directly to the skin. Tigason (etretinate) is used in the treatment of psoriasis. These nutrients are available by prescription and have been found to be very beneficial without the side effects that are common with the large doses of vitamin A. Women who are pregnant or of childbearing age should not take etretinate as it remains in the body for two years and can cause birth defects. Accutane can cause birth defects as well, but it leaves the body within two to three weeks. Alternatives are being researched.

Other nutrients are also helpful. Zinc is an efficient bacterial suppressor and a necessary element in the oil-producing glands of the skin. It has been found to be deficient in many who suffer from acne. Foods high in zinc are wheat germ, peanuts, pecans, shellfish, turkey, and liver. (See the tables of food composition in Section 6.) Daily supplements of zinc picolinate (15 to 45 milligrams chelated daily) have produced successful results in many people. Acne vulgaris is a chronic inflammation that affects many adolescents who are deficient in zinc.

The B-complex vitamins (a high-potency supplement daily is recommended), with extra riboflavin (B_2) and pyridoxine (B_6), if a deficiency is already in place, at 10 milligrams daily is beneficial. Along with pantothenic acid, these nutrients help reduce facial oiliness and blackhead formations.

Vitamin C aids in resisting the spread of acne infection, and vitamin D guards the body's store of calcium from excretion. Vitamin E is important in the treatment of acne and has been found helpful in the prevention of scarring. Vitamin E also enhances the action of vitamin A. In addition, selenium supports vitamin E function and helps prevent the inflammation associated with acne. Supplemental chromium may also be helpful. Research indicates that patients with acne also have an impaired ability to metabolize sugar and that taking chromium improves both glucose tolerance and acne.

Herbs and other natural ingredients also may be helpful. Goldenseal is an herb that has been used topically to treat acne. Blue flag, agrimony, clover, horsetail, lavender, Solomon's seal, tansy, white birch, southernwood, lemon balm, iris, and fumitory may help. Tea tree oil has proven to be beneficial, with a

5 percent solution treating mild acne. Homeopathic therapies are Calcarea silicata 6c, Kali bichromicum 6c, sulphur 6c, and Hepar sulphuris 6c. Burdock, used as a vegetable and in homeopathic medicine, has been used for acne. Aromatherapy may include bergamot, cedarwood, Roman chamomile, cypress, eucalyptus, geranium, juniper, lavender, peppermint, tea tree, rosemary, and sandalwood. These are used as facials and tonics and in baths and saunas or for massages.

Adrenal Exhaustion

Adrenal exhaustion is the progressive lessening of activity of the adrenal glands, which may eventually lead to complete functional failure. Adrenal insufficiency is caused by rapid infection (as sometimes seen in the newborn), severe stress, starvation, overwork, or removal of the glands in surgery. Symptoms are a low energy level in the morning that gradually rises, being highest late at night. The person goes to bed but cannot fall asleep right away; then sleeps soundly but arises exhausted. Adrenal exhaustion is often categorized with insomnia. Other symptoms are weakness, weight loss, mild pigmentation to bronzing of the skin, loss of appetite, vomiting, nausea, abdominal pain, intestinal disorders, salt craving, and sometimes loss of consciousness from acute hypoglycemia.

Vitamins B_2 and B_{12}, folic acid, and pantothenic acid with potassium and sodium stabilize the activity of the adrenal glands. Frequently eating a well-balanced diet will promote good health. A variety of whole foods is recommended. Fresh fruit, vegetables, lean meats, fish, and low-fat dairy products are good choices. Caffeine, alcohol, refined flour, and sugars (white and brown) should be strictly avoided.

AIDS

AIDS (*Acquired*—acquired by association with the environment; *Immune*—the body's system of defense; *Deficiency*—abnormal functioning; *Syndrome*—signs and symptoms that occur together) is a serious illness in which people lose their ability to fight off disease. In America, there were approximately 950,000 people with HIV/AIDS in 2004, an increase of 50,000 since 2001. And globally, an estimated 38 million individuals, almost half of whom are females between the ages of 15 and 25, are living with HIV.

AIDS is believed to be caused by the human immunodeficiency virus (HIV). The immune system that protects the body against germs, bacteria, viruses, and cancers is destroyed by the HIV virus. HIV is a retrovirus, entering the cell as a piece of RNA (ribonucleic acid) and then replicating into a new piece of DNA (deoxyribonucleic acid), which incorporates itself into the cell's DNA. Since the virus is in the DNA, it is not possible to extract it from the genetic code of the cell once it has incorporated itself.

At one time, the only available tests for HIV were the enzyme-linked immunosorbent assay (ELISA) blood test that measured antibodies to the virus, and the Western blot test that looked for HIV proteins. Individuals tested had to wait up to two weeks for results, a stressful procedure. But now there are two highly accurate tests that produce results in as little as twenty minutes. In addition, there is a U.S. Food and Drug Administration (FDA) approved home test, the Home Access HIV Test marketed by Home Access Health, that is as accurate as a clinical test. The person mails a sample of blood to a laboratory and results come in three to five business days. With the use of a code number, anonymity and privacy are assured.

HIV/AIDS testing can be either anonymous or confidential. If confidentiality is the standard, positive results are likely to be reported to a state health department but to no one else. With anonymous testing, a person is not required to give his or her name. While most states provide some form of confidential testing, not every state allows anonymous testing.

Individuals with AIDS develop so-called opportunistic infections, illnesses caused by commonly found organisms that are harmful only to individuals with low immune function. These individuals also are susceptible to cancers from which most people with a healthy immune system are protected. The two most frequently reported diseases among AIDS patients are a common protozoan infection of the lungs called *Pneumocystis carinii* pneumonia, which 52 percent of AIDS patients develop, and a rare form of cancer called Kaposi's sarcoma (KS), the most common form of cancer in HIV-positive patients.

Being infected with HIV does not necessarily mean a person will develop full-blown AIDS. In fact, most infected people remain in good health for lengthy periods of time. After ten years or more, 5 percent of HIV patients (called nonprogressors) never display any symptoms of AIDS and remain in good health. These individuals show no signs of deterioration. By contrast, some people acquire AIDS without getting HIV and experience a wide range of diseases. It has recently been found that the long-term survival of some with HIV may be due to high levels in their blood of DHEA, the most dominant steroid hormone in the body and produced by the adrenal glands. In HIV patients, AIDS did not develop until the DHEA blood levels dropped. The body converts this mother hormone to whatever particular hormone is needed at any specific time. Phytochemicals and meditation increase DHEA levels and are highly recommended.

Long-term survivors of AIDS—those who live longer than three years after being diagnosed—are few but are being studied for insights into the eventual destruction of this disease. Sensible eating habits that include natural foods, a mostly vegetarian diet, hard work, exercise, spirituality, meditation, enlightenment, a group-healing circle, positive thinking, and other alternative approaches such as imagery are some of the aspects of these people's lives that they feel are responsible for their longevity. In one case, a woman had no remaining signs of the disease in her body after making use of these forms of treatment. Some refrained from taking prescription drugs and many still do. Researchers believe that these people may have unusually powerful immune systems or that the virus they received was a defective one. From this information, a vaccine may be developed. The latest thought is that the HIV is not dormant for all those years, but that the body constantly fights the virus, sometimes for years, until the HIV exhausts itself.

Alternative methods along with medical care may be helpful. Drugs that kill the virus are a high risk because they can damage the cell's own DNA in the process. An infected person's response to drug therapy and a reduced susceptibility to HIV infections may be helped with diet. There is also increasing scientific evidence that supplements can enhance the functioning of the immune system above its normal level. Oxygen therapies as well as thymic and transfer factor therapies are possible aids for the disease.

Malnutrition plays an important role in the course of and outcome of AIDS. Dr. Charles Halsted, chief of the internal medicine department at the University of California–Davis Medical School, found that AIDS attacks the intestinal cells that absorb vital nutrients during the early stages of the disease. He went on to state that "poor absorption of nutrients can be one of the early causes of malnutrition in patients." The goal of a vitamin supplement for HIV-infected people is to ensure absorption by oversupplying the nutrients that are necessary for the immune system to function at its very best all the time.

Long-term effects of a healthy diet will strengthen the immune system. Also, with a natural diet, the body is prevented from being exposed to artificial chemicals that may negatively affect the body's functioning. With HIV, the body has an unusually high metabolic requirement; therefore, the diet must contain more than the normal amounts of carbohydrates and protein as well as a necessary amount of fat, for essential energy, bodybuilding, and body maintenance needs. For an HIV- or AIDS-infected person, the diet should consist of whole grains at least once a day, fruits as a natural source of energy (instead of processed sugar products), an abundance of vegetables, and adequate amounts of protein (dairy products should be monitored for health effects).

Without adequate protein, infections slow the healing of wounds, increase chances of weight loss, and cause a lack of vigor over time. If a person is under a "moderate" amount of stress, the recommended amount of protein is 0.4 gram per pound. So, a 165-pound individual would require an intake of 66 grams per day. Foods that are high in protein are liver, fish, chickpeas, lentils, peanuts, cottage cheese, cheese, grains, and sesame seeds, to name a few. Protein can be supplemented.

Eating plenty of onions, garlic, and ginger may be beneficial. Natural soups, teas, and warm beverages (excluding caffeinated beverages) should be increased in the diet, since they are additional ways to add to the level of soothing nutrients in the body. Cold beverages demand energy that could otherwise be used by the immune system. The best oils to be used are olive and sesame. Raw foods such as oysters, clams, marinated fish, and sushi as well as very rare meats and undercooked or raw eggs (present in authentic Caesar salad) should be avoided since they may contain infectious bacteria as well as certain agents that may hinder absorption. To keep the diet alkaline, more grains and vegetables should be eaten than fruits.

Vegetables are especially healthful when added to soups because the nutrients contained within the cells can dissolve into a warm and easily digestible broth. The absorption of nutrients from soups goes straight to the body's systems. Adding reishi or shiitake mushrooms may increase the production of T-helper cells, which are lymphocytes and an essential part of the immune system. T-helper cells, specifically T_4, are most vulnerable to infection by the AIDS virus that destroys them.

Whole grains provide fiber, vitamins, and trace minerals that are important for keeping the immune system healthy. Fiber stimulates the immune-enhancing cells called Peyer's patches, found in the lining of the intestines. These cells, when stimulated, help activate and strengthen the immune system by producing antibodies, which are the body's first line of defense against disease in the intestinal tract. The fiber in whole grains also stimulates the blood flow to these cells, thus enhancing their ability to function. Fiber also helps to prevent parasites and other intestinal infections.

In addition, most fruits are high in vitamins, minerals, and fiber. An HIV-infected person may notice that sugar from fruit and fruit juice may lead to an overgrowth of thrush, a common oral infection in HIV-positive people and caused by the yeast *Candida albicans*. Too much fruit on a daily basis may cause thrush to accelerate or make it appear for the first time. If thrush is a problem, processed sugar should be eliminated from the diet. If the problem still occurs, fruit and fruit juices should be eliminated.

The immune system can be weakened when there is an excessive consumption of sugar, caffeine, and alcohol, especially if breakfast is skipped and an inadequate amount of protein is consumed. The white blood cells, including the T-helper cells, are adversely affected by excessive amounts of sugar in the bloodstream. In one study, white blood cells that were exposed to high levels of sugar had a decreased ability to engulf bacteria (phagocytosis). In other studies, evidence shows that protein molecules can be adversely affected by elevated levels of sugar in the bloodstream. Excess sugar binds with molecules, which can interfere with immune function, lead to blurred vision, and cause damage to the kidneys and the lungs.

A high dose of sugar will cause the digestive system to work harder to prevent the sugar from entering the bloodstream all at once. The pancreas must also work extra hard to produce sufficient insulin for processing the sugar, which depletes precious energy from the immune system. Sweeteners for foods can be fruit juices, small amounts of honey, pure maple syrup, and molasses.

Constant consumption of caffeine does not allow the body to heal, because the caffeine blocks the cell's ability to regenerate its energy resources. Roasted whole grain coffee substitutes may be used instead. In addition, alcohol depresses the nervous system, inhibits the bone marrow's ability to regenerate blood cells, depletes B vitamins with beta-carotene, may cause liver damage, and causes dehydration. Alcohol poisons every system in the body, and for an HIV-infected individual, it should be consumed in small amounts or avoided completely. Taking lots of water or other liquids is recommended before and after drinking alcohol to dilute and replace the fluids lost because of the dehydrating effects of alcohol.

Nutrients may be helpful. AL 721, an immune stimulant, inhibits the replication of the HIV virus. Immunomodulators naltrexone and ampligen are natural drugs that may help. Heparin may help, too. A pineapple and pancreatic enzyme, Wobe-Mugos, may be of benefit. Lipid encapsulated superoxide dismutase (LIPSOD), monolaurin, and isoprinosine are also used.

Vitamins C and E, selenium, and beta-carotene are antioxidants that have been shown to have a beneficial effect on the functioning of the immune system. Vitamin C boosts the immune system against viral infections. A study conducted by Steve Harakeh, Raxit Jariwalla, and Dr. Linus Pauling was published in the *Proceedings of the National Academy of Sciences* in 1990. Entitled "Suppression of Human Immunodeficiency Virus Replication by Ascorbate in Chronically and Acutely Infected Cells," the study provided evidence that vitamin C directly inhibits the growth and replication of HIV.

Vitamin C increases interferon levels and functions as a potent antioxidant. Dr. Pauling recommends dosages approaching 20,000 milligrams per day (although most studies show significant antiviral benefit occurring between 2,000 and 6,000 milligrams per day). High doses of vitamin C can aggravate or even cause loose bowel movements and diarrhea. Consult a physician before trying any new therapy.

A study researched by Simin Meydani, a nutritionist for the U.S. Department of Agriculture, showed the immune-stimulating effects of vitamin E. The results indicated that the group receiving the vitamin E supplement had a significant increase in immune response when compared with the unsupplemented group.

A 1982 study published in *Basic and Clinical Immunology* showed that while small increases in dietary vitamin A may stabilize the cells so their immune abilities are enhanced, an excess of vitamin A may be harmful to the immune response. Vitamin A should be replaced with beta-carotene for this reason. As an antioxidant, beta-carotene has its own potential to fight disease, and the body is able to excrete any excess amounts of this water-soluble nutrient that are not being used, eliminating the risk of the toxicity experienced with fat-soluble vitamin A. In test tube work, beta-carotene can stimulate immune cells so that they are better able to fight off such infections as *Candida albicans* (yeast infections commonly known as thrush), the type of infections that often multiply in AIDS patients. More than double the kill rate of *Candida albicans* was found when beta-carotene was added to suspensions of immune cells called neutrophils.

A majority of HIV-positive people will have some form of digestive imbalance at some time. Daily acidophilus supplementation is suggested to help prevent digestive problems from occurring. Production of significant amounts of B-complex vitamins, folic acid, and vitamin B_{12} as well as reduction of intestinal gas and diarrhea and improved digestion of dairy products from an increased production of lactase are additional benefits of acidophilus.

Some individuals who are infected with HIV, ARC (pre-AIDS), and AIDS have reported that using certain minerals has helped them. Dr. Asai's organic germanium compound may inhibit the reproduction of HIV in the test tube, although tests are ongoing. Organic germanium compounds have also been shown to have immune-enhancing properties. To date, no significant toxic effects have been noted.

A report has shown that blood selenium levels were significantly diminished in a group of twelve males with AIDS. Selenium appears to be a key element in the immune system. All AIDS patients should see a nutritionist for an assessment, including attention to selenium status. Interactions with vitamin E and other nutrients should be considered. Consult with a skilled physician.

In mice, a copper deficiency has been shown to result in a decreased antibody response that may affect the immune system, although research continues. The strength of the T-helper cells may be diminished by a lack of iron, which must be available for DNA synthesis. Zinc has been reported to be low in those with AIDS. In HIV patients, zinc supplementation has enhanced immune function and improved weight.

An additional aid in keeping HIV dormant is the use of herbs. The herbs listed here are recommended to address a particular problem: strengthening the immune system, digestive system, sleeping habits, and so on. Herbal remedies should not be used as the only treatment for HIV or AIDS.

One or more of the following may be chosen for a particular ailment: aloe vera (works like the drug AZT without the side effects), astragalus (for the immune system), echinacea and bee and flower pollen (boost immunity), and capsicum (hot peppers for pain of peripheral neuropathies). Other beneficial herbs to look into include goldenseal root, myrrh, ginseng, mistletoe, St. John's wort, red seaweed like Irish moss, chamomile, slippery elm, peppermint, spearmint, catnip, nervines, Chinese tonic herbs, schizandra, ligus-

trum, ganoderma, white atractylodes, codonopsis, and licorice.

The healing process works best when the body is relaxed and energy is concentrated inward. A part of being able to relax and allow this to happen is exercise and meditation, which not only enhance general well-being but also aid in the overall health of the immune system. The National AIDS Hotline (1-800-232-4636) is hosted by the Centers for Disease Control, and it answers questions about HIV/AIDS and how to protect yourself.

Alcoholism

Alcohol is a drug that has given people pleasure and relaxation for five thousand years. This beverage affects moods, sensations, and behavior. Taken in moderation, alcohol can reduce inhibitions and encourage social interactions. People differ in their tolerance levels, so it is impossible to name an exact amount per day that is "allowable" for everyone. According to the *Dietary Guidelines for Americans 2005*, those who choose to drink alcoholic beverages should do so sensibly and in moderation, which is defined as up to one drink per day for women and up to two drinks per day for men. One drink is defined as 12 fluid ounces of regular beer, 5 fluid ounces of wine, or 1.5 fluid ounces of 80-proof distilled spirits. These amounts are intended as an average over several days rather than the amount consumed on any single day.

This level of moderate drinking, in recent years, has been touted as good for heart health, with antioxidant flavonoids in red wine cited as one of the reasons for such benefits. However, in 2006, a team of researchers at the University of Victoria in British Columbia and the University of California–San Francisco reanalyzed dozens of studies thought to support this idea and found a flaw in the evidence. While such studies show a higher death rate for abstainers than for moderate drinkers, many of the abstainers were doing so because of poor health. When individuals who, by choice rather than because of poor health, did not drink alcohol were compared with drinkers, there was no difference in the rates of heart disease.

But whether or not having a glass or two is beneficial or causes harm, such moderation is not even a choice for certain people. Unfortunately, many people drink excessively and cannot control their behavior, giving alcohol the distinction of being the most widely abused drug in the world. The disease associated with this abuse is alcoholism, a dependence on or an addiction to alcohol. It is chronic, progressive, and potentially fatal. According to the U.S. National Longitudinal Alcohol Epidemiological Study, 7.5 to 9.5 percent of the U.S. adult population abuses and is dependent upon alcohol. For those who live in an alcoholic world, the effects are astounding. Life becomes a roller coaster of events that are dictated by a liquid beverage that interferes with sound logical and critical thinking. The lives of everyone touched by the individual—and even of those not involved—are affected. The destruction that occurs is social, political, and personal, and it touches every aspect of our civilization.

Alcohol-addicted people may be able to drink normally at times, but they are unpredictable. At other times, they drink far too much and lose control. Others drink continuously because of a physical addiction and/or mental addiction, as if their lives were missing something vital without it. Drinking in spite of not wanting to, and then feeling remorse at having failed to abstain, is one of the signs of alcoholism. If alcohol has adversely affected friendships or relationships, has interfered with daily routines or responsibilities, has affected health, or has preoccupied the mind so that everything revolves around its presence, alcoholism is definitely a threat and should be addressed.

There should not be a feeling of inferiority about alcohol addiction. Something happens internally that makes those who are predisposed to this disease react differently from those who do not become addicted. Environment, nutrition, and heredity all contribute. It has been found that those who "flush" when drinking carry a gene that allows for a buildup of acetaldehyde in the body.

The body's outward reaction to alcohol suggests that the drug acts as a stimulant, producing aggressive social behavior such as increased boldness. In fact, alcohol is a depressant that acts to decrease the basic speed of all bodily functions, including muscle contractions, speed of reaction time, digestion, and thinking processes. The increased activity familiar to drinkers is due to the decreased inhibition of behavior. Mental depression is chronic in alcoholics and, among other behaviors, is responsible for many situations that require counseling and treatment for family members, friends, employers, and employees.

Fetal alcohol syndrome (FAS) is a collection of physical and behavioral abnormalities that appears to be caused by the consumption of alcohol by the mother during the developmental stages of the fetus. Physical characteristics are growth retardation both before and after birth, small head circumference, small eyes, retarded development of the midfacial area (lips and area above them), flattened bridge within the mouth, and shortened nose. Psychological differences are abnormal neonatal behavior, mental retardation, and other neurobehavioral development. Heart murmurs, birthmarks, eye and ear defects, undescended testicles, abnormal fingerprints, and palmar creases (difficulty straightening out the ring and little finger) are other effects.

Diagnosis of FAS is made using several of these symptoms and a drinking history. Not all children of drinking mothers display these characteristics, but varying degrees of FAS may still be present. No one is certain what the prime periods are for the development of fetal abnormalities, but the first three months are vital and should be treated as critical.

The occurrence of FAS is about 23 to 29 per 1,000 births among women who are problem drinkers. The rate for heavy-drinking women is from 80 to 200 births per 1,000. Less than 20 percent of babies from heavy-drinking mothers have FAS, and about 5 percent of those display the outward characteristics. Even though the sperm quality of the father is also in question, these statistics give maternal alcohol use the distinction of being the most frequent cause of environmental mental retardation in the Western world. Spontaneous abortion is also twice as likely for heavier drinkers. It is impossible to set a safe limit for the consumption of alcohol; however, given the fact that genetics may also play a part in where the severities lie, abstinence is the best policy during pregnancy. Those who feel that they cannot live without alcohol during pregnancy should give the issue very deep thought and turn to someone for help. It may ease their life and that of their baby forever.

For binge drinkers, another effect of excessive alcohol is a temporary and marked increase in blood pressure. For regular drinkers, there are ulcers of the stomach and intestines; colitis; deterioration of the muscles, including the heart; and premature fatigue when exercising. Increased lung infections, including emphysema, and cancer of the lung, throat, and mouth are common in those who also smoke. The high amount of carbohydrate in the alcohol may cause hypoglycemia, which may contribute to further craving for alcohol.

Mental disorders occur (even schizophrenia in some). Kidney, bladder, and prostate damage, loss of function of the testicles, damage to the adrenal glands leading to feminization and sexual impotence in men, and failure of the ovaries and early menopause in women are all repercussions of excessive alcohol intake. It has long been known that equal doses of alcohol lead to higher peak alcohol concentrations in women than in men. Proposed reasons for this include that women may have fewer enzymes in the gastrointestinal tract required for the metabolization of alcohol or the lower body water content in the female body, compared with men, results in higher blood alcohol concentrations.

Alcoholics older than age sixty-five who have been heavy drinkers all of their lives are subject to a severe condition called Korsakoff's syndrome, marked by a loss of short-term memory and an inability to learn new information. This condition is far worse in long-term drinkers than for elderly people who begin drinking in later life. Within two years, however, the same results are apparent for beginning elderly drinkers as for those who have been drinking all their adult lives. After three weeks of not drinking, new drinkers can begin to rebuild damaged brain cells.

Prolonged dependence on alcohol may result in severe problems in the pancreas, liver, and gastrointestinal tract. The brain shrinks with even moderate use of alcohol, with damage being limited to the amount taken. Because the liver is able to regenerate itself, the early stages of liver disease are reversible. Abstinence and an adequate diet are necessary for this transformation.

Alcohol enters the bloodstream directly through the walls of the stomach and begins to act upon the central nervous system by changing the most basic mental functions through the destruction of brain cells. This tissue loss is thought to be directly related to alcohol toxicity, in which cells are killed because of the withdrawal of necessary water from brain tissues. Wernicke's disease is caused by a deficiency of thiamin; the symptoms are confusion, ataxia, abnormal eye movements, and walking abnormalities. It usually coexists with Korsakoff's symptoms. Wernicke-Korsakoff syndrome is mostly irreversible; however, test results show conflicting results with certain tasks. There is greater hope for recovery for the younger alcoholic.

The liver works to neutralize the effects of drinking upon the body by breaking down the composition of the alcohol. Under normal circumstances, especially if there is food in the stomach, the liver can effectively perform the task if not more than one drink per hour is consumed (recent evidence shows this time allowance can stretch up to two hours in some people). However, when the liver is overworked, it must compensate by creating microsomal enzymes that allow for an increased tolerance for alcohol.

After a time, the liver cannot handle the large amounts and begins to compensate less rapidly. The liver then becomes fatty because it cannot break down the glucose and fat and is less able to metabolize the alcohol. Fat accumulates and causes the fatal disease cirrhosis, and less alcohol is needed to produce intoxication. As drinking continues, the fat cells grow and rupture, killing the liver cells and leaving scars.

Detoxification in the liver involves a two-step enzymatic process, and alcohol is broken down in the first phase of this sequence. Nutrients that play a role in Phase I detoxification include niacin, vitamin B_1, and vitamin C. The phytochemical limonene is also useful. Another nutrient, pantothine, speeds up the body's detoxification process by lowering the blood levels of acetaldehyde, a major negative factor in long-term alcohol consumption. Selenium is also known for its detoxifying effects for alcohol, as well as heavy metals, drugs, cigarette smoke, and peroxidized fats. It is thought that selenium may guard against fatty liver.

The intestine also becomes damaged in alcoholism, which then interferes with the absorption of *all* nutrients, causing many deficiencies of different kinds. Vitamin C, which is often deficient in alcoholics, is needed to prevent scurvy. A zinc deficiency may occur, making the alcoholic more prone to cirrhosis of the liver and preventing vitamin K, a blood-clotting agent, from being absorbed into the body. Iron is needed to correct the anemia that often develops. A magnesium deficiency can contribute to the occurrence of delirium tremens. A deficiency of potassium may also occur in alcoholics, and supplements may be necessary.

The liver sends all its folic acid into the blood and then to the kidneys to expel it when alcohol is consumed, which causes a deficiency. A thiamin deficiency is one factor underlying alcohol-induced brain damage and also can lead to the thiamin deficiency disease beriberi, which affects the nervous system. Symptoms are mental confusion, visual disturbances, paralysis of some of the eye muscles, staggering gait, footdrop, and decreasing sensation in the feet and legs. For these symptoms, recommended doses of thiamin are large, from 10 up to 100 milligrams a day.

Vitamin and mineral interactions show that alcohol interferes with or diminishes the stores of thiamin, riboflavin, niacinamide, pyridoxine, folic acid, calcium, iron, zinc, magnesium, selenium, and vitamins B_{12}, C, A, and D. Alcohol consumption impairs the absorption of the enzymes in the liver that activate these vitamins. Thiamin is the one nutrient that alcohol interferes with the most; therefore, it is essential to supplement.

Vitamins B_6, B_{12}, and A are metabolically altered by alcohol. B_6 is let go from its protein binding and is destroyed. The intrinsic factor of B_{12} is inhibited, which does not allow the vitamin to be absorbed. Vitamin A is still absorbed, but even when moderate amounts of alcohol are consumed, its stores are depleted from the liver. Zinc, magnesium, and potassium are excreted in water from the kidneys, creating deficiencies. Beta-carotene and heavy smoking (more than one pack per day) along with alcohol caused liver damage in animal studies. To possibly reduce liver damage, moderate drinkers can take antioxidants four hours before or after drinking.

Severe deficiencies of many nutrients occur not only because of the absorption problems, but also because the alcohol itself satisfies the body's caloric needs. Alcohol contains about 70 calories per ounce and is pure carbohydrate, but it contains no vitamins or minerals needed for carbohydrate metabolism. In order for carbohydrate breakdown to occur, vitamins and minerals are taken from other parts of the body, leading to many deficiencies and tissue depletion.

There are many natural aids for the alcoholic. Phosphatidylcholine and AL 721 (an active lipid that includes phosphatidylcholine) may aid in the withdrawal from addiction. Niacinamide by mouth and sodium ascorbate (vitamin C) by vein benefit the alcoholic even psychologically. Alcohol craving may be due to a nutritional deficiency. Two grams of L-glutamine and 1 gram of L-carnitine daily may be important to reduce the craving for alcohol. Tryptophan may also have the same effect.

Alcoholic hepatitis C, or non-A and non-B, can be helped by the aid of 3 grams of phosphatidylcholine, which repairs liver cells. Hepatic encephalopathy, impaired function of the central nervous system caused by liver damage, may be reversed by branched-chain amino acids (L-leucine, L-isoleucine, and L-valine). Vitamin A is an anti-infective agent for upper respiratory infections such as tuberculosis and pneumonia, both of which are common in alcoholics. The vitamin B complex is essential for the prevention and treatment of alcoholic neuritis, pellagra, and delirium tremens. Choline aids in the decomposition of fat in the liver and helps maintain health in kidneys jeopardized by heavy drinking.

Diets containing only alcohol produce euphoria that, among other things, depresses appetite. Even if the drinker tries to eat well, large amounts of alcohol will impair ingestion, digestion, absorption, metabolism, and excretion of nutrients. The intestine becomes damaged, further interfering with absorption. Alcohol affects every organ, and complications can develop that change nutrient requirements. Also, since there is biochemical individuality for each person, different nutritional approaches to the diet will be needed.

Protein is necessary for tissue regeneration, particularly when cirrhosis occurs. Protein synthesis is inhibited in the brain. The liver is kept from releasing its protein nutrients, which along with a poor diet can cause a protein deficiency. Amino acid transport is interfered with, so even if protein is consumed, little true nutrition is being used. Protein deficiencies lead to infection, and fat is deposited in the arteries, heart, and liver.

Large amounts of alcohol in the body also change the way that carbohydrates and fats are metabolized. Drinking too much alcohol, which is pure carbohydrate without vitamins and minerals, can contribute to obesity but with prolonged use the opposite can happen. Refined carbohydrates are poor choices for the diet. Rats placed on the typical American highly refined carbohydrate diet eventually avoided the water bowl in favor of the bowl of whiskey.

Complications that can interfere with alcohol recovery are concurrent drug use and hypoglycemia. Food allergy additions may also be a factor. Permanent brain damage from alcoholism may not respond to nutrient therapy. Aspirin, ibuprofen, and acetaminophen in any dose should not be taken in combination with any amount of alcohol over any period of time.

Herbs that are helpful with alcoholism are milk thistle, which contains silymarin, a flavonoid complex. Silymarin is beneficial for the treatment of a wide range of alcohol-related liver diseases, from relatively mild forms to cirrhosis. Other herbs used in the treatment of alcoholism include primrose oil (for mood swings and liver damage), and ginseng, valerian root, goldenseal, skullcap, motherwort, and lavender (for withdrawal). A homeopathic remedy is Quercus mother tincture. Aromatherapy treatment includes aspen, agrimony, and olive oil.

Allergies

An allergy is a sensitivity to a particular substance that is ordinarily harmless to some people but can cause a reaction in others. An allergy indicates that the immune system is trying to fight foreign substances that enter the body from the environment—substances such as dust, pollen, cosmetics, metals, animal dander, smoke, perfumes, molds, and certain foods.

Almost any food may pose a threat to anyone at any particular time.

The body's allergic reaction to the allergen may manifest itself as hay fever, asthma, hives, high blood pressure, abnormal fatigue (one of the causes of chronic fatigue syndrome may be allergic reactions), constipation, stomach ulcers, dizziness, headache, mental disorders, hyperactivity, hypoglycemia, nausea, cramps, and even shock.

Susceptibility to an allergen depends on several factors, including heredity and the condition of the body's immune system. Stress, poor diet, insufficient sleep, emotional traumas, and infections can predispose the body to allergic reactions. A healthy body can resist allergens, but a lack of any one nutrient can increase cell permeability allowing easy entrance by foreign substances.

Allergens enter the body in numerous ways. They may be injected from drugs or vaccines; they may enter through the skin from cosmetics, soaps, dyes, leather, animal substances, metals, insect bites, poison oak, or poison ivy; they can be taken in by the mucous membranes of the nose from pollen, dust, smoke, perfumes, and airborne chemicals, which bring on sneezing, coughing, and breathing problems; or they can be absorbed through the intestinal tract from foods, bacteria, molds, or drugs.

Sometimes the sun can cause an allergic reaction, as can excessive cold. The body can also be allergic to itself. Many allergens are transitory; the effects are felt at some times and not at others. A food may cause a reaction when a person is emotionally upset, and yet the same person may experience no reaction when in a tranquil mood. Inhalant allergies are those related to pollen, dust, molds, smoke, perfumes, malodorous substances, dander, and mites.

Nutrients may help. Vitamin B_{12} at 500 to 1,000 micrograms daily may aid with the prevention and treatment of respiratory allergies in general. A bioflavonoid substance used widely in the United States for allergy treatment is sodium cromoglycate (whose ingredients are in an herb that has been used in Egyptian medicine for many centuries). Dissolving one to two tablets in warm water before eating has helped some people with their food sensitivities (lactose contents used as a filler may be a problem for some).

There are several forms of this bioflavonoid substance: cromolyn sodium, which can be prescribed; intel, used for the treatment of allergic asthma, which involves wheezing, coughing, and chest tightness (allergic asthma can also be helped with 1 gram of vitamin C and 50 to 100 milligrams of vitamin B_6 daily

and may respond to lozenges or injections of B_{12}); nasalcrom, used for allergic rhinitis, which is a runny, itchy, congested nose; and opticrom, used for conjunctivitis, or itchy, runny allergic eye problems.

Vitamin C has been used to treat hay fever, 500 milligrams two to three times daily. Timed-release may work for some. Test tube studies with quercetin, quercetin derivatives, and bioflavonoids suggest an anti-allergy role that prevents histamine and other mediators involved in allergic reactions.

Allergies to food in the diet, as well as inhalants and chemicals, can cause a brain reaction mimicking typical psychological problems of young people, from listlessness, insomnia, and irritability to more severe symptoms such as migraine headaches, depression, poor memory, violent outbursts, and hallucinations.

Recent research has related schizophrenia to high histamine levels in relation to food allergies. Sometimes the brain's sensitivity to certain foods can be an allergy and an addiction at the same time. Cystic breast disease and symptoms of discomfort in the breast during the menstrual period and in menopause are thought to be affected by food allergies.

Food allergies can be discovered by using the elimination diet. About 90 percent of food allergies are caused by only a few substances: the proteins in cow's milk, egg whites, shellfish, wheat, soybeans, and peanuts, the latter being the most common trigger. Often considered allergenic, chocolate, tomatoes, and strawberries, in fact, rarely cause an immunologic reaction.

A sensitivity to wheat may indicate that there may also be a sensitivity to meat products, canned goods, and bakery products that have dry milk added. Also, hydrolyzed protein may contain wheat, corn, eggs, or milk. Fortunately, a wide range of whole grains and grain products is now available in standard supermarkets and natural food stores, giving the consumer many alternatives to wheat. These alternatives include oats, buckwheat, barley, millet, rice, rye, sorghum, corn, and quinoa.

Food allergies trigger an acute response, causing symptoms such as nausea, vomiting, diarrhea, skin rashes, or difficulty breathing. Fatal shock may occur in severe cases. In contrast, a food intolerance, which may be caused by, for instance, lactose (milk sugar) in milk, results in chronic problems such as gas, diarrhea, and stomach cramps. Individuals who are lactose intolerant need to avoid milk but seem able to tolerate yogurt because of the bacteria it contains that produce lactase, which breaks down the lactose. Sensitivity to gluten, a protein in wheat, rye, and barley, also produces gastrointestinal upset. This condition is known as celiac disease. In addition, certain food dyes and sulfites used to preserve vegetables in salad bars and processed foods such as dried fruit also can trigger asthma attacks.

If a food allergy is suspected, consult a physician certified by the American Board of Allergy and Immunology. Allergy is assessed using skin tests in which a liquid extract of the possible allergenic food is placed on the arm or back, which is then pricked or scratched with a needle. If itchy swelling occurs within twenty minutes, the test is positive. Allergy can also be determined by laboratory testing of a mix of the patient's blood with food extracts, called the RAST test. This is less accurate than the skin test, but even the skin test is not totally reliable. A third way to assess allergy is the elimination diet in which all but very well-tolerated foods are eliminated from meals and possible allergens are reintroduced into the diet one at a time, monitoring for a negative response to each.

Herbs may help allergies. Devil's claw and dong quai are herbal tea ingredients that have been used to treat allergies. Ginkgo and skullcap are also used as antiallergic herbal treatments. Mua huang, or ephedra, has been used as an antiasthmatic and antiallergy treatment. However, in 2004, the FDA prohibited the sale of ephedra because of significant health risks, including serious potential cardiovascular events or death.

Alzheimer's Disease

Alzheimer's disease is the major form of mental impairment in older people and is characterized by the deterioration of brain tissue over an extended period of time. The parts of the brain that control thought, memory, and language are affected, with the loss of memory being the earliest noticeable symptom. Confusion, not recognizing close friends and relatives, and the inability to carry out daily tasks are others. Problems with speech or understanding math, reading, and writing are more serious symptoms. In later stages, personality and behavioral changes become apparent, including mood swings, insomnia, aggression, and wandering that requires eventual total care. Another form of this kind of illness is vascular dementia, or sudden changes due to the quick death of brain cells, which may also be found at the same time as Alzheimer's.

Alzheimer's is named for a German psychiatrist who described the changes in the brain tissue of a woman he thought had died from an unknown men-

tal disorder. He found abnormal plaque deposits and tangles of nerve fibers that are now the identifying characteristics of Alzheimer's disease. Loss of nerve cells in several areas of the brain that are vital to memory and other mental abilities and reduced amounts of neurotransmitters that relay vital messages in the brain are other deteriorations.

At this point in time, there is no known cause and there is no cure; however, research has identified the chemical component of plaque in the brain as a protein called beta-amyloid and another protein called tau as the component of the nerve tangles. Scientists are researching how these abnormal proteins can be blocked. Others are working on keeping the brain cells from being destroyed. The possible links between environmental toxins, aluminum (abnormal amounts are found in those with Alzheimer's), and a particular virus are also being explored. Healthy brain cell transplants are being researched. Drugs to enhance memory and other thought processes are being investigated. Other research is in the area of aiding the caregiver with the difficult situations that arise, such as incontinence, wandering, and agitation in the patient.

In addition, research is showing that certain ailments increase the risk of developing dementia. Conditions such as high blood pressure, diabetes, and metabolic syndrome are cited. According to the Rotterdam Study, started in 1990 and conducted in the Netherlands, individuals with diabetes had almost twice the risk of dementia.

It is estimated that 4.5 million people in the United States have Alzheimer's disease. Alzheimer's usually strikes after the age of sixty, although it has been found in younger people as well. The prevalence of Alzheimer's doubles every five years beyond age sixty-five. Recent estimates are that 5 percent of people age sixty-five to seventy-four have the disease, and nearly half of those who are eighty-five or older may also have it. Alzheimer's is, however, not a normal part of aging; it is a disease. The behavior of those who suffer from this condition is caused by brain damage, not by the intention of the ill person.

There is no unique test for Alzheimer's. An autopsy is the only way to positively identify the tangles and plaque that mark the disease. However clinicians do have various means of assessment to differentiate between true dementia and depression. Facets of clinical assessment include taking a detailed history; neurological, physical, and psychological examination; testing for the degree of mental impairment; and laboratory tests that include electrocardiogram (EKG), electroencephalogram (EEG), and computerized tomography (CT). Abnormal fingerprints are also associated with Alzheimer's disease.

Other conditions must be ruled out that may cause memory or abnormal thought processes, such as fever, gland or hormone problems, small strokes, poor nutrition, depression, brain tumors, head injuries, drug reactions, and blood vessel disease that causes dementia in the brain. There is 80 percent to 90 percent accuracy in the diagnosis rate today, with the goal being to develop, through research, a skin or blood test that can slow the illness in time for intervention and possibly prevention.

Treatment ranges from person to person, with the disease lasting from five to twenty years. Maintaining a quality of life with normal function as much as possible is the goal for many. Some people do not need medication, but for others, experimental drugs relieve such symptoms as sleeping problems, anxiety, depression, and agitated behavioral and mental states. The drug tetrahydroaminoacridine (THA) stops the breakdown of the memory chemical acetylcholine. This may be especially helpful for those in the early stages, but the side effect is that it may cause liver damage and it does not halt the disease, only slows it. Continuing to use the mind will keep brain cells working. A loving and understanding family and friends along with a caring professional are very helpful. Some training and preparation for the major caregiver is important.

After a period of time, the task of caring for the patient can become too much for family and friends and help must be found. Assistance is available through the Alzheimer's Association, which provides information on educational programs and support groups for caregivers and family members. They can be contacted at: Alzheimer's Association, National Office, 225 N. Michigan Ave., Fl. 17, Chicago, IL 60611-7633. Information can be found through the Alzheimer's Association website: alz.org. The association also has a toll-free, 24/7 helpline, 1-800-272-3900, for information, assistance, care consultation, and referrals.

Diet can play a role in the prevention of Alzheimer's. According to a 2006 study conducted by Columbia University Medical Center in New York, a Mediterranean-style diet that appears to cut the risk of heart disease also helps protect against Alzheimer's. This diet includes eating lots of vegetables, legumes, fruits, cereals, and fish, while limiting intake of meat and dairy products, drinking moderate amounts of alcohol, and emphasizing monounsaturated fats, such as those in olive oil, over saturated fats.

Antioxidants such as vitamin C, vitamin E, and beta-carotene plus the minerals selenium and zinc also offer significant protection. While more research is needed in this area, antioxidants likely protect against Alzheimer's in the same way these nutrients help prevent heart disease, Parkinson's, and other ailments associated with excessive oxidation. Antioxidant-containing foods such as citrus fruits, green leafy vegetables, tomatoes, potatoes, seeds, wheat germ, orange vegetables, cheddar cheese, lentils, liver, and lean meats should be consumed. In addition, staying away from sources of free radicals such as rancid fats, cigarette smoke, pollution, and radiation is recommended.

Avoiding sources of aluminum is also advised. Alzheimer's patients have significantly higher levels of aluminum in their brains than normal people, and chelation of this mineral over time has resulted in a slowing of the progression of the disease. Sources include food, antacids, deodorants, and, in particular, drinking water. Animal research has shown that aluminum in water is more bioavailable and readily enters the animal's brain tissue.

An herbal treatment, ginkgo biloba extract (GBE) standardized to contain 24 percent ginkgo flavonglycosides, is proving to be of benefit in treating Alzheimer's, at least in the disease's early stages. This substance seems to work by enhancing brain function and normalizing receptors for acetylcholine. Lipotropes increase blood flow and oxygen to the brain. Phosphatidylcholine and choline can increase the level of the neurotransmitter acetylcholine in the brain, thereby enhancing memory. Phosphatidylserine has been shown to improve memory and decrease dementia in six months in patients with severe Alzheimer's. Lipid encapsulated superoxide dismutase (LIPSOD) is an enzyme that may be helpful in Alzheimer's. Hydergine (involved in electrical nerve signals) is thought to retard the aging of the brain. Piracetam has been shown to enhance learning ability, and amaricetam has been used to treat dyslexic children in Switzerland with variable results. Studies are being conducted. Centrophenoxine, vasopressin, and ethoxyquin are other memory enhancers.

Taking a daily walk may help delay the onset of Alzheimer's, according to a report in 2006 in *Alzheimer's & Dementia*.

Anemia

Anemia is a reduction of the amount of hemoglobin in the bloodstream and/or a reduction in the number of red blood cells themselves. This lowers the amount of oxygen available to all body cells, which in turn reduces energy levels. Carbon dioxide accumulates in the cells, causing decreased efficiency and slowing the rate of body processes. When the brain cells are deprived of oxygen, dizziness may result. Additional symptoms of anemia are general weakness, fatigue, paleness, white eyelid linings, brittle nails, loss of appetite, mood changes, headaches, heart palpitations, and abdominal pain.

Anemia often arises from recurrent infections and/ or diseases involving the entire body. It can be caused by certain drugs that destroy vitamin E and other nutrients necessary for the health of the blood cells. Some insecticides damage bone marrow, often resulting in anemia. The most likely cause is iron-deficiency anemia, or too little iron in the blood. This kind of anemia can creep into one's life hardly noticed; when iron is added to the diet the feeling of increased wellness is quite remarkable. It may also be caused by inadequate intake or impaired absorption of nutrients or by excessive blood loss through such conditions as heavy menstruation or peptic ulcers. It has been shown that excess amounts of vitamin K in the diet during pregnancy may cause anemia in newborn infants.

A diet rich in iron is essential for the reversal of anemia. There are two types of iron: heme and nonheme. Heme iron is found in meats (lean red meat, turkey, chicken, and seafood such as tuna, salmon, oysters, shrimp, clams, and haddock), is easily absorbed, and can increase absorption of nonheme iron in cereals, vegetables, and salads that might accompany a meal. Nonheme iron is not easily absorbed; however, vitamin C taken with this form of iron aids in absorption. Eating meat and vegetables that contain vitamin C accomplishes this task. Tea and coffee, if consumed at all, should not be taken until an hour after eating, because they interfere with iron absorption.

Iron-deficiency anemia can occur even if the diet is rich in iron. A lack of vitamin B_1, vitamin B_2, niacin, pantothenic acid, or choline results in iron malabsorption. These nutrients are essential for the secretion of hydrochloric acid, which dissolves the iron before it is absorbed. Iron absorption can also be adversely affected by diarrhea, chronic use of laxatives, and malabsorption diseases such as sprue and celiac disease. Vitamin E may be needed to help maintain the health of red blood cells. Pica, a disease characterized by cravings for strange substances such as laundry starch, cigarette ashes, hair, earth, and plaster, may be caused by iron-deficiency anemia. Sometimes these cravings are the cause of iron-deficiency anemia.

Pernicious or megoblastic anemia is a form that results from a deficiency of vitamin B_{12} or folic acid. It is a severe form of anemia in which there is a gradual reduction in the number of red blood cells because the bone marrow fails to produce them. Pernicious anemia probably arises from an inherited inability of the stomach to secrete intrinsic factor, which is necessary for the intestinal absorption of vitamin B_{12} as in the case of Crohn's disease. This form of anemia can also be caused by the inability of those with celiac disease to absorb nutrients because of a gluten sensitivity factor.

Pernicious anemia occurs in both sexes. Its occurrence is rare in persons under the age of thirty, but susceptibility increases with age. Vegetarians are particularly susceptible to this type of anemia because sufficient vitamin B_{12} is found mainly in animal foods. In addition, the high levels of folic acid contained in vegetarian diets can mask a B_{12} deficiency. Good sources of vitamin B_{12} are meat, eggs, and dairy products. (See the table of food composition in Section 6.)

Symptoms of pernicious anemia include weakness and gastrointestinal disturbances causing a sore tongue, slight yellowing of the skin, and tingling of extremities. In addition, disturbances of the nervous system may occur, such as partial loss of coordination of the fingers, feet, and legs; some nerve deterioration; and disturbances of the digestive tract, such as diarrhea and loss of appetite.

Pernicious anemia may be fatal without treatment. Vitamin B_{12} injections together with a highly nutritious diet supplemented with large amounts of desiccated liver are the recommended treatment. Studies have shown that for less serious cases, the body will absorb enough vitamin B_{12} from a large dose to be effective, but a physician must be consulted first. Intake of the entire vitamin B complex will help maintain the health of the nervous system, although folic acid should not be taken in amounts exceeding 0.1 milligram daily. Folic acid has the effect of concealing the symptoms of pernicious anemia, allowing the unseen destruction of the nervous system to continue until irreparable damage is done. A diet rich in protein, calcium, vitamins C and E, and iron is recommended.

Sickle cell anemia is characterized by red blood cells that become bent and hard, clogging the circulation system and depriving the body tissues of oxygen. It has been observed that sickle cell patients seem to have a high requirement for folic acid and have responded to ingestion of 5 milligrams or more of this vitamin per day. When iron stores are depleted, it is hard for the body to replenish them with diet alone; supplements are recommended. Iron is less irritating when taken with meals. People with a condition called hemochromatosis can overload on iron and must consult with a physician before taking any supplements.

Nutrients may be helpful. Iron, copper, selenium, folic acid, and vitamins B_6 (deficiencies may cause anemia) and riboflavin (riboflavin and iron deficiencies may occur at the same time) are needed to prevent anemia. Protein and vitamins B_{12}, E, and C are all necessary for the formation of red blood cells, and a deficiency in any of these nutrients can cause anemia. Large doses of vitamin B_1 (thiamin) may help thiamin-responsive anemia syndrome or unexplained anemias, and lipid encapsulated superoxide dismutase (LIPSOD), an enzyme, is used for unresponsive anemia. Molybdenum mobilizes an enzyme called xanthine oxidase that helps absorb and use the storage form of iron.

Infants, adolescents, and women, particularly during pregnancy and lactation, are often deficient in iron. Iron supplements should be taken alone or with vitamin C between meals for optimal absorption. Zinc, antacids, and calcium (especially in women) interfere with the absorption of iron and should be taken at different times. Iron toxicity may cause stomach disorders and constipation. Infants and children are especially affected by overdoses of iron, which may even cause death. (See the tables of food composition in Section 6.)

The diet should contain foods that are high in easily absorbed iron such as liver (raw is best), lean red meats, fish, chicken, leafy greens, peas, soybeans, kidney beans, egg yolks, broccoli, kelp, parsley, raisins, prunes, rice bran, corn flour, brewer's yeast, and blackstrap molasses. Foods such as asparagus, chocolate, rhubarb, soda, spinach, beets, kale, Swiss chard, most nuts (cashews), and beans that contain oxalic acid should be limited as they interfere with iron absorption. The tannins in some teas (black tea) also interfere with absorption. In addition, some additives in soda pop, beer, candy bars, and dairy products interfere with the absorption of iron. Finally, cadmium in cigarette smoke, lead in some products, and the polyphenols in coffee inhibit absorption.

Herbs that may be helpful are fenugreek, comfrey, ginseng, gui pi wan, milk thistle (for hemolytic anemia), mullein, angelica (aids in absorption), dandelion, red raspberry, alfalfa (only under the supervision of a physician), and nettle. Homeopathic tissue salt remedies are Ferr. Phos. 6x, and Calc. Phos. 6xsa.

Aneurysm

An aneurysm is a permanent ballooning of an artery that is caused by unhealthy walls and abnormally high blood pressure. This condition can exist undetected for years. There is no cure, and the focus of treatment is prevention.

Dietary recommendations are to limit salt and saturated fats, including red meats and dairy products, and increase the intake of fatty fish such as sardines, herring, and salmon. Careful, regulated exercise is recommended. A person diagnosed with an aneurysm is advised to consult a physician.

Arteriosclerosis, Atherosclerosis, Angina, and Coronary Heart Disease

A thickening and hardening of the walls of the arteries is known as arteriosclerosis and is caused by a gradual deposit of calcium in the artery walls, resisting the flow of blood to the body's cells. A second, more advanced type of arteriosclerosis called atherosclerosis is due to the buildup of not only calcium but also cholesterol or fatty deposits in the artery walls. Atherosclerosis usually affects the aorta, heart, and brain arteries as well as the other blood vessels of the body and extremities. Both types affect the circulatory system in about the same manner. Angina, usually the first sign of atherosclerosis, and coronary heart disease are the result of the blockages caused by these kinds of blood flow restrictions.

Fat molecules are normally absorbed through the artery walls. With atherosclerosis, excess fatty material resists blood flow, and the fatty globules begin to appear in between the layers of the artery walls. As more and more of this fat is introduced, the artery walls thicken, which eventually causes strokes, angina, and high blood pressure. Angina attacks occur when there is any restriction of blood flow around the heart; the artery walls begin to lose their elasticity and become hard and brittle. Hemorrhages from small vessels located in the arterial wall beneath the plaques may cause the cholesterol deposits to break free from the wall, or a clot may form as blood passes over the rough edge of a plaque. A clot can form anywhere in the body and work its way to the brain or heart. The plaques, clots, or a combination of these may cause a total block in the vessel, known as myocardial infarction or coronary occlusion (heart attack), resulting in death.

Lack of sufficient blood to the brain may cause such symptoms as confusion and senility. Partial blockage causing a limited blood supply can result in cataracts. Coldness, numbness, weakness, heaviness, and pain in the hips and extremities (arteriosclerosis obliterans), sometimes leading to gangrene, are also symptoms of blocked blood supplies. Another symptom is claudication, which is characterized by a relief of pain when sitting down after walking.

Later symptoms of atherosclerosis are hypertension (high blood pressure), cramping or paralysis of muscles, a sensation of heaviness or pressure in the chest, and pains that radiate from the chest to the left arm and shoulder. Factors that enhance the tendency to develop atherosclerosis are obesity, lack of exercise, high blood pressure, smoking, heredity, stress, and poor diet.

Diet is important in many ways. Stress uses up nutrients that are needed for fat utilization. Some physicians believe that stress alone may cause atherosclerosis regardless of blood fat levels. The greatest stress is placed where the arteries branch and curve; the faster the blood flows during stress, the more injury that occurs at these particular sites. And an inadequate diet lays the groundwork for cholesterol to accumulate.

Studies have shown that not only the amount of fat but also the kinds of fat in the diet determine the risk of developing atherosclerosis. Monounsaturated fats help prevent arterial disease, while saturated fats promote such conditions. Saturated fat in the diet also raises cholesterol in the blood and can even have more of an impact on cholesterol levels than dietary cholesterol itself. The amount of cholesterol in the diet may not have any relation to the cholesterol in the blood. In addition, if the body does not receive enough cholesterol for its needs, the liver begins to produce what it is lacking. Trans fatty acids also raise cholesterol. They are present in fried foods and in partially hydrogenated vegetable oils widely used in a variety of food products, particularly baked goods. The ability of the body to metabolize fat, which varies among individuals, is also a factor in the risk of heart disease.

Studies by Dr. Dean Ornish, assistant clinical professor at the University of California in San Francisco, have shown that diet and behavior changes can reverse coronary heart blockage in a year. The diet they studied is extreme and a physician should be consulted first. No animal foods are allowed. Only whole grain cereals, cooked dried beans and peas, sprouts, egg whites, and fresh or dried fruits and vegetables are part of the regimen, which allows for just 10 percent of calories from fat per day. Walking for thirty minutes to one hour daily and meditation and yoga fill out the program.

Other diets recommended include the previously mentioned foods, sources of plant-based protein, as well as low-fat animal foods such as white meat chicken and turkey. Fish rich in the heart-healthy omega-3 fatty acids, such as salmon and sardines, are also recommended. Red meat and high-fat dairy products should be avoided. According to a study of nearly one thousand healthy middle-aged adults published in 2006 in the *American Journal of Clinical Nutrition*, whole grains cut the risk of heart disease. The benefits may be in part due to the fiber, minerals, vitamins, and antioxidants such foods contain. Cooking oils should be the kind that lower the undesirable low-density lipoprotein (LDL) form of cholesterol and raise the levels of the desirable high-density lipoprotein (HDL) cholesterol, which carts excess cholesterol to the liver where it can be broken down on its way out of the body. (See "Cholesterol Level, High.") Olive and canola oils are good sources. (See Section 2, Table 2.2, "Fat Content of Common Cooking Oils.")

Excess sugar and alcohol also need to be minimized because when not utilized as a source of energy by the body, these substances eventually turn into saturated fat. In addition, alcohol does not appear to protect against heart disease, as once thought. (See "Alcoholism.") If hypertension accompanies atherosclerosis, a diet low in sodium and high in potassium and magnesium is indicated.

Nutrients may be helpful. Vitamins E and C will aid in increasing the oxygen supply to the bloodstream. Iodine taken with vitamin E has been shown to stimulate the thyroid gland, aiding in the metabolism of fats, which helps those with atherosclerosis. Vitamin E also helps prevent free-radical damage of cholesterol, lowering the risk of cholesterol accumulating and forming dangerous plaque. Large doses of vitamin C have inhibited atherosclerosis in animals that were deficient in the vitamin. Nicotinic acid, a form of B_3 or niacin, may be able to reverse atherosclerosis for those who are genetically vulnerable to high blood levels of cholesterol. Having adequate selenium levels is also necessary, as a deficiency is associated with blockage of the arteries.

People with atherosclerosis that is considered hereditary may have an abnormally high genetic requirement for nutrients that properly metabolize fats. Atherosclerosis needs nutrients that will fight cholesterol deposits that threaten to clog the arteries. The more saturated fats in the diet, the more the body needs linoleic acid and lecithin. Linoleic acid appears to be necessary for the utilization of saturated fats and cholesterol. Polyunsaturated oils are good sources of linoleic acid. However, these oils oxidize easily in the bloodstream, so taking the antioxidant vitamin E along with the oil is recommended. Lecithin breaks down cholesterol and fats in the blood, allowing them to be effectively utilized by the cells of the body. Nutrients vital for the production of lecithin are choline, inositol, vitamin B$_6$, and magnesium.

Vitamin K, which coagulates the blood, can promote the formation of blood clots, triggering a heart attack or stroke. Therefore, consuming an abnormally large amount of vitamin K should be avoided. A daily aspirin, a blood thinner, is often prescribed to reduce the risk of suffering a fatal heart attack. However, at all recommended dosages, 300 milligrams, 150 milligrams, and 75 milligrams, there is an increased risk of gastrointestinal bleeding due to peptic ulcers.

Herbs that may be helpful for arteriosclerosis are hot red peppers, ginger, ginkgo biloba extract (for peripheral vascular disease), hawthorn berries, chickweed herb, and cayenne. Foods such as onion and garlic are also useful. Charcoal has been found to lower undesirable LDL cholesterol, but should not be taken for an hour before or after a meal. Dextran sulfate, a polysaccharide and an anticoagulant, is also useful for atherosclerosis. Lipoic acid has prevented atherosclerosis in animals. Liposomes that do not carry drugs have been shown to clean out cholesterol from atherosclerotic plaque in animals.

Exercise is essential but does not have to be strenuous. It is important, however, that exercise be regular. The American Heart Association recommends exercising thirty to sixty minutes most days of the week. Meditation and yoga can also be of benefit, relaxing muscles, reducing stress, and, in some cases, even lowering blood pressure.

Arthritis

An autoimmune disease, arthritis results in inflammation and soreness of the joints. It has been suggested that the condition is related to the body's immune system, which is unable to produce enough antibodies to prevent viruses from entering the joints; or the antibodies that are produced are unable to differentiate between viruses and healthy cells (the immune system mistakes the healthy cells for diseased ones), thereby destroying both. Arthritis may also result from an allergy to certain foods.

Osteoarthritis and rheumatoid arthritis are the two main types of the disease, but another type known as gouty arthritis is also prevalent. (See "Gout.") Osteoarthritis, usually found in elderly people, develops as a result of the continuous wearing away of the cartilage in a joint. Cartilage, which is a smooth, soft, pearly tissue, covers the ends of the bones at the joints. It provides a smooth surface for the bones to slide against, allowing easy movement of the joints. As a result of injury or years of use, cartilage becomes thin and may disappear. When enough cartilage has worn away, the rough surfaces of the bones rub together, causing pain and stiffness. Osteoarthritis usually affects the weight-bearing joints, such as the hips and knees. Symptoms of osteoarthritis include body stiffness and pain in the joints, especially during damp weather, in the morning, or after strenuous activity.

Rheumatoid arthritis affects the entire body instead of just one joint. Onset of the disease is often associated with physical or emotional stress; however, poor nutrition or bacterial infection may be just as likely a cause. Rheumatoid arthritis destroys the cartilage and tissues in and around the joints and often the bone surfaces themselves. The body replaces the damaged tissue with scar tissue, causing the spaces between the joints to become narrow and fuse together. This in turn causes the stiffening and crippling of the disease. Symptoms of rheumatoid arthritis include swelling and pain in the joints, fatigue, anemia, weight loss, and fever. These symptoms often disappear and recur at a later date.

Most rheumatoid arthritics have high serum copper and low iron levels, although the joints and lymph nodes have excess iron that may be responsible for the painful joints. The high copper levels are now thought to be the body's gathering of the mineral to a site of inflammation so it can do its work. Supplements containing iron may encourage swelling and joint deterioration. Natural food sources should be used instead.

Gouty arthritis is found mostly in overweight people who eat a diet full of foods rich in fats and refined carbohydrates and who drink alcohol quite heavily. Uric acid accumulates in the small joints in the hands and feet; men are more prone to this form of arthritis than women.

Many nutritional cures for arthritis have been claimed; research still continues. It is recommended that the arthritic have a well-balanced diet in order

...pantothenic acid may combat arth... Rheumatoid arthritis may benefit from L-histidine, another amino acid. Yet another amino acid, L-phenylalanine, is used in the treatment of chronic pain from arthritis. Osteoarthritis may be aided by lipotropes (important in lipid metabolism) such as SAM-e (S-adenosylmethionine), which is thought to ease symptoms. A fatty acid imbalance of the omega-3s and omega-6s may cause arthritis and other degenerative diseases. When injected into affected joints, a sulfated polysaccharide called hyaluronic acid lubricates and relieves discomfort.

When injected, superoxide dismutase (SOD) has been found to be effective for the relief of the stiffness, pain, and swollen joints in arthritis. A member of a group of enzymes found mainly in the fluids inside the cells, SOD protects against damage caused by free radicals. Dimethyl sulfoxide (DMSO) is another radical scavenger that relieves the stiffness and pain. Its effects are enhanced when taken with other vitamins and minerals such as A, B complex, C, E, zinc, and selenium. Dimethyl sulfoxide has been used topically to treat arthritis. Thymosin, a group of hormones produced by the thymus gland, provides significant relief to rheumatoid arthritis sufferers. Adenosine, a nucleic acid derivative, may reduce the stiffness of arthritis.

A vegetarian diet has been found beneficial for arthritis sufferers. Meat has a form of fat that encourages the formation of inflammatory agents in the body. Fats can regulate eicosanoids, which control inflammation, pain, and other symptoms of arthritis.

Reducing the omega-6 oils seems to help. Canola oil is the best fat to use, since it contains a balance of both pro-inflammatory omega-6s and anti-inflammatory omega-3s. Flax oil contains almost twice as much omega-3 fatty acids as does fish oil. Salad dressings that combine canola oil and flax are recommended. Olive oil, a monounsaturated fat, is also acceptable.

Food allergies may be a cause of the pain for some individuals, especially if there is no arthritis but occasional joint pain. The elimination diet will isolate the food or foods that may be causing the problem. The following should be avoided: eggs, milk, cheese, butter, coffee, sugar, corn, wheat, oats, rye, soya, malt, tomato, green pepper, white potato, eggplant, oranges, grapefruit, lemon, peanuts, beef, bacon/pork, and lamb.

Natural ingredients may help. Fish oils and royal bee jelly, rich in pantothenic acid, are reportedly helpful for arthritic people. Oil of evening primrose, which is rich in gamma-linoleic acid (GLA) and aids in anti-inflammatory action, is also useful. In addition, alfalfa, parsley, celery seed, ginger (which is anti-inflammatory), *hot* peppers, and garlic are also helpful for arthritis.

Herbs such as comfrey, burdock, brigham, black cohosh, valerian root, chaparral, yucca extract, gotu kola, chickweed, nettle (may cause side effects if taken as tea), devil's claw, dong quai, and feverfew are helpful for arthritis. Rheumatoid arthritis is helped by Wobe-Mugos, enzymes obtained from pineapple. Aromatherapy recommends coriander, clary sage, eucalyptus, ginger, lavender, lemon, juniper, sweet marjoram, rosemary, vetiver, cedarwood, and cypress.

Other natural ingredients are a bath of Arnica tincture, rosemary, basil, and lavender to promote relaxation and relieve pain. Aromatherapy includes roman chamomile, ginger, juniper, lemon, marjoram, lavender, eucalyptus, coriander, rosemary, and cypress. Skin brushing may stimulate the lymphatic system, which may help the arthritic.

Exercise is important in both the prevention and treatment of arthritis because unused joints tend to stiffen. Proper exercise instruction is essential as great harm can be done with what could be a normally easygoing activity. Swimming, water exercise, yoga, and tai chi (a martial arts program) have been found to be slow and careful enough to loosen joints without causing additional discomfort.

Good posture is also important to prevent stiffness and crippling. Poor posture can cause body weight to be distributed unevenly, placing more stress on certain joints, resulting in unnecessary pain for the arthritic person. Overweight and obesity also affect the weight-bearing joints, which become irritated and stressed by having to carry too much of a load.

Some drugs used to treat the symptoms of arthritis may interfere with the absorption of valuable nutrients. Consult with a physician about alternative medications or with a nutritionist about replacing missing food or using supplements.

Asthma

Asthma is a chronic respiratory condition whose close relation to allergies is characterized by difficulty breathing, frequent coughing, and a feeling of suffocation. An attack of asthma is often precipitated by physical or emotional stress, respiratory infections, air pollution, changes in temperature or humidity, or exposure to fumes such as those of gasoline or paint, sulfur dioxide, and sulfites. Attacks may also be related to low blood sugar, disorders of the adrenal glands, or specific allergies.

At the first sign of an attack, the muscles clench, causing inflammation that then causes further attacks. Symptoms of asthma are tightness in the chest and difficulty in breathing that is usually accompanied by a wheezing or whistling sound. Violent coughing often occurs as the lungs attempt to expel mucus. An attack can last from several minutes to several days depending on individual situations and agents involved. In almost all cases, asthma does not cause any serious damage to the lungs or the heart. However, an acute asthma attack can be a medical emergency, requiring a consultation with a physician or going to an emergency room immediately.

Skin tests are often given to pinpoint the patient's allergic tendencies. Common offenders are pollen, animal hair, dust, and certain foods. Proper nutrition is necessary, and the asthmatic should eliminate from the diet those foods that may bring on an attack. Meat, eggs, and dairy products can trigger allergens. Nuts, chocolate, colas, milk, and monosodium glutamate (MSG) are also triggers. Metabisulfate, a food preservative that is sprayed on fruits and vegetables and found in wine, may cause an attack. It is all right to ask waiters for information about food content and preparation when eating out. Allergens such as dust mites in carpets, roaches, cats, and dogs can all bring on an attack. Other triggers are exercise, viral infections, and sinusitis.

Nutrients may be beneficial. Vitamin A is necessary for the general health of the lungs, as is vitamin E, which guards against visible and invisible air pollutants. A person should have a diet sufficient in the vitamin B complex to avoid deficiency symptoms of nervousness, which might bring on an attack. Vitamin B_6 helps prevent and treat asthmatic symptoms. Vitamin B_{12} is good for the treatment of respiratory allergies across the board. The need for vitamin C is increased by stress and exposure to hot or cold weather, cigarette smoking, and industrial air pollution. This vitamin also prevents some symptoms of allergic asthma. Cromolyn sodium, a bioflavonoid-like derivative of an Egyptian herb, is a prescription drug used to treat asthma. Magnesium deficiency may play a role in the cause of asthma. (See the tables of food composition in Section 6.)

In addition to nutrients, natural ingredients may be helpful. Fish oil may lessen attacks in some people. Avoid oils that are high in omega-6 fatty acids, such as safflower and sunflower; a mix with flax oil is a good idea. Canola oil has a balance of both omega-6 and omega-3 oils. Other foods that may help are onions (possibly due to their content of mustard oils), garlic, and fruits and vegetables rich in vitamin C. A vegetarian diet benefits those with asthma. Hot foods such as chili peppers at least three times a week may help breathing. The caffeine in coffee will dilate bronchial tubes and may be used during an attack. A high fluid intake and the inhalation of steam may help liquefy mucus and make it easier to expel it from the air passages. Avoid smoking or being around smokers.

Herbs that are helpful are chickweed, echinacea, propolis, horsetail, pau d'arco tea, nettle (may have side effects), juniper berries, damiana tea to calm nerves, licorice root, slippery elm bark tablets, and thai ginger. Snakeweed or euphorbia acts as an expectorant but may be toxic to the kidneys. Ginkgo is helpful for all diseases of the lung, preventing the onset of asthma and reducing inflammation. Lobelia aids during an attack, red clover is an expectorant, and schizandra is a Chinese herb that acts as an astringent.

Oil of eucalyptus and sandalwood massaged into the back and chest are helpful. Frankincense is also good. A great deal of mucus requires myrrh. Homeopathic remedies include Antimonium tartaricum 6c, Bryonia 6c, Drosera 6c, Spongia 6c, and Corallium rubrum 6c for varying kinds of coughing discomfort.

Exercise for those with asthma is helpful to keep breathing efficient. Activities in warm, humid environments, and those that use short bursts of energy may be best. Pretreatment with an inhaler and warm-up and cool-down periods are essential.

Attention Deficit/ Hyperactivity Disorders

Attention deficit/hyperactivity disorders (ADHD) (sometimes still only referred to as attention deficit disorder [ADD]) is the term currently used to refer to several conditions such as "hyperactive child syndrome," "hyperkinetic reaction of childhood," "hyperkinetic syndrome," and "minimal brain dysfunction." Attention deficit disorder with associated hyperactivity affects school-age children, beginning about age three although the child may be older by the time the condition is diagnosed. In some cases, ADHD continues into adulthood. The hyperactive child may show symptoms of being fidgety, disruptive, tearful, aggressive, impulsive, easily frustrated, and unable to concentrate. He or she has a short attention span, is clumsy, sleeps poorly, and has poor school grades despite an average or above-average IQ. While debate continues over the causes of hyperactivity, there is a solid body of evidence pointing to food additives, allergic reactions to food and sugar in the diet. Some other known causes are heredity, oxygen deprivation at birth, prenatal trauma, smoking during pregnancy, and air pollution. The disorder may also be a result of boredom or feelings of insecurity.

All foods, medicines, cosmetics, and toothpaste that contain dyes and artificial flavorings (tartrazine and E 102) should be avoided. Food additives commonly cause adverse responses; the hyperactive child does not have the natural body defenses necessary to ward them off. These substances may be very small in quantity, but a susceptible individual can get a reaction from an infinitesimal molecular amount. Phosphate additives are thought to be responsible for a condition called *hyperkinesis*, which is exaggerated muscle activity.

Foods that each individual has allergies to will also cause changes in behavior. Carbonated beverages, foods that contain the preservative butylated hydroxytoluene (BHT), processed or manufactured foods, and foods that contain natural salicylates such as almonds, all berries, apples, peaches, apricots, tomatoes, oranges, prunes, and cucumbers should not be eaten.

A diet containing refined carbohydrates such as sugar is not healthful for anyone but is even worse for those with hyperactivity. Aggressive behavior and restlessness have been significantly correlated with intake of sucrose. Sensitivity to sugar was demonstrated in one study in which a high percentage of hyperactive children were found to be hypoglycemic, having difficulty managing blood sugar. Hypoglycemia triggers the release of adrenal stress hormones and because these spur a person into action, hyperactivity can result. A menu full of whole foods that include lean meat (not for those who need to restrict phosphorus) and fish, fresh fruit, and vegetables is recommended. Bottled or distilled water is best.

Nutrients may be beneficial. Zinc supplements have been found to be helpful. GABA (gamma-aminobutyric acid) is thought to decrease hyperactivity and a tendency to violence. Large doses of vitamins B_1, B_2, niacin, pantothenic acid, folic acid, and choline, and the minerals magnesium and manganese, have successfully treated the underlying causes of hyperactivity and adjusted the chemical imbalance of the brain. A minimum of three to six months is required before substantial results are manifest; however, a general slowing of the hyperactivity and increased concentration may initially be observed.

Another form of ADHD that does not include hyperactivity is learning disability. Poor concentration and brief attention span are symptoms. Recurrent ear infections, nutritional deficiencies of many sorts (even minor ones), and heavy metal toxicity can lead to this condition. Accumulation in the body of lead, copper, and heavy metals such as mercury and cadmium appears to affect behavior and can be tested for by a hair analysis. (Measuring blood levels tests only for recent exposure, not long-term accumulation.) Vitamin C can aid the body in removing heavy metals. Too much copper has been shown to affect behavior. Herbs that may help are evening primrose oil and valerian root.

Children have been treated in a clinical setting for hyperactivity with the following nutrients in quantities directed by age and weight (between 35 and 45 pounds): vitamin B complex, thiamin, and riboflavin, vitamin B_{12}, vitamin C, pantothenic acid, folic acid, choline, L-cysteine, zinc, GABA, manganese, calcium, magnesium, and brewer's yeast. In addition, 200 to 400 milligrams per day of vitamin B_6 is also part of this protocol. (For a child fewer than 35 pounds, quantities were adjusted as follows: 1 gram niacin; vitamin C in 500-milligram doses twice a day, increased to one 2-gram dose a day if tolerated; and 100 milligrams of B_6 and pantothenic acid twice a day, increased to 200 milligrams twice a day. For a child 45 pounds plus, vitamin C and niacin were gradually increased to 3 grams a day.)

Autism

Autism is a spectrum of neuropsychiatric disorders characterized by difficulties with communication and social interaction. Repetitive and unusual behavior is also typical. Some persons with autism are nonverbal. The severity of symptoms ranges from mild to severe and mimics retardation. Autism is normally diagnosed in children before they reach age six and is also identified in infants. Incidence of autism prior to 1970 was 1 in 2,000. By 1996, this had increased to 1 in 500 and, according to the Centers for Disease Control and Prevention, the current figure is closer to 1 in 166. There is debate over whether this highly dramatic increase in known cases of autism is due to better detection of autism as well as changes in the way developmental delay is classified. However, the "diagnosis shifting" theory was refuted by a 2005 study conducted by the National Alliance for Autism Research, which also found that autism prevalence is increasing in successively younger children.

Some researchers looking into the causes of autism believe the condition has a strong genetic component. Boys are more likely to develop autism than girls, but females tend to have more severe symptoms. One hypothesis is that once normal intestinal flora is disrupted by the use of broad-spectrum antibiotics, resulting changes in flora may allow the growth of particular neurotoxin-producing bacteria. But the proposal that has drawn the greatest attention and the most heated controversy is the possible link between mercury poisoning and autism. Mercury is a known toxin, affecting neurological and immune systems. Symptoms of mercury poisoning and autism are strikingly similar, with mercury damaging those parts of the brain also affected in autism.

In children, the prime source of mercury is childhood vaccines that contain thimerosal, a preservative that is 49.6 percent ethylmercury by weight. Mercury-containing vaccines are given to infants and toddlers at a time when the blood-brain barrier is not completely developed and is more likely to allow toxins to pass into brain tissue. In addition, detoxification processes in the liver are suboptimal, bile production is minimal, and the vaccines can trigger immune reactions that increase the permeability of the gut and the blood-brain barrier. In the 1990s, infants were given routine and repeated vaccines, in particular hepatitis B, starting at birth and continuing for fifteen to eighteen months, receiving a total dose of mercury, based on body weight, that far exceeded supposed "safety limits" for this toxin. A child can also be exposed to mercury in mother's milk, if the mother has mercury-containing amalgam tooth fillings. Not all children develop autism when exposed to such vaccines, but those who do may have an inability to eliminate mercury from their systems. More research is needed to explore the link between mercury and autism.

To assess mercury toxicity and possible damage to body systems, hair is screened for mercury and urine is analyzed after a challenge of an oral chelator. Blood and stool are also tested. High levels of lead are also often found; this metal increases the toxicity of mercury in the brain. Treatment may involve oral chelation therapy and supplements to remove heavy metals. Patients may also receive additional nutrients needed to support cellular chemistry, probiotics to normalize the gastrointestinal tract, a protocol to support liver detoxification function, and a dietary plan. With such treatment, children have shown significant, steady improvement.

A research psychologist in San Diego, California, Dr. Bernard Rimland has had positive results in treating autism with megavitamin therapy. In his study, 50 percent of the children tested improved significantly by showing a reduction in tantrums, increased alertness, improved speech, better sleep patterns, and greater sociability. The vitamins that were most prominent were niacin, pantothenic acid, B_6, and C. For the children not responding to the treatment, the doctor suggested an increase in the dosage of vitamin B_6, and improvement was then noted; 3 percent of the children in the study got worse with the treatment, with noticeable side effects such as bed-wetting and extreme sensitivity to noise. Because B_6 in large quantities can deplete magnesium from a person with a marginal supply of the mineral, the children were given a magnesium supplement and the side effects disappeared. When the vitamin treatment was discontinued, the illness regressed.

Backache

Backache may be a symptom of a variety of disturbances in the muscles, tendons, ligaments, bones, or underlying organs. The most common disturbances are caused by some type of sprain in the muscles or tendons and are treated by doctors more often than any other condition except the common cold. Very few back problems become serious; however, they are debilitating when they happen. Some stresses to the back are unavoidable, and everyone should be prepared for those situations. Vital to a healthy back are the midsection of the body, good posture, weight control, alignment, rest, and stress management.

The many underlying causes of backache may be one or several conditions, including arthritis, osteoporosis, infection and fever, tumor, weak stomach muscles, peptic ulcer, emotional tension or stress, gynecological problems, slipped or ruptured disks or other spinal cord injury, abnormal curvature of the spine, and disorders of the urinary system. Muscle strain or sprain results from excessive or improper physical exertion, incorrect posture, sleeping on soft beds, or incorrect lifting. Overweight and obesity, flat feet, and unequal leg length are other factors that may be responsible for back pain. Muscles contract together in spasms that are very painful. A backache that is accompanied by fever or headache should receive medical attention.

The most painful back malady is the slipped, ruptured, or herniated disk. When a disk or its supporting ligaments become weakened, the disk slips out of alignment and presses against delicate spinal nerves, causing shooting pain and possibly loss of bladder control.

Back pain may be the result of localized tender spots of the muscles called "trigger points." Some physicians inject these sore spots with procaine, killing the pain. An exercise program is then recommended. Trigger points and slipped disks can have many of the same symptoms, confusing diagnosis. Trigger points do not cause reflex or sensory loss, numbness, or weakness, which are common in disk injury. If the skin itself is sensitive to touch, a condition called fibrositis may be indicated, which may be successfully treated by a pinching massage given regularly over a period of weeks or months.

Natural therapies may help. Massage around the vertebral area is relaxing and relieves muscle tension. Relaxation techniques will lessen pain and aid in healing. Numerous treatments, varying according to the exact reason for the back pain, have helped many people. They include chiropractic manipulation of the backbone, use of hot and cold packs, injection of anestheticlike compounds into the painful areas, application of radio-frequency beams that eliminate nerve pain surrounding a slipped disk, and acupuncture. Surgery seems to be necessary only in extreme circumstances.

Exercise is thought to be the one way not only to prevent backaches but also to cure back problems (80 percent) within short periods of time. Weak, unused, and tense muscles are responsible for most back problems. By exercising the key postural muscles, one can rejuvenate the support system to counter many of the causes of the pain and function at a prime level again. Active

people have less back pain, and aerobic, stretching, and strengthening exercises are recommended. Walking with arms in motion is one of the best exercises for the lower back. Exercising later in the day is advisable, since the disks take on extra fluid during the night.

Exercises to firm stomach muscles can relieve the strain of daily exertions placed on the lower back region. Many back pain sufferers do not have sufficient strength in their muscles to support their own weight. In particular, Pilates, a currently popular set of exercises developed in the early 1900s and rediscovered in the 1980s, has proven to significantly relieve nagging back pain. Pilates focuses on the development of deep muscles of the back and abdomen to strengthen support of proper posture and improve spinal alignment. Even in disk cases, exercises that retrain weak muscles can many times adequately improve the condition of the spinal column.

To protect the back from strain, it is also important to make sure to properly lift heavy objects by bending at the knees instead of at the waist. Avoiding unnecessary physical or emotional stress or strain can help as can maintaining ideal weight for one's height. Not smoking is also essential, since smoking limits the blood supply to the disks.

Certain nutrients are essential for maintaining a healthy back. Protein is necessary for firm supporting tissue but animal sources will contain uric acid and are best avoided until the back is healed. Other protein sources are soy and combinations of grains and legumes. The B-complex vitamins, especially niacin, provide strength and health for nerve tissues. Vitamins C and D together with calcium are important in the development and maintenance of bones and nerve function. (See "Osteoporosis.")

Bromelain, an enzyme found in pineapple and available as a supplement, can ease pain associated with inflammation. Herbs for backache are Arth-X, which is a combination of nutrients for the bones and joints; white willow bark; slippery elm; horsetail; and burdock. Agrimony and hornbeam are flower therapies. Homeopathic remedies are Calc Fluor., Calc Phos., Kali Phos., and Nat Mur.

Baldness (Alopecia)

Baldness is the partial or complete loss of hair from the scalp, resulting from heredity, hormonal factors, aging, or local or systemic diseases. One possible cause is stress and shock, which trigger a hormonal imbalance that overproduces androgen, a male hormone in both male- and female-pattern baldness. Hair loss in women that occurs in cycles may be due to stress, diseases, surgery, childbirth, abortion, or discontinuance of oral contraceptives. It also may occur after menopause. Some women lose hair after childbirth because of hormonal changes that allow the loss. Certain medicines can cause hair loss in both men and women. They include antibiotics such as penicillin and sulfonamides, the hyperthyroid drug carbimazole, and the anticoagulant drug heparin.

Male-pattern baldness comprises 90 percent of hair-loss cases. The hair usually starts to recede at the hairline, in a circle on the crown of the head, or at the back of the head. In male-pattern baldness, hair follicles spend more time in a resting phase than in a growing cycle. However, hair continues to fall out. Researchers have discovered a substance that will stimulate the follicles to regrow hair. Rogaine, a prescription drug that contains minoxidil, has been found to stimulate hair growth in varying amounts in certain people. Younger men who are just beginning to lose hair or lose hair in spots are helped more readily by Rogaine than those who have receding hairlines. Minoxidil is at least a preventive measure against male-pattern baldness. Hair transplants are an alternative.

Studies have shown that dihydrotestosterone, a hormone resulting from the metabolism of testosterone, causes the hair follicles to remain in the resting stage. Other causes of baldness are poor circulation, starvation or poor-quality dieting, skin disease, diabetes, chemotherapy, stress, vitamin and mineral deficiencies, iron deficiencies, and severe or prolonged illness. Treatment consisting of large amounts of a testosterone-compound salve (such as cypionate) applied topically to the scalp can slow or even halt male-pattern baldness by preventing the formation of dihydrotestosterone. Reclining with the head lowered for a period of time each day will allow blood to reach the follicles in the scalp. A daily massage will also help keep the scalp stimulated. Overbrushing is not a good idea, since it will promote hair loss more quickly.

Nutrients may be helpful. Myoinositol and para-aminobenzoic acid (PABA) protect hair follicles, preventing hair loss and often premature graying. Biotin also may slow hair loss. The B-complex vitamins for stress should be taken daily. Pantothenic acid regenerates and restores luster and color to the hair. Zinc restores hair to those with a disease called alopecia areata totalis (complete lack of body hair). Vitamin C found in fresh fruits and vegetables such as citrus fruits, broccoli, green pepper, and parsley is good. Increased intake of protein foods such as meat, fish, liver, beans and peas, dairy foods, and eggs aids regeneration.

Herbs may be beneficial. Sage and burdock tea are thought to stimulate hair growth. Fleece flower root, wolfberry fruit, and mulberry fruit are Chinese remedies that treat the liver and kidney, which nourish the blood.

Other natural ingredients are apple cider, applied directly, as a growth stimulant. It has been reported that cayenne pepper rubbed into the scalp has resulted in hair regrowth, possibly because of its stimulative effect on the cells. Homeopathic remedies are Lycopodium 6c, Phosphoric acid 6c, and Sepia 6c for varying kinds of stress.

Beriberi

Beriberi is a disease caused by a thiamin deficiency. The disease seldom occurs outside the Far East, where the principal diet consists of polished rice, which does not supply sufficient thiamin. Rare cases of beriberi in the United States are usually associated with stressful conditions, such as hypothyroidism, infections, pregnancy, lactation, and chronic alcoholism, which increase the body's need for thiamin.

Symptoms of beriberi in infants are convulsions, respiratory difficulties, and gastrointestinal problems such as nausea, vomiting, constipation, diarrhea, and abdominal discomfort. Adult symptoms are fatigue, visual disturbances, mental confusion, paralysis of the eye muscles, diarrhea, appetite and weight loss, disturbed nerve function causing paralysis and wasting of the limbs, edema, and heart failure.

Nutrients may be helpful. The administration of thiamin will prevent and cure the disease. Because of the diarrhea that accompanies beriberi, the diet must be rich in liquids and all nutrients.

Bone Abnormalities

Broken, inflamed, infected, decalcified, weak, or brittle bones require sufficient amounts of many nutrients to repair and heal properly. Osteitis, osteomyelitis, and osteitis deformans, of which Paget's disease is a form, are bone inflammation diseases characterized by swelling, tenderness, pain, and often infection.

In some cases, bone abnormalities are caused by immobilization of a part or all of the body, increasing the urinary loss of many nutrients. In osteitis deformans, stress causes a rapid loss of minerals from the bone and prevents the forming of new proteins essential for building up the bone. Cortisone can cause a depletion of calcium from the bone.

Nutrients may help. Calcium is released from its storage areas in the bone and used for repair. Lack of adequate calcium in the diet will prevent this repair process because the calcium that is taken in will not be stored but will be used first by the soft tissues of the body. Slow healing is often an indication of low levels of calcium.

Magnesium and vitamin D are essential for the absorption of calcium. Bone repair depends on protein and all the nutrients needed for protein metabolism. Digestive enzymes and hydrochloric acid may be necessary to ensure sufficient digestion and absorption of needed vitamins and minerals. Vitamin E can prevent stiffness and scarring; vitamin C helps heal and prevent infection. (See "Osteoporosis.")

To reduce the inflammation that is associated with these conditions, supplementing with curcumin can be beneficial. Increasing intake of the omega-3 fatty acids can also be helpful. Conversely, avoiding red meat and trans fatty acids is important. (See "Inflammatory Conditions.")

Aromatherapy includes roman chamomile, eucalyptus, lavender, ginger, peppermint, marjoram, tea tree, and rosemary.

Bronchitis

Bronchitis is not an infection but an inflammation of the tissues lining the air passage leading to the lungs. Chronic bronchitis can eventually lead to emphysema. Factors that can cause or increase susceptibility to bronchitis are asthma and other respiratory diseases, air pollution, cigarette smoking, fatigue, chilling, and malnutrition. Food allergies may also be a cause. Chest x-rays may be taken to rule out other diseases such as pneumonia or cancer. A new long-lasting kind of bronchitis has been found mainly in women and can be treated with antibiotics.

Symptoms of bronchitis are a slight fever, back and muscle pain, sore throat, and difficulty breathing. A dry cough is followed by the coughing up of mucus as the inflammation becomes more severe. Ribs have been broken from this cough. Smoking makes recovery from bronchitis impossible because the irritant will not allow air passages to clear. Children, whose lungs are not mature yet, are especially susceptible to contracting bronchitis from the smoke around them.

Treatment for bronchitis includes rest, adequate fluid intake, and a well-balanced diet; antibiotics are not used, because most cases are caused by viral infection. Meals should include vegetable juices, soups, and herbal teas, as well as ingredients high in vitamin C, vitamin A, beta-carotene, zinc, and bioflavonoids. Vitamin A is essential to the health of the lung tissues. Vitamin C, an antioxidant, helps fight infection, protects the lungs from damage, and promotes healing. There is 70 percent less chance of contracting both asthma and bronchitis if vitamin C is taken. Smokers need three times as much vitamin C per day as others, even without bronchitis. Bioflavonoids enhance the action of vitamin C, while beta-carotene is a precursor of vitamin A. Zinc enhances immune function. Sugar should be kept to a minimum.

Certain foods can be helpful in treating bronchitis, such as garlic and onions, which contain allicin, a phytonutrient that fights infection. Crushing raw garlic releases compounds that combine to form allicin. When cooking with raw garlic, it is important to set aside the crushed garlic before use because this chemical process requires ten to fifteen minutes to complete. Baked garlic does not supply the active compound. Chicken soup fights congestion, especially when the soup includes garlic and hot red pepper, which open airways. In addition, chicken meat contains cysteine. Doctors prescribe a form of cysteine, acetylcysteine (which thins mucous), to treat bronchitis. If a patient with bronchitis is suffering from malnutrition, special attention should be paid to adequate intake of protein along with all the other nutrients.

Herbal treatments include black cohosh, chickweed, damiana tea, wild cherry bark infusion tea, cayenne tea, elecampane infusion tea, horehound, peppermint, black radish, echinacea, slippery elm bark, ginkgo (ginkgolide B), mullein flowers, Iceland moss, myrrh, wheatgrass, fenugreek, coltsfoot, reishi mushrooms, and ganoderma, which has immune-enhancing activity. (See "Asthma" for more natural therapies). The protein-digesting enzyme bromelain suppresses coughing and thins mucous. Aromatherapy includes cedarwood, black pepper, basil, eucalyptus, cypress, tea tree, Scots pine, juniper, ginger, grapefruit, marjoram, lavender, lemon, orange, peppermint, and sandalwood.

Bruises

A bruise is an injury that involves the rupture of small blood vessels, causing discoloration of underlying tissues without a break in the overlying skin. Bruises are frequently the result of falling or bumping into objects. However, frequent bruising with no apparent cause, or a bruise that applies pressure to a neighboring portion of the body, requires medical attention.

Factors that may cause or make one susceptible to bruising are hemophilia, overweight and obesity, anemia, and time of menstrual period. Frequent bruising without apparent cause may signal that the materials needed for clotting may not be present in the blood. Leukemia and excessive doses of anticlotting drugs also can cause frequent or large bruises. Excessive bruising may indicate a lack of vitamin D, a natural blood-clotting agent.

Vitamin C, bioflavonoids, and zinc help maintain capillary walls, strengthening these small blood vessels. A deficiency results in easier bruising. Excellent sources of vitamin C include sweet peppers, strawberries, and citrus fruits. Bioflavonoids are found in citrus fruits, green peppers, and buckwheat. Zinc is found in whole grains, eggs, lentils, meats, and cheese. (See the tables of food composition in Section 6 for more information.) Colorful fruit supplies flavonoids, a group of pigments in plants that also help stabilize cell walls. If the cause of bruising is anemia, there should be an increased intake of iron in the diet. If obesity appears to be a cause of bruising, a well-balanced reducing diet is indicated. Applied externally, dimethyl sulfoxide (DMSO) may prevent the discoloration of bruises; it acts as a scavenger of free radicals that are produced when blood vessels are damaged. Vitamins A, B_1, B_5, B_6, and the antioxidants C and E as well as zinc and selenium should be taken in conjunction with DMSO. Enzyme therapy is also recommended. According to research, bromelain as well as papain, an enzyme found in papaya, have successfully been used to treat bruises due to sports injuries.

Black eyes can be treated by homeopathy with Arnica 6c, Bellis perennis, and Ledum 6c. Immediate use of an ice pack for five minutes will discourage the blood from bleeding into the area and causing the eye to turn black. Cold witch hazel may help. Aromatherapy is sweet marjoram and lavender.

Bruxism (Teeth Grinding)

Bruxism, or teeth grinding, usually occurs during sleep and results in teeth that are loosened in their sockets, which causes tooth loss and gum recession. Two University of Alabama doctors believe that bruxism is a nutritional problem that can be helped with increased dosages of calcium and pantothenic acid.

Calcium is effective for treating involuntary movement of muscles, and pantothenic acid is important for maintaining proper motor coordination. Both nutrients are also antistress formulas. Another reported cause of bruxism, as expressed by a Swiss dental scientist, is a change in the central nervous system caused by nervous tension or a conflict situation.

Burns

A burn is a tissue injury caused by heat, electricity, radiation, or chemicals. There are three degrees of burn severity. A first-degree burn appears reddened, a second-degree burn includes blister formation, and a third-degree burn involves destruction of the entire thickness of skin and possibly of the underlying muscle. Since there is tissue destruction with third-degree burns, massive losses of body fluids, proteins, sodium, potassium, and nitrogen can occur. Because large amounts of fluids are lost in extensive burns, the possibility of shock exists. Infection is another threat to the burn victim.

Immediate treatment measures for burns include cold applications to reduce pain and swelling, cleansing, and covering of the burn to minimize the possibility of bacterial infection. Ointments, salves, or butter should not be applied to burns. They tend to promote infection and prevent circulation of air to the wound by retaining heat within the body. Treatment of chemical burns may include application of an antidote specific to the offending agent. Ice will help remove any tar, wax, or plastic that may have melted on the skin. Elevating the affected area will reduce swelling.

Diet is very important to burn victims, especially to those with extensive burns. A diet high in calories for energy and high in protein for tissue repair is recommended. Adequate intake of fluids in proportion to the amount of fluids lost is also essential.

Nutrients may be beneficial. Vitamin C may aid healing (large doses speed the healing of burns in the cornea of the eye), and the B vitamins are necessary to meet the body's increased metabolic demands. Intake of vitamin A, necessary for the health of the skin, should be increased, as well as the intake of potassium. Dr. Frederick Klenner of Reidsville, North Carolina, recommends that 30 to 100 grams of vitamin C be given intravenously to burn victims until healing has taken place. His studies have also shown that this treatment will supply the tissues with sufficient oxygen to make skin grafting unnecessary and can remove any smoke poisoning in fire victims. Some authorities indicate that vitamin E relieves pain and promotes healing in burns, but this has not been proved. Thermal burns create a deficiency of zinc in the body.

Natural ingredients also may be helpful. Fresh aloe vera gel speeds up the healing of burns when applied immediately to first-degree burns and, after healing is started, to second- and third-degree burns. Baking soda mixed with olive oil aids in healing and prevents scarring. Capsicum or hot peppers cool the inflammatory reactions that happen when there is a burn. Ginger can be applied directly to burns and may serve as an antiseptic. L-arginine stimulates the growth hormone, which accelerates wound healing. Alginates or seaweed (calcium alginate) is used in wound dressing and may also benefit the treatment of burns. A substance taken from brewer's yeast called skin respiratory factor (SRF) has been applied to skin-graft sites and has brought about significantly faster healing times.

Other natural healing aids that can be administered directly to the wound or taken internally as tea are the herbs white oak bark, beriberi leaves, sumac leaves, and sweet gum. The herb melaleuca has antiseptic and antifungal properties that aid the healing of burns. Oil of Roman chamomile (an herbal extract) in water is used as an antiseptic.

Homeopathy therapies are Hypericum and Calendula for a punctured blister, and Rhus toxicodendron 6c for an itchy, swollen, and red blister. Aromatherapy includes lavender and geranium.

Bursitis

Bursitis arises from an inflammation of the liquid-filled sac, called a bursa, found within the joints, muscles, tendons, and bones. The bursa helps promote muscular movement and reduce friction. Bursitis is commonly found in the hip or shoulder joints, elbows, or feet and is more commonly known as frozen shoulder, tennis elbow, or bunion.

Bursitis may be caused by stretched muscles, shoes that are too tight, injury such as a bump or bruise, or irritation from calcium deposits found in the bursa wall. It may also be the result of metabolic inefficiency caused by stress, which prevents proper absorption and utilization of food that is eaten.

Symptoms include swelling, tenderness, and agonizing pain in the affected area, which frequently limits motion. Treatment involves removing the cause of the injury, making adjustments in how physical functions are performed, clearing up any underlying infection, and surgically removing calcium deposits. Reducing inflammation is another treatment goal, accomplished through diet and nutritional supplementation. (See "Inflammatory Conditions.") Other measures include rest and immobilization of the affected part. Posture will affect bursitis, stretching is good, and exercise is also important.

Nutrients may be beneficial. Vitamin E has also been found to be beneficial in the treatment of bursitis. The need for protein and vitamins A and C increases during infection, and extra amounts of these nutrients are required for bursitis victims. In one uncontrolled study, intramuscular injections of vitamin B_{12} relieved pain in the majority of patients.

Cancer

Cancer cells appear as immature, persistently dividing cells that do not fulfill their natural functions. These cells invade surrounding tissue and rob neighboring normal cells of their essential nutrients, causing a severe wasting away of the cancer patient. Cancer cells are capable of migrating and planting themselves in any part of the body, resulting in abnormal growth or tumors. Cancers are categorized according to the type of tissue from which they originate.

The importance of early detection in treating cancer cannot be overemphasized. Early detection is the only chance for successful treatment of the disease. It is now thought that intestinal cancer begins its journey to full-blown disease as much as twenty years before it is noticed. Self-testing is vitally important. One must always be alert to the American Cancer Society's seven warning signs: unusual bleeding or discharge, appearance of a lump or swelling, hoarseness or cough, indigestion or difficulty in swallowing, change in bowel or bladder habits, a sore that does not heal, or a change in a wart or a mole. To test for colon cancer, a physician performs either a low gastrointestinal series (barium enema x-ray) or the more accurate colonoscopy to diagnose and locate the tumor. Symptoms and their severity vary with the type and location of the cancer. Obesity in women has been found to be a contributing factor to uterine, cervical, breast, and gallbladder cancer. Fat affects female hormones that encourage cell division, which starts the cancer process. In men, obesity encourages colorectal cancer. It has been reported that males who have had a vasectomy have three times the chance of getting prostate cancer.

For the treatment of cancerous growths or tumors, surgery, radiation, and certain drugs have proved beneficial. Surgical operations remove the original growth and any secondary ones. Drugs, although unable to completely cure cancer, are used to reduce the growth or to delay the appearance of secondary growths. Radiation is often used to destroy cancer cells and to prevent them from spreading.

Nutrients may be beneficial. The ill side effects from chemotherapy and radiation therapy, such as vomiting and diarrhea, can be lessened or prevented by vitamins C, E, and B complex. It is important to begin taking these vitamins several days before the treatment starts. The psychological stress of cancer greatly increases the need for vitamin C and B complex. Vitamin E should be taken before a meal. Vitamin injections ensure absorption into the blood and should be used whenever possible.

X-rays and other radiation treatments suppress the immune system and destroy vitamins A, C, E, K, and B complex as well as unsaturated fatty acids. Large amounts of E can protect vitamin A and the unsaturated fats. As malignant tissues are being destroyed, harmful by-products are made. The liver is able to neutralize these substances if adequate amounts of vitamins C and E, protein, and the amino acid methionine are present. Vitamin E can prevent radiation burns, relieve pain, and reduce scarring.

In animals, spontaneous cancers, especially those of the thyroid, develop with iodine-deficient diets. Iodine deficiency also has been implicated in female breast cancer. Iron deficiency is thought to leave those with Plummer-Vinson syndrome (a condition in middle-aged women characterized by cracks around the mouth and sore tongue and esophagus) more vulnerable to cancer of the esophagus and the stomach. A zinc deficiency may lead to prostate, esophageal, and bronchogenic cancer. Liver damage of any kind increases the susceptibility to cancer.

Testing of animals shows that vitamins A, C, E, B_3, and B_6 inhibit the growth of cancer cells. They do this by stimulating the body's immune system and acting as free-radical scavengers. Lipotropes protect the cells from the transformation to cancer cells. Superoxide dismutase (SOD) has also been shown to destroy free radicals. Free radicals are chemicals produced by the body when it is exposed to harmful substances such as radiation, food and drink contaminants, rancid fats, and air pollution. Free radicals damage parts of the human cell, especially DNA and RNA, which in part direct the actions of each cell. Once this process is disturbed, cancer can develop. Supplementation of several substances may be desirable. L-arginine inhibits the growth of tumors. Vitamin K has been found to protect against certain cancer-causing substances. Large amounts of folic acid have helped against precancerous cervical cells and, with B_{12}, precancerous bronchial cells in smokers. Oral folic acid prevents breaks in cancer-related chromosomes, which decreases the risk of cancer. Proper maintenance of the intestinal flora may be a factor in cancer and can be accomplished by taking generous amounts of yogurt or acidophilus culture.

In normal and high-risk individuals who have family histories of colorectal cancer, calcium with vitamin D was found to have a preventive effect. Germanium has anticancer activity that functions with the immune system. Trace elements are important to maintain a level that prevents cancer-causing agents from invading. Molybdenum-enriched soil guards against esophageal cancer. Vitamin B_2 (riboflavin) also guards against the disease. Selenium protects against a wide number of cancers, including skin and colon cancer. In a 2005 study, published in the *Journal of the National Cancer Institute*, individuals with higher blood levels of selenium had a 34 percent lower risk of developing colon cancer than those with lower levels. Iodine is also cancer-protective. Additional amounts of copper given to animals in a laboratory test significantly retarded cancer development.

Thymosin, one of several hormones secreted by the thymus gland that controls the maturation of T cells, may shrink tumors. There is hope that someday one of the most promising health discoveries, dehydroepiandrosterone (DHEA), will not only prevent cancer but also cure it. This substance is produced by the adrenal glands and is what all other hormones that are involved in all bodily functioning are made from. Transfer factor involves the extraction of healthy cells from a healthy donor to the body of an unhealthy person and has had considerable success when combined with other therapies. There is evidence that aspirin may be helpful in the treatment of some cancers such as mouth, throat, and esophagus cancers as well as bowel and lung cancers. Iron supplementation should be avoided since it tends to inhibit the cancer-fighting abilities of macrophages and T- and E-cell activity.

To reduce the risk of cancer, the *Dietary Guidelines for Americans*, published jointly by the Department of Health and Human Services (HHS) and the Department of Agriculture (USDA), recommends a diet that provides 20 percent to 35 percent of calories from fat, with saturated fat contributing less than 10 percent of total calories. Trans fats are to be trimmed to as little as possible. In addition, whole grains and plenty of fruits and vegetables, a minimum of nine one-half-cup servings a day, are advised. In the 1990s, in a combined effort, the American Institute for Cancer Research and its affiliate, the World Cancer Research Fund in the United Kingdom, undertook a review of 4,500 studies on cancer and diet from around the world. From an analysis of these studies it became evident that a diet that predominates in plant foods, combined with exercising regularly and maintaining a healthy weight, cuts the risk of cancer 30 percent to 40 percent. As a teaching tool, they developed the New American Plate, a diagram of the ideal dinner plate, with a minimum two-thirds filled with vegetables, fruit, whole grains, and beans. The remaining portion of the plate—one-third or less—is filled with fish, poultry, or red meat. On this plan, no tobacco is to be used in any form.

A good diet for cancer is important not only for those with the disease but also for those who are interested in prevention of the disease. A variety of whole, unrefined foods is essential, with the avoidance of processed foods highly recommended. A high intake of dietary fat encourages the growth of cancer cells. Red meats and dairy products should be kept to a minimum. Dark green leafy vegetables, deep orange and red fruits such as watermelon and berries, and vegetables such as orange winter squash and tomatoes are needed. In a large, comprehensive study conducted by Harvard School of Medicine, involving nearly fifty thousand prostate-cancer-free male health professionals, lycopene, a phytonutrient plentiful in tomatoes, was found to significantly reduce the risk of developing prostate cancer. Beverages that contain caffeine should be avoided or limited.

Dietary fiber has long been recommended as a means of preventing colon cancer, but a meta-analysis of thirteen studies involving more than 725,000 health professionals, published in the *Journal of the American Medical Association* in 2005, found no link between colorectal cancer and fiber intake. However, these findings contradict two earlier large studies that demonstrated that fiber had cancer-protective effects. Whichever conclusion is correct, foods high in fiber are still an excellent addition to the diet, promoting normal elimination, lowering cholesterol, and adding bulk to make meals more satisfying.

Breast cancer has been slowed with the use of fish oils. Broiled, oily fish should be consumed two to three times a week, and yogurt may slow tumor growth. Soy products such as tofu are also good since they help balance hormones and can reduce estrogen levels. Higher estrogen level is linked to a greater risk of both breast and uterine cancer. A study published in 2001 in *Fertility and Sterility* found that drinking four or five cups of coffee daily raised blood levels of estrogen in women. Dark-colored fruit juices are beneficial, as are vegetable juice combinations such as carrot, beet, cabbage, and asparagus. Foods rich in potassium, such as whole grains, dried fruits, legumes, and sunflower seeds, contain other substances that aid in the fight against cancer. (People with kidney failure should not take potassium or eat excessive amounts of potassium-rich foods.) Dairy products that supply vitamin D are recommended for women living in northern latitudes who are not exposed to sufficient sunlight in winter months. According to research conducted by the American Cancer Society and published in 2006, vitamin D may cut the risk of breast cancer in postmenopausal women.

Almonds are rich in laetrile, which (although not confirmed) is thought to be a cancer-fighting agent. Vegetarian diets in any degree are beneficial, as are macrobiotic diets. Kelp as a substitute for salt, blackstrap molasses or pure maple syrup to sweeten foods, and whole wheat instead of white flour are all alternatives. Only purified water for drinking is recommended.

Rancid and reheated oils are cancer-causing. A balance of the omega-3 and omega-6 oils must be adhered to. Besides fish oil, flax oil is three times richer in the omega-3s and can be mixed with other omega-6 oils (such as corn and safflower) to achieve a balance. Canola has a fairly even balance of both.

It is also thought that barbequed foods that are charred or burned trigger chemical reactions during the cooking process that create carcinogens, which are then consumed along with the food. Avoiding foods preserved by pickling, smoking, and nitrite curing is advised. It has been well established that people who smoke or drink have a higher incidence of cancer. The chemical acetaldehyde, found in cigarette smoke and made in the liver from alcohol, is known to be a carcinogen and a free-radical producer. It also destroys cysteine, an antioxidant. No more than three to five alcoholic drinks per week should be consumed.

Herbs and other natural ingredients may be helpful. Astragalus, an herb, counters the effects of cancer treatments, including radiation. Bee and flower pollens inhibit cancer. Fucoidin from seaweed is an active anticancer ingredient. An algae called spirulina contains beta-carotene and other natural substances that fight cancer. Onion and garlic (both contain bioflavonoids) are beneficial as they are known anticarcinogens. Burdock is used to treat a number of cancers in China, as is fo-ti.

Chaparral has an antioxidant effect. Chickweed, high in vitamin C, is an aid. Echinacea destroys cancer cells because it contains macrophages, which stimulate the immune system. Wobe-Mugos (enzymes from the pineapple and the pancreas) is an anticancer agent. Ginseng is used for cancer. Goldenseal contains beriberine sulfate, which is an anticancer (tumor) agent. Comfrey (as a poultice), horsetail grass, Jason Winters tea, nettle, carnivora, suma, black radish, pau d'arco (also as a poultice), dandelion, and licorice are used.

Ragwood and wood sage (as a poultice), wheatgrass/barleygrass, and quinine have been used for cancer. Mistletoe or iscador stimulates immunity and inhibits tumor growth. Extracts from the shiitake and reishi mushrooms have antitumor capabilities. Spirulina, which is rich in beta-carotene and other natural substances, is an anticancer substance.

Nutrients and other natural substances may be helpful. Enemas to keep the colon free from residues that could become toxic may be advisable. Avoiding radiation from microwaves and x-rays and sitting at least three to four feet away from the television set are advised. Cookware should be of the glass or ceramic-coated types. Exposure to chemicals such as fresh paint, hairspray, cleaning agents, and pesticides promotes the formation of free radicals; the body expends energy fighting the toxic substances instead of fighting the cancer.

Exercise is important as inactivity is linked to cancer. Studies show a lesser rate of the disease in those who are physically active compared with those who do not exercise regularly.

For the terminally ill cancer patient, specific food needs depend on the location of the tumor. Generally, however, a high-protein, high-calorie diet is necessary to maintain and help restore normal cells. Dietary iron (from food sources of the heme kind) may prevent anemia, which is a frequent complication of cancer.

Cataracts

A leading cause of impaired vision and blindness, cataracts are white, opaque blemishes on the lens of the eye. Cataracts occur when the protein structure of the eye becomes damaged. The lens of the eye controls focus and allows us to see objects both near and far; as cataracts develop, these visual functions diminish. Cataracts may occur at any time in life but are usually associated with degenerative changes that occur with age. Cataracts in young people are usually congenital (present at birth) but may be caused by a nutritional disorder or inflammatory condition in the eye. There is a high incidence of cataracts among diabetics. High blood sugar levels, as in diabetes, can cause cataract formation.

Drugs, air pollution, smoking, rancid fats, and chemicals also may produce this condition. Improper deposition of calcium or cholesterol contributes to cataract formation by slowing circulation to the eyes. Stress and an inadequate diet can be the cause.

Research has shown that a reduction of vitamin C, riboflavin, and selenium in the lens of the eye contributes to the development of cataracts. Infants who are lactose intolerant develop cataracts due to riboflavin deficiency because the inability to break down galactose, a component of lactose or milk sugar, increases the need for this vitamin. In addition, low levels of folic acid predict cataracts. Low levels of calcium in the blood can also cause cataracts.

Symptoms of cataracts include painless, progressive blurring and loss of vision, sensitivity to bright light, and the appearance of halos around lights. In the early stages of the development of cataracts, several clinical studies have demonstrated that high doses of vitamin C can stop further progression of cataracts and even improve vision. In addition, in animal experiments, cataracts disappeared after the animals were given riboflavin, pantothenic acid, vitamin E, and the essential amino acids. However, once cataracts develop, in order to restore normal vision and prevent blindness, the standard treatment is surgical removal of the lens, one of the most frequently performed procedures in the United States. A drug that contains hyaluronic acid, a sulfated polysaccharide, is used to protect the cornea during cataract surgery and lens implantation.

Shading the eyes throughout life from ultraviolet light is one of the best measures one can take to prevent cataracts. The Z80.3 designation on the lenses of sunglasses means that 95 percent of the sun's ultraviolet light is being filtered out. Brimmed hats are also recommended.

Having adequate levels of certain nutrients protects against the development of cataracts. These include vitamin C and vitamin E, beta-carotenes, and selenium, all of which have antioxidant activity, preventing free-radical damage of lens tissue. Vitamin B_6 may also protect against cataracts.

Another antioxidant, glutathione, a small protein composed of the amino acids glycine, glutamic acid, and cysteine, also helps prevent cataracts. Valuable food sources include avocado, asparagus, watermelon, and oranges. Cataract patients also have low levels of the antioxidant superoxide dismutase (SOD). While supplemental SOD is of little benefit, precursor minerals that allow the body to manufacture SOD are useful. These minerals are copper, manganese, and zinc.

Other natural ingredients may also be helpful. Consuming spinach protects against getting cataracts and consuming foods rich in carotenoids reduces the risk of getting cataracts by 40 percent. Drinking teas that have high antioxidant content has been successful in countering cataracts. Hachimijiogan, a combination of Chinese herbs, is used both to prevent and treat cataracts. Eating three and one-half servings of fruits and vegetables a day will lower the chances of getting cataracts.

Homeopathy recommends that Cineraria maritima mother tincture in fifty parts water be applied to the eyes twice daily for three weeks.

Celiac Disease

Celiac disease is a disease of the digestive tract that damages the small intestine. Celiac disease is also known as celiac sprue, nontropical sprue, and gluten-sensitive enteropathy. Individuals with celiac disease do not tolerate gluten, a protein present in wheat (including spelt, triticale, and kamut), rye, barley, and possibly oats. Some individuals with celiac disease appear to tolerate oats. Ingestion of gluten irritates and flattens the villi in the intestinal lining, interfering with the absorption of nutrients in food.

Celiac disease is hereditary and can be triggered by pregnancy, childbirth, first-time surgery, severe emotional stress, parasites, or a viral or intestinal infection. In addition, protein deficiencies that occur on reducing diets or the excessive use of laxatives can alter the intestinal tract to the extent that absorption of gluten is impaired. Allergies to milk are also suspect. The amount of gluten one eats may also be a factor.

Celiac disease is more common in the United States than once thought, with about two million people afflicted with this condition.

Diagnosis of celiac disease can be difficult because symptoms are similar to those of other conditions such as irritable bowel syndrome, iron deficiency anemia, Crohn's disease, diverticulitis, chronic fatigue syndrome, and intestinal infections. Recently, researchers discovered that individuals with celiac disease have abnormally high levels of autoantibodies in their blood. Measuring the amount of these in the blood is now used as a diagnostic indicator of the presence of the disease.

Celiac disease is considered both an autoimmune disease and a disease of malnutrition. Persons with celiac disease may be deficient in fat, protein, and carbohydrates as well as a variety of vitamins and minerals. Common vitamin deficiencies include low levels of vitamins A, B complex, C, D, and E. It has been found that people with celiac disease are extremely deficient in vitamin B_6. A lack of this vitamin causes diarrhea, vomiting, gas, and eczema. Common mineral deficiencies include calcium, magnesium, and zinc. Iron, folic acid, and vitamin B_{12} can be used to correct the anemia that usually accompanies celiac disease. Kinesiology is used to determine whether gluten is the problem.

An individual with celiac disease may or may not experience symptoms. When these do occur, they can range from weight loss, diarrhea, steatorrhea (unabsorbed fat particles in the stool), gas, bloated stomach, constipation, and abdominal pain to anemia, mood swings, fatigue, depression, constipation, infertility, and skin disorders. Malnutrition often accompanies this disorder because of the greatly reduced absorption of nutrients. The interference of protein absorption causes edema. Blood-clotting abnormalities due to a vitamin K deficiency lead to a tendency to bleed easily. Tetany and bone pain are caused from the lack of calcium. In infants, celiac disease can cause failure to thrive.

Celiac disease may be a causative factor in schizophrenia. The mental symptoms of celiac patients were greatly improved when they were placed on gluten-free diets. Cancers of the intestine, osteoporosis, miscarriage, congenital malformation, and short stature also may result secondary to this condition.

Some physicians believe that weaning infants to gluten-containing cereals at too early an age may be responsible in part for those who have a family history or are otherwise predisposed to this affliction. Breast-feeding to four months is suggested and then introduction of rice and millet in a form suitable for infants. After one year, wheat products may be introduced.

The only treatment for celiac disease is following a gluten-free diet. Meals should also be well balanced, high in calories and proteins, and moderate in fats. Fiber is obtained from fruits, vegetables, nuts, and dried fruits such as figs and raisins. Improvement can begin within days of starting the diet. When gluten is removed from the diet, reversal of this condition is complete. However, in order to stay well, the celiac patient must avoid gluten for the rest of his or her life.

While wheat, rye, and barley must be strictly avoided, the celiac diet includes many other grains such as corn, hominy, rice, buckwheat (which is not related to wheat), millet, teff, amaranth, and quinoa. Flour and meal made from soy, tapioca, arrowroot, potatoes, and flax are also allowed. Gluten-free bread and pasta are also available. Herbs that are helpful are papain and slippery elm.

The celiac patient must also be vigilant in avoiding hidden sources of gluten. Many processed foods such as ice cream, salad dressings, and canned foods contain fillers made from wheat flour; check the food labels. Gluten is also found in nonfood items such as the glue used on stamps and envelopes and in certain medicines and vitamins.

According to author Adelle Davis, celiac patients may have an unusually high requirement for nutrients that are needed for gluten utilization. The B vitamins should be generously supplied.

There are various organizations offering information and support for this condition. These include the Celiac Sprue Association/USA Inc. in Omaha, Nebraska; the Gluten Intolerance Group of North America in Seattle, Washington; and the National Foundation for Celiac Awareness in Ambler, Pennsylvania.

Chicken Pox

Chicken pox is a highly contagious viral disease, the chief symptom being skin eruptions similar to blisters. One attack usually protects against the disease for life. It is not curable; however, a recent discovery has produced a vaccine called acyclovir, which lessens the severity of the disease and is now available for children and adults who are susceptible or who work in areas that expose them to the virus.

About twenty-four to thirty-six hours before the first series of eruptions, the patient may have a headache and low fever. The rash then appears as red bumps containing drops of clear fluid, usually on the face and trunk of the body. The fluid breaks out, forming a crust, and the eruptions continue in cycles for three or four days.

Treatment may be soothing lotions that are applied for the relief of itching. At the first sign of infection, a bath to thoroughly clean the body should be administered. Fingernails should be cut short to prevent scratching, which could cause more infection and scarring. Because the blisters are so contagious, the patient should be kept clean with frequent soaking in a bath of baking soda or oatmeal. This also relieves itching, keeps the infection from spreading (pus in the blisters is the infectious agent), and is quite soothing. The patient should be isolated for as long as the patient has weeping pustules—about ten days. When the blisters have scabbed over, returning to activities is considered safe. Varicella zoster, the virus that causes chicken pox, is the same virus that causes shingles, so it is important to keep infected children away from the elderly.

Nutrients may help with symptoms. Fevers increase the body's need for calories, fluids, and vitamins A and C. Extra protein is needed for the repair of tissues. Protein powder and brewer's yeast can be added to juice. Dr. Frederick Klenner dries up chicken pox with intravenous injections of up to 400 milligrams per kilogram of body weight of vitamin C given two or three times in a twenty-four-hour period. Fruits and vegetables rich in vitamin C should be consumed in the form of juices as well as in whole forms.

Herbs that are beneficial include red clover, honeysuckle tea, pau d'arco, cimicifuga tube tea, ginger (as a bath), catnip tea, lobelia herb extract, safflower tea, and goldenseal. Herbal tea baths are recommended. Oil of peppermint, chickory, cherry plum, and hornbeam will soothe the blisters. Cool wet towels are also soothing. Homeopathic therapies include: Rhus toxicodendron 6c, Antimonium tartaricum 6c, and Pulsatilla 6c.

Cholesterol Level, High

Cholesterol is a waxy, fatty substance that is essential for maintaining healthy cell membranes and is needed to form sex and adrenal hormones, vitamin D, and bile salts. It has a vital function in the brain and nerves. Cholesterol is transported in the blood by carrier substances known as lipoproteins. Low-density lipoproteins carry cholesterol to the arteries, while high-density lipoproteins cart cholesterol from the arteries to the liver where it can be broken down and readied for excretion. The terms *HDL cholesterol* and *LDL cholesterol* refer to their carrier lipoproteins.

Most of the cholesterol in the body is made in the liver. It is also made in the intestines and all the cells in the body. This production averages about 1 to 2 grams daily and takes place even if there is no cholesterol consumed. The body makes less cholesterol as more is consumed and when a person is fasting.

Eating foods that contain cholesterol such as liver, egg yolks, and meats may increase levels of cholesterol in the body. However, the major dietary factor that increases blood cholesterol levels is saturated fat that the body is able to use to manufacture cholesterol. Dietary saturated fat has a greater impact on blood cholesterol levels than dietary cholesterol.

Certain fats, when substituted for saturated fat in the diet, can lower cholesterol. Monounsaturated fats such as olive oil can lower LDL cholesterol and stabilize or even raise HDL cholesterol levels. When replacing saturated fats, polyunsaturated fats such as safflower and canola oil lower LDL cholesterol. The omega-3 polyunsaturated fish oils protect the heart in other ways, for instance, reducing the risk of blood clots and lowering triglyceride levels. According to studies, stearic acid, a saturated fat present in chocolate, can lower LDL cholesterol in some individuals.

Trans fatty acids, man-made fats present in partially hydrogenated vegetable oil, should be minimized or eliminated from the diet. They do more damage to the heart than saturated fat because trans fats both raise LDL and lower HDL. The U.S. Food and Drug Administration (FDA) now requires manufacturers of food products to state on their labels the amount of trans fats a serving of the product contains. Commercial baked goods and cereals often contain partially hydrogenated oils.

When cholesterol levels in the blood become abnormally high, fatty deposits composed of both cholesterol and calcium tend to accumulate in the arteries, including those of the heart—a situation that increases one's susceptibility to heart attacks and other complications. Cholesterol deposits occur mostly in parts of the blood vessels that have been weakened by high blood pressure or undue strain. Another collection point for fatty cholesterol deposits and plaque, one of the first signs of heart disease in men, may be in the arteries that supply the penis, making it less full during an erection.

Epidemiological studies reveal that the incidence of atherosclerosis is higher in countries where diets are high in saturated fats. However, vegetarians whose diets are low in saturated fats may develop atherosclerosis, and Eskimos who eat large amounts of saturated fats seldom develop the disease. This indicates there are other factors besides saturated fat that affect the cholesterol level of the blood, including stress, anxiety, cigarette smoking, overeating, lack of exercise, and high consumption of refined carbohydrates. Some people may not efficiently metabolize saturated fats. Other factors may include high blood pressure, diabetes, and gout.

Various foods can be helpful in reducing cholesterol levels. Those that contain the soluble fiber found in such foods as oats and beans soak up cholesterol in the intestines and escort it out of the body. Several studies have confirmed that pectin can limit the amount of cholesterol accumulation in the bloodstream. Pectin is found in many fruits and berries, notably apples.

Antioxidant nutrients such as beta-carotene, vitamins E and C, zinc, and selenium in fruits and vegetables prevent LDL cholesterol from being oxidized. Oxidation increases cholesterol's ability to produce artery-blocking plaque. Cholesterol-lowering fats are supplied by foods such as olive and canola oils, almonds, and walnuts. Garlic and onion lower cholesterol.

High dietary cholesterol foods such as liver, eggs, caviar, and some seafood are not the kind that are necessarily bad, because they do not contain the concentrated forms of saturated animal fat that create the LDLs. The liver balances dietary cholesterol levels and, therefore, *if consumed in moderation*, these foods are excellent sources; however, too much of even this type has been shown to shorten the life span.

It is also known that too low a fat content in the diet, below 10 percent, will lower both LDL and the desirable HDL cholesterol. This situation will leave one just as vulnerable to heart disease as will too high an LDL level. Other consequences of a cholesterol level lower than 160 are brain hemorrhages from weakened vessels or bleeding stroke, obstructive lung disease, suicide (low levels of cholesterol are associated with depression in older men), alcoholism, colon and liver cancer, and a variety of other physical problems. A higher monounsaturated fat diet such as the Mediterranean diet is recommended. Restricting omega-6 types of oils such as corn and safflower, which are found in margarine, vegetable shortenings, and many processed foods, is thought to be beneficial. Particles from these oils incorporate themselves into LDL and become oxidized, leaving them vulnerable to buildup in the body's arterial system.

The harmful forms of cholesterol are animal fats of the saturated types that are usually visible to the eye (on the top of soup, the cheese on pizza, the skin and yellow globules of fat on chicken, and the white fat on meat) found in meat, poultry, and dairy products. Butter, cheese, whole milk, poultry skin, and beef and pork fat are sources. Cutting back on these fats will give the greatest degree of a noticeably lowered cholesterol level.

There are other foods that alter cholesterol levels. Filtered as opposed to percolated coffee is recommended because the agent in coffee that appears to raise cholesterol levels is screened out. Decaffeinated coffee appears to raise cholesterol levels by 10 percent because of the stronger bean used in the process.

Nutrients may be helpful. Choline, vitamin B_{12}, biotin, lecithin, methionine, and possibly inositol are lipotropic substances that must be present to prevent accumulation of fat in the liver. Since the liver regulates cholesterol, these vitamins may be essential. Deficiencies of magnesium, potassium, manganese, copper, zinc, vanadium, chromium, or selenium, or of vitamins C, E, niacin, folic acid, and B_6 may also be significant. Many of these nutrients are necessary for fat utilization. Supplemental niacin (1.5 grams/day) lowers LDL cholesterol and raises HDL cholesterol. The safest form is inositol hexaniacinate. Pantethine, a form of vitamin B_5, also lowers cholesterol and has no significant side effects.

Cholesterol in the blood must be kept in solution to prevent deposits from forming. Lecithin seems to help the bile do this. Lecithin is contained in many fatty foods, but when these fats are hydrogenated as in margarines, the lecithin is lost. Adequate supplies of unsaturated fatty acids (especially linoleic acid) and vitamin E seem to help control the cholesterol level of the blood and may prevent atherosclerosis. Vitamin C aids in preventing the formation and deposition of cholesterol. Chromium raises the HDL levels of cholesterol.

Herbs and natural substances that may be helpful are hawthorn berries, goldenseal, cayenne, cinnamon, and kelp.

Cirrhosis of the Liver

Cirrhosis of the liver is a chronic disease characterized by degeneration and hardening of liver cells. Scar tissue replaces normal liver tissue, disrupting the functioning of this vital organ. Cirrhosis may be caused by alcoholism, malnutrition, viral hepatitis, chronic inflammation, or obstruction of the blood through certain ducts in the liver. Certain drugs used to treat high blood pressure, tuberculosis, Parkinson's disease, and cancer can also lead to cirrhosis.

Of the 13.8 million people in the United States who meet the diagnostic criteria for alcoholism, two million of these likely have alcoholic liver disease and fourteen thousand people die each year due to cirrhosis of the liver. Cirrhosis due to alcohol can be stopped if found early enough and if no more alcohol is consumed. For people who stop drinking, the five-year survival rate is about 90 percent; those who continue to drink have a survival rate of 70 percent. Women who drink 18 ounces and men who drink 36 ounces of beer daily for a period of ten to fifteen years are at risk for cirrhosis.

Early symptoms of cirrhosis include fever, indigestion, diarrhea or constipation, and weakness. Palms become red due to capillary dilation, and skin may turn yellow (jaundice). Later symptoms include edema (swelling), anemia, and bleeding disorders characterized by the presence of spider-shaped bruises. A deficiency of the B complex and vitamins A, C, and K may also occur.

Optimal nutrition provides the key to recovery from the disease. A high-protein diet (1 gram of protein per kilogram of body weight, or approximately 75 to 100 grams of protein per day) is prescribed to promote regeneration of the liver cells. High-quality proteins from vegetable sources are recommended. However, in the case of coma associated with alcoholic encephalopathy, protein should be restricted. In addition, the diet needs to be high in calories (2,500 to 3,000 calories per day) and high in complex carbohydrates (300 to 400 grams per day) to increase the storage of glycogen, to ensure that protein is used for regeneration rather than as a source of energy, and to compensate for weight losses caused by fever.

Fresh vegetable juices such as beet, dandelion, and carrot are good. Raw fruits and vegetables taken with the juices for two weeks if severe cirrhosis is evident may be helpful.

Animal fat or saturated fats, milk and cheese, spices, caffeine and colas, refined rice, refined carbohydrate foods such as pastries and candy, rancid nut oils, refined grains, and all processed foods should be avoided. Cold-pressed oils are best. Fresh nuts supply magnesium, as do dried beans and green leafy vegetables. If nausea is present, frequent or small meals are better tolerated than three large meals.

Nutrients may be beneficial. A common complication of cirrhosis is the failure of the liver to make vitamins available in an active form in the body. For this reason, the diet should be high in B-complex vitamins as well as vitamins C, D, and K. The amino acid cysteine with vitamin C protects against the damage caused by alcohol. Foods that are rich in vitamin A, such as fish, are also recommended but in limited quantities because excessive intake of this nutrient or its precursor, beta-carotene, can become toxic to the liver when coupled with even moderate amounts of alcohol. The zinc content in fish is useful. If jaundice is present, special attention should be paid to fat-soluble vitamins A, D, E, and K because absorption of these nutrients may be interfered with. If edema is present, sodium, which causes the body to retain water, should be restricted.

Alcohol greatly reduces the absorption of the B vitamins and other nutrients. A deficiency state can result, leading to liver injury despite an adequate diet. A deficiency of B vitamins produces confusion, memory loss, heart irregularities, and gastrointestinal problems. Damage to the liver from long-term excessive drinking is irreversible. Further damage can be prevented by abstaining from alcohol, eating a nutritious diet, and taking vitamin and mineral supplements. All alcohol should be strictly avoided.

Herbs that are helpful include milk thistle because of its active ingredient silymarin, which promotes detoxification of the liver. Other herbal treatments are evening primrose oil (prevents damage), burdock, red clover, Irish moss, fennel, dandelion, celandine, barberry, chionanthus, thyme, rose hips, sumac, goldenseal, hops, black radish, suma, and echinacea. Natural-form enemas are useful to keep the colon clean of toxins that tax the kidney and liver. Wheatgrass and coffee enemas are thought to detoxify the liver.

Colds

The common cold is a general inflammation of the mucous membranes of the respiratory passages caused by a variety of viruses. Colds are highly contagious. On the average, Americans contract two or three colds per year. Poor nutrition, resulting in a poorly functioning immune system, is one of the most prevalent causes of colds.

The difficulty modern medicine has had in finding a cure for the common cold may lie in the fact that there are so many different types of viruses that change in size and shape. In addition, each new generation of viruses changes slightly in its chemical makeup. At the start of a cold, the body's immune system produces a chemical called an antibody that attacks the virus, preventing harm to healthy cells. For the body to effectively fight a virus, an antibody that exactly matches the virus must be produced. The body is just not able to produce antibodies that can copy all the slight variations of each new virus. Factors that lower the body's resistance to virus infection are fatigue, overexposure to cold, recent or present infections, allergic reactions, and inhalation of irritating dust or gas. A virus can even reinfect the person carrying the virus. However, a small percentage of the population with strong immune systems are able to resist infections and they never have colds.

Once a person becomes infected with a cold virus, symptoms appear after about two days. These include nose and throat irritations, watery eyes, headaches, fever, chills, muscle aches, and possible temporary loss of smell and taste.

Prevention of colds includes adequate sleep and a well-balanced diet that reinforces the immune system. A low-fat, high-fiber diet full of a variety of whole foods is recommended. Treatment includes adequate fluids (hot kinds except milk are the best), including mineral water and juices, to sustain the losses that occur with fever and evaporation from breathing through the mouth. Milk causes a thickening of mucous and should be avoided. Chicken soup does wonders if sipped. Yogurt will build immunity to ward off colds and hay fever. Eating garlic, which has antiviral and antibacterial properties, at the first sign of a sore throat may prevent the cold from developing any further. Consuming alkaline foods, rather than acidic, will ease a sore throat.

Nutrients may be helpful. Reports on the role of vitamin C in the treatment of the common cold are contradictory. However, many authorities claim that taking vitamin C in amounts from 1 to 2 grams daily is effective in lessening the duration and severity of a cold. Another source indicates that at the onset of a cold, vitamin C taken in amounts of 600 to 625 milligrams every three hours may be successful for treatment. The amount of vitamin C recommended for the prevention and treatment of a cold varies from individual to individual. Vitamin C taken with the bioflavonoid quercetin protects against colds. Zinc, if taken at the first sign of infection, will avoid or shorten the duration of a cold. Unsaturated fatty acids reduce the incidence and duration of colds. Vitamin B_6 helps in the production of antibodies that defend the body against infection. Vitamin A is necessary to maintain the health of the mucous membrane of the respiratory passages. Some individuals have found that vitamin D is also helpful in the prevention of colds.

Natural ingredients that may be beneficial include Russian horseradish toddy with one tablespoon of fresh horseradish, one teaspoon of honey, and one teaspoon ground cloves in a glass of warm water. Licorice root tea soothes throats and suppresses coughs, but may raise blood pressure if too much is consumed. Other useful remedies are onion cough syrup, which is six white chopped onions in a double boiler with half a cup of honey cooked slowly for two hours and strained; potato peeling broth, boiled for twenty minutes and then cooled; and sage gargle made by steeping sage leaves in water that has been heated to a boil (not recommended for children under the age of two). One drop each of oil of tea tree and lemon in a steamer will fight infection, and oil of peppermint or eucalyptus with a bit of honey will encourage sweating and soothe the throat (avoid steaming if asthma is a problem).

Herbs that are beneficial for colds are bayberry root bark, quinine, St. John's wort, slippery elm, pau d'arco, bark of the butternut walnut, and yarrow tea. A catnip tea enema is good for fever. Echinacea and goldenseal work well for children.

Homeopathic remedies are Gelsemium 6c, Nux vomica 6c, Hepar sulphuris 6c, Allium cepa 6c, and Mercurius solubilis 6c. (See "Bronchitis" for cough therapies.) Aromatherapy is cedarwood, basil, black pepper, eucalyptus, cypress, ginger, grapefruit, juniper, marjoram, lavender, lemon, myrrh, orange, peppermint, Scots pine, sandalwood, and tea tree.

Colitis and Crohn's Disease

Ulcerative colitis and Crohn's disease are conditions that affect the intestinal tract and are referred to collectively as inflammatory bowel disease (IBD). At one time, these conditions were referred to as ileitis and enteritis, respectively. In ulcerative colitis, the lining of the colon or large intestine is inflamed and has bloody diarrhea as its main symptom. Crohn's disease can affect any area of the digestive tract in the same manner and is characterized by abdominal pain, diarrhea or constipation, and weight loss. If healing aids are unsuccessful, surgery is almost always necessary. This condition often strikes teenagers who need emotional support.

Although the cause of the disease is unknown, there is usually a correlation between colitis and lifestyle, with depression or anxiety playing a part. The degree of a person's emotional stress often will indicate the severity of the colitis. Deficiency of vitamin K is linked to ulcerative colitis. Deficiencies of pantothenic acid cause abdominal distress, vomiting, and cramps. Deficiency of phosphorus also is likely with these diseases.

In early stages, the symptoms of colitis are abdominal cramps or pain, diarrhea, and the need to eliminate several times daily. These symptoms are accompanied by rectal bleeding as the condition becomes more severe. Instead of being absorbed by the body, water and minerals are rapidly expelled through the lower digestive tract, resulting in a loss of weight and possibly dehydration or anemia. Because of this rapid expulsion and decreased absorption of water and nutrients, the entire nutritional status of the colitis patient is in jeopardy. Anorexia will often accompany this disease because of the symptoms.

A therapeutic diet for these conditions varies from one individual to the next because of foods that irritate, but the diet should basically be low in fat and high in fiber (except during flare-ups), protein, and unsaturated fatty acids to restore lost or worn-down tissues. Yeast found in bread and other related foods including pastries has been found to irritate the bowels of IBD sufferers.

Recent studies have isolated the following foods as being especially allergic to the intestines: dairy products, cruciferous vegetables like cabbage and cauliflower, corn, wheat, tomatoes, citrus fruits, and eggs. Omega-6 vegetable oils should be monitored for a balance with the omega-3s, such as fish and flax oil. Flax oil can be mixed with omega-6 oils for a balance. Canola has both. Saturated fats (omega-6s) encourage inflammation and diarrhea. Frequent, small meals are recommended. Trying different foods and eliminating the ones that are irritants is the best way to establish a healthful pattern of eating for each individual. Foods high in roughage such as raw fruits and vegetables and whole grains that do not irritate (brown rice, if others do) are good sources of fiber. Adding rice or other grain brans to cereals or juice, putting raw or steamed vegetables through a blender first, or consuming junior baby foods will ease irritation of intestinal walls while providing adequate nutrition. Large amounts of garlic, best taken raw or in capsule form, kill infection.

Pure water or club soda may be used to replace fluids lost to diarrhea. Sometimes milk and dairy products are not tolerated and a calcium supplement may be necessary; however, lactose-free milk is available. High-fat milk and cheeses are to be avoided as are seeds and nuts. Avoid fats in cooking by broiling or baking foods. Some fruits that contain fructose, such as peaches, pears, plums, prunes, and apple juice, can irritate the lining of the bowel and, therefore, should be eaten with other foods or after a meal. Fatty red meats, sugar substitutes, processed foods, caffeine, tea, chocolate, colas, and all foods that irritate should be avoided.

Acidophilus is useful in the upkeep of the intestine. Iron is necessary to deter the development of anemia, and vitamin C is needed to aid in the absorption of iron. Vitamin B_6 along with magnesium is given intravenously to relax the muscles and control the spastic colon.

Exercise is of importance, with stretching being of particular benefit in helping improve digestion. The strength of the abdomen is also important. Staying active is beneficial in all aspects of life, especially in improving the fragile emotional status of the IBD sufferer.

Herbs are chamomile (overuse causes diarrhea), lobelia tea, slippery elm (soothes the colon), red clover, bee pollen (regulates bowels and lessens prostate problems), pau d'arco, charcoal for gas (must be taken one hour before or after other supplements or medicines), parsley (also for gas), fennel seed, ginger, juniper, dandelion, comfrey (for gastritis), feverfew, capsicum or red peppers (for pain and inflammation), catnip, and yarrow. Skullcap is a natural sedative to combat nervousness, and valerian root will calm a nervous stomach and intestine.

Comfrey, pepsin, senna-based thistle, and triphala are laxatives for those whose colitis causes constipation. Aloe vera juice for ulcerative colitis will aid in healing the colon. A wheatgrass enema will relieve the pain of gaseous buildup and clean the colon of otherwise leftover waste material. Alfalfa is useful for gas pains. Gamma-linolenic acid (GLA) or evening primrose oil is good for gastrointestinal function. Alginates (seaweed) are a natural form of antacid. Homeopathic remedies are Mercurius corrosivus 6c, Arsenicum album 6c, and Podophyllum 6c.

Conjunctivitis (Pink Eye)

Conjunctivitis, commonly called pink eye, is an inflammation of the mucous membrane that lines the eyelids and covers the white portion of the eye.

Symptoms of conjunctivitis include redness, swelling, itching, and pus in the membrane. This condition may be caused by contact lens solution, allergy, bacteria, virus, smoke, dust, Reiter's syndrome in men, or chemical irritants such as chlorine, smog, or those found in makeup. Pink eye is highly contagious when the cause is a virus and is spread in the same manner that the common cold is. If not treated, the condition can lead to bronchitis or pneumonia because of drippage from the eye into the nasal passages and down the throat.

A deficiency of vitamin A, vitamin B_6, or riboflavin may cause conjunctivitis symptoms. The diet should be adequate in these nutrients to help prevent the condition. Certain forms of conjunctivitis are the result of a calcium deficiency. In addition, meals should include those foods that dampen inflammation. (See "Inflammatory Conditions.")

Helpful nutrients are vitamin D, magnesium, and phosphorus, which aid in the absorption of calcium. For viral conjunctivitis, warm compresses dilate blood vessels and bring white blood cells to the area (do not irrigate, since it may spread the infection). For irritant conjunctivitis, cold tea compresses are good. Helpful herbs are raspberry leaf tea to alleviate redness and irritation, chrysanthemum tea, fennel, red eyebright (an astringent that may irritate), and chamomile. The potato, another natural astringent, may also have a healing effect. Homeopathic remedies are Argentum nitricum 6c, Apis 6c, Arnica Montana, Euphrasia, Aconite, Sulfur, Belladonna, Pulsatilla 6c, Arsenicum album, and Euphrasia.

Constipation

Constipation is a disorder characterized by decreased frequency of bowel movements, resulting in waste matter remaining in the colon and becoming dry and difficult to expel. This condition regularly affects more than four million people in the United States. Constipation may stem from a variety of causes. A poor diet lacking in fiber is the most common cause of constipation. Not taking in sufficient fluids and not exercising enough are also important factors. Insufficient muscle tone in the intestinal or abdominal wall due to a lack of exercise, repeated failure to heed the signal to eliminate, or excessive fatigue, nervousness, anxiety, stress, or excitement may also result in constipation. Medications such as diuretics, antacids, and drugs that treat Parkinson's disease may also promote this condition. Consuming too much milk may cause children to be constipated.

It is important that the bowels move at least three times a week, since toxins will accumulate and may cause problems. Ailments that are caused by constipation are diverticulosis, hemorrhoids, hernia, boils, bowel cancer, cellulite, indigestion, obesity, varicose veins, headaches, bad breath, insomnia, and gas. The continued use of laxatives rather than correcting poor elimination with proper exercise, rest, and diet may result in dependency and merely perpetuate the problem.

Diet can cure and prevent constipation, but if the cause is chronic and not related to diet, a physician should be consulted. Six to eight glasses of water a day are necessary to avoid fecal impaction. The more fiber contained in the diet from fruits, vegetables, legumes, and whole grains, the softer and the larger the amount of feces that will pass. Fiber also reduces transit time and the amount of toxins reabsorbed into the system from the stool. Bran is the safest, least expensive, and most natural means of taking care of healthy elimination of bodily waste. Prunes and prune juice are also effective. Ground psyllium seeds are an excellent concentrated source of fiber; they are sold in health food stores and used in some commercial products designed to treat constipation. Chemical laxatives will stimulate the bowel nerves and eventually weaken the muscles, whereas bran bulks the waste and activates the nerve reflexes that signal healthy elimination.

Foods containing fats may be useful in the treatment of constipation because of their lubricating effect on the mucous walls of the colon. Other foods that may be helpful are garlic (the allicin in garlic stimulates the walls of the intestines), linseed oil (2 or 3 tablespoons daily), yogurt or acidophilus, and fruits—especially apples, papaya, pineapple, prunes, and figs. Milk and cheese cause constipation in some people.

Herbs and other natural therapies that are beneficial are barley juice, blessed thistle, comfrey, holly, goldenseal, chickweed, flaxseed, fo-ti, wheatgrass, pepsin, nettle, and psyllium seed. Herbs that function as laxatives are alfalfa, cascara sagrada, dandelion (weak), senna leaf, dong quai for chronic cases, and euphorbia (strong). Coffee is a natural laxative but may cause constipation in certain individuals who drink too much. Enemas are useful if movement is stopped. Fasting periodically is a good idea. Foul-smelling stools may indicate acidosis.

Aromatherapy includes black pepper, sweet marjoram, rose otto, and rosemary. Exercise is very important, since it moves the waste through the intestines without allowing any toxins to accumulate. Aerobic exercise such as walking, swimming, and bicycling are recommended. Certain poses in yoga that massage the intestinal tract can also be very helpful.

To retrain bowel function, use the minimum dose necessary of a natural stimulant laxative such as senna or cascara daily at bedtime. The next week, reduce the dosage by half and continue this procedure. Normal bowel regularity will likely be established in four to six weeks.

Croup

Croup encompasses a variety of symptomatic conditions in which there is a high-pitched cough and wheezing called stridor, difficulty in breathing, and constricted lungs. Fever may or may not accompany the disorder. Croup usually affects children under the age of five. Conditions that may bring on the symptoms of croup are allergies, viruses that cause colds, lung infections, diphtheria, a foreign body in the throat, and swelling from a throat infection.

Croup may vary greatly in severity depending on its cause. Treatment involves taking care of any underlying infections or removing any obstruction in the throat. The breathing of warm moist air from a humidifier or hot shower often brings relief from coughing.

Nutritional treatment for croup involves a well-balanced diet high in protein that promotes the growth and repair of tissues. If fever is present, the need for vitamins A and C is increased. Increased fluid intake is also essential, especially when croup occurs in very small children or infants. Herbs that are good are echinacea (for fever), elecampane (an expectorant), thyme, goldenseal, comfrey, and eucalyptus oil (for the inhaler). A ginger herb bath is good, and hot onion packs are also soothing. Homeopathy recommends Aconite 6c for night cough.

Cystic Fibrosis

Cystic fibrosis is a hereditary disease affecting certain glands and organs in the body (both exocrine and endocrine), such as the liver, gallbladder, pancreas, heart, small intestine, male reproductive organs, lungs, and sweat glands. The sweat glands produce an unusually salty perspiration, draining the body of salt and making the patient susceptible to heat exhaustion. The mucous glands in the lungs, which normally aid in moistening the air passages, produce thick mucus that blocks the passages and promotes the growth of harmful bacteria. The disease is inherited and usually begins during infancy, though symptoms may manifest themselves later in life. Researchers have recently discovered the gene that causes this disease and are now closer to developing a cure.

The greatest danger at the onset of cystic fibrosis is malnutrition from an obstruction of pancreatic juices to the intestine caused by thick mucus in the ducts. As a result, along with all foods, fats are poorly digested and absorbed and a deficiency may occur. Rather than restrict fat intake, pancreatic enzymes may be taken. Ox bile can also be beneficial. Protein-digestion enzymes derived from pineapple (bromelain) and from papaya (papain) are not as effective.

The recommended diet is high in calories, the majority of calories coming from protein and starches, which are nutritionally better than sugars. Mucus-forming foods should be avoided. The intake of fluids and salt should be increased, particularly during hot weather. Infants who are on formula need enzyme replacements.

Since there is poor absorption of nutrients, additional vitamins—A, the B complex, C, D, E (vitamin E deficiency can lead to cystic fibrosis), and K—should be included in the diet. Fat-soluble vitamins should be taken in a water-mixable form. Taurine, an amino acid, may help cystic fibrosis; research continues. Taste sensitivity in cystic fibrosis is caused by a zinc deficiency. Adequate blood levels of selenium should be maintained. Wobe-Mugos, a pancreatic enzyme, helps in malabsorption syndrome, including cystic fibrosis.

New Zealand physician Dr. Robert B. Elliot based his treatment on the fact that people afflicted with cystic fibrosis have abnormally low blood levels of linoleic acid. He gave periodic infusions of soy oil, which contains a large amount of linoleic acid, to several groups of children. Oral supplementation was not effective. The results showed that at least one of the characteristic biochemical abnormalities of the disease improved in all children tested.

At the University of Pennsylvania School of Medicine and the Wistar Institute, researchers gave thirteen children afflicted with cystic fibrosis dietary supplements of corn oil, vitamin E (to prevent oxidation), and pancreatic enzymes. After a year on the diet, all the children gained weight, grew taller, and seemed healthier and happier. In individual cases, the supplements relieved symptoms such as diarrhea, sodium loss, and general problems associated with poor nutrition.

Running and walking exercises were also part of the program. Regular exercise helped patients keep their lungs clear of mucus and may be a factor in slowing the deterioration of lung function.

Herbal remedies are ginger, yarrow, goldenseal, and echinacea.

Cystitis (Bladder Infection)

Cystitis is an inflammation of the urinary bladder found mostly in women; it is much less common in males, except in infants. Infection is easily transmitted because of the close proximity of the anus, vagina, and urethra. Cystitis is most frequently caused by bacteria that ascend from the urinary opening, but it may also be caused by infected urine sent from the kidneys to the bladder. Sexually transmitted diseases can cause cystitis as well. Oral contraceptives, bruising during intercourse, stress, and diet are causes. Taking antibiotics may also promote this condition. After a bowel movement, wiping from the front to the back lessens the possibility of infection and a shower for both partners before intercourse also lessens the possibility. Avoiding douching and other vaginal preparations is advised.

Symptoms of cystitis are chilliness, pain in the lower abdomen and back, and frequent, urgent, and painful urination. Diagnosis involves microscopic examination of the urine to see if it is infected with high levels of white blood cells and bacteria. Fever may possibly accompany these symptoms. Home tests are now available. Treatment for cystitis includes increasing the fluid intake to at least eight glasses a day. In particular, cranberry juice and blueberry juice are effective tonics, reducing the ability of the bacteria *Escherichia coli* (*E. coli*) from adhering to the lining of the bladder and urethra. Maintaining a well-balanced diet, high in alkalizing fruits and vegetables, is also recommended. In addition, taking alkalizing compounds such as potassium citrate or sodium citrate have provided symptomatic relief in the majority of cases in various clinical studies.

Several nutrients may be helpful, including dimethyl sulfoxide (DMSO), which is used in the treatment of interstitial cystitis (fibrosis of the bladder) mainly in women over age forty. Vitamin B complex helps maintain the muscle tone in the gastrointestinal tract and liver. Vitamin C helps ward off and clear up the infection. Vitamin E maintains proper functioning of the liver. If antibiotics are taken for a bladder infection, a deficiency of vitamin K is likely.

Herbs that are helpful are juniper berries, horsetail grass, rose hips, uva ursi, burdock root, damiana, marshmallow root, yarrow infusion (three times a day), and goldenseal (not for use during pregnancy). Homeopathic remedies are Nux vomica, Cantharus 6c, Apis 6c, Staphysagria 6c, Mercurius corrosivus 6c, and Sarsaparilla 6c. Juniper, sandalwood, and lavender oils are soothing in a bath.

Dandruff

Dandruff may simply be dry flakes of skin that brush off the hair or it may be a more serious situation that causes an inflamed, waxy, and itchy condition that can travel to the eyebrows, ears, and other areas of the body. This is called seborrheic dermatitis and results from sebaceous glands that have become overactive. Emotional traumas, illness, or hormonal imbalance can aggravate and worsen seborrheic dermatitis. It appears that, for some people, there is no cure for dandruff, but it can be controlled.

Studies have shown that causes of dandruff include not washing the hair and scalp often enough, an inadequate diet, and inefficient carbohydrate metabolism. Investigations have found a severe dandruff that is caused by a fungus called *Pityrosporum ovale*; it can be killed by using a cream containing ketoconazole, but the scales will still remain. Severe dandruff can lead to hair loss and possibly baldness. Food allergies may cause the problem. Consuming too many citrus fruits is thought to contribute to dandruff. Eating lots of sugar often triggers the condition, as does not brushing the hair enough. Poor circulation within the scalp has been thought to contribute to the problem. Products that are alkaline may be a cause. Extreme cases may also be due to psoriasis.

Dandruff can be substantially controlled by diet, including vitamins and minerals and other natural ingredients. Unrefined carbohydrates, B-vitamin supplements, and the antioxidant nutrients vitamin C, vitamin E, beta-carotene, and selenium are also helpful. Vitamin A and the trace mineral zinc are needed, and warm olive or mineral oil or vitamin E and lemon oil massaged into the scalp to loosen existing scales is good (leave on for several hours and then shampoo). A daily dry massage to the scalp is useful since it increases circulation. Along with the diet, shampoos designed to control dandruff (those containing selenium sulfide or zinc pyrithione) must be used. Dark-haired people can use tar, which has salicylic acid to soften and remove itchy scales. Prescription cleansing lotions are also available.

Helpful herbs are red clover, dandelion, juniper, goldenseal, and rosemary and sage tea used as a rinse. Rinsing the hair in chaparral may be helpful. Aromatherapy includes Roman chamomile, cedarwood, eucalyptus, juniper, lavender, rosemary, and tea tree.

Deafness

Sound travels through three different sections of the ear. The outer ear passes incoming sound waves to the eardrum, located in the middle ear. The middle ear transfers these sounds through three tiny bones that vibrate a fluid in the cochlea, which is located in the inner ear. The cochlea has tiny hairs protruding from its walls that relay the sound vibrations as electrical impulses to the brain. The brain then interprets these impulses as sound.

The quality of hearing depends on the condition of the eighth cranial nerve, located in the inner ear, where sound is transferred to the brain. Perceptive (nerve damage from aging, loud noise, disease, and injury) and conductive (from ear blockage) deafness are two common types of hearing damage that affect this area. In children, ear infections are often a cause. (See "Ear Infection/Earache.")

Perceptive deafness occurs in the inner ear and the neural pathways to the brain. Examples of this type of deafness are gradual hearing loss from aging (presbycusis), congenital problems, Ménière's syndrome, and damage from drugs, excessive noise, or infectious diseases such as mastoiditis. A deficiency of the B vitamins in the diet may be a very important factor in perceptive deafness.

Presbycusis is associated with the aging process. It is gradual and often not noticed for years. The higher tones are lost first; eventually understanding conversation becomes difficult. Because this disease is one of the results of aging, nutrients involved in slowing the aging process—vitamins B and C and selenium, for example—are important in its prevention. At a hearing clinic in Alabama, hard-of-hearing patients improved markedly when given yeast and liver (sources of the B complex), vitamin C, and glutamic acid.

Exposure to 85 decibels or more for prolonged periods can cause ear damage. Excessive noise contracts the tiny blood vessels in the ear, and repeated exposure progressively increases the time required for them to return to normal, eventually resulting in injury, possibly permanent. Normal conversation registers at 60 decibels, a loud motorcycle at 110, and rock music amplified to its peak registers at 120 decibels. The noise level is too loud if a person needs to shout to be heard by someone standing a few feet away. This form of hearing loss is one of the easiest to prevent; ear plugs for those who work in settings where there is noise is highly advisable. Hearing aids are available for those with permanent damage.

Conductive deafness is caused by an obstruction that prevents the transmission of sounds to the inner ear. A physician should be consulted to determine the obstruction. Sounds may still be sent but distinguishing them is difficult. Otosclerosis, wax accumulation (cerumen), and boils on the ear canal are causes of this type of deafness. In otosclerosis, the tiny bones in the middle ear become hard and overgrown, interfering with sound transmission. Once the disease occurs, surgery appears to be the only alternative. However, vitamin A (by injection) has been shown to improve this condition in humans; and in animals, a lack of the vitamin is thought to be a cause.

Earwax, or cerumen, is a naturally occurring substance, a secretion formed from sebaceous and sweat glands that are located in the outer section of the ear canal. The wax is made of water, fats, and lecithin, and functions as a lubricant and trap for such particles as bacteria and dust. Its importance should not be underestimated; for example, dust on the eardrum would distort sound and without lubrication, infections could become serious and even life-threatening. Cerumen is excreted by the motions of the jaws while eating and talking; it eventually falls out during sleep. Symptoms of impacted cerumen include tinnitus (a ringing in the ears), earache, reflex cough, dizziness, an echo sensation, and disturbances in behavior seen especially in mental patients. If the wax is left too long in the ear, it can become a medium for bacterial and fungal growth. Excessive pollutants also build up on the wax, increasing the susceptibility to infection and causing difficult expulsion. Two major causes of impacted earwax are air pollution and refined foods, which need little chewing action.

Excessive fat in the diet appears to collect in the blood vessels of the ear, causing obstruction. Controlled experiments have been conducted between people who consumed a high-fat diet and others on a low-fat diet. The patients on the low-fat diet experienced better hearing. In other studies, many patients with hearing loss and ear problem symptoms had elevated cholesterol levels, showed abnormal glucose tolerance (diabetes), and were overweight. Their hearing was significantly improved by reducing dietary fats and refined foods and losing weight.

Herbs that are used are peppermint, plantain seed, thorowax root, and chrysanthemum flowers. Parsley extracts in large doses appear to aid in the hearing process.

Depression/Bipolar Mood Disorder

Depressive disorders are long-lasting feelings of sadness and despair. What was previously pleasurable has become of little interest. Mood disorders are a form of mental illness that occurs when a person is no longer able to cope effectively with emotional or physical stress. Bipolar mood disorder (formerly known as manic-depressive disorder) is the back-and-forth feeling of either mania (euphoric, mental highs) or depression. The problems facing one person may not necessarily be more serious than the problems facing another, but the affected person who has any of these disorders has less ability to deal with the stress. Of special concern is how disruptive to the person's life the condition has become.

Symptoms of depression are insomnia, reduced appetite, lack of energy, sluggish movement and speech, lack of sexual desire, irritability, anxiety, headaches, brooding, low self-esteem, crying bouts, constipation, and feelings of hopelessness, dejection, and guilt. People who have mild symptoms are diagnosed as having dysthymic disorder. During a manic episode, symptoms are hyperactivity and sleeplessness. Rapid speech, changing topics quickly and often, and a mind that speeds uncontrollably are characteristics. Compulsive gambling, sexual activity, and extravagant spending habits often accompany a manic period. Mild bipolar disorder is called cyclothymic disorder.

Causes of depression and bipolar mood disorder have been linked to both genetic and psychological origins. A genetic vulnerability to bipolar illness (not the illness itself) has been isolated in a study of the Amish, who have kept records through generations and have an unusually high incidence of this condition. The environment that the individual lives in seems to determine whether the illness is manifest or not.

Another theory is that chemical changes in the brain cause mood disorders; however, many of these changes may depend on and be triggered by a person's environment. How a person interprets and thinks about situations and others is also a cause of depression. Depressed people usually will analyze a happening with a "jumping off the deep end" kind of thinking—in other words, in a manner that allows no going back to fix the situation. The failure is devastating because there is no resolution and depression eventually takes over.

Inadequate social skills resulting from inexperience, shyness, involvement with alcohol and/or drugs at an early age with continued dependence into late adulthood, or a challenging family background that left the person with inadequate social confidence may contribute to making the individual vulnerable to depression. Stress seems to be a major factor in starting the process for certain people. Stress can build up within a month of the onset of the illness. It has recently been noted that depression is contagious. Persons who associate with individuals who are depressed may themselves begin to feel blue, leaving the depressed individual even more alone as they begin to avoid the ill person. Postnatal depression, with its accompanying inability to care for the child along with the other symptoms of depression, is thought to come from deficiencies of nutrients.

Psychological treatment involves several kinds of psychotherapy. Short-term therapy concentrates on the obvious problem unlike psychoanalysis, which can continue for months or years and delves into the origins of a problem in a person's past experiences. The most popular of the new styles of short-term therapy is cognitive therapy, which examines how the thought process or way of thinking perpetuates the depression and how to change those patterns. The period of therapy is not longer than six weeks. Another brief therapy is interpersonal therapy, which uses relationships to help discover why and where the depression came from. This kind of therapy uses the stages of life and human development to point out changes in needs and wants. Longer psychotherapy sessions that deal with lifelong stresses, after an initial recovery period, may be desirable for prevention of future episodes.

Medical treatment encourages the use of certain medications that interfere with the chemical reactions of the neurotransmitters in the brain. All these medications have side effects. Candid discussion of symptoms with a physician is beneficial to determine the best treatment. Monoamine oxidases (MAO), used to treat chronic depression, may cause severe hypertension and headaches and may raise blood pressure to fatal levels. If taking these drugs, avoid the amino acid tyrosine, as it raises blood pressure.

One theory is that low levels of certain neurotransmitters, chemicals in the brain that transmit signals from one nerve cell to another, can cause depression. Low levels of serotonin, a mood-elevating and tranquilizing neurotransmitter produced by the brain, are associated with depression. Oral contraceptives and steroid drugs lower serotonin levels. A deficiency of serotonin causes sleeplessness, irritability, and forgetfulness.

Diet directly affects these disorders. A raw fruit and vegetable diet with lots of complex carbohydrates is important. However, certain of these foods tend to rapidly raise blood sugar in sensitive persons, a concern because hypoglycemia can result and its symptoms mimic those of depression. If control of blood sugar is an issue, adding foods with a low glycemic index and low glycemic load, such as legumes, nuts, and animal protein, can be of benefit. Also important is including foods that supply nutrients commonly deficient in depressed individuals, specifically vitamin B_6, vitamin B_{12}, and folic acid. Green leafy vegetables such as spinach are high in folic acid, which is good for depression because it raises serotonin levels in the brain.

Depression is also linked to inadequate intake of omega-3 fatty acids; research has suggested that these fats may reduce the development of depression. Walnuts, flaxseed, and fish are excellent sources. (See Section 5 for additional sources of these needed nutrients.) Food allergies are thought to have a good deal to do with depression in some people. Avoid phenylalanine foods, as they often cause allergic reactions for those who are depressed. (See Section 5.) Choline, arginine, and ornithine are other natural substances that should be avoided by those with bipolar disorder. Whole grains, low-fat dairy products, cereals, and fish are recommended. New evidence has shown that low levels of cholesterol in elderly men help induce depression. A level that does not go below 160 is recommended. Blues caused by premenstrual syndrome (PMS) and winter blues caused by seasonal affective disorder (SAD) are best fought with carbohydrates, preferably the complex kind.

Nutrients may be beneficial. Magnesium aids in fighting depression. Taking 200 to 500 milligrams of folic acid per day may raise serotonin levels. Studies have shown that vitamin C is helpful in the management of bipolar disorder. Seafood is high in the trace mineral selenium, known to elevate moods depending on deficiency level in the individual. A single Brazil nut, higher in selenium than any other nut, will supply the daily requirement; however, selenium is also found in grains and meat. Hydergine affects enzyme systems at serotonin receptor sites and is thought to aid in depression. Selenium is known to be toxic so consumption should be monitored.

High levels of vanadium are negatively associated with bipolar illness; high doses of vitamin C will reduce those levels. Black pepper and dill are high in vanadium. Allergies, malabsorptive conditions, and hypoglycemic and thyroid conditions may interfere with the absorption of folic acid and vitamin B_{12}, which may lead to depression. High doses of choline may induce further depression in those who are already depressed.

Other natural supplements and sources may be helpful. The amino acid L-glutamine is thought to counter depression. Another amino acid, tryptophan, a precursor of serotonin, may relieve depression when taken with carbohydrates. Tryptophan is present in foods such as chicken, turkey, fish, dried beans and peas, soybeans, nuts, peanut butter, and brewer's yeast. It is also available as a supplement. Supplemental tryptophan for a time was taken off the market because the product coming from a certain producer was contaminated and caused health problems. While tryptophan is once again available, a form of tryptophan called 5-hydroxytryptophan is proving safer and more effective in treating depression. Another amino acid called DL-phenylalanine (DLPA) relieves depression but should not be taken if one has high blood pressure. With a physician's consent, a gradual amount may be tried—100 to 500 milligrams is recommended daily. Lipotropes (injection form) are used in severe depression to increase the flow of blood and oxygen to the brain.

Women with postnatal depression are often found to be deficient in the B-complex vitamins, especially B_2 and B_6. Taking 125 milligrams of zinc daily and 300 milligrams of magnesium daily, and eating a complex carbohydrate food every three hours may also be helpful. Useful herbs for postnatal depression are primrose oil and skullcap infusion.

Natural substances are helpful. Garlic will give a feeling of well-being, and the capsaicin in hot chili peppers can precipitate a temporary mental high by tricking the brain into releasing natural painkillers in the form of endorphins. The more peppers, the more endorphins the brain produces. Caffeine can cause temporary depression in those who are sensitive to it or who are in withdrawal; but it is a well-known, mild food source antidepressant for some people. Alcohol acts as a depressant in various ways, disrupting brain chemistry, interfering with sleep, and making a person more prone to hypoglycemia. Licorice and honey are natural antidepressants. Oats may help but this has not been confirmed.

Herbs that are beneficial are ginger, kava, gingko biloba, and St. John's wort, which takes effect after several months. St. John's wort should not to be taken by pregnant or nursing women or those who are using MAO drugs; consult a physician. Yohimbine may lessen anxiety and depression associated with erectile failure. Oil of clary sage is soothing. Flower remedies are mustard and sweet chestnut. Homeopathy recommends Pulsatilla 6c, Natrum muriaticum 6c, and Sepia 6c. Aromatherapy includes bergamot, basil, coriander, clary sage, Roman chamomile, geranium, frankincense, lavender, grapefruit, lemon, orange, orange blossom, patchouli, pettigrain, rose otto, sandalwood, and ylang-ylang.

Exercise pulls the mind away from its negative thoughts and allows new and positive experiences to enter. Studies have shown that jogging for thirty minutes three times a week accomplishes as much as therapy sessions do in the treatment of depression. Always consult a physician before attempting any exercise program.

Dermatitis

Dermatitis is an inflammatory skin reaction that is usually recurring. It can be caused by contact with an irritating agent found in the environment such as poison oak or ivy, detergents, rubber (in gloves and condoms), makeup, some medicines, and jewelry metals. Another cause is ingesting a food that triggers an allergic reaction. Continued exposure to these agents could result in the spreading of and the continued deterioration of the affected area. Dermatitis may be caused by or associated with hereditary allergic tendencies and may be aggravated by emotional stress and fatigue.

Atopic dermatitis is known as eczema. Eczema is hereditary and is most commonly triggered by an allergic reaction to a particular food, such as peanuts, eggs, or milk. Skin eruptions are characterized by tiny blisters that weep and crust. It is most likely found in the creases of the armpits, elbows, and knees. Tight bra straps cause eczema flare-ups. Chronic forms are characterized by scaling, flaking, eventual thickening, and color changes of the skin. Itching is almost always present.

Certain treatments may be helpful. Exposing the skin to a moderate amount of sunlight is helpful, but too much will worsen the condition. Staying comfortable enough not to sweat will discourage an outbreak. Using a humidifier will keep the dryness off the skin. Moisturizing often will keep the skin supple. Cool baths (including whirlpools) taken often will keep the skin moist. Sleeping with gloves covering moisturized or treated hands is suggested. Loose, natural-fiber clothes are more comfortable than clinging synthetic types. If the irritating agent is a food item, the elimination diet should be used to identify the irritant. Certain dairy products, fats, processed foods, and gluten found in grains may be irritants.

Nutrients may be helpful. A deficiency of any of the B vitamins can cause dermatitis, and these vitamins should, therefore, be present in the diet in adequate amounts. Niacin should be added in greater amounts, since a deficiency affects the skin and mucous membranes. Zinc may be needed since many eczema patients are deficient and this mineral plays a role in the metabolization of essential fatty acids (EFAs). The EFAs in fish oils, EPA and DHA, have proven beneficial in the treatment of this skin condition, so a supplement should be considered. Vitamin C and the bioflavonoids will relieve inflammation. (See "Inflammatory Conditions.") Selenium sulfate lotions inhibit all forms of dermatitis. Linoleic acid (unsaturated fat) and vitamin B_6 have been found to cure infants who have dermatitis caused by a fat-free diet. Vitamin A is also essential for maintaining healthy skin tissue. A protein deficiency can cause chronic eczema. A manganese deficiency produces scaly dermatitis.

Herbs that may be beneficial are dandelion, red clover, comfrey, Chinese gentian, Oriental wormwood, pau d'arco, peony root, myrrh gum, coleus forskohlii, and licorice. Primrose oil for infants as well as all others is useful. Primrose may be taken in capsule form and may produce results within three to six months. Chickweed and seaweed are useful for eczema. Colloidal oatmeal in the bath will soothe. Aloe vera can alleviate certain skin conditions related to dermatitis, especially that which is caused by radiation. Fish oil is good for atopic dermatitis. Chamomile and chaparral may cause dermatitis.

Homeopathic remedies are Sulphur 6c, Petroleum 6c, and Graphite 6c. Aromatherapy includes Roman chamomile, cedarwood, lavender, and geranium. The therapy also uses foot and hand baths for specific skin conditions.

Diabetes

The body normally breaks down carbohydrates into glucose, the body's main energy source. Insulin, a hormone produced in the pancreas, is essential for the passage of this glucose into cells where it is converted into energy. Diabetes is a metabolic disorder characterized by the breakdown of this process, resulting in the decreased ability (or complete inability) of the body to utilize carbohydrates.

There are two types of diabetes. In type I diabetes, also called insulin-dependent diabetes mellitus (IDDM) and formerly referred to as *juvenile onset diabetes*, the pancreas produces insufficient insulin, decreasing the amount of glucose the cells take in and keeping blood sugar levels high. This form of diabetes can occur at any age but usually first occurs in people under the age of thirty. The disease is chronic and because there is no cure, lasts a lifetime. It is estimated that 5 percent to 10 percent of individuals with diabetes have this form. While a person may have a genetic predisposition to developing type I diabetes, this disease can be triggered by viral infection, an autoimmune disease in which the immune system attacks and destroys the insulin-producing cells in the pancreas, and even a diet high in smoked or cured meats.

In type I diabetes, there is rapid onset of symptoms and these can be severe. Common symptoms include excessive thirst, frequent urination, increased appetite, fatigue, and loss of weight. Other symptoms, though less characteristic of type I diabetes, are muscle cramps, itching of the skin, and poorly healing wounds. Acute complications may include hypoglycemia and diabetic ketoacidosis.

In type II diabetes, also called non-insulin-dependent diabetes mellitus (NIDDM), either the body does not produce enough insulin or cells cease to readily respond to insulin, a condition known as *insulin resistance*. In this form of diabetes, blood levels of both glucose and insulin may be elevated. About 90 percent of all diabetic patients have the non-insulin type and about 90 percent of these are obese. Being overweight is a major contributing factor to the development of type II diabetes. Other conditions that contribute to its development are high intake of fat and especially saturated fat, chromium deficiency, pregnancy, surgery, and physical or emotional stress.

Complications of both forms of diabetes range in severity from low resistance to infections, especially in the extremities, to more serious consequences such as heart attack, stroke, kidney failure, impaired vision or blindness, nerve damage, and even amputation.

Type II diabetes at one time occurred predominantly in adults only after age forty, but in recent years, cases of type II diabetes have been on the rise among teenagers. In addition, teenagers are now at higher risk for gestational diabetes, a condition that occurs during pregnancy and usually disappears once a woman gives birth. Being overweight and having insufficient exercise are considered the prime reasons for these changes in demographics and the modern-day "epidemic" of diabetes.

The incidence of diabetes has dramatically increased in recent years. From 1980 to 2004, the number of Americans with diagnosed diabetes has more than doubled, increasing from 5.8 million to 14.7 million. And the Centers for Disease Control and Prevention predict that one in three Americans born in 2000 will develop diabetes sometime during his or her lifetime. Diabetes has become a disease of prime concern, with an economic cost in 2002 of $132 billion.

Patients with type I diabetes require insulin, and even type II diabetics may need insulin therapy if their condition cannot be controlled with diet alone, though such treatment may be of limited usefulness. However, for both types of diabetes, diet is a fundamental part of any treatment plan. The standard therapeutic diabetic diet incorporates three meals a day plus snacks between meals and at bedtime. Goals include weight loss, if required, as well as stabilization of blood sugar.

Meals should be well-balanced and rich in high-fiber fruits, vegetables, and whole grains and low in fat and animal foods. The emphasis should be placed on whole foods that are naturally high in vitamins and minerals that the diabetic especially requires. Refined ingredients such as white flour must be avoided. While refined white sugar has no place in a diabetic diet, moderate amounts of fruit and fructose (the form of sugar in fruit) are much better tolerated. Being aware of the glycemic index and glycemic load of various foods is essential in designing a diabetic diet plan to focus on those ingredients that only minimally raise blood sugar levels. (See Section 2, Table 2.1, "Glycemic Index and Glycemic Load of Common Foods.")

The diabetic diet emphasizes fatty fish, poultry, and soy products rather than red meats to meet the protein requirements. Low-fat and nonfat dairy products are recommended. Sources of fiber, such as fruits and vegetables, as well as oats and legumes that provide soluble fiber, should make up 30 percent to 40 percent of the daily food intake. Vegetables such as garlic, onions, lettuce, cabbage, root types, avocados, broccoli, and brussels sprouts are good. Antioxidant-containing foods should be consumed. (See Section 2,

Table 2.4, "Antioxidants and Antioxidant Foods.") The total amount of fat should be less than 30 percent of the day's total calories, with saturated fat contributing less than 10 percent of total calories. Use infant formulas for babies, not cow's milk since it is thought to be the cause of type I diabetes in later years. Alcohol and caffeine should be avoided.

Certain nutrients—vitamins B_1 (a deficiency of), B_2, B_3 (in glucose metabolism), B_6 (a deficiency of), B_{12}, pantothenic acid, vitamins A and C (for wound healing), protein, and potassium—and small frequent meals, each containing some carbohydrate, can stimulate insulin production within the body. The time involved in stimulating insulin production will vary with individuals. These methods will have the same effect as insulin injections, so symptoms of insulin shock must be watched and dosages must be adjusted as necessary.

L-carnitine may protect against diabetes. But L-cysteine and fish oil supplements may interfere with insulin and should not be taken without the advice of a physician. Chromium helps normalize blood sugar levels in all people, especially in the elderly, and also aids in weight loss in diabetics. Diabetes has been reversed with vanadium in studies with diabetes induced in rats. Magnesium must be replaced in those with diabetes. Zinc is involved with insulin at several stages as well as in wound healing and in immune responses that fight infection. This mineral could possibly reduce many diabetic-related complications and, because of decreased absorption owing to the disease as well as age, zinc should be supplemented.

A deficiency of myoinositol is linked to diabetic peripheral neuropathy (tingling, pain, and numbness of the feet and legs), which is one of the most serious side effects of diabetes. Diabetic retinitis, a hemorrhaging of the eye, is often a complication of diabetes. It is apparently brought on by stress and may be prevented with substantial amounts of protein and the vitamin B complex, extra vitamin B_{12}, vitamin C, and pantothenic acid.

Exercise is as vital a factor in diabetes treatment as diet because in some cases exercise can help reduce the need for insulin, reduce the cholesterol level, and guard against overweight and obesity. Engaging in physical activity thirty minutes on five or more days of the week is recommended. This amount, plus a small amount of weight loss (5 percent to 7 percent of total body weight) has proven to delay and possibly prevent diabetes in high-risk persons, according to a major, federally funded study, the Diabetes Prevention Program.

Herbs and other natural substances that help are ginseng and fenugreek seed (lowers blood sugar levels), damiana, huckleberry, lilyturf, lotus seed, devil's claw, buchu leaves, triphala, golden root, grassy privet, cinnamon (balances sugars in sweets), and Chinese yam. Iraqis use barley bread to treat diabetes, while from Mexico comes another antidiabetic food, nopales (cactus paddles). Juniper berries, coriander, and alfalfa are used in other cultures. Many of these herbs, spices, and foods have compounds that will lower blood sugar levels. Aromatherapy for circulation includes black pepper, coriander, cypress, ginger, juniper, lavender, lemon, sweet marjoram, orange, rose otto, rosemary, and vetiver.

Diarrhea

Diarrhea is a condition causing frequent elimination of stools that are abnormally watery in nature. This condition is fairly common and can exist alone or as a symptom of other diseases. Diarrhea may be accompanied by vomiting, increased thirst, abdominal cramps and bloating, intestinal rumbling, and loss of appetite. If the condition persists, consult a physician.

Because of the decreased appetite associated with diarrhea and rapid expulsion of food through the lower digestive tract, an individual with diarrhea does not properly absorb nutrients and, therefore, can develop nutrient deficiencies. In addition, the change in consistency of the stool causes the body to lose a great amount of water, a loss that can cause dehydration as well as the loss of minerals and water-soluble vitamins.

The most frequent cause of diarrhea is the presence in the colon of bacteria foreign to the intestinal tract. Bacteria may come from pathogens in food that cause food poisoning or from poorly refrigerated, undercooked, or partially rancid food. Radiation therapy or antibiotics can destroy friendly bacteria in the intestines. Emotional stress, such as anxiety, is another major cause of diarrhea. Diarrhea can also be brought about by food allergies or a diet that is overly abundant in roughage, which increases the movement of food through the intestines. Milk, food additives, alcohol, and unripe fruits are other causes. Infection, a diseased pancreas, antacids, prolonged use of laxatives, caffeine, colitis, cancer, and parasites are other causes.

Replacing fluids and electrolytes is the most essential aspect of the treatment for diarrhea. It is important to replace the water that is lost in the stools, thereby preventing dehydration, and to replenish the various minerals that are depleted as well. Sodium, magnesium (in the form of magnesium gluconate), and potassium are bound closely to water, which the body loses as it becomes dehydrated. This is vitally important especially for infants and the elderly. Fluids that supply electrolytes, such as vegetable juices, hot carob, or boiled water with lemon or orange juice and table salt added are healthful. Electrolyte replacement drinks, with healthy ingredients, are sold in natural food stores.

While the usual recommendation is to avoid solid foods during the acute phase of diarrhea, in actuality, continuing to eat shortens this ailment if the foods consumed provide bulk. An often recommended dietary regimen is the BRAT diet—bananas, rice, applesauce, and toast. Certain foods, dairy products, and sugar need to be avoided as they will irritate the condition. As more foods are reintroduced, these should be high in fiber and rich in protein, carbohydrates, oils, vitamins, and minerals to compensate for the loss of all nutrients that occurs with diarrhea. Digestive enzymes should be taken with meals. Yogurt with *Lactobacillus acidophilus* will replace the helpful bacteria that have been destroyed.

The diet should be supplemented with nutrients, including the water-soluble B-complex vitamins, vitamin C, and the electrolytes sodium, magnesium, and potassium. Vitamin A resists bacteria that may cause diarrhea.

Herbs that are helpful are slippery elm, chamomile tea, goldenseal infusion, bayberry root bark, blackberry root, raspberry leaves, black walnut bark (helps control), cayenne, yellow dock, ginger tea (for cramps), schizandra (for chronic diarrhea), haritaki, and quinine. Homeopathic remedies are Croton tiglium, Chamomilla 6c for irritable bowels, and Arsenicum album, Veratrum album, Podophyllum, Colocynthis, Dulcamara, and Sulphur 6c for soreness. For camp diarrhea, Pyrogen is used; for infants, Nux vomica is good. Nitric acid for antibiotic-induced diarrhea is used for prompt relief.

Diverticulitis

Diverticulitis is the inflammation of the small sacs (diverticula), or outpouchings, found along the esophagus and small or large intestine (colon). It is caused mainly by small bubbles of the inner lining of the colon that bulge out at weak points when extra pressure, irregular bowel movements, or constipation occurs. This condition is very common among those ages sixty and older. When empty, the diverticula remain dormant and without complication. However, when food particles get trapped in the sacs and are digested by the bacteria normally present in the colon for this purpose, the digested food particles become stagnant, causing inflammation and infection. Diverticulitis may be hereditary, or it may accompany old age when the muscles of the colon are weakened from years of use.

As diverticulitis becomes more severe, the infection can spread out of the sacs to the rest of the colon and to other organs of the abdomen. In very severe cases, the disease can result in perforation of the wall of the colon, causing severe bleeding for which immediate surgical attention is necessary. Prevention and treatment by following a high-fiber diet is very helpful.

Diverticulitis can manifest itself in a short but severe attack or in a long-term, less severe problem. Symptoms of the disease include cramps and pain in the lower abdomen accompanying bowel movements, abdominal bloating, and the frequent urge to eliminate followed by constipation. If infection occurs, fever can develop in more severe cases. Some people never experience any discomfort.

Diverticulitis is treated with a high-fiber diet providing 25 to 30 grams of fiber per day. However, this is not recommended at times when there is a flare-up of this condition, which would then require a low-fiber diet. Good sources of fiber are whole grains, certain brans, fruits, steamed vegetables, dried peas, and beans. Drinking six glasses of fluids a day is also recommended. Both fiber and fluids help prevent constipation, which increases the likelihood that diverticulitis will develop. In addition, a low-carbohydrate, high-protein diet rich in vegetables and fish is beneficial. Refined carbohydrates should be avoided. Acidophilus, present in active-bacteria yogurt, will prevent further accumulation of food in the diverticula. The texture of food should also be considered when planning meals. Grains, seeds, and nuts that look like they may become lodged in the pockets should be avoided or chewed very well. Liquid vitamins and foods that are mashed or ground may be necessary when there is a flare-up.

Nutrients may be beneficial. Since some of the B vitamins are manufactured by the intestinal bacteria, a deficiency may occur if these bacteria are destroyed by the infection. It is therefore necessary that the diet provide adequate amounts of the B vitamins, especially folic acid. Acidophilus will destroy putrefactive bacteria in the colon and aid in the growth of beneficial bacteria and the manufacture of B vitamins. Herbs and other natural substances that are helpful are psyllium (cleans and softens), garlic, yarrow tea, chamomile, cayenne, and slippery elm (soothes inflammation). Clay tablets, papaya, charcoal (to relieve trapped gas), and garlic are good. Cleansing enemas may clear food remnants and relieve pain. Massage of the abdomen each morning may help.

Dizziness/Vertigo

Dizziness is characterized by a sensation of giddiness, unsteadiness, or light-headedness. Vertigo and dizziness are often used interchangeably, but true vertigo is a sensation of spinning or a feeling that the floors are sinking or rising. It is usually accompanied by nausea, vomiting, perspiration, and headache.

Dizziness and vertigo may be caused by infections of or injuries to the inner ear, which normally helps maintain the body's sense of balance. A physical injury such as a concussion or skull fracture may harm the inner ear. In this type of injury, dizziness may occur long after the injury is supposedly healed. Brain tumors, misalignments of the spine, Ménière's disease, anemia, high or low blood pressure, lack of oxygen or glucose in the blood, fears associated with phobias or other psychological stress, and nutritional deficiencies or malnutrition may be other causes of vertigo.

Nutrients may be helpful. A deficiency of vitamin B_6 or niacin may cause dizziness. Including B-complex vitamins in the diet may prevent and alleviate dizziness, and the B vitamins plus salt in hot climates may also help. Herbs that may be helpful are mulberry fruit, dasdrodia tube, wolfberry, and Chinese angelica. Homeopathic remedies are Bryonia 6c, Cyclamen 6c, Theridion 6c, and Gelsemium 6c. Chiropractic may be useful.

Ear Infection/Earache

An ear infection can occur in any of the three sections within the ear. One section, the outer ear, is the visible portion plus the ear canal, a skin-lined tube that ends at a disk known as the eardrum. Another section, the middle ear is composed of three small bones that lie on the inward side of the eardrum. These bones connect with the inner ear, the third section, which changes sound waves into nerve impulses and sends them to the brain.

Infection in the outer ear is usually caused by swimming in contaminated water, water that stays in the ear canal and becomes contaminated, too high humidity, impacted ear wax, contaminated hot tubs, or damage to the wall of the ear canal. Symptoms of the infection are swelling, severe pain, and drainage, possibly accompanied by fever. Prevention is the best policy by using ear plugs or by adding a few drops of mineral oil or rubbing alcohol in each ear before swimming and afterward draining the ear.

Infection in the middle ear is most frequently due to the spread of bacteria from infection in the nose and throat; however, food allergies may play a part. Symptoms include earache, a feeling of fullness in the ear, diminished hearing, and fever. "Airplane ear" is a vacuum in the middle ear that presses the eardrum inward and is caused from too rapid a change in air pressure from the outside. Recommendations are that one not fly with a cold or any disease involving stuffiness that might block normal pressure changes within the ear. Do not use a decongestant before takeoff. One technique for counteracting airplane ear that is sometimes effective is swallowing and yawning to relieve the pressure. However, pinching the nose and gently blowing—a technique used by pilots—seems to be more effective.

Infection in the inner ear usually arises from meningitis, the spread of a middle ear infection, or a broken eardrum. Symptoms include loss of hearing, dizziness, nausea, vomiting, and fever. An eardrum can be broken by a foreign object (such as a Q-tip) if it enters the ear and protrudes through the eardrum. It can also be caused by diving, hearing a loud noise such as a gun shot, or being slapped on the ear. Eardrums usually heal themselves; however, some conditions may need medical help. Severe ear infections may result in permanent scarring and partial or total loss of hearing.

A well-balanced diet adequate in protein is necessary to help the body fight infection and repair damaged tissue. Various nutrients support the healing process. If fever is associated with earache, additional vitamin A and vitamin C will be needed. Breast-fed infants experience fewer earaches than those who are not. A large study conducted at the University of Arizona found that feeding infants solely breast milk for the first four months of life cut the incidence of earaches in half compared with infants who were not breast-fed. Warm olive or garlic oil in the ear may help relieve pain. Herbs that may be helpful are St. John's wort infusion and lobelia tincture with oil.

Homeopathic remedies are Belladonna 6c, Mullein oil, Aconite 6c, Plantago majus tincture, Ferrum phosphoricum, and Chamomilla 6c. Warmth to the ear is soothing.

Eating Disorders

A normal desire to look good is healthy; however, for some people this natural desire becomes distorted and results in abnormal eating habits in an effort to lose weight. Women in particular fall victim to this compulsion. Ninety percent of those with eating disorders are women between the ages of twelve and twenty-five. Stated another way, among young women in the United States 1 percent to 4 percent suffer from anorexia nervosa and 1 percent to 3 percent of this group are bulimic. Anorexia and bulimia exist because the sufferer has a fear of being fat. Research has isolated the family background as one of the major causes of this phenomenon, along with a certain personality type that is inherited. A childhood environment that includes alcoholism, strong parental or sibling opinions, depression, sexual abuse, divorce, or constant challenges contributes toward this condition. Outward appearance for acceptance and love becomes a necessity, leaving little time or energy for inner growth and development of true self-esteem.

To contribute to the problem, women have been exposed to ultraslim images for the last few decades. However, it has been recently reported that the number of men who are becoming anorexic and bulimic is rising as well. This is due in part to the new fitness and bodybuilding images found in advertisements and magazines and in gyms.

- **Anorexia** is thought to be the most dangerous of the eating disorders, because 10 percent of these individuals die an early death. Wasting of the muscles as protein is being used for energy, dangerously low blood pressure, dehydration from laxative use, weak resistance to infection from lowered immunity, heart attacks and heart damage from potassium deficiencies, digestive tract immobility, and degeneration are some life-threatening side effects of the disease. Missed periods (17 percent to 22 percent of body fat must be maintained for normal periods, although in severe cases menstruation may be lost forever), loss of sexual function (including sterility in men and women), anemia, increased body hair, dry skin, coldness, abnormal electric brain activity, disturbed sleep patterns and bad dreams, and depression resulting from nutrient deficiencies are all consequences. Anorexia needs professional help. Since the anorexic is unlikely to respond to the physical need for nutrition by eating and does not see that there is a problem, both medical and psychological aspects of the person should be considered. A twelve-step approach is being used as well as other programs in which treatment involves love and understanding in combination with psychological, medical, nutritional, and other helpful therapies. Consult a qualified physician.

- **Bulimia.** Bulimics will binge and then throw up, or purge, the eaten food in order to keep calories from becoming incorporated into their systems, which they fear will make them fat. Bulimia and anorexia are both used to maintain thinness. Bulimia is different from anorexia in that it is more common and there is more control over how much food is consumed. Some bulimics are aware that what is happening is not right and that there is a need to eat to remain alive. For others, the problem is much more severe. Similar to the anorexic, there is a feeling that thin is never thin enough and the condition will be pushed to the limit. Near-anorexic conditions are very possible, and the same consequences mentioned for anorexics apply to the severely suffering bulimic as well. With bulimia, constant vomiting can cause instant weakness because of an electrolyte imbalance that also causes kidney damage. Chronic tiredness and dehydration are common, and esophageal and throat scarring may occur. Drugs that induce vomiting can cause heart failure, and stomach acid erodes tooth enamel. Bulimics, similar to anorexics, will use laxatives to hurry food through the digestive tract so as few calories as possible are absorbed. Some 90 percent of bulimics are clinically depressed, with drug and alcohol abuse being involved. Depression that often involves suicidal thoughts is a major problem for both disorders. Treatment for bulimia may also call for hospitalization, especially if depression is involved and where both physical and psychological help that combine therapies are available. There are also many support groups that may be of benefit, but just telling someone who is understanding may help. College groups and peer counseling for those who are in school are also good ideas. Nutritional counseling adapted to each individual's need is very helpful and motivating.

Diet for those suffering from severe conditions includes one that introduces foods carefully and gradually back into the system. Brewer's yeast is good. Foods that help increase appetite are radish seeds, wheat sprouts, loganberries, and rice as well as foods that supply zinc. (See Section 5 for additional sources of zinc.) A well-balanced, high-fiber diet that is low in sugar and white- and refined-flour products, along with a good multivitamin supplement, may be helpful. Tube feedings that contain nutrients may be necessary under some circumstances. High doses of PABA may cause anorexia. Herbs that may be helpful for the appetite are gotu kola, gingerroot, peppermint, and ginseng.

Eczema

Eczema is a skin condition characterized by inflammatory itching and the formation of scales. (See "Dermatitis.") Sometimes eczema is related to an allergic reaction. Vitamins A and C together with the B-complex vitamins are helpful in preventing and healing eczema. Homeopathic remedies for the scalp are Natrum muriaticim, sulfur, and Calcarea carbonica. For skin eruptions, Natrum sulphuricum, Arsenicum, and petroleum are used. Graphites are used for weeping lesions. Aromatherapy includes Roman chamomile, cedarwood, geranium, lavender, and tea tree.

Edema (Fluid Retention)

Edema, referred to as dropsy in the past, is a condition in which excess fluid is retained by the body, either localized in one area or generalized throughout the body. This retention of fluids appears as swelling, which is most often seen in the hands, in the feet, or around the eyes. But the swelling may be located in any area of the body. This puffiness may be a symptom of high blood pressure or preeclampsia.

Disorders that can cause edema include poor kidney function, poor bladder function, congestive heart failure, liver problems, protein or thiamin deficiency, varicose veins, phlebitis, PMS, and sodium retention. Other factors that may cause edema are flying (since movement on an airplane is restricted and a person may be required to stay in a seated position for several hours), standing for long periods of time, pregnancy, the use of oral contraceptives, injury to an area of the body (such as a sprain), and allergic reactions (such as to insect bites). Edema is often indicative of adrenal exhaustion, which affects hormone production.

Diet should include as many raw foods as possible to eliminate the salt in cooking processes as well as to ensure a high fiber intake. Broiled fish and poultry and low-salt dairy products are good protein sources. Sodium, as found in table salt as well as in many other processed products, is often restricted in diets of individuals who are prone to edema because excess amounts cause the body to retain water. Soy sauce, pickled products, gravies, and alcohol also should be limited for this reason. Caffeine, tobacco, chocolate, and refined sugar and flour are not beneficial for the edemic person.

Nutrients such as vitamin B$_6$ reduce fluid retention, and vitamin D increases salt excretion. Sufficient sources of pantothenic acid and calcium also encourage salt excretion, whereas a high-carbohydrate diet retains salt and water in the tissues. L-carnitine at 2,000 milligrams daily may reduce the bloating associated with PMS. If edema is the result of protein or thiamin deficiency, correction of the deficiency is essential. Taking certain medications for fluid retention leads to the loss of potassium via the urine and is one reason to include foods high in this mineral in meals each day. (See Section 5 for additional sources of potassium.)

Herbs that may be beneficial are corn silk, juniper berries (mild), mua huang, astragalus, kava kava (mild), horsetail (mild), blessed thistle (mild), burdock (mild), alfalfa, dandelion root (mild), butcher's boom (mild), buchu (mild), pau d'arco tea, uva ursi (mild but not to be used by those who are pregnant or by children), and lobelia. Garlic, kelp, and parsley (mild) are also helpful.

Licorice will cause swelling of the ankles, which can be dangerous for those with diabetes or high blood pressure, stroke-vulnerable people, pregnant and nursing women, and those with glaucoma. Exercising regularly is very important in edema. Individuals who are prone to edema should try to promote good circulation by elevating the legs while at rest, avoiding restrictive clothing, and refraining from crossing the legs.

Emphysema

Emphysema is characterized by abnormal swelling and destruction of the tiny air sacs of the lungs. These sacs become thin and stretch, thus losing their elasticity. Exhaling is extremely difficult, resulting in an accumulation of used air in the lungs that leads to a decreased ability to utilize fresh air. Therefore, the body is robbed of the precious exchange of oxygen and carbon dioxide that it must have to survive.

Smoking is responsible in the majority of emphysema cases. Other factors that may contribute to or cause the onset of this disease include exposure to air pollution from cars and factories, various dusts, bronchitis, asthma, and other respiratory diseases. For some individuals, a deficiency of protein in the blood is the cause. Symptoms of emphysema include wheezing, shortness of breath and difficulty in breathing, and coughing, often accompanied by mucus. Weight loss occurs as the condition progresses, and the victim may develop a characteristic "barrel chest."

Research has developed a laser form of treatment that destroys the cysts that form in the lungs and rob the person of the life-giving oxygen. Another treatment involves drugs that arrest the disease at whatever level it has reached, and future treatments may keep the disease from forming at all.

Nutrients may be helpful. Vitamins A and C provide some protection against emphysema by helping to maintain healthy tissues in the respiratory passage. The vitamin B complex and protein are necessary to strengthen the deteriorating tissue. Since the emphysema victim suffers from a lack of oxygen, many authorities suggest that vitamin E may be beneficial. Vitamin E also acts as an antioxidant, preventing the oxidation of vitamin A and the unsaturated fatty acids. Selenium is known to be useful for prevention and for all aspects of optimal health. Potassium may be needed to replace what has been lost by the use of diuretic medications. It has been reported that a copper deficiency can produce emphysema in animals and is thought to be a free-radical fighter, helping prevent lung damage in those who are chronically exposed to cigarette smoke or air pollution.

Even though eating may be difficult, diet is very important to maintain strength. Foods consumed should aid in the clearing of mucus from the body. Chicken soup is good for emphysema because the chicken contains cysteine, which thins mucus and is useful for all respiratory problems. Tabasco sauce, chili peppers, and garlic in foods are recommended at least three times a week. All antioxidant foods (dark green and orange vegetables) are recommended.

Olive oil may aid in the removal of toxic waste from the gallbladder and large intestine. Onion is good and raw foods are also beneficial. Tobacco and foods that encourage the formation of mucus, such as dairy products, meat, eggs, and processed foods, should be avoided. Salt should be used sparingly. Gas-forming foods particular to each person should be avoided.

Herbs and other natural ingredients that may be helpful are coltsfoot, fresh horseradish, rosemary, ginkgo (increases oxygen), comfrey with fenugreek, mullein tea, and thyme. Exercising moderately and working out will strengthen the heart and breathing muscles. Walking and calisthenics are good, but always consult a physician for a safe regimen.

Endometriosis

Endometriosis is a condition in which cells from the uterus break away and implant themselves in various places within the pelvis such as the ovaries, ligaments of the uterus, cervix, appendix, bladder, and bowel. Endometria are also found in some cases as far away from the pelvis as the armpit and the lungs. Similar to the regular lining of the uterus, these implants of uterine tissue respond to normal hormonal changes and can begin to feel painful in the two weeks leading up to menstruation. They also can cause bleeding when menstruation begins. But in this case, blood accumulates not in the uterus where blood can exit the body through the vaginal opening, but rather in tissues where the blood becomes trapped. Pools of blood form, resulting in inflammation, scar tissue, or cysts, harming organs and tissues. The severity of this condition at times can completely overtake the ovaries, fallopian tubes, and other areas of the pelvis.

It is estimated that 5.5 million American women have endometriosis. The ages that are most affected are between twenty and forty-five. However, some cases have been found in teenagers, and there may be recurrences in postmenopausal women. The two most common symptoms of endometriosis are pain and infertility. Menstrual cramps progressively worsen, causing abdominal and lower back pain. Patients also suffer from chronic pelvic pain, constipation or painful bowel movements, and pain during intercourse. Some 60 percent to 70 percent of patients experience considerable pain and have their lives altered because of it. In addition, 30 percent to 40 percent of women with endometriosis become infertile, making endometriosis one of the top three causes of infertility. Other symptoms include frequent urination, blood in the urine during menstruation, rectal bleeding, premenstrual spotting, and excessive flow during the

period. Some cysts are full of blood and can leak, causing pain.

Besides medical treatment, which gives supplemental hormones and drugs to lower estrogen levels and consequently diminishes pain, diet may be able to accomplish the same objective with no side effects. A high-fiber, vegetarian-based diet is the best that has been found. The elimination of fats from animal sources such as meat and dairy products has been found to be most beneficial. Avoid caffeine, salt, sugar, and high-fat dairy products. Yogurt is good. Antioxidant foods such as sweet potatoes, apricots, cantaloupes, carrot juice, spinach, broccoli, and kale are good sources. Whole grains, beans, peas, and liver are sources of the B vitamins. Citrus fruits have both the bioflavonoids and vitamin C, which work well together. Grain and seed oils such as soybean are sources of vitamin E. Fatty fish contain natural prostaglandins, which help to reduce cramps.

Nutrients also may be beneficial. Beta-carotene, vitamin C (also works against stress and helps curb the spread of the disease; 1,000 to 4,000 milligrams daily is advised), and bioflavonoids (regulate estrogen levels in menopausal women and are a companion to vitamin C) aid in excessive bleeding. The B complex (50 to 150 milligrams per day) helps the liver keep estrogen levels down. Vitamins B_1, B_2, and B_3 along with the entire complex works for those with other high-estrogen-level complications such as fibrocystic breast disease, PMS, and heavy menstrual flow; B_6 (up to 300 milligrams daily) relaxes the uterus and should also be supplemented. Calcium and magnesium help reduce cramps.

Vitamin E aids in endometriosis and other estrogen-related problems. It is generally recommended to increase dosage slowly starting with 400 IU per day. Essential fatty acids work as muscle and blood vessel relaxants that can reduce cramps. Magnesium, zinc, niacin, and vitamins C and B_6 must all be present to transform the fatty acids into the necessary components to accomplish this task. Other factors that could interfere with the conversion of fatty acids are alcohol, too much cholesterol, diabetes, eczema, allergies, and stress.

Herbs that may be helpful are white willow bark (which contains the chemical precursor of aspirin), meadow sweet (for cramps), fennel, false unicorn root, raspberry leaves, licorice, blessed thistle, black cohosh, dong quai, Siberian ginseng, and anise. Homeopathic remedies are Silica, Mag. Phos., and Kali. Phos. Moderate exercise is recommended.

Environmental Pollution

Our bodies are being continually exposed to pollutants in the food we eat, the water we drink, and the air we breathe. The human system has evolved metabolic processes that can effectively assimilate toxins that are ingested periodically. However, when chronic or continual exposure occurs or when new substances are encountered that the system cannot detoxify, adverse reactions can manifest. Chronic effects are muted, often invisible, and not immediately experienced. They can result in cancer that may be latent for ten to thirty years; metabolic and genetic changes that affect growth, health, behavior, and resistance to disease; and birth defects or premature births from a delayed response to built-up toxins.

- **Lead** is found in the air, in dust particles, and in drinking water from lead water pipes. Lead suppresses the body's immune system and interferes with the actions of the free-radical scavengers. Vitamin C removes lead from bone and the brain. Experiments have shown that susceptibility to lead accumulation in the body correlates with the nutritional status of the individual. In animals, lead absorption is greatly diminished when dietary calcium is adequate.
- **Polynuclear aromatic hydrocarbons (PAH)** are carcinogenic compounds that are formed from the burning of organic substances such as wood, coal, oil, and tobacco. The antioxidants—vitamins B_1, C, and E; calcium; pantothenic acid; L-cysteine (an amino acid); selenium; and zinc—protect the body from damage by these hydrocarbons.
- **Radioactive metals**, released from coal-burning power plants as fly ash, concentrate in the bones and remain for life. These concentrated substances create free radicals in the body that may be inactivated with the antioxidant vitamins A, C, and E and the antioxidant enzyme SOD. Strontium 90 is a product of nuclear reactions that chemically resembles calcium and can replace the mineral in the body if sufficient calcium is not present. Strontium 90 also inhibits certain actions of vitamin D.
- The lungs are damaged by **cigarette smoke**, which prevents the cilia (hairlike projections in the lungs) from expelling pollutants. Smoke adversely affects the immune system. The nonsmoker who breathes in the smoke is an involuntary victim of this pollutant. Carbon monoxide is a component of cigarette smoke as well as of the air in traffic areas. This chemical inhibits the oxygen-carrying capacity of the blood to the brain. Symptoms are headache, dizziness, irritability, nausea, and decreased mental alertness; loss of consciousness and death result from excessive doses. The pollutant has the same density as air and, therefore, stays at the surface level of city streets. Heavy exercising near city streets and eating at sidewalk restaurants can subject an individual to added levels. Vitamins A, C, and E; selenium; and zinc may help protect against the harmful effects.
- **Chlorine**, used as a water disinfectant, is an oxidizing agent and destroys vitamins C and E. Hexavalent chromium, an air, water, and cigarette smoke pollutant, produces gastrointestinal hemorrhage and possibly cancer. Vitamin C is able to convert this toxic form of chromium into the innocuous form, trivalent chromium. Copper is found in drinking water as a result of industrial waste leachate and corroded plumbing. It is also sometimes added to the water supply for algae control. Excessive copper causes irritation of the gastrointestinal tract and mental disorders; zinc function is impaired; and molybdenum, manganese, and magnesium are depleted. Vitamin C aids in the stabilization of the trace metals.
- **Nitrates** and **nitrites**, used to prevent bacterial growth in meat, can combine with amines, forming carcinogenic nitrosamines. Vitamin C in adequate doses can prevent this transformation. Selenium and vitamin C effectively protect against mercury poisoning.
- Protection from **ozone**, an oxidizing chemical found in city air and green countrysides, can be obtained from vitamin A, vitamin E, and PABA. A high-protein diet, including vitamin E and the sulfur-containing amino acids such as cysteine, can effectively reduce the toxicity of carbon monoxide. Cadmium, found in refined foods, coffee, tea, artists' oil paints, cigarette smoke, and the air (as a result of automobile exhaust), can cause hypertension and heart disease. The metal depletes the body of zinc and iron.

Epilepsy

Epilepsy is a disease characterized by seizures that are caused by electrical impulses that build up and suddenly discharge, leaving the surrounding cells overwhelmed. There are many kinds of seizures that range from a jerk of an arm or a sudden daydream-like moment to a full convulsion. Both males and females are at equal risk for this disease. Children have mild seizures; adults are more prone to have the larger ones. An individual may experience only one seizure in a lifetime or several seizures per day. Factors that may precipitate a seizure are fatigue, overeating or overdrinking, emotional tension or excitement, fever, new environmental stresses, illness, or menstruation.

There are two forms of seizures. One form, referred to as *petit mal*, is a sensory seizure involving only a change in sensation or a minor loss of consciousness as in a daydream. The other form, known as *grand mal*, is a severe convulsive seizure (convulsion) characterized by abnormal muscular behavior.

The cause of epileptic seizures is sometimes unknown, but two of the most common circumstances are head injuries and an abnormality in the development of the fetus. Another reason is an electrical disturbance in the nerve cells in one section of the brain that may be the result of infection, rabies, tetanus, meningitis, rickets, lack of oxygen, lead and aluminum poisoning, malnutrition, hypoglycemia or low blood sugar, stroke, arteriosclerosis, and fever. Aspartame, found in sugar substitutes and in many diet food products, has also been associated with seizures.

Treatment options for epilepsy include antiepileptic drugs, epilepsy surgery, and the vagal nerve stimulator as well as diet and exercise. The epileptic should maintain a well-balanced whole food diet, including leafy green vegetables, carrots, beets and their tops, beans, and peas. Taking in excessive amounts of food or fluid at one time should be avoided; small meals throughout the day are best. Alcoholic beverages should also be avoided because they can increase the number and severity of seizures. Yogurt, vegetable juices, eggs, raw nuts and seeds, soybeans, red grapes, and raw milk and cheese are good food choices. Peanuts and tea have been shown to trigger attacks. Caffeine and nicotine are to be avoided.

Children with migraine headaches and epilepsy (not just epilepsy alone) have been helped when they avoided foods they were allergic to. The foods that were the most responsible were cow's cheese and milk, eggs, pork, chocolate, tomatoes, corn, citrus fruit, and wheat. Vitamin E helps control seizures in children. In addition, a special diet for treating epilepsy in children has been developed. The ketogenic diet is high in fat and low in carbohydrate and protein, designed to increase the body's use of fat in the form of ketones (the breakdown products of fat), rather than glucose for energy. This way of eating metabolically mimics

the fasting state that has been noted to reduce seizures. The ketogenic diet gained attention in recent years because antiepileptic drugs are not effective in preventing seizures in 20 percent to 30 percent of children. This highly specialized diet must be initiated under the supervision of a team of health professionals experienced with the diet, because the diet must be customized to the patient, it is deficient in some nutrients, and there are side effects.

Nutrients may be beneficial as research has demonstrated a link between manganese deficiency and convulsions in humans. Pregnant women with a deficiency of manganese may give birth to epileptic children and should receive prenatal care that includes a vitamin and mineral supplement. Pregnant rats maintained on a low-manganese diet delivered young with poorly coordinated movements and a susceptibility to convulsions. Magnesium, zinc, and calcium all have anticonvulsive properties. Taking 450 milligrams daily of magnesium successfully controlled attacks. Zinc and calcium levels in multivitamin supplements are sufficient. Taurine, an amino acid, has been shown to help control seizures (50 to 100 milligrams per day). Vitamin E may help control seizures in adults; studies are continuing.

Excellent results have been obtained by administering vitamin B_6. If there are no results from this vitamin, its poor absorption may be the reason. When large doses of B_6 are given alone, the other B vitamins should accompany it, especially vitamins B_2 and pantothenic acid so that there is no further damage. A lack of vitamins D and B_6 is closely associated with convulsions, which may often be prevented by an adequate supply of these nutrients in the diet. If the proper nutrients are given, anticonvulsant drugs can often be discontinued.

Herbs that may be helpful are valerian, lobelia, black cohosh, and hyssop. Evening primrose oil aggravates temporal lobe epilepsy. Regular exercise when physical conditions are stable is highly recommended, with the gentle kind being the most desirable. Consult a physician before beginning any form of exercise program. Adequate rest should be encouraged.

Eye Disorders

Many eye defects or abnormalities can be traced to faulty nutrition, and many more could be prevented. Eye problems are often the first indicators of unhealthy conditions in other parts of the body, for example, allergies (eyes watery and itchy), colds, sleeplessness (dark circles under the eyes), liver disease (yellow color of the white areas), gallstone blockage, high blood pressure and diabetes (blurred vision), myasthenia gravis (droopy eyes), and pupils that are different sizes (a tumor in another part of the body).

The good health of the mother during pregnancy is essential for healthy eye development in the fetus. Factors that may cause eye problems are tooth infections (because of common nerves and blood vessels) and oral contraceptives. One of the side effects of the pill is the possible formation of blood clots that form most often in small blood vessels such as those found in the eye.

Deficiencies of vitamins may cause eye problems. Even a slight deficiency of vitamin A can cause easy tiring of the eyes, sensitivity to light variations, dry eyelids, susceptibility to eye infections, and possible ulcerations and irreversible blindness. An insufficiency of B-complex vitamins results in paralyzed eye muscles, itching, burning, light sensitivity, bloodshot eyes, and watering eyes. Protruding or bulging eyes may be a sign of thyroid problems or vitamin E deficiency. A thiamin deficiency can cause paralysis of the muscles in the eye. A deficiency of zinc may be responsible for macular degeneration, a disease that strikes the elderly and can lead to blindness.

- **Amblyopia** is a dimness of sight. Vitamin B is used to correct it.
- **Bitot's spots** are characterized by white, elevated, and sharply outlined patches, or spots, on the whites of the eyes, caused by a deficiency of vitamin A and protein.
- **Cataracts** may be helped with the use of aspirin for both treatment and prevention. Although not proved, vitamin B_6 may protect the lens of the eye from clouding up. Vitamin C is thought to do the same. Hyaluronic acid may be injected into the eye to protect against corneal loss during surgery.
- **Conjunctivitis**, an inflammation of the eyelid, may be helped with the use of eyebright tincture, and barberry and herbal therapy.
- **Corneal ulcers** can result in scar tissue, causing permanent damage if not properly treated. They may be healed by vitamins B_2, B_6, and C; pantothenic acid; and protein.
- **Eyestrain** occurs when the eyes have been abused by using them excessively in improper light. Too little light, glaring light and reflections, shadows on work areas, and flickering light such as that from some fluorescent tubes cause the eyes to make numerous unnecessary adjustments that may lead to eyestrain. Eyestrain may also be a result of uncorrected eyesight; eyes should be checked regularly by an eye specialist for any adjustments that should be made. Frequent relaxation of the eyes, especially by changing the range of focus by looking up and away from your work toward a distant object, may alleviate strain caused by improper light and headaches caused by nervous tension. Adequate intake of the vitamins necessary for eye health is helpful. An herbal remedy is the capsule form of eyebright taken orally, or the leaf form as a tea.

- **Farsightedness**, or **hyperopia**, is characterized by being able to see far away but not clearly up close. If proper eyewear is not used, itchy, red, and tired eyes result.
- **Glaucoma tension** and hardening of the eyeball with progressive loss of sight may be helped with vitamin C. (See "Glaucoma/Age-Related Macular Degeneration.")
- **Nearsightedness** often results from stress. Tension can appear when there is an undersupply or poor absorption of calcium. Adolescents are particularly susceptible to this eye disorder because of the stress of growth, allergies, and often an inadequate diet. Symptoms of nearsightedness are eyestrain, squinting, dizziness, fatigue, headaches, and possibly low blood pressure. The disorder may be prevented or alleviated with vitamins B_2, C, D, and E as well as pantothenic acid, calcium, protein, and the unsaturated fatty acids.
- **Night blindness** is the inability to see well in dim or dark light. The major cause of night blindness is deficiency of vitamin A. Vitamin A is necessary for the formation of visual purple, the substance in the eyes that enables them to adjust from bright light to darkness. Other causes of night blindness are fatigue, emotional disturbances, or hereditary factors. Adequate intake of vitamin A will protect against night blindness. Riboflavin, niacin, thiamin, and zinc have been reported to relieve night blindness when vitamin A has not produced a response, and attention, therefore, should be paid to ensure their adequate intake. Retinitis pigmentosa is a gradual degeneration of the retina resulting in blindness. The early stages are characterized by night blindness and other vitamin-A-deficient disorders. It appears that people with this disorder absorb vitamin A very poorly. Improvement has been accomplished by vitamin A injections and by

water-based vitamin A, unsaturated fatty acids, bile tablets, lecithin, and vitamin E, all taken daily.

- **Photophobia** is a condition in which the eyes are extra sensitive to light. People with green eyes are unusually vulnerable to photophobia.
- **Xerophthalmia** is a disease that is characterized by dryness from an inflammation of the covering of the eye.

Nutrients may be beneficial. Vitamins A, B complex, C, and E as well as protein are especially important for good eye health. Vitamin B_2, specifically, has corrected eye symptoms such as color disturbance, inability to see part of an image or printed page, halos around lights or objects, and spots floating in front of the eyes. Vitamin C and rutin are necessary to prevent or clear up infections. They also help prevent capillary fragility and tissue hemorrhaging; in addition, vitamins B_2 and E and niacin may be beneficial for retinal hemorrhage. The B complex may prevent the thinning of eyelashes.

Studies have shown that vitamin E can improve eyesight. Supplements of vitamin E have resulted in decreased severity and duration in the acute stage of retrolental fibroplasia. In combination with vitamin A or C, vitamin E may relieve cases of abnormal eye movement and of eye conditions that do not respond to any single vitamin. Arteriosclerosis of the eye has been reversed with the use of vitamins C and E. A deficiency of vitamin E is possibly a factor in detached retina. Use of vitamin E has also relieved weak eye muscles, crossed eyes, blurred vision, and double vision; taking the B complex may also be helpful. Visual acuity improved when folic acid was given to elderly diabetic and peripheral vascular disease patients. A childhood cancer called retinoblastoma may be helped with vitamin B_2. Sufficient protein, essential for the health of the lens, is necessary for healing and preventing infections, retinitis, and myopia.

Diet is especially important for pregnant women for the development of the fetus. Antioxidant foods should be taken regularly. A combination of sugar, caffeine, and nicotine can temporarily alter sight. Sufficient protein, essential for the health of the lens, is necessary for healing and preventing infections, retinitis, and myopia.

Herbs and other natural substances that may be helpful for eye problems are goldenseal (not to be taken in large amounts when pregnant), bayberry bark, cayenne, and red raspberry leaves. Eyebright as an eye rinse is not recommended since it may irritate and cause swelling. A bioflavonoid-like substance called sodium cromoglycate, sold under the name of Opticrom, is used for allergic eye problems. This substance is a derivative of an herb that has been used in Egyptian medicine for centuries. Homeopathic remedies are Graphites, Pulsatilla, and Mercurius for inflamed eyelids, and Ruta graveolens and Arnica montana for eyestrain. Styes are treated with Pulsatilla, sulfur, and Sulphuris calcareum.

Fatigue and Chronic Fatigue Syndrome (CFS)

Fatigue as well as chronic fatigue, which is caused by the Epstein-Barr virus, is a feeling of physical and mental weariness that may be brought on by a variety of conditions, such as digestive problems, *Candida albicans*, anemia, physical exertion, nutrient deficiencies, poor nutrition (the number 1 cause), sleep disorders, weight loss, obesity or overweight, boredom and depression, allergies, food allergies (possibly wheat, rye, oats, and milk), smoking, alcohol, drugs, stress or emotional tension, or almost any disease process.

In general, obesity contributes to fatigue in that more energy is needed to maintain that weight. In addition, those who are overweight may be eating the wrong foods and lack the nutrients necessary to convert food to energy. For those with CFS, weight loss lessens the symptoms. However, for the slim person, consuming fewer than 1,000 to 1,200 calories per day may cause fatigue.

In addition to a feeling of weariness, symptoms of fatigue include headache, backache, irritability, and indigestion. A thorough physical checkup by a qualified physician to determine the cause of fatigue is essential before any treatment is attempted. CFS is a type of fatigue that does not respond to normal methods of treatment and takes time to diagnose, has flulike symptoms that include joint achiness, headache, sore throat, exhaustion, burning eyes, fever, chills, and muscle pain. Eventually, confusion and short-term memory loss become noticeable. In this kind of fatigue, any physical activity will drain the individual of needed energy stores and is not recommended. Extensive testing is required to isolate this illness.

There are many different kinds of tiredness and just as many different causes. (See "Mononucleosis.") Most people do not know the reason for their tiredness, and those who do may not wish to make the changes necessary to help remedy their situation. In either case, when one is tired of being sick and tired, there is help. Lifestyle changes that include diet, exercise, and nutrition are all important. Handling stress is also of great importance.

A mild deficiency of magnesium can result in fatigue. A diet insufficient in potassium causes muscular weakness, irritability, and a tired feeling. Deficiencies of the vitamin B complex (especially thiamin), vitamins C and D, and iron may cause fatigue. Overdosing on vitamins and minerals is also linked to fatigue, so consulting a physician is necessary to establish proper levels for each individual. Vitamin and mineral needs vary from age to age and from one gender to the other.

A well-balanced diet can prevent, relieve, or lessen the symptoms of fatigue, while a nutritionally impoverished diet promotes fatigue. The carbohydrate portion of the diet should be made up of whole grains, legumes, and vegetables that are starchy—foods that promote longer-lasting energy rather than a quick burst that is soon over. If quick energy is needed, fruit is ideal. The sugar in fruit, fructose, is a ready source of energy but has a more gentle effect on blood sugar than glucose, the energy source in cookies and colas. And unlike sweets with their empty calories, fruit provides a range of beneficial vitamins, minerals, and phytonutrients.

Not only is protein needed to convert food into energy, but the body can also use protein to produce energy when other sources are not available. Lean meats, more white fish, some eggs, cheeses that are low or void in fat, and combinations of various grains (check for allergies) and legumes are good sources of protein. (In some cases of chronic fatigue and immune deficiency syndrome [CFIDS] and allergies, dairy products can be detrimental.)

The body must have some fat to function, and fat makes the stomach feel full longer. However, too much for the person who is fatigued can be tiring. Napping or a desire to nap may be common in those whose diets contain high levels of fat. Between 20 percent and 30 percent (45 to 50 grams) of daily calories should come from fat, with saturated types amounting to no more than 10 percent. The body tends to use fat for reserve energy; therefore, fat should be consumed less because this storage form is what adds weight to the body.

Nutrients and other natural ingredients are important. High doses of vitamins C and B_{12} have been given with encouraging results. Thiamin, riboflavin,

B_6, biotin, niacin, vitamin E, and folate are helpful. Benefits may also be provided by iron, iodine, magnesium, brewer's yeast, AL 721, the memory enhancer aniracetam, the mineral germanium, isoprinosine, and L-aspartic acid (no more than 1.5 grams daily).

Exercise is thought to be the most important aspect of curing fatigue because it boosts vitality, and the endorphins released during physical exertion rid the mind of depression that may be associated with fatigue. Except for those who have been diagnosed with CFS, whatever the reason for the fatigue that an individual is experiencing, physical exertion sets into motion the changes that will eventually overtake fatigue. Exercise that promotes weight loss for those who need it is essential, since energy levels are lower for overweight people.

Herbs that may be helpful are schizandra, ginkgo biloba extract, damiana, gotu kola, cayenne, Siberian ginseng, guarana, black cohosh, and acacia.

Fever

Fever is the elevation of body temperature above normal. Normal temperature varies from individual to individual, although normal is generally considered to be within the range of 97° to 99°F. When the body temperature is raised not more than 5 degrees, the rise does not completely interfere with bodily functions. However, when fever reaches 106°F, convulsions are common, and if fever should reach 108°F, irreversible brain damage frequently results. Fever is thought by some to be a sign of healing as opposed to a symptom of a coming disease. A restorative effect noticed after a fever may be proof of this theory.

Fever accompanies a wide variety of diseases ranging from mild to severe and can be considered a warning that something is wrong within the body. Symptoms associated with fever include flushed face, headache, nausea, body aches, little or no appetite, and occasionally diarrhea or vomiting. The skin may be either hot and dry or warm to the touch with some degree of perspiring. Perspiration is the natural result of the body's attempt to lower its temperature. Cool cloths or a cool bath in emergency situations to lower the body temperature is recommended.

Diet should be restricted until the fever drops. Since fever has depleted the body's energy stores, caloric needs are high and intake should be adjusted accordingly. Additional protein is also needed to replace and rebuild the damaged and used-up body tissue and to form new antibodies—substances manufactured by the body to fight infection. A high fluid intake is necessary to compensate for the loss that occurs with fever. Sodium and potassium are lost when fluid is lost; therefore, their replacement is also necessary when fever occurs. Lemon and honey in water is a good replacement.

Nutrients may be helpful. The increased energy expenditure that occurs during fever increases metabolism. Because vitamin A, the B complex, and vitamin C are involved in the process of metabolism, deficiencies of these nutrients may arise also. The vitamin B complex especially should be increased during an extended fever, since these vitamins may stimulate the appetite. Additional calcium may also be required because of its decreased absorption during fever. Iron should *not* be taken during a fever, since the body's defense mechanisms have pulled all the reserves out and more would only add strain to the body. Zinc is not absorbed during a fever.

Herbs that may be beneficial are dandelion tea, licorice root, bayberry root bark, black cohosh, lobelia extract, blackthorn, ginger, fenugreek seed, hyssop, blessed thistle, devil's claw, fo-ti, quinine, poke root, cat mint infusion, echinacea root, yarrow tea, thyme, and seaweed. Catnip enemas are good. Homeopathy includes Belladonna 6c, Arsenicum album 6c, and Aconite 6c.

Flatulence (Intestinal Gas)

Flatulence is the most common digestive disturbance. Most people have some gas; however, if the gas begins to cause discomfort, it may be an indication of a more complex problem.

Two causes of flatulence are swallowed air and gases liberated by fermentation or bacteria that are living on undigested food. Both often occur simultaneously. Excessive swallowing of air can occur while eating or drinking, eating too fast, or eating when anxious or upset. The air passes into the stomach and becomes trapped in the intestines, where it expands and stretches nerve endings, causing discomfort. Eating too much food overwhelms the digestive enzymes. The undigested food becomes a breeding ground for putrefactive bacteria, which form gas. Efficient digestion depends upon hydrochloric acid, bile, and other digestive secretions and enzymes.

Other causes of flatulence are milk products because some people lack the enzyme needed to break down lactase, a milk sugar. For many people, beans cause flatulence due to a lack of the enzyme needed to digest certain sugars in these foods. Fortunately, a product that supplies the missing enzyme is sold in tablet and liquid form in most natural food stores, so these nutritious legumes can be enjoyed in meals without worry. Certain vegetables and fruits such as cucumbers, cabbage, apples, and whole grains may also be a problem for some people. The high fiber in these foods remains undigested, fermenting in the intestine. Fried foods and the concentrated sugars of dried fruits can cause gas. (The sugars can be diluted by boiling or soaking the dried fruits.) Combining in one meal foods that digest quickly, such as a melon, with foods that break down slowly, such as meat, can result in flatulence. If no reason can be found for digestive disturbances, psychological problems may be the factor.

Nutrients may be helpful. Pantothenic acid has been shown to relieve intestinal gas and distension when there is no physical cause. Gas pains were relieved in postoperative patients and prevented in others when they were given 250 milligrams of pantothenic acid daily. Pantothenic acid aids in bowel motility and efficient digestion. Without pantothenic acid, acetylcholine cannot be produced. This chemical transmits messages to nerves that control the motor and secretory activities of the intestine. Charcoal tablets are relief for gas.

Fermented foods such as yogurt and buttermilk aid in the digestion of high-fiber and other foods by increasing friendly bacteria in the colon. They are also well tolerated by people who have a lactase deficiency. Other foods that may be helpful are lemon juice and cider vinegar. Soy sauce, cheese, and alcohol should be avoided. Carbonated drinks only add more air. To counter the effects of some foods, there are natural products on the market that neutralize flatulence.

Carminative herbs stimulate digestion by increasing gastric juices, decreasing the amount of putrefactive bacteria, and stimulating intestinal motility. These include garlic, magnolia bark, sweet flag infusion, anise, fennel, ginger infusion, orange or lemon peel, and caraway. In traditional cuisines found in various countries, certain classic dishes include herbs considered to reduce gas. For instance in Mexican cooking, beans are cooked with the native herb epazote. Homeopathic remedies are Argentum nitricum 6c, Lycopodium 6c, and Arsenicum album 6c. Exercise stimulates intestinal peristalsis and helps break down large gas bubbles.

Flu (Influenza)

Flu can refer to two different conditions. The first is stomach flu, or gastroenteritis, which is the inflammation of the lining of the stomach. This inflammation has a variety of causes, such as food poisoning, certain viruses, alcohol intoxication, sensitivity to drugs, and allergies. The second type of flu is influenza, which is an acute viral infection of the respiratory tract. It is highly contagious and easily spread by sneezing and coughing.

Symptoms of gastroenteritis include diarrhea, vomiting, possible fever, chills, and abdominal cramps that vary in severity, but recovery is usually within one or two days. Treatment for stomach flu includes bed rest and abstention from food until the stomach settles. A regular well-balanced diet should then be introduced. Repeated vomiting and diarrhea can cause potassium and fluid loss, which should be corrected as soon as possible. If fever is present, intake of vitamins A and C should be increased.

Symptoms of influenza include sudden chills, high fever, sore throat, headache, abdominal pain, hoarseness, cough, enlarged lymph nodes, aching of the back and limbs, and frequent vomiting and diarrhea. Serious complications can develop, including pneumonia, sinus infections, laryngitis, bronchitis, meningitis, pharyngitis, strep throat, and ear infections.

Influenza vaccines are available that help the body become immune to the virus. Many doctors recommend that elderly people, pregnant women, and those with heart, kidney, or lung disease have these vaccinations. The protection from respiratory infection is greatly enhanced when vitamin C is taken along with the vaccine.

There is no specific treatment for influenza other than to treat its symptoms and try to prevent complications. Nutrients may be helpful. Vitamin B complex helps metabolize calories. Infections accompanied by fever increase the need for vitamins A and C. Vitamin A is especially important in influenza for the immune system and also the health of the lining of the throat. Vitamin C stimulates the production of interferon, a virus killer that will lessen the duration and intensity of a cold or flu. Zinc will aid in antibody production and also in the circulation of the T-cells that are part of the immune system; zinc should be taken after a fever has broken. Iron is also an important part of the immune system since the production of antibodies that must be built up depend on having adequate dietary iron.

The diet should include a variety of whole foods to maximize nutrients, with an emphasis on plant foods to alkalize the system. Refined grains and sugars, fast foods, and fried foods should be avoided because they are typically low in nutrients and acidifying. (See Section 5, Table 5.3, "Acid- and Alkaline-Forming Foods.") Special healing foods should also be included such as onions and garlic. Raw garlic and onion deliver more flu-counteracting benefits than cooked. Use of garlic products that have the active ingredient allicin removed may not be effective. Blueberries fight viral infection and are high in a natural form of aspirin. Bananas curb diarrhea, which may be associated with flu. Carrots are high in vitamin A, which supports immune function. Chili peppers ease breathing due to congestion and are a plentiful source of natural aspirin. Cranberries, licorice, mustard, onion, pineapple, plum, raspberry, rice, soybeans, strawberries, and black, oolong, and green tea all have flu-fighting chemicals in them. Fever usually accompanies influenza and requires additional calories to be taken in several small meals and additional protein foods for the repair of tissues destroyed by fever. Increased fluid intake is essential in the event of fever.

Smoking, caffeine, and alcohol should be avoided. Proper rest is essential in prevention. Stress is responsible in part for the reduction in the immune system's ability to fight colds and flu.

Herbs and other natural substances may be beneficial. Echinacea, slippery elm, ginger, catnip tea enemas, lobelia tincture, and pau d'arco are helpful. Echinacea and goldenseal as a tincture is good for children. Aromatherapy includes basil, black pepper, cedarwood, eucalyptus, ginger, grapefruit, lemon, orange, juniper, lavender, marjoram, myrrh, peppermint, Scots pine, tea tree, and sandalwood. Relaxation and positive thinking release anti-flu interleukins into the body.

Fracture (Broken Bone)

A fracture is any break in a bone. When the bone breaks but the skin remains intact, the fracture is called *closed*, or *simple*. When the bone breaks through the skin, an opening for bacteria is created and the fracture is called *open*, or *compound*.

Most fractures are caused by an accident, but some occur because of tumors, osteoporosis, or deficiencies of vitamin D or calcium. Fracture symptoms include limb deformities, limited limb functioning, shortening of the limb in fractures of long bones, pain, a grating sensation if the broken bone ends rub against each other, and swelling and discoloration of the skin overlying the fracture area.

First-aid treatment for fractures should include covering any wound and immobilizing or splinting the broken part in its original position. Medical treatment involves repositioning the bone pieces in their normal location.

Nutrients may aid in healing. In the healing process, a bridge of tissue composed largely of protein fibers grows across the ends of the broken bones. Calcium and phosphorus leave deposits among these protein fibers to form a new bone, so the diet must be high in protein and adequate in calcium and phosphorus. High calcium intake may promote kidney stone formation during the immobile period while the cast is on. Vitamin D intake must be adequate because it is essential for maintaining normal blood levels of calcium.

Vitamin K is used for healing bone fractures and is good for those who are postmenopausal and have osteoporosis. (See "Osteoporosis" for more about needed nutrients.) Calcium is known to decrease the incidence of bone fractures in postmenopausal women. Potassium is required for cell formation, vitamin C is necessary for the maintenance and development of bones, and vitamin A helps increase the rate of bone growth.

The diet should be high in calories to provide the energy necessary for new bone cell formation. Foods that are preserved and contain phosphorus may lessen bone strength and allow for increased fractures.

An herbal remedy that may be beneficial is comfrey, taken orally.

Gallbladder Disorders

The gallbladder is a small pear-shaped sac hanging between the lobes of the liver, and it stores bile made in the liver. Bile is composed of cholesterol, bile salts, lecithin, and other substances and is necessary for the digestion of fats. As fat-containing foods in the diet enter the small intestine, the gallbladder empties its bile, and simultaneously the liver begins to produce more.

Diet is important for this condition. Too little protein or too much refined carbohydrate in the diet prevents adequate bile production. Consequently, fats remain in large undigested particles and the fat-soluble vitamins, A, D, E, and K, are left unabsorbed. Some of these undigested fats combine with calcium and iron, preventing their absorption, which leads to hard stools and constipation. Eventually this condition can cause anemia and also porous, easily fractured bones. Undigested fats also melt and coat protein and carbohydrate foods, preventing them from enzyme digestion and absorption. Intestinal bacteria thrive on all the undigested food and cause the release of gas in the intestines.

The cholesterol in the bile can sometimes crystallize and form gallstones, which vary in size from a grain of sand to 1 inch in diameter. (See "Gallstones.") These stones can block the passages where bile leaves the gallbladder to go to the intestine, causing the pain, vomiting, and nausea. Fatty foods may trigger this painful condition. Overeating and gallbladder disease go hand in hand. Losing weight too rapidly can be a cause of gallbladder problems. An inflamed gallbladder also can be caused by drugs, chemicals, or bacteria.

Although a low-fat diet may be temporarily adhered to, such a diet should generally be avoided by people with gallbladder diseases, because it does not supply sufficient amounts of the necessary nutrients.

Nutrients may help with gallbladder function. A diet supplying sufficient B vitamins aids the emptying of the gallbladder. The liver should be supplied with complete proteins and the B, C, and E vitamins to aid detoxification. Herbs that may be helpful are gingerroot, parsley, cramp bark, catnip, dandelion, barberry root bark, horsetail, and wild yam.

Gallstones

Gallstones develop when deposits of cholesterol or calcium combine with bile. Bile is a secretion produced by the liver to emulsify fats so that they can be digested. Most of the bile manufactured by the liver is stored in the gallbladder until the small intestine calls for it when fat has been ingested. However, some bile travels directly from the liver to the small intestine. Gallstones may form in the passages between the liver and gallbladder, between the liver and intestine, or in the gallbladder itself.

The risk of developing gallstones increases if foods routinely eaten are low in fiber, are deficient in vitamin C or vitamin E, trigger food allergies, or are high in cholesterol or sugar. In addition, gallstones are more frequently found in diabetics, obese people, the elderly, and women who are overweight—by even as few as ten pounds—and who are forty years of age and older, especially if these women have not had children.

Gallstone formation begins to appear when cholesterol crystallizes and forms stones. Nearly half of all gallstone patients are without symptoms. It is when a stone obstructs any of the bile passages that problems begin. These symptoms characteristically include nausea, vomiting, and severe right upper abdominal pain that may radiate to the right shoulder or back. The symptoms commonly occur a few hours after eating a heavy meal of fatty or fried foods. If the stone totally obstructs one of the bile passages, jaundice (a yellowish cast to the skin and eyeballs), dark urine, clay-colored stools, and itching of the skin may also occur.

Too rapid a loss of weight (which occurs when consuming 600 or fewer calories per day) may trigger an attack, but several teaspoons of olive oil per day may remedy the situation. And fasting can lead to gallstone formation. Skipping breakfast can bring on an attack as can both caffeinated and decaffeinated coffee.

Gallstones can be prevented and sometimes dissolved by following the right diet. Certain foods can act to dissolve the cholesterol and keep it from crystallizing. As little as one-third ounce per day of alcohol is thought to reduce the level of bile salts. In studies, bran added to the diet (especially oat) has lowered the cholesterol concentration of the bile. Low-sugar and high-fiber diets show low levels of cholesterol in the gallbladder. High-fiber fruits and vegetables are recommended, in particular those that supply soluble fiber, such as beans, peas, lentils, lima beans, and oats. Cutting down on fatty foods after gallstones have formed will not remedy the painful situation.

Following a gallstone attack, solid food should be avoided for the first two days. As food is reintroduced, pear and apple juices are a good beginning. Shredded raw fruits and vegetables can eventually be added. To help pass the gallstones, olive oil and lemon juice may be taken before retiring and then again upon awakening. Drinking six to eight glasses of water per day is advised. Many stones will pass in the stool using this method.

Nutrients may be helpful. Lecithin (phosphatidylcholine) may be used to prevent and treat gallstones. Taking adequate amounts of vitamins A, B complex, and E may help dissolve stones. Lecithin reduces cholesterol levels; the B vitamins increase the body's production of lecithin and also stimulate the emptying of the gallbladder. Chenodeoxycholic acid, a substance particularly abundant in goose liver and goose bile, has been used medically to dissolve gallstones. It aids in the conversion of cholesterol into bile acids.

Herbs that may be beneficial are burdock, balmony with fringe tree, lysimachia, rhubarb, pyrrosia leaf, and seaweed.

Gastritis

Gastritis is a disease in which the mucous lining of the stomach becomes irritated and inflamed. (See "Colitis and Crohn's Disease" and "Ulcers.") If gastritis is prolonged, the stomach walls become very thin and secretions are made up almost entirely of mucus, with very little digestive acid. In this condition the stomach is unable to produce the intrinsic factor, a substance necessary for the absorption of vitamin B_{12}, which the body needs for the formation of red blood cells. Thus the gastritis patient is in danger of developing pernicious anemia.

Symptoms of gastritis include indigestion (dyspepsia), vomiting, headache, coated tongue, and abnormal increase or decrease in appetite. Diarrhea and abdominal cramps also may occur. The cause of gastritis appears to be overindulgence in alcohol, smoking, coffee, or highly seasoned or fried foods, all of which increase the activity of the stomach. Eating rancid foods can cause bacterial infection, which may cause gastritis. Recurring cases of gastritis may be the result of peptic ulcers or of the buildup of poisonous body wastes from such diseases as chronic uremia or cirrhosis of the liver. Any condition causing stress can bring on the symptoms of gastritis. The ailment has been experimentally induced by the same deficiencies that result in ulcers.

Diet for gastritis is to avoid fried foods and highly seasoned foods. A low-fat diet is necessary for those with a chronic condition. Frequent small meals are easier for the stomach to digest than fewer large meals. Acidic foods such as citrus, tomatoes, pineapple, and spicy foods can irritate a sore stomach just as they would a sore on your skin, so these foods should be avoided. Alcohol, coffee, caffeinated sodas, carbonated drinks, aspirin, and other substances that irritate the stomach lining must be eliminated. Antacids may help.

An increase of alkalizing, noncitrus juices, such as papaya, can be helpful. In addition, fresh papaya contains the enzyme papain that helps in digesting protein and some starches and can also guard against the development of ulcers caused by taking large doses of aspirin. Other recommended foods are brown rice, pasta, potatoes, and yogurt with active-culture acidophilus. Whole grains are preferred to the refined white flour of cakes and cookies because whole grains trigger a slower secretion of gastric acid and contain protein, which helps neutralize this acid. Chewing food thoroughly and relaxing when eating meals will do wonders for the stomach.

Nutrients may be beneficial. If gastritis is severe, iron supplements and injections of vitamin B_{12} may be helpful for preventing pernicious anemia. Herbs that may be helpful are goldenseal infusion and white willow as a substitute for aspirin with none of the side effects to the stomach (pregnant women should not take this herb). Homeopathic therapies are Nux vomica 6c, Bryonia 6c, Anacardium 6c, and Phosphorus 6c. Exercise is very good for the stomach; any kind of enjoyable activity is recommended.

Glaucoma/Age-Related Macular Degeneration

Glaucoma is characterized by an increase in pressure of the fluid within the eyeball and a hardening of the surface of the eyeball. The disease is the second leading cause of blindness. It is found more typically in those who are over age forty and in women more than men.

The causes are many but the most general is poor nutrition and anxiety or stress. It also may be due to tumor, trauma, infection, (in one type) heredity, allergy, and hormone disorders. Symptoms include eye discomfort or pain, especially in the morning, blurred vision, halos or rainbow rings around lights, inability to adjust to a darkened room, and loss of vision at the sides (peripheral). Early detection of glaucoma can substantially reduce the incidence of blindness resulting from it.

Glaucoma cannot be cured, but it can be controlled through the use of prescribed eyedrops (there are side effects). Laser treatment may also be a choice before surgery is elected.

Macular degeneration is another leading cause of blindness and the first in all new cases diagnosed. There are two types: dry (most common) and wet (more serious and may be helped with laser surgery).

Those who are sixty-five and older are vulnerable to this disease, which runs in families. There is no known cause (although exposure to light, such as blue and ultraviolet, is one theory) and no known cure, and it affects ten out of every one hundred people. Everyone who lives long enough will experience some macular degeneration; however, in some it becomes severe. The symptoms are blurring of central vision, distortion of straight lines into wavy ones, and blind spots. One or both eyes may be affected.

A diet of antioxidant foods, including those containing beta-carotene, vitamins D and E, and the phytochemicals, is helpful for macular degenerative disease as well as for general overall health. (See Section 5 for food sources of these needed nutrients.) New research has shown that two phytochemicals, lutein and zeaxanthin, are especially effective in preventing age-related macular degeneration. These nutrients are also pigments, a yellow hue that blocks out blue light, the kind that is most damaging to the macula. The two nutrients are the only carotenoids present in the macula. Vitamin A foods such as liver, eggs, cheese, cod liver oil, and dairy products may be consumed and are essential for eye tissue health. Bioflavonoids also strengthen eye tissues and are found in foods such as citrus fruits (in the skin and pith), red onions, blue or red berries, and leafy vegetables.

If the symptoms of anxiety are related to a B-vitamin deficiency, then correction of this deficiency will decrease the susceptibility of an individual to glaucoma. Alcohol, tobacco, chocolate, coffee, and tea (all caffeinated drinks) should be avoided since they decrease circulation to the eye. Small amounts of liquids at a time are recommended for glaucoma. Watching television or reading may aggravate the situation.

Nutrients may be helpful. Fish oils appear to reduce the pressure on the fluids in the eye. Studies are continuing on the value of this substance to the human body. Italian physicians have significantly reduced the intraocular pressure in the eyes of glaucoma patients by administering large doses of vitamin C (500 milligrams per 2.2 pounds of body weight). Glaucoma is often an indication of adrenal exhaustion; therefore, nutrients necessary for the adrenals should be taken. (See "Adrenal Exhaustion.") Vitamin C is helpful, and bioflavonoids strengthen the tissues of the eye. Injections of B-complex vitamins may be useful if stress is a major cause. The nutrients that meet the demands of stress should also be emphasized.

Herbs that may be helpful are fennel bulb as an eyewash, eyebright, and chamomile.

Goiter

A goiter is an enlargement of the thyroid gland, which is located at the base of the neck. It secretes a fluid, the hormone thyroxine, which is made from iodine and tyrosine, an amino acid. Through the thyroxine hormone, the thyroid regulates metabolism (the burning of food), growth, and body temperature and influences mental and emotional balance; it is also a factor in the function of the reproductive system.

Thyroid disorders are caused by an inadequate intake of iodine, resulting in insufficient thyroxine production, or a disorder elsewhere in the body that requires more thyroxine than the gland can manufacture. It can also develop if there is overactivity or underactivity of the thyroid gland.

One of the earliest symptoms of goiter is dry hair. Others are a swelling at the base of the neck, weight loss, changes in menstruation, palpitations, hoarseness, irritability, bulging eyes, change in the rate of metabolism, and, in extreme cases, difficulty in swallowing and breathing.

Nutrients and other natural treatments of goiter vary with the cause. If goiter is due to an iodine deficiency, increasing the intake of iodine will prevent further enlargement of the gland and, in some cases, reduce its size. Vitamin A is necessary for the proper metabolism of iodine; this vitamin is also important for the functioning of the pituitary gland, which secretes a substance that regulates the thyroid. Tyrosine, a component of the thyroid hormone, cannot be used without vitamins B_6 and C. Vitamin E increases the absorption of iodine. The use of iodized salt has helped eliminate goiter in many locations where iodine does not occur naturally in foods. Seaweed is used worldwide for the treatment of goiter. Kelp is an excellent source of iodine, is low in sodium, and is better retained by the body than potassium iodide.

Diet can influence the state of those with goiter. Foods that interfere with the absorption of iodine are turnips, cassava root, cabbage, mustard, soybeans, millet, peanuts, and pine nuts. Herbs that may be helpful are bugleweed, bayberry root bark, and bladderwrack (a seaweed).

Gout

Gout is a type of arthritis characterized by an excess of uric acid salts that crystallize in the tissue around the joints, especially in the fingers and the toes. (See "Arthritis.") Gout can also occur in the heel, knee, hand, ear, or any joint in the body. Gout results when certain crystals are formed as an end product of improper protein metabolism. These crystals are deposited in a joint, forming a bump or growth that irritates, causing the joint to become inflamed; thus an attack of gout occurs.

There are several causes of this disease. Gout often appears to be hereditary; however, factors such as obesity, increasing age, temperament, and improper diet increase an individual's susceptibility to gout. Alcohol, a large meal that includes purine-rich foods, or any physical or emotional stress also may bring on an attack of gout.

Treatment for gout emphasizes an adequate intake of fluids to expel crystals and prevent their buildup in the kidneys and urinary tract. A gradual weight-reduction program for those who need it will help prevent gout attacks, but a rapid weight loss may bring on attacks, owing to the stressful effect on the body. Drugs are available to treat the pain and other symptoms of gout, but they all carry side effects and none are a cure.

The diet most often recommended for gout restricts foods that contain purines, substances from which uric acid is formed. Alcohol must be avoided, since it stimulates the production of uric acid, as do caffeine drinks and chocolate. Other foods that contain purines and should not be eaten are meat gravies and stocks, organ meats, sweetbreads, shellfish, anchovies, sardines and herring, mussels, mushrooms, and asparagus. Meat, white flour and sugar products, cakes and pies, yeast products, fish, oatmeal, cauliflower, poultry, dried beans, spinach, and peas should also be avoided. Some investigators believe that the amount of uric acid in foods is too small to cause gout and that the cause really lies in the inefficient breakdown of proteins by the body. A diet of incomplete proteins or one too high or too low in isolated amino acids that make protein can produce too much uric acid. However, if a low-purine diet is preferred, generous supplemental amounts of all vitamins and minerals, especially the B-complex vitamins and vitamin E, should be taken.

Fruits, vegetables, and juices aid uric acid excretion. Foods that neutralize uric acid are strawberries, cherries (one-half pound per day), and celery juice (increases excretion of uric acid). Seeds, nuts, vegetable juices, and grains are good.

Nutrients may be helpful. Pantothenic acid is necessary for the conversion of uric acid into the harmless compounds urea and ammonia. Many gout patients are deficient in this B vitamin, resulting in uric acid accumulation. Vitamin B$_6$ plays a role in protein synthesis. Stress rapidly depletes pantothenic acid as well as other B vitamins. A lack of vitamin E allows excessive formation of uric acid.

Herbs and other natural ingredients that may be helpful are burdock, chickwood, horsetail grass, seaweed, and nettle (relieves pain). Walnuts used externally are helpful. Charcoal tablets will reduce uric acid levels. Homeopathic remedies are Colchicum 6c, Ledum 6c, Urtica urens, and Arnica 30c.

Hair Problems

Healthy hair is dependent on blood quality and circulation, which in turn are dependent on nutrition. Partial lack of any nutrient can cause hair problems such as drying and dulling of the hair, hair loss, and graying. A well-balanced diet is important to maintaining healthy hair, although hereditary graying and balding cannot be completely prevented by nutritional means. (See "Baldness.")

Hair is composed primarily of protein. A deficiency of protein in the diet can result in a temporary change of hair color and texture, resulting in dull, thin, dry hair. If the protein deficiency is corrected, the hair will return to its normal condition.

Biotin may promote healthy hair and prevent graying and baldness. RNA and DNA supplement formulas are thought to benefit the hair. Myoinositol may fight hair loss. A deficiency of vitamin A may cause hair to become dull, dry, and lusterless and eventually fall out. However, an excess of vitamin A may cause similar problems. A deficiency of manganese may slow the growth of hair.

Hair loss occurs during stress or when the diet is inadequate in the B vitamins, especially B$_6$, biotin, inositol, folic acid, magnesium, sulfur, or zinc. An underactive thyroid causes the hair to fall out. Excess copper results in hair loss in women who take oral contraceptives. Women lose more hair after giving birth because of hormones that inhibit loss of hair during pregnancy. Intoxication by heavy metals such as mercury, lead, and cadmium causes hair loss. Radiation, skin disease, poor circulation, surgery, sudden weight loss, diabetes or thyroid disease, iron deficiency, and acute illness are all causes of hair loss.

Graying hair can indicate a deficiency of nutrients in other parts of the body. A return of normal hair color has been accomplished by supplements of copper, folic acid, pantothenic acid, and/or para-aminobenzoic acid (PABA); 5 milligrams of folic acid and 300 milligrams of PABA and pantothenic acid along with the B-complex vitamins have been shown to prevent hair loss and to restore hair color in some people. Graying hair at an early age is related to family genetics, not to biological aging. Good hygiene is also important for healthy hair. This includes brushing the hair properly and washing it with a mild shampoo. Exposure to wind and sun may cause early graying and cause brittle, broken hair. Herbs that may be helpful are sage (as a rinse), ligustrum (slows graying), burdock (promotes hair growth), and fo-ti (keeps hair black).

Halitosis

Halitosis, or bad breath, is an unpleasant odor of the breath. It may be caused by improper diet, poor mouth hygiene, nose or throat infections, extensive tooth or gum decay, smoking, a yeast infection of the digestive tract, or the presence of bacteria that are foreign to the mouth.

Diabetes or nervous tension may be the cause of bad breath. Other sources are chemicals that may be present in the body such as arsenic, lead, bismuth, and methane. Most often, however, bad breath can be attributed to putrefactive bacteria living on undigested food, which release gas through expelled air.

All nutrients necessary for efficient digestion are essential, as well as digestive enzymes. Yogurt with live acidophilus improves the intestinal bacteria and is also helpful when yeast infections are the cause of the halitosis. Acidophilus is also available as a supplement. Other treatments for halitosis involve proper mouth hygiene, including regular tooth and tongue brushing. Often the use of dental floss is recommended.

A carefully balanced diet is essential for the prevention of halitosis. Avoiding excessive consumption of carbohydrates (sugar) may help prevent tooth decay, which can cause bad breath. Vitamin C helps keep gums healthy and prevents gingivitis. Vitamin A is necessary for the overall development and health of the gums and teeth. A diet of raw foods may help.

Herbs and other natural substances that may be helpful are peppermint, parsley, sage (as a rinse), fenugreek, tea tree, oriental worm root, hyssop, rosemary, radish seeds, and myrrh (to brush the teeth with). Lemon water fasts may help cleanse the system. Homeopathic remedies are Petroselinum and Nux vomica 6c.

Hangovers

Hangovers are a very unpleasant side effect of drinking alcohol. Their severity and whether they include headaches or not depend on inherited genetic characteristics. Distilled spirits that have more flavor to them contain substances (congeners) that cause hangovers. Red wine has similar substances that certain people are sensitive to, as does beer. The less taste there is to a kind of alcohol, the fewer the congeners and the better one will feel in the morning. Vodka and gin contain the least, while bourbon, rum, and pure malt scotch have the most. Alcohol leaves the body quite rapidly but congeners take their time—as many hours as the number of drinks consumed the night before. There is only one cure for a hangover—time.

Hangover symptoms are headache, nausea, dizziness, irritability, and depression. Many of these effects are caused from dehydration and can be remedied by taking water while drinking alcohol, and also taking large amounts before going to sleep. Raising blood sugar levels with a snack of fruit before bed will also help. Another pain-saving tip is never to drink on an empty stomach (eating protein foods such as cheese, whole milk, meat, and peanut butter is helpful) and to take a B-complex supplement ahead of time. Mixing different kinds of drinks is not good, nor is using a carbonated mixer (enters the system, along with the alcohol, too fast). Water and juice as mixers are best, and beer and wine will absorb more slowly than distilled spirits.

For those who do not drink often, the liver may be slow to do its work; getting tipsy too rapidly may be a result. Also, the smaller a person is, the harder the effects of alcohol will be, including the hangover. Women metabolize alcohol more completely than men do, and their concentrations of alcohol are highest just before menstruation. Drinking and doing drugs can be fatal when normal amounts of each are taken together. Drinking under tense or guilt-ridden circumstances seems to generate the worst hangovers. Fatigue also contributes; getting enough sleep is very important. Coffee and a cold shower do not get rid of congeners any more quickly than does time.

Diet may help. Eating carbohydrates replenishes nutrients and aids in relieving the symptoms. A banana (replenishes potassium) milkshake (soothes the stomach) with honey (raises lowered blood sugar levels in the brain) is good. Having a broth made with meats and vegetables replenishes fluids and electrolytes. Useful supplements include B-complex vitamins, vitamin C, and cysteine.

Herbs that may help are willow bark and cayenne. Homeopathic remedies are Nux vomica 6c, Bryonia 6c, and Sulphur 6c.

Hay Fever (Allergic Rhinitis)

Hay fever is a reaction of the mucous membranes of the eyes, nose, and air passages to seasonal pollens and dust, feathers, animal hair, and other irritants. Large numbers of antibodies are produced to attack the allergen; however, these antibodies also release histamine, which makes the capillaries more permeable to fluid accumulation, resulting in swelling and irritation.

Hay fever symptoms include itching of the eyes, nose, and throat; a clear, watery discharge from the nose and eyes; frequent sneezing; and nervous irritability. Alcoholic beverages and stressful situations may precipitate a hay fever attack.

The most effective treatment for hay fever is to avoid the irritant. This can be accomplished by covering the mattress, vacuuming, using air conditioning, closing windows, keeping animals outside, and repairing leaks in one's living space that can result in waterlogged walls and other surfaces where mold can grow.

In addition, diet may help. Eating yogurt before the pollen season (three months) may lessen the symptoms of hay fever. Onions contain a substance called quercetin (a flavonoid) that quells allergic reactions. Hot foods such as chili peppers open clogged passageways and should be consumed at least three times a week. Citrus fruits are rich in both vitamin C and bioflavonoids, which are in the pith. There is a supplement combining these two nutrients. Carotenoid foods are also recommended.

Nutrients may offer benefits. Vitamin A is essential for the general health of the respiratory system. Some authorities believe that vitamin C can relieve hay fever. Vitamin C with bioflavonoids acts as an antihistamine.

Dr. Mitsuo Kamimura, of the department of dermatology at the Sapporo Medical College in Japan, has tested the antihistamine effect of vitamin E on both animals and humans. His studies reveal that the vitamin prevents the symptoms of allergies, is more effective if given before symptoms begin than after the fact, and can reduce itching and redness when applied topically. He believes vitamin E decreases the permeability of the capillaries and depresses the release of histamine.

Herbs that may be helpful are nettle and parsley (both can deplete potassium stores after prolonged use), licorice, and a combination of inula, a sweet essential oil, with almond oil or jojoba. Homeopathic remedies are Allium cepa, Ambrosia, Euphrasia officinalis, Pulsatilla, and Naphthalin.

Headache

A headache is a pain or ache in any portion of the head. All headaches are treated the same as migraines; they just vary in degrees of severity. Diet along with stress is thought to be the main trigger to the headache family. Genetics is the other major determinant as to how serious the individual condition will be.

Most commonly, headaches and their causes fall into one of three categories: tension headaches, resulting from a contraction of the neck, scalp, or forehead muscles; vascular headaches, caused by uneven dilation rates of the blood vessels in the brain; and sinus headaches, caused by inflamed mucous membranes of the nose. Sinus headaches are often brought on by changes in the weather, onset of menstruation, or a head cold.

There are many other possible causes of headache, such as diseases of the eye, nose, or throat; trauma to the head; air pollution; drugs, alcohol, and tobacco; fever; generalized body infections; disturbances of the digestive tract and circulatory system; brain disorders; incorrect eyewear or eyestrain; anemia; low blood sugar; niacin or pantothenic acid deficiency; an overdose of vitamin A; mold or other allergies; salt; excessive carbohydrates; allergenic foods (wheat, citric acid, marinated foods, fermented foods, and foods containing MSG); oral contraceptives or other sources of estrogen; constipation or bowel problems; bruxism (grinding teeth); improper bite; the chewing of gum; food additives such as nitrites in meats; aspartame; stuffy rooms (caused by an electrical imbalance of the ion count of the air); and PMS (possibly a result of water retention in the brain tissues, which can be relieved by vitamin B_6).

A migraine is a particular type of headache that is usually on one side of the head, caused by the alternating constriction and dilation of the blood vessels in the brain. It is often hereditary. Symptoms are sensitivity to light, food allergies, pressure behind the eyes or in the facial sinus, throbbing head and temples, and all-over head pain. Migraine headaches can be triggered by shock, anxiety, low blood sugar, depression, food allergies, and overexertion as well as changes in diet, climate, or daily lifestyle. There are two types of migraine: classic migraine, which is preceded by light-headedness, flashing lights, and supersensitivity to noise, and common migraine, accompanied by nausea, a general feeling of ill-being, and sometimes depression and irritability. The face may be pale, swollen, and sweaty. A migraine attack may last for hours or days. Feverfew is an herb that is used to prevent migraine attacks (may take two to three months). Tablets are available.

Cluster headaches, a variant of the migraine, are sudden and severe, usually located on one side of the face or head, producing sweating and tearing. Vigorous exercise or the inhalation of pure oxygen has alleviated the pain in many individuals. Many people with this type of headache have unusually high copper levels in the body, which can be lowered by zinc supplements.

Treatment for headache depends upon the underlying cause. Spinal alignment through chiropractic treatment may be a choice. Repeated headaches may be the result of stress or may be a symptom of a serious disorder and, therefore, deserve attention. Learning better ways of coping with stress and relieving nervous tension is often the most effective treatment for headaches and migraines. Acupuncture has been shown to be effective in preventing or lessening the severity of headaches in many people. Massage, a hot bath, moist heat, or cold packs can help tension headaches. To alleviate sinus headaches, the inflamed, congested membranes of the nose can be drained by using steam humidifiers or warm packs applied over the eyes and cheekbones. Acupressure has also helped some individuals.

Vitamin therapy may take a period of time, from six months to two years in some people, before headache symptoms disappear or diminish substantially. Special attention should be paid to preventing deficiencies of iron, niacin, and pantothenic acid. Niacin may be used at the first sign of a migraine headache to try to prevent it from worsening. Vitamin A may also prove helpful to headache victims. The B complex, especially niacin, is a very important factor in maintaining normal dilation of the blood vessels. Copper appears to ward off headaches. Niacin, calcium (taken in the morning), zinc, magnesium, and sometimes potassium and tryptophan (an amino acid), along with relaxation, may help the pain of migraine.

Diet is an important factor. Fish oils and ginger may alleviate headaches. Acidophilus is helpful for establishing the friendly intestinal bacteria from which the body produces the B vitamins. Oysters, lobster, and green olives are rich in copper.

Foods that may trigger migraines in children are oranges, cheese, peanuts, wheat, rye, eggs, milk, coffee, fish, pork, beef, soy products, bacon, tartrazine, yeast, benzoic acid, and tomato. Foods that do the same for adults are red wine, figs, dates, raisins, chocolate, nuts, hard cheeses, yogurt, sour cream, nitrates in cured or processed meats, dishes that contain MSG, herring, sauerkraut, and citrus fruit. Coffee can zap a small headache for some, but for others it can be a major trigger. Use the elimination diet to determine which foods are triggers for you.

Helpful herbs are feverfew and ginger. Homeopathic remedies are Iris versicolor 6c, Spigelia 6c, Sanguinaria 6c, and Natrum muriaticum 6c. Exercise has been shown to reduce migraine attacks. Aromatherapy for migraines includes basil, Roman chamomile, lavender, sweet marjoram, peppermint, rose otto, and rosemary.

Heart Disease/ Cardiovascular Disease

The heart is the chief organ of the circulatory system and the most delicate (weighing only 10 ounces). Yet it is the most durable because it is made of the toughest muscle fibers of the body. The heart is a very efficient pump, beating one hundred thousand times daily to force one thousand gallons of blood through sixty thousand miles of blood vessels. More than a million Americans die of heart disease each year. The most common causes of congestive heart failure are coronary heart disease (blockage that kills muscle cells) and high blood pressure (enlarged heart muscle). Research has given us an understanding of coronary heart disease and high blood pressure, and we now have the knowledge to prevent them. Proper exercise and nutrition are essential to maintaining a healthy heart. (See "Arteriosclerosis, Atherosclerosis, Angina, and Coronary Heart Disease" and "Hypertension.")

The arteries supplying the heart with blood are formed around the heart like a crown, or corona, giving the names *coronary arteries* and *coronary artery disease*. These arteries supply blood with oxygen to smaller arteries that branch over the heart. If the circulation in these small arteries has been decreased to such an extent that very little of the oxygen reaches the heart muscle, pain signaling angina or silent ischemia results. Silent ischemia is similar to angina except that there is no pain. It is thought to be more dangerous because it gives no warning of what may be about to happen. An electrocardiogram will show the abnormalities. Ischemic attacks may be caused by a heavy meal, unaccustomed physical exertion, stress, emotional tension, or exposure to cold. The frequency and duration of attacks vary and may range from several attacks per day to one attack every few years.

The pain varies greatly in severity from a mild pressure to an intolerable agony. It usually starts in the upper chest or throat and radiates to the left shoulder and down the left arm. The patient is pale, sweaty, and very apprehensive. These symptoms are similar to those of a heart attack but can be differentiated in that the pain lasts only for minutes and can be relieved by rest. However, if the blood supply is insufficient enough, angina pectoris can progress to a heart attack.

If atherosclerosis has impaired circulation to the point where a coronary artery becomes completely plugged and no oxygen reaches the heart, the death of heart cells results and what occurs then is technically called a myocardial infarction, or heart attack. Unlike angina, heart attacks occur suddenly with no warnings. They are usually caused by ruptures or clots. Fatty deposits take years to build up in the artery walls; however, when a blood clot forms, it can clog an artery and quickly cut off oxygen in people with atherosclerosis at any age (including children).

Each year, three hundred thousand people die from heart attacks before they can make it to the hospital; 10 percent of those who die do so within three days. One out of five that survive will have another attack within four years. Classic symptoms of a heart attack are excruciating pain in the lower chest or upper abdomen. The pain often spreads to the neck and shoulders, down the arms, especially to the left side and possibly to the back. Sometimes, however, pain may be felt in only one of these locations. The pain increases in severity and is not relieved by rest or nitroglycerin, a medication often prescribed for patients with mild angina. Additional heart attack symptoms include perspiration and pale skin, a decrease in blood pressure, weak and rapid pulse, and possibly nausea and vomiting. A moderate fever usually appears twenty-four to forty-eight hours after the onset of the attack. Sometimes a heart attack (15 percent), like silent ischemia, has no pain—only symptoms such as weariness and a feeling of dread or intense anxiousness are manifest.

These are the classic symptoms of heart attack, but in recent years it has come to light that the way a woman may experience a heart attack can be significantly different from the way a heart attack feels to a man. Females have a greater tendency to have atypical chest pain or to complain of abdominal pain, nausea, unexplained fatigue, and difficulty breathing. In addition, women have poorer outcomes following a heart attack.

When a heart attack does occur, immediate medical attention is necessary and can best be obtained at a coronary care unit in a hospital setting. Usually the patient will be given an electrocardiogram, or EKG, a test designed to detect changes in heart function or damage to some part of the heart. But often this test will not show the heart damage until hours or days after the attack. A blood test is also often done to help detect if a myocardial infarction, or heart attack, has occurred.

During the first three weeks of treatment, the patient runs a great risk of suffering further irregularities in heart function. The immediate goal of treatment is for the patient to obtain rest, to decrease the workload of the heart. Pain medication and oxygen therapy are often applied. Because the workload of the heart increases after meals, the diet during the first few days often consists of six small feedings. Cold fluids should be avoided because they may trigger irregularities in heart function. Protein intake must be adequate to replace protein lost by damaged heart cells. By six weeks the healing is almost complete and increased amounts of activity can be tolerated.

Another concern is that a heart already weakened or damaged by diseases such as rheumatic fever, heart attack, hypothyroidism, arteriosclerosis, or beriberi is unable to properly pump the blood through the body. This inefficient circulation, which leads to congestion of many organs with blood and other tissue fluids, is called congestive heart failure. Early symptoms of congestive heart failure are abnormal fatigue and shortness of breath following work or exercise. Swelling, particularly in the ankles and feet, is a further symptom. Congestion of the abdominal organs causes nausea, lack of appetite, and gas. Fluid in the lungs impairs breathing and in some cases causes a persistent cough.

A damaged heart requires a special diet. Poor appetite, inefficient digestion, and excessive nutrient loss from the body after heart failure can result in a state of malnutrition. A well-balanced diet high in protein foods, fresh vegetables and fruits, and whole grains should be substituted for high intake of refined starches, sweets, hydrogenated fats, and cholesterol. Natural, whole foods provide fiber, which is very important for heart health. Protein is essential to the strength of all muscles, including the heart. A low-sodium diet is recommended, particularly if there are symptoms of congestive heart failure and edema.

A low-fat diet has long been considered a given of heart-healthy diets. An overconsumption of fat has been thought to harm the heart, possibly weakening arteries by reducing their elasticity and clogging them with cholesterol. But in recent years the dangers of fat have been reexamined. The focus is now on the type of fats in the diet more than on the amount consumed. Support for this premise comes from the Lyon Diet Heart Study, conducted in 1988 with more than five years of follow-up, involving patients who had had a first heart attack. Those on a Mediterranean-style diet, which included healthy unsaturated olive oil and fish, had far fewer second heart attacks as compared with participants who followed a standard low-fat diet that cut back on all forms of fat, both saturated and unsaturated. And more recently, a very large-scale and well-designed trial published in the *Journal of the American Medical Association* in 2006 found that a low-fat diet per se did not prevent heart attacks and strokes. Oils such as olive and canola that raise HDL levels should be consumed.

In the past several years, new risk factors for heart disease have been identified. Elevated levels of homocysteine, an amino acid in the blood, are associated with an increased risk of heart attacks, stroke, and peripheral artery disease. Supplemental folic acid can lower homocysteine. A safe dosage ranges from 400 to 2,500 micrograms of folic acid daily. Along with folic acid, 50 milligrams a day of vitamin B_6 can be taken for further lowering of homocysteine. And because folic acid can mask the signs of pernicious anemia, adding 1 milligram of vitamin B_{12} daily to the supplement protocol is advised.

Other new risk factors are elevated fibrinogen levels, a component of blood clotting, and elevated blood levels of C-reactive protein used to track inflammation, now known to be a component of heart disease. (See "Inflammatory Conditions.")

Nutrients may be beneficial. Vitamin E strengthens the heart muscle. At times it acts as a diuretic to rid the body of excess fluid, decreases elevated blood pressure, helps keep oxygen in the blood, has similar actions as digitalis, and may be as effective as anticoagulant drugs in preventing clots. (Vitamin E temporarily raises blood pressure, so heart patients should begin with low doses, perhaps 100 IU daily. Its use may be hazardous in individuals with rheumatic heart disease.) As an antioxidant, it helps protect arteries and prevent the accumulation of plaque. (Increased omega-3 and omega-6 oil consumption, fats that oxidize more readily than saturated fat, should be accompanied by increased vitamin E.)

Despite all these benefits, the usefulness of taking vitamin E supplements continues to be debated. A review of two large trials, published in 2006 in the *Journal of the American Medical Association*, found no significant differences in heart attack risk or strokes between the group taking vitamin E and the placebo group. In addition, while one of the trials noted an unexpected increase in risk of heart failure in vitamin E users, the other found that supplemental vitamin E resulted in a significant decline in cardiovascular-related deaths. However, many earlier studies, such as those conducted at Harvard School of Public Health, have found that vitamin E does dramatically lower the risk of heart attack. In addition, the work of Drs. Wilfrid and Evan Shute in the late 1940s documents the usefulness of treating thousands of patients with high dosages of vitamin E above 800 IU a day.

A deficient operation of the thyroid gland may be involved in some cases of faulty fat metabolism. Vitamins A (beta-carotene), C, and B complex (especially niacin) and the minerals zinc and selenium are necessary for the maintenance of arterial health and repair as well as protection against atherosclerosis. Chromium assists the metabolism of blood fats, and superoxide dismutase (SOD) possibly aids the restoration of the heart tissue. Copper levels appear to be extremely low in people who develop an aneurysm, leading to a rupture of the artery and death. Copper is also important for vessel strength and elasticity. Aspirin aids against blood clotting.

Overweight and obesity can be a contributing factor to both high pulse rate and high blood pressure; excess pounds greatly tax the heart and the circulatory system in general. A properly balanced diet will lead to reduction of pounds without the adverse symptoms experienced when eating only one or two foods, as is common in many fad diets. Exercise is vital and should be done with the help of a physician. Sedentary people increase their risk of heart attack by 190 percent.

Stress may raise blood pressure as well as pulse rate. Fluctuations of blood pressure against artery walls contribute to arterial injury and hardening. Exercise is an excellent way to deal with stress and improve muscle tone of the heart and entire body. Unless otherwise advised by your physician, begin walking for ten minutes a day and gradually increase up to one hour. Walking should be at a brisk pace but must be begun slowly. Strenuous exercise (work or recreation) to which one is not accustomed should be avoided

because the heart may not be able to meet the unusual requirements made upon it.

To lower a pulse rate, reduce the intake of food, avoid emotional stress, and curtail use of drugs, alcoholic drinks, and tobacco products. Substances to which one is allergic will raise the pulse rate, producing further stress on the heart.

Hemophilia

Hemophilia is a rare, hereditary blood disease characterized by a prolonged coagulation time. The blood fails to clot, and abnormal bleeding occurs. Hemophilia is a sex-linked hereditary trait, transmitted by normal females carrying the recessive gene. This disease occurs almost exclusively in males. There is no known cure for hemophilia. Transfusion of fresh whole blood or plasma is required in emergencies to provide the necessary coagulation factors. AIDS is a threat for the hemophiliac.

Anemia is common in the hemophiliac and has been successfully corrected with vitamins C and E. Vitamin E, if taken continuously, may shorten the clotting time and prevent hemorrhaging in hemophiliacs. Foods that contain vitamin K have blood-clotting agents in them. Sources of vitamin K are green leafy vegetables, egg yolks, liver, broccoli and cauliflower, and alfalfa. (See Section 5 for additional sources of vitamin K.)

Hemorrhoids (Piles)

Hemorrhoids, or piles, are ruptured or distended veins located around the rectum that may extend out of the anus. The most common cause of hemorrhoids is strain on the abdominal muscles from factors such as heavy or improper lifting, pregnancy, overweight and obesity, constipation, or an extremely sedentary life. The flow of blood through the vessels of the anus is particularly sensitive to the pressure and strain of pregnancy and constipation. The blood collects in these vessels and the pressure against the weakest sections causes tiny bulges or piles. They may itch, tear, and bleed, causing pain.

Treatment for severe hemorrhoids may involve surgical removal. Injections of a sclerosing agent may seal them off, which causes them to eventually shrivel up without surgery. Laser technology is being used.

Breathing normally when the body is under any type of strain will eliminate abdominal pressure, lessening the risk of hemorrhoids. A diet that includes fiber and fluids is beneficial; cleanliness is also an important preventive measure.

Nutrients may be helpful. The bioflavonoids, especially troxerutin, strengthen the capillaries. Vitamin E can prevent and dissolve blood clots. Ointments containing vitamins A and D or E or vitamin E suppositories can lubricate and relieve pain. Vitamin K, a blood-clotting agent, may be helpful with bleeding hemorrhoids.

In countries where diets are high in fiber and whole unrefined foods, hemorrhoids are rare. Cereals, low-fat protein, and fruits and vegetables are recommended. Insoluble fibers such as wheat, rye, corn, and rice are helpful, as are soluble fibers found in certain fruits and legumes. On the other hand, spices, alcohol, coffee, and colas can irritate.

Herbal remedies are blackberry, collinsonia root, butcher's broom, chickweed, mullein, goldenseal (topically), witch hazel, red grapevine root, gotu kola, elderberry (poultice), buckthorn bark, pillwort ointment, stone root, yarrow, and triphala (in the form of ointments or suppositories). Natural ingredients that are helpful include brewer's yeast (skin respiratory factor isolated from the yeast is used in over-the-counter preparations). Psyllium is a natural laxative that may relieve pain, itching, and bleeding from hemorrhoids and is also used in over-the-counter drugs. Cayenne and garlic enemas will clean the rectum, and potatoes cut to conform with the rectum can be held against it to help shrink the distentions. Homeopathy remedies are Sepia 6c, Tatanhia 6c, Hamamelis 6c, and Sulphur 6c.

Hepatitis

Hepatitis is an inflammation of the liver caused by infection or toxic agents. It begins with flulike symptoms of fever, aching muscles, weakness, drowsiness, abdominal discomfort, and headache, possibly accompanied by jaundice, and is contagious two weeks before and one week after jaundice is apparent. Soon extreme fatigue and loss of appetite occur. The liver is unable to eliminate the poisons, which then build up in the system to the point that the liver can no longer store and process certain nutrients vital for the body.

There are two types of viral hepatitis. Hepatitis A is caused by the ingestion of contaminated water, inhalation of airborne virus from infected people, consumption of contaminated shellfish (prevented by cooking for at least six minutes), or transfer of virus from the hands to the mouth or from person to person. Hepatitis B is more serious and sometimes fatal. It is contracted from blood-sucking insects, contaminated blood transfusions, injections using unsterilized needles, bodily fluids contracted during some forms of sexual contact, or contaminated chemicals taken into the system by injection. Hepatitis non-A and non-B cause hepatitis C, which is chronic active hepatitis. There is no cure.

Treatment for hepatitis involves abstention from alcohol, a diet adequate in all nutrients, and rest. Reduced intake of saturated fats and refined carbohydrates, and an increase in fiber along with large doses of vitamins (under the supervision of a physician or a professional naturopath) are advised. Phosphatidylcholine repairs the membranes of liver cells. Raw vegetables and fruit, as well as juices made from these are good. Distilled water should be consumed. Vitamin B_{12} and folic acid may help shorten recovery times. A high-protein and/or a high-carbohydrate diet along with nutrients, unsaturated fatty acids, fluids, and vitamins B complex, C (improves viral hepatitis), and E should be continued long after recovery because sensitivity to toxic materials may persist.

Herbs that may help are St. John's wort (for hepatitis B), dandelion (for the liver), red clover, milk thistle (to regenerate the liver), gardenia fruit, black radish, yarrow tea, globe artichoke (stimulates the release of bile), wormwood, licorice, skullcap (for the liver), and reishi mushroom (immune enhancer).

Hernia/Hiatal Hernia

A bulging and tenderness in the groin area may be a hernia (consult a physician for an accurate diagnosis). The soft tissues of organs such as the intestine may protrude through a defect in the muscle walls. This condition is found most commonly in men, and in rare cases can cause death. Coughing, heavy lifting, laughing, and constipation are all causes. Prevention is the most likely form of treatment and is relatively simple. Lifting properly with the knees and leg muscles is important. Avoiding constipation, exercising the abdomen, and quitting smoking (which causes coughing) are ways to avoid getting a hernia. Treatment may be to wear a truss; however, most hernias get larger with time and surgery is often the final solution. Weight loss reduces stress on the muscles. Exercise is needed to strengthen stomach muscles.

A hiatal hernia is a condition in which a portion of the stomach pokes through the diaphragm via an opening called the esophageal hiatus. When this happens, the sphincter, a muscle at the base of the esophagus, tends not to contract and close. The result is that food, mixed with stomach acid, backs up into the esophagus causing gastroesophageal reflux. Symptoms are discomfort behind the breastbone, heartburn, and burping. Treatment for hiatal hernia includes small meals throughout the day, eating slowly to prevent swallowing air and then belching up the air mixed with acid, and keeping the body vertical after eating to allow gravity to keep food and acids in the stomach. Fried foods and chocolate relax the sphincter; smoking and mint also cause a lax sphincter. Citrus juice, alcohol, coffee, tomatoes, and other foods that are allergenic or can irritate should be avoided. Losing weight will help release pressure on muscles.

Herbs that may help are goldenseal root, comfrey, pepsin (for short periods), and red clover. Tissue salts are Calc. Fluor. 6x.

Herpes Simplex I and II

Herpes Simplex I (characterized by cold sores and skin eruptions, sometimes infecting the genital area) and Herpes Simplex II (found in the genital area and sexually transmitted) are two of five types of human herpes simplex viruses. (The other three cause chicken pox, mononucleosis, and shingles.) The herpes virus moves into healthy cells, reprogramming them to work for the virus. It will remain in some form in the body for life; however, with time the body eventually becomes more efficient in suppressing it.

Most of the time, the virus will remain dormant and will not be contagious. However, the virus will become active when the body's immune system is weakened—whether from stress, another disease, or an environmentally related factor.

Other than being very inconvenient, the virus can become serious in two situations. If it is transmitted to the eyes, blindness can result; therefore, it is important that the hands be washed after contact with the lesions. Second, pregnant women who have Herpes Simplex II need to take special precautions upon delivery; if the virus is active at the time, a caesarean will have to be performed.

Recognizing the symptoms that indicate that the virus is becoming active is very important in preventing exposure to other people. The early warning sign that an outbreak is about to occur is a numbing or tingling sensation around the mouth, which may last for a day or two before the blister appears. Within about forty-eight hours the blister ruptures and begins to heal. Herpes Simplex I primarily results in cold sores on the mouth, eyes, or nose. It is mainly contracted by kissing or sharing a utensil containing moist saliva of the infected person. During the early warning signs, the virus is active beneath the skin and is just as contagious as when the lesions actually appear. Once the blisters form, they will last typically one to five days. They will then rupture and form a scab, the final stage. At this healing stage the virus is probably not contagious, because it has run its course and is gone.

Herpes Simplex II (HSV II) is sexually transmitted. The lesions of HSV II that occur in men are usually located on the penis, scrotum, or, rarely, inside the urinary tube. The early warning signs are an itching or numb feeling about the penis. The testicles and groin area may be tender. Fatigue and an ill feeling may be experienced. Intercourse during outbreaks will transfer the disease and should be avoided. The virus can be spread by using the same towels, same lipsticks, and the like.

The early warning signs of HSV II in women are similar to those in men. The area around the outside of the vagina begins to itch or tingle, the upper inner thighs become tender, and headaches, fever, or a sick feeling may occur. Most women have the infection inside the vagina as well, with the symptoms of irritation and a watery discharge. The blisters will appear on the inner or outer lips of the vagina, around the clitoris, or around the anal area. Women with herpes have been found to have a higher incidence of cervical cancer and should have a Pap smear test taken yearly.

Outbreaks of herpes can be prevented or greatly limited in frequency and duration by following certain guidelines. Safe sex should be adhered to faithfully. Medications are available to lessen the severity of the symptoms. Other treatment basically involves diet and nutrients that strengthen the immune system, which will not only prevent herpes activation but will also raise the body to a higher state of health.

In addition, nutrients and diet may help. Foods that contain good amounts of the amino acid lysine are recommended because, according to laboratory studies, lysine blocks arginine, the amino acid required for replication of the virus. Food sources of lysine include fish and shellfish, turkey, chicken, bean sprouts, brewer's yeast, beans, and fruits and vegetables. In turn, during outbreaks, foods that contain arginine should be avoided. These include gelatin; wheat germ; cereals or grains such as rye, corn, oats, and barley; soybeans; nuts such as almonds, peanuts, walnuts, and cashews; and carob and chocolate. Citrus foods may also irritate. Other foods that should be avoided are refined carbohydrates, whole grain and white flour and sugar, colas and coffee, alcohol, and processed foods.

Stress has a strong link with the onset of herpes outbreaks. Certain supplements that have been shown to have a direct effect on the virus are lysine in cream form; vitamins B complex, C, and E; and zinc. Topical treatments that may aid the healing of lesions are vitamin E oil (applied at the beginning of symptoms through the last stage), povidone-iodine solution (obtained at drugstores), a cream containing lithium carbonate (available at health food stores), and ice (applied for an hour and a half or two hours). Cotton underwear is helpful for circulation of air.

Stress lowers the resistance to disease and decreases immune system activity. Therefore, stress management is of utmost importance. Stress not only comes from a psychological origin; it can also result from fatigue, lack of adequate sleep, menstruation, sunburn, fever, drugs, alcohol, caffeine, inadequate diet, refined carbohydrates, sugar, and tap water. Many of these factors cause stress on the body by depleting it of essential nutrients or loading it with harmful substances.

Herbs and other natural treatments are St. John's wort, goldenseal, ginseng (for the immune system), hyssop (inhibits viral growth), alfalfa, aloe vera (inhibits reproduction of herpes), echinacea, licorice, peppermint oil, red clover, marjoram, goldenseal, and myrrh. One of the most popular topical preparations incorporating herbs is Melissa cream, available in Europe and the United States, and made with *Melissa officinalis*, the botanical name for lemon balm. Epsom salts, oatmeal, or baking soda baths also may help. Eating seaweed seems to shrink and remove herpes. Monolaurin, isoprinosine, and AL 721 are lipids that have shown antiviral capabilities. The bioflavonoids hesperidin, catechin, and quercetin have antiviral activities against Herpes Simplex I. Transfer factor (injecting healthy cells into an infected person) is being used to fight herpes. Homeopathic remedies for cold sores, which are the outward signs of the herpes simplex virus, are Rhus toxicodendron, Lycopodium, and Natrum muriaticum.

Hypertension (High Blood Pressure)

Hypertension, an abnormal elevation of blood pressure, is found in one in three American adults. Of these, two in five African Americans have hypertension, one in five Hispanics, and one in six Native Americans. And of those with hypertension, more than 30 percent don't know they have it. The cause is generally unknown, but hypertension often accompanies arteriosclerosis and kidney disease.

Blood pressure is the force exerted by the blood against the walls of the blood vessels. The pressure can temporarily rise after physical activity or emotional tension but after a period of relaxation will return to normal. An abnormal condition arises when the pressure does not return to normal and remains high. This is called *essential hypertension*, meaning independent of local cause or disease without apparent cause. There are two blood pressure readings: a systolic, pressure taken at its highest while the heart is pumping; and a diastolic, pressure taken at its lowest in the rest between heartbeats. Neither reading should be high, with 110/70 to 140/90 being the normal range.

Even though there is no known cause for hypertension, it is known that lifestyle contributes with too much alcohol (binge drinking elevates blood pressure considerably), dietary fat, body fat, salt, and stress coupled with not enough fiber, exercise, potassium, and calcium. If this hypertension persists, it can cause heart disease (congestive heart failure, coronary artery disease, and diseases of the aorta), kidney disease, eye damage, or stroke.

In approximately 10 percent of hypertension cases, a physical disorder such as a kidney infection, an obstruction of an artery of the kidney, diabetes, a disorder of the adrenals, hyperthyroidism, sleep apnea, or a constriction of the aorta of the heart is present. Hypertension of these origins can usually be corrected. However, exact reasons for hypertension in most people may be difficult to find.

Atherosclerosis can contribute to hypertension because the blood has great difficulty in passing through arteries that are plugged with fatty substances; consequently, the blood pressure becomes high. Other factors that drive up blood pressure are obesity, cigarette smoking, excessive use of stimulants such as coffee and tea (especially when stressed) and drugs, and use of oral contraceptives.

Stress is an important factor to be considered in hypertension. Stress and tension cause the arterial walls to contract and become smaller. Many people drive themselves too hard and consequently become hypertensive. These people must learn to avoid stressful conditions by changing their lifestyle. They should eat regular, unhurried meals; try to avoid worry; allow themselves plenty of leisure time; take vacations; and generally use moderation in all things. If their occupations involve excessive emotional and physical stress, they may have to consider changing jobs or make adjustments to make their work less stressful. Steps should be taken to alleviate the prolonged stress of unexpressed emotions. Some people, because of their personality characteristics, overreact to emotional situations, causing more frequent and longer-lasting elevations of blood pressure. If this is not corrected, sustained hypertension may result.

A person with hypertension may have no symptoms or may experience headache, nervousness, insomnia, nosebleeds, blurred vision, edema, shortness of breath, dizziness, ringing in the ears, and eventually hemorrhaging in the eyes.

Diet is very important for hypertension and should be the first choice for treatment. A vegetarian diet full of fruits, vegetables, and grains has been found to be most helpful for lowering or eliminating high blood pressure. If that is not an option, animal fat must be severely reduced and sugar and salt must be reduced. Sodium is a primary contributor of hypertension because it causes fluid retention, which adds additional stress to the heart and circulatory system. In the Dietary Approaches to Stop Hypertension (DASH) trial, conducted by the National Institutes of Health and the National Heart, Lung, and Blood Institute, more than four hundred participants were fed high, medium, or low sodium diets. Dropping from high to low sodium intake reduced blood pressure from 6.7 over 3.5 points. Benefits are greatest in people who already have high blood pressure. The DASH diet, which is especially high in fruits and vegetables and low-fat dairy products, has proven beneficial. This way of eating increases the intake of fiber as well as minerals such as potassium and magnesium associated with lower levels of blood pressure. Potassium foods such as fish, bananas, potatoes, tomatoes, peaches, avocados, and orange juice should be consumed. Magnesium foods should also be eaten and may be found in cooked dried beans and peas, dark green leafy vegetables, nuts, soybeans, and seafood. Calcium foods such as skim or low-fat milk, spinach, and broccoli are also needed. Foods that have been known to lower blood pressure are celery, garlic, onion, fatty fish (salmon, sardines, tuna, herring, and mackerel three times a week) or fish oil, and olive oil.

Nutrients may help with hypertension. Increasing the potassium, calcium, and vitamin D intake will cause the body to excrete more sodium. Vitamin C and bioflavonoids can help maintain the health of the blood vessels, which are strained by the greater pressure placed on them by the hypertension. Bioflavonoids reduce cerebral hemorrhage that leads to death in hypertensives. Magnesium is also important. Aspirin may prevent a form of high blood pressure in pregnant women called preeclampsia. Niacin may reduce blood pressure. However, L-tyrosine, phenylalanine, and vitamin E may be harmful and should not be taken. If taking MAO-inhibitor drugs, do not use tyramine and tyrosine, since the combination will raise blood pressure. For those with hard-to-control blood pressure, the use of aspirin is not advised as it may cause stroke; consult a physician.

Herbs that may be helpful are fennel, black cohosh, cayenne, hawthorn, rosemary, suma tea, chrysanthemum flowers, lavender bath (for relaxation), chamomile, astragalus, parsley, reishi mushrooms, and peony root.

Regular, gentle exercise and weight loss for those who need it are essential in preventing and treating high blood pressure in order to keep the circulatory system healthy. Walking, slow swimming, and casual cycling are good choices. Promoting a tranquil outlook on life is of primary importance in reducing and preventing hypertension. Yoga will relax, stretch, and improve overall health and well-being. Sexual intercourse should be easygoing and may be dangerous to the hypertensive patient. Consult a physician.

Hyperthyroidism

Hyperthyroidism is overproduction of hormones by the thyroid gland, which also influences the pituitary, parathyroid, and sex glands. Symptoms of the condition are nervousness, irritability, fatigue, weakness, loss of weight and hair, separation of nails, goiter, insomnia, fluctuating moods, tremor of the hands, easy perspiring, protruding eyeballs, intolerance of heat, and rapid pulse or heartbeat. Hyperthyroidism can be caused by hereditary factors, emotional stress, or other unknown factors.

The excess production of thyroid hormones speeds up all body processes and malabsorption occurs. As a result, all nutrients in the body are depleted at a greater rate. The diet should therefore be increased in all nutrients. Eating a wide variety of whole foods is important. If weight loss has been great, additional protein may be necessary to replace muscle tissue that may have been lost. Coffee and tea containing caffeine should be avoided, because caffeine increases the metabolic rate, thereby resulting in more calories being expended. These beverages deplete nutrients because they are diuretics and increase vitamin and mineral loss via the urine. Nicotine and the initial effects of alcohol also increase the metabolic rate and should be avoided.

With respect to nutrients, particular attention should be paid to the adequate intake of the vitamin B complex because it is needed for the metabolism of the extra carbohydrates and protein.

Hypoglycemia (Low Blood Sugar)

Hypoglycemia is an abnormally low level of glucose, or sugar, in the blood. There are three general types of hypoglycemia. Two of them are rare organic forms involving the pancreas, tumors of the pancreas, and enlargement of the island of Langerhans. The third and most common form is called functional hypoglycemia (FH) and is caused by an inadequate diet that is too high in refined carbohydrates or that results in impaired absorption and assimilation of ingested food. An overconsumption of carbohydrates causes the blood sugar level to rise rapidly, stimulating the pancreas to secrete an excess of insulin. This excess insulin removes too much sugar from the blood, resulting in an abnormally low blood sugar level.

Although hypoglycemia is precipitated most often by an inadequate diet, susceptibility to it may be hereditary. In some people, hypoglycemia can contribute to other illnesses such as epilepsy, allergies, asthma, ulcers, arthritis, impotence, and mental disorders. Functional hypoglycemia is often found in people with such disorders as schizophrenia, alcoholism, drug addiction, juvenile delinquency, hyperactivity, and obesity. Hypoglycemia can also result from taking diabetes medication.

Symptoms of FH are episodic and have a direct relationship to the time and type of meal that was last eaten. They include fatigue, shakiness, weakness in legs, sweating, swollen feet, tightness in chest, constant hunger, eye ache, migraine, pains in various parts

of the body, nervous habits, mental disturbances such as brain fog, depression, irritability, confusion, and insomnia. Rapid fluctuations in blood sugar level can give rise to many bizarre symptoms that may suggest mental disorder. A glucose tolerance test will ascertain the amount of sugar in the blood at a given time. Poor adrenal function and impaired carbohydrate and protein metabolism are present. Functional hypoglycemia may be subclinical, which means the symptoms are subtle and difficult to diagnose. The patient may have a low but acceptable blood sugar level that does not drop until the last hours of a prolonged test.

The therapeutic diet for hypoglycemia is high in protein and fiber, low in carbohydrates, and moderate in fat. (A diet high in unrefined complex carbohydrates with moderate protein has also been used successfully.) The diet may be supplemented with high-protein between-meal snacks. Cruciferous vegetables should be limited or avoided because they suppress thyroid function. For instant relief, in an emergency, a small amount of sweet fruit, such as a few raisins, will quickly raise blood sugar. Milk can also help, raising blood sugar more slowly than, for instance, a piece of candy. Smaller, more frequent meals are called for with this condition, and not skipping meals will help.

Heavily sugared foods should be avoided, and foods with high natural sugar content should be restricted. Carbohydrates should include only the complex kinds that are slowly absorbed, such as fruits, vegetables, and whole grain products, so that the change in the blood sugar level will be gradual. Fructose, the form of sugar in fruit, has a less dramatic effect on blood sugar than glucose found in common white table sugar. Drink distilled water. Caffeine, alcohol, tobacco, and other stimulants should be avoided because they are capable of precipitating an attack of hypoglycemia.

Nutrients may be beneficial in controlling hypoglycemia. Vitamin and mineral supplementation is necessary to supply tissues that are markedly depleted. Digestive enzymes may be needed to ensure proper absorption of food. Chromium normalizes blood sugar metabolism.

For herbal therapy, fenugreek may help.

Hypotension (Low Blood Pressure)

The blood vessel walls of a person with hypotension are usually very relaxed and possibly flabby or stretched. Few nutrients or little oxygen can reach body tissues from vessels in this condition. This disease is often accompanied by hypoglycemia, hypothyroidism, or anemia. Symptoms of low blood pressure are fatigue, lack of endurance, sensitivity to heat and cold, development of a rapid pulse on exertion, and little interest in sex. The individual requires more sleep than normal people and often wakes up tired.

Systolic blood pressure as low as 100 or 80 may be considered healthy as long as that has always been normal for that person. However, if the systolic pressure has suddenly dropped to that level or if an individual has any of the symptoms just mentioned, hypotension may be the cause.

Mild deficiencies of calories, protein, or vitamins C and B complex (especially pantothenic acid) have produced low blood pressure. Adrenal exhaustion is commonly associated with the disease.

The diet should be sufficient in all nutrients, with emphasis on complete proteins and the vitamins B complex, C, and E. Since excessive amounts of salt may be excreted because of an undersupply of pantothenic acid, salty foods should be eaten daily until the pressure has reached normal.

Hypothyroidism

Found mostly in women, hypothyroidism is the underproduction of hormones by the thyroid gland. This condition impacts many body systems. Cellular metabolism slows, decreasing the rate at which the body uses carbohydrates, fats, and proteins. Hypothyroidism affects the hair, skin, and nails as well as the heart and skeletal system. A low thyroid level may cause night blindness and even deafness. Men may become impotent and have a low sperm count. Women's sex drive is lowered, ovulation may cease, and menstruation may be excessive or irregular. The brain cells are affected and intellectual capacity is impaired. Depression can result. A newborn baby may develop mental retardation unless thyroid hormone is quickly supplied. If an adult has additional forms of stress such as infection or surgery, a coma may result.

Hypothyroidism comes on gradually and is difficult to diagnose. Early symptoms such as fatigue, lack of zest, and sensitivity to cold may be attributed to other sources, such as stress. In the elderly, hypothyroidism is often mistaken for senility, exhibiting similar symptoms of depression, poor memory, and impaired mental condition Other symptoms include accumulation of fluid under the eye, decreased appetite, gaining weight even when not eating, constipation, sleeplessness, weak or aching muscles, lack of concentration, slurred speech, clumsiness, numbness and tingling in the hands and feet, and dull, dry hair and skin.

Measuring basal body temperature at one time was the standard test for hypothyroidism, but laboratory measurement of thyroid hormone levels in the blood has replaced this. However, the thyroid-stimulating hormone (TSH) blood test misses mild cases of hypothyroidism, which are most common, and is not sensitive enough for early detection. Many mild cases, such as may occur in postmenopausal women, go undiagnosed.

A person can self-test by collecting the first urine of the morning in a Styrofoam cup in which has been placed a basal temperature thermometer. (Using a Styrofoam cup will hold the heat of the urine and maintain its temperature.) Leave the urine in the cup for three minutes and record the temperature of the urine. For most reliable results, this procedure should be repeated every morning for a month. In women who are still menstruating, the most accurate readings are taken the fifth to the seventh day after their period begins. If the temperature of the urine is consistently below 98°F, the thyroid may be underactive. Results need to be confirmed by a physician.

Many cases are caused by autoimmune disease, in which the body attacks its own thyroid cells. Genetics seems to play a role, and the condition may also result from a deficiency of iodine.

Hypothyroidism is the easiest thyroid disease to reverse. An adequate diet supplying all nutrients at an optimal level is essential. Foods rich in iodine such as iodized salt, seafood, shellfish, and seaweed are needed. Avoid foods that inhibit the absorption of iodine, including peanuts, cabbage, soybeans, pine nuts, mustard, and turnips.

Nutrients may be beneficial. Vitamin A (beta-carotene may not be broken down), vitamins C and E, riboflavin, niacin, pyridoxine, and zinc may help. Treatment for hypothyroidism may include administration of thyroid hormone (thyroxine). Exercise is important because it stimulates the production of the thyroid hormones.

An herbal remedy that may be beneficial is bladderwrack. Natural ingredients may also help. Organic iodine, such as that found in kelp, may be better retained in the body and less likely to be readily excreted than potassium iodide.

Indigestion (Dyspepsia)

Indigestion, or dyspepsia, is imperfect or incomplete digestion, manifesting itself in a sensation of fullness or discomfort in the abdomen accompanied by pain or cramps, heartburn, nausea, and large amounts of gas in the intestines. Dyspepsia may be a symptom of a disorder in the stomach or small or large intestine, or it may be a complaint in itself. If indigestion occurs frequently and with no recognizable cause, medical investigation is advised. (See "Gastritis.")

Dyspepsia may be caused by psychological stresses, anxiety, worry, or disappointment, which disturb the nervous mechanism that controls the contractions of stomach and intestinal muscles. Other causes are over-eating or eating too rapidly; improper diet, such as a diet overabundant in carbohydrates at the expense of other nutrients; or overconsumption of stimulants such as coffee, tea, and alcohol. Smoking before or during a meal or swallowing too much air with meals, as when nervous or anxious, can also bring about indigestion.

Too little hydrochloric acid impairs the absorption of several vitamins and minerals and the digestion of protein. Insufficient amounts of hydrochloric acid can be brought about by a lack of vitamins A and B complex and low protein intake. This condition also results in a decreased amount of digestive enzymes and impaired stomach movements necessary to mix the food with the enzymes.

Heartburn, or acid or sour stomach, usually is caused by eating too fast or when exhausted or emo-tionally upset. Swallowing air during meals, especially easy when anxious, can result in heartburn. The air warms to body temperature, expands, and is belched with enough force to push stomach acid into the esophagus where it irritates membrane tissues, caus-ing discomfort. Antacids that contain magnesium and alkalizers are possibly more destructive (by causing diarrhea) than helpful. They neutralize all the acid in the stomach, preventing efficient digestion and thus interfering with vitamin and mineral absorption.

In treating dyspepsia, the diet should be nutrition-ally well balanced and high in fiber. Carbohydrates are usually the foods that create the gas. Foods should be monitored from individual to individual, since each person has his or her own sensitivities and some foods may need to be avoided, such as lentils and beans, dairy products, spicy and fatty foods, junk and pro-cessed foods, peanuts, tomatoes, carbonated bever-ages, and soybeans.

Acidophilus to increase friendly bacteria in the gut can be beneficial. The individual should eat slowly and avoid eating when overtired or upset. Hydrochloric acid tablets and digestive enzymes may be helpful. Papaya contains enzymes that can break down protein and other foods in the stomach. Pancreatic enzymes are also helpful. Peppermint has a soothing effect on the digestive tract and stimulates digestive secretion. Rice and barley broths may help with gas, bloating, and heartburn. Apple cider vinegar before meals may help with digestion. Charcoal tablets are good for gas but must be taken separately from meals—preferably not within one hour before or after a meal. Exercise will always aid the digestive process.

Herbs that may help are comfrey, chamomile, fen-nel, catnip, fenugreek, and goldenseal root. Slippery elm enemas may be used for colorectal inflammation.

Infections

Infections are the starting point of many illnesses and often they are not serious enough for medical atten-tion. However, besides the kind that can come from normal everyday wear and tear like cuts and minor wounds, infections can result in a wide variety of serious illnesses, including swollen glands or tonsils, sore throat, colds, hay fever, gangrene, encephalitis, and viral pneumonia. White blood cells, lymph cells, and antibodies mobilize to prevent any bacteria, virus, or toxin from entering the body. A nutritious diet is essential for the maintenance and reinforce-ment of these defenses. Symptoms of an infection may be fever, aching joints, redness, inflammation, and pus.

Nutrients may be helpful. Antioxidant nutrients such as vitamins C and E, beta-carotene, the B-complex vitamins, selenium, zinc, and magnesium are all ben-eficial, and supplements of these and other depleted vitamins and minerals should be considered.

Stress rapidly depletes the body of many nutrients, including the B-complex and C vitamins that are vital for the formation of antibodies. In addition, vitamin C directly destroys bacteria, viruses, and toxins. It aids the adrenal glands in stimulating the production of antibodies and white blood cells.

Vitamin A also supports the production of immune cells and prevents and clears up infections of the skin, the cornea of the eye, and the mucous mem-branes that line all body cavities. The vitamin A blood level drops very low during infections and often much is lost in the urine. Cortisone and other drugs given for infections can deplete the body of this vitamin. If antibiotics are taken, acidophilus is another necessary supplement. It will replace the intestinal bacteria that are destroyed.

Diet is important as the body's natural defensive substances are made of protein. Therefore, recovery from any infection will be prevented unless sufficient amounts of complete protein are consumed. Limiting nicotine, alcohol, and food additives in the diet is recommended, since these impair immunity. Broccoli, strawberries, tomatoes, dark leafy greens, orange vegetables, whole grains, oysters, liver, beans (lentils), cheddar cheese, eggs, mackerel, pork, oranges, black currants, and green peppers are all good choices. Following an anti-inflammatory diet is also important. (See "Inflammatory Conditions.")

Infections that result in minor respiratory illness, such as colds, sore throats, and bronchitis, are often a sign that the patient's system has become overly acidic. Restoring the body to a slightly alkaline state can be beneficial. Eating a more alkaline diet that emphasizes plant foods can begin to accomplish this. (See Section 5, Table 5.3, "Acid- and Alkaline-Forming Foods.") Taking small amounts of sodium bicarbonate in water can also be helpful.

Herbs that may help are alfalfa (fungal), aloe, crushed apple leaves, balm (streptococci), barberry (streptococci and staphylococci), crushed bay leaf, boneset (viral-like flu), burdock (bacteria and fungi), catnip (garden mishaps), chamomile compresses, cinnamon (decay- and disease-bearing fungi and viruses), clove (intestinal parasites), coriander and marshmallow (minor wounds and cuts), cranberry and dill (urinary tract infection), dandelion and echinacea (yeast infection), garlic (women's bladder, yeast infection, and flu virus), ginger (infectious diseases), goldenseal (bacterial, protozoan, and fungal infections), hops (bacterial infection), kelp (bacteria and fungi), licorice (streptococci, staphylococci, and *Candida albicans*, or yeast infection), peppermint oil (herpes virus), red pepper (boosts resistance), rosemary (minor cuts and wounds), St. John's wort and turmeric (wound treatment), tarragon (garden first aid), and uva ursi (wound healing and, in cream form, oral herpes and vaginal infections).

Homeopathic remedies for dental infection include Pyrogen 12x or 30x and Hepar sulph at no less than 30x.

Exercise, particularly yoga, is recommended.

Infertility/Impotence

A diagnosis of infertility is only given after a couple has had no success in conceiving after twelve months of regular, unprotected intercourse. About 10 percent to 15 percent of couples are considered to have some form of infertility. Male infertility is the cause in about 40 percent of the cases and by far the most common reason is low sperm count and/or poor sperm quality. Problems with a woman's reproductive system are responsible for another 40 percent of cases. And in the remaining instances, infertility is due to reproductive problems in both partners.

Couples having difficulty conceiving a child should consult a physician. A fertility specialist will perform tests to determine the problem and test for fertility, assessing sperm count. At one time, 40 million/mL of semen was considered the minimum necessary for a man to be fertile, but this minimum has now dropped to 10 million/mL as it has become evident that quality of sperm and not just quantity is important. In addition, the worries over a possible decline in male fertility in various populations now appear to have been unmerited. A large study in 2000 found no change in sperm count from a study fifty years earlier. Reasons for the discrepancy may be that sperm count can fluctuate by the season and year and also can vary according to region. In addition, a new test for assessing fertility is the postcoital test, which measures the ability of sperm to penetrate the cervical mucus after intercourse. Another test gives a reading on the presence of antisperm antibodies, usually a sign of infection in the male reproductive tract.

There are dozens of causes of infertility. In men, low sperm count may be due to abuse of alcohol, use of recreational drugs, certain prescribed medications, and exposure to toxins such as pesticides. Even small amounts of alcohol may cause impotence and infertility in certain males. Caffeinated products and smoking interfere with sperm production and contribute to impotence because of inhibited blood flow. Royal jelly or bee pollen and pumpkin seeds may interfere with conception. Accumulation of heavy metals such as mercury and lead in the system can lead to low sperm count. Presence of heavy metals is assessed using hair analysis.

Falling sperm count may also be caused by wearing tight underwear or taking a hot bath, which raises temperature of the scrotum and kills sperm. Infection, lack of sleep, and stress may also be at the root of the problem. Or a man may be allergic to the woman's natural lubricants with infertility the consequence. Using condoms intermittently for a month at a time can be helpful.

In women, infertility may be caused by problems with ovulation, endometriosis, adhesions, or obstructed fallopian tubes owing to scars from infections. An infection that blocks the fallopian tubes is pelvic inflammatory disease (PID). This includes other sexually or nonsexually contracted infections, but the most common is chlamydia. Symptoms are mild or severe pain during intercourse, pelvic pain, or abscesses in the tubes. The disease should be treated aggressively. Mild cases are treated with antibiotics; severe cases are usually treated with hospitalization. The disease can damage fallopian tubes to the point where in vitro fertilization is the only method of conception.

Another condition that interferes with conception in women is fibroid tumors. These tumors may grow and compress the fallopian tubes or disturb the lining of the uterus. They may also cause spontaneous abortion. Improving the diet and reducing stress are advisable. Fibroids may be shrunk with the supplementation of nutrients. Vitamins A, C, and E; the B-complex vitamins; bioflavonoids; and essential fatty acids are recommended. Chinese acupuncture treatment is known to shrink fibroids in some women.

Impotence is the inability to achieve and maintain an erection. Impotency may be caused by guilt, stress, anxiety, drugs, alcohol, fatigue, and depression; 10 percent is caused by disease or structural problems in the spinal cord. Older men have fewer erections because of lessened circulation and decreased levels of testosterone. Yoga is recommended.

If all else fails in attempting to conceive, there are several possible medical treatments, including in vitro fertilization and artificial insemination. However, before those methods are resorted to, there are some practical methods to try. The best times to conceive are the thirteenth, fourteenth, and fifteenth days before the next menstrual cycle. There are kits on the market that help determine the best time to conceive. Abstaining from sexual intercourse for several days beforehand will ensure a healthy sperm count. Avoiding tight clothing and hot baths for the male also can help. Egg whites should be used as a lubricant during intercourse, since this encourages sperm movement. For the female, lying down for at least thirty minutes after intercourse will allow the sperm to move freely. Women should not douche immediately after intercourse.

Nutrients may be beneficial. Vitamin B_6 helps infertility in women. Vitamin C "unclumps" sperm cells and helps other important minerals such as zinc (essential for sperm formation), magnesium, copper, and potassium, which are also vital to sperm functioning. By stimulating the pituitary gland, PABA may restore fertility. A chromium deficiency as well as a glucose intolerance in animals was accompanied by a decreased sperm count. A selenium deficiency gives rise to infertility. The amino acid arginine is vital to sperm production (4 grams orally daily). Birth defects have been shown to be reduced with 0.4 milligrams of B_6 daily. Another substance that may help is testosterone for those who suffer from erectile impotence and who show a deficiency.

Diet is important. Whole foods and a variety of them are always good. Fresh fruits and vegetables, dried beans and peas, lean meat, fish, and canola and olive oils are the best choices. Vitamin E foods are seeds, nuts, and wheat germ. Oysters, which are high in zinc, have long been considered an aphrodisiac. Oats have been shown to have aphrodisiac properties. Soy is recommended as an excellent source of phytoestrogens, which help balance hormones. Both men and women are exposed to estrogens and estrogenic compounds in the water supply, air, and food, which can interfere with sexual function. Isoflavonoids, the phytoestrogens in soy that have less of an estrogenic effect than human estrogen, bind with estrogen receptor sites, preventing the more potent form of estrogen from affecting reproductive function.

Exercise should be gentle, since increased activity appears to lower sperm count and lessen ovulation. Yoga is recommended to lessen stress, which inhibits conception for many reasons.

Herbs that may help are cibot root, ginseng (sexual desire), kava kava (heightens sexuality, although heavy use over a long period produces side effects), yohimbe (sexual depression over erectile problems), dong quai, burdock (impotence and sterility), gotu kola, and damiana (impotence and sterility). Aromatherapy includes ylang-ylang, sandalwood, and clary sage.

Inflammatory Conditions

Inflammation is associated with a wide range of conditions from sinusitis to rheumatoid arthritis as well as emphysema. (The suffix -*itis* is of Greek origin and means "inflammation of.") It is a nonspecific immune response that occurs in reaction to any type of bodily injury, including physical trauma, a foreign body, or a pathogenic organism. Getting a splinter from walking barefoot or cutting a finger while cooking will trigger an inflammatory response. Telling signs are redness, heat, swelling, and pain. The process involves an increase in blood flow to the injured area and then increased vascular permeability to allow plasma to pass out of the capillaries and into the tissues. At this stage there is edema and possibly pain. Next, various components of the immune system travel from the bloodstream to the injured tissues to destroy the pathogen or control any tissue damage that has occurred. Acute inflammation is of rapid onset and quickly resolves, likely within twelve hours, while chronic inflammation is less intense and lasts for an extended period of time. It is this latter form of inflammation that in recent years has drawn the attention of the medical community. Research is showing that chronic inflammation touches many diseases not strictly considered inflammatory, including diabetes, obesity, cancer, Alzheimer's disease, and heart disease. This sort of inflammation ages the body, what Italian researchers have termed "inflamaging."

The standard blood test to assess inflammation has long been to measure the sedimentation rate, which indicates how quickly red blood cells settle and form a sediment. Blood cells settle faster when inflammation is present. The downside of this test is that it is an extremely general indicator. However, a new and inexpensive test, high-sensitivity C-reactive protein (CRP), though not currently part of routine lab work, is available. It is a more accurate indicator of chronic, systemic inflammation. Researchers at Harvard Medical School and Brigham and Women's Hospital in Boston monitored more than twenty-eight thousand healthy, postmenopausal women for three years and found that CRP was the most accurate predictor of heart disease compared with eleven other factors, including LDL cholesterol.

Systemic, chronic inflammation can be triggered by a variety of toxins and allergens as well as problems with blood sugar, physical injury, oxidation, stress, and a deficiency of oxygen in tissues. Toxins include such synthetic compounds as pollutants in the air, household chemicals, medications, and pesticides, naturally occurring compounds such as microbes and plant toxins, heavy metals and toxins in the body such as secondary bile acids, and ammonia. Any food that may lead to an allergic reaction, including dairy products, nuts, and grains such as wheat and oats, can also trigger inflammation.

These triggers release mediators of inflammation within the body, such as neurotransmitters, hormones, reactive oxygen species, cytokines, and eicosanoids. A complex chemistry is involved in the formation and release of these substances. For instance, prostaglandins, a type of eicosanoid and classified in series, either promote inflammation (series 2) or are anti-inflammatory (series 1). How much of one type of prostaglandin versus another the body produces depends upon the mix of omega-6 fatty acids (safflower oil) and omega-3 fatty acids (flax oil) in the diet. (See Section 3 for information on the fatty acid composition of oils.) The omega-6 fatty acids produce arachidonic acid and in turn, the series 2 prostaglandins are derived from these, while omega-3 fatty acids reduce the synthesis of the pro-inflammatory series 2 compounds. Diet can also be used to inhibit the synthesis of compounds.

Foods that participate in this chemistry and have an anti-inflammatory effect include those that supply the omega-3 fatty acids, such as fish, walnuts, flaxseeds, and canola oil, as well as certain specially balanced cooking oils that can be found in natural food stores. Onion, garlic, and ginger are anti-inflammatory, blocking the pro-inflammatory effect of arachidonic acid. It is also important to avoid dietary sources of arachidonic acid such as beef fat and egg yolk. The spice turmeric used in curries, because of its active ingredient curcumin longa, is anti-inflammatory. The herbs wintergreen and boswellia dampen inflammation.

Specific nutrients have an anti-inflammatory effect. These include lipoic acid, vitamin C, vitamin E, and flavonoids. The phytonutrient quercetin, found in onions and available as a supplement, inhibits inflammation. Supplementing with tripeptide glutathione, cysteine or N-acetylcysteine, or selenium may be helpful.

Kwashiorkor

Kwashiorkor is a severe malnutritional disease caused by a diet that supplies adequate calories through carbohydrates but is seriously lacking primarily in protein but also in zinc and other nutrients. Kwashiorkor commonly develops in children who are between the ages of one and five and who are weaned from mother's milk to a diet of primarily starches and sugars.

Symptoms of kwashiorkor include changes in the skin and hair, retarded growth, diarrhea, loss of appetite, and nervous irritability. The belly bulges with a fatty liver, and there is swelling known as edema. Severe infections and many vitamin deficiencies often accompany kwashiorkor.

The initial treatment for the disease is aimed at correcting the protein deficiency. Because of the patient's poor ability to tolerate fat, a skim milk formula is often used in treatment. Gradually, additional foods are added until the patient progresses to a well-balanced diet. Vitamin deficiencies, if they exist, must be corrected.

Leg Cramp and Charley Horse

A leg cramp is an involuntary contraction or spasm of a muscle in the leg or foot. Cramps most commonly occur at night when the limbs are cool and there is poor circulation, particularly after a day of unusual exertion. They happen more frequently in the elderly, the young, and people with arteriosclerosis. These cramps seem to be caused by an imbalance in the body of potassium and sodium, or calcium and magnesium. Another cause may be unnatural positions or repetitive actions that impair the blood supply, causing the muscles to abnormally contract. People who use a lot of diuretics, such as those with high blood pressure, may experience cramping and may need potassium supplements.

A cramp usually lasts only a few seconds or minutes. Treatment is to drink fluids immediately and begin stretching the contracting muscle. If a cramp occurs while a person is walking, it may be a signal of seriously impaired circulation, but a cramp that occurs while a person is resting does not indicate this severity.

Nutrients may be deficient. Leg cramps may signify a variety of nutritional deficiencies. The most common is lack of calcium, which is necessary for normal muscle contraction. Other deficiencies indicated are vitamin E, thiamin, pantothenic acid, biotin, and magnesium. Occasionally a sodium loss, such as occurs in heavy perspiration or diarrhea, may result in muscle cramps. A vitamin C deficiency also can be responsible for pains in the muscles and joints.

Nutrients may help. Calcium should be increased and vitamin D is needed for absorption of calcium. Vitamin E (300 IU) and bioflavonoids are good for night cramps.

Although there is no prevention, treatment for leg cramps should include an adequate diet containing sufficient amounts of dark green leafy vegetables, milk, cheese, yogurt, canned fish, liver, egg yolk, broccoli, and sesame products.

A charley horse is a pulled and bruised muscle that results in soreness and stiffness. It is usually caused by a blow or a forceful stretch of the leg during athletic activity. A fifteen-minute warm-up before exercising will help eliminate cramping. A person who has suffered a charley horse should have a high intake of protein to rebuild stressed tissues. Regular exercise will also help prevent cramps.

Herbal remedies are ginkgo, dong quai, chaparral, quinine, horsetail grass, silica, saffron, and elderberry extract. Alfalfa, brewer's yeast, kelp, and chlorophyll are helpful. Homeopathy recommends Cuprum metallicum 6c.

Liver Disorders

The liver, located under the diaphragm just above the stomach, is the largest organ of the body. Countless chemical reactions take place in the liver every day, including the synthesis of amino acids, sugar conversion and storage, and storage of some vitamins and minerals. It also produces lecithin, cholesterol, enzymes, and bile and detoxifies harmful substances such as pesticides, food additives, and environmental pollutants. The liver is the only organ that can regenerate itself if it is damaged. Liver damage can result from chronic alcoholism, overweight and obesity, drug or chemical ingestion, or improper diet. (See "Cirrhosis of the Liver" and "Hepatitis.")

Slight liver injury may go largely unnoticed, producing vague symptoms such as digestive disturbances and fatigue. Long before actual damage is detected, the liver may have degenerated cells, fat accumulation, scar tissue, and greatly reduced enzymes and bile, resulting in poor utilization of nutrients. Starch is neither formed nor stored, which causes chronic fatigue, excessive weight, and obesity. Lecithin is not properly synthesized, and fats are inefficiently used. When the liver cannot metabolize certain enzymes needed to inactivate various hormones, such conditions as water retention, hypoglycemia, hyperthyroidism, and excessive male or female hormones in the opposite sex can result.

Deficiencies of the B-complex vitamins, vitamins C and E, and certain amino acids limit enzyme synthesis. A severe vitamin C, vitamin E, and protein deficiency may result in massive cell death and hemorrhaging of the liver. Liver damage in animals has occurred when they are fed diets high in refined carbohydrates, high in saturated fats, or low in magnesium, calcium, and the sulfur-containing amino acids.

Diet and nutrients may help. The liver can usually regenerate if the diet is adequate, supplying all essential nutrients, including complete proteins, the B complex, and vitamins C and E. Branched-chain amino acids may reverse hepatic encephalopathy. Lipotropes and myoinositol help prevent fatty deposits in the liver. Phosphatidylcholine may be used in the treatment of viral hepatitis.

Vitamins A, C, and E (protects against chronic liver disease) and choline aid the liver in detoxifying harmful drugs and chemicals. Vitamin B$_6$, magnesium, acidophilus, digestive enzymes, and lecithin can prevent the accumulation and formation of ammonia, which results from a damaged liver's inability to properly break down proteins. Garlic helps the liver detoxify chemicals. Herbs that may help with liver problems are reishi mushrooms (for hepatitis), burdock, indigo, blessed thistle, milk thistle, seaweed, sweet woodruff, licorice, Oregon grape, tumeric, dandelion, ginseng (detoxifies), parsley, schizandra, and yarrow.

In some cases of liver disease, liquid accumulates in the abdomen, a condition called *ascites*. The liver does not produce enzymes needed to inactivate a urine-controlling hormone, and insufficient urine is formed. Ascites can be helped by an adequate diet and 2 tablespoons of brewer's yeast after each meal.

Measles

Measles is a viral disease most commonly affecting school-age children, although adults contract the disease as well. There are two main varieties: German measles and common measles. There is an immunization but if there are existing conditions, there may be complications. Consult a physician to be safe.

German measles (rubella) is caused by a virus and has a rapid recovery period, but the disease must run its course and there is little that can be done medically for its treatment. German measles is a mild illness, alarming only to pregnant women. If a woman contracts German measles during the early months of pregnancy, the newborn can suffer from such malformations as heart defects, deafness, mental retardation, and blindness.

Symptoms of German measles may include fever, headache, and stiff joints (mainly in the neck), although most people seldom complain of any symptoms. A rash that lasts for about three days appears on the arms, chest, and forehead. Lotions may be applied to the rash to relieve itching, and the patient should stay away from other people to avoid spreading the disease. A well-balanced diet rich in all nutrients is recommended. One attack of the disease (or a vaccination for it) will usually produce lifelong immunity against German measles.

Common measles (rubeola) is a highly contagious disease spread by droplets from the nose, throat, and mouth. The first symptoms of common measles are a fever that lasts for a couple of days, followed by a cough, runny nose, and inflammation of the eyes. Stomach pains, diarrhea, and vomiting may also occur. Within twenty-four to forty-eight hours, small red spots with white centers appear on the inside of the cheeks. A rash, which is first seen on the face and upper neck and then spreads down the back and trunk and then to the limbs, usually appears three to five days after the onset of the first symptoms. As the rash spreads, fever goes down. After about five days, the rash fades in the same order it appeared. Common measles may have many serious complications, such as ear infections, pneumonia, encephalitis, and injury to the nervous system.

Treatment for common measles is isolation in a well-ventilated room that is darkened if the patient is sensitive to light. Nutrients and diet may be helpful. Fevers increase the body's need for fluids, calories, and vitamins A (strengthens cells) and C. Increasing fluids in any form, such as water or fruit and vegetable juices, is good. Eventually, soups and cereals may be introduced. Frequent small meals and special foods may be beneficial.

Herbs that may be helpful are yarrow, goldenrod, catnip, echinacea decoction, safflower, honeysuckle, peppermint, lobelia (for pain), and aloe vera. Baking soda baths are soothing. Homeopathic remedies are Belladonna 6c, Aconite 6c, Pulsatilla 6c, and Euphrasia 6c.

Ménière's Syndrome

Ménière's syndrome is a disease of the inner ear in which an increase of fluids leads to recurrent attacks of deafness, tinnitus (ringing in either or both ears), vertigo (balance), nausea, vomiting, sound distortion, and a feeling of pressure in the inner ear.

Conditions in the inner ear that may cause this disease are hemorrhage, poor circulation, fluid imbalance, clogged arteries, or a spasm of a blood vessel subsequently leading to vasodilation and an increased flow of blood. Allergies, premenstruation, eye or mental strain, stress, alcohol, tobacco, or an inadequate diet, especially a deficiency of the B vitamins, can precipitate Ménière's attacks. Ménière patients have been found to be chronically deficient in the B vitamins, possibly due to defective utilization of the B complex. Gallbladder disease occurs in these patients at twice the rate of the general population.

Nutrients may be helpful. Nicotinic acid, or niacin, because of its vasodilator action, has been shown to be effective in controlling Ménière's syndrome caused by vasodilation.

Diet for Ménière's syndrome should be low salt (or salt free), low in fats, and high in fiber. Since attacks often follow an illness in which antibiotics are given, adequate intake of all nutrients is recommended. Except for water, fluids may be reduced. Raw vegetables, beans, seeds, nuts, seaweed, fish, and low-fat yogurt are good choices. Acidophilus aids in the restoration of beneficial intestinal bacteria and also in the manufacture of the B vitamins.

Substances to avoid are caffeine, present in chocolate, cola, tea, and coffee; fried foods; processed and refined foods; alcohol; and food additives and preservatives.

Herbs that may help are butcher's broom and ginkgo. Exercise keeps the blood in circulation.

Menopause

Menopause is the period in a woman's life marked by glandular changes that bring on the end of her menstrual cycle and reproductive years. Menopause usually results from a decreased production of female sex hormones when a woman is between the ages of forty-two and fifty-two.

Poor diet, lack of exercise, and emotional stress may exaggerate the symptoms and discomfort of menopause. Fatigue is the most commonly reported symptom of menopause. As the body changes gear, it is a time for rest. In addition, menopause-related insomnia and night sweats interfere with sleep. Some women experience severe nervous symptoms and become irritable, anxious, or depressed. They may have headaches, abdominal pains, or rushes of blood to the head and upper body that are known as "hot flashes." Hot flashes trigger sweats and as the perspiration evaporates from the skin, the woman's body

will feel cold. Other symptoms include backaches, leg cramps, nosebleeds, frequent bruises, varicose veins, dry skin, brittle hair, poor concentration, tearfulness, rheumatic symptoms such as arthritis, constipation, and irregular menstrual bleeding. The onset of such ailments occurs during perimenopause, which encompasses the years leading up to menopause. Problems such as hot flashes are thought to be triggered not by reduced production of estrogen but rather by changing hormone levels that dramatically rise and fall. However, some women experience few or any of these conditions; they sail through menopause untroubled, with only perhaps the occasional hot flash.

Usually within a few months or a year or two, the body adjusts and the symptoms disappear. Although the menstrual periods cease, a woman's normal sexual needs remain after menopause, and accelerated aging is not the norm.

Diet changes at the onset of symptoms can help. Many foods are estrogenic, in particular, soybeans and flaxseed, which have been shown to raise estrogen levels. Soy products that qualify are tofu, soy milk, tempeh, and textured soy protein. The mineral boron has an estrogenic effect. Foods that are rich in boron are grapes, dates, peaches, almonds, hazelnuts, honey, apples, pears, and raisins. Wheat bran, legumes, and cruciferous vegetables such as broccoli, brussels sprouts, cauliflower, and cabbage are also estrogenic foods. In general, a diet high in plant foods delivers a good supply of estrogenic compounds. Taking hormone replacement therapy (HRT) can also help balance hormones and reduce some symptoms of menopause but not without risk of developing certain types of cancers. If considering HRT, consult with an informed physician about the benefits and alternatives.

Whole grain cereals and fruit and vegetables are good choices to help with symptoms. Vitamin E foods are wheat germ and nuts, peaches, whole grain cereals, broccoli, dried prunes, spinach, avocados, vegetable oils, and seeds. B vitamins are found in wheat germ and are good when taken with a fruit and a B-complex supplement. Three servings of calcium-rich foods, including green leafy vegetables such as kale and mustard greens, cooked dried beans, and whole grain cereals are recommended. The use of dairy sources of calcium needs to be monitored as dairy products can increase cramping and fluid retention, PMS-like symptoms of perimenopause. Reducing the amount of red meat in the diet is recommended. Caffeine, alcohol, chocolate, and refined and processed foods are not good choices.

If long-term nutrient deficiencies have left the body unprepared for the stress of menopause, and particularly if symptoms are severe, all nutrients needed for coping with a stressful situation and for stimulating the adrenals, such as vitamin A, the B vitamins, and vitamin C, should be taken. (See "Stress" and "Adrenal Exhaustion.") Nutrients that support the adrenal glands are important at this time because as ovarian production of estrogen gradually decreases, the adrenal glands assume this function and start making both estrogens and androgens, taking over many actions of the ovarian hormones.

The vitamin E requirement (up to 1,200 IU daily) is exceptionally high during menopause, and supplements have relieved night sweats, hot flashes, backaches, fatigue, nervousness, insomnia, dizziness, shortness of breath, and heart palpitations in many women. If supplemental estrogen is taken, the need for the vitamin increases further. Vitamin E foods are wheat germ and nuts, peaches, whole grain cereals, broccoli, dried prunes, spinach, avocados, vegetable oils, and seeds.

At menopause, calcium is absorbed less and excreted more. A deficiency can cause nervousness, irritability, insomnia, headaches, and depression. Vitamin D and magnesium are needed for proper calcium absorption: 2 grams of calcium, 1,000 IU of vitamin D, and 1 gram of magnesium daily have been used effectively in a clinical setting. The calcium-phosphorus balance should be carefully maintained during the mature years.

Vitamins A and C, the B complex, and zinc are important for skin maintenance. The B complex, especially pantothenic acid and PABA, relieves nervous irritability. Vitamin C together with bioflavonoids increase capillary strength, helping prevent heavy menstrual flow that sometimes occurs during perimenopause.

The herb dong quai, widely used in Europe, documented in sound research and readily available in the United States as the supplement Remifemin, can relieve some of the symptoms of menopause such as hot flashes. Siberian ginseng has been found to be successful in treating hot flashes, night sweats, anxiety, and vaginal dryness. Peony root, Chinese angelica, and thorowax may also help.

Aerobic exercise is vital to the health of menopausal women and is best when combined with yoga. Walking, swimming, and any enjoyable activity that raises the heartbeat to the individual target rate is good. In addition, acupuncture treatments can lessen symptoms of menopause.

Mental Illness and Schizophrenia

Our conception of mental and emotional normality and abnormality is shaped in part by research and scientific knowledge, social attitudes and trends, and cultural values. Change in these areas is ongoing. Stereotyped images of mental illness are being modified, and individuals with mental illness are no longer being labeled as emotionally weak, incurable, dangerous, or abnormal. The realization that they share our environment with a view that differs in varying degrees from the norm is becoming more acceptable. (See "Depression/Bipolar Mood Disorder.")

Certain personality types combined with environmental influences trigger mental instability, possibly causing biological and chemical changes within. What is evident from the information from years of studies is that mental illness stems from *a personality type that is genetic or inherited and that is extraordinarily sensitive to the surrounding environment*. An individual's stress reactions (environmental) and a vulnerability (genetic) to the disorder are important. The immediate surroundings of those who succumb to this disease are often challenging, even if mildly so. Science has also isolated the aspect of family communication as one contributor to schizophrenia. Negative parenting techniques and attitudes that are passed on from generation to generation may be a problem. There is also a growing body of research linking nutritional deficiencies with a variety of mental disorders.

Under the listing of mental illness, there are six disorders. They are anxiety, somatoform, dissociative, mood, schizophrenic, and personality.

- **Anxiety** disorders may be of the generalized type, which includes feelings that are not connected to anything specific; phobic, or a persistent and irrational fear of an object or a situation that represents no danger; panic disorder, which involves recurrent attacks of overwhelming anxiety that occur suddenly and also includes agoraphobia, or fear of public places; and obsessive-compulsive disorder, or the persistent and uncontrollable intrusion of unwanted thoughts (obsessions) and urges to engage in senseless rituals (compulsions).

- **Somatoform** disorders are more severe and are physical complaints that appear to be psychological in origin. They are a conversion disorder, or loss of physical function with no physical reason. Symptoms are partial or complete loss of vision, partial or complete loss of hearing, partial paralysis, severe laryngitis or mutism, and loss of feeling or function in the limbs. Hypochondriasis is a preoccupation with health concerns that often appears alongside other disorders such as anxiety and depression.

- **Dissociative** disorders are psychogenic amnesia, which is the sudden loss of personal information that is extensive, and multiple personality disorder, which involves the coexistence of more than one complete personality in one body.

- **Mood** disorders show a distortion in emotions, and schizophrenia shows a distortion in thought resulting in changes in personality and behavior. Thoughts become disassociated with the physical reality of the body and what is truly going on within the immediate environment.

- Five main biotypes of **schizophrenia** have been identified: histapenia, characterized by low blood histamine with excess copper; histadelia with high blood histamine and low copper; pyroluria, which is a familiar double deficiency of zinc and vitamin B_6; cerebral allergy, which includes wheat-gluten allergy; and nutritional hypoglycemia or low blood sugar. Symptoms of one or the other of these types of schizophrenia include hallucinations, hearing commanding voices, illusions, delusions, depression, tension, insomnia, fatigue, faulty thinking, deterioration of social behavior, and paranoia. Other features of schizophrenia are social withdrawal, disturbed sense of self, and hesitant speech.

- **Personality** disorders are marked by traits that cause distress in social and occupational functioning. They are anxious-fearful (avoidant, dependent, passive-aggressive, and mild obsessive-compulsive), odd-eccentric (schizoid and paranoid), and dramatic-impulsive (histrionic, narcissistic, borderline, and antisocial).

Extensive research, over time, indicates that there is no direct genetic, chemical, or biological cause of mental illness. No gene has been discovered, and chemical and neurotransmitter theories are riddled with problems and are not nearly as convincing as once thought to be. No one is born with mental illness; it appears to be induced.

Some types of mental illness may be a direct result of poor nutrition. Brain cells must be properly nourished to function efficiently. Deficiencies of nutrients appear to have a great deal to do with creating the symptoms of the disease. Deficiencies of the B vitamins, ascorbic acid (vitamin C), and phosphorus are known to decrease the metabolic rate of the brain. Irritability and listlessness are also symptoms of vitamin C deficiency.

A vitamin B-complex deficiency results in loss of appetite, depression, irritability, confusion, loss of memory, inability to concentrate, fear, and sensitivity to noise. Deficiency of niacin may cause symptoms of deep depression often seen in psychosis. Symptoms of a severe vitamin B_6 deficiency are headache, irritability, dizziness, extreme nervousness, and inability to concentrate. Signs of a thiamin deficiency are lack of energy, constant fatigue, loss of appetite, and irritability. A prolonged thiamin deficiency may result in brain damage, contributing to emotional upsets characterized by overreaction to normal stress. Folic acid levels have been found to be low in a large percentage of psychiatric patients.

A person with a magnesium deficiency is apt to be uncooperative, withdrawn, apathetic, or belligerent. Defective adrenal function may contribute to depression and other forms of mental illness. A shortage of thyroxine (the iodine-carrying hormone) generally results in a slowdown of both physical and mental activity. An unbalanced blood sugar level and hypothyroidism (which leads to a deficiency of thyroxine in the blood) are acknowledged causes of emotional disturbances.

A deficiency of pantothenic acid can cause such reactions as becoming upset, irritable, depressed, tense, dizzy, and numb. Calcium deficiency results in tenseness, insomnia, and fatigue. Insufficient amounts of minerals can cause fatigue, weakness, apathy, poor equilibrium, hyperactivity, and uncoordinated movements. Inadequate protein causes depression, apathy, irritability, and a desire to be left alone.

Allergy specialists and psychiatrists have successfully treated patients by isolating foods and chemicals in the environment. Symptoms that vary from fatigue and dizziness to hyperactivity, catatonia (a complete loss of voluntary motion), and hallucinations have all been helped.

Allergic reactions may be a factor in criminal behavior. Allergens are able to get into the bloodstream and circulate through the brain. Besides immediate reactions that affect the brain, there is another response called masked food allergy that does not produce negative symptoms until hours after ingestion of the offensive food.

An example of a mental disorder that is caused by food allergies involves a patient of Dr. H. L. Newbold of New York who had spent nearly five years in a psychiatric hospital diagnosed as schizophrenic. The doctor placed the patient on a five-day spring water fast to cleanse her body of allergens. Her worst symptoms began to disappear. The doctor then began a refeeding program and watched for any foods that would cause a reaction. This particular patient was found to be allergic to sugar, which rapidly brought back her previous illness. Other patients have been found to be allergic to wheat, corn, milk, and cigarette smoke.

Many allergists feel that the typical modern diet, which is high in nonnutritive sugar and refined foods, does not provide optimal nutrition for the human body and therefore lowers resistance to allergies. Sweets should be taken minimally. Excellent vitamin B-complex food choices that are especially rich in niacin are tuna, tomatoes, carrots, chicken, turkey, eggs, beans, peas, sunflower seeds, brewer's yeast, peanut butter, halibut, low-fat dairy products such as milk and cheese, soybeans, nuts, and cereals with corn, millet, rice, and potato products.

Wheat and products containing wheat should be avoided since the gluten may be an allergen. Avoid alcohol and caffeine in all products, including chocolate, tea, colas, and coffee. Food additives, preservatives, pesticide residues on food, air pollution, household cleaning items, and chlorine and fluorine in drinking water have been found to precipitate allergic reactions. Excess amounts of uric acid have been found in children who feel the need to mutilate themselves. Foods that contain purines like gravies, consommé, stocks, organ meats, sweetbreads, shellfish, anchovies, sardines, herring, mussels, mushrooms, and asparagus should be avoided.

One of the symptoms of schizophrenia and paranoid personality disorder is a fear that food has been poisoned—a fear that may contribute to the malnutrition of the individual. Education on what to eat and what not to, along with allowing the person his or her private method of consumption, may be helpful.

Nutrients also may help. This is the premise of the Princeton Brain Bio Center, founded by pioneering research nutritionist Carl C. Pfeiffer, Ph.D., M.D. The center has treated thousands of patients through the years using orthomolecular medicine. Zinc, vitamin B_6, and manganese have been used to treat one form of schizophrenia. A protocol for addressing mental illness caused by food allergy makes use of zinc, manganese, vitamin B_6, and vitamin C.

Supplemental nutrients work to correct the source rather than to disguise it, so the response may be slow. Sometimes three to six months at least are necessary for changes to become apparent. It has been shown that megavitamin therapy for psychological disorders doubled the recovery rate and may help eliminate the suicide rate in schizophrenics. Megadoses of vitamins B_3, B_6, C, and E may be recommended.

Vitamins A, B_1, B_2, B_3, B_6, C, D, and E, and pantothenic acid have been found to be effective in lessening or blocking allergic reactions and promoting overall health. Amino acid supplementation may be needed. The proper phosphorus-to-calcium ratio (1:2) is essential for nourishment of the entire nervous system.

Pantothenic acid is essential for the body's ability to handle stressful situations. A lack of oxygen is involved in many cases of mental disturbance, since the brain is dependent upon an uninterrupted supply of oxygen not only to function properly but also to stay alive. Vitamin E is an oxygen conserver and increases the amount of oxygen available to the brain.

Scientists at the Massachusetts Institute of Technology have found that choline has a direct and almost immediate effect on brain function. Because of this discovery, choline has been used successfully for the treatment of a neurological disease called tardive dyskinesia (caused in some people by the medications prescribed for schizophrenia that cause tremors and other involuntary bodily movements) and for manic-depressives. It may also be a factor in improving the memory of the aged. The high copper level present in many schizophrenics can be reduced by dietary intake of zinc and manganese.

Aromatherapy for anxiety includes basil, bergamot, cedarwood, Roman chamomile, clary sage, cypress, frankincense, geranium, juniper, lemon, sweet marjoram, myrrh, orange blossom, orange, patchouli, petitgrain, rose otto, sandalwood, vetiver, and ylang-ylang.

Mononucleosis

Mononucleosis is an infectious disease caused by the Epstein-Barr virus (EBV) or the cytomegalovirus (CMV). It affects primarily the lymph tissues or glands located in the neck, armpits, and groin. The lymph glands remove many microscopic materials such as bacteria and viruses, thus helping prevent the infection from spreading throughout the body. Mononucleosis is spread by coughing, sharing utensils, sneezing, and kissing (hence its nickname the "kissing disease"). However, mononucleosis is far less contagious than commonly thought, and the vast majority of infections don't develop into the disease. Adolescents and young adults (between ages ten and twenty-five) are the ones most likely to contract "mono"; and when it is present, it is severe, sometimes lasting three months or longer. The following year, tiredness may return and last a year, but when that is over, the immune system has learned to fully control the virus and the disease cannot be contracted again, according to the Centers for Disease Control and Prevention.

Symptoms of mononucleosis appear four to seven weeks after infection and include sore throat, fever, chills, swollen glands, and extreme fatigue. In one study, people who had a particular antigen in their blood to fight the virus were immune to mono.

Adequate rest and a well-balanced, whole foods diet is essential for the maintenance of general health and for treatment and prevention of mononucleosis. Low-fat dairy products; cod liver oil; egg yolks; liver; kidney; dark green, yellow, and orange vegetables and fruits; wheat germ; whole wheat bread; nuts; vegetable oil; seeds; brewer's yeast; soybeans; lean meat; fish; brown rice; oatmeal; and poultry are recommended. Avoid alcohol and smoking. Drinking plenty of fluids is important. Protein is needed to stimulate the formation of antibodies—substances that protect against other infections that may accompany or follow mononucleosis.

Nutrients may be beneficial. Potassium and vitamin C supplements (500 milligrams three times a day) may be needed to compensate for the loss that occurs during fever. The B complex (50 milligrams daily) will also help. Vitamin A (beta-carotene) is needed for the health of the tissue lining of the throat. Vitamin E, copper, zinc, and selenium are all important. If there is a deficiency of thiamin, riboflavin, or biotin, supplementing these nutrients in the diet may prevent fatigue and headaches.

Herbs that may help are myrrh, dandelion, honeysuckle, echinacea, red peony, goldenseal, dyer's woad leaf, forsythia fruit, pau d'arco, and chrysanthemum flowers. Homeopathic remedies include Mercurius 6c, Ailanthus 6c, and Phytolacca 6c.

Mouth and Tongue Disorders

A deficiency of the B vitamins in particular can manifest in various abnormalities of the mouth, gums, and tongue. A sore mouth is one of the first indications of a B_6 deficiency; a lack of folic acid causes the development of ulcerated lips and sore mouth, throat, and esophagus. The mouth, throat, esophagus, tongue, and gums become sore from insufficient niacin. The gums become puffy, tender, and bleed easily as a result of inadequate vitamin C. The oral membranes become susceptible to canker sores when vitamins C and niacin are undersupplied. (See "Tooth and Gum Disorders, Gingivitis, and Periodontitis" and "Halitosis.")

Mouth ulcers and sores may be white, yellow, or gray spots; may cluster or appear singly; and can be very painful. They can be a sign of digestive problems, stress, a virus, or irritations from dental work or braces. A diet of juices, fruits, and vegetables followed later by whole grains and raw and cooked vegetables is desirable (food may be liquefied). Nutrients that may help are vitamin A (750 IU daily), vitamin E (250 IU daily), and vitamin B_2 (riboflavin, 10 milligrams daily). Herbs that may help are myrrh, blackberry, and rose (rosaceae) petals. Aromatherapy for mouth ulcers is cypress, geranium, myrrh, and tea tree.

The tongue of a healthy person is smooth and an even red color. "Geographic tongue" occurs from a prolonged deficiency of the B vitamins; the taste buds clump together and create fissures and ridges. Inadequate B_2 can discolor the tongue, turning it purplish while insufficient niacin can color it bright red. A smooth, shiny tongue indicates a B_{12} or folic acid deficiency. An enlarged beefy-looking tongue can result from a lack of pantothenic acid. A coated tongue can indicate putrifactive bacteria that are allowed to grow in the intestinal tract. Including acidophilus in the diet will aid the growth of beneficial bacteria as well as create a medium for the manufacture of B vitamins.

Multiple Sclerosis

Multiple sclerosis (MS) is a chronic, nonfatal disease that causes the deterioration of the protective covering of the nerve cells (myelin sheath) in the brain and spinal cord. This results in the hardening of various parts of the nervous system and the development of scars or lesions on the disturbed nerves. One theory is that MS is an autoimmune disease in which the body attacks itself because of some kind of message mistake.

Most of the research into the origins and treatment of multiple sclerosis focuses on the immune system and T-lymphocytes in order to find a way to alter the immune response. In addition, glial cells, which produce myelin, are being researched for their role in supplying healthy cells after disease. It appears that myelin deteriorates faster than the glial cells can replace it. Genetic research continues. There is no single gene for MS; instead of one gene, there may be many. However, there does appear to be an inherited susceptibility to the disease, although this risk is small. Dietary links are also being carefully considered.

Multiple sclerosis is one of the most common neurological disorders among young adults (between the ages of twenty and forty) and affects between 250,000 and 350,000 of these people in America. More young women than men are struck, and those with a northern European heritage are more vulnerable. Children and older people have also been known to have the disease. The cause of the disease is still unknown, although it has been seen to follow malnutrition, emotional stress, and infections. This gives rise to the theory that there may be something in the environment and the way each individual handles that environment that contributes to MS.

Multiple sclerosis varies in severity and in length of time in both its longevity and its attacks and remissions. The disease may progress slowly and disappear for periods of time but return intermittently, usually in a more severe form.

Symptoms also vary from person to person. They usually begin with fatigue, visual problems (double vision and blind spots), numbness and tingling, speech disturbances, dizziness, bowel and bladder disorders, weakness, lack of coordination (difficulty walking, foot dragging), paralysis, loss of balance, and emotional instability. Also of special interest is the fact that a deficiency of magnesium in normal people results in muscle spasms, weakness, twitching, and an inability to control the bladder, all characteristics of MS. Lyme disease may mimic the same symptoms as MS.

Nutrients and other natural ingredients have been found to slow or even prevent the advancement of MS. Autopsy studies have shown a great deficiency of lecithin in the brain and the myelin sheath that covers the nerves. The small amounts of lecithin that were present were abnormal, containing saturated instead of unsaturated fatty acids. Nutrients that are necessary for the manufacture of lecithin are probably needed by the MS patient: vitamin B_6 (50 milligrams daily), choline, inositol, the essential fatty acids, and magnesium (50 milligrams daily).

Wobe-Mugos, a group of pancreatic enzymes and an enzyme extracted from pineapple, has been shown to help MS. The amino acid glycine has been demonstrated to aid muscle control, and carnitine helps those with muscle weakness. Superoxide dismutase (SOD), lipid encapsulated superoxide dismutase (LIPSOD), and Poly(A)/Poly(B), synthetic polyribonucleic acid derivatives, may help MS.

Vitamin E (100 IU three times a day), B complex (25 milligrams daily), vitamin C (1 gram three times a day), and zinc (15 milligrams daily) are helpful. In some cases of the disease, vitamin B_{12} has been used to increase stability when standing and walking.

An inherited need for vitamin D may lead to MS. This vitamin is vital for the proper development of the nervous system, and poorly constructed neural tissues may break down in later years. Calcium is dependent on vitamin D for its utilization. Long-term sufferers of MS cannot benefit from the vitamin; however, in the young patient starting to exhibit symptoms, it may possibly slow or even stop the progress of the disease.

Pregnant women deficient in linolenic acid can pass the same deficiency to the fetus, making the brain and spinal cord susceptible to the destruction of the sheaths around their nerve fibers. The defect may not manifest until the child is fifteen or sixteen years old, when the brain has fully developed.

To treat MS, Dr. Frederick Klenner of Reidsville, North Carolina, used massive doses of the B vitamins as well as other nutrients, including minerals, unsaturated fatty acids, and amino acids.

A diet rich in fish, vegetables, fruits, whole grains, and vitamin and mineral supplements (minerals preferably in the orotate form) and very limited in saturated fats (under 15 grams per day), sugar, and processed (especially with saturated fats) and refined foods is extremely beneficial for the MS patient. Foods such as packaged cake mixes, cheeses, pastries, and other processed items, because they contain hidden or unknown quantities of saturated fat, are not recommended. A low-fat diet (nonfat dairy products) started before disability set in allowed 95 percent of those tested to live longer with no symptoms. Less than 15 grams of saturated fat daily yielded even greater results. High fiber is important for managing constipation, which can be alleviated by drinking adequate amounts of water and following a diet high in unrefined roughage foods.

Increase essential fatty acids found in seed oils (omega-6s), especially safflower, wheat germ, sunflower, corn, soybean, sesame, and primrose (500 milligrams daily), all of which are rich in linolenic acid. These are important for the development and integrity of the brain and spinal cord. Daily supplements of 2 tablespoons of seed oil have been reported to reduce the severity and increase the period of remission in

MS victims. A balance of omega-3s is also important; 1,000 milligrams of fish oil helps relieve symptoms of MS and also balances the omega-6 oils. Canola, which has omega-6s and omega-3s, and flax oil, which has more omega-3s than fish oil, may also be used.

Allergies to particular foods should be taken into consideration and the offending food eliminated from the diet; milk and gluten in wheat are common offenders. Avoid chocolate, spicy foods, coffee, and salt. Alcohol and smoking should also be avoided. Alcohol interferes with unsaturated fatty acid conversion, increases the saturated-fat blood count, destroys various B vitamins, and worsens MS symptoms. Smoking adversely affects a diet high in unsaturated fatty acids, lowers blood levels of vitamin C, and temporarily worsens MS symptoms. In a recent study, published in 2005 in the journal *Brain*, researchers at Harvard concluded that smoking is a risk factor for MS and likely contributes to the disease's progression.

Adequate rest and exercise are especially important. Physical activity for the MS patient is to relieve fatigue, not create it. Body heat should remain steady, so gentle swimming in cool water is suggested. Consult a physician before attempting any physical exertion. Yoga helps to keep muscles supple and is a wise choice.

There are reports of successful treatment of MS patients with a daily high-potency vitamin supplement, minerals, and a controlled diet. Patients are also advised to take wheat germ or vitamin E to keep the unsaturated oils from becoming rancid or oxidized once inside the body.

Observed results of the patients have been a reduction in relapses, more energy, the ability to continue walking and working, and an increase in life expectancy. Also, when the treatment was started in the early stages of the disease with little evident disability, 90 percent to 95 percent of the cases remained unchanged or improved during the following twenty years.

Herbs that may help are a compress of horseradish (for stiffness) and a bath (for stiff muscles and aching joints) of sage, mugwort, or strawberry leaves, or equal parts of chamomile, mugwort, and agrimony; another combination is 1 ounce each of mugwort, comfrey leaf, burdock root, and sage in 1 quart water.

For more information and support for the MS sufferer as well as the family, contact the National Multiple Sclerosis Society at 733 Third Ave., New York, NY 10017-3288. The toll-free information line is 1-800-344-4867.

Muscle Weakness and Disorders

Strong and normally functioning muscles are reflected in an individual's movement. Weak muscles can be seen in every age group, from the infant's wobbly neck to the old man's stoop. Poor muscle tone interferes with blood circulation, lymph flow, and digestion.

Nutrients may be helpful in maintaining muscle control. Muscles are largely made up of protein and essential fatty acids; however, almost every nutrient is involved in their contraction (calcium and potassium), relaxation (magnesium), and repair. Potassium, which is very low in diets high in fats and refined foods, is necessary for the contraction of every muscle in the body. Besides a poor diet, a potassium deficiency can be brought on by stress, diarrhea, kidney damage, diuretics, or cortisone therapy. The results of insufficient amounts of the minerals are fatigue, gas distention, spasms or twisting of the bowel, constipation, and possibly inability to pass urine.

Vitamin E is essential for the formation of the nuclei of muscle cells and of enzymes that are needed for muscular contractions. A deficiency of this vitamin increases the need for oxygen in the muscles, interferes with the metabolism of certain amino acids, and causes the loss of phosphorus in the urine and the B vitamins by rancidity. This allows too much calcium to be left to settle in muscle tissue. A deficiency of B_1 results in muscle weakness. Pregnant women often have difficult deliveries because of the lack of enzymes needed for muscle contraction. Vitamin E is useful for cramps. A deficiency can also be suspected if a child cannot sit up well at three months old.

Branched-chain amino acids (BCAAs) may increase muscle mass, coenzyme Q10 may strengthen muscles, and iron deficiency is associated with weak muscles. The amino acids lysine, arginine, and ornithine increase growth hormone, which builds muscle and may also help burn fat. Leucine (promotes growth hormone and can convert to glucose), isoleucine, and valine are also involved with metabolic reactions in the muscle. They are essential, which means that they must be obtained from food. Seafood, chicken, turkey, lentils, peas, and other beans are sources. High-quality proteins such as eggs, soy meal, beef, and fish are recommended for building muscles.

Another amino acid, taurine, regulates muscle systems. People with muscle-weakening diseases have been shown to be deficient in the amino acid carnitine, which may be supplemented. Other nutrients that may help in building muscle mass are branched-chain keto acids (BCKAs), ornithine alpha-ketoglutarate (OKG), boron, chromium picolinate, and L-carnosine. A deficiency of magnesium is associated with muscle weakness and may be supplemented.

Abnormal muscular movements may be aided by choline and phosphatidylcholine. When there is a deficiency, the mineral phosphate will boost athletic energy. Selenium aids muscular atrophy, and SOD and LIPSOD guard against hardening of muscles in autoimmune diseases, including the heart. Vitamin C guards against muscle wasting. Steroid drugs are masculinizing and muscle-building; however, the side effects are considerable and a physician should be consulted before any therapy is begun.

Herbs that may be helpful for muscle aches are agrimony, arnica, bay, cayenne pepper, juniper, mugwort, oregano, uva ursi, wintergreen, and witch hazel. Aromatherapy for overworked and aching muscles includes bergamot, black pepper, Roman chamomile, coriander, cypress, eucalyptus, ginger, juniper, lemon, lavender, sweet marjoram, peppermint, Scots pine, and rosemary.

Muscular Dystrophy

Muscular dystrophy (MD) is the progressive wasting and weakening of the muscles. There are nine major forms of MD, each with its own pathology. The various types of MD differ in whether males or both genders are affected, at what age onset occurs, how quickly symptoms appear, and what area of the body is involved along with the related problems that result. MD is caused by genetic defects, but the genes responsible have been identified for only some of the forms.

The most severe type is Duchenne muscular dystrophy (DMD), which affects young boys. The cause is the absence of a protein, dystrophin, which is involved in maintaining the integrity of muscle. The affliction starts between 3 and 5 years of age. Progressive muscle weakness usually begins in the legs and gradually spreads to all muscles, causing severe disability. Most boys are unable to walk by age 12, and later they need a respirator to breathe. In families with DMD, girls have a 50 percent chance of inheriting and passing the defective gene to their children. A blood test can determine if one is a carrier.

A form of muscular dystrophy similar to Duchenne is Becker MD, but Becker is less severe. Other forms of MD include myotonic dystrophy, facioscapulohumeral MD, limb-girdle MD, oculopharyngeal MD, congenital MD, distal MD, and Emery-Dreifuss MD. The common, major symptom of all of these types of MD is muscle weakness, manifesting as leg weakness, unsteadiness, and permanent muscle tightening (contractures). The patient has trouble walking. A child may have problems raising hands above the head or regaining an upright position after falling, and general clumsiness may be noted (inability to climb stairs, falling easily, and walking with feet wide apart). Muscles appear large because fat replaces wasting muscle tissue.

The act of eating may also become difficult if the muscles of the face and neck have become weak because of MD. In some cases there is malposition of teeth and a limited ability to open the jaw adding to eating problems. Chewing, swallowing, and self-feeding become a challenge, leading to loss of weight and increasing the risk of dehydration as well as choking and acid reflux when acidic stomach contents backflow and reach the esophagus. Weak muscle tone in the stomach may make a child feel full quickly so that he or she takes in less nourishment.

A useful strategy to make the eating process easier for the patient is to limit mealtime to twenty to thirty minutes to prevent the muscles involved in eating from becoming tired. Additional food can be given as between-meal snacks. To increase calorie intake, nutrient-dense foods such as peanut butter and full-fat yogurt are recommended. Mashed and chopped foods that require less chewing may be appropriate. Sauces on food makes it easier to swallow. It may also be important to give the patient thickened liquids that move more slowly through the throat and are less likely to go down the wrong way and cause aspiration. Instructing the patient on safe swallowing procedures is also useful—sitting upright after meals and dry swallowing rather than rinsing foods down with liquids.

Nutrients may be beneficial. Some time before MD can be detected, amino acids and a substance called creatine are lost in the urine. This indicates that muscle tissue is breaking down. If the degeneration has not advanced too far, supplemental vitamin E has prevented further progression. It is speculated that the hereditary factor of the disease may be an abnormally high genetic requirement for vitamin E, which is essential for the formation of the nucleus of every cell. In animal studies, dystrophy has been produced from a deficiency of protein; vitamins A, B_6, and E as well as choline. A selenium deficiency has been known to lay a solid foundation for muscular dystrophy formation.

In dystrophic tissue, the oxygen requirement is tremendously increased, many enzymes necessary for muscle function are greatly reduced, and the essential fatty acids that form the structural part of the muscle are destroyed. The cell membrane becomes increasingly permeable, allowing nutrients to leak out into the blood. Eventually the muscles are replaced by scar tissue.

The diet of a person with muscular dystrophy should be adequate in all essential nutrients, including complete proteins and vegetable and omega-3 (fish and flax) oils. Meal-replacement shakes, high in calories and protein, are useful. In the early stages in some cases, muscular wasting may be arrested and remissions prolonged by an adequate diet. Vitamin E and choline, found primarily in the germ of cereals, are easily deficient in diets of refined foods because of their removal during the refining process. (They are not replaced as are some nutrients.) Chlorine in drinking water and rancid fats also destroy vitamin E.

Myasthenia Gravis

Myasthenia gravis is a neurological disorder that affects muscles in any part of the body but most often the muscles of the face and neck. In this disease, there is an underproduction of acetylcholine, a compound that transmits nerve impulses to the muscles. The disease is characterized by exhaustion and progressive paralysis.

Symptoms include abnormal weakness, muscle fatigue, double vision (diplopia), drooping eyelids (ptosis), choking, and difficulty in breathing, swallowing, and talking (imperfect articulation, stammering, and stuttering). The cause is thought to be from faulty nerve impulses to the muscle. The onset is especially strong following infection, during pregnancy, or with immunologic abnormalities such as thyroid activity, rheumatoid arthritis, and tumors of the thymus.

Recovery from myasthenia gravis has occurred in many cases—if the diet is adequate and includes nutrients that are needed for the production of acetylcholine. These include vitamin B complex, protein, and potassium foods and supplements. (See Section 5, "Food Lists," for additional sources of these required nutrients.) An adequate diet including a wide variety of *whole* foods that contain all of the food groups while avoiding alcohol, caffeine, processed and refined foods, food additives, and preservatives constitutes excellent overall nutrition. Vitamin E aids the utilization of acetylcholine; if the vitamin is undersupplied, acetylcholine is destroyed by oxygen.

For herbs and other natural aids, see "Muscle Weakness and Disorders."

Nail Problems

Nails are composed almost entirely of protein. Abnormal or unhealthy nails may be the result of a local injury, fungal infection, a glandular deficiency such as hypothyroidism, nail biting, or a deficiency of certain nutrients. Nails grow about 0.5 to 1.2 millimeters a week.

Many nail problems are due to deficiencies of nutrients. A protein deficiency can cause opaque white bands to appear on the nails or cause the nails to become dry, brittle, and very thin. Insufficient amounts of complete proteins and/or vitamin A slow down the rate of nail growth (which is also affected by various drugs). A shortage of vitamin A or calcium in the diet also may cause dryness and brittleness. A lack of the B vitamins causes nails to become fragile, with horizontal or vertical ridges appearing. Splitting nails show a deficiency of hydrochloric acid (HCl). A vitamin B-complex deficiency is also a factor in fungus infestation, which is found underneath the nails.

Frequent hangnails usually indicate an inadequate intake of vitamin C, folic acid, and protein. An iron deficiency can disturb the growth of the nails, causing dryness, brittleness, thinning, flattening, and eventually the appearance of spoon-shaped nails. White spots can be caused by a zinc and vitamin B_6 deficiency. Discolored nails may be due to prolonged illness, allergies, smoking, stress, or discoloration from coloring with nail polish.

The condition of the nails may provide signs of what is happening within the body. Flat nails may indicate Raynaud's disease; thick nails may mean circulation problems; red moons may be a sign of heart problems; blue nails may be a signal of lung trouble; white nails may indicate anemia or liver or kidney problems; white lines may mean liver disease; and wide, square nails may be a symptom of hormonal disorders.

Most abnormalities indicate that the diet is not adequate, and one that supplies all essential nutrients is recommended. Protein foods such as eggs and non-fat dairy products are good. Iron food sources are red meats, fish, poultry, and green leafy vegetables. Citrus fruits are sources of vitamin C, while liver, cod-liver oil, and carrot juice are sources of vitamin A. Brewer's yeast, live yogurt, and acidophilus should be taken daily for fungal infections. Whole grain cereals, brewer's yeast, and wheat germ are also excellent additions for white spots in the nail. Homeopathy remedy is Lilica 6x. Exercising the fingers will aid in the growth of the nail tissue.

Nausea and Vomiting

Nausea and vomiting can indicate the presence of many diseases, including an infected appendix, low blood sugar, and food poisoning. Other causes are drinking too much alcohol, eating foods that are too rich, migraines, stress, motion sickness, pregnancy, shock, and side effects of some drugs. If the symptoms persist, a physician should be consulted.

Nutrients may be beneficial. If there is a vitamin B_6 deficiency, an unsettled stomach and burning stomach pain, bloating, abdominal soreness and cramps, and the passing of gas both orally and rectally will accompany the sickness. Vitamin B_6 has been successfully used to alleviate the nausea and vomiting that can occur with pregnancy, radiation treatments, and motion (car, sea, or air) sickness. Vomiting babies may also be helped by magnesium and yeast or wheat germ (vitamin B_6 sources).

Bananas can help alleviate nausea and vomiting. Whole grain cereals, soups, and steamed vegetables are also good, provided they can be eaten. Drinking plenty of fluids—clear liquids, including distilled or bottled water—and munching occasionally on soda crackers may help. Avoid coffee and juices, especially citrus drinks.

Herbs that may help are mint, black horehound (for stress), red raspberry, chamomile, St. John's wort, bee balm, and ginger (for most kinds). Homeopathic remedies include Ipecac 3x or 6x, Nux vomica 6c, Lactic acid 6c, Sepia 6c, and Tobacum 3x or 30x.

Nephritis (Bright's Disease)

Nephritis, also called Bright's disease, is the inflammation of one or both of the kidneys. There is a hereditary type but one of the most common forms of nephritis, pyelonephritis, occurs during childhood and pregnancy. It may be caused by bacteria from the stools being introduced into the urinary opening by wiping in a forward direction, allowing the bacteria to travel to the bladder and finally to the kidney. Another form of nephritis, caused by streptococcal bacteria, is glomerulonephritis, which comes from a strep infection in the throat. Infections in the valves of the heart and certain drugs cause another type of nephritis.

Symptoms of nephritis may be nonexistent, or they may include blood and/or albumin in the urine, fatigue, lower back or abdominal pain, fever, chills, headache, edema (swelling of the face, eyes, and legs), nausea and vomiting, loss of appetite, dark urine, and frequent urge to urinate. Anemia and high blood pressure may accompany severe nephritis.

Deficiencies may be a cause. Nephritis has been produced in animals deficient in choline. The capillaries are damaged and severe hemorrhages occur. Urine formation is decreased, and circulation is inhibited. Insufficient vitamin E can result in tubules plugged with dead cells, decreasing the amount of urine that can pass.

Medical treatment of nephritis is essential and includes antibiotics, bed rest, protein restriction if kidney failure occurs, and, possibly, fluid restriction. Generally, however, 2 quarts of liquid a day are recommended. Nutrients also may help. Kidney function has markedly improved when vitamin A has been taken. Vitamin E protects the kidneys from toxic substances, prevents scarring, and increases the flow of urine. Zinc supplements will replace the zinc removed from the urine by albumen. Because cortisone is often given for nephritis, nutrients that increase the body's natural production of cortisone, including the vitamin B complex, pantothenic acid, vitamin C, and complete protein, are recommended.

Neuritis

Neuritis is the inflammation or deterioration of a nerve or group of nerves. Symptoms of neuritis vary with its cause. Some symptoms are a severe, sharp pain occurring along the course of the nerve (neuralgia), tenderness, tingling and loss of the sensation of touch in the affected nerve area, redness and swelling of the affected area, and, in severe cases, convulsions.

Causes of neuritis include injury to a nerve, such as in a direct blow or a nearby bone fracture; infection involving a nerve; diseases such as diabetes, gout, and leukemia; poisons such as mercury, lead, and methyl alcohol; and dietary deficiency of the vitamin B complex, especially thiamin. A thiamin deficiency results in the impairment of nerve tissue so that the tissue cannot properly utilize carbohydrates for energy. Sciatica, peripheral neuropathy, low back pain, facial pain, glossopharyngeal neuralgia after an attack of herpes or shingles, and trigeminal neuralgia are some conditions that cause nerve pain. Sometimes neuritis may be purely mechanical, caused by pressure on the nerves when sleeping in a cramped position or possibly on too soft a mattress.

Treatment for neuritis varies with the cause. For severe cases, a neurologist should be consulted. If neuritis is caused by poisons, exposure to them should be ended, and if it is caused by a specific disease or trauma, treatment should be given. Nutrients may be helpful. A vitamin B complex should be taken daily. When a thiamin or vitamin B-complex deficiency is responsible, administration of these vitamins will result in recovery within three to four days. Adequate intake of the B vitamins is necessary even when a deficiency does not exist, since they are needed for the general health of nerve tissue.

A well-balanced diet is important to the individual with neuritis for the maintenance and repair of muscles and nerves. If infection is present, protein, calorie, and fluid intake should be increased. Pork, oranges, peas and dried beans, brewer's yeast, wheat germ, green leafy vegetables, milk, mushrooms, avocados, broccoli, asparagus, liver, egg yolks, soybeans, peanuts, bananas, and oatmeal are all sources rich in the B vitamins. Coffee should be avoided. For the type that involves herpes, abstinence from chocolate and nuts is advised. These foods contain arginine, which exacerbates herpes. Herbs that may be helpful are horseradish, St. John's wort (painkiller), valerian (tension reducer), wormwood, willow, and oil of lavender and basil bath with a drop of valerian. Homeopathic remedies are Hypericum 6c and Aconite 6c.

Osteoporosis (Brittle Bones)

Osteoporosis is a reduction of the total mass of bone, with the remaining parts being left fragile or "brittle." Primarily a disease of the aged, osteoporosis usually begins at about age fifty. After the age of thirty, bone mass is no longer made and maintaining what mass there is should then be the focus. Women past menopause lose the most bone mass; however, some elderly men suffer the same condition. It is a disease in which minerals are being depleted more rapidly than they can be replaced, but with treatment such as diet, hormones, and exercise, the quality of life can be improved. There are drugs on the market that can slow or reverse bone loss. Foods high in calcium as well as many other important vitamins and minerals important for bone health, along with weight-bearing exercise, fill different density areas in the bone; all are needed to maintain complete optimal health of the skeletal system.

There are 1.3 million fractures from osteoporosis each year, with 250,000 of those being of the hip. Some 80 percent of those occur in women age sixty-five and older who have osteoporosis. One-quarter of those will die from complications such as pneumonia and blood clots within the first year, and another third will be impaired to the point where they are no longer self-sufficient. Besides bone fracture, osteoporosis is responsible for gum and jaw loss, dowager's hump, back pain, wrist fractures, and loss of height. These fractures and conditions occur even when no undue strain is put on bones. Some may happen when there is no trauma at all. Risk factors are racial background, family history, lifestyle, natural early menopause, childlessness, and removal of the ovaries. Women who are sedentary or small boned, have a fair complexion, and present no known health condition are also at risk.

Heredity has been established as the number 1 determinant of who will get the disease. After that, other causes include inadequate diet over a period of years, an inability to absorb sufficient calcium through the intestine, calcium-phosphorus imbalance, lack of exercise, steroid use, and lack of certain hormones.

Calcium is the major mineral in bones and needs to be adequately present in the diet. The best sources of calcium are dairy products such as yogurt, skim milk, buttermilk, skim mozzarella cheese, fortified soy milk, and canned sardines and salmon, which contain softened bones. Some greens have readily absorbable calcium, including dandelion and mustard greens, turnip and beet greens, kale, bok choy, and broccoli. Research shows that having sufficient calcium usually guards against osteoporosis, but not in all cases. Preventing calcium deficiency alone may not prevent or help treat the condition. Bones require a range of nutrients, with many other minerals, as well as vitamins, needed to maintain the dynamic and complex tissue that makes up the skeletal system. Other essential minerals are magnesium, manganese, boron, zinc, strontium, copper, and silicon. A diet rich in plant foods provides many of these. Boron is found in nuts such as almonds, Brazil nuts, and hazelnuts; dried fruits such as figs and prunes are a source of boron and calcium. Other boron-rich foods are apples, grapes, dates, raisins, pears, peaches, soybeans, molasses, and honey. Boron in the diet may explain why fewer cases of osteoporosis are found in vegetarians. The diet must also be adequate in protein.

Supplemental nutrients can be helpful such as calcium citrate, calcium lactate, or calcium phosphate (1,000 milligrams daily or 1,500 milligrams for postmenopausal women not on estrogen; more than 2,500 milligrams daily can contribute to kidney stones); boron (prevents magnesium and calcium loss); magnesium citrate (500 milligrams daily); copper (osteoporosis is a symptom of a deficiency); manganese; zinc (essential for normal bone formation); phosphorus; strontium (makes bone more resistant to resorption); silicon (supports calcification of bone); folic acid (1 milligram daily); vitamin C; vitamin B_6 (100 milligrams daily); vitamin K (for calcification of bones); and vitamin D.

For those who use lots of sunscreen, vitamin D may be a problem since, without it, bones cannot harden. Milk is fortified with vitamin D and supplements are also available. Calcium should be taken alone at night and more should be taken if diuretics, thyroid pills, or blood-thinning drugs are also being taken. Thiazide diuretics may be responsible for kidney stones and should not be taken with calcium and vitamin D. Trace amounts of fluorides from foods or drinking water (1 milligram per liter) also protect against bone decomposition.

Beer and alcoholic drinks are the bones' worst enemies because they directly interfere with the absorption of calcium as do coffee, soft drinks, and nicotine. In addition, a diet that predominates in foods that acidify the system can increase the risk of osteoporosis. Some health experts point to the many acid-forming foods in the standard American diet as a significant factor in the high rate of osteoporosis in Western societies. This compares with more traditional cultures where osteoporosis is not an epidemic and processed and refined foods, as well as milk, are only minimally consumed if at all. Refined sugar and flour, colas, coffee, tea, meats, and salt metabolize to acid compounds that the body must buffer in order to maintain normal pH balance in cells and the fluid between cells. Alkalizing minerals are required and the body draws on its major reservoir of these, the bones, depleting the skeletal structure of calcium. (See Section 5 for Table 5.3, "Acid- and Alkaline-Forming Foods.")

Herbs that may help are horsetail, angelica bark, shavegrass, licorice, feverfew, birch (osteoarthritis pain), seaweed, cibot rhizome, oatstraw, and eucommia bark.

There is overwhelming evidence that exercise is vitally important for bone health. Weight-bearing exercise and exercise that involves impact on bones such as racket sports encourage bones to thicken. It has also been found that weight lifting benefits the bones in areas where the muscle attaches to the bones. Those who cannot do certain kinds of exercise may still benefit by engaging in any kind of activity, such as walking, running, and aerobics, since it seems that some exercise is better than none. In general, a variety of exercises is recommended to maintain all the areas of the body.

Overweight and Obesity

Overweight and obesity are among the major nutritional and health problems in the United States today. These conditions are defined clinically in terms of the body mass index (BMI), which is a person's weight in kilograms divided by the square of his or her height in meters. A BMI of 25 or higher indicates overweight, a BMI of 30 or higher defines obesity, and a BMI of 40 or higher is extreme obesity. Of great concern to health professionals and national policy planners is that the weight gain trend is on the rise. For instance, according to the Centers for Disease Control and Prevention (CDC), in 2000, 20 percent of adults were obese but by 2004, one-third of adults qualified as obese and another third qualified as overweight. The data for overweight in young people are also being closely monitored. The ranks of those who are overweight have more than tripled since 1980. Of children and teens age six to nineteen more than nine million, or 16 percent, are overweight.

According to the CDC, in 2000, poor diet and a lack of exercise led to four hundred thousand deaths, a 33 percent increase as compared to 1990. Many ailments stem from being overweight: hypertension, high cholesterol and triglycerides, type II diabetes, heart disease, stroke, gallbladder disease, osteoarthritis, sleep apnea and respiratory problems, complications of pregnancy, and some cancers such as breast, colon, and endometrial cancer. Statistics show that people of average weight have a longer life span, more energy, and usually feel better than those people who are overweight.

Some general causes of overweight may be glandular and hormonal malfunctions, malnutrition, emotional tension, boredom, habit, and love of food. Another source of overeating may be food sensitivities or substances in the environment that can influence the hypothalamus, an area of the brain that regulates the desire to eat. Certain medications (such as tranquilizers), viral infections, nutritional deficiencies, or brain injuries can also adversely affect these cells. A well-balanced, whole foods diet high in all essential nutrients and absent the offending substances can gradually result in weight reduction.

Another aspect of an insatiable appetite may be its emotional nature. What is being fed may not be the body, but the need for love and comfort. It is very possible that all the nutritional information anywhere would not be enough to replace the true root of the problem. Food has been a source of emotional acceptance from birth, and for some, the attachment is ongoing. Reaching out to groups or to a professional is highly recommended, since many people in society understand those needs and can help.

Having a low resting metabolism, preventing a person from quickly burning calories, has been an often cited reason for being overweight, but the results of a 2000 study published in *Obesity Research* challenges this assumption. Researchers at the University of Alabama at Birmingham compared two groups of women with identical resting metabolic rates and fat-free mass, one group living in the United States and the other living in Nigeria. Those in the United States had an average body fat of 41.3 percent and a body mass index of 31.4, while the Nigerian women had an average body fat of 29.1 percent and a body mass index of 23.3. The researchers concluded that factors in the environment, not genetics, underlie the current epidemic of weight gain in America.

Eating habits are a major source of the weight problem, in particular, the popularity of large portion sizes and simply eating too much. In 2000, individuals consumed 1,775 pounds of food per year, an increase from 1,497 pounds per year in 1970.

Calories are needed for the body to function; they are the body's fuel. The body requires a certain number of calories to run normal body functions. Daily activities and exercise use up additional calories. For example, one hour of average office work probably uses up 10 to 15 calories, whereas moderate housework may require 70 calories per hour more than basal metabolism requirements. Brisk walking uses up

about 110 calories per hour; driving a car uses about 40. Strenuous exercise and hard physical labor may require more than 400 calories per hour.

But after the body burns a certain amount of food, converting it into calories needed for energy, the body converts the remaining food into glycogen, which is stored all over the body as fat. When the number of calories consumed is greater than the number of calories burned, increased body fat results. One pound of stored fat is equal to 3,500 calories. Many successful weight-loss programs focus on this simple equation, cutting calories so that none need be stored as fat. A daily decrease of 1,000 calories results in approximately two pounds of weight loss per week.

Another approach to weight loss focuses on the kinds of foods consumed, as well as the number of calories. There are high-protein diets, such as Dr. Arthur Agatston's South Beach Diet, that limit intake of carbohydrates because the body readily stores carbohydrates as fat. These diets also consider the type of carbohydrate, favoring those with a low glycemic index. The glycemic index of an item indicates how quickly the body can digest and absorb a food. High glycemic foods enter the bloodstream rapidly, quickly delivering more calories than are needed at the time as fuel; consequently, some of the food entering the system ends up as fat. Low glycemic foods enter the system more slowly.

Whole grains, which digest slowly, can be part of such a diet while table sugar, baked goods made with white flour, potatoes, white rice, and food products made with high-fructose corn syrup should be avoided. Another reason to favor unrefined foods is that they contain all the nutrients necessary for efficient energy production. In addition, because they contain fiber, they are filling and are less likely to be overeaten.

Considering a carbohydrate's glycemic load goes one step further in fine-tuning food intake that some of the newest diets incorporate. These diets factor in typical portion sizes along with glycemic index. Under this system, carrots, which have a high glycemic index, become a very acceptable addition to a weight loss diet. (See Table 2.1 in Section 2.)

High protein–low carb diets, which include meats, fish, poultry, and nuts, allow a certain amount of fat. The typical calorie-counting diet limits fat because 1 gram contains more than twice as many calories as 1 gram of protein or carbohydrate. In contrast, high protein–low carb diets, which include meats, fish, poultry, and nuts, allow a certain amount to make meals tasty and satisfying, one way in which such diets curb appetite. But guidelines for eating healthy fats should still be followed. When buying packaged and canned foods, it is important to check fat content by reading labels. Labels show the number of grams of total fat, saturated fat, and trans fat. They also give the percent daily value, indicating the percent fat a single serving provides, based on the needs of a 2,000-calorie diet. Be sure to check the serving size stated on the label, which is sometimes much smaller than the amount normally eaten.

Certain label terms can also be misleading. Words such as *light* or *lite* mean that there is something in the product that is less than the original. This can be color, flavor, alcohol content, texture, sodium, or fat content. If the content is fat, the amount that is referred to would be one-third fewer calories, or no more than half the fat of the original product. A label of "95% fat free" may be deceptive as the percentage may have been taken from the weight of the product, not the calorie content. *Low-fat* meat must be no more than 10 percent fat by weight, and *low-fat* milk must contain between 0.5 percent and 2 percent milk fat.

When there is inadequate intake of all essential nutrients, fat is not readily or efficiently burned. Fat is burned only if sufficient energy is produced. Energy production depends upon almost every known nutrient.

Nutrients may help as the actions of the body during weight loss create an increased need for a number of these. Supplementation of a natural, overall vitamin-and-mineral formula is recommended. The B vitamins are important for energy production. Fat is burned at a greatly reduced rate if pantothenic acid and protein are undersupplied. Vitamin B_6 is necessary for the energy conversion of stored fat. It is also a factor in the utilization of protein and fat.

Proteins are needed for the proper functioning of many energy-producing enzymes. Protein itself cannot be effectively used without many other nutrients, including choline and vitamin B_6. Sufficient vitamin E doubles fat utilization. Lecithin aids the cells to burn fat; any deficiency of the nutrients necessary for lecithin production, specifically choline and inositol, results in poor fat utilization. A potassium-magnesium phosphate supplement will increase metabolic rate, which helps burn excess body fat.

Dehydroepiandrosterone (DHEA) is thought to be an antiobesity substance that may inhibit fat production. The amino acid phenylalanine (100 to 500 milligrams at night on an empty stomach) aids in weight reduction. A combination of the amino acids L-arginine, L-lysine, and L-ornithine is thought to burn fat by releasing a growth hormone that is not normally found in adults. Chromium picolinate is said to raise metabolism and burn fat; however, the study that made this claim possible has not been able to be replicated. Moreover, it is not known what excess chromium in the body may do over time.

Liver damage is common in overweight people. When the liver is injured, sufficient amounts of energy-producing enzymes are unable to be synthesized. A diet including complete proteins, the vitamin B complex, choline, vitamin B_{12}, vitamins C and E, and lecithin aids the restoration of the liver.

Salt in excess causes the body to retain water, which adds weight to the body and is not healthy. No more than 2,400 to 3,000 milligrams daily is recommended. Use salt-free, low-salt, and reduced-salt products. Citrus juice, spices, hot peppers, low-sodium soy sauce, and other condiments are other choices. Drinking at least eight glasses of water per day is important, especially if the diet is rich in fiber. Water is a nutrient that is essential for the body to perform at its optimal level. Hunger could just turn out to be thirst, so try drinking first.

Diets that are temporary may have a purpose, but "going on a diet" to lose general weight is no longer considered healthful or practical. A rapid weight loss from consuming fewer than 600 calories per day can cause gallstones in up to 50 percent of dieters. Intermittently dieting and then resuming normal eating habits is also not recommended. According to the "set-point" theory, a built-in genetic mechanism in the body reads a dramatic loss in weight as a signal to slow down metabolism in case the supposed "famine" continues. As the person resumes his or her usual eating habits, the now slower metabolic rate persists and the person gains weight as more calories are stored as fat.

In order to lose weight safely, a person must set up a sensible, long-term lifestyle plan. This plan should include plenty of whole foods that contain all the essential nutrients and minerals along with weekly activities that increase the individual heart rate to promote a healthy metabolism.

Some basic good advice is never to go grocery shopping on an empty stomach. The temptation is to buy forbidden foods, and more of them. Not consuming food later on in the day has worked wonders for many people who have difficulty maintaining an ideal weight. Put less on the plate, eat slowly, and never chew gum (it tells the body to get ready to eat) are some helpful habits. Alcohol should be avoided, since it is highly caloric and a pure carbohydrate that contains no nutrition to metabolize that energy. All foods that need to be heated should be baked, broiled, or steamed without any added oils. Comfort foods that fit diet restrictions must be substituted for sugary, high-caloric items. Planning relaxing times and events that show self-caring and self-love is recommended. Aromatherapy, massage, yoga, and other techniques should become part of one's daily routine.

Exercise is vital for weight loss, as it speeds up metabolism, burns calories, and may even reduce the appetite. Activity that brings a change in the heart rate is good. In general, losing weight is a matter of consciously curbing the amount of food eaten, regulating the types of food eaten, and increasing daily activity.

Herbs that may help control weight are chickweed and yohimbe. Homeopathic remedies are Fucus 3x and Phytolacca berry tincture. Aromatherapy for cellulite includes cedarwood, cypress, geranium, grapefruit, juniper, lavender, lemon, patchouli, and rosemary.

Parkinson's Disease

Parkinson's disease, also called shaking palsy or paralysis agitans, is a slowly progressive disease of the nervous system in which an essential type of nerve cell located in a small part of the brain is destroyed. The cause of the disease is unknown, but there is speculation that a deficiency of vitamin E early in life may be responsible. Symptoms begin when there is an imbalance of two chemicals in the brain, dopamine and acetylcholine. These substances transfer messages between nerve cells that control muscle function. In Parkinsonism, the amount of dopamine is diminished, creating an imbalance that confuses nerve signals. Approximately 1 percent of Americans over age sixty-five suffer from Parkinson's.

Symptoms of Parkinson's disease include muscular rigidity (first the legs, then the arms) and cramping, involuntary tremors that include a characteristic pill-rolling movement of the thumb and forefinger as they rub against each other, excessive salivation, impaired speech, a staring facial expression, drooling, and a short, shuffling gait. Despite these symptoms, sensation and mental activity are not impaired. Parkinson's can affect digestion, causing constipation and early satiety. There is often a loss of appetite and some weight loss, giving rise to the possibility of malnutrition developing. Chronic constipation may complicate the condition.

There is no cure for the disease, although drugs, in particular levodopa (L-dopa), are prescribed to alleviate the symptoms. However, L-dopa has many side effects (nausea, involuntary movements, mental changes such as paranoia and hallucination, cardiac irregularities, and urinary retention) and should not be taken with B_6. The B vitamins, especially B_6, tend to diminish the effectiveness of L-dopa. Vitamin C may help alleviate these reactions. Zinc may also be needed to make sure the B_6 does not interfere with the effectiveness of L-dopa. Manganese poisoning can mimic the final stages of Parkinson's disease.

Along with medication, alternative therapies are sometimes included in treatment. A small, well-designed study found coenzyme Q10 effective in slowing the progression of Parkinson's in the early stages of the disease. A dose of 1,200 milligrams/day was found to be safe and well tolerated. Massive doses of vitamin E may help slow the disease. Some patients have been helped with leucine (10 grams daily), a branch-chain amino acid, but follow-up tests are needed. Lipotropes work by increasing blood flow and oxygen to the brain. Supplemental choline and phosphytidylcholine have proved effective. Creatine and minocycline are two other substances under investigation for their effectiveness in reducing the clinical signs of early Parkinson's. In 2006, researchers at the University of Rochester in New York State published encouraging results in the journal *Neurology* that warrant further study. However, they noted that while neither substance caused major side effects, minocycline was not well tolerated. When using an alternative therapy, a physician should be consulted.

In her book *Let's Get Well*, Adelle Davis reported that vitamin B_6 when taken with the other B vitamins and magnesium resulted in progressive improvement. Patients begin to feel stronger and walk with a steadier gait. They also had better bladder control, a greater sense of well-being, better mental alertness, and a decrease in muscular cramps, trembling, and rigidity. Sometimes improvement is not noticed in people who have had a severe case of the disease for several years.

Modification of the diet and treatment of constipation may also be helpful. Whole grain cereals, fruits and vegetables, low-fat protein, fiber for constipation, and broad and fava beans (contain levodopa, the drug used to treat Parkinson's disease) are good choices. Consuming a large amount of protein all at one time can slow the absorption of levodopa; consequently, having a small amount of protein at each meal throughout the day is recommended. Seeds, nuts, and salad oils are rich in vitamin E. Frequent small meals, to compensate for early satiety, will increase the patient's nutrient and caloric levels, thus preventing malnutrition. A marked increase in fluid intake is also necessary because the normal secretions of the intestines may be lessened by some of the prescribed drugs. High-fiber food will assist in alleviating constipation.

Herbs that may help are fleece flower root, uncaria stem, and wolfberry. Exercise helps with flexibility, mobility, balance, and coordination. Gentle activities such as stretching, using a rowing machine or cycling machine, and walking are recommended. Yoga and tai chi are parts of some treatment programs. In treating Parkinson's, physical activity is meant to strengthen, not exhaust. Short sessions several times a day with bad days as rest times are recommended. Passive exercise with a therapist, friend, or relative will help muscle shortening. Therapeutic massage and acupuncture may also be useful.

Pellagra

Pellagra is a disease caused by a long-term deficiency of the B vitamins, particularly riboflavin, niacin, and thiamin. The disease occurs frequently in populations whose diets consist mainly of corn. Although the disease is seldom found in the United States, its rare occurrence affects people with gastrointestinal disturbances or chronic alcoholism.

Symptoms of pellagra are diarrhea, loss of appetite and weight, reddened and swollen tongue, weakness, depression, and anxiety. Itchy dermatitis on the hands and neck is a prominent characteristic of the disease. Subclinical pellagra may be mistaken for mental illness.

A diet that is adequate in the B vitamins and protein will prevent pellagra. A diet rich in the B vitamins niacin, thiamin, riboflavin, and folic acid and vitamin B_{12} will cure the disease. The amino acid tryptophan is necessary for the synthesis of niacin. Foods rich in niacin and other B vitamins are tuna, turkey, chicken, beans, peas, brewer's yeast, peanut butter, cheese, milk, soybeans, halibut, and tomatoes.

Pernicious Anemia

Pernicious anemia, or Addison's anemia, results from a deficiency of vitamin B_{12}. It is a severe form of anemia in which there is a gradual reduction in the number of blood cells because the bone marrow fails to produce mature red blood cells. Pernicious anemia probably arises from an inheritable inability of the stomach to secrete a substance called the intrinsic factor, which is necessary for the intestinal absorption of vitamin B_{12}.

Pernicious anemia occurs in both sexes. Its occurrence is rare in people under the age of thirty, as susceptibility increases with age. Symptoms of pernicious anemia include weakness and gastrointestinal disturbances causing a sore tongue, slight yellowing of the skin, and tingling of the extremities. In addition, disturbances of the nervous system, such as partial loss of coordination of the fingers, feet, and legs; some nerve deterioration; and disturbances of the digestive tract, such as diarrhea and loss of appetite, may occur.

Pernicious anemia may be fatal without treatment. Nutrients may help. Megadose injections of vitamin B_{12} together with a highly nutritious diet supplemented with large amounts of desiccated liver allow complete recovery. Intake of the entire vitamin B complex will help maintain the health of the nervous system, although folic acid should not be taken in amounts exceeding 0.1 milligram daily. Folic acid has the effect of concealing the symptoms of pernicious anemia, allowing the unseen destruction of the nervous system to continue until irreparable damage is done.

A diet rich in protein, calcium, vitamin C, vitamin E, and iron is recommended. If iron, vitamin C, and hydrochloric acid are taken with each meal to ensure absorption, the production of the intrinsic factor may be stimulated enough so that people with a mild case of the disease can decrease the doses of vitamin B_{12}.

Phlebitis

Phlebitis, the inflammation of a vein wall, is usually found in the legs and can be a complication of varicose veins. Symptoms of phlebitis include reddening and cordlike swelling of the vein, increased pulse rate, slight fever, and pain accompanying movement of the afflicted area.

A complication that may occur in individuals with phlebitis is thrombophlebitis, the formation of a clot in the inflamed vein. If this clot should break loose from the vein wall and lodge in a blood vessel that supplies some vital area with blood, serious and possibly fatal damage may occur. In some cases, the use of oral contraceptives has been related to the occurrence of thrombophlebitis.

Factors that seem to encourage the onset of phlebitis are operations, especially in the lower abdomen, childbirth, and infections resulting from injuries to veins. Phlebitis can be prevented by the treatment of varicose veins so that inflammation does not set in. Infections in the legs or feet, especially fungus infections of the toes, should be given immediate attention as a safeguard against phlebitis.

Supplementing the diet with niacin, part of the vitamin B complex, may be useful to help prevent clot formation. Vitamin C can help strengthen the blood vessel walls. Some research indicates that vitamin E may dilate blood vessels, thus discouraging the formation of varicose veins and phlebitis. Regular exercise is a further preventive measure. (See "Inflammatory Conditions.")

Pneumonia

Pneumonia is an ailment in which the tiny air sacs in the lungs become inflamed and filled with mucus and pus. The primary causes of pneumonia are bacteria, viruses, and fungi. It is not contagious. Factors that contribute to the onset of pneumonia are colds and flu, chemical irritants, allergies, alcoholism, malnutrition, seizure or stroke, smoking, kidney failure, foreign matter in the respiratory passages, and malnutrition. Symptoms of the disease vary from mild in children to severe in the elderly, but they usually include sharp pains in the chest, enlarged lymph glands, fever and chills, sore throat, fatigue, rapid respiration, bluish-colored nails, and cough that produces either yellow or green phlegm and sometimes blood.

Vitamin A is necessary for maintaining the health of the lining of the respiratory passages. A deficiency of the vitamin increases susceptibility to respiratory infections, which in turn can lead to pneumonia. Bacterial pneumonia is very serious and is most common in children under age twelve. Symptoms are chills, high temperature, and shakiness with fatigue and weakness lasting for four to eight weeks. Consult a physician since a chest x-ray is the only way to positively identify the condition.

Nutrients may be helpful. Since protein loss accompanies high fever and because protein is necessary for the repair of body tissue, its intake should be increased during the illness. Water and fluid intake should be increased to prevent dehydration that can result from fever and perspiration. Vitamin C intake is required to fight infection. Because deficiency of the vitamin B complex usually occurs with pneumonia, an increased intake is necessary. Some research shows a correlation between vitamin E deficiency and lung disease.

An individual is more susceptible to developing pneumonia when his or her system is overly acidic, making alkalizing foods the diet of choice in treating this condition. Unrefined and unprocessed foods of plant origin alkalize the body while animal foods and refined food products such as white flour and white sugar increase acidity. (See Section 5, Table 5.3, "Acid- and Alkaline-Forming Foods.") Diet should include plenty of fluids like fruit and vegetable juices. However, it should be noted that tomatoes and pineapples, and the juice made from these, are highly acidic foods.

Herbs that may be beneficial are bloodroot, coltsfoot, and raw garlic. Steam inhalations for chest congestion and pain are good. Eucalyptus works well. Homeopathic remedies are Ferrum phosphoricum 6c, Bryonia 6c, and Aconite 6c. Aromatherapy includes basil, black pepper, cedarwood, cypress, eucalyptus, ginger, grapefruit, juniper, lavender, lemon, sweet marjoram, myrrh, orange, peppermint, Scots pine, tea tree, and sandalwood.

Polio

Polio is a virus infection of the spinal cord that destroys the nerves controlling muscular movement, resulting in paralysis of certain muscles. Due to an extremely successful public health campaign, polio was eradicated from the West years ago. But recently, flare-ups of the disease have occurred in Africa and Asia, and several cases have been identified even in a farming community in central Minnesota.

There are two stages of this disease: the infectious stage, when the virus is active, and the noninfectious, or recovery, stage. Symptoms of the infectious stage include fever, nausea, diarrhea, headache, and irritability.

During the infectious stage, the diet of the polio patient should be high in protein and potassium to replace that which is lost because of the rapid destruction. Caloric intake should also be increased because of the increased energy expenditure during fever, and additional B vitamins are necessary to help metabolize the additional calories. Fever creates the need for additional sodium because of the loss through perspiration. Fluid intake should also be increased during fever to compensate for loss and to dilute toxic substances produced by the virus. Nutrients may help. Fever and the accompanying increase in metabolism also increase the need for vitamins A and C. Bioflavonoids act against the virus that causes polio. An extract of the licorice root called glycyrrhizin acts against the polio type 1 virus.

Dr. Frederick Klenner of Reidsville, North Carolina, used massive amounts of vitamin C (injections) in treating polio. Calcium should accompany vitamin C treatment because it increases the effectiveness.

Pregnancy

Pregnancy is the state a mother is in when developing offspring in her uterus. It is a stressful condition involving numerous physical and mental changes in the mother's body as the fetus develops. The tissues in the breasts and uterus increase, the blood supply increases, there is a frequent urge to urinate, there is slight nausea in the morning or even later in the day, the menstrual period is absent, and the need for sleep and fluids is increased. Because of these changes, dietary supplementation is advised, since all nutritional requirements of the mother increase in preparation for the newborn baby. A woman who has maintained a nutritionally balanced diet throughout her life has the best chance of remaining in good health while bearing a healthy child capable of developing to his or her full genetic potential.

The fetus takes nutrients from the mother; therefore, if the mother does not eat properly, both may suffer the consequences. Expectant mothers should be free to gain weight, within reason, on a diet full of wholesome foods containing all vital nutrients.

Morning sickness from nervous conditions will probably respond to additional amounts of the B vitamins, vitamin C, and vitamin K. Recommendations for vitamin B_6 are 25 milligrams with each meal for nausea and 250 milligrams or more daily for vomiting. Pineapple juice, chamomile tea, soda crackers, and small meals, as well as juices, soup, milk, and nuts to maintain blood sugar levels are helpful. Fresh ginger tea may help. Homeopathic remedies are Mercurius 6c, Phytolacca 6c, and Ailanthus 6c.

The B-vitamin complex and enzyme supplements (papaya) may relieve heartburn and digestive upsets. One cup of chamomile, peppermint, and fennel infusion after meals may help. Eating carbohydrates and protein together may cause indigestion. Try carbohydrates and vegetables or vegetable proteins instead. Fruit is less irritating when taken in the morning.

Miscarriage can result from infections, malnutrition or nutrient deficiency, fetal abnormalities, hormonal imbalances, structural problems in the uterus, weak cervical muscles, falls, and hazardous chemicals in the environment. Symptoms of a miscarriage are lower abdominal cramps and bleeding or spotting.

Studies have shown that women susceptible to miscarriage may be able to carry a fetus to full term if sufficient amounts of vitamin C are taken (500 milligrams to 4 grams, increasing to as much as 10 to 15 grams at the end of pregnancy), along with bioflavonoids to increase the vitamin's effectiveness. Hemorrhaging, which is due to capillary fragility, can also be caused by a deficiency of vitamin C and the bioflavonoids. Vitamin E (up to 200 IU with each meal) and folic acid have been shown to be helpful in preventing miscarriages. Oral antibiotics can destroy B vitamins and vitamin K. Lack of vitamin K can cause hemorrhaging in the placenta. Homeopathic remedies are Arnica 6c and Hypericum 6c. Exercise should be gentle swimming, stretching, and yoga.

Doctors have found that edema (puffiness in the feet, ankles, fingers, and face) in well-nourished, nontoxemic pregnant women may actually be protective for mother and fetus; therefore, a physician should be consulted and low-salt diets and diuretics should be taken carefully. Vitamins C and E are known to have diuretic actions. Potassium-rich foods such as meats, potatoes, avocados, orange juice, and apricots are good. Dandelion leaves in simmered water will help reduce swelling. Baking soda and some antacids contain sodium and may cause fluid retention if used excessively.

Toxemia, characterized by sudden weight gain, headache, and high blood pressure, occurs in the late months of pregnancy and can result in the death of the newborn baby. The illness may be attributed to the overuse of diuretics or poor nutrition. Laboratory animals developed a condition similar to toxemia when fed diets deficient in magnesium, vitamin B_6, choline, and protein. Vitamin E may prevent toxemia. Vitamin B_6 has been found to be effective in regulating fluid retention associated with the development of toxemia.

Birth defects can be a disease of heredity, but they are just as likely to result from drugs, environmental pollutants, viral or bacterial infections, parasites, or inadequate nutrition. Poor diets lacking any vitamin, mineral, or enzyme for the mother deprive the fetus of necessary building materials. A shortage of any nutrient may result in a stillbirth, a premature infant of low birth weight, a baby with brain damage (including impaired intelligence and psychological disturbances), or a baby with weak immunity to infection.

In the mother, a deficiency of folic acid, now fortified in some foods such as cereal and bread, has caused such birth defects as spina bifida and anencephaly, which may leave an infant with brain damage and paralysis. Only 0.4 milligram of folic acid a day will dramatically reduce the chance of abnormalities, and several servings of cereals, orange juice, spinach and other green leafy vegetables, and dried beans should help. Excess of preformed vitamin A has been linked to birth defects in animals (beta-carotene should be used instead). Some vitamin A derivatives used for skin problems should not be taken. Pregnant women should not take any vitamin, minerals, or drug without consulting a knowledgeable physician.

Ingestion by the mother of nicotine, alcohol, chemical food additives, and drugs can interfere with the fetal enzyme system and growth factors. Any interference with the B-complex metabolism in the fetus will produce deformities or abnormalities, and iodine deficiency during pregnancy may cause mental retardation.

Diet and nutrients are important. Protein, calcium, and iron are especially important to the development of bones, soft tissues, and blood. Protein of both animal and plant origin should be included in the diet because the body can make the fullest use of these products in combination. Protein is also needed to provide for the 20 percent increase in blood volume during pregnancy.

Together with calcium (found in milk, other dairy products, and bonemeal), the B vitamins (60 milligrams a day) may help relieve leg, back, and joint pains often associated with pregnancy. Muscle cramps may benefit from calcium, magnesium, and vitamin B_6 if there is a deficiency. Vitamin E (200 IU daily), found in vegetable oils, wheat germ, nuts, and seeds, may help restless legs. Severely limiting caffeine food choices is advisable. Vitamin E and zinc are helpful to normalize nervousness and emotional states that occur frequently during and after pregnancy.

An adequate supply of vitamin D is needed to ensure proper absorption and utilization of calcium and phosphorus. Additional iron is essential to prevent anemia in both mother and baby and to guard the mother against excessive blood loss during birth. Adequate iron also guards against miscarriage and fetal malformation. Sources of iron are lean red meat, fish, poultry, green leafy vegetables, and dried fruits. Vitamin C, vitamin K, and the bioflavonoids are necessary to strengthen blood vessels and to prevent excessive bleeding.

There are nutrients for the delivery process that may be helpful. In late pregnancy and postdelivery, thiamin requirements are greatly increased. The vitamin B complex is found in wheat germ and brewer's yeast. Since calcium, with vitamin D to ensure proper absorption, is known to decrease sensitivity to pain, the mineral may ease the pain of labor. Taking 2,000 milligrams between the beginning of labor and the time of arrival at the hospital has resulted in easier deliveries for many women. Vitamin E also has desensitizing properties and increases the elasticity and expandability of the vaginal tissues, making delivery easier and shorter. Zinc may help ease the difficulties of birth, and muscles can be kept strong with sufficient protein, magnesium, potassium, and unsaturated fatty acids.

Exercise is very important; walking and swimming are recommended. The end results of proper prenatal nutrition are a more comfortable pregnancy and easier delivery, a healthier baby, and a greater chance of successfully nursing the baby.

Premenstrual Syndrome

Premenstrual syndrome (PMS) is a cluster of physical and emotional symptoms that affects 8 percent to 29 percent of women. The onset of PMS is typically one to two weeks before a woman's period begins, that is, in the late ovulatory phase of the menstrual cycle. What causes PMS is unknown, but it appears that there are many triggers and that the interaction of neurohormones and other brain chemicals is involved. Premenstrual syndrome is often associated with elevated levels of estrogen and a deficiency of progesterone; however, several studies have found that women who suffer from PMS can have normal hormone levels. Other factors may be depressed levels of serotonin, an excess of prolactin, a deficiency of vitamin B_6, or problems with glucose metabolism.

Typical symptoms of PMS include fatigue, breast tenderness and swelling, menstrual cramps, water retention, weight gain, acne, cold sores, constipation, diarrhea, nausea, backaches, insomnia, mood swings, anxiety, and crying spells. There also may be food cravings, particularly for sweet and salty foods. Premenstrual syndrome occurs most often in women in their thirties, seems to worsen with age, and is often more severe during stressful times. Symptoms commonly worsen until menstruation begins and then usually rapidly end.

Nutrients may be beneficial. Vitamin B_6 is helpful for overall symptoms, vitamin E is useful for breast tenderness, magnesium is good for tension and weight gain, and fiber and the B-complex vitamins are helpful for constipation.

Diet is helpful in that foods may ease some of the symptoms. Complex-carbohydrate foods have a calming effect, counteracting low serotonin levels, and should be eaten often. Foods such as pasta, vegetables, whole grain breads, and cereals are examples. Soy foods that are high in plant estrogens can help balance hormones, normalizing estrogen levels. They are also a source of various nutrients including calcium, which is also found in dark leafy greens. New research suggests that PMS may be the result of calcium deficiency. In a 2005 study conducted at the University of Massachusetts in Amherst, women with debilitating PMS for a few days a month were 30 percent less likely to develop symptoms by consuming about 1,200 milligrams of calcium per day as compared with women who had only 530 milligrams per day. Vitamin D produced comparable results. In the study, women who consumed four servings a day of low-fat or skim milk had a 46 percent reduction in the risk of PMS.

However, there are drawbacks in using dairy products as a source of calcium to ameliorate symptoms. Dairy foods contain a form of fat that can worsen menstrual cramps; cheese may be high in sodium, encouraging bloating; and these foods interfere with the absorption of magnesium, which can help stabilize mood swings. Other foods to minimize or eliminate from the diet are cookies, candies, all refined carbohydrates, red meats, and fried and fatty foods. Caffeine, colas, alcohol, and chocolate should also be avoided.

Herbs that may help are blessed thistle, skullcap, sarsaparilla, primrose oil, poria, dong quai, Chinese angelica, cayenne, white peony, kelp, raspberry leaves, and squaw vine. Homeopathic remedies are Nux vomica, Sepia, and Pulsatilla. Moderate aerobic exercise several weeks before the menstrual period is essential to a healthy body and mind. Brisk walking or swimming are aerobic exercises that are good choices for PMS. Natural painkillers are released from the brain during exercise.

Prostatitis and Prostate Enlargement

Prostatitis is the inflammation of the prostate, a male sex gland located just below the bladder and surrounding the top portion of the tube (urethra) that drains urine from the bladder. The condition is common in older males but is also present at every age. It results in partial or total blockage of the flow of urine, causing retention. The usual cause of prostatitis in young men is a bacterial infection, from the urethra or from the bladder, which has invaded the prostate. Prostatitis can also be sexually transmitted.

Symptoms of acute prostatitis are pain between the scrotum and rectum, fever, frequent urination accompanied by a burning sensation, and flulike aches in the back, rectum, and between the legs. As prostatitis becomes more advanced, these symptoms continue, and men also suffer from premature ejaculation, blood or pus in the urine, and loss of potency. Urinating becomes increasingly difficult.

Treatment for prostatitis involves increasing the fluid intake to meet the increased needs during infection and to stimulate urine flow, thus preventing retention of urine. Urinary retention can result in cystitis and possibly kidney infection. Nutrients may help. A well-balanced diet rich in vitamin A, the B complex, and vitamin C is important during fever and infection. Increased protein and calories are needed during fever and infection to replace lost body tissues and energy. Zinc (orotate, 100 milligrams every other day) has been shown to clear up the condition. Fish oil, which is anti-inflammatory, will replenish fatty acid deficiencies. (See "Inflammatory Conditions.")

An enlarged prostate, or benign prostatic hyperplasia (BPH), is a condition usually found in older males. While the prostate gland grows from about the size of a pea to the size of a walnut from birth to young adulthood, a second period of growth begins when a man is in his mid- to late forties. About half of men in their sixties have prostate enlargement and up to 90 percent of men in their seventies and eighties, according to the Mayo Clinic. The cause of BPH is unclear but one theory is that this gland becomes more susceptible to the effects of testosterone. Current risk factors include heredity, national origin with Americans and Europeans at greater risk than Asians, and being married.

This condition must be diagnosed by a physician. A checkup may include a digital rectal exam, a urine test, and a blood test to measure the level of prostate-specific antigen (PSA). Additional assessment may include a questionnaire, urine flow test, postvoid residual volume test, ultrasound, urodynamic studies, cystoscopy, and x-ray of the urinary tract.

Standard recommendations for self-care are to stop drinking all beverages after 7:00 P.M. to reduce the need to urinate during the night and to empty the bladder fully when urinating. Limiting alcohol intake, which irritates the bladder, is also advised. Staying active and keeping warm are also beneficial. Be aware that over-the-counter decongestants can cause difficulty with urination.

Diet and supplements can play a role in reducing symptoms. Zinc is a critical nutrient for prostate health. Foods rich in zinc are pumpkin and sunflower seeds, oatmeal, clams, herring, oyster, and wheat bran. Organic foods are important as pesticides can undermine prostate health. Foods that supply essential fatty acids, such as fish and walnuts, are beneficial and research supports the use of these in supplement form. Some sources advocate the avoidance of alcoholic beverages, spicy foods, and exposure to very cold weather if prostatitis is present.

The use of an extract of flower pollen, Cernilton, has been found to be very effective in reducing symptoms of BPH. The pollen reduces inflammation and has been shown to contract the bladder while relaxing the urethra. Another benefit of the extract is that it contains a compound that inhibits the growth of prostate cells. Lower cholesterol relieves symptoms.

Various herbs have been used to treat enlarged prostate, including stinging nettle, pygeum, and saw palmetto, which has been shown to significantly reduce symptoms in numerous clinical studies.

Pruritus Ani

Pruritus ani is a form of contact dermatitis characterized by an itching or burning of the rectum. This area is covered and often moist, two good conditions for germ and fungal growth. Moisture in the rectal area is often present because its sweat glands are connected to the sexual glandular system. These sweat glands are highly responsive to emotion or sexual excitation and a large amount of perspiration is released. This moisture, high in protein and carbohydrates, is a favorable environment for bacterial growth. The moisture can also cause the release of dyes from clothing worn in this region, which can aggravate the condition.

Nutrients may help. Pruritus ani has been associated with a deficiency of vitamins A and B complex and iron. Diabetics often have this rash because of the high sugar content of the skin; sugar is another good breeding ground for fungal growth. The diet should

not contain chocolate, nuts, and caffeine. Overeating hot chili peppers may be a problem.

Adequate B vitamins, vitamin A, and iron are necessary. Acidophilus may be helpful. Excessive amounts of citrus juices should be avoided. In addition, the area should be kept as dry as possible and good hygiene practices should be followed.

Psoriasis

Psoriasis is a chronic skin disease of scaling and inflammation and is often hereditary. The disease is not contagious. It is characterized by eruptions on the skin of thick, red, circular patches of all sizes covered with dry, silvery scales. The patches enlarge slowly, forming more extensive patches. Psoriasis appears mainly around the legs, arms, scalp, ears, and lower back. The condition seems to come and go and there is no cure. People between the ages of fifteen and thirty-five appear to be the most vulnerable. In the United States, between 5.8 and 7.5 million people, equally men and women and primarily adults, have psoriasis. Of these, one million suffer from psoriatic arthritis in which there is inflammation of the joints. In one-third of these cases, there is no associated skin condition. It appears that psoriasis may be caused by faulty signals in the immune system.

Symptoms are toenails and fingernails that are pitted and dull with ridges, and itchy patches of red and inflamed skin. Conditions that may cause or bring on psoriasis are poison ivy, surgery, stress or tension, viral and bacterial infections, sunburn, cuts, lithium, beta blockers, chloroquine, and illness.

Current medical treatments for psoriasis include topical medications, a first line of defense; systemic treatments; and phototherapy, which includes UVB, PUVA, and lasers. In phototherapy, the skin is exposed to wavelengths of ultraviolet light under medical supervision. Home phototherapy is also available. Care must be taken to limit the risk of skin cancer when using such therapy. Consult a physician.

Exposure to natural sunlight or ultraviolet light reduces the scaling and redness of psoriasis, which seems to lessen during the summer months. Nutrients may be helpful. Vitamin A (10,000 IU three times a day for six days), the B complex (100 milligrams morning and night), vitamin C, and vitamin D (normal levels), all of which play a part in skin health, have been found to be useful in treating some cases of the disease. Some researchers have also found vitamin E to be effective in healing psoriasis. Zinc (15 to 30 milligrams per day) and fish oil (cut back on omega-6 oils to keep a balance with the omega-3s) are also beneficial.

Diet may be helpful. An increase of fiber, present in foods such as whole grain cereals, cooked dried beans and peas, fruits, and vegetables, has been found to be advantageous. Oily fish such as mackerel and salmon are good, as is primrose oil and linseed oil (1 to 2 tablespoons per day). Zinc foods such as oysters, pumpkin seeds, wheat bran, oatmeal, herring, clams, and sesame seeds are beneficial. A reduction in animal protein (red meat and eggs), fat, sugar, and alcohol can be useful for treating psoriasis. Dairy products such as whole milk, butter, and cream may produce allergic reactions in the form of psoriasis in some persons.

Herbs that may help are sarsaparilla (not for children under age two), burdock (ointment), comfrey (ointment), Oregon grape (tincture), yellow dock, celery seed (use in consultation with a physician; not for children under age two), dandelion, milk thistle, gotu kola (cream), lavender (for bath), ginger (bath), tropical periwinkle (ointment), and oatmeal (bath). Aerobic exercise helps improve circulation.

Pyorrhea (Periodontal Disease)

Pyorrhea is an infectious disease of the gums and tooth sockets characterized by the formation of pus and by the loosening of the teeth. Gum disorders such as puffiness, tenderness, soreness, and bleeding are often related to vitamin C and bioflavonoid deficiencies that cause increased capillary fragility. Calcium, folic acid, and/or niacin are also usually deficient. All nutrients that fight infection and rebuild bones should be emphasized. (See "Tooth and Gum Disorders, Gingivitis, and Periodontitis.")

Rhinitis

Rhinitis is the inflammation of the nasal mucosa, causing nasal congestion with increased secretion of mucus, or simply runny nose.

Treatment is Nasalcrom, a bioflavonoid-like substance; general measures include rest, adequate fluid intake, and a well-balanced diet. Vitamin A and vitamin C have been used successfully in the treatment of rhinitis. (See "Allergies," "Hay Fever," and "Sinusitis.")

Rickets and Osteomalacia

Rickets is primarily a childhood disease of malnutrition in which there is a deficiency of vitamin D, calcium, and/or phosphorus. The chief symptom of rickets is an inability of the bones to retain calcium. This causes them to become soft, which results in deformities when the bones are called upon to support weight that they are too weak to support. Such deformities include bowlegs, knock-knees, protruding breastbone, narrowed rib cage, and bony beads along the ribs. Other symptoms of rickets include tetany (muscle spasms caused by too little calcium or vitamin D), leg cramps, pain in the bones (mainly the legs, neck, ribs, and hips), numbness in the extremities, general weakness, pain in joints, easily decaying teeth that are malformed, and, in babies, an enlarged head. However, weight gain and growth are generally normal in children with rickets.

The adult form of rickets is known as *osteomalacia*. It is most likely to occur at times of bodily stress such as multiple pregnancies or during breast-feeding. Also susceptible are those who have absorption problems, those who are malnourished or have poor diets, and older people who do not go outside to absorb the necessary vitamin D from sunlight to absorb calcium.

Causes may be a kidney defect or disease, a deficiency of calcium or phosphorus, or an inability to use vitamin D. Rickets may occur in people who get little sunshine or in those on diets so low in fats that inadequate bile is made and vitamin D is not absorbed.

Nutrients may help. Vitamin D, calcium, and phosphorus work together to form strong bones; if one of these nutrients is missing, the result is rickets or osteomalacia. Vitamin D is needed for proper absorption and use of calcium and phosphorus, which harden the bones. A deficiency of vitamin C can make the bones less able to retain calcium and phosphorus. To stimulate bile flow, oils should be used instead of solid fats; lecithin and digestive enzymes should also be included. (See "Osteoporosis.")

Diet should include low-fat dairy products, green leafy vegetables, sesame products, yogurt, and raw fruits and vegetables. Avoid junk foods. Biochemical tissue salts are Calc. Phos. 6x, which promotes the absorption of calcium and phosphorus.

Sciatica

Sciatica refers to severely painful spasms along the sciatic nerve of the leg. This nerve runs from the back of the buttock and thigh, down the inside of the leg to the ankle. Among the possible causes of sciatica are trauma or inflammation of the nerve itself, sprained joints or structural damage in the lower back, rupture of a disk between the spinal bones, and neuritis. There is numbness and tingling.

Treatment for sciatica includes rest and hot or cold, wet or iced applications to the affected leg for the relief of pain and inflammation. Massage, acupuncture, chiropractic treatment, and hydrotherapy may help. The vitamin B complex is essential for the health of nerve tissue. (See "Neuritis.")

Scurvy

Scurvy is a malnutrition disease caused by a diet deficient in vitamin C. Symptoms of adult scurvy include swelling and bleeding of the gums; tenderness of joints and muscles; rough, dry, discolored skin; poor healing of wounds; and increased susceptibility to bruising and infection. Because vitamin C facilitates the absorption of iron, scurvy may be complicated by anemia.

An infant with scurvy experiences joint pain that causes the child to assume a position called the "scrobutic pose," in which he or she is comfortable only when lying on his or her back with knees partially bent and thighs turned outward. The vitamin C deficiency makes the infant's bones less capable of retaining calcium and phosphorus, causing them to become weak and eventually brittle.

Nutrients may be beneficial. Scurvy responds dramatically, usually in two or three days' time, to the daily administration of 100 to 200 milligrams of vitamin C. In treating complications such as anemia and bone changes, a well-balanced diet high in protein, iron, calcium, vitamin D, and magnesium is also necessary to promote tissue repair.

Shingles (Herpes Zoster)

Shingles (herpes zoster) is an infection that is left over from childhood chicken pox. After the chicken pox has run its course, the virus exits to the nerve endings near the brain and the spinal cord, where it lays dormant for many years until there is a weak moment within the system. Then it attacks again. A weak immune system seems to account for the disparity. If there has been chicken pox, the chance for contracting shingles is 40 percent. Adult chicken pox is very dangerous, and anyone who has not had the childhood kind should avoid anyone who has them. As many as one million people a year get shingles. For those over age fifty, postherpetic neuralgia (PHN) may become a problem. The blisters never really heal and there are sensation problems (itching, pain, and numbness) for months or even years.

The disease is characterized by symptoms such as blisters and crust formations and severe pain along the involved nerve, which may last for several weeks. There is deep pain where there is an attack, usually on one side involving the arm or leg and sometimes the face or eyes (see an ophthalmologist since shingles may cause blindness). Fever and fatigue often accompany the pain. Blisters filled with pus appear, usually on the abdomen under the ribs, but they may appear anywhere several days later. The blisters take ten to fourteen days to dry up and become noncontiguous. If the right nutrients are taken at the first sign of blisters, they will dry and heal faster. Nutrients may help. The B vitamins (25 milligrams daily) are necessary for the proper functioning of the nerves. Intramuscular injections of thiamin hydrochloride and vitamin B_{12} have successfully been used in the treatment of herpes zoster. Vitamins A and C (1,000 milligrams four times a day) help promote healing of the skin lesions characteristic of the disease. Massive doses of vitamin C can boost the immune system and limit the infection of shingles. Calcium and magnesium are important for the transmission of nerve impulses and protection of sensitive nerve endings. Vitamin E (up to 1,600 IU daily) has been shown to relieve long-term symptoms. Vitamin E oil applied to the area is thought to help. Lysine (500 milligrams three or four times per day) may help if the postviral neuralgia is already present. Adenosine, a nucleic acid derivative, may relieve symptoms of shingles. AL 721 interferes with the infectivity of the virus.

A well-balanced diet of vegetable protein or lean meat, fish, low-fat dairy products, and fruits and vegetables is recommended. Foods to fight the virus and keep the immune system at its optimum are essential. Vitamin C foods such as citrus fruits, vegetables such as brussels sprouts, fruits such as strawberries, brewer's yeast, brown rice, and whole grains are good. Chocolate, gelatin, nuts, and other foods high in arginine should be avoided.

Herbs and natural ingredients that may be beneficial are hot red peppers, parsley, wormwood, licorice, and Chinese gentian. Cornstarch and baking soda compresses or baths are soothing. Coolness numbs nerve endings in the skin and interferes with messages for pain and itch to the brain. Electric hand massagers can also interfere with messages to the brain. Regular exercise can help one cope with pain. Medically, antidepressants are used to help the brain handle the pain. Homeopathic remedies are Mezereum 6c, Rhus toxicodendron 6c, Ranunculus bulbosus 6c, and Variolinum 30c for prevention.

Sinusitis

Sinusitis is the blocking of the sinus passageways because of inflammation or excess mucus. These passageways are located in the bones surrounding the eyes and nose. Symptoms are nasal congestion and foul-smelling discharge, fatigue, headache, earache, pain around the eyes and face (including the upper jaw and toothaches), mild fever, cough, and an increased susceptibility to infection.

Sinusitis may be the result of an injury, viral or bacterial infection such as a cold, sore throat, tonsillitis, allergies, swimming, or poor oral hygiene. Recurrent attacks could mean that the cause is an allergy. Recent studies indicate that a deficiency of vitamin A, which helps maintain the health of the mucous membrane of the nose and throat, may cause the condition. Smoking, damp weather, or the ingestion of spicy foods or alcohol may aggravate sinusitis.

Nutrients may be beneficial. Adequate intake of vitamin A may be useful in the treatment of sinusitis, especially if a deficiency exists. Vitamin C can help fight the infections that may occur with this condition, and protein will help restore damaged sinus tissues. Potassium, calcium, vitamin A, and zinc, which is necessary for vitamin A mobilization from the liver, aid the work of the cilia. (Cilia are tiny "fingers" in the nasal passages that help the expulsion of mucus.)

The bacteria and viruses that cause sinusitis thrive in an acidic environment. For this reason, the diet should emphasize those foods that help alkalize the system, that is, those that are unrefined and unprocessed and of plant origin. Diet should be free of dairy products and limited in refined carbohydrates like white flour and white sugar. (See Section 5, Table 5.3, "Acid- and Alkaline-Forming Foods.") Included should be lots of raw, green vegetables; hot, spicy foods at least three times a week are recommended. Chicken soup is very good for thinning mucus. Steamer inhalations may help. Drinking any fluid thins mucus, air conditioners keep pollen out, and saline and water nose sprays help. Keeping hands clean and postponing plane travel are other helpful tips. Herbs that may help are marjoram, honeysuckle, xanthium fruit, goldenseal infusion with bromelain, peppermint, fritillary bulb, tangerine peel, and garlic (raw as much as possible).

Homeopathic remedies are Kali bichromicum 30c, Sticta pulmonaria 6c, and Mercurius solubilis 6c. Aromatherapy includes basil, black pepper, cedarwood, cypress, eucalyptus, ginger, grapefruit, juniper, lavender, lemon, sweet marjoram, myrrh, orange, peppermint, Scots pine, tea tree, and sandalwood.

Skin Problems

- **Bites**, **stings**, and **poisons** adversely affect many people, especially those who are allergic to bites. More people die of bee stings than from poisonous insects. People with these known allergies should carry vitamin C with them and, if bitten, should take large amounts of the vitamin immediately and frequently thereafter. Dr. Frederick Klenner of North Carolina successfully used large doses of vitamin C (4 grams every few hours) to treat the bites of black widow spiders, highland moccasins, and rattlesnakes. His patients made complete recoveries in as short a time as thirty-eight hours. He recommends calcium be taken with the vitamin to increase the effectiveness of the treatment and decrease the sensitivity to pain. Following any bite, sting, or poison, pantothenic acid should be increased and vitamin E applied topically to reduce the pain. A reaction to poison oak or ivy can be alleviated by taking large quantities of calcium and vitamin C. Homeopathic remedies are Ledum palustre for insect bites or stings and human or animal bites; Hypericum perforatum for puncture wounds; and gunpowder, pyrogen, and Hepar sulph for infection.

- A **boil**, or **furuncle**, is an infected nodule on the skin with a central core of pus surrounded by inflamed and swollen tissue. A boil forms when skin tissue is weakened by chafing, lowered resistance as a result of disease, or inadequate nutrition. Boil symptoms include itching, mild pain, and localized swelling. Proper hygiene is essential for the treatment of boils. The infected areas should be washed several times daily and swabbed with antiseptic. Hot compresses can relieve pain and promote healing. The person should receive adequate rest and pay special attention to eating a well-balanced diet. Nutrients may help. Vitamins A, C, and E are necessary for healthy skin. Vitamin A can also be applied locally. Sufficient zinc in the diet (30 milligrams per day) may actually prevent boils from occurring. Homeopathic remedies are Hypericum perforatum tincture and Tarentula cubensis.

- **Canker sores** are shallow, open sores found anywhere on the mouth. They are usually located on the mucous membrane inside the lips and cheeks, and are often hard to distinguish from cold sores or Herpes Simplex I. Canker sore symptoms are a sensation of burning and tingling and a slight swelling of the mucous membrane. The sore, a white center surrounded by a red border, is tender to pressure and is painful when acids or spicy foods are eaten. The sore lasts from four to twenty days and heals spontaneously, leaving no scar. The specific cause of canker sores is unknown, although they appear to be brought on by anxiety, other emotional stress, or sensitivity to various foods and substances that produce allergic-type reactions. When the system becomes overly acidic, a person is more vulnerable. Nutrients may help. Because stress is the most common instigator, the B complex taken in large doses often reduces the active time of the sores. Oral doses (50 milligrams) and topical application of zinc have successfully prevented or shortened the duration of canker sores; magnesium and vitamins B_1 and B_2 were also included in several of the tests. Other studies have shown that many canker sore patients are likely to be deficient in iron, folic acid, and vitamin B_{12}. The sores have cleared quickly when acidophilus tablets or yogurt was eaten several times a day. Vitamins A and D are necessary for maintaining the condition of mouth tissue and may also be applied locally. The B complex helps in the general condition of the skin, tongue, and digestive system. A well-balanced diet that provides adequate amounts of these vitamins protects against the formation of canker sores.

- A **carbuncle** is a painful localized infection producing pus-filled areas in the deeper layers of the skin tissues. It commonly appears as a group of boils but is usually more painful, deeper, and slower-healing than an ordinary boil. Carbuncles are formed when bacteria enter lesions in the skin, causing infection. Symptoms of carbuncles include fever and chills, fatigue, and weight loss. Treatment for carbuncles demands proper hygiene, including frequent washing of the infected areas with soap and water and application of an antiseptic. Hot compresses can relieve pain and promote healing. Bed rest is beneficial, and a well-balanced diet is essential. Nutrients may help. Vitamins A, D, and C are necessary for healthy skin. If a fever is present, vitamin E may reduce scarring. Calorie and nutrient levels should be increased. Vitamin A or E may be applied locally. Homeopathic remedies are echinacea and Hypericum.

- **Dry skin** can result from a deficiency of vitamins A, C, or B complex. (See "Dermatitis.") Because the oils of the skin are largely unsaturated, the unsaturated fatty acids are needed for moist skin. Vitamin A is necessary for natural skin growth and repair, and pantothenic acid is required for the synthesis of the fats and oils essential for proper skin function. The skin's natural moisturizer, NA-PCA (the sodium salt of pyrrolidone carboxylic acid), which decreases with age, is available as a spray or cream for topical application. Aromatherapy includes lavender, ylang-ylang, rose otto, chamomile, neroli, and sandalwood.

- **Fungus** infestations can refer to athlete's foot, ringworm (appearing on any part of the body), infestations on or around the genitals and anus or around the mouth (causing thrush), or inflammations on the fingers or under the fingernails. The most common cause of these infestations is the destruction of beneficial bacteria by antibiotics, drugs, or radiation, resulting in the takeover by undesirable fungi. Besides being taken as a drug, antibiotics often are found in the food supply because antibiotic supplements are given to animals as treatment for diseases and also as a feed additive. People with any type of fungal infestation should establish an adequate diet, including generous amounts of vitamins A, B, and C; raw fruits; vegetables; whole grains; and yogurt or acidophilus. Aromatherapy includes lavender, myrrh, patchouli, and tea tree.

- **Ichthyosis** resembles fish skin in appearance (*ichthus* is Greek for "fish") and is characterized by widespread patches of dry skin that turn dark and scaly. Physicians in Egypt have discovered that niacin completely clears the disease after a period of treatment. Niacin should be accompanied by the other B vitamins. In other cases, vitamins A (150,000–200,000 IU daily) and C (up to 10 grams daily) have cleared up the skin with no signs of vitamin A toxicity.

- **Impetigo** is a skin disease caused by bacterial infection. The disease occurs primarily in children, especially in those who are undernourished. Impetigo symptoms are pus-filled skin lesions located mainly on the face and hands. These lesions rupture and form a honey-yellow crust over the infected area. The disease is spread by scratching the lesions and contaminating other skin areas with the fingers. Strict hygiene is essential to prevent spread of the infection to other body parts of the body or to other people. Neglected impetigo in adults may result in boils, ulcers, or other complications. Nutrients may help. Vitamin A is necessary for the health of skin tissue, and vitamins C, D, and E may be helpful in aiding the skin in its recovery from impetigo. The disease often disappears after topical application of vitamins A and E.

- **Intertrigo** is caused by skin areas that are rubbed together, resulting in redness and chafing. Areas such as between the thighs, under the breast, under bra straps, under the arms, and in the groin area are most likely sites, but intertrigo can appear anywhere that there is friction. These areas are then perfect breeding grounds for bacteria and fungus to invade. Garlic and acidophilus products may help.

- **Itching skin** often arises from an iron deficiency, especially if there is no other disease present. Numbness and tingling sometimes accompany the itching, indicating slight nerve dysfunction. Vitamin B_6 is helpful. Lip problems, including sore lips, whistle marks, and cracks at the corners of the mouth, usually indicate a vitamin B-complex deficiency—specifically vitamins B_2, B_6, folic acid, or pantothenic acid. Unsaturated fatty acids may also be undersupplied. When adequate amounts of these nutrients are taken, the conditions should disappear quite easily, although whistle marks may take some time. Cosmetic surgery can help this condition. Smoking causes these tiny wrinkles and should be avoided.

- **Lupus erythematosus** primarily affects the connective tissue. The disease is characterized by anemia, joint stiffness, and signs of adrenal exhaustion. Large doses of the B complex and all essential nutrients, especially vitamin E (900 to 2,000 IU) and pantothenic acid (4,900 milligrams to 15 grams), have been reported to result in complete recovery with no recurrence unless the vitamins were discontinued. Also recommended is 50 milligrams of manganese taken morning and evening.

- **Moles** are normally harmless; however, large, flat ones with jagged edges and mottled color should be seen by a physician. A mole that has a crust, bleeds, or has an extreme color change needs immediate attention to check for cancer.

- **Oily skin** (and hair) occurs when there are hormonal imbalances. The condition may develop during pregnancy and when taking oral contraceptives. Other factors are stress and poor diet. Avoiding fatty foods and eating raw fruits and vegetables is helpful. Oily skin has been produced in people who are only slightly deficient in vitamin B_2. Doses of 15 milligrams daily have cleared up the condition; the entire B complex may be beneficial. Whole grains, liver, and brewer's yeast are good sources. Zinc helps regulate the oil glands and can be found in lean meat, poultry, fish, organ meat, and whole grains. Herbs are calendula, lavender, chamomile, and peppermint. Aromatherapy includes juniper, lavender, lemon, eucalyptus, cedarwood, bergamot, geranium, patchouli, rosemary, cypress, and tea tree.

- **Pigmentation** of the skin commonly appears as spots across the forehead, sometimes coinciding with the stress of pregnancy and then referred to as *pregnancy cap*. The skin of affected individuals may become deeply pigmented. The disease is connected with an inadequate diet; vitamins A, B complex, C, D, and E are needed. The discoloration has disappeared after folic acid (5 milligrams), pantothenic acid, and/or niacin (100 milligrams) were taken with each meal. Pigmentation may be due to high copper levels. Zinc will cause the secretion of copper from the body.

- **Prickly heat** is a rash consisting of tiny inflamed pimples that itch, sometimes quite severely. Research has suggested that the disease occurs when the sweat glands no longer function in a particular part of the body, probably because of fatigue. The rash develops wherever there is excessive sweating, such as the inside of the thighs or under a tight diaper on a baby. Cornstarch is effective as an allaying compound. Studies have shown that vitamin C (1 gram daily) can prevent or cure prickly heat. It apparently has a connection with the enzyme systems that relate to the sweat glands.

- **Purpura** is characterized by spontaneous bruising or bleeding and tiny bumps in the skin and mucous membranes. The disease has been considered rare but is now seen more frequently, especially in women. Researchers believe it may be due to the heavy use of estrogen, both in oral contraceptives and as a treatment during menopause. Estrogen (as well as other drugs, chemicals, and infections) destroys vitamin E, which is essential for capillary integrity. Doses of the vitamin (400 to 600 IU daily) have been shown to prevent or result in recovery from purpura.

- **Rosacea** is caused by dilated blood vessels. It begins with a flush over the forehead, nose, chin, and cheekbones and progresses to tiny bumps and spider veins that worsen over time. Rosacea can be disfiguring and psychologically devastating. Financier J. P. Morgan and entertainer W. C. Fields are known to have had the disease. Rosacea attacks fair-skinned people and appears to run in families. Men appear to carry the most devastating symptoms, but more women get the disease. The condition is most likely to appear between the ages of thirty and fifty and can be inexpensively treated. Antibiotics (as an anti-inflammatory) and laser surgery are quite successful (physical appearance is greatly improved). Its cause is thought to be *Helicobacter pylori*, a bacterium that also causes peptic ulcers. Poor hygiene and alcoholism may worsen the situation but are not the cause of the condition. And allergies are not suspect. Acne and cortisone medication worsens rosacea. The national hotline, sponsored by the National Rosacea Society, is 1-888-NO-BLUSH (662-5874) and provides information about rosacea and the opportunity to speak to someone about this condition.

- **Scabies** is an itchy rash caused by a parasite or itch mite. It is highly contagious and is usually found in day-care or nursing home situations. The drug lindane is used to cure the condition. Aromatherapy includes lavender, peppermint, rosemary, and tea tree.

- **Scars** have been prevented and removed by vitamin E. For example, an excessive amount of scar tissue called a keloid, which causes pain and itching, has been relieved by 1,200 IU of vitamin E taken daily. Sufficient zinc in the diet can help prevent keloids. At doses of 200 to 300 IU daily, vitamin E has removed scars from the fingers and palms in a condition called Dupuytren's contrac-

ture; the same amount has corrected Peyronie's disease, which is characterized by abnormal scar tissue on the penis that causes pain on erection and impotence. The vitamin is effective when taken orally as well as applied topically. Stretch marks can appear on teenagers and males as well as previously overweight people and pregnant women. These marks can be prevented and sometimes removed by vitamin E (up to 600 IU daily), the B complex, pantothenic acid (up to 300 milligrams daily), and an adequate intake of zinc and vitamin C. In addition, laser surgery is now used to remove these scars.

- **Ulcers** of the skin heal more rapidly when vitamin E (400 IU daily) is taken and also applied topically. All nutrients are necessary to stimulate healing of the sore, including vitamin C, pantothenic acid, folic acid, and the unsaturated fatty acids.

- **Vitiligo** is a condition in which the skin is unable to manufacture a pigment, melanin, in certain areas, resulting in light patches of skin marked by a dark border. An adequately nutritious diet is especially important in the disease, and it has been helped with supplements of hydrochloric acid and digestive enzymes that ensure proper absorption. The B complex, pantothenic acid (150 to 300 milligrams per day), PABA (100 to 1,000 milligrams per day)—all also applied topically—and vitamins B_6 and C, zinc, and manganese have all aided in the improvement and cure of this condition. Injections of the vitamins along with the tablets may be necessary.

- **Warts** are possibly of viral origin and occur when the body's immune system is low. Doses of 25,000 to 50,000 IU of vitamin A have caused warts to disappear. Vitamin E (500 IU), taken orally and also applied topically, is also beneficial. A homeopathic remedy is Thuja occidentalis for all warts. Antimonium is for plantar warts; Causticum and Graphites are for warts under and around the fingernails; and nitric acid is for yellow, painful, and bleeding warts. Use of all three alternates also works.

- **Wrinkles** and the **loss of elasticity** result from the sun, smoking, expressed emotions, and genetics and gravity (loss of elasticity). A damaged cross-linking mechanism, in which proteins are bonded together and prevented from functioning properly, is a deeper cause. Cross-linking can be slowed down or prevented by taking antioxidants such as vitamins A, B_1, B_2, C, and E (400 IU, not the di-tocopherol kinds) as well as copper, zinc, and 100 micrograms of selenium daily. A calcium deficiency may age the skin. Dimethyl sulfoxide (DMSO) is an anti-aging substance that is good for skin diseases. RNA/DNA are good for aging and the skin. Treatments for more youthful skin vary: topically applied fruit acids may reduce fine-line wrinkles; chemical peels, aided by a physician, can reduce deeper wrinkles; glycosphingolipids (GSL) temporarily puff up the top layer of skin; Retin-A improves sun-damaged skin; alpha-lipoic acid lessens wrinkles. Overall nutrients may be helpful. A biotin deficiency causes dry, flaky skin with a rash around the nose and mouth. Brewer's yeast aids collagen formation. Superoxide dismutase (SOD) is used for skin disorders where there is hardening. Overall diet should include lots of water, and cold-pressed oils are recommended. Avoid fried foods, soda, chocolate, junk foods, and animal fat. Food allergies that cause a rash may be started by eating milk, wheat, eggs, peanuts, meat, poultry, and fish. Vegetable protein may be used. Sulfur improves appearance of skin and is found in eggs, garlic, onions, and asparagus or can be taken in supplemental form.

Herbs for oily skin: witch hazel, licorice, rosebuds, calendula, and lemongrass; for oily and dry skin: peppermint, lavender, and chamomile. Other remedies: chaparral (for skin cancer), garlic and black walnut (for ringworm), gotu kola (for skin ulcers), green magma, bee pollen (for skin renewal), burdock, bayberry (for boils, carbuncles, and cankers), ligustrom (retards aging), eucalyptus, soapwort, marshmallow, slippery elm (soothes irritated tissues), melaleuca (for bacterial/fungal infections), and yellow dock. *Homeopathic remedies*: Apis 6c for stinging skin; Sulphur 6c (silicea or silicon dioxide) for hot, burning, and itchy skin; Graphites 6c, Natrum muriaticum 6c, and Petroleum 6c for chapping. *Aromatherapy for sensitive skin*: half-strengths of chamomile, rose otto, and lavender; *puffy skin*: geranium, juniper, patchouli, cypress, and lavender; *combination of skin ailments*: lavender, neroli, geranium, and rose otto; *dehydrated skin*: clary sage, rose otto, lavender, and chamomile; *normal skin*: frankincense, lavender, neroli, geranium, chamomile, and rose otto.

Sore Throat

Sore throat is the common name for inflammation of the pharynx, larynx, or tonsils. The condition is often associated with the common cold or breathing through the mouth. Symptoms of sore throat may include pain on swallowing, scratchiness of the throat, a red throat with swollen tonsils, and swollen and tender lymph nodes in the neck. Symptoms are typically worse in the morning and lessen as the day advances. Ninety percent of sore throats are caused by viruses. Strep throat, a more serious condition that often includes fever, is caused by bacterial infection and can lead to rheumatic fever.

Gargling several times a day with warm salt water, using ½ teaspoon salt in 1 cup of warm water, can ease a sore throat. Sore throat may be associated with vitamin C deficiency. Supplementing with vitamin C buffered with alkaline minerals, bioflavonoids, and the herbs goldenseal and echinacea may be beneficial. Following a diet rich in alkaline foods rather than acidic is recommended as the virus thrives in an acidic environment. (See Section 5, Table 5.3, "Acid- and Alkaline-Forming Foods.")

Stress

Stress is any physical or emotional strain on the body or mind. Physical stress occurs when an external or natural change or force acts upon the body. Extreme heat, cold, or activity; injuries; malnutrition; and exposure to drugs and poisons are examples of physical stress. Emotional stress may be a result of fear, hate, love, anger, tension, grief, joy, frustration, and/or anxiety.

Physical and emotional stress can overlap, as in special body conditions such as pregnancy, adolescence, and aging. During these times, body metabolism is increased or lowered, changing the body's physical functions, which in turn affects the person's mental and emotional outlook on life. A certain amount of stress is useful as a motivating factor, but when it occurs in excess or is of the wrong kind, the effect can be detrimental. Society today is high energy and high tech and stress is ever present. Love, life, finances, working, raising a family, violence, commuting, and computers are all areas of known daily stress that have negative effects on the body.

Symptoms of stress may be high blood pressure, neck and backaches, dizziness, diarrhea, tearfulness, fatigue, insomnia, lack of concentration, sexual problems, irritability, and loss of appetite or overeating. Frequent illness due to an immune system that is overworked is common.

The metabolic response of the body to either physical or emotional stress is to produce more adrenal hormones. These adrenal hormones are secreted by glands that lie above the kidneys. When released into the blood, these hormones prepare the body for action by increasing blood pressure and heartbeat and by making extra energy available. These body responses are useful when physical action is needed, as in the fight-or-flight dilemma, but in our modern civilization there is usually little physical outlet for the overload. The body must react to stress by channeling the body's responses inward to one of the organ systems, such as the digestive, circulatory, or nervous system. When this happens, the system reacts adversely, and conditions such as ulcers, hypertension, backache, atherosclerosis, allergic reactions, asthma, fatigue, and insomnia often develop.

Anxiety, a fearful or distressful feeling, is responsible for the stress of many individuals. Anything that threatens a person's body, job, loved ones, or values may cause anxiety. If the person cannot cope with the situation, stress on the body is increased, resulting in many of the disorders associated with stress. Change in attitude or lifestyle may be necessary to eliminate the needless strain and allow the body to resume normal functioning. Some people manage to create stress even if there isn't any. Long-term stress causes the body to break down.

Nutrients may help in relieving stress. The increase in the production of adrenal hormones increases the metabolism of protein, fats, and carbohydrates, producing instant energy for the body to use. As a result of this increased metabolism, there is also an increased excretion of protein, potassium, and phosphorus and a decreased storage of calcium. DHEA relieves stress. B-complex vitamins (especially B_{12}) are needed for the nervous system. L-tyrosine taken before a stressful event acts as a stress reliever.

Many of the disorders related to stress are a direct result not of the stress itself, but of nutrient deficiencies caused by increased metabolic rate during periods of stress. For example, vitamin C is utilized by the adrenal gland during stressful conditions, and any stress that is sufficiently severe or prolonged will cause a depletion of vitamin C in the tissues.

People experiencing stress need to maintain a nutritious, well-balanced diet with special emphasis on replacing the nutrients that may be depleted during stress. Whole grain breads and cereals, fruits and vegetables, and enough protein to sustain cellular rejuvenation are recommended. Honey and all carbohydrates (pasta, potatoes, beans, bread, and cereal) have a calming effect on the brain, with the effect being stronger the older the person is. Beverages high in sugar, a carbohydrate, work more quickly because the dissolved carbohydrate is rapidly absorbed. However, the metabolism of sugar requires some of the same nutrients required by the adrenals during stress, but sugar does not supply these. Onions induce relaxation and drowsiness.

Refined and junk foods create stress on the system, as do refined sugar and flours. Dairy foods may be an allergen. Caffeine may trigger panic and anxiety disorders. Alcohol should not be used to handle stress, because it can cause panic attack in some people in the twelve-hour withdrawal period after drinking, in any amount.

Other aspects of stress management are exercise, relaxation techniques such as meditation and self-hypnosis, music, conversations with friends, hot baths, biofeedback, massage, yoga, prayer, and, in serious situations, consultation with a professional. High stress levels have been associated with a greater tendency to choose less healthy and more passive ways of relieving stress, including eating, drinking, and watching TV.

Herbs that may help ease stress are goldenseal (muscle relaxer), lady slipper, melissa, pau d'arco, hops, peony root, bee pollen, schizandra fruit, ginseng, passion flower, catnip, skullcap, chamomile, lavender, thorowax, valerian root, Siberian ginseng, rose hips, and rosemary. Homeopathic remedies are Gelsemium (for weak anxiety) and Arsenicum album, Ignatia, Argentum nitricum, Calcarea carbonica, and Aconite (for strong anxiety). For children, Chamomilla and Coffea cruda are recommended.

As a natural releaser of tension, exercise is important. Under stress, the body feels a need to be active. Aerobic exercise and yoga are excellent ways to relax. Biofeedback teaches the body how to handle stress and is also very beneficial.

Stroke

A stroke, or cerebrovascular accident, occurs when the blood supply of an area of brain cells is cut off for a long period of time, resulting in the death of the deprived cells from lack of oxygen and nutrients. The process is similar to that of a heart attack, the difference being that in the heart, cell death is in the muscle as opposed to the brain cells that die during a stroke. The blood vessels may be blocked by atherosclerosis, clotting, or hemorrhaging. Predisposing factors are untreated high blood pressure, atherosclerosis, diabetes, old age, obesity, and cigarette smoking. Recent discoveries have provided a medication that, when administered within the first four to five hours after a stroke, will increase survival rates considerably.

Typical symptoms include impaired memory and attention span, tingling or lack of feeling in limbs, a feeling of heaviness in the limbs, and loss of movement. Symptoms are often restricted to one side of the body, as seen in the frequent right- or left-sided paralysis. Strokes may be so small that they are not even noticed or so severe as to be fatal. It is difficult to tell the extent of injury or cell death at the time the stroke occurs, and the long-term outlook depends on the area and extent of the brain damage. Physical and speech therapy are often helpful in rehabilitating the patient.

Nutrients may help. All nutrients should meet the demands of stress and should lower blood cholesterol if it is too high. The B vitamins and vitamin C (500 milligrams daily) are good because they are needed for general health of the blood vessels. Niacin, or B_3, lowers cholesterol. Vitamin E (400 IU daily), which thins blood, can be of help in preventing clots. Six 500-milligram tablets of primrose oil divided through the day and 3 grams of fish oil, also a blood-thinner, daily are recommended; 5 to 10 grams of lecithin is also good. Garlic supplements thin the blood. One aspirin daily is known to limit strokes. In addition, DMSO is being studied as an aid for cerebral stroke. Daily doses of 400 milligrams of magnesium, selenium, and potassium protect against stroke. Taking a higher dosage of these natural blood-thinning agents or blood-thinning medication, or a combination of the two, can result in a tendency to bleed and bruise easily. Regular testing of prothrombin time of the blood can help tailor the treatment to current needs.

The diet should be well balanced with whole grains, fruits, and vegetables, and complete low-fat proteins should be emphasized. Preventive dietary measures include restricting sodium intake to reduce high blood pressure and reducing cholesterol, saturated fat, and trans fatty acid intake to prevent further cholesterol buildup in blood vessels. However, the recommended amount of cholesterol must be maintained, since too little can cause weakened vessels to blow out, resulting in a hemorrhage or bleeding stroke. Blood levels much below 160 are not recommended.

One piece daily of potassium-rich fruit such as a banana will help prevent stroke. Dried apricots and cantaloupe are good choices as well. Five servings of carrots per week may reduce the risk, as will spinach. These are antioxidant vegetables. Other vegetables that are good are avocado, potato (with the skin), and beans. Shiitake mushrooms prevent strokes. Garlic lowers cholesterol levels and thins the blood. Onions are also very good. Use olive and canola oil. Fatty fish such as sardines and mackerel as well as other seafood such as salmon two or three times a week is suggested. Fish intake needs to be limited because of possible mercury and other heavy metal content. Green tea has been connected with stroke prevention.

Fatty meat, salt (induces mini-strokes even if it does not raise blood pressure), and high-fat dairy products should be avoided. Smoking and alcohol consumption (no more than two drinks per day) need to be limited if not stopped, and coffee for those with irregular heartbeats should also be avoided. Reduction of overweight and obesity by sensible dieting is of the utmost importance.

Herbs that may help are yarrow, alfalfa, ginger, ginkgo, tarragon, and turmeric. Homeopathic remedies are Arnica 200c, and Arnica 6c with Kali mur. 6x. Gentle exercise is recommended immediately after an attack. Muscles must be kept supple.

Sudden Infant Death Syndrome (SIDS)

Sudden infant death syndrome (SIDS) is the sudden death of an infant that cannot be explained after all known causes have been painstakingly ruled out. An autopsy, family history, and death scene investigation are aspects that are all considered. Crib death, or SIDS, is the number 1 killer of children between the ages of one month and one year, and the third leading cause of death overall among infants less than one year of age. Since the mid-1990s, thanks to increased knowledge about how to prevents SIDS and outreach to inform the public, the incidence of SIDS has declined significantly. However, in 2002, the number of reported SIDS deaths still numbered 2,295 in infants under twelve months, occurring in all races, ethnic groups, and socioeconomic segments of society.

In studying SIDS, researchers have identified three possible areas of origin: (1) intrinsic abnormalities in cardiorespiratory control, (2) a critical period of development of homeostatic control mechanisms, and (3) the existence of stresses such as mild upper respiratory infection and gastrointestinal illness, as well as changes in the immediate microenvironment of the child involving temperature or air content of oxygen or carbon dioxide. A combination of causes is suspected.

Symptoms in babies may be apparent a day or so before death, and constant communication with a physician about the baby's behavior is advisable. There may be coughing, wheezing, vomiting, diarrhea, and poor appetite. Other symptoms may be restlessness or irritability, and the child may appear pale and listless. Progressively, the child will experience a bluish skin color with cold hands and feet and have difficulty in breathing. Internally, the lungs and respiratory tract become swollen and inflamed. Water and blood collect in the lungs and the tubes connecting the lungs to the bloodstream become spastic.

In the late 1980s and early 1990s, based on a body of evidence, the position in which an infant sleeps began to emerge as a highly significant risk factor for SIDS. Studies in Great Britain, New Zealand, Scandinavia, and Australia found that risk was highest for infants sleeping tummy-down in a prone position, intermediate for side-sleeping infants, and lowest for those lying with their faces upward. Based on this research, the first alert to health care providers and the general public to place infants supine for sleep was issued in 1992. At that time, the rate of prone sleeping for infants was 75 percent but by 1999, this rate had dropped to 14 percent. During this same period, incidence of SIDS declined 43 percent.

Through her own studies, Dr. Joan L. Caddell, a pediatric cardiologist, believes the cause of crib death may be a magnesium deficiency. A borderline yet critical deficiency of the mineral in the mother during pregnancy, and secondarily in the infant's diet, may precipitate crib death.

It is known that the period of greatest risk for SIDS is during the second and fourth months of life, the most rapid growth period for newborns. Rapid growth depletes magnesium. A magnesium deficiency also is a factor in the release of histamine, which is a substance that increases the permeability of the capillaries, allowing nutrients and oxygen to leak out and collect in sites such as the lungs.

Dr. Frederick Klenner suggested that adequate daily intake of vitamin C may prevent SIDS attributed to suffocation, of which the symptoms may be as slight as congested nasal passages. He also treated infants suffering from crib syndrome, a less acute condition, with calcium gluconate and massive injections of vitamin C. He attributed this syndrome to a possible brain trauma at birth. The symptoms are similar to those of a cold. He stated that adequate amounts of vitamin C taken by the mother during pregnancy might prevent this condition. Researchers and physicians have also linked the pregnant mother's cigarette smoking and a deficiency of vitamins B and E to infant crib death.

Some other measures to take include not smoking around the baby, avoiding overheating the infant, and using firm bedding instead of placing the baby on items such as foam pads, cushions, beanbags, sheepskins, sofa cushions, or synthetic-filled adult pillows. Breast-feeding when possible is desirable. Babies who are premature, have low birth weights, or are twins or triplets are at risk. Other factors that seem to make a difference are the age of the mother (the younger, the greater the risk), the season (cold-weather months have higher rates), the sex of the baby (boys are at a higher risk), and the baby's age.

At this date, there is no known cause of this baffling condition, and no one should feel guilty for not doing enough, either before the child is born or after, to prevent SIDS from happening. A woman who is pregnant should always be given a prenatal vitamin and mineral supplement. The best that parents can do is the best that they know how, and the rest should be left to science to discover just what it is that is taking the lives of so many newborns.

The American SIDS Institute provides a nationwide, twenty-four-hour toll-free number for those who wish to discuss their concerns with a SIDS counselor, request additional information, or be connected to the local SIDS affiliate for support services in their area: 1-800-232-SIDS.

Sunburn

Sunburn is caused by excessive exposure to ultraviolet rays or sunlight, which actually burn up surface skin and later the lower cells. The amount of exposure to ultraviolet rays that causes burning depends basically on four factors: the individual, place, time, and atmospheric conditions.

Caution should be used in exposing oneself to the sun for extended periods of time between 10 A.M. and 2 P.M., when most of the ultraviolet rays are present. Reflections from water, metal, sand, or snow may double the amount of rays one absorbs. Long-term effects of this exposure are premature aging and skin cancer.

Sunburns may be classified in three degrees. First-degree sunburn causes reddening of the skin and possibly slight fever. Second-degree sunburn causes reddening of the skin accompanied by water blisters. Third-degree sunburn causes lower cell damage and the release of fluid, resulting in eruptions and breaks in the skin where bacteria and infection can enter. Consult a physician for third-degree burns.

Fair and young skin seems to be the most vulnerable; however, all colors are affected. Sunscreens are advised. A gradual approach to getting a tan is more sensible, since the damage will be limited. The less the burn, the more safe the exposure.

Nutrients may be beneficial. Vitamins A, C, and E are recommended for treatment of sunburn. Cold compresses and fresh aloe vera may help a severe burn. Baking soda, oatmeal, or vinegar in a cool bath will soothe. PABA is used as a sunscreen. Retin-A may lessen the signs of years of aging by the sun. Diet for sunburn should include protein foods for regeneration of damaged cells. Fluids may be taken, since there will be some dehydration. Herbs that may help are melaleuca (topical) and quinine.

Swollen Glands

Swollen glands is a term commonly used to describe enlargement of the lymph nodes, or glands of the neck, on both sides of the throat. Technically, however, it can also describe enlargement of any of the lymph glands, such as those located in the armpit or groin. The enlargement of lymph glands is usually a signal of an infection in the area, because the lymph glands function to filter out microscopic material, such as bacteria, in order to prevent the spread of infection.

Symptoms include enlarged or swollen glands that may be hard or soft. These symptoms may be accompanied by heat, tenderness, and reddening of the overlying skin, and fever.

Swollen glands may simply indicate a localized infection or may be a symptom of a more serious disease. Swollen gland conditions may occur with such disorders as mononucleosis, measles, chicken pox, leukemia, cancer, tuberculosis, bulimia, and syphilis.

Treatment includes maintaining a well-balanced diet and fighting the particular infection or condition that is causing the lymph node enlargement. In general, infection requires an increased intake of protein, fluids, and calories. Nutrients may help. If the infec-tion is accompanied by fever, the diet should be rich in vitamins A, C, and the B complex.

Syndrome X (Metabolic Syndrome)

Syndrome X, or metabolic syndrome, is a newly recognized collection of conditions, all associated with high blood insulin levels, that place people at high risk for coronary artery disease. These conditions can include type II diabetes, obesity, high blood pressure, and a poor lipid profile. Other names for Syndrome X include *insulin resistance syndrome*, *dysmetabolic syndrome X*, and *Reaven syndrome*.

Normally, after the body has broken food down into various component parts in the intestine, the glucose that is produced is absorbed into the system and begins circulating in the blood. Then the pancreas goes into action, secreting the hormone insulin, which ushers this glucose into certain cells where it can fuel the various tasks the cells perform. In Syndrome X, however, the cells do not readily respond to insulin. Type II diabetes also involves this "insulin resistance." But Syndrome X differs from type II diabetes in a significant way. In type II diabetes the pancreas does not produce sufficient insulin to overcome insulin resistance, keeping blood sugar levels high. In Syndrome X, to overcome insulin resistance the pancreas shifts into high gear, producing more and more insulin until all the glucose has been safely stored in the cells. This results in very high blood levels of insulin.

This scenario can eventually lead to type II diabetes as the overworked pancreas begins to lose its ability to produce insulin. But of more immediate concern is that Syndrome X can set the stage for the development of heart disease. High levels of insulin in the blood can lead to the many risk factors for Syndrome X and heart disease. These include impaired glucose tolerance, low HDL cholesterol, and smaller, more dense LDL cholesterol, an increase in blood fats, slow clearance of fat from the blood, a greater risk of blood clots, and high blood pressure.

It is estimated that sixty to seventy-five million Americans experience Syndrome X. Susceptibility to developing Syndrome X is in part due to genetics. Lifestyle factors also play a role, including obesity, lack of physical exercise, cigarette smoking, and a diet high in carbohydrates and low in fat. Prevention and treatment of Syndrome X requires the reverse, according to

Dr. Gerald Reaven, the pioneering Stanford University physician who first described Syndrome X. The makeup of the diet needs to be as follows: 45 percent carbohydrate, 40 percent fat (contributed by 30 percent to 35 percent polyunsaturated and monounsaturated fats and only 5 percent to 10 percent saturated fats), and 15 percent protein. Limiting substances that can reduce insulin sensitivity is also important. In a 2002 study conducted in the Netherlands and published in *Diabetes Care*, researchers found that caffeine can decrease an individual's sensitivity to insulin.

Tics, Tremors, Twitches, and Tourette's Syndrome

Tics, tremors, and twitches begin somewhere around the age of seven and are not considered serious since most people outgrow them. They run in families and may be caused by an imbalance of minerals, an excess of lead in the body, an allergic reaction to food or chemicals, or drugs and medication.

Nutrients may help. The most common cause is a deficiency of potassium and/or magnesium. These minerals are essential for the conduction of nerve impulses that pass to a muscle and control its movement. Sometimes the B-complex vitamins, necessary for the health of the nervous system, are found to be deficient, and when the B complex is taken, symptoms disappear. If an excess of lead is found, calcium or zinc can effectively leach this toxic metal out of the body.

When simple tics become more severe, such as vocal barking, grunting, coughing, or uttering of swear words, the condition becomes known as Tourette's syndrome. Besides the nutrients that may help, tranquilizers do dramatically reduce tics, but there are side effects. Consult a physician.

Tonsillitis

Tonsillitis, found mostly in children, is an inflammation of the tonsils, which are glands of lymph tissue located on either side of the entrance to the throat. For the first three years of life, the tonsils trap germs and develop antibodies to help fight off future infections. In some people, after the usefulness of the tonsils is over, they continue to trap bacteria (including streptococcal, which may respond to antibiotics) and viruses (harder to treat) and become infected; the result is tonsillitis when the body's resistance is lowered and cannot fight back. With each repeated episode, the likelihood of a cure lessens. In cases of severe tonsil infection, surgical removal may be necessary. One reason for the infection may be that there is an improper diet that is high in carbohydrates and low in protein and other nutrients essential for the immune system.

Symptoms of tonsillitis include pain, a white coating, redness and swelling in the back of the mouth, difficulty in swallowing, hoarseness, and coughing. Headache, earache, fever and chills, nausea, bad breath, vomiting, nasal obstruction and discharge, and enlarged lymph nodes throughout the body are additional symptoms of tonsillitis.

Nutrients may be beneficial. The regular intake of vitamin C may help prevent tonsillitis. The most effective means of prevention for tonsillitis is maintaining a well-balanced diet that is adequate in protein, vitamins, and minerals. Anti-inflammatory foods should be included. (See "Inflammatory Conditions.")

Diet during the illness is to take plenty of fluids from fruit and vegetable sources. Steamed vegetables and broth are also good. When able to eat, avoid dairy products and refined carbohydrates such as pastries and sweets, including white sugar and flour. Junk foods should be replaced with whole grain cereals, fruits, and vegetables—foods that alkalize the system.

Herbs that may help are sage (warm as a gargle), pau d'arco, thyme, echinacea, and honeysuckle flower tea. Gargling with warm salt water may be soothing. Humidifiers may keep the throat moist. Homeopathic remedies for pharyngitis and laryngitis are Apis mellifica, Hepar sulphuris, Calcareum, Lachesis, Aconite, Belladonna, Lycopodium, and Phytolacca.

Tooth and Gum Disorders, Gingivitis, and Periodontitis

Cavities (dental caries) are the primary dental problem in the United States. Most cavities are caused by persistent eating of refined sugars and starches, which mix with saliva to form an acid that erodes tooth enamel. One can control cavities by avoiding such items. Eating dried fruit, high in sugar, also increases the risk of developing cavities because the fruit is sticky and clings to the teeth. Brushing immediately after eating is necessary. Other helpful strategies to prevent cavities are to eat a nutritionally balanced diet, refrain from smoking or drinking alcohol, and properly cleanse the mouth, including brushing teeth *and* gums. Besides cleanliness, other causes of cavities and gum disease are illness, blood disease, and glandular disorders. Cleansing between the teeth with dental floss following meals and snacks is an extra precaution that prevents loss of the teeth from gum diseases.

Gum disease begins as a condition known as gingivitis, which can lead to a condition known as periodontitis, an irreversible disease that accounts for the loss of more teeth than do cavities. Three out of four Americans will experience gum disease in one or another of the forms. Gum disease begins with plaque, a mixture of food, bacteria, and mucus that attaches to the spaces between the teeth and the gums. This substance, if not properly removed from the base of the teeth through brushing and flossing or dental visits, hardens into a substance called calculus that irritates and infects the gums.

In early stage gingivitis, the gums react to the presence of calculus by reddening, swelling, and having a tendency to bleed. If not treated, gingivitis can lead to pyorrhea, characterized by further gum inflammation from pockets created between the teeth from the already irritated area. This condition is accompanied by a continuous discharge of pus, gum recession, and loosening of teeth. Cementum is the area of the root of the tooth that becomes exposed as a result of gum disease and is highly sensitive to hot and cold when eating. Two symptoms of gum disease are bad breath and a not so fresh taste in the mouth. (See "Pyorrhea.")

Periodontitis, as it progresses, can lead to deterioration of the bones that surround and support the teeth and may be accompanied by mouth and upper respiratory infections. Causes include inadequate diet, poor cavity fillings, and poorly fitting dentures as well as the improper cleansing of teeth and gums.

Nutrients may help. Bioflavonoids that are found in vitamin C foods help bleeding gums. Although all vitamins and minerals are essential for the proper formation and continued health of the teeth, an adequate vitamin C intake is especially helpful for the prevention of gingivitis and pyorrhea. A severe deficiency of vitamin C causes teeth to loosen and break down. Vitamin A seems to control the development and general health of the gums; a lack of this vitamin often results in gum infection. Vitamin A is also necessary for the formation and maintenance of tooth development in children. Minerals important for healthy teeth are sodium, potassium, calcium, phosphorus, iron, and magnesium. Vitamin D is essential for the absorption of calcium.

A varied diet of fresh vitamin C fruits and vitamin C green leafy vegetables as well as raw vegetables, which requires lots of chewing, will provide the teeth and gums with needed exercise and supply the body with vitamins and minerals essential for dental health. Meat and whole grain bread also provide essential nutrients. Smoking doubles the risk of gum disease by suppressing the immune system.

Herbs that may help are chaparral mouthwash (toothache, decay, and gum disease), red sage leaves, myrrh tincture (found in European toothpaste), cardamom seeds (chew), sanguinaria from the bloodroot plant (as a mouthwash), marshmallow (infusion for mouth and gum pain), yellow dock (gum disease), bayberry (spongy gums), walnut leaves, tea tree (toothpaste and mouthwash), and fresh aloe vera leaf rubbed directly on the gum (for denture or other irritation). Homeopathic remedies are Hypericum for nerve pain, Phosphorus 6c, Saliva officinalis for dry socket, and Mercurius solubilis 6c. Pain remedies are Chamomilla, Plantago majus tincture, Hypericum, and Belladonna.

Aromatherapy for gingivitis is cypress, myrrh, and tea tree.

Ulcers

About one in ten people in the United States develop ulcers. There are many causes of ulcers, and stress is only one of them. Although it still plays a part, stress has been found not to be the culprit that it once was thought to be. Corporate executives get ulcers at similar rates as those whose lives are relatively free of stress. There is a physical vulnerability to ulcers that appears to run in families. Those who regularly take steroid or nonsteroid painkillers, including aspirin, ibuprofen, and other anti-inflammatory drugs, seem to be more susceptible as well. It has recently been discovered that the bacterium *Helicobacter pylori* (*H. pylori*) may be the cause of ulcers. Researchers are studying the infectant for a possible cure.

To form the ulcer, the defense of the lining of the stomach is inadequate and damage results; the stomach is unable to secrete sufficient mucus to protect against the strong acid essential for digestion. *Gastric* ulcers occur in the stomach; *peptic* ulcers appear in the intestines; and *duodenal* ulcers are found in the duodenum, the top part of the small intestine that the stomach empties into. A hemorrhaging ulcer occurs when the ulcer has penetrated a blood vessel, causing it to bleed. Symptoms of an ulcer vary and can include stomach pain (blunt or gnawing), low back pain, pain in passing stool, headaches, choking sensations, and itching. Taking food or an antacid usually alleviates the symptoms. Surgery is rarely needed any longer, except for bleeding or perforating ulcers. The first line of treatment is antibiotics to treat *H. pylori*. Physicians will also sometimes prescribe antacids to reduce symptoms.

Recent studies have shown that cayenne pepper will actually strengthen the lining of the stomach. Spicy foods were found not to interfere with stomach ulcers or the stomach lining, which may indicate differences from individual to individual. Milk does not coat the stomach and is not good for ulcers; however, it may be taken in small amounts for its nutrient value. A nutrient that may be beneficial is L-glutamine, which helps speed the healing of peptic ulcers. It has been found that 150 milligrams of zinc daily, in people who were not deficient in zinc, helped to heal ulcers more quickly. Studies have shown that the ulcerated stomach processes almost all foods impartially.

Since a deficiency of almost any nutrient can cause the development of ulcers, the diet should be well balanced, meet all the demands of stress, and promote healing. Foods should be chosen according to physical reactions; if a certain food causes discomfort, then the food should not be eaten.

Ulcers are made worse by foods that stimulate acid secretions. Some of them are fatty foods, fruit juices, colas, and cocoa. Coffee (caffeinated or not), cigarettes (inhibit healing), chocolate, carbonated drinks, more than an ounce a day of alcohol (especially beer), and strong tea increase the amount of stomach acid and should be avoided. Decaffeinated green teas are good. Other foods that are acid-encouraging are eggs, fish, bread, heavy starches, and sugary foods. For protein needs, use cheese instead of meat, since it encourages less acid secretion. Foods that have temperatures that are too hot will lay the groundwork for ulcers. Foods that are too cold will upset the stomach.

High-fiber carbohydrate foods are encouraged. Fresh fruits and vegetables are alkaline foods, and lots of them are recommended. (See Section 5, Table 5.3, "Acid- and Alkaline-Forming Foods.") Cottage cheese, avocados, blue grapes, potatoes, squash, and yams are foods that are good for ulcers. Foods that strengthen the stomach lining are bananas and plantains, cabbage or the juice, broccoli, brussels sprouts, turnips, cauliflower, kale, green tea, and figs. Red and white beans and unpolished rice soak up acid in the stomach. A tablespoon of apple cider vinegar after meals may help digestion (if there is not enough stomach acid). Baby foods for a bleeding ulcer are good.

Herbs that may help are chamomile (prevents and heals), licorice (soothes gastric and duodenal ulcers), slippery elm, fennugreek seeds, ginger, reishei mushrooms, scented geranium, comfrey, alfalfa (peptic ulcer), burdock (peptic ulcer), dandelion juice, noto ginseng, bayberry root bark, and marshmallow root. Homeopathic remedies are Anacardium 6c, Nox vomica 6c, Kali bichromicum 6c, Bryonia 6c, and Phosphorus 6c. Yoga and biofeedback are recommended for relaxation.

Underweight

Underweight develops when more calories are utilized by the body than are consumed. Underweight without a lack of nutrients may or may not be serious, depending upon the degree of underweight and metabolic state. A thin person is probably less apt to suffer from heart diseases and certain other ailments and will live longer than a person who is overweight.

Malnutrition occurs when an individual is deficient in the nutrients necessary for life. Individuals with this problem are very susceptible to infections, lack nutrient reserves for times of stress, and are easily fatigued. When underweight and malnutrition are severe, there is starvation. The body's stores of nutrients and fats are depleted, and muscle tissue is broken down to provide energy for bodily functions.

Symptoms that may accompany underweight are weakness, fatigue, sensitivity to cold, hunger, dizziness, and loss of ambition. Underweight may be caused by poor eating habits, mental problems, nervous conditions, overactivity, illness, heredity problems, or poorly functioning digestion and absorption processes.

Underweight can be corrected by removal of the underlying causes and improvement of the diet. Food presentation and how it smells is important. Red seems to stimulate the appetite and may be used in either the food or the utensils used to serve the food. The diet should be well balanced, consisting of 300 grams of complex carbohydrates, 100 grams of protein, and 2,500 to 3,000 calories per day. Whole, unrefined foods, many of which should be high calorie, including cheeses, olive oil, nuts, seeds, and avocados, are good choices. Extra protein is needed to rebuild tissues. Sources are eggs, turkey, chicken, fish, lean meat, and vegetable proteins. Other food choices are rice, wheat sprouts, safflower oil, beans, potatoes, and vegetable and fruit juices.

Foods that supply zinc, such as oysters and pumpkin seeds, can be helpful. Zinc regulates appetite and a deficiency may reduce the sensation of taste, contributing to loss of appetite. High-calorie snacks are encouraged. Frequent smaller feedings may be of help in weight gain. Exercise is important during weight gain so that muscle tissues are healthy and properly formed. Weight should not be gained at the rate of more than a pound or two per week. Any vitamin deficiencies should be corrected as quickly as possible. Herbs that may help are fenugreek (appetite stimulant), radish seeds, and loganberries.

Vaginitis

Vaginitis is an inflammation of the vagina that is usually caused by bacterial or yeast infection. Women who are more likely to be at risk are those who have hormonal problems (especially during pregnancy), are diabetic, use antibiotics or oral contraceptive, douche excessively, forget to remove a tampon, have allergies, are postmenopausal, have a vitamin B deficiency, or have intestinal worms. The condition is also sexually transmitted. Symptoms of vaginitis include a burning or itching sensation, redness, odor, and an abnormal vaginal discharge that is white or yellow or curdish (for a yeast infection). Yeast infections (*Candida albicans*) are more common in women of child-bearing age.

Similar infections are *Gardnerella vaginalis*, which has a foul-smelling, milky, and frothy white or gray discharge, and *Trichomonas vaginalis*, which is sexually transmitted and has a yellow or green discharge with an offensive odor. Vaginal infection can be transferred to the male partner as urethritis, which is a painful but not serious condition. Antibiotics are needed, and both parties need to be treated.

Adequate rest and a healthful diet are important for the treatment of vaginitis. A container of yogurt a day that has active *Lactobacillus acidophilus* (which is also available as a supplement) is good. Heating or cooking the yogurt kills the helpful bacteria. Lots of whole grain breads and cereals, fruits and vegetables, and lean meat and fish are recommended. Garlic is an antifungal and can be purchased in capsule form. Coffee and sugar should be avoided since they upset the alkali balance; sugar also creates food for fungal infections.

Treatment involves keeping the genital area clean, especially for both partners before intercourse. Wiping from front to back, avoiding talcs, and using fragrance-free soaps and vaginal deodorants are also recommended. Cotton underwear is sometimes recommended because it allows for free circulation of air. Tight clothes inhibit the circulation of air. Medications are available both by prescription and over the counter. Consult a physician.

Nutrients may be beneficial. Vaginal itching may be prevented by the intake of vitamin A and the B complex if a deficiency is present. Vitamin E ointment applied topically may give relief to an inflamed area. Herbs that are helpful are oil of tea tree and myrrh bath as a douche, apple cider or baking soda in the bath as a douche, goldenseal and myrrh as a douche (not during pregnancy), and chickweed (for itch).

Varicose Veins and Spider Veins

Varicose veins are blue veins that have become enlarged, twisted, and swollen. They may be located anywhere in the body, but they are most commonly found in the legs and in the anal area as hemorrhoids or as varicocele in the testes. (See "Hemorrhoids.") Valves prevent blood from returning to the heart, pooling the blood, which stretches the lower veins and stagnates there. Spider veins are smaller versions of varicose veins and are more an annoyance than they are painful or harmful. Varicose and spider veins are not a part of the aging process.

Factors that inhibit blood circulation, thus causing the condition, are constipation, weight lifting, obesity, certain hereditary conditions, tight clothing, sitting with crossed legs, menopause, long periods of standing, and a sedentary occupation. A pregnant woman or one who has had several pregnancies is usually more prone to varicose veins than are other women. Symptoms are heaviness, tiredness, and aching in the calves and in the legs. Night cramps and restless legs are also symptoms. Legs may be itchy and sore. On rare occasions, varicose veins may indicate a deeper blood clot.

Elevating the legs while resting can be a preventive measure. Yoga is recommended for improvement in breathing. Gentle running techniques are suggested, and weight lifting should be done with care. Sitting longer than three hours will contribute to the susceptibility to varicose veins. Support hose for small veins and gradient stockings for severe cases are recommended. Sclerotherapy is injecting a solution into the vein to dissolve it. Ultrasound has made this method quite successful; however, there may be recurrences. Surgery is used for severe cases. Consult a physician.

The diet for varicose veins should consist of fish and fresh fruits and vegetables. Foods that contain rutin, which keeps veins elastic, are cherries, rose hips, citrus fruits, blackberries, apricots, and buckwheat. Raw beets are also good. Smoking constricts the veins. Foods to avoid are junk foods, alcohol, salt, fried foods, and refined and processed foods.

Nutrients may help. Bioflavonoids are used for varicose veins, strengthening capillary walls. Skin respiratory factor (SRF, an ingredient in Preparation H) is used for varicose veins and hemorrhoids. Adequate amounts of the B vitamins and vitamin C are necessary in the diet for the maintenance of strong blood vessels. Some research has indicated that vitamin E (400 IU daily) can dilate blood vessels and improve circulation.

Herbs that may help are gotu kola (for circulation), white oak bark bath, butcher's broom, red grapevine, buckthorn bark, marigold leaves in a bath, stone root, parsley, rose hips (which contain rutin), collinsonia root, and uva ursi. Aromatherapy for spider veins includes cypress, rose otto, chamomile, and lemon.

It is essential that individuals who are at risk receive adequate exercise. Stretching activities help circulation. Dancing, brisk walking, and skipping are good.

Venereal Disease/ Sexually Transmitted Diseases (STDs)

Sexually transmitted diseases (STDs) can be contracted by anyone. They are totally controllable, and education about these conditions is of vital importance. Safe sex should be practiced at all times. Latex condoms are good; others may deteriorate under normal circumstances.

Some STDs are curable and the severity of some symptoms in others can be lessened. Sexual intercourse, which includes oral sex, or intimacy associated with sexual intercourse, is only one manner in which to get STDs. Each condition has its own methods of contraction and some of them are through open wounds, anal methods, by being anatomically close, and by using the same towels, clothes, and other items. Getting an exam before starting a sexual relationship is advised, since there may be silent STDs present.

Genital warts are sexually transmitted and in some cases are found inside the vagina or around the opening, on the cervix, and around the anus. In men they can be found on the penis or under the foreskin. These warts have been connected to cervical cancer in women. Cervical dysplasia, a precancerous condition, is caused by the same virus as genital warts. Treatment is to remove them surgically or to use chemicals; however, they do recur. Rubbing garlic on the warts as well as eating garlic will help.

Gonorrhea ("the clap") is one of the most frequently reported STDs and is transmitted through sexual intimacy or from the mother to the newborn as the infant passes through an infected birth canal. Gonorrhea is highly contagious and dangerous and may display no symptoms. Its cause is the bacterium *Neisseria gonorrhoeae*, which thrives in the mouth, urinary tract, cervix, and rectum.

Within three to fourteen days after contact, males experience burning, pain, and discharge of pus upon urination. Complications of gonorrhea in males may include prostatitis and testes infection. Females may have increased painful urinary frequency and a yellowish discharge from the vagina, but there are usually no immediate symptoms until the infection has included all the reproductive organs of the pelvic region. If not treated, the symptoms for a woman may degenerate into bleeding between periods, abdominal pain, and vomiting and fever. Complications of gonorrhea may result in sterility in both sexes. Latex condoms are the best protection. Herbs for gonorrhea are burdock, horsetail grass, and nettle.

In addition to obtaining medical treatment, an afflicted person should maintain a well-balanced diet high in protein to help repair the tissue damage that has occurred. Homeopathic remedies may be Thuja mother tincture and Natrum muriaticum 6c.

Nonspecific urethritis (NSU) is extremely common. Men are more likely to experience this disease, but women who do contract the infection may suffer infertility. Inflammation, discharge, and pain during urination are the symptoms. Treatment should be cleanliness before and after sex and practicing safe sex. Antibiotics are used.

Pubic lice cause itching in the pubic area. "Crabs" are not necessarily contracted from sexual intercourse;

a person can be exposed to these in bedding, towels, and clothes. Treatment involves the entire family, and sexual contacts should be treated as well. Insecticide lotions are used.

Scabies is itching in the pubic area where mites have burrowed into the skin and have laid eggs. Closeness is the method of transference, not necessarily sexual activity. The sore rash is around the trunk, fingers, wrists, and genital area. Homeopathy recommends Sulphur 6c.

Treatment for syphilis includes massive injections of antibiotics, usually penicillin, to rid the body of the venereal organism. Early treatment is essential to prevent complicating tissue damage. To prevent spreading venereal disease, an afflicted person should abstain from sexual intercourse and intimacy until the disease has been cured. Herbs that may help syphilis are goldenseal, sarsaparilla, burdock, echinacea, gotu kola, pau d'arco, St. John's wort, suma, and yellow dock.

Thrush is a yeast infection that affects the mouth or vagina. The discharge is creamy, white, and curdlike or is a white coating in the mouth. The condition happens when the immune system is down and the acid-alkali balance in these areas is disrupted. Besides sexual contact, douching, spermicides, and scented bath products may allow the environment to reproduce the yeast. Antibiotics are also responsible.

Diet for thrush is especially important. Sugar, including the sugar in fruit, maple syrup, honey, and alcohol, will allow thrush to thrive. Foods containing yeast—such as mushrooms, blue cheese, MSG foods, smoked foods, vinegar, and bread—are to be avoided. Other food substances to avoid are coffee, tea, and chocolate. Foods to boost the immune system should be consumed. Some are raw and steamed vegetables, brown rice, fish, and lean meat. Live yogurt, olive oil, and garlic are good. Acidophilus supplements may help as well as douches in the form of powder (not for pregnant women). Caprylic acid from coconuts is an antifungal agent that comes in capsule form. Homeopathic remedies are (for the mouth) Arsenicum album 6c, Capsicum 6c, and Borax 6c.

Only women get trichomoniasis, a parasitic infection of the vagina. Symptoms are discomfort, itch and irritation, discharge from the vagina, and frequent urination. Diet may help. Cranberry juice and active yogurt are good. Fruits and vegetables will help fight infection. Nutrients may help: vitamin A (10,000 IU daily), vitamin C (1,000 milligrams daily), vitamin E (800 IU daily), and zinc (50 milligrams daily). An antiparasitic is used to medicate. Vinegar or acidophilus

douches may help balance out the bacteria and acidity, but do not douche during pregnancy.

Worms and Intestinal Parasites

Worms irritate the intestinal lining and, therefore, cause poor absorption of nutrients. There are several types of parasitic worms that can live in human intestines. The most common are pinworms, tapeworms, hookworms, and roundworms. Worms irritate the gastrointestinal lining, causing poor absorption of nutrients. Symptoms of worms include rectal itching (spreads the condition), diarrhea and other colon disorders, hunger pains, appetite loss, weight loss, and anemia. Causes are meat that has been infected and not properly cooked, human waste that is not properly treated or disposed of, and eating dirt (pica) or coming in contact with contaminated soil. Diagnosis can be made by examining the stools or, occasionally, by inducing vomiting. The extent of the intestinal damage is then determined by the type of worm, the size of the worm, and the number of worms present.

- **Pinworms**, or **threadworms**, are the most common parasite worms in the United States. The chief symptom of this small, threadlike worm is rectal itching, especially at night. Personal hygiene is most important for the control of pinworms. Pinworms lodge under the fingernails as a person scratches an infected area, and if that person then handles food, the food becomes contaminated with the worms. Vacuuming carpets, especially around beds, is recommended.
- **Tapeworms** can be contracted from eating insufficiently cooked meats, especially beef, pork, and fish. The most common tapeworm in the United States, beef tapeworm, grows to a length of 15 to 20 feet in the intestines.
- **Hookworms** are often found in the soil or sand in moderate climates. They can enter the body by boring holes in the skin of the bare feet, or they can enter by mouth if food contaminated by dirty hands is eaten.
- **Roundworms** are most common in children and have the fewest symptoms until they have multiplied. These worms can leave the intestines and settle in different areas of the body, causing diseases such as pneumonia, jaundice, and periodontitis.

A diet high in refined carbohydrates that supplies few nutrients increases a person's susceptibility to infestation. A well-balanced diet that is high in calories and sodium (for one to two weeks) with whole foods is important. Eating garlic and onions, figs, pumpkin seeds, and sesame seeds may create an uninhabitable environment for parasites. Since the absorption in the intestine is impaired, large amounts of all nutrients are recommended.

Nutrients may be helpful. When a person is afflicted with parasites, the body's supply of all nutrients is depleted to the point that supplementation is necessary to restore normal health. Nutrients of special importance are vitamin A; the B complex, especially thiamin, riboflavin, B_6, B_{12}, and pantothenic acid; vitamins C, D, and K; and calcium, iron, and protein. Acidophilus is especially helpful for amebic dysentery and possibly for all intestinal infestations. Sufficient stomach acid destroys parasites contained in food.

Herbs and other natural ingredients that may be beneficial are clove, bark of black walnut or extract (a poultice will aid in ringworm), elecampane, wormseed and wormwood, turmeric, pinkroot, male fern tea, oregano, areca nut, St. John's wort, seaweed, and chaparral tea. Homeopathic remedies are Teucrium 6c and Cina 6c.

Food Lists

Foods with Pharmacological Activity

The first two tables in this section are Table 5.1, "Foods with Analgesic, Antibacterial, Anticancer, and Anticoagulant Activities," and Table 5.2, "Foods with Antioxidant, Antiviral, Cholesterol-Lowering, Salicylate, and Sedative Activities." More information about the pharmacological activity of various foods can be obtained from the U.S. Department of Agriculture (USDA) and Natural Products Alert, or NAPRALERT, a database of more than one hundred thousand studies at the University of Illinois in Chicago.

Acid- and Alkaline-Forming Foods

The foods in Table 5.3 are arranged in approximate descending order from most acidic or most alkaline to least. However, health professionals have differing opinions about which category some items belong in. And some nutritionists include a third list of "bal-

anced" foods that are neither very acidic nor very alkaline. These would be the items toward the bottom of the two lists of foods in this table. And there is debate where dairy products belong. Dairy products are classified as "buffer" foods in some nutrition systems but are considered moderately acidic in others. Further confusion enters because a food is categorized as acidic or alkaline based on the kind of residue it leaves when metabolized, not its initial acid content. Hence, acidic lemons that taste tart are often referred to as alkaline fruit because they eventually leave an alkaline residue. However, drinking lemonade first adds acid to the stomach.

In general, most individuals need alkalizing foods since the typical Western diet predominates in acid-forming foods. And whole foods are more alkaline than refined foods.

Rich Food Sources of Nutrients

To increase intake of particular nutrients, use the food and nutrient lists in Tables 5.4–5.15 as a guide. These foods are especially abundant sources of the specified vitamins and minerals.

Table 5.1

Foods with Analgesic, Antibacterial, Anticancer, and Anticoagulant Activities

Analgesic Activity	Antibacterial Activity	Anticancer Activity	Anticoagulant Activity
chili peppers	apples	asparagus	amaranth
cinnamon	bananas	barley	cinnamon
cloves	basil	basil	cumin
coffee	beets	berries	fish oil
garlic	blueberries	broccoli	garlic
ginger	cabbage	brussels sprouts	ginger
licorice	carrots	cabbage	grapes
onions	cashews	cantaloupe	melons
peppermint	celery	carrots	mushrooms, tree ear
	chili peppers	cauliflower	onions
	chives	celery	Swiss chard
	coconut	chili pepper	tea
	cranberries	chives	watermelon
	cumin	citrus fruits	
	daikon	cucumber	
	dill	daikon	
	flaxseed	eggplant	
	garlic	fennel	
	ginger	fenugreek	
	honey	flaxseed	
	horseradish	garlic	
	licorice	ginger	
	lime	lentils	
	nori	licorice	
	nutmeg	melons	
	olive	mints	
	onions	miso	
	papayas	mushrooms, enoki, shiitake, maitake	
	plums	mustard greens	
	purslane	oats	
	radishes	olive oil	
	sage	onions	
	seaweed	oregano	
	tea, black, green, oolong	papaya	
	umeboshi	parsley	
	watermelon	parsnips	
	yogurt	peppers	
		potatoes	
		rice, brown	
		rosemary	
		rutabagas	
		sage	
		seafood	
		soybeans	
		tarragon	
		tea, black, green, oolong	
		thyme	
		tomatoes	
		turmeric	
		turnips	
		whole wheat	
		winter squash	

Table 5.2

Foods with Antioxidant, Antiviral, Cholesterol-Lowering, Salicylate, and Sedative Activities

Antioxidant Activity	Antiviral Activity	Cholesterol-Lowering Activity	Salicylate Activity	Sedative Activity
apricots	apples	almonds	almonds	anise
asparagus	barley	apples	apples	celery seed
avocados	black currants	avocados	blueberries	clove
basil	blueberries	barley	cherries	cumin
berries	chives	beans, dry	currants	fennel
Brazil nuts	coffee	carrots	curry powder	garlic
broccoli	collards	garlic	dates	ginger
brussels sprouts	cranberries	grapefruit	licorice	honey
cabbage	dandelion	mushrooms, shiitake	oranges	marjoram
carrots	dill	oats	paprika	onions
cauliflower	flaxseed	olive oil	peppers	parsley
chili peppers	garlic	rice, brown	persimmons	sage
cloves	ginger	soybeans	pineapple	spearmint
collards	gooseberries	walnuts	prunes	
cumin	grapefruit		raspberries	
fish	grapes		tea, black, green, oolong	
garlic	lemons			
ginger	mushrooms, shiitake			
grapefruit, pink	onions			
grapes, red	oranges			
kale	peaches			
licorice	pineapple			
marjoram	plums			
nutmeg	raspberries			
oats	sage			
olive oil, extra virgin	seaweed			
onion, red or yellow	spearmint			
oranges	strawberries			
peanuts	tea, black, green, oolong			
peppers				
peppermint				
pumpkin				
sage				
sesame seeds				
spearmint				
spinach				
sweet potatoes				
tomatoes				
vegetables, green leafy				
watermelon				

Table 5.3

Acid- and Alkaline-Forming Foods

Acid-Forming Foods	Alkaline-Forming Foods
vinegar	most vegetables
wine	lettuce
berries	mushrooms
pineapple	brussels sprouts
tomatoes	carrots
refined flour	most fruits
refined sugar	melons
fats and oils	dates
beans, lentils	figs
coffee	papaya
milk	maple syrup
most cheeses	brown-rice syrup
fish	honey
poultry	whole grains
meat	cocoa
eggs	

Table 5.4

Foods Rich in Vitamins A, B₁, and B₂

Vitamin A	Vitamin B$_1$ (Thiamin)	Vitamin B$_2$ (Riboflavin)
liver	brewer's yeast	organ meats
eggs	whole grains	fish and pork
orange fruits/vegetables	wheat germ	eggs
carrots	pine nuts	cheese
squash	whole grain flour	milk
mangoes	rice bran	yogurt
dandelion greens	blackstrap molasses	almonds
kale	brown rice	chicken
tuna	flaxseed	kidney (beef)
mackerel	macadamia nuts	brewer's yeast
whole milk/milk products	organ meats	wheat germ
fish-liver oil	meats, fish, poultry	
	salmon	
	pork	
	egg yolks	
	legumes	
	chickpeas	
	kidney beans	
	navy beans	
	soybeans	
	sunflower seeds	

Table 5.5

Foods Rich in Vitamins B₃, B₆, and B₁₂

Vitamin B$_3$ (Niacin)	Vitamin B$_6$ (Pyridoxine)	Vitamin B$_{12}$ (Cyancobalamin)
beets	avocados	beef liver
brewer's yeast	bananas	cheese
pork	carrots	eggs
turkey	lentils	fish
chicken	brown rice	clams
veal	beef liver	milk and milk products
lamb	bran (wheat and rice)	
fish	soybeans	
salmon	sunflower seeds	
swordfish	filberts	
tuna	tuna	
sunflower seeds	shrimp	
peanuts	wheat germ	
	whole grain flour	

Table 5.6

Foods Rich in Bioflavonoids, Biotin, and Fluoride

Bioflavonoids	Biotin	Fluoride
citrus fruits	egg yolks	tea
fruits	liver	seafood
black currants	unpolished rice	fluoridated water
buckwheat	brewer's yeast	
	whole grains	
	sardines	
	legumes	

Table 5.7

Foods Rich in Vitamins C, D, E, and K

Vitamin C	Vitamin D	Vitamin E	Vitamin K
guava	eel	cold-pressed oils	kale
papaya	catfish	eggs	Swiss chard
bell peppers	salmon	almonds	chicory
citrus fruits	sardines	wheat germ	spinach
rose hips	herring	organ meats	dark leafy greens
acerola cherries	mackerel	molasses	egg yolks
alfalfa seeds, sprouted	tuna	sweet potato	safflower oil
black currants	vitamin D fortified milk	leafy vegetables	blackstrap molasses
grapefruit	milk products	sunflower seeds	cauliflower
lemons	egg yolks	peanuts	
orange juice	organ meats	Brazil nuts	
tomatoes	fish-liver oils	cashews	
pimientos	bonemeal	pecans	
cantaloupe		almonds	
strawberries		hazelnuts	
kiwi fruit		wheat germ	
broccoli		soybeans	
brussels sprouts		lima beans	
cabbage			
cauliflower			
kale			
peas			

Table 5.8

Foods Rich in Calcium, Choline, Chloride, and Iodine

Calcium	Choline	Chloride	Iodine
milk/milk products	egg yolks	table salt	seafood
yogurt	organ meats	seafood	kelp
ricotta	brewer's yeast	meats	
parmesan	wheat germ	ripe olives	
dark leafy greens	soybeans	rye flour	
bok choy	orange juice	dulse	
spinach	watermelon		
collards	fish		
broccoli	legumes		
soybeans	lecithin		
garbanzo beans			
okra			
shellfish			
mackerel			
salmon			
sardines			
molasses			
almonds			
chestnuts			

Table 5.9

Foods Rich in Chromium, Cobalt, Coenzyme Q10, and Copper

Chromium	Cobalt	Coenzyme Q10	Copper
broccoli	organ meats	spinach	liver
orange juice	seafood	broccoli	oysters
honey	nuts	peanuts	sesame seed
grapes	legumes	tuna	mushrooms, shiitake
raisins	molasses	sardines	wheat germ
corn oil	raisins	beef	barley
clams		chestnuts	lentils
whole grain cereals		walnuts	Brazil nuts
brewer's yeast		vegetable oils	cashews
			walnuts
			filberts
			peanuts
			oatmeal
			molasses

Table 5.10

Foods Rich in Folic Acid, Inositol, Iron, and Potassium

Folic Acid	Inositol	Iron	Potassium
spinach	beans (most kinds)	organ meats	lean meats
romaine lettuce	chickpeas	meats	red snapper
asparagus	brown rice	clams	salmon
turnip greens	nuts (most kinds)	lentils	yogurt
brussels sprouts	whole grains	eggs	whole grains
lima beans	whole grain flour	fish and poultry	potatoes
soybeans	oatmeal	blackstrap molasses	beet greens
organ meats	citrus fruits (except lemons)	cherry juice	acorn squash
chicken liver	cantaloupe	green leafy vegetables	avocados
brewer's yeast	brewer's yeast	dried fruits	bananas
root vegetables	molasses	desiccated liver	cantaloupe
whole grains	beef		tomato juice
enriched white rice	veal		orange juice
wheat germ	pork		peaches
bulgur wheat	calf's liver		prunes
kidney beans	milk		soybeans
white beans	vegetables		lima beans
oysters	lentils		Swiss chard
salmon	lecithin		yams
orange juice			spinach
avocados			dried fruits
milk			blackstrap molasses
			sunflower seeds

Table 5.11

Foods Rich in L-Carnitine, L-Methionine, L-Taurine, and L-Tryptophan

L-Carnitine	L-Methionine	L-Taurine	L-Tryptophan
eggs	eggs	eggs	pumpkin seeds (roasted)
fish	meats (all types)	meats (all types)	sunflower seeds (dried)
meats (all types)	poultry (all types)	pork	turnip greens
milk	milk	lamb	collard greens
		fish (all types)	potato (baked with skin)
		shellfish	seaweed (kelp and spirulina)
		milk	milk

Table 5.12

Foods Rich in Magnesium, Manganese, Molybdenum, and Niacin

Magnesium	Manganese	Molybdenum	Niacin
seafood	pecans	lentils	lean meats
almonds	Brazil nuts	whole grains	brewer's yeast
cashews	almonds	cauliflower	poultry and fish
whole grains	whole grains	milk	peanuts
buckwheat	dark leafy greens	kidney	milk/milk products
rye	legumes	liver	rice bran
dark leafy greens	pineapples	dark green vegetables	
blackstrap molasses	raisins		
nuts	egg yolks		
bonemeal			

Table 5.13

Foods Rich in Pantothenic Acid (Vitamin B₅), Para-Aminobenzoic Acid (PABA), Phosphorus, and Phytonutrients

Pantothenic Acid (Vitamin B₅)	Para-Aminobenzoic Acid (PABA)	Phosphorus	Phytonutrients
brewer's yeast	organ meats	fish, meats, poultry	soybeans
blue cheese	wheat germ	eggs	soy products
corn	yogurt	legumes	hot chili peppers
lentils	molasses	milk/milk products	tomatoes
egg yolks	green leafy vegetables	nuts	broccoli
organ meats		whole grain cereals	citrus fruits
liver			berries
meats (all types)			apricots
peas			garlic
peanuts			onions
soybeans			
sunflower seeds			
whole grain flour			
lobster			
whole grains			
wheat germ			
salmon			

Table 5.14

Foods Rich in Polyphenols, Selenium, Sodium, and Sulfur

Polyphenols	Selenium	Sodium	Sulfur
yam	butter	seafood	fish
onions	Brazil nuts	table salt	hot chili peppers
nuts	tuna	baking powder	garlic
strawberries	herring	baking soda	onion
apple	oysters	celery	eggs
coffee	salmon	processed foods	meats
tea, green, black	clams	milk products	cabbage
wine	chicken liver	kelp	brussels sprouts
	brewer's yeast		horseradish
	wheat germ and bran		
	whole grains		
	wheat flour		
	puffed wheat		
	sesame seeds		

Table 5.15

Foods Rich in Unsaturated Fatty Acids, Vanadium, and Zinc

Unsaturated Fatty Acids	Vanadium	Zinc
vegetable oils	buckwheat	pumpkin seeds
walnuts	oats	squash seeds
flaxseed	rice	sunflower seeds
sunflower seeds	corn	seafood
	green beans	oysters
	carrots	crabmeat
	cabbage	herring
	mushrooms	organ meats
	spinach	mushrooms
	parsley	brewer's yeast
	beer	soybeans
	wine	eggs
	shellfish	wheat germ
	soybeans	meats
	vegetable oils	liver
	fish	turkey

Tables of Food Measurements and Composition

Weights and Measures

Metric Conversions

1 teaspoon	= 5 milliliters (ml)
1 tablespoon	= 15 milliliters
1 ounce	= 30 milliliters
1 cup	= 235 milliliters or ¼ liter
1 quart	= 0.95 liter
1 gallon	= 3.8 liters

Weights

1 microgram	= 1/1,000,000 gram
1000 micrograms	= 1 milligram
1 milligram	= 1/1000 gram
1000 milligrams	= 1 gram
1.00 ounce	= 28.35 grams
3.57 ounces	= 100.00 grams
0.25 pound	= 113.00 grams
0.50 pound	= 227.00 grams
1.00 pound	= 16.00 ounces
1.00 pound	= 453.00 grams

Capacity Measurements

1 quart	= 4 cups
1 pint	= 2 cups
1 cup	= ½ pint
1 cup	= 8 fluid ounces
1 cup	= 16 tablespoons
2 tablespoons	= 1 fluid ounce
1 tablespoon	= ½ fluid ounce
1 tablespoon	= 3 teaspoons

Approximate Equivalents

1 average serving	= about 4 ounces
1 ounce fluid	= about 28 grams
1 cup fluid	
Cooking oil	= 200 grams
Water	= 220 grams
Milk, soups	= 240 grams
Syrup, honey	= 325 grams
1 cup dry	
Cereal flakes	= 50 grams
Flours	= 100 grams
Sugars	= 200 grams
1 tablespoon fluid	
Cooking oil	= 14 grams
Milk, water	= 15 grams
Syrup, honey	= 20 grams
1 tablespoon dry	= ⅙ ounce
Flours	= 8 grams
Sugars	= 12 grams
1 pat butter	= ½ tablespoon
1 teaspoon fluid	= about 5 grams
1 teaspoon dry	= about 4 grams
1 grain	= about 65 milligrams
1 minim	= about 1 drop water

Abbreviations and Symbols Used in the Tables

avg	average
cal	calorie
C	cup
ckd	cooked
diam	diameter
enr	enriched
g	gram
IU	International Unit
lb	pound
lge	large
mcg/µg	microgram
med	medium
mg	milligram
mL	milliliter
oz	ounce
reg	regular
sm	small
sq	square
svg	serving
t	trace
T	tablespoon
tsp	teaspoon
unsw	unsweetened
w	with
w/o	without
whl grd	whole ground
—	reliable data lacking
/	of; with; per
"	inches

Recommended Dietary Intake Chart

For more than fifty years, nutrition experts have produced a set of nutrient and energy standards known as the Recommended Dietary Allowances (RDA). A major revision is currently under way to replace the RDA. The revised recommendations are called Dietary Reference Intakes (DRI) and reflect the collaborative efforts of both the United States and Canada. Until 1997, the RDA were the only standards available and they will continue to serve health professionals until DRI can be established for all nutrients. For this reason, both the 1989 RDA and the 1997 DRI for selected nutrients are presented here.

Recommended Dietary Intakes

1989 Recommended Dietary Allowances (RDA) / 1997 Dietary Reference Intakes (DRI)

Age, yr	Energy, kcal	Protein, g	Vitamin A, μg RE	Vitamin E, mg α-TE	Vitamin K, μg	Vitamin C, mg	Thiamin, mg	Riboflavin, mg	Niacin, mg NE	Vitamin B6, mg	Folate, μg	Vitamin B12, μg	Iron, mg	Zinc, mg	Iodine, μg	Selenium, μg	Age, yr	Vitamin D, μg	Calcium, mg	Phosphorus, mg	Magnesium, mg	Fluoride, mg
Infants																	**Infants**					
0.0–0.5	650	13	375	3	5	30	0.3	0.4	5	0.3	25	0.3	6	5	40	10	0.0–0.5	5	210	100	30	0.01
0.5–1.0	850	14	375	4	10	35	0.4	0.5	6	0.6	35	0.5	10	5	50	15	0.5–1.0	5	270	275	75	0.5
Children																	**Children**					
1–3	1300	16	400	6	15	40	0.7	0.8	9	1.0	50	0.7	10	10	70	20	1–3	5	500	460	80	0.7
4–6	1800	24	500	7	20	45	0.9	1.1	12	1.1	75	1.0	10	10	90	20	4–8	5	800	500	130	1.1
7–10	2000	28	700	7	30	45	1.0	1.2	13	1.4	100	1.4	10	10	120	30						
Males																	**Males**					
11–14	2500	45	1000	10	45	50	1.3	1.5	17	1.7	150	2.0	12	15	150	40	9–13	5	1300	1250	240	2.0
15–18	3000	59	1000	10	65	60	1.5	1.8	20	2.0	200	2.0	12	15	150	50	14–18	5	1300	1250	410	3.2
19–24	2900	58	1000	10	70	60	1.5	1.7	19	2.0	200	2.0	10	15	150	70	19–30	5	1000	700	400	3.8
25–50	2900	63	1000	10	80	60	1.5	1.7	19	2.0	200	2.0	10	15	150	70	31–50	5	1000	700	420	3.8
51+	2300	63	1000	10	80	60	1.2	1.4	15	2.0	200	2.0	10	15	150	70	51–70	10	1200	700	420	3.8
																	71+	10	1200	700	420	3.8
Females																	**Females**					
11–14	2200	46	800	8	45	50	1.1	1.3	15	1.4	150	2.0	15	12	150	45	9–13	5	1300	1250	240	2.0
15–18	2200	44	800	8	55	60	1.1	1.3	15	1.5	180	2.0	15	12	150	50	14–18	5	1300	1250	360	2.9
19–24	2200	46	800	8	60	60	1.1	1.3	15	1.6	180	2.0	15	12	150	55	19–30	5	1000	700	310	3.1
25–50	2200	50	800	8	65	60	1.1	1.3	15	1.6	180	2.0	15	12	150	55	31–50	5	1000	700	320	3.1
51+	1900	50	800	8	65	60	1.0	1.2	13	1.6	180	2.0	10	12	150	55	51–70	10	1200	700	320	3.1
																	71+	10	1200	700	320	3.1
Pregnant	+300	60	800	10	65	70	1.5	1.6	17	2.2	400	2.2	30	15	175	65	Pregnant	*	*	*	+40	*
Lactating																	**Lactating**	*	*	*	*	*
1st 6 mo	+500	65	1300	12	65	95	1.6	1.8	20	2.1	280	2.6	15	19	200	75						
2nd 6 mo	+500	62	1200	11	65	90	1.6	1.7	20	2.1	260	2.6	15	16	200	75						

*Values are the same as for other women of comparable age.

†1 μg (1 mcg) is 1 microgram. To convert 1-μg RE (microgram of retinol equivalent) to IUs (International Units), multiply 1-μg RE by 3.33. To convert 1-mg α-TE (alpha tocopherol equivalent) to IUs, multiply 1-mg α-TE by 1.49.

Source: RDA reprinted with permission from *Recommended Dietary Allowances,* 10th edition © 1989 by the National Academy of Sciences. Courtesy of the National Academy Press, Washington, D.C.: Committee on Dietary Reference Intakes, *Dietary Reference Intakes for Calcium, Phosphorus, Magnesium, Vitamin D, and Fluoride* (Washington, D.C.: National Academy Press, 1997).

Dietary Reference Intakes: Recommended Intakes for Individuals

Life stage group	Calcium, mg/d	Phosphorus, mg/d	Magnesium, mg/d	Vitamin D, μg/d[a,b]	Fluoride, mg/d	Thiamin, mg/d	Riboflavin, mg/d	Niacin, mg/d[c]
Infants								
0–6 mo	210*	100*	30*	5*	0.01*	0.2*	0.3*	2*
7–12 mo	270*	275*	75*	5*	0.5*	0.3*	0.4*	4*
Children								
1–3 y	500*	**460**	**80**	5*	0.7*	**0.5**	0.5	6
4–8 y	800*	**500**	**130**	5*	1*	**0.6**	0.6	8
Males								
9–13 y	1300*	**1250**	**240**	5*	2*	**0.9**	0.9	12
14–18 y	1300*	**1250**	**410**	5*	3*	**1.2**	1.3	16
19–30 y	1000*	**700**	**400**	5*	4*	**1.2**	1.3	16
31–50 y	1000*	**780**	**420**	5*	4*	**1.2**	1.3	16
51–70 y	1200*	**700**	**420**	10*	4*	**1.2**	1.3	16
>70 y	1200*	**700**	**420**	15*	4*	**1.2**	1.3	16
Females								
9–13 y	1300*	**1250**	**240**	5*	2*	**0.9**	0.9	12
14–18 y	1300*	**1250**	**360**	5*	3*	**1.0**	1.0	14
19–30 y	1000*	**700**	**310**	5*	3*	**1.1**	1.1	14
31–50 y	1000*	**700**	**320**	5*	3*	**1.1**	1.1	14
51–70 y	1200*	**700**	**320**	10*	3*	**1.1**	1.1	14
>70 y	1200*	**700**	**320**	15*	3*	**1.1**	1.1	14
Pregnancy								
≤18 y	1300*	**1250**	**400**	5*	3*	**1.4**	1.4	18
19–30 y	1000*	**700**	**350**	5*	3*	**1.4**	1.4	18
31–50 y	1000*	**700**	**360**	5*	3*	**1.4**	1.4	18
Lactation								
≤18 y	1300*	**1250**	**360**	5*	3*	**1.4**	1.6	17
19–30 y	1000*	**700**	**310**	5*	3*	**1.4**	1.6	17
31–50 y	1000*	**700**	**320**	5*	3*	**1.4**	1.6	17

Note: This table presents Recommended Dietary Allowances (RDAs) in **bold type** and Adequate Intakes (AIs) in ordinary type followed by an asterisk (*). RDAs and AIs may both be used as goals for individual intake. RDAs are set to meet the needs of almost all (97 to 98%) individuals in a group. For healthy breastfed infants, the AI is the mean intake. The AI for other life-stage and gender groups is believed to cover needs of all individuals in the group, but lack of data or uncertainty in the data prevent being able to specify with confidence the percentage of individuals covered by this intake.

[a]As cholecalciferol. 1-mg cholecalciferol = 40-IU vitamin D.

[b]In the absence of adequate exposure to sunlight.

[c]As niacin equivalents (NE). 1 mg of niacin = 60 mg of tryptophan; 0–6 months = preformed niacin (not NE).

Dietary Reference Intakes: Recommended Intakes for Individuals (*Continued*)

Vitamin B$_6$, mg/d	Folate, µg/d[d]	Vitamin B$_{12}$, µg/d	Pantothenic acid, mg/d	Biotin µg/d	Choline[e], mg/d	Vitamin C, mg/d	Vitamin E[f], mg/d	Selenium, µg/d	Life stage group
									Infants
0.1*	65*	0.4*	1.7*	5*	125*	40*	4*	15*	0–6 mo
0.3*	80*	0.5*	1.8*	6*	150*	50*	5*	20*	7–12 mo
									Children
0.5	150	0.9	2*	8*	200*	15	6	20	1–3 y
0.6	200	1.2	3*	12*	250*	25	7	30	4–8 y
									Males
1.0	300	1.8	4*	20*	375*	45	11	40	9–13 y
1.3	400	2.4	3*	25*	550*	75	15	55	14–18 y
1.3	400	2.4	5*	30*	550*	90	15	55	19–30 y
1.3	400	2.4	5*	30*	550*	90	15	55	31–50 y
1.7	400	2.4[g]	5*	30*	550*	90	15	55	51–70 y
1.7	400	2.4[g]	5*	30*	550*	90	15	55	>70 y
									Females
1.0	300	1.8	4*	20*	375*	45	11	40	9–13 y
1.2	400[h]	2.4	5*	25*	400*	65	15	55	14–18 y
1.3	400[h]	2.4	5*	30*	425*	75	15	55	19–30 y
1.3	400[h]	2.4	5*	30*	425*	75	15	55	31–50 y
1.5	400	2.4[g]	5*	30*	425*	75	15	55	51–70 y
1.5	400	2.4[g]	5*	30*	425*	75	15	55	>70 y
									Pregnancy
1.9	600[i]	2.6	6*	30*	450*	80	15	60	≤18 y
1.9	600[i]	2.6	6*	30*	450*	85	15	60	19–30 y
1.9	600[i]	2.6	6*	30*	450*	85	15	60	31–60 y
									Lactation
2.0	500	2.8	7*	35*	550*	115	19	70	≤18 y
2.0	500	2.8	7*	35*	550*	120	19	70	19–30 y
2.0	500	2.8	7*	35*	550*	120	19	70	31–50 y

[d]As dietary folate equivalents (DFE). 1 DFE = 1 µg (mcg) food folate = 0.6 µg of folic acid from fortified food or as a supplement consumed with food = 0.5 µg of a supplement taken on an empty stomach.

[e]Although AIs have been set for choline, there are few data to assess whether a dietary supply of choline is needed at all stages of the life cycle, and it may be that the choline requirement can be met by endogenous synthesis at some of these stages.

[f]As α-tocopherol. α-Tocopherol includes RRR-α-tocopherol, the only form of α-tocopherol that occurs naturally in foods, and the 2R-stereoisomeric forms of α-tocopherol (*RRR-*, *RSR-*, *RRS-*, and *RSS-*α-tocopherol) that occur in fortified foods and supplements. It does not include the 2S-stereoisomeric forms of α-tocopherol (*SRR-*, *SSR-*, *SRS-*, *SSS-*α-tocopherol) also found in fortified foods and supplements.

[g]Because 10 to 30% of older people may malabsorb food-bound B$_{12}$, it is advisable for those older than 50 years to meet their RDA mainly by consuming foods fortified with B$_{12}$ or a supplement containing B$_{12}$.

[h]In view of evidence linking folate intake with neural tube defects in the fetus, it is recommended that all women capable of becoming pregnant consume 400 µg (mcg) from supplements or fortified foods in addition to intake of food folate from a varied diet.

[i]It is assumed that women will continue consuming 400 µg from supplements or fortified food until their pregnancy is confirmed and they enter prenatal care, which ordinarily occurs after the end of the periconceptional period—the critical time for formation of the neural tube.

Source: Food and Nutrition Board, Institute of Medicine—National Academy of Sciences.

Tables of Food Composition

The foods in the following tables have been divided according to food groups. All figures are averages of different food samples. The dash (—) indicates that meaningful analysis of the food for that nutrient is lacking. The zero confirms the absence of a nutrient. The content of trace minerals depends on the soil in which the foods are grown and where they are grown and will vary significantly in foods from area to area. Updated values are from the U.S. Department of Agriculture *Nutrient Database for Standard Reference*, Release 13, November 1999.

Food Groups

Beverages

	Beer, reg.	Coffee, reg.	Coffee substitute, cereal grain	Cola	Tea, brewed
Measure	12 oz	6 oz	6 oz	12 oz	6 oz
Weight, g	356	178	180	370	178
Calories	146	6	9	152	1.8
Protein, g	1.1	0.18	0.18	0	0
Carbohydrate, g	13	0.71	1.8	39	0.53
Fiber, g	0.7	0	0	0	0
Vitamin A, IU	0	0	0	0	0
Vitamin B_1, mg	0.02	0	0.01	0	0
Vitamin B_2, mg	0.09	0	t	0	0.03
Vitamin B_6, mg	0.18	0	0.02	0	0
Vitamin B_{12}, mcg	0.07	0	0	0	0
Niacin, mg	1.6	0.4	0.4	0	0
Pantothenic acid, mg	0.21	t	0.02	0	0.02
Folic acid, mcg	21	0.18	0.54	0	9.3
Vitamin C, mg	0	0	0	0	0
Vitamin E, IU	0	0	0	0	0
Calcium, mg	18	3.6	5	11	0
Copper, mg	0.03	0.01	0.02	0.04	0.02
Iron, mg	0.11	0.09	0.01	0.11	0.04
Magnesium, mg	21	9	7	4	0.3
Manganese, mg	0.04	0.05	0.03	0.13	0.4
Phosphorus, mg	43	1.8	13	44	1.8
Potassium, mg	89	96	43	4	66
Selenium, mcg	4.3	0.18	0.36	0.37	0
Sodium, mg	18	3.6	7	15	5
Zinc, mg	0.1	0.04	0.05	0.04	0.04
Total lipid, g	0	0	0	0	0
Total saturated, g	0	t	0.01	0	t
Total unsaturated, g	0	0	0.04	0	t
Total monounsaturated, g	0	t	t	0	t
Cholesterol, mg	0	0	0	0	0
Tryptophan, g	0.01	—	t	—	0
Threonine, g	0.02	—	t	—	0
Isoleucine, g	0.02	—	t	—	0
Leucine, g	0.02	—	t	—	0
Lycine, g	0.03	—	t	—	0
Methionine, g	t	—	t	—	0
Cystine, g	0.01	—	t	—	0
Phenylalanine, g	0.02	—	t	—	0
Tyrosine, g	0.05	—	t	—	0
Valine, g	0.03	—	t	—	0
Arginine, g	0.03	—	t	—	0
Histidine, g	0.02	—	t	—	0
Alanine, g	0.04	—	t	—	0
Aspartic acid, g	0.04	—	t	—	0
Glutamic acid, g	0.11	—	0.03	—	0
Glycine, g	0.03	—	t	—	0
Proline, g	0.11	—	0.01	—	0
Serine, g	0.02	—	t	—	0

Beverages

	Tea, herb, brewed	Wine, table, red	Wine, table, white
Measure	6 oz	3.5 oz	3.5 oz
Weight, g	178	103	103
Calories	1.8	74	70
Protein, g	0	0.21	0.1
Carbohydrate, g	0.36	1.8	0.8
Fiber, g	0	0	0
Vitamin A, IU	0	0	0
Vitamin B_1, mg	0.02	0.01	t
Vitamin B_2, mg	t	0.03	0.01
Vitamin B_6, mg	0	0.04	0.01
Vitamin B_{12}, mcg	0	0.01	0
Niacin, mg	0	0.08	0.07
Pantothenic acid, mg	0.02	0.04	0.02
Folic acid, mcg	1	2	0.2
Vitamin C, mg	0	0	0
Vitamin E, IU	0	—	—
Calcium, mg	3.6	8	9
Copper, mg	0.03	0.02	0.02
Iron, mg	0.14	0.44	0.33
Magnesium, mg	1.8	13	10
Manganese, mg	0.08	0.62	0.47
Phosphorus, mg	0	14	14
Potassium, mg	16	115	82
Selenium, mcg	0	0.21	0.21
Sodium, mg	1.8	5	5
Zinc, mg	0.07	0.09	0.07
Total lipid, g	0	0	0
Total saturated, g	t	0	0
Total unsaturated, g	t	0	0
Total monounsaturated, g	t	0	0
Cholesterol, mg	0	0	0
Tryptophan, g	—	—	—
Threonine, g	—	—	—
Isoleucine, g	—	—	—
Leucine, g	—	—	—
Lycine, g	—	—	—
Methionine, g	—	—	—
Cystine, g	—	—	—
Phenylalanine, g	—	—	—
Tyrosine, g	—	—	—
Valine, g	—	—	—
Arginine, g	—	—	—
Histidine, g	—	—	—
Alanine, g	—	—	—
Aspartic acid, g	—	—	—
Glutamic acid, g	—	—	—
Glycine, g	—	—	—
Proline, g	—	—	—
Serine, g	—	—	—

Cheese

	Blue	Brick	Brie	Camembert	Cheddar
Measure	1 oz	1 oz	1 oz	1 oz	1 oz
Weight, g	28	28	28	28	28
Calories	100	105	95	85	114
Protein, g	6.07	6.59	5.88	5.61	7.06
Carbohydrate, g	0.66	0.79	0.13	0.13	0.36
Fiber, g	0	0	0	0	0
Vitamin A, IU	204	307	189	262	300
Vitamin B_1, mg	0.008	0.004	0.02	0.008	0.008
Vitamin B_2, mg	0.108	0.1	0.147	0.138	0.106
Vitamin B_6, mg	0.047	0.018	0.067	0.064	0.021
Vitamin B_{12}, mcg	0.345	0.356	0.468	0.367	0.234
Niacin, mg	0.288	0.033	0.108	0.179	0.023
Pantothenic acid, mg	0.49	0.082	0.196	0.387	0.117
Folic acid, mcg	10	6	18	18	5
Vitamin C, mg	0	0	0	0	0
Vitamin E, IU	0.27	0.21	0.28	0.28	0.15
Calcium, mg	150	191	52	110	204
Copper, mg	0.011	0.007	t	0.022	0.031
Iron, mg	0.09	0.12	0.14	0.09	0.19
Magnesium, mg	7	7	5.7	6	8
Manganese, mg	0.003	0.003	0.01	0.011	0.003
Phosphorus, mg	110	128	53	98	145
Potassium, mg	73	38	43	53	28
Selenium, mcg	4	4	4	4	3.9
Sodium, mg	396	159	178	239	176
Zinc, mg	0.75	0.74	0.68	0.68	0.88
Total lipid, gm	8.15	8.41	7.85	6.88	9.4
Total saturated, gm	5.3	5.32	5	4.33	5.98
Total unsaturated, gm	0.23	0.22	0.23	0.21	0.27
Total monounsaturated, gm	2.2	2.4	2.3	2	2.66
Cholesterol, mg	21	27	28	20	30
Tryptophan, g	0.089	0.092	0.091	0.087	0.091
Threonine, g	0.223	0.25	0.213	0.203	0.251
Isoleucine, g	0.319	0.322	0.288	0.275	0.438
Leucine, g	0.545	0.636	0.547	0.522	0.676
Lycine, g	0.526	0.602	0.525	0.501	0.588
Methionine, g	0.166	0.16	0.168	0.16	0.185
Cystine, g	0.03	0.037	0.032	0.031	0.035
Phenylalanine, g	0.309	0.349	0.328	0.313	0.372
Tyrosine, g	0.368	0.316	0.34	0.325	0.341
Valine, g	0.442	0.417	0.38	0.362	0.471
Arginine, g	0.202	0.248	0.208	0.199	0.267
Histidine, g	0.215	0.233	0.203	0.194	0.248
Alanine, g	0.183	0.19	0.243	0.232	0.199
Aspartic acid, g	0.408	0.45	0.383	0.365	0.454
Glutamic acid, g	1.47	1.56	1.24	1.18	1.72
Glycine, g	0.115	0.124	0.112	0.107	0.122
Proline, g	0.596	0.73	0.697	0.665	0.796
Serine, g	0.318	0.366	0.331	0.316	0.413

Cheese

	Cheshire	Colby	Cottage, creamed, sm curd	Cottage, low-fat, 1%	Cream
Measure	1 oz	1 oz	1 C	1 C	1 oz
Weight, g	28	28	225	226	28
Calories	110	112	232	164	99
Protein, g	6.62	6.74	28	28	2.14
Carbohydrate, g	1.36	0.73	5.6	6	0.75
Fiber, g	0	0	0	0	0
Vitamin A, IU	279	293	367	83	405
Vitamin B$_1$, mg	0.013	0.004	0.05	0.05	0.005
Vitamin B$_2$, mg	0.083	0.106	0.37	0.37	0.056
Vitamin B$_6$, mg	0.02	0.022	0.15	0.15	0.013
Vitamin B$_{12}$, mcg	0.23	0.234	1.4	1.4	0.12
Niacin, mg	0.02	0.026	0.28	0.29	0.029
Pantothenic acid, mg	0.12	0.06	0.48	0.49	0.077
Folic acid, mcg	5.2	5.2	27	28	4
Vitamin C, mg	0	0	0	0	0
Vitamin E, IU	—	0.15	0.4	0.37	0.4
Calcium, mg	182	194	135	137	23
Copper, mg	0.01	0.012	0.06	0.06	0.011
Iron, mg	0.06	0.22	0.32	0.32	0.34
Magnesium, mg	6	7	12	12	2
Manganese, mg	t	0.003	t	t	0.001
Phosphorus, mg	131	129	297	302	30
Potassium, mg	27	36	190	193	34
Selenium, mcg	4	4	20	20	0.68
Sodium, mg	198	171	910	917	84
Zinc, mg	0.8	0.87	0.83	0.86	0.15
Total lipid, g	8.68	9.1	10	2.3	9.89
Total saturated, g	5.5	5.73	6.4	1.5	6.23
Total unsaturated, g	0.25	0.27	0.3	0.07	0.36
Total monounsaturated, g	2.5	2.6	2.9	0.66	2.8
Cholesterol, mg	29	27	34	10	31
Tryptophan, g	0.085	0.087	0.313	0.312	0.019
Threonine, g	0.236	0.24	1.25	1.24	0.091
Isoleucine, g	0.411	0.418	1.65	1.65	0.113
Leucine, g	0.635	0.645	2.9	2.88	0.207
Lycine, g	0.551	0.561	2.3	2.27	0.192
Methionine, g	0.173	0.176	0.846	0.843	0.051
Cystine, g	0.033	0.034	0.26	0.26	0.019
Phenylalanine, g	0.349	0.355	1.5	1.5	0.119
Tyrosine, g	0.32	0.325	1.5	1.5	0.102
Valine, g	0.442	0.45	1.7	1.7	0.125
Arginine, g	0.25	0.254	1.3	1.28	0.081
Histidine, g	0.233	0.236	0.93	0.93	0.077
Alanine, g	0.187	0.19	1.46	1.45	0.065
Aspartic acid, g	0.426	0.433	1.9	1.9	0.151
Glutamic acid, g	1.62	1.64	6	6.1	0.486
Glycine, g	0.114	0.116	0.6	0.6	0.042
Proline, g	0.747	0.759	3.3	3.2	0.195
Serine, g	0.387	0.394	1.6	1.6	0.113

Cheese

	Edam	Feta	Fontina	Gjetost	Gouda
Measure	1 oz	1 oz	1 oz	1 oz	1 oz
Weight, g	28	28	28	28	28
Calories	101	75	110	132	101
Protein, g	7.08	4	7.26	2.74	7.07
Carbohydrate, g	0.4	1.16	0.44	12	0.63
Fiber, g	0	0	0	0	0
Vitamin A, IU	260	127	333	316	183
Vitamin B_1, mg	0.01	0.04	0.006	0.09	0.009
Vitamin B_2, mg	0.11	0.24	0.058	0.4	0.095
Vitamin B_6, mg	0.022	0.12	0.024	0.07	0.023
Vitamin B_{12}, mcg	0.435	0.48	0.48	0.69	0.44
Niacin, mg	0.023	0.28	0.043	0.23	0.018
Pantothenic acid, mg	0.08	0.27	0.122	0.95	0.096
Folic acid, mcg	5	9	1.7	1	6
Vitamin C, mg	0	0	0	0	0
Vitamin E, IU	0.31	t	0.15	—	0.15
Calcium, mg	207	140	156	113	198
Copper, mg	0.008	—	t	0.023	0.01
Iron, mg	0.12	0.18	0.06	0.15	0.07
Magnesium, mg	8	5	4	20	8
Manganese, mg	0.003	t	t	0.01	t
Phosphorus, mg	152	96	98	126	155
Potassium, mg	53	18	18	400	34
Selenium, mcg	4	4.3	4	4	4
Sodium, mg	274	316	227	170	232
Zinc, mg	1.06	0.82	0.99	0.32	1.11
Total lipid, g	7.88	6	8.83	8.37	7.78
Total saturated, g	4.98	4.24	5.44	5.43	4.99
Total unsaturated, g	0.19	0.17	0.47	0.27	0.19
Total monounsaturated, g	2.3	1.3	2.5	2.2	2.2
Cholesterol, mg	25	25	33	27	32
Tryptophan, g	0.1	0.06	0.1	0.038	0.1
Threonine, g	0.264	0.18	0.27	0.111	0.264
Isoleucine, g	0.371	0.23	0.4	0.147	0.370
Leucine, g	0.720	0.4	0.76	0.281	0.727
Lycine, g	0.754	0.35	0.66	0.231	0.752
Methionine, g	0.204	0.1	0.2	0.09	0.204
Cystine, g	0.07	0.024	0.074	0.016	0.07
Phenylalanine, g	0.406	0.2	0.424	0.153	0.406
Tyrosine, g	0.413	0.19	0.43	0.154	0.412
Valine, g	0.513	0.3	0.55	0.217	0.512
Arginine, g	0.273	0.133	0.24	0.093	0.273
Histidine, g	0.293	0.113	0.27	0.083	0.293
Alanine, g	0.217	0.18	0.23	0.092	0.216
Aspartic acid, g	0.495	0.22	0.4	0.201	0.494
Glutamic acid, g	1.74	0.69	1.46	0.563	1.74
Glycine, g	0.138	0.03	0.13	0.054	0.137
Proline, g	0.922	0.4	0.94	0.334	0.92
Serine, g	0.439	0.33	0.42	0.133	0.438

Cheese

	Gruyere	Limburger	Monterey Jack	Mozzarella	Mozzarella, part skim
Measure	1 oz	1 oz	1 oz	1 oz	1 oz
Weight, g	28	28	28	28	28
Calories	117	93	106	80	72
Protein, g	8.45	5.68	6.94	5.5	6.88
Carbohydrate, g	0.1	0.14	0.19	0.63	0.78
Fiber, g	0	0	0	0	0
Vitamin A, IU	346	363	269	225	166
Vitamin B$_1$, mg	0.017	0.023	t	0.004	0.005
Vitamin B$_2$, mg	0.079	0.143	0.111	0.069	0.086
Vitamin B$_6$, mg	0.023	0.024	0.02	0.016	0.02
Vitamin B$_{12}$, mcg	0.454	0.295	0.23	0.185	0.232
Niacin, mg	0.03	0.045	0.03	0.024	0.03
Pantothenic acid, mg	0.159	0.334	0.06	0.018	0.022
Folic acid, mcg	3	16	5	2	2
Vitamin C, mg	0	0	0	0	0
Vitamin E, IU	0.15	0.27	0.15	0.15	0.18
Calcium, mg	287	141	212	147	183
Copper, mg	t	t	0.009	t	0.008
Iron, mg	0.05	0.04	0.2	0.05	0.06
Magnesium, mg	10	6	8	5	7
Manganese, mg	t	0.01	0.003	t	0.003
Phosphorus, mg	172	111	126	105	131
Potassium, mg	23	36	23	19	24
Selenium, mcg	4	4	4	4	4.1
Sodium, mg	95	227	152	106	132
Zinc, mg	1	0.6	0.85	0.63	0.78
Total lipid, g	9.17	7.72	8.58	6.12	4.51
Total saturated, g	5.36	4.75	5.4	3.73	2.87
Total unsaturated, g	0.5	0.14	0.26	0.22	0.13
Total monounsaturated, g	2.85	2.44	2.5	1.86	1.3
Cholesterol, mg	31	26	25	22	16
Tryptophan, g	0.119	0.082	0.089	0.08	0.1
Threonine, g	0.309	0.209	0.247	0.21	0.262
Isoleucine, g	0.457	0.346	0.431	0.264	0.33
Leucine, g	0.88	0.593	0.665	0.537	0.671
Lycine, g	0.768	0.475	0.578	0.559	0.699
Methionine, g	0.233	0.176	0.182	0.154	0.192
Cystine, g	0.086	0.03	0.035	0.033	0.041
Phenylalanine, g	0.494	0.316	0.365	0.287	0.359
Tyrosine, g	0.503	0.339	0.335	0.318	0.398
Valine, g	0.636	0.408	0.463	0.344	0.430
Arginine, g	0.276	0.198	0.262	0.236	0.295
Histidine, g	0.317	0.164	0.244	0.207	0.259
Alanine, g	0.272	0.189	0.196	0.168	0.21
Aspartic acid, g	0.466	0.419	0.446	0.399	0.498
Glutamic acid, g	1.69	1.27	1.69	1.28	1.6
Glycine, g	0.151	0.116	0.12	0.105	0.132
Proline, g	1.09	0.691	0.782	0.567	0.708
Serine, g	0.487	0.324	0.406	0.321	0.401

Cheese

	Muenster	Neufchatel	Parmesan, hard	Parmesan, grated	Port du salut
Measure	1 oz	1 oz	1 oz	1 T	1 oz
Weight, g	28	28	28	5	28
Calories	104	74	111	23	100
Protein, g	6.64	2.82	10	2	6.74
Carbohydrate, g	0.32	0.83	0.91	0.19	0.16
Fiber, g	0	0	0	0	0
Vitamin A, IU	318	321	171	35	378
Vitamin B$_1$, mg	0.004	0.004	0.011	0.002	t
Vitamin B$_2$, mg	0.091	0.055	0.094	0.019	0.068
Vitamin B$_6$, mg	0.016	0.012	0.026	0.005	0.015
Vitamin B$_{12}$, mcg	0.418	0.075	0.34	0.07	0.425
Niacin, mg	0.029	0.036	0.077	0.016	0.017
Pantothenic acid, mg	0.054	0.16	0.128	0.026	0.06
Folic acid, mcg	3	3	2	t	5
Vitamin C, mg	0	0	0	0	0
Vitamin E, IU	0.19	—	0.34	0.06	0.21
Calcium, mg	203	21	336	69	184
Copper, mg	0.009	t	0.101	0.018	t
Iron, mg	0.12	0.08	0.23	0.05	0.12
Magnesium, mg	8	2	12	3	6.9
Manganese, mg	0.002	t	0.006	t	t
Phosphorus, mg	133	39	197	40	102
Potassium, mg	38	32	26	5	39
Selenium, mcg	4	0.85	6.4	1.3	4
Sodium, mg	178	113	454	93	151
Zinc, mg	0.8	0.15	0.78	0.16	0.74
Total lipid, g	8.52	6.64	7.32	1.5	8
Total saturated, g	5.42	4.2	4.65	0.95	4.73
Total unsaturated, g	0.19	0.18	0.16	0.03	0.21
Total monounsaturated, g	2.5	1.9	2	0.44	2.7
Cholesterol, mg	27	22	19	4	35
Tryptophan, g	0.093	0.025	0.137	0.028	0.097
Threonine, g	0.252	0.12	0.373	0.077	0.248
Isoleucine, g	0.325	0.149	0.537	0.11	0.41
Leucine, g	0.641	0.274	0.979	0.201	0.704
Lycine, g	0.606	0.253	0.937	0.192	0.563
Methionine, g	0.161	0.068	0.272	0.056	0.208
Cystine, g	0.037	0.025	0.067	0.014	0.04
Phenylalanine, g	0.352	0.157	0.545	0.112	0.375
Tyrosine, g	0.318	0.135	0.566	0.116	0.403
Valine, g	0.42	0.166	0.696	0.143	0.484
Arginine, g	0.25	0.107	0.373	0.077	0.235
Histidine, g	0.235	0.101	0.392	0.08	0.194
Alanine, g	0.191	0.086	0.297	0.061	0.224
Aspartic acid, g	0.454	0.199	0.634	0.13	0.497
Glutamic acid, g	1.57	0.641	2.32	0.477	1.51
Glycine, g	0.125	0.056	0.176	0.036	0.137
Proline, g	0.735	0.258	1.18	0.243	0.82
Serine, g	0.368	0.149	0.586	0.12	0.385

Cheese

	Provolone	Ricotta	Ricotta, part skim	Romano	Roquefort
Measure	1 oz	1 C	1 C	1 oz	1 oz
Weight, g	28	246	246	28	28
Calories	100	428	340	110	105
Protein, g	7.25	27.7	28	9	6.11
Carbohydrate, g	0.61	7.48	12.6	1	0.57
Fiber, g	0	0	0	0	0
Vitamin A, IU	231	1205	1063	162	297
Vitamin B$_1$, mg	0.005	0.032	0.052	0.01	0.011
Vitamin B$_2$, mg	0.091	0.48	0.455	0.105	0.166
Vitamin B$_6$, mg	0.021	0.106	0.049	0.024	0.035
Vitamin B$_{12}$, mcg	0.415	0.831	0.716	0.32	0.182
Niacin, mg	0.044	0.256	0.192	0.022	0.208
Pantothenic acid, mg	0.135	0.52	0.6	0.12	0.491
Folic acid, mcg	3	30	32	2	14
Vitamin C, mg	0	0	0	0	0
Vitamin E, IU	0.15	1.34	0.79	0.3	—
Calcium, mg	214	509	669	302	188
Copper, mg	0.007	0.085	0.08	t	0.01
Iron, mg	0.15	0.94	1.08	0.22	0.16
Magnesium, mg	8	28	36	12	8
Manganese, mg	0.003	0.024	0.03	t	0.009
Phosphorus, mg	141	389	449	215	111
Potassium, mg	39	257	308	25	26
Selenium, mcg	4	36	41	4	4
Sodium, mg	248	207	307	340	513
Zinc, mg	0.92	2.85	3.3	0.73	0.59
Total lipid, g	7.55	31.9	19.4	7.64	8.69
Total saturated, g	4.84	20.4	12.1	4.8	5.46
Total unsaturated, g	0.22	1	0.63	0.17	0.37
Total monounsaturated, g	2.1	8.9	5.7	2.2	2.4
Cholesterol, mg	20	124	76	29	26
Tryptophan, g	0.1	0.31	0.31	0.12	0.086
Threonine, g	0.278	1.27	1.28	0.33	0.274
Isoleucine, g	0.309	1.45	1.46	0.48	0.345
Leucine, g	0.651	3	3.03	0.87	0.6
Lycine, g	0.75	3.29	3.32	0.834	0.524
Methionine, g	0.194	0.69	0.698	0.24	0.16
Cystine, g	0.033	0.243	0.246	0.06	0.036
Phenylalanine, g	0.365	1.36	1.38	0.49	0.3
Tyrosine, g	0.431	1.45	1.46	0.5	0.29
Valine, g	0.465	1.7	1.72	0.62	0.46
Arginine, g	0.29	1.55	1.57	0.33	0.2
Histidine, g	0.316	1.12	1.14	0.35	0.17
Alanine, g	0.2	1.22	1.24	0.26	0.275
Aspartic acid, g	0.494	2.44	2.47	0.56	0.335
Glutamic acid, g	1.76	6	6.08	2.1	1
Glycine, g	0.123	0.725	0.733	0.16	0.04
Proline, g	0.784	2.62	2.65	1.1	0.6
Serine, g	0.417	1.41	1.43	0.52	0.5

Cheese

	Swiss	Tilsit	Processed, American	Processed, Swiss	Cheese spread, American
Measure	1 oz	1 oz	1 oz	1 oz	1 oz
Weight, g	28	28	28	28	28
Calories	107	96	106	95	82
Protein, g	8.06	6.92	6.28	7	4.65
Carbohydrate, g	0.96	0.53	0.45	0.6	2.48
Fiber, g	0	0	0	0	0
Vitamin A, IU	240	296	343	229	223
Vitamin B_1, mg	0.006	0.017	0.008	0.004	0.014
Vitamin B_2, mg	0.103	0.102	0.1	0.078	0.122
Vitamin B_6, mg	0.024	0.02	0.02	0.01	0.033
Vitamin B_{12}, mcg	0.475	0.595	0.197	0.348	0.113
Niacin, mg	0.026	0.058	0.02	0.011	0.037
Pantothenic acid, mg	0.122	0.098	0.137	0.074	0.194
Folic acid, mcg	2	5.67	2	1.7	2
Vitamin C, mg	0	0	0	0	0
Vitamin E, IU	0.21	0.3	0.19	0.28	—
Calcium, mg	272	198	174	219	159
Copper, mg	0.036	t	0.017	t	t
Iron, mg	0.05	0.06	0.11	0.17	0.09
Magnesium, mg	10	4	6	8	8
Manganese, mg	0.005	t	t	t	t
Phosphorus, mg	171	142	211	216	202
Potassium, mg	31	18	46	61	69
Selenium, mcg	3.6	4	4.1	4.5	3.2
Sodium, mg	74	213	406	388	381
Zinc, mg	1.11	0.99	0.85	1.02	0.73
Total lipid, g	7.78	7.36	8.86	7.09	6.02
Total saturated, g	5.04	4.76	5.58	4.55	3.78
Total unsaturated, g	0.276	0.2	0.28	2.18	0.18
Total monounsaturated, g	2.1	2	2.54	—	1.76
Cholesterol, mg	26	29	27	24	16
Tryptophan, g	0.114	0.1	0.092	0.102	0.07
Threonine, g	0.294	0.255	0.204	0.227	0.178
Isoleucine, g	0.436	0.421	0.29	0.324	0.236
Leucine, g	0.839	0.722	0.555	0.62	0.505
Lycine, g	0.733	0.578	0.623	0.696	0.427
Methionine, g	0.222	0.214	0.162	0.181	0.152
Cystine, g	0.082	0.04	0.04	0.045	0.03
Phenylalanine, g	0.471	0.385	0.319	0.356	0.264
Tyrosine, g	0.48	0.413	0.344	0.384	0.252
Valine, g	0.606	0.497	0.376	0.42	0.387
Arginine, g	0.263	0.241	0.263	0.293	0.155
Histidine, g	0.302	0.2	0.256	0.286	0.144
Alanine, g	0.259	0.23	0.157	0.176	0.171
Aspartic acid, g	0.445	0.51	0.386	0.431	0.313
Glutamic acid, g	1.61	1.55	1.3	1.45	0.985
Glycine, g	0.144	0.141	0.103	0.115	0.088
Proline, g	1.04	0.842	0.639	0.713	0.658
Serine, g	0.465	0.395	0.303	0.338	0.294

Cream

	Half and half	Coffee	Whipping, light	Whipping, heavy	Whipped, pressurized
Measure	1 C	1 T	1 C	1 C	1 C
Weight, g	242	15	239	238	60
Calories	315	29	699	821	154
Protein, g	7.16	0.4	5.19	4.88	1.92
Carbohydrate, g	10.4	0.55	7.07	6.64	7.49
Fiber, g	0	0	0	0	0
Vitamin A, IU	1050	108	2694	3499	548
Vitamin B$_1$, mg	0.085	0.005	0.057	0.052	0.022
Vitamin B$_2$, mg	0.361	0.022	0.299	0.262	0.039
Vitamin B$_6$, mg	0.094	0.005	0.067	0.062	0.025
Vitamin B$_{12}$, mcg	0.796	0.033	0.466	0.428	0.175
Niacin, mg	0.189	0.009	0.1	0.093	0.042
Pantothenic acid, mg	0.699	0.041	0.619	0.607	0.183
Folic acid, mcg	6	t	9	9	1.56
Vitamin C, mg	2.08	0.11	1.46	1.38	0
Vitamin E, IU	0.4	0.03	2.1	2.2	0.54
Calcium, mg	254	14	166	154	61
Copper, mg	0.024	0.033	0.02	0.014	t
Iron, mg	0.17	0.01	0.07	0.07	0.03
Magnesium, mg	25	1	17	17	6
Manganese, mg	t	0	t	t	t
Phosphorus, mg	230	12	146	149	54
Potassium, mg	314	18	231	179	88
Selenium, mcg	4.4	0.09	1.2	1.2	0.84
Sodium, mg	98	6	82	89	78
Zinc, mg	1.23	0.04	0.6	0.55	0.22
Total lipid, g	27.8	2.9	73.8	88	13
Total saturated, g	17.3	1.8	46.2	54.8	8.3
Total unsaturated, g	1	0.11	2	3.3	0.5
Total monounsaturated, g	8	0.84	22	25	3.9
Cholesterol, mg	89	10	265	326	45.6
Tryptophan, g	0.101	0.006	0.073	0.069	0.027
Threonine, g	0.323	0.018	0.234	0.22	0.087
Isoleucine, g	0.433	0.025	0.314	0.295	0.116
Leucine, g	0.702	0.04	0.508	0.478	0.188
Lycine, g	0.568	0.032	0.411	0.387	0.152
Methionine, g	0.18	0.01	0.130	0.122	0.048
Cystine, g	0.066	0.004	0.048	0.045	0.018
Phenylalanine, g	0.346	0.02	0.25	0.236	0.093
Tyrosine, g	0.346	0.02	0.25	0.236	0.093
Valine, g	0.479	0.027	0.347	0.327	0.129
Arginine, g	0.259	0.015	0.188	0.177	0.07
Histidine, g	0.194	0.011	0.141	0.132	0.052
Alanine, g	0.247	0.014	0.179	0.168	0.066
Aspartic acid, g	0.543	0.031	0.393	0.37	0.146
Glutamic acid, g	1.5	0.085	1.08	1.02	0.402
Glycine, g	0.152	0.009	0.110	0.103	0.041
Proline, g	0.694	0.039	0.502	0.473	0.186
Serine, g	0.39	0.022	0.282	0.265	0.104

Cream Frozen Desserts Milk

	Sour cream	Ice cream, vanilla	Sherbet, orange	Whole, 3.25% milkfat	Low-fat, 2% added vitamin A
Measure	1 C	½ C	½ C	1 C	1 C
Weight, g	230	66	74	244	244
Calories	493	133	102	150	121
Protein, g	7.27	2.3	0.8	8.03	8.12
Carbohydrate, g	9.82	15.6	23	11.37	11.7
Fiber, g	0	0	0	0	0
Vitamin A, IU	1817	543	56	307	500
Vitamin B$_1$, mg	0.081	0.03	0.02	0.093	0.095
Vitamin B$_2$, mg	0.343	0.16	0.06	0.395	0.403
Vitamin B$_6$, mg	0.037	0.03	0.02	0.102	0.105
Vitamin B$_{12}$, mcg	0.69	0.26	0.14	0.871	0.888
Niacin, mg	0.154	0.08	0.044	0.205	0.21
Pantothenic acid, mg	0.828	0.38	0.133	0.766	0.781
Folic acid, mcg	25	3.3	3.7	12	12
Vitamin C, mg	1.98	0.4	2.3	2.29	2.32
Vitamin E, IU	1.9	0	0.09	0.36	0.25
Calcium, mg	268	85	40	291	297
Copper, mg	0.04	0.02	0.02	0.02	0.02
Iron, mg	0.14	0.06	0.1	0.12	0.12
Magnesium, mg	26	9.2	5.9	33	33
Manganese, mg	t	t	t	0.01	t
Phosphorus, mg	195	69	30	228	232
Potassium, mg	331	131	71	370	377
Selenium, mcg	5.1	1.7	0.96	4.9	5.4
Sodium, mg	123	53	34	120	122
Zinc, mg	0.62	0.46	0.36	0.93	0.95
Total lipid, g	48.2	7.3	1.48	8.15	4.68
Total saturated, g	30	4.48	0.86	5.07	2.92
Total unsaturated, g	1.8	0.27	0.06	0.3	0.17
Total monounsaturated, g	14	2.1	0.4	2.35	1.35
Cholesterol, mg	102	29	4.4	33	18
Tryptophan, g	0.1	0.03	0.01	0.113	0.115
Threonine, g	0.33	0.1	0.03	0.362	0.367
Isoleucine, g	0.44	0.13	0.04	0.486	0.492
Leucine, g	0.71	0.21	0.07	0.786	0.796
Lycine, g	0.58	0.17	0.06	0.637	0.644
Methionine, g	0.184	0.05	0.02	0.201	0.204
Cystine, g	0.067	0.02	0.007	0.074	0.075
Phenylalanine, g	0.35	0.1	0.036	0.388	0.392
Tyrosine, g	0.35	0.1	0.035	0.388	0.392
Valine, g	0.485	0.14	0.05	0.537	0.544
Arginine, g	0.26	0.08	0.03	0.291	0.294
Histidine, g	0.2	0.06	0.02	0.218	0.22
Alanine, g	0.25	0.08	0.03	0.277	0.28
Aspartic acid, g	0.55	0.17	0.06	0.609	0.616
Glutamic acid, g	1.5	0.45	0.15	1.68	1.7
Glycine, g	0.154	0.06	0.016	0.17	0.172
Proline, g	0.7	0.22	0.074	0.778	0.787
Serine, g	0.4	0.117	0.04	0.437	0.442

Milk

	Low-fat, 1%, added vitamin A	Nonfat, added vitamin A	Buttermilk, low-fat	Whole, dry	Nonfat, dry
Measure	1 C	1 C	1 C	1 C	1 C
Weight, g	244	245	245	128	120
Calories	102	86	99	635	435
Protein, g	8	8.35	8.11	33.6	43.4
Carbohydrate, g	11.8	11.8	11.7	49	62.3
Fiber, g	0	0	0	0	0
Vitamin A, IU	500	500	81	1180	43
Vitamin B$_1$, mg	0.095	0.088	0.083	0.362	0.498
Vitamin B$_2$, mg	0.41	0.343	0.377	1.54	1.86
Vitamin B$_6$, mg	0.11	0.098	0.083	0.387	0.433
Vitamin B$_{12}$, mcg	0.9	0.926	0.537	4.16	4.84
Niacin, mg	0.212	0.216	0.142	0.827	1.14
Pantothenic acid, mg	0.79	0.806	0.674	2.9	4.28
Folic acid, mcg	12.4	13	12.3	47	60
Vitamin C, mg	2.4	2.4	2.4	11	8.11
Vitamin E, IU	0.15	0.15	0.22	2	0.04
Calcium, mg	300	302	285	1168	1508
Copper, mg	0.024	0.027	0.027	0.1	0.05
Iron, mg	0.1	0.1	0.12	0.6	0.38
Magnesium, mg	34	28	27	108	132
Manganese, mg	t	t	t	0.05	0.024
Phosphorus, mg	235	247	219	993	1162
Potassium, mg	381	406	371	1702	2153
Selenium, mcg	2.2	5	4.9	21	32.7
Sodium, mg	123	126	257	475	642
Zinc, mg	0.95	0.98	1.03	4.28	4.9
Total lipid, g	2.59	0.44	2.16	34.2	0.92
Total saturated, g	1.6	0.287	1.34	21.4	0.6
Total unsaturated, g	0.095	0.017	0.08	0.95	0.036
Total monounsaturated, g	0.75	0.115	0.62	10	0.24
Cholesterol, mg	9.8	4	9	124	24
Tryptophan, g	0.112	0.118	0.088	0.475	0.612
Threonine, g	0.364	0.377	0.386	1.52	1.96
Isoleucine, g	0.486	0.505	0.5	2.03	2.62
Leucine, g	0.786	0.818	0.807	3.3	4.25
Lycine, g	0.637	0.663	0.679	2.67	3.44
Methionine, g	0.2	0.21	0.198	0.845	1.08
Cystine, g	0.07	0.077	0.076	0.312	0.401
Phenylalanine, g	0.39	0.403	0.427	1.62	2.1
Tyrosine, g	0.39	0.403	0.339	1.62	2.1
Valine, g	0.54	0.559	0.596	2.25	2.9
Arginine, g	0.29	0.302	0.309	1.22	1.57
Histidine, g	0.22	0.227	0.233	0.914	1.17
Alanine, g	0.276	0.288	0.292	1.16	1.49
Aspartic acid, g	0.61	0.634	0.647	2.55	3.29
Glutamic acid, g	1.68	1.74	1.57	7.05	9.08
Glycine, g	0.17	0.177	0.178	0.713	0.918
Proline, g	0.78	0.809	0.819	3.26	4.2
Serine, g	0.44	0.454	0.422	1.83	2.36

Milk

	Nonfat, dry, instant	Condensed, sweetened	Evaporated	Evaporated, nonfat	Chocolate
Measure	1 C	1 C	½ C	½ C	1 C
Weight, g	68	306	126	128	250
Calories	244	982	169	99	208
Protein, g	23.8	24.2	8.58	9.63	7.92
Carbohydrate, g	35.5	166	12.6	14.4	25.8
Fiber, g	0	0	0	0	0.15
Vitamin A, IU	18.3	1004	306	500	302
Vitamin B$_1$, mg	0.281	0.275	0.059	0.057	0.092
Vitamin B$_2$, mg	1.18	1.27	0.398	0.394	0.405
Vitamin B$_6$, mg	0.235	0.156	0.063	0.07	0.1
Vitamin B$_{12}$, mcg	2.71	1.36	0.205	0.305	0.835
Niacin, mg	0.606	0.643	0.244	0.222	0.313
Pantothenic acid, mg	2.2	2.29	0.804	0.941	0.738
Folic acid, mcg	34	34	10	11	12
Vitamin C, mg	3.79	7.96	2.37	1.58	2.28
Vitamin E, IU	0.02	0.98	0.34	0.009	0.34
Calcium, mg	837	868	329	369	280
Copper, mg	0.03	0.046	0.02	0.02	0.16
Iron, mg	0.21	0.58	0.24	0.37	0.6
Magnesium, mg	80	78	30	34	33
Manganese, mg	0.014	0.018	t	t	0.19
Phosphorus, mg	670	775	255	248	251
Potassium, mg	1160	1136	382	423	417
Selenium, mcg	18.6	45.3	2.89	3.2	4.75
Sodium, mg	373	389	133	147	149
Zinc, mg	3	2.88	0.97	1.15	1.02
Total lipid, g	0.49	26.6	9.53	0.26	8.48
Total saturated, g	0.32	16.8	5.78	0.155	5.26
Total unsaturated, g	0.02	1.03	0.31	0.008	0.31
Total monounsaturated, g	0.127	7.4	2.94	0.079	2.48
Cholesterol, mg	12	104	37	5	30
Tryptophan, g	0.337	0.341	0.121	0.136	0.112
Threonine, g	1.07	1.09	0.387	0.435	0.358
Isoleucine, g	1.44	1.46	0.519	0.582	0.479
Leucine, g	2.33	2.37	0.841	0.943	0.776
Lycine, g	1.89	1.92	0.681	0.763	0.629
Methionine, g	0.599	0.607	0.215	0.241	0.199
Cystine, g	0.221	0.224	0.079	0.089	0.073
Phenylalanine, g	1.15	1.16	0.414	0.465	0.383
Tyrosine, g	1.15	1.16	0.414	0.465	0.383
Valine, g	1.59	1.62	0.574	0.644	0.53
Arginine, g	0.864	0.876	0.311	0.349	0.287
Histidine, g	0.647	0.656	0.233	0.261	0.215
Alanine, g	0.823	0.835	0.296	0.332	0.273
Aspartic acid, g	1.81	1.83	0.651	0.73	0.601
Glutamic acid, g	4.99	5.07	1.79	2.01	1.66
Glycine, g	0.505	0.512	0.182	0.204	0.168
Proline, g	2.31	2.34	0.831	0.932	0.768
Serine, g	1.29	1.31	0.467	0.524	0.431

	Milk			**Yogurt**	
	Eggnog	Goat	Human, mature	Plain, whole milk	Plain, low-fat
Measure	1 C	1 C	1 C	1 C	1 C
Weight, g	254	244	246	227	227
Calories	342	168	171	139	144
Protein, g	9.68	8.69	2.53	7.88	11.9
Carbohydrate, g	34.4	10.9	17	10.5	16
Fiber, g	0	0	0	0	0
Vitamin A, IU	894	451	593	279	150
Vitamin B$_1$, mg	0.086	0.117	0.034	0.066	0.1
Vitamin B$_2$, mg	0.483	0.337	0.089	0.322	0.486
Vitamin B$_6$, mg	0.127	0.112	0.027	0.073	0.111
Vitamin B$_{12}$, mcg	1.14	0.159	0.111	0.844	1.27
Niacin, mg	0.267	0.676	0.435	0.17	0.259
Pantothenic acid, mg	1.06	0.756	0.549	0.883	1.34
Folic acid, mcg	2	1	13	17	25
Vitamin C, mg	3.81	3.15	12.3	1.2	1.82
Vitamin E, IU	0.86	0.33	3.3	0.32	0.15
Calcium, mg	330	326	79	274	415
Copper, mg	0.033	0.112	0.12	0.022	0.03
Iron, mg	0.51	0.12	0.07	0.11	0.18
Magnesium, mg	47	34	8	26	40
Manganese, mg	0.013	0.044	0.064	0.01	0.01
Phosphorus, mg	278	270	34	215	326
Potassium, mg	420	499	126	351	531
Selenium, mcg	10.7	3.4	4.43	5.4	8.1
Sodium, mg	138	122	42	105	159
Zinc, mg	1.17	0.73	0.42	1.34	2.02
Total lipid, g	19	10	10.7	7.38	3.52
Total saturated, g	11.3	6.51	4.94	4.76	2.27
Total unsaturated, g	0.86	0.36	1.22	0.225	0.108
Total monounsaturated, g	5.67	2.7	4.08	2.18	1.04
Cholesterol, mg	149	28	31	29	14
Tryptophan, g	0.137	0.106	0.041	0.044	0.067
Threonine, g	0.444	0.398	0.112	0.323	0.489
Isoleucine, g	0.583	0.505	0.137	0.43	0.65
Leucine, g	0.937	0.765	0.233	0.794	1.2
Lycine, g	0.758	0.708	0.168	0.706	1.06
Methionine, g	0.222	0.196	0.052	0.232	0.351
Cystine, g	0.097	0.113	0.047	0.078	0.118
Phenylalanine, g	0.463	0.377	0.113	0.43	0.65
Tyrosine, g	0.462	0.437	0.129	0.398	0.601
Valine, g	0.643	0.585	0.156	0.652	0.986
Arginine, g	0.378	0.291	0.105	0.237	0.359
Histidine, g	0.24	0.218	0.057	0.195	0.295
Alanine, g	0.346	0.287	0.089	0.337	0.51
Aspartic acid, g	0.74	0.512	0.201	0.625	0.945
Glutamic acid, g	1.95	1.52	0.414	1.54	2.33
Glycine, g	0.213	0.123	0.064	0.19	0.288
Proline, g	0.89	0.899	0.203	0.933	1.41
Serine, g	0.55	0.441	0.107	0.488	0.738

Yogurt　　Eggs

	Plain, nonfat	Fruit, low-fat	Whole, raw	White, raw	Yolk, raw	Whole, dried
Measure	1 C	1 C	1 lge	1 lge	1 lge	1 T
Weight, g	227	227	50	33	17	5
Calories	127	225	79	16	63	30
Protein, g	13	9.04	6.07	3.35	2.79	2.29
Carbohydrate, g	17.4	42.3	0.6	0.41	0.04	0.24
Fiber, g	0	0.27	0	0	0	0
Vitamin A, IU	16	111	260	0	313	98
Vitamin B_1, mg	0.109	0.077	0.044	0.002	0.043	0.015
Vitamin B_2, mg	0.531	0.368	0.15	0.094	0.074	0.059
Vitamin B_6, mg	0.120	0.084	0.06	0.001	0.053	0.02
Vitamin B_{12}, mcg	1.39	0.967	0.773	0.021	0.647	0.5
Niacin, mg	0.281	0.195	0.031	0.029	0.012	0.012
Pantothenic acid, mg	1.45	1.01	0.864	0.08	0.753	0.319
Folic acid, mcg	28	19	32	5	26	9
Vitamin C, mg	1.98	1.36	0	0	0	0
Vitamin E, IU	0.018	0.11	0.78	0	0.78	0.33
Calcium, mg	452	314	28	4	26	11
Copper, mg	0.037	0.194	0.007	0.102	0.004	0.009
Iron, mg	0.2	0.14	1.04	0.01	0.95	0.39
Magnesium, mg	43	30	6	3	3	2
Manganese, mg	0.012	0.157	0.012	0.001	0.015	0.006
Phosphorus, mg	355	247	90	4	86	34
Potassium, mg	579	402	65	45	15	24
Selenium, mcg	8.8	6.86	15.4	5.8	7.5	5.98
Sodium, mg	174	121	69	50	8	26
Zinc, mg	2.2	1.52	0.72	0.01	0.58	0.27
Total lipid, g	0.41	2.61	5.58	0	5.6	2.09
Total saturated, g	0.264	1.68	1.67	0	1.68	0.63
Total unsaturated, g	0.012	0.081	0.68	0	0.698	0.29
Total monounsaturated, g	0.12	0.774	1.9	0	1.9	0.767
Cholesterol, mg	4	10	212	0	212	86
Tryptophan, g	0.073	0.051	0.097	0.051	0.041	0.037
Threonine, g	0.534	0.371	0.298	0.149	0.151	0.113
Isoleucine, g	0.709	0.493	0.380	0.204	0.16	0.143
Leucine, g	1.31	0.911	0.533	0.291	0.237	0.201
Lycine, g	1.16	0.81	0.41	0.206	0.189	0.155
Methionine, g	0.383	0.266	0.196	0.13	0.071	0.074
Cystine, g	0.127	0.08	0.145	0.083	0.05	0.055
Phenylalanine, g	0.709	0.493	0.343	0.21	0.121	0.129
Tyrosine, g	0.656	0.456	0.253	0.134	0.12	0.095
Valine, g	1.07	0.748	0.437	0.251	0.17	0.165
Arginine, g	0.391	0.272	0.388	0.195	0.193	0.147
Histidine, g	0.322	0.224	0.147	0.076	0.067	0.055
Alanine, g	0.557	0.387	0.354	0.216	0.14	0.134
Aspartic acid, g	1.03	0.717	0.602	0.296	0.233	0.227
Glutamic acid, g	2.54	1.77	0.773	0.467	0.341	0.292
Glycine, g	0.314	0.218	0.202	0.125	0.084	0.076
Proline, g	1.54	1.07	0.241	0.126	0.116	0.091
Serine, g	0.805	0.559	0.461	0.247	0.231	0.174

Fats and Oils

	Almond	Apricot kernel	Avocado	Beef tallow	Butter
Measure	1 T	1 T	1 T	1 T	1 T
Weight, g	13.6	13.6	14	12.8	14.1
Calories	120	120	124	115	101
Protein, g	0	0	0	0	0.12
Carbohydrate, g	0	0	0	0	0.008
Fiber, g	0	0	0	0	0
Vitamin A, IU	0	0	0	0	433
Vitamin B$_1$, mg	0	0	0	0	t
Vitamin B$_2$, mg	0	0	0	0	0.004
Vitamin B$_6$, mg	0	0	0	0	t
Vitamin B$_{12}$, mcg	0	0	0	0	0.018
Niacin, mg	0	0	0	0	0.006
Pantothenic acid, mg	0	0	0	0	0.016
Folic acid, mcg	0	0	0	0	0.375
Vitamin C, mg	0	0	0	0	0
Vitamin E, IU	7.96	1.76	—	0.52	0.33
Calcium, mg	0	0	0	0	3.37
Copper, mg	0	0	0	0	0.004
Iron, mg	0	0	0	0	0.022
Magnesium, mg	0	0	0	0	0.25
Manganese, mg	0	0	0	0	0.006
Phosphorus, mg	0	0	0	0	3.25
Potassium, mg	0	0	0	t	3.62
Selenium, mcg	0	0	0	0.03	0.142
Sodium, mg	0	0	0	t	117
Zinc, mg	0	0	0	0	0.007
Total lipid, g	13.6	13.6	14	12.8	11.5
Total saturated, g	1.1	0.857	1.62	6.4	7.15
Total unsaturated, g	2.37	3.99	9.5	0.512	0.43
Total monounsaturated, g	9.51	8.16	1.88	5.35	3.33
Cholesterol, mg	0	0	—	14	31
Tryptophan, g	0	0	—	0	0.002
Threonine, g	0	0	—	0	0.005
Isoleucine, g	0	0	—	0	0.007
Leucine, g	0	0	—	0	0.011
Lycine, g	0	0	—	0	0.009
Methionine, g	0	0	—	0	0.003
Cystine, g	0	0	—	0	0.001
Phenylalanine, g	0	0	—	0	0.005
Tyrosine, g	0	0	—	0	0.005
Valine, g	0	0	—	0	0.008
Arginine, g	0	0		0	0.004
Histidine, g	0	0	—	0	0.003
Alanine, g	0	0	—	0	0.004
Aspartic acid, g	0	0	—	0	0.009
Glutamic acid, g	0	0	—	0	0.025
Glycine, g	0	0	—	0	0.002
Proline, g	0	0	—	0	0.011
Serine, g	0	0	—	0	0.006

Fats and Oils

	Canola	Chicken fat	Coconut	Cod liver	Corn
Measure	1 T	1 T	1 T	1 T	1 T
Weight, g	14	12.8	13.6	13.6	13.6
Calories	124	115	117	123	120
Protein, g	0	0	0	0	0
Carbohydrate, g	0	0	0	0	0
Fiber, g	0	0	0	0	0
Vitamin A, IU	0	0	0	13,600	0
Vitamin B_1, mg	0	0	0	0	0
Vitamin B_2, mg	0	0	0	0	0
Vitamin B_6, mg	0	0	0	0	0
Vitamin B_{12}, mcg	0	0	0	0	0
Niacin, mg	0	0	0	0	0
Pantothenic acid, mg	0	0	0	0	0
Folic acid, mcg	0	0	0	0	0
Vitamin C, mg	0	0	0	0	0
Vitamin E, IU	4.37	0.52	0.057	—	4.28
Calcium, mg	0	0	0	0	0
Copper, mg	0	0	0	0	0
Iron, mg	0	0	t	0	0
Magnesium, mg	0	0	0	0	0
Manganese, mg	0	0	0	0	0
Phosphorus, mg	0	0	0	0	0
Potassium, mg	0	0	0	0	0
Selenium, mcg	0	0.026	0	0	0
Sodium, mg	0	0	0	0	0
Zinc, mg	0	0	0	0	0
Total lipid, g	14	12.8	13.6	13.6	13.6
Total saturated, g	0.994	3.8	11.8	3.08	1.7
Total unsaturated, g	4.14	2.68	0.245	3.07	7.98
Total monounsaturated, g	8.25	5.7	0.79	6.35	3.3
Cholesterol, mg	0	11	0	77.5	0
Tryptophan, g	—	0	0	—	0
Threonine, g	—	0	0	—	0
Isoleucine, g	—	0	0	—	0
Leucine, g	—	0	0	—	0
Lycine, g	—	0	0	—	0
Methionine, g	—	0	0	—	0
Cystine, g	—	0	0	—	0
Phenylalanine, g	—	0	0	—	0
Tyrosine, g	—	0	0	—	0
Valine, g	—	0	0	—	0
Arginine, g	—	0	0	—	0
Histidine, g	—	0	0	—	0
Alanine, g	—	0	0	—	0
Aspartic acid, g	—	0	0	—	0
Glutamic acid, g	—	0	0	—	0
Glycine, g	—	0	0	—	0
Proline, g	—	0	0	—	0
Serine, g	—	0	0	—	0

Fats and Oils

	Cottonseed	Grapeseed	Hazelnut	Margarine	Olive
Measure	1 T	1 T	1 T	1 T	1 T
Weight, g	13.6	13.6	13.6	14.1	13.5
Calories	120	120	120	101	119
Protein, g	0	0	0	0	0
Carbohydrate, g	0	0	0	0	0
Fiber, g	0	0	0	0	0
Vitamin A, IU	0	0	0	465	0
Vitamin B_1, mg	0	0	0	0	0
Vitamin B_2, mg	0	0	0	0.006	0
Vitamin B_6, mg	0	0	0	0	0
Vitamin B_{12}, mcg	0	0	0	0.012	0
Niacin, mg	0	0	0	0.003	0
Pantothenic acid, mg	0	0	0	0.012	0
Folic acid, mcg	0	0	0	0.24	0
Vitamin C, mg	0	0	0	0.024	0
Vitamin E, IU	7.75	—	—	2.68	2.49
Calcium, mg	0	0	0	4.23	0.02
Copper, mg	0	0	0	0	0
Iron, mg	0	0	0	t	0.05
Magnesium, mg	0	0	0	0.36	t
Manganese, mg	0	0	0	—	—
Phosphorus, mg	0	0	0	3.24	0.16
Potassium, mg	0	0	0	5.97	—
Selenium, mcg	0	0	0	0	0
Sodium, mg	0	0	0	133	t
Zinc, mg	0	0	0	0	0.01
Total lipid, g	13.6	13.6	13.6	11.4	13.5
Total saturated, g	3.5	1.31	1	2.2	1.8
Total unsaturated, g	7.1	9.51	1.39	3.57	1.13
Total monounsaturated, g	2.4	2.2	10.6	5.04	9.95
Cholesterol, mg	0	0	0	0	0
Tryptophan, g	0	0	0	0.003	0
Threonine, g	0	0	0	0.006	0
Isoleucine, g	0	0	0	0.006	0
Leucine, g	0	0	0	0.012	0
Lycine, g	0	0	0	0.009	0
Methionine, g	0	0	0	0.003	0
Cystine, g	0	0	0	0	0
Phenylalanine, g	0	0	0	0.006	0
Tyrosine, g	0	0	0	0.006	0
Valine, g	0	0	0	0.009	0
Arginine, g	0	0	0	0.003	0
Histidine, g	0	0	0	0.003	0
Alanine, g	0	0	0	0.003	0
Aspartic acid, g	0	0	0	0.009	0
Glutamic acid, g	0	0	0	0.024	0
Glycine, g	0	0	0	0.003	0
Proline, g	0	0	0	0.012	0
Serine, g	0	0	0	0.006	0

Fats and Oils

	Palm	Palm kernel	Peanut	Safflower	Sesame
Measure	1 T	1 T	1 T	1 T	1 T
Weight, g	13.6	13.6	13.5	13.6	13.6
Calories	120	117	119	120	120
Protein, g	0	0	0	0	0
Carbohydrate, g	0	0	0	0	0
Fiber, g	0	0	0	0	0
Vitamin A, IU	0	0	0	0	0
Vitamin B_1, mg	0	0	0	0	0
Vitamin B_2, mg	0	0	0	0	0
Vitamin B_6, mg	0	0	0	0	0
Vitamin B_{12}, mcg	0	0	0	0	0
Niacin, mg	0	0	0	0	0
Pantothenic acid, mg	0	0	0	0	0
Folic acid, mcg	0	0	0	0	0
Vitamin C, mg	0	0	0	0	0
Vitamin E, IU	4.4	0.77	2.59	6.97	0.83
Calcium, mg	0	0	0.01	0	0
Copper, mg	0	0	0.001	0	0
Iron, mg	t	0	0	0	0
Magnesium, mg	0	0	0.01	0	0
Manganese, mg	0	0	—	0	0
Phosphorus, mg	0.02	0	0	0	0
Potassium, mg	0	0	0	0	0
Selenium, mcg	0	0	0	0	0
Sodium, mg	0	0	0.01	0	0
Zinc, mg	0	0	t	0	0
Total lipid, g	13.6	13.6	13.5	13.6	13.6
Total saturated, g	6.7	11	2.3	0.84	1.9
Total unsaturated, g	1.27	0.22	4.3	1.95	5.67
Total monounsaturated, g	5	1.55	6.24	10	5.4
Cholesterol, mg	0	0	0	0	0
Tryptophan, g	0	0	0	0	0
Threonine, g	0	0	0	0	0
Isoleucine, g	0	0	0	0	0
Leucine, g	0	0	0	0	0
Lycine, g	0	0	0	0	0
Methionine, g	0	0	0	0	0
Cystine, g	0	0	0	0	0
Phenylalanine, g	0	0	0	0	0
Tyrosine, g	0	0	0	0	0
Valine, g	0	0	0	0	0
Arginine, g	0	0	0	0	0
Histidine, g	0	0	0	0	0
Alanine, g	0	0	0	0	0
Aspartic acid, g	0	0	0	0	0
Glutamic acid, g	0	0	0	0	0
Glycine, g	0	0	0	0	0
Proline, g	0	0	0	0	0
Serine, g	0	0	0	0	0

Fats and Oils

	Soybean	Sunflower	Vegetable shortening	Walnut	Wheat germ
Measure	1 T	1 T	1 T	1 T	1 T
Weight, g	13.6	13.6	12.8	13.6	13.6
Calories	120	120	115	120	120
Protein, g	0	0	0	0	0
Carbohydrate, g	0	0	0	0	0
Fiber, g	0	0	0	0	0
Vitamin A, IU	0	0	0	0	0
Vitamin B$_1$, mg	0	0	0	0	0
Vitamin B$_2$, mg	0	0	0	0	0
Vitamin B$_6$, mg	0	0	0	0	0
Vitamin B$_{12}$, mcg	0	0	0	0	0
Niacin, mg	0	0	0	0	0
Pantothenic acid, mg	0	0	0	0	0
Folic acid, mcg	0	0	0	0	0
Vitamin C, mg	0	0	0	0	0
Vitamin E, IU	3.68	1.3	0.23	0.65	39
Calcium, mg	0.01	0.03	0	0	0
Copper, mg	0	0	0	0	0
Iron, mg	t	t	0	0	0
Magnesium, mg	t	0.03	0	0	0
Manganese, mg	0	0	0	0	0
Phosphorus, mg	0.03	0	0	0	0
Potassium, mg	0	0	0	0	0
Selenium, mcg	0	0	0	0	0
Sodium, mg	0	0.01	0	0	0
Zinc, mg	0	0	0	0	0
Total lipid, g	13.6	13.6	12.8	13.6	13.6
Total saturated, g	2	1.4	5.2	1.24	2.6
Total unsaturated, g	7.9	5.45	1.4	8.6	8.4
Total monounsaturated, g	3.17	6.17	5.68	3.1	2.05
Cholesterol, mg	0	0	7.2	0	0
Tryptophan, g	0	0	0	0	0
Threonine, g	0	0	0	0	0
Isoleucine, g	0	0	0	0	0
Leucine, g	0	0	0	0	0
Lycine, g	0	0	0	0	0
Methionine, g	0	0	0	0	0
Cystine, g	0	0	0	0	0
Phenylalanine, g	0	0	0	0	0
Tyrosine, g	0	0	0	0	0
Valine, g	0	0	0	0	0
Arginine, g	0	0	0	0	0
Histidine, g	0	0	0	0	0
Alanine, g	0	0	0	0	0
Aspartic acid, g	0	0	0	0	0
Glutamic acid, g	0	0	0	0	0
Glycine, g	0	0	0	0	0
Proline, g	0	0	0	0	0
Serine, g	0	0	0	0	0

Fruits and Fruit Juices

	Apple, med	Apple, dried	Apple juice	Applesauce, unsw.	Apricot
Measure	1	10 rings	1 C	1 C	3
Weight, g	138	64	248	244	105
Calories	81	155	116	106	51
Protein, g	0.27	0.59	0.15	0.4	1.48
Carbohydrate, g	21	42	29	27.5	11.7
Fiber, g	3.7	5.57	0.52	2.9	2.5
Vitamin A, IU	74	0	2	70	2769
Vitamin B$_1$, mg	0.023	0	0.052	0.032	0.032
Vitamin B$_2$, mg	0.019	0.102	0.042	0.061	0.042
Vitamin B$_6$, mg	0.066	0.08	0.074	0.063	0.057
Vitamin B$_{12}$, mcg	0	0	0	0	0
Niacin, mg	0.106	0.593	0.248	0.459	0.636
Pantothenic acid, mg	0.084	0.16	0.156	0.232	0.254
Folic acid, mcg	3.9	0	0.2	1.4	9.1
Vitamin C, mg	7.8	2.5	2.3	2.9	10.6
Vitamin E, IU	0.66	0.52	0.04	0.036	1.39
Calcium, mg	10	9	16	7	15
Copper, mg	0.057	0.122	0.055	0.063	0.094
Iron, mg	0.25	0.9	0.92	0.29	0.58
Magnesium, mg	6	10	8	7	8
Manganese, mg	0.062	0.058	0.28	0.183	0.084
Phosphorus, mg	10	25	18	18	21
Potassium, mg	159	288	296	183	313
Selenium, mcg	0.7	0.83	0.25	0.488	0.42
Sodium, mg	1	56	7	5	1
Zinc, mg	0.05	0.13	0.07	0.06	0.28
Total lipid, g	0.49	0.2	0.28	0.12	0.41
Total saturated, g	0.08	0.033	0.047	0.02	0.029
Total unsaturated, g	0.145	0.06	0.082	0.034	0.027
Total monounsaturated, g	0.021	0.01	0.012	0.005	0.06
Cholesterol, mg	0	0	0	0	0
Tryptophan, g	0.003	0.006	—	0.005	0.016
Threonine, g	0.01	0.021	—	0.015	0.05
Isoleucine, g	0.011	0.024	—	0.015	0.043
Leucine, g	0.017	0.036	—	0.024	0.082
Lycine, g	0.017	0.037	—	0.024	0.103
Methionine, g	0.003	0.006	—	0.005	0.006
Cystine, g	0.004	0.008	—	0.005	0.003
Phenylalanine, g	0.007	0.017	—	0.012	0.055
Tyrosine, g	0.006	0.011	—	0.007	0.031
Valine, g	0.012	0.028	—	0.02	0.05
Arginine, g	0.008	0.019	—	0.012	0.048
Histidine, g	0.004	0.01	—	0.007	0.029
Alanine, g	0.01	0.021	—	0.015	0.072
Aspartic acid, g	0.047	0.104	—	0.068	0.333
Glutamic acid, g	0.028	0.062	—	0.041	0.166
Glycine, g	0.011	0.024	—	0.015	0.042
Proline, g	0.01	0.02	—	0.015	0.107
Serine, g	0.011	0.024	—	0.017	0.088

Fruits and Fruit Juices

	Apricot, dried	Apricot nectar	Avocado	Banana, med.	Blackberries
Measure	10 halves	1 C	1	1	1 C
Weight, g	35	251	272	175	144
Calories	83	141	324	105	74
Protein, g	1.28	0.92	3.99	1.18	1.04
Carbohydrate, g	21.6	36	14.8	26.7	18.3
Fiber, g	3.15	1.5	10	2.8	7.6
Vitamin A, IU	2534	3304	1230	92	237
Vitamin B_1, mg	0.003	0.023	0.217	0.051	0.043
Vitamin B_2, mg	0.053	0.035	0.245	0.114	0.058
Vitamin B_6, mg	0.055	0.055	0.563	0.659	0.084
Vitamin B_{12}, mcg	0	0	0	0	0
Niacin, mg	1.05	0.653	3.86	0.616	0.576
Pantothenic acid, mg	0.264	0.24	1.95	0.296	0.346
Folic acid, mcg	3.6	3.3	124	21.8	49
Vitamin C, mg	0.8	1.4	15.9	10.3	30.2
Vitamin E, IU	0.775	0.3	0.4	0.55	1.52
Calcium, mg	16	17	22	7	46
Copper, mg	0.15	0.183	0.527	0.119	0.202
Iron, mg	1.65	0.96	2.05	0.35	0.83
Magnesium, mg	16	13	79	33	29
Manganese, mg	0.096	0.08	0.454	0.173	1.86
Phosphorus, mg	41	23	83	22	30
Potassium, mg	482	286	1204	451	282
Selenium, mcg	0.77	0.5	0.8	1.5	0.864
Sodium, mg	3	9	21	1	0
Zinc, mg	0.26	0.23	0.84	0.19	0.39
Total lipid, g	0.16	0.23	30.8	0.55	0.56
Total saturated, g	0.011	0.015	4.9	0.21	0.02
Total unsaturated, g	0.03	0.043	3.9	0.12	0.32
Total monounsaturated, g	0.07	0.095	19.3	0.056	0.055
Cholesterol, mg	0	0	0	0	0
Tryptophan, g	0.023	—	0.042	0.014	—
Threonine, g	0.046	—	0.133	0.039	—
Isoleucine, g	0.039	—	0.143	0.038	—
Leucine, g	0.075	—	0.247	0.081	—
Lycine, g	0.089	—	0.189	0.055	—
Methionine, g	0.006	—	0.074	0.013	—
Cystine, g	0.004	—	0.042	0.019	—
Phenylalanine, g	0.053	—	0.137	0.043	—
Tyrosine, g	0.03	—	0.098	0.027	—
Valine, g	0.047	—	0.195	0.054	—
Arginine, g	0.049	—	0.119	0.054	—
Histidine, g	0.021	—	0.058	0.092	—
Alanine, g	0.063	—	0.239	0.044	—
Aspartic acid, g	0.293	—	0.569	0.129	—
Glutamic acid, g	0.129	—	0.416	0.127	—
Glycine, g	0.04	—	0.167	0.042	—
Proline, g	0.076	—	0.155	0.046	—
Serine, g	0.074	—	0.163	0.054	—

Fruits and Fruit Juices

	Blueberries	Boysenberries, frozen	Cherimoya w/o skin, seeds	Cherries, w/o pits	Cherry, sour
Measure	1 C	1 C	1	1 C	1 C
Weight, g	145	132	547	145	103
Calories	82	66	514	104	51
Protein, g	0.97	1.46	7	1.74	1
Carbohydrate, g	20.5	16	131	24	12.5
Fiber, g	3.9	3.56	13	3.3	1.65
Vitamin A, IU	145	89	55	310	1322
Vitamin B_1, mg	0.07	0.07	0.547	0.073	0.031
Vitamin B_2, mg	0.073	0.049	0.6	0.087	0.041
Vitamin B_6, mg	0.052	0.074	—	0.052	0.045
Vitamin B_{12}, mcg	0	0	0	0	0
Niacin, mg	0.521	1.01	7	0.58	0.412
Pantothenic acid, mg	0.135	0.330	—	0.184	0.147
Folic acid, mcg	9.3	83.6	—	6.1	7.73
Vitamin C, mg	18.9	4.1	49	10.2	10
Vitamin E, IU	2.16	0.885	—	0.28	0.134
Calcium, mg	9	36	126	21	16.5
Copper, mg	0.088	0.106	—	0.138	0.11
Iron, mg	0.24	1.12	2.7	0.56	0.33
Magnesium, mg	7	21	—	16	9.27
Manganese, mg	0.409	0.722	—	0.133	0.115
Phosphorus, mg	15	36	219	28	15.5
Potassium, mg	129	183	—	325	178
Selenium, mcg	0.87	0.79	—	0.87	0.412
Sodium, mg	9	2	—	1	3.1
Zinc, mg	0.16	0.29	—	0.09	0.103
Total lipid, g	0.55	0.35	2.2	1.39	0.309
Total saturated, g	0.046	0.012	—	0.313	0.07
Total unsaturated, g	0.24	0.195	—	0.419	0.093
Total monounsaturated, g	0.078	0.033	—	0.38	0.084
Cholesterol, mg	0	0	0	0	0
Tryptophan, g	0.004	—	—	—	—
Threonine, g	0.026	—	—	—	—
Isoleucine, g	0.03	—	—	—	—
Leucine, g	0.058	—	—	—	—
Lycine, g	0.017	—	—	—	—
Methionine, g	0.016	—	—	—	—
Cystine, g	0.01	—	—	—	—
Phenylalanine, g	0.035	—	—	—	—
Tyrosine, g	0.012	—	—	—	—
Valine, g	0.041	—	—	—	—
Arginine, g	0.049	—	—	—	—
Histidine, g	0.015	—	—	—	—
Alanine, g	0.041	—	—	—	—
Aspartic acid, g	0.075	—	—	—	—
Glutamic acid, g	0.12	—	—	—	—
Glycine, g	0.041	—	—	—	—
Proline, g	0.036	—	—	—	—
Serine, g	0.029	—	—	—	—

Fruits and Fruit Juices

	Crabapple, slices	Cranberries	Currants, black	Dates	Elderberries
Measure	1 C	1 C	1 C	10	1 C
Weight, g	110	95	112	83	145
Calories	0.83	46	71	228	105
Protein, g	0.44	0.37	1.57	1.63	0.95
Carbohydrate, g	21.9	12	17.2	61	26.6
Fiber, g	—	4	—	6.2	10
Vitamin A, IU	44	44	258	42	870
Vitamin B$_1$, mg	0.033	0.029	0.056	0.075	0.102
Vitamin B$_2$, mg	0.022	0.019	0.056	0.083	0.087
Vitamin B$_6$, mg	—	0.062	0.074	0.159	0.334
Vitamin B$_{12}$, mcg	0	0	0	0	0
Niacin, mg	0.11	0.095	0.336	1.82	0.725
Pantothenic acid, mg	—	0.208	0.446	0.647	0.203
Folic acid, mcg	—	1.6	—	10.4	8.7
Vitamin C, mg	8.8	12.8	202	0	52.2
Vitamin E, IU	—	0.14	0.167	0.012	2.16
Calcium, mg	20	7	61	27	55
Copper, mg	0.074	0.055	0.096	0.239	0.088
Iron, mg	0.39	0.19	1.72	0.96	2.32
Magnesium, mg	7	5	27	29	7.25
Manganese, mg	0.127	0.149	0.287	0.247	—
Phosphorus, mg	17	8	66	33	57
Potassium, mg	213	67	361	541	406
Selenium, mcg	—	0.57	—	0.158	0.87
Sodium, mg	1	1	2	2	8.7
Zinc, mg	—	0.12	0.3	0.24	0.16
Total lipid, g	0.33	0.19	0.45	0.37	0.73
Total saturated, g	0.053	0.016	0.038	0.016	0.033
Total unsaturated, g	0.097	0.084	0.2	0.003	0.358
Total monounsaturated, g	0.013	0.027	0.065	0.012	0.116
Cholesterol, mg	0	0	0	0	0
Tryptophan, g	0.004	—	—	0.042	0.019
Threonine, g	0.015	—	—	0.043	0.039
Isoleucine, g	0.018	—	—	0.039	0.039
Leucine, g	0.028	—	—	0.073	0.087
Lycine, g	0.028	—	—	0.05	0.038
Methionine, g	0.004	—	—	0.018	0.02
Cystine, g	0.006	—	—	0.037	0.022
Phenylalanine, g	0.012	—	—	0.046	0.058
Tyrosine, g	0.009	—	—	0.025	0.074
Valine, g	0.021	—	—	0.055	0.048
Arginine, g	0.014	—	—	0.055	0.068
Histidine, g	0.007	—	—	0.025	0.022
Alanine, g	0.015	—	—	0.083	0.044
Aspartic acid, g	0.077	—	—	0.105	0.084
Glutamic acid, g	0.046	—	—	0.177	0.139
Glycine, g	0.018	—	—	0.079	0.052
Proline, g	0.015	—	—	0.088	0.036
Serine, g	0.018	—	—	0.055	0.046

Fruits and Fruit Juices

	Fig	Fig, dried	Gooseberries	Grapefruit, med.	Grapefruit juice
Measure	1	10	1 C	½	1 C
Weight, g	64	190	150	128	247
Calories	47	480	67	38	96
Protein, g	0.48	5.7	1.32	0.75	1.24
Carbohydrate, g	12.2	122	15.2	9.7	22.7
Fiber, g	2.1	23	6.5	1.4	0.247
Vitamin A, IU	91	248	435	149	17.3
Vitamin B_1, mg	0.038	0.133	0.06	0.043	0.099
Vitamin B_2, mg	0.032	0.165	0.045	0.024	0.049
Vitamin B_6, mg	0.072	0.419	0.12	0.05	0.049
Vitamin B_{12}, mcg	0	0	0	0	0
Niacin, mg	0.256	1.3	0.45	0.3	0.494
Pantothenic acid, mg	0.192	0.813	0.429	0.34	0.321
Folic acid, mcg	3.84	14.1	9	12.2	25.7
Vitamin C, mg	1.3	1.6	41.6	41.3	93.9
Vitamin E, IU	0.85	—	0.826	0.26	0.185
Calcium, mg	22	269	38	14	22
Copper, mg	0.045	0.585	0.105	0.056	0.082
Iron, mg	0.23	4.18	0.47	0.1	0.49
Magnesium, mg	11	111	15	10	30
Manganese, mg	0.082	0.726	0.216	0.014	0.049
Phosphorus, mg	9	128	40	10	37
Potassium, mg	148	1332	297	167	400
Selenium, mcg	0.384	2.47	0.9	1.79	0.247
Sodium, mg	1	20	1	0	2
Zinc, mg	0.09	0.94	0.18	0.09	0.13
Total lipid, g	0.19	2.18	0.87	0.12	0.25
Total saturated, g	0.038	0.438	0.057	0.017	0.035
Total unsaturated, g	0.092	1.06	0.475	0.031	0.057
Total monounsaturated, g	0.042	0.49	0.076	0.017	0.032
Cholesterol, mg	0	0	0	0	0
Tryptophan, g	0.004	0.049	—	0.002	—
Threonine, g	0.015	0.187	—	—	—
Isoleucine, g	0.015	0.174	—	—	—
Leucine, g	0.021	0.249	—	—	—
Lycine, g	0.019	0.228	—	0.019	—
Methionine, g	0.004	0.047	—	0.002	—
Cystine, g	0.008	0.094	—	—	—
Phenylalanine, g	0.012	0.138	—	—	—
Tyrosine, g	0.02	0.247	—	—	—
Valine, g	0.018	0.215	—	—	—
Arginine, g	0.011	0.131	—	—	—
Histidine, g	0.007	0.08	—	—	—
Alanine, g	0.029	0.344	—	—	—
Aspartic acid, g	0.113	1.34	—	—	—
Glutamic acid, g	0.046	0.552	—	—	—
Glycine, g	0.016	0.193	—	—	—
Proline, g	0.031	0.376	—	—	—
Serine, g	0.024	0.282	—	—	—

Fruits and Fruit Juices

	Grapes, slipskin	Grapes, seedless	Grape juice	Guava	Kiwi, med.
Measure	1 C	1 C	1 C	1	1
Weight, g	92	160	253	90	76
Calories	62	114	155	45	46
Protein, g	0.58	1.06	1.41	0.74	0.75
Carbohydrate, g	15.7	28.4	37.8	10.7	11.3
Fiber, g	0.92	1.6	0.25	5.04	2.6
Vitamin A, IU	92	117	20	713	133
Vitamin B$_1$, mg	0.085	0.147	0.066	0.045	0.015
Vitamin B$_2$, mg	0.052	0.091	0.094	0.045	0.038
Vitamin B$_6$, mg	0.1	0.176	0.164	0.129	0.068
Vitamin B$_{12}$, mcg	0	0	0	0	0
Niacin, mg	0.276	0.48	0.663	1.08	0.38
Pantothenic acid, mg	0.022	0.038	0.104	0.135	—
Folic acid, mcg	3.6	6.3	6.5	12.6	29
Vitamin C, mg	3.7	17.3	0.2	165	74.5
Vitamin E, IU	0.466	1.67	—	1.5	1.27
Calcium, mg	13	17	22	18	20
Copper, mg	0.037	0.144	0.071	0.093	0.119
Iron, mg	0.27	0.41	0.6	0.28	0.31
Magnesium, mg	5	10	24	9	23
Manganese, mg	0.661	0.093	0.911	0.13	—
Phosphorus, mg	9	21	27	23	31
Potassium, mg	176	296	334	256	252
Selenium, mcg	0.184	0.32	0.25	0.54	0.456
Sodium, mg	2	3	7	2	4
Zinc, mg	0.04	0.09	0.13	0.21	0.129
Total lipid, g	0.32	0.92	0.19	0.54	0.34
Total saturated, g	0.105	0.302	0.063	0.155	0.022
Total unsaturated, g	0.094	0.27	0.056	0.228	0.183
Total monounsaturated, g	0.013	0.037	0.008	0.05	0.03
Cholesterol, mg	0	0	0	0	0
Tryptophan, g	0.003	0.005	—	0.006	—
Threonine, g	0.016	0.029	0.04	0.028	—
Isoleucine, g	0.005	0.008	0.018	0.027	—
Leucine, g	0.012	0.022	0.03	0.05	—
Lycine, g	0.013	0.024	0.025	0.021	—
Methionine, g	0.019	0.035	0.003	0.005	—
Cystine, g	0.009	0.018	—	—	—
Phenylalanine, g	0.012	0.022	0.03	0.002	—
Tyrosine, g	0.01	0.019	0.008	0.009	—
Valine, g	0.016	0.029	0.025	0.025	—
Arginine, g	0.042	0.078	0.119	0.019	—
Histidine, g	0.021	0.038	0.018	0.006	—
Alanine, g	0.024	0.045	0.218	0.037	—
Aspartic acid, g	0.071	0.13	0.056	0.047	—
Glutamic acid, g	0.121	0.221	0.278	0.096	—
Glycine, g	0.017	0.032	0.03	0.037	—
Proline, g	0.019	0.035	0.04	0.023	—
Serine, g	0.028	0.051	0.033	0.022	—

Fruits and Fruit Juices

	Kumquat	Lemon juice	Lime juice	Loganberries, frozen	Loquat
Measure	1	1 T	1 T	1 C	1
Weight, g	19	15.2	15.4	147	13.6
Calories	12	3	4	80	6.4
Protein, g	0.17	0.06	0.07	2.23	0.06
Carbohydrate, g	3.12	0.99	1.39	19	1.65
Fiber, g	1.25	0.06	0.06	7.2	0.23
Vitamin A, IU	57	2	2	52	208
Vitamin B_1, mg	0.015	0.006	0.003	0.074	0.003
Vitamin B_2, mg	0.019	0.001	0.002	0.05	0.003
Vitamin B_6, mg	0.01	0.007	0.007	0.096	0.014
Vitamin B_{12}, mcg	0	0	0	0	0
Niacin, mg	0.095	0.03	0.015	1.23	0.024
Pantothenic acid, mg	—	0.014	0.021	0.359	—
Folic acid, mcg	3	1.5	—	37.8	1.9
Vitamin C, mg	7.1	3.8	4.5	22.5	0.136
Vitamin E, IU	0.07	0.02	0.02	4.8	0.18
Calcium, mg	8	2	1	38	2
Copper, mg	0.02	0.006	0.005	0.172	0.004
Iron, mg	0.07	0.02	0	0.94	0.03
Magnesium, mg	2	1	1	32	1
Manganese, mg	0.016	0.003	0.001	1.83	0.015
Phosphorus, mg	4	1	1	38	3
Potassium, mg	37	15	17	213	36
Selenium, mcg	0.114	0.016	0.015	0.88	0.08
Sodium, mg	1	3	0	1	0.136
Zinc, mg	0.02	0.01	0.01	0.5	t
Total lipid, g	0.02	0	0.02	0.46	0.02
Total saturated, g	0.003	0	0.002	0.016	0.004
Total unsaturated, g	0.005	0	0.008	0.259	0.01
Total monounsaturated, g	0.002	0	0.003	0.044	0.001
Cholesterol, mg	0	0	0	0	0
Tryptophan, g	—	—	—	—	0.001
Threonine, g	—	—	—	—	0.002
Isoleucine, g	—	—	—	—	0.002
Leucine, g	—	—	—	—	0.004
Lycine, g	—	—	—	—	0.003
Methionine, g	—	—	—	—	0.001
Cystine, g	—	—	—	—	0.001
Phenylalanine, g	—	—	—	—	0.002
Tyrosine, g	—	—	—	—	0.002
Valine, g	—	—	—	—	0.003
Arginine, g	—	—	—	—	0.002
Histidine, g	—	—	—	—	0.001
Alanine, g	—	—	—	—	0.003
Aspartic acid, g	—	—	—	—	0.008
Glutamic acid, g	—	—	—	—	0.008
Glycine, g	—	—	—	—	0.003
Proline, g	—	—	—	—	0.004
Serine, g	—	—	—	—	0.003

Fruits and Fruit Juices

	Lychee	Mango	Melon, cantaloupe, sm.	Melon, casaba	Melon, honeydew
Measure	1	1	1	⅒	⅒
Weight, g	16	207	441	164	125
Calories	6	135	154	43	46
Protein, g	0.08	1.06	3.9	1.48	0.59
Carbohydrate, g	1.59	35	37	10	11.8
Fiber, g	—	3.7	3.5	1.3	0.77
Vitamin A, IU	—	8060	14217	49	52
Vitamin B_1, mg	0.001	0.12	0.159	0.098	0.099
Vitamin B_2, mg	0.006	0.118	0.09	0.033	0.023
Vitamin B_6, mg	—	0.277	0.5	0.197	0.076
Vitamin B_{12}, mcg	0	0	0	0	0
Niacin, mg	0.058	1.21	2.5	0.656	0.774
Pantothenic acid, mg	—	0.331	0.56	—	0.267
Folic acid, mcg	—	29	75	28	7.5
Vitamin C, mg	6.9	57.3	186	26.2	32
Vitamin E, IU	—	3.46	0.66	0.367	0.28
Calcium, mg	0	21	49	8	8
Copper, mg	0.014	0.228	0.19	0.066	0.053
Iron, mg	0.03	0.26	0.93	0.66	0.09
Magnesium, mg	1	18	49	13	9
Manganese, mg	0.005	0.056	0.2	—	0.023
Phosphorus, mg	3	22	75	11	13
Potassium, mg	16	322	1363	344	350
Selenium, mcg	—	1.24	1.76	0.49	0.5
Sodium, mg	0	4	40	20	13
Zinc, mg	0.01	0.07	0.71	0.26	—
Total lipid, g	—	0.57	1.23	0.16	0.13
Total saturated, g	—	0.137	0.313	0.041	0.031
Total unsaturated, g	—	0.106	0.485	0.064	0.049
Total monounsaturated, g	—	0.209	0.031	0.003	0.003
Cholesterol, mg	0	0	0	0	0
Tryptophan, g	0.001	0.017	—	—	—
Threonine, g	—	0.039	—	—	—
Isoleucine, g	—	0.037	—	—	—
Leucine, g	—	0.064	—	—	—
Lycine, g	0.004	0.085	—	—	—
Methionine, g	0.001	0.01	—	—	—
Cystine, g	—	—	—	—	—
Phenylalanine, g	—	0.035	—	—	—
Tyrosine, g	—	0.021	—	—	—
Valine, g	—	0.054	—	—	—
Arginine, g	—	0.039	—	—	—
Histidine, g	—	0.025	—	—	—
Alanine, g	—	0.106	—	—	—
Aspartic acid, g	—	0.087	—	—	—
Glutamic acid, g	—	0.124	—	—	—
Glycine, g	—	0.043	—	—	—
Proline, g	—	0.037	—	—	—
Serine, g	—	0.046	—	—	—

Fruits and Fruit Juices

	Mulberries	Nectarine	Orange	Orange juice	Papaya
Measure	1 C	1	1	1 C	1
Weight, g	140	136	131	248	304
Calories	61	67	62	111	117
Protein, g	2.02	1.28	1.23	1.74	1.86
Carbohydrate, g	13.7	16	15.4	25.8	30
Fiber, g	2.4	2.2	3.1	0.49	5.5
Vitamin A, IU	35	1001	269	496	6122
Vitamin B$_1$, mg	0.041	0.023	0.114	0.223	0.082
Vitamin B$_2$, mg	0.141	0.056	0.052	0.074	0.097
Vitamin B$_6$, mg	0.07	0.034	0.079	0.099	0.058
Vitamin B$_{12}$, mcg	0	0	0	0	0
Niacin, mg	0.868	1.34	0.369	0.992	1.02
Pantothenic acid, mg	—	0.215	0.328	0.471	0.663
Folic acid, mcg	8.4	5.1	39.7	75	116
Vitamin C, mg	51	7.3	69.7	124	187
Vitamin E, IU	0.94	1.8	0.468	0.33	5
Calcium, mg	55	6	52	27	72
Copper, mg	0.08	0.099	0.059	0.109	0.049
Iron, mg	2.59	0.21	0.13	0.5	0.3
Magnesium, mg	25	11	13	27	31
Manganese, mg	—	0.06	0.033	0.035	0.033
Phosphorus, mg	53	22	18	42	16
Potassium, mg	271	288	237	496	780
Selenium, mcg	0.84	0.54	0.655	0.248	1.8
Sodium, mg	14	0	0	2	8
Zinc, mg	0.168	0.12	0.09	0.13	0.22
Total lipid, g	0.55	0.62	0.16	0.5	0.43
Total saturated, g	0.038	0.069	0.02	0.06	0.131
Total unsaturated, g	0.29	0.313	0.033	0.099	0.094
Total monounsaturated, g	0.057	0.237	0.03	0.089	0.116
Cholesterol, mg	0	0	0	0	0
Tryptophan, g	—	—	0.012	0.005	0.024
Threonine, g	—	—	0.02	0.02	0.033
Isoleucine, g	—	—	0.033	0.02	0.024
Leucine, g	—	—	0.03	0.032	0.049
Lycine, g	—	—	0.062	0.022	0.076
Methionine, g	—	—	0.026	0.007	0.006
Cystine, g	—	—	0.013	0.012	—
Phenylalanine, g	—	—	0.041	0.022	0.027
Tyrosine, g	—	—	0.021	0.01	0.015
Valine, g	—	—	0.052	0.027	0.03
Arginine, g	—	—	0.085	0.117	0.03
Histidine, g	—	—	0.024	0.007	0.015
Alanine, g	—	—	0.066	0.037	0.043
Aspartic acid, g	—	—	0.149	0.186	0.149
Glutamic acid, g	—	—	0.123	0.082	0.1
Glycine, g	—	—	0.123	0.022	0.055
Proline, g	—	—	0.06	0.109	0.03
Serine, g	—	—	0.042	0.032	0.046

Fruits and Fruit Juices

	Passion fruit	Peach	Peach, dried	Peach nectar	Pear
Measure	1	1	10 halves	1 C	1
Weight, g	18	98	130	249	166
Calories	18	42	311	134	98
Protein, g	0.4	0.69	4.69	0.67	0.65
Carbohydrate, g	4.21	9.65	79.7	34.6	25
Fiber, g	1.97	2	10	1.5	4
Vitamin A, IU	126	524	2812	643	33
Vitamin B$_1$, mg	0	0.015	0.003	0.007	0.033
Vitamin B$_2$, mg	0.023	0.036	0.276	0.035	0.066
Vitamin B$_6$, mg	0.018	0.016	0.087	0.017	0.03
Vitamin B$_{12}$, mcg	0	0	0	0	0
Niacin, mg	0.27	0.861	5.68	0.717	0.166
Pantothenic acid, mg	—	0.148	0.73	0.169	0.116
Folic acid, mcg	2.5	3	0.39	3.5	12.1
Vitamin C, mg	5.4	6.5	6.3	13.1	6.6
Vitamin E, IU	0.3	1.17	—	0.037	1.24
Calcium, mg	2	5	37	13	19
Copper, mg	0.015	0.059	0.473	0.172	0.188
Iron, mg	0.29	0.1	5.28	0.47	0.41
Magnesium, mg	5	6	54	11	9
Manganese, mg	—	0.041	0.397	0.047	0.126
Phosphorus, mg	12	11	155	16	18
Potassium, mg	63	193	1295	101	208
Selenium, mcg	0.11	0.46	2.86	0.5	1.2
Sodium, mg	5	0	9	17	1
Zinc, mg	0.018	0.12	0.75	0.2	0.2
Total lipid, g	0.13	0.08	0.99	0.05	0.66
Total saturated, g	0.011	0.009	0.107	0.005	0.037
Total unsaturated, g	0.074	0.044	0.48	0.027	0.156
Total monounsaturated, g	0.015	0.033	0.36	0.02	0.139
Cholesterol, mg	0	0	0	0	0
Tryptophan, g	—	0.002	0.013	—	—
Threonine, g	—	0.023	0.183	—	0.017
Isoleucine, g	—	0.017	0.135	—	0.018
Leucine, g	—	0.035	0.265	—	0.033
Lycine, g	—	0.02	0.151	—	0.023
Methionine, g	—	0.015	0.113	—	0.008
Cystine, g	—	0.005	0.038	—	0.007
Phenylalanine, g	—	0.019	0.148	—	0.017
Tyrosine, g	—	0.016	0.122	—	0.005
Valine, g	—	0.033	0.256	—	0.023
Arginine, g	—	0.016	0.12	—	0.012
Histidine, g	—	0.011	0.087	—	0.007
Alanine, g	—	0.037	0.28	—	0.022
Aspartic acid, g	—	0.102	0.783	—	0.128
Glutamic acid, g	—	0.092	0.712	—	0.046
Glycine, g	—	0.021	0.164	—	0.018
Proline, g	—	0.025	0.198	—	0.018
Serine, g	—	0.028	0.217	—	0.023

Fruits and Fruit Juices

	Pear, Asian	Pear, dried	Pear nectar	Persimmon	Pineapple
Measure	1	10 halves	1 C	1	1 C
Weight, g	275	175	250	168	155
Calories	116	459	149	118	77
Protein, g	1.4	3.28	0.27	0.98	0.6
Carbohydrate, g	29	122	39.4	31.2	19.2
Fiber, g	10	13	1.5	6	1.9
Vitamin A, IU	0	6	1	3640	35
Vitamin B$_1$, mg	0.025	0.014	0.005	0.05	0.143
Vitamin B$_2$, mg	0.028	0.254	0.033	0.034	0.056
Vitamin B$_6$, mg	0.06	0.126	0.035	0.168	0.135
Vitamin B$_{12}$, mcg	0	0	0	0	0
Niacin, mg	0.6	2.4	0.32	0.168	0.651
Pantothenic acid, mg	0.19	0.268	0.055	—	0.248
Folic acid, mcg	22	—	3	12.6	16.4
Vitamin C, mg	10.5	12.3	2.7	12.6	23.9
Vitamin E, IU	1.38	—	0.253	1.48	0.23
Calcium, mg	11	59	11	13	11
Copper, mg	0.14	0.649	0.168	0.19	0.171
Iron, mg	0	3.68	0.65	0.26	0.57
Magnesium, mg	22	58	6	15	21
Manganese, mg	0.17	0.572	0.075	0.596	2.55
Phosphorus, mg	30	103	7	28	11
Potassium, mg	333	932	33	270	175
Selenium, mcg	1.65	7.9	1.25	1	0.93
Sodium, mg	0	10	9	3	1
Zinc, mg	0.06	0.68	0.16	0.18	0.12
Total lipid, g	0.63	1.1	0.03	0.31	0.66
Total saturated, g	0.03	0.061	0.003	0.034	0.05
Total unsaturated, g	0.15	0.259	0.007	0.072	0.226
Total monounsaturated, g	0.135	0.231	0.007	0.062	0.074
Cholesterol, mg	0	0	0	0	9
Tryptophan, g	0.014	—	—	0.017	0.008
Threonine, g	0.036	0.086	—	0.05	0.019
Isoleucine, g	0.038	0.095	—	0.042	0.02
Leucine, g	0.069	0.165	—	0.071	0.029
Lycine, g	0.047	0.116	—	0.055	0.039
Methionine, g	0.017	0.039	—	0.008	0.017
Cystine, g	0.014	0.032	—	0.022	0.003
Phenylalanine, g	0.036	0.086	—	0.044	0.019
Tyrosine, g	0.011	0.028	—	0.027	0.019
Valine, g	0.049	0.116	—	0.05	0.025
Arginine, g	0.025	0.056	—	0.042	0.028
Histidine, g	0.014	0.035	—	0.02	0.014
Alanine, g	0.047	0.109	—	0.049	0.026
Aspartic acid, g	0.27	0.644	—	0.096	0.088
Glutamic acid, g	0.1	0.236	—	0.128	0.07
Glycine, g	0.04	0.095	—	0.042	0.026
Proline, g	0.044	0.089	—	0.037	0.02
Serine, g	0.05	0.117	—	0.037	0.039

Fruits and Fruit Juices

	Pineapple juice	Plantain	Plum	Plum, sapotes	Pomegranate
Measure	1 C	1 C	1	1	1
Weight, g	250	148	70	225	154
Calories	139	181	36	302	104
Protein, g	0.8	1.92	0.52	1.8	1.47
Carbohydrate, g	34.4	47.2	8.59	76	26.4
Fiber, g	0.5	3.4	0.99	5.9	0.92
Vitamin A, IU	12	1668	213	923	0
Vitamin B$_1$, mg	0.138	0.077	0.028	0.022	0.046
Vitamin B$_2$, mg	0.055	0.08	0.063	0.045	0.046
Vitamin B$_6$, mg	0.24	0.443	0.053	—	0.162
Vitamin B$_{12}$, mcg	0	0	0	0	0
Niacin, mg	0.643	1.01	0.330	4.1	0.462
Pantothenic acid, mg	0.25	0.385	0.120	—	0.918
Folic acid, mcg	57.7	32.6	1.4	—	9.24
Vitamin C, mg	26.7	27.2	6.3	45	9.4
Vitamin E, IU	0.075	0.6	0.59	—	1.26
Calcium, mg	42	4	2	88	5
Copper, mg	0.225	0.12	0.028	—	0.108
Iron, mg	0.65	0.89	0.07	2.25	0.46
Magnesium, mg	34	55	4	68	4.6
Manganese, mg	2.47	—	0.032	—	—
Phosphorus, mg	20	50	7	63	12
Potassium, mg	334	739	113	774	399
Selenium, mcg	0.25	2.22	0.33	—	0.92
Sodium, mg	2	6	0	23	5
Zinc, mg	0.29	0.21	0.06	—	0.185
Total lipid, g	0.2	0.55	0.41	1.35	0.46
Total saturated, g	0.013	0.212	0.032	—	0.059
Total unsaturated, g	0.07	0.102	0.088	—	0.097
Total monounsaturated, g	0.022	0.047	0.268	—	0.071
Cholesterol, mg	0	0	0	0	0
Tryptophan, g	—	0.022	—	0.052	—
Threonine, g	—	0.05	0.011	0.131	—
Isoleucine, g	—	0.053	0.011	0.103	—
Leucine, g	—	0.087	0.014	0.189	—
Lycine, g	—	0.089	0.011	0.216	—
Methionine, g	—	0.025	0.004	0.036	—
Cystine, g	—	0.03	0.003	—	—
Phenylalanine, g	—	0.065	0.011	0.119	—
Tyrosine, g	—	0.047	0.004	0.124	—
Valine, g	—	0.068	0.013	0.173	—
Arginine, g	—	0.16	0.009	0.124	—
Histidine, g	—	0.095	0.009	0.095	—
Alanine, g	—	0.075	0.019	0.259	—
Aspartic acid, g	—	0.16	0.164	1.2	—
Glutamic acid, g	—	0.172	0.024	0.486	—
Glycine, g	—	0.067	0.008	0.128	—
Proline, g	—	0.074	0.022	0.128	—
Serine, g	—	0.061	0.013	0.511	—

Fruits and Fruit Juices

	Prickly pear	Prune	Prune juice	Quince	Raisins packed
Measure	1	10	1 C	1	1 C
Weight, g	103	84	256	92	165
Calories	42	201	181	53	488
Protein, g	0.75	2.19	1.55	0.37	4.16
Carbohydrate, g	9.86	52.7	44.6	14	12.9
Fiber, g	3.7	6	2.5	1.56	6.6
Vitamin A, IU	53	1669	9	37	0
Vitamin B$_1$, mg	0.014	0.068	0.041	0.018	0.185
Vitamin B$_2$, mg	0.062	0.136	0.179	0.028	0.3
Vitamin B$_6$, mg	0.062	0.222	0.558	0.037	0.31
Vitamin B$_{12}$, mcg	0	0	0	0	0
Niacin, mg	0.474	1.64	2.01	0.184	1.83
Pantothenic acid, mg	—	0.386	0.274	0.075	—
Folic acid, mcg	6.2	3.1	1	2.76	5.5
Vitamin C, mg	14.4	2.8	10.6	13.8	9
Vitamin E, IU	0.015	3.28	0.04	0.75	1.7
Calcium, mg	58	43	30	10	46
Copper, mg	0.08	0.361	0.174	0.12	0.498
Iron, mg	0.31	2.08	3.03	0.64	4.27
Magnesium, mg	88	38	36	7	49
Manganese, mg	—	0.185	0.387	—	0.441
Phosphorus, mg	25	66	64	16	124
Potassium, mg	226	626	706	181	1362
Selenium, mcg	0.62	1.93	1.54	0.55	1.15
Sodium, mg	6	3	11	4	47
Zinc, mg	0.124	0.45	0.52	0.037	0.3
Total lipid, g	0.53	0.43	0.08	0.09	0.9
Total saturated, g	0.069	0.034	0.008	0.009	0.294
Total unsaturated, g	0.219	0.009	0.018	0.046	0.223
Total monounsaturated, g	0.077	0.029	0.054	0.033	0.03
Cholesterol, mg	0	0	0	0	0
Tryptophan, g	—	—	—	—	—
Threonine, g	—	—	—	—	—
Isoleucine, g	—	—	—	—	—
Leucine, g	—	—	—	—	—
Lycine, g	—	—	—	—	—
Methionine, g	—	—	—	—	—
Cystine, g	—	—	—	—	—
Phenylalanine, g	—	—	—	—	—
Tyrosine, g	—	—	—	—	—
Valine, g	—	—	—	—	—
Arginine, g	—	—	—	—	—
Histidine, g	—	—	—	—	—
Alanine, g	—	—	—	—	—
Aspartic acid, g	—	—	—	—	—
Glutamic acid, g	—	—	—	—	—
Glycine, g	—	—	—	—	—
Proline, g	—	—	—	—	—
Serine, g	—	—	—	—	—

Fruits and Fruit Juices

	Raspberries	Rhubarb	Straw-berries	Tangerine (mandarin)	Tangerine juice	Water-melon
Measure	1 C	1 C	1 C halves	1	1 C	1 C
Weight, g	123	122	152	84	247	160
Calories	61	26	45	37	106	50
Protein, g	1.11	1.09	0.91	0.53	1.24	0.99
Carbohydrate, g	14.2	5.53	10.4	9.4	25	11.5
Fiber, g	8.4	2.2	3.5	1.9	0.5	0.77
Vitamin A, IU	160	122	41	773	1037	585
Vitamin B$_1$, mg	0.037	0.024	0.03	0.088	0.148	0.128
Vitamin B$_2$, mg	0.111	0.037	0.098	0.018	0.049	0.032
Vitamin B$_6$, mg	0.07	0.029	0.088	0.056	0.104	0.23
Vitamin B$_{12}$, mcg	0	0	0	0	0	0
Niacin, mg	1.1	0.366	0.343	0.134	0.247	0.32
Pantothenic acid, mg	0.295	0.104	0.507	0.168	0.31	0.339
Folic acid, mcg	32	8.7	26.4	17.1	11.4	3.4
Vitamin C, mg	30.8	9.8	84.5	26	76.6	15.4
Vitamin E, IU	0.82	0.364	0.32	0.3	0.22	0.34
Calcium, mg	27	105	21	12	44	13
Copper, mg	0.091	0.026	0.073	0.024	0.062	0.051
Iron, mg	0.7	0.27	0.57	0.09	0.49	0.28
Magnesium, mg	22	14	16	10	20	17
Manganese, mg	1.24	0.239	0.432	0.027	0.091	0.059
Phosphorus, mg	15	17	28	8	35	14
Potassium, mg	187	351	247	132	440	186
Selenium, mcg	0.74	1.34	1.06	0.42	0.247	0.154
Sodium, mg	0	5	2	1	2	3
Zinc, mg	0.57	0.13	0.19	0.202	0.06	0.11
Total lipid, g	0.68	0.24	0.55	0.16	0.49	0.68
Total saturated, g	0.023	0.065	0.03	0.018	0.059	0.074
Total unsaturated, g	0.385	0.121	0.28	0.031	0.099	0.225
Total monounsaturated, g	0.065	0.048	0.079	0.029	0.089	0.165
Cholesterol, mg	0	0	0	0	0	0
Tryptophan, g	—	—	0.01	0.005	0.002	0.011
Threonine, g	—	—	0.028	0.008	0.015	0.043
Isoleucine, g	—	—	0.021	0.014	0.012	0.03
Leucine, g	—	—	0.046	0.013	0.025	0.029
Lycine, g	—	—	0.037	0.027	0.017	0.099
Methionine, g	—	—	0.001	0.011	0.005	0.01
Cystine, g	—	—	0.007	0.006	0.01	0.003
Phenylalanine, g	—	—	0.027	0.018	0.015	0.024
Tyrosine, g	—	—	0.031	0.009	0.007	0.019
Valine, g	—	—	0.027	0.023	0.02	0.026
Arginine, g	—	—	0.039	0.037	0.084	0.094
Histidine, g	—	—	0.018	0.01	0.005	0.01
Alanine, g	—	—	0.046	0.029	0.027	0.027
Aspartic acid, g	—	—	0.206	0.065	0.131	0.062
Glutamic acid, g	—	—	0.134	0.054	0.059	0.101
Glycine, g	—	—	0.036	0.054	0.017	0.016
Proline, g	—	—	0.028	0.026	0.077	0.038
Serine, g	—	—	0.034	0.018	0.022	0.026

Grains

	Amaranth	Barley, pot or scotch	Barley, pearled	Buckwheat groats	Bulgur
Measure	1 C	1 C	1 C	1 C	1 C
Weight, g	195	184	200	164	140
Calories	729	651	704	567	478
Protein, g	28	23	20	19	19
Carbohydrate, g	129	135	155	123	106
Fiber, g	30	32	31	17	25
Vitamin A, IU	0	41	44	0	0
Vitamin B$_1$, mg	0.16	1.19	0.38	0.37	0.32
Vitamin B$_2$, mg	0.41	0.5	0.23	0.44	0.16
Vitamin B$_6$, mg	0.44	0.59	0.52	0.58	0.48
Vitamin B$_{12}$, mcg	0	0	0	0	0
Niacin, mg	2.5	7.4	9	8.4	7.8
Pantothenic acid, mg	2	0.52	0.56	2	1.5
Folic acid, mcg	96	40	46	69	38
Vitamin C, mg	8.2	0	0	0	0
Vitamin E, IU	2.98	1.64	0.39	2.5	0.33
Calcium, mg	298	68	58	28	49
Copper, mg	1.5	0.92	0.84	1	0.47
Iron, mg	15	5.4	5	4	3.4
Magnesium, mg	519	245	158	362	230
Manganese, mg	4.4	3.6	2.6	2.7	4.3
Phosphorus, mg	887	485	442	523	420
Potassium, mg	714	832	560	525	574
Selenium, mcg	—	—	75	14	3.2
Sodium, mg	41	22	18	18	24
Zinc, mg	6.2	5	4.3	4	2.7
Total lipid, g	12.7	4	2.3	4.4	2.5
Total saturated, g	3.2	0.88	0.49	0.97	0.34
Total unsaturated, g	5.64	2.1	1.12	1.36	0.76
Total monounsaturated, g	2.8	0.54	0.3	1.36	0.24
Cholesterol, mg	0	0	0	0	—
Tryptophan, g	0.35	0.38	0.33	0.28	0.266
Threonine, g	1.1	0.78	0.67	0.74	0.5
Isoleucine, g	1.14	0.84	0.72	0.723	0.64
Leucine, g	1.7	1.56	1.35	1.2	1.2
Lycine, g	1.46	0.86	0.74	0.976	0.475
Methionine, g	0.44	0.44	0.38	0.25	0.266
Cystine, g	0.37	0.51	0.44	0.33	0.4
Phenylalanine, g	1.1	1.3	1.1	0.756	0.8
Tyrosine, g	0.64	0.66	0.57	0.35	0.5
Valine, g	1.3	1.13	0.97	0.98	0.776
Arginine, g	2.1	1.2	0.99	1.4	0.81
Histidine, g	0.76	0.52	0.45	0.45	0.4
Alanine, g	1.56	0.9	0.77	1.1	0.6
Aspartic acid, g	2.5	1.4	1.24	1.65	0.88
Glutamic acid, g	4.4	6	5.2	2.97	5.43
Glycine, g	3.2	0.8	0.72	1.5	0.7
Proline, g	1.36	2.7	2.4	0.74	1.78
Serine, g	2.24	0.97	0.84	0.99	0.8

Grains

	Cornmeal, degermed, enr.	Cornmeal, whl. grain	Millet	Oats	Pasta, corn
Measure	1 C	1 C	1 C	1 C	1 C
Weight, g	138	122	200	156	105
Calories	505	441	756	607	375
Protein, g	11	10.6	22.6	26	7.8
Carbohydrate, g	107	93	146	103	83
Fiber, g	10	9	17	17	12
Vitamin A, IU	0	0	0	0	179
Vitamin B$_1$, mg	0.987	0.47	0.84	1.2	0.24
Vitamin B$_2$, mg	0.56	0.25	0.58	0.22	0.09
Vitamin B$_6$, mg	0.355	0.37	0.77	0.19	0.216
Vitamin B$_{12}$, mcg	0	0	0	0	0
Niacin, mg	6.95	4.4	9.4	1.5	2.55
Pantothenic acid, mg	—	0.52	1.7	2	0.51
Folic acid, mcg	258	31	170	87	26
Vitamin C, mg	0	0	0	0	0
Vitamin E, IU	0.68	0.6	0.54	1.64	1.58
Calcium, mg	6.9	7.3	16	84	4.2
Copper, mg	0.11	0.24	1.5	0.98	0.212
Iron, mg	5.7	4	6	7.4	0.98
Magnesium, mg	55	155	228	276	125
Manganese, mg	0.145	0.61	3.3	7.7	0.51
Phosphorus, mg	116	294	570	816	266
Potassium, mg	223	350	390	670	309
Selenium, mcg	11	19	5.4	—	8.3
Sodium, mg	4	43	10	3	3.2
Zinc, mg	0.99	2.1	3.4	6.2	1.9
Total lipid, g	2.3	4	8.5	11	2.18
Total saturated, g	0.31	0.46	1.4	1.9	0.3
Total unsaturated, g	0.98	2	4.3	3.95	0.97
Total monounsaturated, g	0.57	1.2	1.55	3.4	0.57
Cholesterol, mg	0	0	0	0	0
Tryptophan, g	—	0.07	0.24	0.365	0.056
Threonine, g	—	0.37	0.7	0.9	0.3
Isoleucine, g	—	0.36	0.9	1.1	0.28
Leucine, g	—	1.2	2.8	2	0.96
Lycine, g	—	0.28	0.4	1.1	0.22
Methionine, g	—	0.21	0.44	0.49	0.164
Cystine, g	—	0.178	0.4	0.64	0.14
Phenylalanine, g	—	0.49	1.16	1.4	0.384
Tyrosine, g	—	0.4	0.68	0.9	0.32
Valine, g	—	0.5	1.16	1.5	0.4
Arginine, g	—	0.5	0.76	1.9	0.4
Histidine, g	—	0.3	0.47	0.63	0.24
Alanine, g	—	0.7	1.97	1.4	0.6
Aspartic acid, g	—	0.69	1.45	2.26	0.545
Glutamic acid, g	—	1.86	4.8	5.8	1.5
Glycine, g	—	0.41	0.57	1.3	0.32
Proline, g	—	0.87	1.75	1.46	0.684
Serine, g	—	0.47	1.3	1.2	0.37

Grains

	Pasta, couscous	Pasta, macaroni, enr.	Pasta, macaroni, whole wheat, spiral	Pasta, spaghetti, enr.	Pasta, spaghetti, whole wheat
Measure	1 C	1 C	1 C	2 oz	2 oz
Weight, g	173	105	105	57	57
Calories	650	390	365	211	198
Protein, g	22	13	15	7.3	8.4
Carbohydrate, g	134	78	78	43	43
Fiber, g	8.7	2.5	8.7	1.4	—
Vitamin A, IU	0	0	0	0	0
Vitamin B_1, mg	0.28	1.1	0.5	0.59	0.278
Vitamin B_2, mg	0.135	0.67	0.15	0.25	0.08
Vitamin B_6, mg	0.19	0.1	0.23	0.06	0.13
Vitamin B_{12}, mcg	0	0	0	0	0
Niacin, mg	6.04	7.9	5.4	4.3	2.9
Pantothenic acid, mg	2.2	0.45	1.03	0.25	0.56
Folic acid, mcg	35	243	60	132	33
Vitamin C, mg	0	0	0	0	0
Vitamin E, IU	—	0.2	—	0.13	—
Calcium, mg	42	19	42	10	23
Copper, mg	0.43	0.27	0.48	0.145	0.26
Iron, mg	1.9	4.1	3.8	2.2	2
Magnesium, mg	76	50	150	27	82
Manganese, mg	1.35	0.73	3.2	0.4	1.7
Phosphorus, mg	294	158	271	86	147
Potassium, mg	287	170	226	92	123
Selenium, mcg	—	65	—	3.5	42
Sodium, mg	17	7.4	8.4	4	4.6
Zinc, mg	1.44	1.3	2.5	0.7	1.4
Total lipid, g	1.11	1.66	1.47	0.9	0.8
Total saturated, g	0.2	0.24	0.27	0.13	0.147
Total unsaturated, g	0.44	0.68	0.58	0.37	0.317
Total monounsaturated, g	0.15	0.2	0.21	0.11	0.111
Cholesterol, mg	0	0	0	0	0
Tryptophan, g	0.28	0.17	0.197	0.09	0.11
Threonine, g	0.58	0.355	0.4	0.19	0.22
Isoleucine, g	0.85	0.52	0.6	0.28	0.325
Leucine, g	1.5	0.92	1.05	0.5	0.57
Lycine, g	0.42	0.26	0.34	0.14	0.185
Methionine, g	0.34	0.21	0.25	0.11	0.135
Cystine, g	0.62	0.38	0.32	0.21	0.174
Phenylalanine, g	1.1	0.65	0.76	0.354	0.415
Tyrosine, g	0.58	0.35	0.4	0.19	0.22
Valine, g	0.94	0.57	0.667	0.31	0.36
Arginine, g	0.8	0.495	0.54	0.27	0.295
Histidine, g	0.45	0.27	0.36	0.15	0.196
Alanine, g	0.65	0.39	0.48	0.2	0.26
Aspartic acid, g	0.9	0.55	0.69	0.3	0.376
Glutamic acid, g	7.96	4.84	5.33	2.63	2.9
Glycine, g	0.7	0.4	0.56	0.23	0.3
Proline, g	2.43	1.48	1.64	0.8	0.9
Serine, g	0.75	0.63	0.75	0.34	0.41

Grains

	Popcorn, oil popped	Rice, brown	Rice cake, brown, plain	Rice, flour, brown	Rice, white, enr.
Measure	1 C	1 C	1	1 C	1 C
Weight, g	11	196	9	158	195
Calories	54	704	35	574	708
Protein, g	0.99	14.8	0.74	11	13.1
Carbohydrate, g	6.3	152	7	121	157
Fiber, g	1.1	6.5	0.38	7.3	2.7
Vitamin A, IU	17	0	4	0	0
Vitamin B_1, mg	0.015	0.68	t	0.7	1.1
Vitamin B_2, mg	0.02	0.08	0.015	0.13	0.09
Vitamin B_6, mg	0.03	1	0.013	1.2	0.3
Vitamin B_{12}, mcg	0	0	0	0	0
Niacin, mg	0.17	9.2	0.7	10	9.9
Pantothenic acid, mg	0.034	2.1	0.09	2.5	2.6
Folic acid, mcg	1.9	32	1.9	25	450
Vitamin C, mg	0	0	0	0	0
Vitamin E, IU	0.02	1.86	0.1	1.7	0.38
Calcium, mg	1	64	1	17	17
Copper, mg	0.04	0.4	0.04	0.36	0.2
Iron, mg	0.4	3.2	0.13	3	8.5
Magnesium, mg	12	272	12	177	68
Manganese, mg	0.1	7.1	0.34	6.3	2.1
Phosphorus, mg	28	502	32	532	211
Potassium, mg	25	509	26	457	168
Selenium, mcg	0.8	43	2.2	—	29
Sodium, mg	97	7.6	29	13	1.95
Zinc, mg	0.3	3.6	0.27	3.9	2.5
Total lipid, g	3.09	5.1	0.25	4.4	1.5
Total saturated, g	0.538	1	0.05	0.88	0.31
Total unsaturated, g	1.5	1.8	0.089	1.57	0.3
Total monounsaturated, g	0.9	1.85	0.09	1.59	0.35
Cholesterol, mg	0	0	0	0	0
Tryptophan, g	0.007	0.18	0.009	0.15	0.15
Threonine, g	0.037	0.52	0.027	0.42	0.46
Isoleucine, g	0.036	0.6	0.03	0.48	0.56
Leucine, g	0.12	1.18	0.06	0.95	1.1
Lycine, g	0.03	0.54	0.03	0.44	0.47
Methionine, g	0.02	0.3	0.02	0.26	0.3
Cystine, g	0.02	0.17	0.01	0.14	0.26
Phenylalanine, g	0.05	0.74	0.038	0.59	0.69
Tyrosine, g	0.04	0.5	0.03	0.43	0.4
Valine, g	0.05	0.84	0.04	0.67	0.79
Arginine, g	0.05	1.1	0.056	0.87	1.1
Histidine, g	0.03	0.36	0.02	0.3	0.3
Alanine, g	0.07	0.83	0.04	0.67	0.75
Aspartic acid, g	0.07	1.33	0.07	1.1	1.2
Glutamic acid, g	0.19	2.9	0.15	2.3	2.5
Glycine, g	0.04	0.7	0.04	0.56	0.59
Proline, g	0.086	0.67	0.034	0.54	0.61
Serine, g	0.05	0.73	0.04	0.6	0.67

	Grains		**Breads**	
	Rice, wild	Quinoa	Bagels, enr.	Cracked wheat, enr.
Measure	1 C	1 C	1 (4 in dia.)	1 slice
Weight, g	160	170	89	23
Calories	565	636	245	60
Protein, g	22.6	22	9	2
Carbohydrate, g	121	117	48	12
Fiber, g	9.9	10	2	1.4
Vitamin A, IU	30	0	0	0
Vitamin B_1, mg	0.18	0.337	0.48	0.09
Vitamin B_2, mg	0.42	0.67	0.28	0.06
Vitamin B_6, mg	0.63	0.38	0.045	0.076
Vitamin B_{12}, mcg	0	0	0	0
Niacin, mg	9.9	4.98	4	0.9
Pantothenic acid, mg	1.63	1.78	0.3	0.14
Folic acid, mcg	152	83	78	15
Vitamin C, mg	0	0	0	0
Vitamin E, IU	1.7	—	0.05	0.22
Calcium, mg	30	102	66	11
Copper, mg	0.84	1.4	0.145	0.056
Iron, mg	3	16	3.2	0.7
Magnesium, mg	283	357	26	13
Manganese, mg	2	3.8	0.48	0.34
Phosphorus, mg	692	697	85	38
Potassium, mg	683	1258	90	44
Selenium, mcg	4.5	—	28.5	6
Sodium, mg	11	36	475	135
Zinc, mg	9.5	5.6	0.78	0.3
Total lipid, g	1.7	9.9	1.4	0.98
Total saturated, g	0.25	1	0.24	0.23
Total unsaturated, g	1.1	2.6	0.11	0.17
Total monounsaturated, g	0.25	4	0.144	0.48
Cholesterol, mg	0	0	0	0
Tryptophan, g	0.286	—	0.136	0.03
Threonine, g	0.75	0.78	0.33	0.065
Isoleucine, g	0.99	0.8	0.44	0.085
Leucine, g	1.6	1.34	0.8	0.15
Lycine, g	1	1.25	0.276	0.06
Methionine, g	0.7	0.445	0.21	0.037
Cystine, g	0.28	—	0.25	0.05
Phenylalanine, g	1.2	0.9	0.57	0.1
Tyrosine, g	0.995	0.6	0.33	0.06
Valine, g	1.4	1	0.5	0.1
Arginine, g	1.8	1.56	0.4	0.087
Histidine, g	0.6	0.5	0.25	0.05
Alanine, g	1.3	1.1	0.38	0.076
Aspartic acid, g	2.3	1.6	0.53	0.11
Glutamic acid, g	4	2.65	0.854	0.7
Glycine, g	1.1	1.16	0.41	0.08
Proline, g	0.83	0.7	1.3	0.23
Serine, g	1.25	0.8	0.56	0.1

Breads

	English muffin, enr.	English muffin, whole-wheat	French, enr.	Mixed grain, 7 grain
Measure	1	1	1 slice	1 slice
Weight, g	57	66	20	26
Calories	130	134	58	65
Protein, g	4.4	5.8	1.8	2.6
Carbohydrate, g	26	27	11.1	12
Fiber, g	1.5	4.4	0.75	1.7
Vitamin A, IU	0	0	0	0
Vitamin B_1, mg	0.23	0.2	0.13	0.11
Vitamin B_2, mg	0.136	0.09	0.08	0.09
Vitamin B_6, mg	0.025	0.11	0.01	0.087
Vitamin B_{12}, mcg	0.023	0	0	0
Niacin, mg	2	2.25	1.2	1.14
Pantothenic acid, mg	0.25	0.46	0.08	0.133
Folic acid, mcg	46	32	24	21
Vitamin C, mg	0	0	0	0.078
Vitamin E, IU	0.14	0.69	0.1	0.25
Calcium, mg	99	175	19	24
Copper, mg	0.1	0.14	0.05	0.07
Iron, mg	1.08	1.62	0.6	0.9
Magnesium, mg	12	47	6.8	14
Manganese, mg	0.2	1.2	0.127	0.39
Phosphorus, mg	76	186	26	46
Potassium, mg	75	139	28	53
Selenium, mcg	1.2	27	7.9	7.7
Sodium, mg	265	420	152	127
Zinc, mg	0.4	1.06	0.22	0.33
Total lipid, g	1	1.39	0.64	0.088
Total saturated, g	0.48	0.22	0.14	0.2
Total unsaturated, g	0.51	0.55	0.17	0.24
Total monounsaturated, g	0.17	0.34	0.3	0.4
Cholesterol, mg	0	0	0	0
Tryptophan, g	0.5	0.085	0.025	0.034
Threonine, g	0.14	0.2	0.06	0.08
Isoleucine, g	0.18	0.23	0.085	0.1
Leucine, g	0.32	0.4	0.154	0.18
Lycine, g	0.14	0.2	0.05	0.08
Methionine, g	0.08	0.1	0.04	0.04
Cystine, g	0.09	0.125	0.05	0.056
Phenylalanine, g	0.22	0.275	0.1	0.13
Tyrosine, g	0.13	0.18	0.06	0.074
Valine, g	0.2	0.27	0.1	0.12
Arginine, g	0.17	0.275	0.08	0.115
Histidine, g	0.1	0.135	0.048	0.06
Alanine, g	0.16	0.23	0.07	0.1
Aspartic acid, g	0.23	0.337	0.1	0.15
Glutamic acid, g	1.4	1.7	0.75	0.78
Glycine, g	0.16	0.24	0.078	0.1
Proline, g	0.46	0.55	0.25	0.26
Serine, g	0.2	0.27	0.11	0.13

Breads

	Pita, enr.	Pita, whole wheat	Pumpernickel	Rolls, dinner, enr.
Measure	1 sm.	1 sm.	1 slice	1
Weight, g	28	28	32	28
Calories	77	75	79	85
Protein, g	2.55	2.7	2.9	2.4
Carbohydrate, g	15.6	15	17	14
Fiber, g	0.6	2.1	2.1	0.85
Vitamin A, IU	0	0	0	0
Vitamin B_1, mg	0.17	0.095	0.07	0.14
Vitamin B_2, mg	0.09	0.022	0.04	0.09
Vitamin B_6, mg	0.01	0.07	0.05	0.015
Vitamin B_{12}, mcg	0	0	0	0
Niacin, mg	1.3	0.795	0.99	1.14
Pantothenic acid, mg	0.1	0.23	0.16	0.14
Folic acid, mcg	27	9.8	26	27
Vitamin C, mg	0	0	0	0.03
Vitamin E, IU	0.02	0.38	0.21	0.37
Calcium, mg	24	4.2	27	34
Copper, mg	0.05	0.08	0.09	0.04
Iron, mg	0.7	0.857	0.8	0.9
Magnesium, mg	7.3	19	23	6.5
Manganese, mg	0.14	0.487	0.42	0.13
Phosphorus, mg	27	50	57	33
Potassium, mg	34	48	67	38
Selenium, mcg	7.6	13	7.8	7.7
Sodium, mg	150	149	215	148
Zinc, mg	0.235	0.43	0.365	0.22
Total lipid, g	0.336	0.728	0.9	2.1
Total saturated, g	0.046	0.115	0.14	0.497
Total unsaturated, g	0.15	0.295	0.396	0.34
Total monounsaturated, g	0.029	0.088	0.3	1.05
Cholesterol, mg	0	0	0	0.284
Tryptophan, g	0.029	0.042	0.03	0.028
Threonine, g	0.07	0.08	0.085	0.07
Isoleucine, g	0.1	0.1	0.1	0.1
Leucine, g	0.18	0.19	0.2	0.17
Lycine, g	0.06	0.074	0.08	0.067
Methionine, g	0.045	0.043	0.05	0.043
Cystine, g	0.055	0.064	0.06	0.05
Phenylalanine, g	0.125	0.13	0.135	0.12
Tyrosine, g	0.07	0.08	0.076	0.07
Valine, g	0.11	0.123	0.13	0.1
Arginine, g	0.09	0.127	0.115	0.1
Histidine, g	0.05	0.06	0.06	0.05
Alanine, g	0.085	0.1	0.1	0.08
Aspartic acid, g	0.114	0.14	0.15	0.114
Glutamic acid, g	0.85	0.88	0.87	0.8
Glycine, g	0.09	0.1	0.1	0.08
Proline, g	0.28	0.3	0.304	0.26
Serine, g	0.123	0.13	0.13	0.117

Breads

	Rolls, dinner, whole wheat	Rolls, hamburger/ hotdog, enr.	Rye	Wheat incl. wheatberry
Measure	1	1	1 slice	1 slice
Weight, g	35	40	32	25
Calories	90	119	83	65
Protein, g	3.5	3.3	2.1	2.3
Carbohydrate, g	18.3	21.2	12	12
Fiber, g	2.7	1.16	1.9	1
Vitamin A, IU	t	0	2.24	0
Vitamin B₁, mg	0.12	0.21	0.14	0.1
Vitamin B₂, mg	0.05	0.13	0.11	0.07
Vitamin B₆, mg	0.07	0.02	0.02	0.024
Vitamin B₁₂, mcg	0	0	0	0
Niacin, mg	1.1	1.7	1.22	1
Pantothenic acid, mg	1.76	0.23	0.1	0.11
Folic acid, mcg	11	41	26	19
Vitamin C, mg	0	0.04	0.13	0
Vitamin E, IU	0.73	0.99	0.17	0.2
Calcium, mg	37	60	23	26
Copper, mg	0.086	0.05	0.06	0.05
Iron, mg	0.8	1.4	0.9	0.83
Magnesium, mg	40	8.6	10	12
Manganese, mg	0.8	0.14	0.3	0.26
Phosphorus, mg	98	34	40	38
Potassium, mg	102	61	53	50
Selenium, mcg	18	11	9.9	17
Sodium, mg	197	241	211	133
Zinc, mg	0.7	0.21	0.4	0.26
Total lipid, g	1.69	2.2	1.06	1.1
Total saturated, g	0.3	0.5	0.2	0.224
Total unsaturated, g	0.778	1.08	0.256	0.227
Total monounsaturated, g	0.4	0.36	0.42	0.43
Cholesterol, mg	0	0	0	0
Tryptophan, g	0.048	0.043	0.03	0.03
Threonine, g	0.09	0.1	0.08	0.07
Isoleucine, g	0.12	0.14	0.1	0.09
Leucine, g	0.216	0.26	0.185	0.16
Lycine, g	0.1	0.1	0.075	0.065
Methionine, g	0.05	0.065	0.044	0.04
Cystine, g	0.07	0.078	0.055	0.05
Phenylalanine, g	0.15	0.18	0.132	0.11
Tyrosine, g	0.09	0.1	0.07	0.067
Valine, g	0.145	0.16	0.12	0.1
Arginine, g	0.147	0.133	0.1	0.1
Histidine, g	0.07	0.08	0.06	0.05
Alanine, g	0.113	0.12	0.1	0.08
Aspartic acid, g	0.167	0.168	0.14	0.12
Glutamic acid, g	0.97	1.21	0.8	0.73
Glycine, g	0.125	0.13	0.1	0.086
Proline, g	0.32	0.41	0.3	0.24
Serine, g	0.15	0.177	0.13	0.1

Breads

	White, enr.	Whole wheat	Crackers, graham	Crackers, soda
Measure	1 slice	1 slice	1	1
Weight, g	23	28	14.2	2.8
Calories	62	69	55	12.5
Protein, g	2	2.4	1.1	0.26
Carbohydrate, g	11.6	11	10.4	2
Fiber, g	0.58	1.9	0.22	0.09
Vitamin A, IU	0	0	0	0
Vitamin B$_1$, mg	0.12	0.098	0.01	0.017
Vitamin B$_2$, mg	0.085	0.057	0.03	0.014
Vitamin B$_6$, mg	0.009	0.05	t	t
Vitamin B$_{12}$, mcg	t	0	0	0
Niacin, mg	0.99	1.1	0.2	0.03
Pantothenic acid, mg	0.1	0.174	0.075	0.014
Folic acid, mcg	24	13	8.4	3.7
Vitamin C, mg	0	0	0	0
Vitamin E, IU	0.14	0.3	0.43	0.07
Calcium, mg	20	23	3.4	3.6
Copper, mg	0.05	0.06	0.03	0.006
Iron, mg	0.6	0.9	0.2	0.16
Magnesium, mg	5	25	5.68	0.81
Manganese, mg	0.07	0.65	0.113	0.02
Phosphorus, mg	22	64	21	2.5
Potassium, mg	24	70	55	3.4
Selenium, mcg	6.44	10	1.4	0.59
Sodium, mg	117	148	95	31
Zinc, mg	0.155	0.5	0.113	0.023
Total lipid, g	0.79	1.17	1.3	0.37
Total saturated, g	0.16	0.257	0.3	0.075
Total unsaturated, g	0.475	0.28	0.53	0.05
Total monounsaturated, g	0.18	0.47	0.57	0.19
Cholesterol, mg	0.25	0	0	0
Tryptophan, g	0.024	0.04	0.013	0.004
Threonine, g	0.06	0.08	0.03	0.01
Isoleucine, g	0.08	0.1	0.034	0.01
Leucine, g	0.145	0.19	0.066	0.02
Lycine, g	0.056	0.085	0.023	0.01
Methionine, g	0.036	0.043	0.017	0.005
Cystine, g	0.04	0.06	0.02	0.006
Phenylalanine, g	0.1	0.13	0.05	0.014
Tyrosine, g	0.06	0.08	0.03	0.01
Valine, g	0.1	0.124	0.04	0.01
Arginine, g	0.08	0.126	0.04	0.01
Histidine, g	0.045	0.06	0.02	0.006
Alanine, g	0.07	0.1	0.03	0.01
Aspartic acid, g	0.1	0.15	0.04	0.01
Glutamic acid, g	0.66	0.83	0.32	0.09
Glycine, g	0.07	0.11	0.036	0.01
Proline, g	0.22	0.27	0.1	0.03
Serine, g	0.1	0.13	0.05	0.014

	Breads	**Flours**		
	Crackers, whole wheat	Buckwheat, whole groat	Corn, degermed	Corn, whole grain
Measure	1	1 C	1 C	1 C
Weight, g	4	120	126	117
Calories	17	402	472	431
Protein, g	0.35	15	7	8
Carbohydrate, g	2.7	85	104	89.9
Fiber, g	0.42	12	2.4	16
Vitamin A, IU	0	0	64	548
Vitamin B$_1$, mg	0.01	0.58	0.09	0.23
Vitamin B$_2$, mg	t	0.23	0.07	0.07
Vitamin B$_6$, mg	t	0.578	0.12	0.43
Vitamin B$_{12}$, mcg	0	0	0	0
Niacin, mg	0.18	7.4	3.35	1.6
Pantothenic acid, mg	0.03	0.53	0.07	0.77
Folic acid, mcg	1.1	65	61	29
Vitamin C, mg	0	0	0	0
Vitamin E, IU	0.06	1.85	0.62	0.43
Calcium, mg	2	49	2.5	7
Copper, mg	0.02	0.7	0.18	0.27
Iron, mg	0.12	5	1.15	2.1
Magnesium, mg	4	301	23	109
Manganese, mg	0.09	2.09	0.07	0.54
Phosphorus, mg	12	404	76	318
Potassium, mg	12	682	113	369
Selenium, mcg	0.59	6.8	11	18
Sodium, mg	27	13	1.3	6
Zinc, mg	0.086	3.7	0.47	2
Total lipid, g	0.69	3.7	1.75	4.5
Total saturated, g	0.136	0.8	0.215	0.635
Total unsaturated, g	0.264	1.14	0.876	2.1
Total monounsaturated, g	0.235	1.14	0.345	1.2
Cholesterol, mg	0	0	0	0
Tryptophan, g	0.005	0.22	—	0.057
Threonine, g	0.01	0.58	—	0.31
Isoleucine, g	0.013	0.57	—	0.29
Leucine, g	0.024	0.95	—	0.995
Lycine, g	0.01	0.77	—	0.23
Methionine, g	0.005	0.2	—	0.17
Cystine, g	0.01	0.26	—	0.146
Phenylalanine, g	0.017	0.6	—	0.4
Tyrosine, g	0.01	0.276	—	0.33
Valine, g	0.016	0.775	—	0.4
Arginine, g	0.017	1.12	—	0.4
Histidine, g	0.01	0.35	—	0.25
Alanine, g	0.013	0.85	—	0.6
Aspartic acid, g	0.02	1.3	—	0.56
Glutamic acid, g	0.112	2.34	—	1.5
Glycine, g	0.014	1.18	—	0.33
Proline, g	0.037	0.58	—	0.71
Serine, g	0.017	0.78	—	0.385

Flours

	Rye, dark	Rye, light	White, enr.	Whole wheat
Measure	1 C	1 C	1 C	1 C
Weight, g	128	102	110	120
Calories	419	374	455	400
Protein, g	20.9	8.6	11.6	16
Carbohydrate, g	87.2	81	95	85.2
Fiber, g	29	15	3	15
Vitamin A, IU	0	0	0	0
Vitamin B_1, mg	0.4	0.34	0.98	0.66
Vitamin B_2, mg	0.28	0.09	0.62	0.25
Vitamin B_6, mg	0.6	0.24	0.066	0.41
Vitamin B_{12}, mcg	0	0	0	0
Niacin, mg	5.5	0.82	7.4	5.2
Pantothenic acid, mg	1.7	0.68	0.51	1.32
Folic acid, mcg	77	22	193	65
Vitamin C, mg	0	0	0	0
Vitamin E, IU	4.9	0.85	0.11	2.19
Calcium, mg	69	18	18	49
Copper, mg	0.96	0.3	0.21	0.6
Iron, mg	8	1.8	5.8	4
Magnesium, mg	317	71	28	136
Manganese, mg	8.6	2	0.85	4.6
Phosphorus, mg	808	198	135	446
Potassium, mg	934	238	133	444
Selenium, mcg	45	36	42	77.4
Sodium, mg	1	2	2	4
Zinc, mg	7.2	1.8	0.87	2.88
Total lipid, g	3.3	1.4	1.1	2.4
Total saturated, g	0.42	0.15	0.19	0.386
Total unsaturated, g	0.5	0.576	0.52	0.98
Total monounsaturated, g	0.42	0.16	0.11	0.278
Cholesterol, mg	0	0	0	0
Tryptophan, g	0.2	0.097	0.16	0.254
Threonine, g	0.6	0.3	0.35	0.474
Isoleucine, g	0.7	0.3	0.45	0.6
Leucine, g	1.24	0.6	0.89	1.1
Lycine, g	0.6	0.3	0.285	0.45
Methionine, g	0.27	0.13	0.23	0.25
Cystine, g	0.355	0.17	0.27	0.38
Phenylalanine, g	0.91	0.43	0.65	0.775
Tyrosine, g	0.355	0.17	0.4	0.48
Valine, g	0.9	0.43	0.52	0.74
Arginine, g	0.8	0.4	0.5	0.77
Histidine, g	0.4	0.2	0.29	0.38
Alanine, g	0.74	0.35	0.42	0.58
Aspartic acid, g	1.24	0.59	0.54	0.84
Glutamic acid, g	5	2.4	4.35	5.2
Glycine, g	0.68	0.325	0.464	0.66
Proline, g	1.9	0.92	1.5	1.7
Serine, g	0.98	0.465	0.65	0.775

Legumes

	Adzuki beans, cooked	Black beans, cooked	Blackeyed peas, cooked	Carob, flour	Fava beans, cooked
Measure	1 C	1 C	1 C	1 C	1 C
Weight, g	230	172	165	103	170
Calories	294	227	178	229	187
Protein, g	17	15	13.4	4.8	13
Carbohydrate, g	57	41	29.9	92	33
Fiber, g	17	15	11	41	9
Vitamin A, IU	14	10	26	14	26
Vitamin B_1, mg	0.27	0.42	0.5	0.055	0.17
Vitamin B_2, mg	0.15	0.1	0.18	0.475	0.15
Vitamin B_6, mg	0.22	0.12	0.18	0.38	0.12
Vitamin B_{12}, mcg	0	0	0	0	0
Niacin, mg	1.6	0.87	0.85	1.95	1.2
Pantothenic acid, mg	0.99	0.42	0.66	0.05	0.27
Folic acid, mcg	279	256	357	30	177
Vitamin C, mg	0	0	0.68	0.2	0.5
Vitamin E, IU	—	—	0.72	0.967	0.224
Calcium, mg	64	46	40	358	61
Copper, mg	0.69	0.36	0.46	0.59	0.44
Iron, mg	4.6	3.6	3.5	3	2.5
Magnesium, mg	120	120	90.7	56	73
Manganese, mg	1.3	0.76	0.82	0.5	0.72
Phosphorus, mg	386	241	241	81	213
Potassium, mg	1224	611	428	851	456
Selenium, mcg	2.8	2	4.3	5.46	4.4
Sodium, mg	18	1.7	2	36	8.5
Zinc, mg	4	1.9	3	0.95	1.7
Total lipid, g	0.23	0.93	1.3	0.669	0.68
Total saturated, g	0.08	0.24	0.237	0.09	0.112
Total unsaturated, g	—	0.397	0.387	0.22	0.279
Total monounsaturated, g	—	0.08	0.076	0.2	0.134
Cholesterol, mg	0	0	0	0	0
Tryptophan, g	0.166	0.18	0.16	0.05	0.12
Threonine, g	0.59	0.64	0.51	0.28	0.46
Isoleucine, g	0.7	0.67	0.54	0.22	0.52
Leucine, g	1.45	1.2	1	0.455	0.97
Lycine, g	1.3	1.05	0.9	0.2	0.83
Methionine, g	0.18	0.23	0.19	0.08	0.105
Cystine, g	0.16	0.165	0.15	0.03	0.165
Phenylalanine, g	0.9	0.8	0.776	0.156	0.55
Tyrosine, g	0.52	0.4	0.43	0.124	0.4
Valine, g	0.9	0.8	0.63	0.46	0.58
Arginine, g	1.12	0.94	0.9	0.134	1.2
Histidine, g	0.455	0.43	0.4	0.13	0.33
Alanine, g	1	0.6	0.6	0.6	0.53
Aspartic acid, g	2.05	1.8	1.6	0.52	1.4
Glutamic acid, g	2.7	2.3	2.5	0.37	2.2
Glycine, g	0.66	0.6	0.55	0.275	0.54
Proline, g	0.76	0.65	0.6	0.365	0.54
Serine, g	0.85	0.83	0.67	0.3	0.6

Legumes

	Garbanzos, cooked	Kidney beans, cooked	Lentils, cooked	Lentil sprouts, raw	Lima beans, cooked
Measure	1 C	1 C	1 C	1 C	1 C
Weight, g	164	177	200	77	188
Calories	269	225	212	81	208
Protein, g	15	14.4	15.6	6.9	14
Carbohydrate, g	45	39.6	38.6	17	40
Fiber, g	13	13	15	—	13
Vitamin A, IU	44	0	15	35	0
Vitamin B$_1$, mg	0.19	0.2	0.33	0.176	0.238
Vitamin B$_2$, mg	0.1	0.11	0.12	0.099	0.163
Vitamin B$_6$, mg	0.23	0.2	0.35	0.146	0.328
Vitamin B$_{12}$, mcg	0	0	0	0	0
Niacin, mg	0.86	1.3	2.1	0.869	0.8
Pantothenic acid, mg	0.47	0.4	1.26	0.445	0.8
Folic acid, mcg	282	230	358	76.9	156
Vitamin C, mg	2	2	3	12.7	0
Vitamin E, IU	0.85	0.21	0.325	—	0.5
Calcium, mg	80	50	38	19	32
Copper, mg	0.58	0.43	0.54	0.27	0.519
Iron, mg	4.7	5.2	6.6	2.47	4.2
Magnesium, mg	79	79	71	28	80
Manganese, mg	1.7	0.84	0.98	0.39	0.97
Phosphorus, mg	276	259	356	133	221
Potassium, mg	477	629	730	248	969
Selenium, mcg	6	2	5.5	0.46	8.5
Sodium, mg	11	3.5	4	8	4
Zinc, mg	2.5	1.9	2	1.16	1.34
Total lipid, g	4.3	0.9	0.75	0.43	0.7
Total saturated, g	0.4	0.13	0.1	0.044	0.167
Total unsaturated, g	1.9	0.487	0.35	0.17	0.32
Total monounsaturated, g	0.96	0.069	0.13	0.08	0.06
Cholesterol, mg	0	0	0	0	0
Tryptophan, g	0.14	0.18	0.16	—	0.17
Threonine, g	0.54	0.65	0.64	0.253	0.63
Isoleucine, g	0.6	0.68	0.77	0.251	0.745
Leucine, g	1	1.2	1.3	0.484	0.113
Lycine, g	0.97	1	1.25	0.548	0.98
Methionine, g	0.19	0.23	0.15	0.081	0.18
Cystine, g	0.195	0.17	0.23	0.257	0.16
Phenylalanine, g	0.78	0.8	0.88	0.34	0.84
Tyrosine, g	0.36	0.4	0.48	0.194	0.52
Valine, g	0.6	0.8	0.89	0.307	0.88
Arginine, g	1.4	0.95	1.4	0.47	0.9
Histidine, g	0.4	0.43	0.5	0.198	0.393
Alanine, g	0.6	0.64	0.75	0.274	0.75
Aspartic acid, g	1.7	1.86	1.98	1.1	1.9
Glutamic acid, g	2.5	2.3	2.77	0.969	2
Glycine, g	0.6	0.6	0.73	0.246	0.62
Proline, g	0.6	0.65	0.75	0.274	0.67
Serine, g	0.7	0.84	0.8	0.381	0.98

Legumes

	Miso	Mung sprouts, raw	Natto	Navy beans, cooked	Peanuts, raw
Measure	1 C	1 C	1 C	1 C	1 C
Weight, g	275	104	175	190	144
Calories	566	32	375	224	838
Protein, g	33	3	31	14.8	37.7
Carbohydrate, g	77	6	25	40.3	29.7
Fiber, g	15	1.8	9.45	12	12
Vitamin A, IU	240	22	0	3.6	0
Vitamin B$_1$, mg	0.267	0.088	0.28	0.27	0.46
Vitamin B$_2$, mg	0.688	0.128	0.33	0.13	0.19
Vitamin B$_6$, mg	0.59	0.092	0.23	0.3	0.576
Vitamin B$_{12}$, mcg	0	0	0	0	0
Niacin, mg	2.37	0.778	0	1.3	24.6
Pantothenic acid, mg	0.7	0.396	0.376	0.46	3
Folic acid, mcg	91	63	14	255	350
Vitamin C, mg	0	13.6	23	1.6	0
Vitamin E, IU	0.04	0.015	0.027	—	19
Calcium, mg	181	14	380	95	104
Copper, mg	1.2	0.17	1.17	0.54	0.62
Iron, mg	7.5	0.94	15	5.1	3.2
Magnesium, mg	116	22	201	107	252
Manganese, mg	2.36	0.19	2.67	1	2.17
Phosphorus, mg	421	56	305	281	586
Potassium, mg	451	154	1276	790	1009
Selenium, mcg	4.4	0.6	15	10	10
Sodium, mg	10.029	6	12	2	26
Zinc, mg	9	0.42	5.3	1.8	4.78
Total lipid, g	16.7	0.2	19	1.1	70.1
Total saturated, g	2.4	0.048	2.78	0.269	10
Total unsaturated, g	9.4	0.052	10.9	0.45	22
Total monounsaturated, g	3.7	0.023	4.25	0.1	36
Cholesterol, mg	0	0	0	0	0
Tryptophan, g	0.4	0.038	0.4	0.187	0.453
Threonine, g	1.76	0.08	1.4	0.67	1.09
Isoleucine, g	2.2	0.138	1.63	0.7	1.45
Leucine, g	3.1	0.182	2.6	1.3	2.8
Lycine, g	1.8	0.172	2	1.1	1.45
Methionine, g	0.4	0.036	0.36	0.24	0.384
Cystine, g	0.27	0.018	0.385	0.17	0.48
Phenylalanine, g	1.64	0.122	1.65	0.86	2.14
Tyrosine, g	0.995	0.054	0.97	0.45	1.8
Valine, g	2	0.136	1.78	0.8	1.7
Arginine, g	2	0.2	1.6	0.98	5.05
Histidine, g	0.91	0.072	0.9	0.44	1.09
Alanine, g	1.57	0.102	1.4	0.66	1.65
Aspartic acid, g	3.6	0.498	3.4	1.9	5.04
Glutamic acid, g	5.78	0.168	5.8	2.4	8.9
Glycine, g	1.5	0.066	1	0.62	2.59
Proline, g	2	—	2.5	0.67	1.82
Serine, g	2	0.034	1.96	0.86	2.09

Legumes

	Peanut butter, smooth	Peas, green	Peas, split, cooked	Pinto beans, cooked	Soybeans, cooked	Soybean, flour
Measure	1 T	1 C	1 C	1 C	1 C	1 C
Weight, g	15	146	200	171	172	84
Calories	86	118	230	234	298	366
Protein, g	3.9	7.9	16	14	29	29
Carbohydrate, g	3.2	21	41.6	44	17	29.5
Fiber, g	0.9	7.4	16	15	10	8
Vitamin A, IU	0	934	14	3.4	15	100
Vitamin B_1, mg	0.018	0.387	0.3	0.32	0.27	0.49
Vitamin B_2, mg	0.02	0.193	0.18	0.156	0.5	0.97
Vitamin B_6, mg	0.05	0.247	0.09	0.27	0.4	0.387
Vitamin B_{12}, mcg	0	0	0	0	0	0
Niacin, mg	2.4	3.05	1.8	0.68	0.69	3.6
Pantothenic acid, mg	0.147	0.152	1.2	0.49	0.31	1.34
Folic acid, mcg	7	95	127	294	93	290
Vitamin C, mg	0	58.4	0.78	3.6	3	0
Vitamin E, IU	2.4	0.84	1	2.38	5	1.64
Calcium, mg	6	36	22	82	175	173
Copper, mg	0.022	0.257	0.5	0.44	0.7	2.45
Iron, mg	0.3	2.14	3.4	4.5	8.8	5.35
Magnesium, mg	26	48	71	94	148	360
Manganese, mg	0.257	0.599	0.78	0.95	1.4	1.9
Phosphorus, mg	59	157	194	273	421	415
Potassium, mg	123	357	709	800	885	2112
Selenium, mcg	1.2	2.6	1.18	12	12	6.3
Sodium, mg	75	7	4	3	1.7	11
Zinc, mg	0.47	1.8	2	1.85	2	3.3
Total lipid, g	8.1	0.58	0.76	0.889	15	—
Total saturated, g	1.5	0.1	0.1	0.186	2.2	2.5
Total unsaturated, g	2.2	0.27	0.3	0.32	8.7	9.8
Total monounsaturated, g	3.9	0.05	0.16	0.18	3.4	3.8
Cholesterol, mg	0	0	0	0	0	0
Tryptophan, g	0.055	0.054	0.18	0.167	0.42	0.422
Threonine, g	0.132	0.296	0.58	0.6	1.24	1.26
Isoleucine, g	0.177	0.285	0.67	0.62	1.4	1.4
Leucine, g	0.342	0.472	1.2	1	2.3	3.37
Lycine, g	0.176	0.463	1.2	0.96	2	1.9
Methionine, g	0.047	0.12	0.17	0.2	0.385	0.4
Cystine, g	0.058	0.047	0.25	0.15	0.46	0.467
Phenylalanine, g	0.26	0.292	0.75	0.76	1.5	1.5
Tyrosine, g	0.219	0.165	0.47	0.4	1.1	1.1
Valine, g	0.206	0.343	0.77	0.74	1.4	1.45
Arginine, g	0.613	0.625	1.46	0.87	2	2.25
Histidine, g	0.133	0.156	0.4	0.4	0.77	0.78
Alanine, g	0.201	0.35	0.72	0.59	1.35	1.37
Aspartic acid, g	0.613	0.723	1.9	1.7	3.6	3.6
Glutamic acid, g	1.08	1.08	2.8	2	5.5	5.6
Glycine, g	0.315	0.269	0.7	0.55	1.3	1.34
Proline, g	0.221	0.253	0.67	0.6	1.7	1.7
Serine, g	0.255	0.264	0.72	0.76	1.66	1.68

Legumes

	Soybean sprouts, raw	Soymilk	Tempeh	Tofu, firm
Measure	1 C	1 C		½ C
Weight, g	70	245	100	126
Calories	90	81	193	97
Protein, g	9	6.7	19	10
Carbohydrate, g	7.8	4.4	9.4	3.7
Fiber, g	0.77	3.2	—	0.5
Vitamin A, IU	8	78	0	10
Vitamin B_1, mg	0.238	0.4	0.078	0.12
Vitamin B_2, mg	0.082	0.17	0.358	0.13
Vitamin B_6, mg	0.124	0.1	0.215	0.08
Vitamin B_{12}, mcg	0	0	0.075	0
Niacin, mg	0.804	0.36	2.64	0.01
Pantothenic acid, mg	0.65	0.12	0.278	0.08
Folic acid, mcg	120	3.7	24	42
Vitamin C, mg	10.6	0	0	0.25
Vitamin E, IU	—	0.04	—	—
Calcium, mg	48	9.8	111	204
Copper, mg	0.3	0.3	0.56	0.3
Iron, mg	1.48	1.4	2.7	1.8
Magnesium, mg	50	47	81	58
Manganese, mg	0.492	0.42	1.3	0.9
Phosphorus, mg	114	120	266	185
Potassium, mg	338	346	412	222
Selenium, mcg	0.4	3.2	0.017	12
Sodium, mg	10	29	9	10
Zinc, mg	0.82	0.56	1.14	1.3
Total lipid, g	4.68	4.7	10.8	5.6
Total saturated, g	0.5	0.5	2.2	0.8
Total unsaturated, g	2	2.04	3.83	3.2
Total monounsaturated, g	1	0.8	3	1.24
Cholesterol, mg	0	0	0	0
Tryptophan, g	0.126	0.11	0.28	0.16
Threonine, g	0.32	0.28	0.796	0.4
Isoleucine, g	0.276	0.35	0.88	0.5
Leucine, g	0.464	0.6	1.43	0.77
Lycine, g	0.386	0.44	0.91	0.67
Methionine, g	0.062	0.1	0.174	0.13
Cystine, g	0.03	0.1	0.32	0.14
Phenylalanine, g	0.222	0.37	0.89	0.5
Tyrosine, g	0.182	0.27	0.664	0.34
Valine, g	0.3	0.345	0.9	0.5
Arginine, g	0.266	0.5	1.25	0.67
Histidine, g	0.148	0.17	0.466	0.3
Alanine, g	0.26	0.3	0.96	0.42
Aspartic acid, g	0.8	0.84	2	1
Glutamic acid, g	0.784	1.35	3.3	1.75
Glycine, g	0.214	0.3	0.75	0.4
Proline, g	0.47	0.4	1	0.55
Serine, g	0.414	0.35	1	0.48

Beef[1]

	Chuck roast	Corned, brisket	Dried	Flank steak	Ground beef, lean
Measure	1 lb	1 lb	1 oz	1 lb	4 oz
Weight, g	454	454	28	454	113
Calories	1164	896	47	888	298
Protein, g	83	66.58	8.25	87.4	20
Carbohydrate, g	0	0.63	0.44	0	0
Fiber, g	0	0	0	0	0
Vitamin A, IU	130	—	—	50	22.5
Vitamin B$_1$, mg	0.485	0.195	0.02	0.499	0.057
Vitamin B$_2$, mg	0.794	0.712	0.09	0.680	0.237
Vitamin B$_6$, mg	1.7	1.32	—	1.87	0.28
Vitamin B$_{12}$, mcg	13.7	8.07	0.52	13.4	2.64
Niacin, mg	14.6	16.6	1.06	20.6	5.1
Pantothenic acid, mg	1.4	2.59	—	1.46	0.418
Folic acid, mcg	32	—	—	32	9
Vitamin C, mg	0	0	—	0	0
Vitamin E, IU	—	—	—	—	—
Calcium, mg	32	30	2	22	9
Copper, mg	0.363	0.499	0.045	0.327	0.082
Iron, mg	9.44	7.66	1.28	8.9	1.99
Magnesium, mg	87	66	9	93	20
Manganese, mg	0.054	0.091	—	0.064	0.017
Phosphorus, mg	779	531	49	864	154
Potassium, mg	1374	1348	126	1585	295
Selenium, mcg	—	—	—	—	—
Sodium, mg	266	5519	984	321	78
Zinc, mg	18.06	12.9	1.49	15.7	4.36
Total lipid, g	90	67.6	1.11	57	23.4
Total saturated, g	38.4	21.44	0.45	25.6	9.39
Total unsaturated, g	—	—	—	—	—
Total monounsaturated, g	—	—	—	—	—
Cholesterol, mg	311	245	—	238	85
Tryptophan, g	0.93	0.608	0.067	0.98	0.246
Threonine, g	3.63	2.51	0.346	3.82	0.837
Isoleucine, g	3.74	2.88	0.338	3.9	0.857
Leucine, g	6.57	4.89	0.616	6.9	1.6
Lycine, g	6.9	5.1	0.673	7.27	1.67
Methionine, g	2.13	1.55	0.199	2.24	0.467
Cystine, g	0.93	0.853	0.098	0.98	0.192
Phenylalanine, g	3.24	2.4	0.309	3.4	0.758
Tyrosine, g	2.8	2.17	0.249	2.9	0.624
Valine, g	4.04	2.93	0.379	4.25	0.968
Arginine, g	5.25	4.1	0.557	5.5	1.35
Histidine, g	2.8	2.1	0.239	2.99	0.636
Alanine, g	5.01	4.8	0.545	5.27	1.3
Aspartic acid, g	7.6	6.5	0.733	7.98	1.8
Glutamic acid, g	12.5	10.8	1.19	13.1	3.14
Glycine, g	4.5	5.56	0.612	4.76	1.48
Proline, g	3.67	4.79	0.449	3.86	1.01
Serine, g	3.18	2.68	0.337	3.34	0.774

[1]Beef contains approx. .63 mg vitamin E/100 g; 13.6 mcg biotin/lb; 19 mg zinc/lb (lean, no fat).

Beef[1]

	Ground beef, regular	Liver	Pastrami	Porterhouse steak	Rib roast
Measure	4 oz	4 oz	1 oz	1 lb	1 lb
Weight, g	113	113	28	454	454
Calories	351	161	99	1289	1503
Protein, g	18.8	22.6	4.9	78.8	72.8
Carbohydrate, g	0	6.58	0.86	0	0
Fiber, g	0	0	0	0	0
Vitamin A, IU	40	39941	—	300	310
Vitamin B$_1$, mg	0.043	0.292	0.027	0.44	0.349
Vitamin B$_2$, mg	0.171	3.14	0.048	0.739	0.576
Vitamin B$_6$, mg	0.27	1.06	0.05	1.62	1.39
Vitamin B$_{12}$, mcg	2.99	78.2	0.5	11.85	12.45
Niacin, mg	5.06	14.4	1.44	15.3	12.4
Pantothenic acid, mg	0.39	8.6	—	1.32	1.35
Folic acid, mcg	8	281	—	27	22
Vitamin C, mg	0	25.3	0.9	0	0
Vitamin E, IU	—	1.59	—	—	—
Calcium, mg	10	6	2	29	39
Copper, mg	0.07	3.12	—	0.336	0.259
Iron, mg	1.96	7.71	0.54	7.83	7.63
Magnesium, mg	18	22	5	82	71
Manganese, mg	0.019	0.298	—	0.054	0.054
Phosphorus, mg	146	360	43	770	685
Potassium, mg	258	365	65	1305	1180
Selenium, mcg	23.5	51.5	—	—	—
Sodium, mg	77	82	348	222	241
Zinc, mg	4.01	4.43	1.21	13.64	16.2
Total lipid, g	30	4.34	8.27	105.6	132
Total saturated, g	12.18	1.69	2.95	45.15	57.4
Total unsaturated, g	—	—	—	—	—
Total monounsaturated, g	—	—	—	—	—
Cholesterol, mg	96	400	26	316	326
Tryptophan, g	0.232	0.325	0.045	0.885	0.816
Threonine, g	0.788	1.034	0.185	3.44	3.18
Isoleucine, g	0.806	1.034	0.211	3.54	3.27
Leucine, g	1.5	2.13	0.359	6.23	5.75
Lycine, g	1.56	1.57	0.375	6.56	6.05
Methionine, g	0.438	0.572	0.113	2.02	1.86
Cystine, g	0.181	0.347	0.063	0.885	0.816
Phenylalanine, g	0.712	1.2	0.176	3.08	2.84
Tyrosine, g	0.586	0.897	0.16	2.65	2.44
Valine, g	0.911	1.4	0.215	3.83	3.58
Arginine, g	1.26	1.42	0.302	4.98	4.6
Histidine, g	0.598	0.618	0.156	2.7	2.49
Alanine, g	1.23	1.4	0.352	4.75	4.39
Aspartic acid, g	1.7	2.17	0.479	7.2	6.65
Glutamic acid, g	2.95	3.06	0.796	11.8	10.9
Glycine, g	1.39	1.29	0.408	4.3	3.97
Proline, g	0.953	1.19	0.352	3.48	3.21
Serine, g	0.727	1.09	0.197	3.01	2.78

[1]Beef contains approx. .63 mg vitamin E/100 g; 13.6 mcg biotin/lb; 19 mg zinc/lb (lean, no fat).

Beef[1]

	Round steak	Short ribs	Sirloin steak	Smoked, chopped	T-bone steak	Tenderloin
Measure	1 lb	1 lb	1 lb	1 oz	1 lb	1 lb
Weight, g	454	454	454	28	454	454
Calories	1093	1761	1179	38	1394	1095
Protein, g	88	65.3	82.7	5.7	76	84.1
Carbohydrate, g	0	0	0	0.53	0	0
Fiber, g	0	0	0	0	0	0
Vitamin A, IU	110	—	220	—	300	—
Vitamin B$_1$, mg	0.435	0.322	0.503	0.024	0.422	0.54
Vitamin B$_2$, mg	0.748	0.535	0.88	0.05	0.712	0.97
Vitamin B$_6$, mg	2.02	1.34	1.71	0.1	1.58	1.74
Vitamin B$_{12}$, mcg	12.21	11.6	12.58	0.49	11.6	12
Niacin, mg	15.97	11.6	13.9	1.3	14.8	13.9
Pantothenic acid, mg	1.53	1.09	1.38	0.167	1.27	1.41
Folic acid, mcg	35	21	30	—	26	28
Vitamin C, mg	0	0	0	0	0	0
Vitamin E, IU	—	—	—	—	—	—
Calcium, mg	23	41	34	—	30	30
Copper, mg	0.322	0.24	0.37	—	0.322	0.435
Iron, mg	8.5	7.03	10.2	0.81	7.58	10.9
Magnesium, mg	92	62	89	6	79	93
Manganese, mg	0.059	0.05	0.054	—	0.054	0.059
Phosphorus, mg	846	624	798	51	703	842
Potassium, mg	1434	1053	1331	107	1248	1422
Selenium, mcg	165	—	—	—	—	—
Sodium, mg	232	224	234	357	217	223
Zinc, mg	13.7	14.3	15.5	1.11	13.1	14.2
Total lipid, g	79.5	164	91.5	1.25	118.5	81.6
Total saturated, g	33.73	71.5	39.15	0.51	50.9	34.7
Total unsaturated, g	—	—	—	—	—	—
Total monounsaturated, g	—	—	—	—	—	—
Cholesterol, mg	298	345	315	13	323	313
Tryptophan, g	0.984	0.73	0.925	0.047	0.853	0.943
Threonine, g	3.84	2.85	3.6	0.24	3.33	3.67
Isoleucine, g	3.95	2.93	3.7	0.234	3.42	3.78
Leucine, g	6.95	5.16	6.54	0.428	6.02	6.65
Lycine, g	7.32	5.43	6.88	0.467	6.33	6.99
Methionine, g	2.25	1.67	2.12	0.138	1.95	2.15
Cystine, g	0.984	0.73	0.925	0.068	0.853	0.943
Phenylalanine, g	3.43	2.55	3.23	0.214	2.97	3.28
Tyrosine, g	2.95	2.19	2.78	0.173	2.56	2.83
Valine, g	4.27	3.18	4.02	0.263	3.7	4.09
Arginine, g	5.55	4.13	5.23	0.386	4.81	5.32
Histidine, g	3.01	2.24	2.83	0.166	2.6	2.88
Alanine, g	5.3	3.94	4.99	0.378	4.59	5.07
Aspartic acid, g	8.03	5.96	7.56	0.508	6.95	7.68
Glutamic acid, g	13.2	9.8	12.4	0.825	11.4	12.6
Glycine, g	4.8	3.56	4.51	0.425	4.16	4.59
Proline, g	3.88	2.88	3.65	0.311	3.36	3.72
Serine, g	3.36	2.5	3.16	0.234	2.91	3.22

[1]Beef contains approx. .63 mg vitamin E/100 g; 13.6 mcg biotin/lb; 19 mg zinc/lb (lean, no fat).

Lamb[1]

	Leg	Chops	Liver	Shoulder
Measure	1 lb	1 lb	1 lb	1 lb
Weight, g	454	454	454	454
Calories	845	1146	617	1082
Protein, g	67.7	63.7	95.3	59
Carbohydrate, g	0	0	13.2	0
Fiber, g	0	0	0	0
Vitamin A, IU	0	0	229070	0
Vitamin B$_1$, mg	0.59	0.57	1.81	0.53
Vitamin B$_2$, mg	0.82	0.79	14.9	0.73
Vitamin B$_6$, mg	1.05	1.05	1.36	1.05
Vitamin B$_{12}$, mcg	8.2	8.2	472	8.2
Niacin, mg	19	18.5	76.5	17.1
Pantothenic acid, mg	2	2	32.7	2
Folic acid, mcg	18	18	990	18
Vitamin C, mg	0	0	152	0
Vitamin E, IU	1.4	1.4	—	1.48
Calcium, mg	0.39	35	45	35
Copper, mg	0.27	0.73	25	0.44
Iron, mg	5.1	4.7	49.4	3.9
Magnesium, mg	61	55	64	50
Manganese, mg	0.09	—	1.04	0.086
Phosphorus, mg	593	567	1583	516
Potassium, mg	1083	1019	916	942
Selenium, mcg	94	78	—	87
Sodium, mg	237	223	236	206
Zinc, mg	15	—	—	18
Total lipid, g	77	0.97	19.6	97
Total saturated, g	35	54.3	6.9	42
Total unsaturated, g	6	—	—	7
Total monounsaturated, g	31	—	—	40
Cholesterol, mg	265	270	1361	270
Tryptophan, g	0.95	—	—	0.88
Threonine, g	3.5	—	—	3.2
Isoleucine, g	3.9	—	—	3.6
Leucine, g	6.3	—	—	5.85
Lycine, g	7.2	—	—	6.6
Methionine, g	2.1	—	—	1.9
Cystine, g	0.97	—	—	0.9
Phenylalanine, g	3.3	—	—	3
Tyrosine, g	2.7	—	—	2.5
Valine, g	4.4	—	—	4
Arginine, g	4.8	—	—	4.5
Histidine, g	2.57	—	—	2.4
Alanine, g	4.9	—	—	4.5
Aspartic acid, g	7	—	—	6.6
Glutamic acid, g	11.8	—	—	11
Glycine, g	4	—	—	3.67
Proline, g	3.4	—	—	3.2
Serine, g	3	—	—	2.8

[1]Lamb contains approx. 13.6 mg zinc/lb (lean, no fat); 13.6 mcg biotin/lb.

Pork

	Bacon	Bacon, Canadian style	Feet	Ham	Leg
Measure	1 lb	1 lb	½	1 lb	1 lb
Weight, g	454	454	95	454	454
Calories	2523	714	251	827	1182
Protein, g	39	93.6	21	79.6	77.4
Carbohydrate, g	0.42	7.61	0	14.1	0
Fiber, g	0	0	0	0	0
Vitamin A, IU	0	0	0	0	31
Vitamin B$_1$, mg	1.67	3.4	0.04	3.9	3.24
Vitamin B$_2$, mg	0.472	0.78	0.1	1.14	0.889
Vitamin B$_6$, mg	0.64	1.77	—	1.52	1.81
Vitamin B$_{12}$, mcg	4.2	3.02	—	3.75	2.79
Niacin, mg	12.6	28.2	1.05	23.8	20.5
Pantothenic acid, mg	1.6	2.36	—	2.02	3.04
Folic acid, mcg	9	18	—	15	33
Vitamin C, mg	0	0	0	—	3.2
Vitamin E, IU	0.41	—	—	—	1.9
Calcium, mg	34	36	56	0.32	25
Copper, mg	0.29	0.204	—	0.449	0.295
Iron, mg	2.7	3.07	—	4.5	3.87
Magnesium, mg	39	79	7	85	91
Manganese, mg	0.032	0.104	—	0.141	0.014
Phosphorus, mg	646	1102	52	1122	867
Potassium, mg	631	1560	216	1508	1405
Selenium, mcg	—	—	—	—	133
Sodium, mg	3107	6391	49	5974	214
Zinc, mg	5.23	6.31	—	9.69	8.6
Total lipid, g	261	31.6	17.9	47.9	94.4
Total saturated, g	96.4	10	6.18	15.4	34
Total unsaturated, g	—	—	—	—	9
Total monounsaturated, g	—	—	—	—	38
Cholesterol, mg	306	228	101	259	335
Tryptophan, g	0.376	0.93	0.042	0.957	0.993
Threonine, g	1.5	3.76	0.545	3.54	3.57
Isoleucine, g	1.6	3.53	0.335	3.49	3.63
Leucine, g	2.73	6.6	0.881	6.32	6.23
Lycine, g	2.9	7.37	0.902	6.75	7.55
Methionine, g	0.866	2.54	0.21	2.1	1.86
Cystine, g	0.404	1.17	—	1.2	0.98
Phenylalanine, g	1.5	3.04	0.566	3.44	3.08
Tyrosine, g	1.14	2.83	0.314	2.6	2.67
Valine, g	1.89	3.73	0.483	3.45	4.12
Arginine, g	2.4	5.1	1.59	5.17	5.53
Histidine, g	1.13	3.4	0.252	2.85	3.74
Alanine, g	2.2	4.70	1.76	4.7	4.31
Aspartic acid, g	3.24	7.8	1.46	7.54	6.75
Glutamic acid, g	5.39	13	2.28	13	11.3
Glycine, g	2.8	4.03	3.48	4.14	3.32
Proline, g	2.09	3.5	2.3	3.4	2.75
Serine, g	1.47	3.55	0.839	3.26	2.99

Pork

	Loin, chop	Shoulder	Spareribs
Measure	1 chop	1 lb	1 lb
Weight, g	151	454	454
Calories	345	1249	804
Protein, g	20	73	48
Carbohydrate, g	0	0	0
Fiber, g	0	0	0
Vitamin A, IU	9	30	30
Vitamin B$_1$, mg	0.948	3.08	1.74
Vitamin B$_2$, mg	0.294	1.19	0.768
Vitamin B$_6$, mg	0.45	1.26	1.18
Vitamin B$_{12}$, mcg	0.86	3.25	2.45
Niacin, mg	5.33	16.8	13.6
Pantothenic acid, mg	0.788	2.87	2.23
Folic acid, mcg	4	16	11
Vitamin C, mg	0.8	3	—
Vitamin E, IU	0.48	1.9	—
Calcium, mg	7	24	19
Copper, mg	0.076	0.376	0.239
Iron, mg	0.85	4.59	2.78
Magnesium, mg	21	77	62
Manganese, mg	0.013	0.05	0.028
Phosphorus, mg	224	803	671
Potassium, mg	346	1325	728
Selenium, mcg	28	115	—
Sodium, mg	63	286	212
Zinc, mg	2.09	11.3	7.58
Total lipid, g	28.7	103	66.3
Total saturated, g	10.3	37.3	26.3
Total unsaturated, g	2.8	9	—
Total monounsaturated, g	11.8	36	—
Cholesterol, mg	81	329	218
Tryptophan, g	0.256	0.934	0.647
Threonine, g	0.923	3.38	2.26
Isoleucine, g	0.939	3.43	2.32
Leucine, g	1.6	5.9	3.9
Lycine, g	1.95	7.14	4.73
Methionine, g	0.481	1.75	1.18
Cystine, g	0.253	0.925	0.624
Phenylalanine, g	0.797	2.91	1.92
Tyrosine, g	0.689	2.52	1.71
Valine, g	1.06	3.89	2.57
Arginine, g	1.43	5.24	3.34
Histidine, g	0.963	3.53	2.44
Alanine, g	1.1	4.06	2.84
Aspartic acid, g	1.73	6.36	4.46
Glutamic acid, g	2.9	10.6	7.47
Glycine, g	0.852	3.13	2.19
Proline, g	0.708	2.6	1.82
Serine, g	0.769	2.82	1.97

Veal[1]

	Breast	Chuck	Cutlet	Liver	Rib roast
Measure	1 lb	1 lb	1 lb	1 lb	1 lb
Weight, g	454	454	454	454	454
Calories	828	628	681	635	723
Protein, g	65.6	70.4	72.3	87.1	65.7
Carbohydrate, g	0	0	0	18.6	0
Fiber, g	0	0	0	0	0
Vitamin A, IU	0	0	0	102060	0
Vitamin B$_1$, mg	0.48	0.52	0.53	0.9	0.48
Vitamin B$_2$, mg	0.87	0.94	0.96	12.3	0.87
Vitamin B$_6$, mg	1.22	1.22	1.22	3.04	1.22
Vitamin B$_{12}$, mcg	5.7	5.7	5.7	272	5.7
Niacin, mg	22	23.6	24.2	51.8	22
Pantothenic acid, mg	3.23	3.23	3.23	36.3	3.23
Folic acid, mcg	37	23	23	—	23
Vitamin C, mg	0	0	0	161	0
Vitamin E, IU	—	—	—	—	1.55
Calcium, mg	39	40	41	36	38
Copper, mg	—	—	1.14	36	1.14
Iron, mg	9.7	10.5	10.9	39.9	9.8
Magnesium, mg	81	—	73	73	52
Manganese, mg	0.045	—	—	—	0.136
Phosphorus, mg	652	722	734	1510	664
Potassium, mg	1050	1126	1157	1275	1051
Selenium, mcg	30	—	—	—	37
Sodium, mg	230	246	253	331	230
Zinc, mg	11	—	—	17	15
Total lipid, g	66	36	41	21.3	49
Total saturated, g	29.3	17	19.7	—	23.5
Total unsaturated, g	4	—	—	—	2.8
Total monounsaturated, g	32	—	—	—	15
Cholesterol, mg	254	320	254	1361	254
Tryptophan, g	0.8	—	—	—	0.86
Threonine, g	3.5	—	—	—	3.74
Isoleucine, g	3.9	—	—	—	4
Leucine, g	6.3	—	—	—	6.8
Lycine, g	6.5	—	—	—	7
Methionine, g	1.8	—	—	—	2
Cystine, g	0.9	—	—	—	0.97
Phenylalanine, g	3	—	—	—	3.45
Tyrosine, g	2.5	—	—	—	2.7
Valine, g	4.4	—	—	—	4.7
Arginine, g	4.7	—	—	—	5
Histidine, g	2.9	—	—	—	3
Alanine, g	4.7	—	—	—	5
Aspartic acid, g	6.8	—	—	—	7.4
Glutamic acid, g	12.5	—	—	—	13.5
Glycine, g	4	—	—	—	4.4
Proline, g	3	—	—	—	3.57
Serine, g	2.9	—	—	—	3

[1]Veal contains approx. 12.7 mg zinc/lb (lean, no fat).

	Veal[1]		Wild Game	
	Rump roast	**Sweetbreads**	**Rabbit**	**Venison**
Measure	1 lb	1 lb	1 lb	1 lb
Weight, g	454	454	454	454
Calories	573	426	581	572
Protein, g	68	80.7	75	95
Carbohydrate, g	0	0	0	0
Fiber, g	0	0	0	0
Vitamin A, IU	0	0	136	—
Vitamin B$_1$, mg	0.5	0.37	0.29	1.03
Vitamin B$_2$, mg	0.9	0.76	0.2	2.19
Vitamin B$_6$, mg	1.22	—	1.58	—
Vitamin B$_{12}$, mcg	5.7	63.6	—	—
Niacin, mg	22.8	11.7	45.9	28.6
Pantothenic acid, mg	3.23	—	2.8	—
Folic acid, mcg	23	—	—	—
Vitamin C, mg	0	0	—	0
Vitamin E, IU	—	—	4.5	—
Calcium, mg	38	41	72	45
Copper, mg	—	0.27	—	—
Iron, mg	10	4.54	4.7	22.7
Magnesium, mg	—	68	—	150
Manganese, mg	—	—	—	—
Phosphorus, mg	699	1521	1261	1129
Potassium, mg	1090	1130	1379	1525
Selenium, mcg	—	—	—	—
Sodium, mg	238	281	154	318
Zinc, mg	—	—	—	—
Total lipid, g	31	9.1	29	18
Total saturated, g	14.9	—	11	11
Total unsaturated, g	—	—	—	—
Total monounsaturated, g	—	—	—	—
Cholesterol, mg	254	1135	295	—
Tryptophan, g	—	—	—	—
Threonine, g	—	—	—	—
Isoleucine, g	—	—	—	—
Leucine, g	—	—	—	—
Lycine, g	—	—	—	—
Methionine, g	—	—	—	—
Cystine, g	—	—	—	—
Phenylalanine, g	—	—	—	—
Tyrosine, g	—	—	—	—
Valine, g	—	—	—	—
Arginine, g	—	—	—	—
Histidine, g	—	—	—	—
Alanine, g	—	—	—	—
Aspartic acid, g	—	—	—	—
Glutamic acid, g	—	—	—	—
Glycine, g	—	—	—	—
Proline, g	—	—	—	—
Serine, g	—	—	—	—

[1]Veal contains approx. 12.7 mg zinc/lb (lean, no fat).

Luncheon Meats and Sausage

	Bologna, beef	Bologna, beef and pork	Bologna, pork	Bratwurst, ckd	Braun-schweiger
Measure	1 oz	1 oz	1 oz	1 link	1 oz
Weight, g	28	28	28	85	28
Calories	89	89	70	256	102
Protein, g	3.31	3.31	4.34	12	3.83
Carbohydrate, g	0.55	0.79	0.21	1.76	0.89
Fiber, g	0	0	0	—	0
Vitamin A, IU	—	—	—	—	3984
Vitamin B_1, mg	0.016	0.049	0.148	0.429	0.071
Vitamin B_2, mg	0.036	0.039	0.045	0.156	0.432
Vitamin B_6, mg	0.05	0.05	0.08	0.18	0.09
Vitamin B_{12}, mcg	0.4	0.38	0.26	0.81	5.69
Niacin, mg	0.746	0.731	1.1	2.72	2.37
Pantothenic acid, mg	0.08	0.08	0.2	0.27	0.96
Folic acid, mcg	1	1	1	—	—
Vitamin C, mg	t	t	t	1	t
Vitamin E, IU	—	—	—	—	—
Calcium, mg	3	3	3	38	2
Copper, mg	0.01	0.02	0.02	0.08	0.07
Iron, mg	0.4	0.43	0.22	1.09	2.65
Magnesium, mg	3	3	4	12	3
Manganese, mg	0.008	0.011	0.01	0.039	0.044
Phosphorus, mg	23	26	39	126	48
Potassium, mg	44	51	80	180	57
Selenium, mcg	—	—	—	—	—
Sodium, mg	284	289	336	473	324
Zinc, mg	0.57	0.55	0.57	1.96	0.8
Total lipid, g	8.04	8.01	5.63	22	9.1
Total saturated, g	3.31	3.03	1.95	7.93	3.09
Total unsaturated, g	—	—	—	—	—
Total monounsaturated, g	—	—	—	—	—
Cholesterol, mg	16	16	17	51	44
Tryptophan, g	0.03	0.03	0.042	0.096	0.041
Threonine, g	0.125	0.145	0.182	0.473	0.151
Isoleucine, g	0.143	0.144	0.188	0.437	0.137
Leucine, g	0.244	0.255	0.331	0.802	0.293
Lycine, g	0.254	0.25	0.341	0.91	0.258
Methionine, g	0.077	0.079	0.117	0.291	0.088
Cystine, g	0.042	0.039	0.048	0.121	0.07
Phenylalanine, g	0.119	0.131	0.166	0.4	0.157
Tyrosine, g	0.108	0.102	0.137	0.345	0.122
Valine, g	0.146	0.176	0.209	0.481	0.175
Arginine, g	0.205	0.198	0.285	0.706	0.217
Histidine, g	0.105	0.09	0.137	0.345	0.091
Alanine, g	0.238	0.207	0.278	0.671	0.216
Aspartic acid, g	0.324	0.291	0.398	0.996	0.319
Glutamic acid, g	0.54	0.531	0.651	1.65	0.462
Glycine, g	0.277	0.245	0.305	0.726	0.251
Proline, g	0.238	0.212	0.219	0.558	0.217
Serine, g	0.134	0.144	0.18	0.463	0.167

Luncheon Meats and Sausage

	Brotwurst	Frankfurter, beef	Frankfurter, beef and pork	Italian sausage, ckd	Kielbasa
Measure	1 oz	1	1	1 link	1 oz
Weight, g	28	45	45	67	28
Calories	92	145	144	216	88
Protein, g	4.04	5.08	5.08	13.4	3.76
Carbohydrate, g	0.84	1.08	1.15	1	0.61
Fiber, g	—	0	0	0	0
Vitamin A, IU	—	—	—	—	—
Vitamin B$_1$, mg	0.071	0.023	0.09	0.417	0.065
Vitamin B$_2$, mg	0.064	0.046	0.054	0.156	0.061
Vitamin B$_6$, mg	0.04	0.05	0.06	0.22	0.05
Vitamin B$_{12}$, mcg	0.58	0.74	0.58	0.87	0.46
Niacin, mg	0.936	1.13	1.18	2.79	0.816
Pantothenic acid, mg	0.02	0.13	0.16	0.3	0.23
Folic acid, mcg	—	2	2	—	—
Vitamin C, mg	t	t	t	1	t
Vitamin E, IU	—	—	—	—	—
Calcium, mg	14	6	5	16	12
Copper, mg	0.02	0.03	0.04	0.05	0.03
Iron, mg	0.29	0.6	0.52	1	0.41
Magnesium, mg	4	4	5	12	5
Manganese, mg	0.011	0.015	0.014	0.055	0.011
Phosphorus, mg	38	37	38	114	42
Potassium, mg	80	71	75	204	77
Selenium, mcg	—	—	—	—	—
Sodium, mg	315	461	504	618	305
Zinc, mg	0.6	0.95	0.83	1.6	0.57
Total lipid, g	7.88	13.2	13.1	17.2	7.7
Total saturated, g	2.81	5.38	4.84	6.08	2.81
Total unsaturated, g	—	—	—	—	—
Total monounsaturated, g	—	—	—	—	—
Cholesterol, mg	18	22	22	52	19
Tryptophan, g	0.037	0.046	0.037	0.108	0.039
Threonine, g	0.17	0.192	0.183	0.531	0.122
Isoleucine, g	0.172	0.219	0.218	0.49	0.181
Leucine, g	0.306	0.373	0.369	0.9	0.248
Lycine, g	0.323	0.389	0.407	1.02	0.286
Methionine, g	0.105	0.118	0.103	0.326	0.078
Cystine, g	0.046	0.065	0.058	0.135	0.064
Phenylalanine, g	0.153	0.183	0.162	0.449	0.142
Tyrosine, g	0.126	0.166	0.141	0.387	0.139
Valine, g	0.191	0.223	0.212	0.539	0.181
Arginine, g	0.268	0.314	0.382	0.792	0.267
Histidine, g	0.124	0.162	0.158	0.387	0.089
Alanine, g	0.262	0.365	0.346	0.751	0.240
Aspartic acid, g	0.366	0.497	0.502	1.11	0.345
Glutamic acid, g	0.598	0.827	0.833	1.85	0.459
Glycine, g	0.291	0.424	0.371	0.813	0.295
Proline, g	0.21	0.365	0.244	0.624	0.195
Serine, g	0.167	0.205	0.208	0.519	0.15

Luncheon Meats and Sausage

	Knockwurst	Liver cheese	Liverwurst	Mortadella	Pepperoni
Measure	1 link	1 oz	1 oz	1 oz	1 slice
Weight, g	68	28	28	28	5.5[1]
Calories	209	86	93	88	27
Protein, g	8.08	4.3	4.01	4.64	1.15
Carbohydrate, g	1.2	0.59	0.63	0.87	0.16
Fiber, g	0	—	—	—	0
Vitamin A, IU	—	4958	—	—	—
Vitamin B$_1$, mg	0.233	0.06	0.077	0.034	0.018
Vitamin B$_2$, mg	0.095	0.631	0.292	0.043	0.014
Vitamin B$_6$, mg	0.11	0.13	—	0.035	0.01
Vitamin B$_{12}$, mcg	0.8	6.96	24.2	0.42	0.14
Niacin, mg	1.86	3.33	—	0.758	0.273
Pantothenic acid, mg	0.22	1	0.84	—	0.1
Folic acid, mcg	—	—	8	—	—
Vitamin C, mg	t	1	—	t	0.018
Vitamin E, IU	—	—	—	—	—
Calcium, mg	7	2	7	5	1
Copper, mg	0.04	0.11	—	0.02	0
Iron, mg	0.62	3.07	1.81	0.4	0.08
Magnesium, mg	8	3	—	3	1
Manganese, mg	—	0.057	—	0.008	—
Phosphorus, mg	67	59	65	27	7
Potassium, mg	136	64	—	46	19
Selenium, mcg	—	—	—	—	—
Sodium, mg	687	347	—	353	112
Zinc, mg	1.13	1.05	—	0.6	0.14
Total lipid, g	18.8	7.25	8.09	7.2	2.42
Total saturated, g	6.94	2.54	3	2.7	0.89
Total unsaturated, g	—	—	—	—	—
Total monounsaturated, g	—	—	—	—	—
Cholesterol, mg	39	49	45	16	—
Tryptophan, g	0.073	0.058	0.043	0.043	0.011
Threonine, g	0.326	0.185	0.192	0.179	0.047
Isoleucine, g	0.317	0.179	0.187	0.201	0.05
Leucine, g	0.558	0.377	0.326	0.344	0.087
Lycine, g	0.634	0.334	0.331	0.358	0.09
Methionine, g	0.195	0.097	0.081	0.112	0.029
Cystine, g	0.1	0.093	0.043	0.058	0.014
Phenylalanine, g	0.277	0.203	0.177	0.17	0.043
Tyrosine, g	0.245	0.132	0.104	0.15	0.037
Valine, g	0.35	0.229	0.246	0.208	0.054
Arginine, g	0.482	0.237	0.232	0.291	0.074
Histidine, g	0.245	0.111	0.128	0.147	0.037
Alanine, g	0.459	0.264	0.237	0.326	0.077
Aspartic acid, g	0.687	0.383	0.333	0.448	0.108
Glutamic acid, g	1.1	0.52	0.628	0.742	0.178
Glycine, g	0.478	0.265	0.314	0.374	0.087
Proline, g	0.367	0.203	0.244	0.312	0.067
Serine, g	0.324	0.196	0.199	0.188	0.047

[1] ⅛″ thick.

Luncheon Meats and Sausage

	Polish sausage	Pork and beef sausage	Pork sausage	Salami, hard	Summer sausage	Vienna sausage
Measure	1 oz	1 link	1 link	1 slice	1 slice	1
Weight, g	28	13	28	10[1]	23[2]	16
Calories	92	52	118	42	80	45
Protein, g	4	1.79	3.31	2.29	3.69	1.65
Carbohydrate, g	0.46	0.35	0.29	0.26	0.53	0.33
Fiber, g	0	0	0	0	0	0
Vitamin A, IU	—	—	—	—	—	—
Vitamin B$_1$, mg	0.142	0.096	0.155	0.06	0.039	0.014
Vitamin B$_2$, mg	0.042	0.019	0.046	0.029	0.069	0.017
Vitamin B$_6$, mg	0.05	0.01	0.07	0.05	0.07	0.02
Vitamin B$_{12}$, mcg	0.28	0.06	0.32	0.19	1.06	0.16
Niacin, mg	0.976	0.438	0.804	0.487	0.94	0.258
Pantothenic acid, mg	0.13	0.06	0.11	0.11	0.13	—
Folic acid, mcg	—	—	1	—	—	—
Vitamin C, mg	0	—	—	t	t	0
Vitamin E, IU	—	—	—	—	—	—
Calcium, mg	3	—	5	1	2	2
Copper, mg	0.03	0	0.02	0.01	0.02	0
Iron, mg	0.41	0.15	0.26	0.15	0.47	0.14
Magnesium, mg	4	1	3	2	3	1
Manganese, mg	0.014	—	—	0.004	0.007	0.005
Phosphorus, mg	39	14	34	14	23	8
Potassium, mg	67	—	58	38	53	16
Selenium, mcg	—	—	—	—	—	—
Sodium, mg	248	105	228	186	334	152
Zinc, mg	0.55	0.24	0.45	0.32	0.47	0.26
Total lipid, g	8.14	4.71	11.4	3.44	6.88	4.03
Total saturated, g	2.93	1.68	4.1	1.22	2.77	1.48
Total unsaturated, g	—	—	—	—	—	—
Total monounsaturated, g	—	—	—	—	—	—
Cholesterol, mg	20	—	19	8	16	8
Tryptophan, g	0.039	0.017	0.027	0.021	0.035	0.017
Threonine, g	0.168	0.072	0.131	0.096	0.158	0.057
Isoleucine, g	0.173	0.069	0.121	0.097	0.177	0.089
Leucine, g	0.305	0.127	0.222	0.173	0.241	0.128
Lycine, g	0.315	0.141	0.252	0.182	0.318	0.127
Methionine, g	0.107	0.043	0.081	0.059	0.081	0.042
Cystine, g	0.045	0.018	0.033	0.026	0.045	0.028
Phenylalanine, g	0.153	0.062	0.111	0.087	0.133	0.068
Tyrosine, g	0.126	0.053	0.096	0.071	0.125	0.055
Valine, g	0.192	0.077	0.133	0.108	0.185	0.092
Arginine, g	0.262	0.111	0.196	0.152	0.228	0.113
Histidine, g	0.126	0.054	0.096	0.07	0.108	0.044
Alanine, g	0.256	0.106	0.186	0.148	0.233	0.104
Aspartic acid, g	0.367	0.154	0.276	0.207	0.331	0.161
Glutamic acid, g	0.6	0.259	0.458	0.338	0.507	0.209
Glycine, g	0.281	0.117	0.201	0.164	0.254	0.162
Proline, g	0.202	0.085	0.154	0.119	0.198	0.097
Serine, g	0.166	0.069	0.128	0.094	0.156	0.069

[1] 1/16" thick.
[2] 1/8" thick.

Nuts and Seeds

	Almonds	Brazil nuts	Cashews, dry roasted	Chestnuts, raw, peeled	Coconut, shredded
Measure	1 C	1 C	1 C	1 oz	1 C
Weight, g	142	140	140	28	80
Calories	849	916	785	56	277
Protein, g	26.4	20	24.1	0.46	2.8
Carbohydrate, g	27.7	15.3	41	13	7.5
Fiber, g	17	7.5	4	—	7.2
Vitamin A, IU	14	0	0	7.4	0
Vitamin B_1, mg	0.34	1.34	0.6	0.04	0.04
Vitamin B_2, mg	1.31	0.17	0.35	0.005	0.02
Vitamin B_6, mg	0.142	0.238	0.325	0.1	0.035
Vitamin B_{12}, mcg	0	0	0	0	0
Niacin, mg	5	2.2	2.5	0.3	0.4
Pantothenic acid, mg	0.668	0.323	1.82	0.135	0.16
Folic acid, mcg	41	5.6	94	16	21
Vitamin C, mg	0	0.98	0	12	2
Vitamin E, IU	55	15.9	1.2	—	0.86
Calcium, mg	332	260	53	5.4	10
Copper, mg	1.18	2.14	2.82	0.12	0.368
Iron, mg	6.7	4.8	5.3	0.27	1.4
Magnesium, mg	386	351	374	8.5	37
Manganese, mg	2.7	3.9	—	0.095	1.05
Phosphorus, mg	716	970	522	11	76
Potassium, mg	1098	1001	650	137	205
Selenium, mcg	11	4144	16	—	8
Sodium, mg	6	1	21	0.57	18
Zinc, mg	4.14	7.1	6.1	0.14	0.88
Total lipid, g	77	93.7	64	0.35	28.2
Total saturated, g	6.2	18.7	10.9	0.067	24.3
Total unsaturated, g	17	34	37	0.14	0.29
Total monounsaturated, g	45	32	11	0.122	1.1
Cholesterol, mg	0	0	0	0	0
Tryptophan, g	0.508	0.364	0.325	0.005	0.001
Threonine, g	1.05	0.644	0.813	0.016	0.097
Isoleucine, g	1.23	0.841	1	0.018	0.105
Leucine, g	2.2	1.66	1.76	0.027	0.198
Lycine, g	0.946	0.757	1.12	0.027	0.118
Methionine, g	0.322	1.42	0.376	0.011	0.05
Cystine, g	0.508	0.489	0.389	0.015	0.053
Phenylalanine, g	1.58	1.04	1.09	0.02	0.135
Tyrosine, g	1	0.64	0.673	0.013	0.082
Valine, g	1.46	1.28	1.43	0.026	0.162
Arginine, g	3.54	3.35	2.39	0.033	0.437
Histidine, g	0.792	0.563	0.546	0.013	0.062
Alanine, g	1.34	0.798	0.962	0.03	0.136
Aspartic acid, g	3.33	1.89	2.06	0.08	0.26
Glutamic acid, g	8.43	4.4	4.97	0.06	0.609
Glycine, g	1.75	0.92	1.1	0.024	0.126
Proline, g	1.78	1.07	0.946	0.024	0.11
Serine, g	1.28	1.04	1.17	0.023	0.138

Nuts and Seeds

	Coconut liquid	Hazelnuts	Hickory nuts, dried	Macadamia nuts	Pecans
Measure	1 C	1 C	5	1 C	1 C
Weight, g	240	135	15	134	108
Calories	792	856	101	940	742
Protein, g	8.7	17	2.1	11	9.9
Carbohydrate, g	16	22.5	2	18.4	15.8
Fiber, g	5.3	13	0.95	11	10
Vitamin A, IU	0	144	20	0	83
Vitamin B_1, mg	0.07	0.62	0.08	0.469	0.93
Vitamin B_2, mg	0	0.738	0.02	0.147	0.14
Vitamin B_6, mg	0.045	0.735	0.03	0.368	0.183
Vitamin B_{12}, mcg	0	0	0	0	0
Niacin, mg	0.2	1.2	0.135	2.87	1
Pantothenic acid, mg	0.63	1.54	0.26	1	1.7
Folic acid, mcg	55	152	6	15	24
Vitamin C, mg	7	8	0.3	1.6	2
Vitamin E, IU	2.6	29.8	1.16	1	5.9
Calcium, mg	26	282	9	94	79
Copper, mg	0.9	1.72	0.214	0.397	1.14
Iron, mg	5.4	4.6	0.4	3.23	2.6
Magnesium, mg	67	313	24	155	142
Manganese, mg	3	5.67	0.69	5.5	1.54
Phosphorus, mg	292	455	49	183	312
Potassium, mg	780	950	64	493	651
Selenium, mcg	—	5.4	1.2	4.8	6.48
Sodium, mg	9	3	0.15	6	t
Zinc, mg	2.3	4	0.61	2.29	5.91
Total lipid, g	83	84.2	10.1	98.8	76.9
Total saturated, g	73	4.2	0.9	14.8	5.4
Total unsaturated, g	0.9	11	3.3	2	23
Total monounsaturated, g	3.5	62	4.89	79	44
Cholesterol, mg	0	0	0	0	0
Tryptophan, g	0.1	0.248	0.2	0.09	0.215
Threonine, g	0.32	0.515	0.06	0.352	0.273
Isoleucine, g	0.34	0.653	0.082	0.327	0.348
Leucine, g	0.65	1.27	0.146	0.619	0.562
Lycine, g	0.38	0.459	0.07	0.434	0.315
Methionine, g	0.16	0.189	0.042	0.123	0.201
Cystine, g	0.17	0.263	0.038	0.129	0.226
Phenylalanine, g	0.44	0.789	0.1	0.348	0.442
Tyrosine, g	0.27	0.521	0.064	0.452	0.307
Valine, g	0.53	0.761	0.1	0.43	0.417
Arginine, g	1.43	2.48	0.298	1.2	1.19
Histidine, g	0.2	0.376	0.05	0.225	0.245
Alanine, g	0.44	0.814	0.094	0.441	0.365
Aspartic acid, g	0.85	1.85	0.194	1.1	0.765
Glutamic acid, g	2	4.07	0.409	2.39	1.67
Glycine, g	0.4	0.81	0.1	0.497	0.407
Proline, g	0.36	0.585	0.081	0.531	0.389
Serine, g	0.45	0.769	0.115	0.47	0.406

Nuts and Seeds

	Pine nuts	Pistachios	Pumpkin and squash seeds	Sesame seeds	Sunflower seeds
Measure	1 oz	1 C	1 C	1 C	1 C
Weight, g	28	128	140	150	145
Calories	180	739	774	873	812
Protein, g	3.7	26	40.6	27.3	34.8
Carbohydrate, g	5.8	31.7	21	26.4	28.9
Fiber, g	1.3	13	5.4	17	15
Vitamin A, IU	10	707	100	99	70
Vitamin B_1, mg	0.36	1.05	0.34	0.27	2.84
Vitamin B_2, mg	0.07	0.223	0.442	0.2	0.33
Vitamin B_6, mg	0.031	2	0.31	0.126	1.8
Vitamin B_{12}, mcg	0	0	0	0	0
Niacin, mg	1.3	1.38	3.4	8.1	7.8
Pantothenic acid, mg	0.06	0.67	0.47	1.02	2
Folic acid, mcg	16	74	79	140	327
Vitamin C, mg	0.54	6	2.6	0	2
Vitamin E, IU	1.48	8.8	2	4.87	107
Calcium, mg	3	173	71	1404	174
Copper, mg	0.29	1.52	1.9	2.39	2.57
Iron, mg	1.5	8.67	15.7	3.6	10.3
Magnesium, mg	66	203	738	270	57
Manganese, mg	1.2	0.419	4	3.5	2.9
Phosphorus, mg	171	644	1620	888	1214
Potassium, mg	170	1399	1113	610	1334
Selenium, mcg	4.7	8.8	7.7	8.2	86
Sodium, mg	1	7	24	59	4
Zinc, mg	1.21	1.71	10.3	15.4	7.3
Total lipid, g	14.3	61.9	65.4	80	68.6
Total saturated, g	1.7	7.84	11.8	11.2	8.2
Total unsaturated, g	6	16.7	29	31	13
Total monounsaturated, g	5.4	29	19.6	27	47
Cholesterol, mg	0	0	0	0	0
Tryptophan, g	0.086	0.362	0.595	0.71	0.5
Threonine, g	0.216	0.924	1.25	1.77	1.34
Isoleucine, g	0.265	1.25	1.74	1.93	1.64
Leucine, g	0.491	2.15	2.87	3.22	2.39
Lycine, g	0.256	1.64	2.53	1.24	1.35
Methionine, g	0.122	0.488	0.76	1.34	0.711
Cystine, g	0.124	0.657	0.415	0.785	0.649
Phenylalanine, g	0.261	1.52	1.69	2.28	1.69
Tyrosine, g	0.249	0.914	1.41	1.69	0.959
Valine, g	0.352	1.8	2.72	2.22	1.9
Arginine, g	1.33	2.79	5.57	4.99	3.46
Histidine, g	0.163	0.686	0.94	1.02	0.91
Alanine, g	0.356	1.28	1.6	2.11	1.6
Aspartic acid, g	0.621	2.7	3.42	3.4	3.5
Glutamic acid, g	1.16	6.3	6	7.42	8.03
Glycine, g	0.347	1.4	2.48	2.84	2.1
Proline, g	0.366	1.2	1.4	2.04	1.7
Serine, g	0.289	1.73	1.58	1.97	1.55

	Nuts and Seeds		**Chicken**[1]
	Tahini	**Walnuts, shelled**	**Light meat, from a 1-lb bird**
Measure	1 T	1 C	4 oz
Weight, g	15	100	116
Calories	89	651	216
Protein, g	2.55	14.8	23.5
Carbohydrate, g	3.18	15.8	0
Fiber, g	1.4	6.7	0
Vitamin A, IU	10	30	115
Vitamin B$_1$, mg	0.183	0.33	0.068
Vitamin B$_2$, mg	0.071	0.13	0.1
Vitamin B$_6$, mg	0.022	0.73	0.56
Vitamin B$_{12}$, mcg	0	0	0.39
Niacin, mg	0.818	0.9	10.3
Pantothenic acid, mg	0.1	0.9	0.921
Folic acid, mcg	15	98	5
Vitamin C, mg	0	2	1.1
Vitamin E, IU	0.5	4.4	0.51
Calcium, mg	64	99	13
Copper, mg	0.242	1.39	0.046
Iron, mg	1.34	3.1	0.92
Magnesium, mg	14	131	27
Manganese, mg	0.22	1.8	0.021
Phosphorus, mg	110	380	189
Potassium, mg	62	450	237
Selenium, mcg	0.25	4.6	19
Sodium, mg	17	2	76
Zinc, mg	0.69	2.26	1.08
Total lipid, g	8.06	64	12.8
Total saturated, g	1.13	4.5	3.66
Total unsaturated, g	3.5	47	2.7
Total monounsaturated, g	3	8.9	5.24
Cholesterol, mg	0	0	78
Tryptophan, g	0.056	0.227	0.263
Threonine, g	0.106	0.538	0.973
Isoleucine, g	0.11	0.679	1.17
Leucine, g	0.195	1.19	1.71
Lycine, g	0.082	0.466	1.92
Methionine, g	0.084	0.336	0.628
Cystine, g	0.051	0.414	0.313
Phenylalanine, g	0.135	0.754	0.914
Tyrosine, g	0.107	0.527	0.760
Valine, g	0.143	0.868	1.14
Arginine, g	0.378	2.52	1.47
Histidine, g	0.075	0.431	0.693
Alanine, g	0.133	0.731	1.36
Aspartic acid, g	0.237	1.77	2.09
Glutamic acid, g	0.569	3.37	3.44
Glycine, g	0.175	0.906	1.49
Proline, g	0.116	0.664	1.12
Serine, g	0.139	0.938	0.828

[1]Chicken contains approx. .25 mg vitamin E/100 g; 4.54 mcg biotin/lb.

Chicken[1]

	Dark meat, from a 1-lb bird	Light meat, w/o skin, from a 1-lb bird	Dark meat, w/o skin, from a 1-lb bird	Back, bone removed
Measure	5.6 oz	3 oz	3.8 oz	½
Weight, g	160	88	109	99
Calories	379	100	136	316
Protein, g	26.7	20.4	21.9	13.9
Carbohydrate, g	0	0	0	0
Fiber, g	0	0	0	0
Vitamin A, IU	273	25	78	248
Vitamin B_1, mg	0.98	0.06	0.084	0.05
Vitamin B_2, mg	0.234	0.081	0.201	0.115
Vitamin B_6, mg	0.39	0.48	0.36	0.19
Vitamin B_{12}, mcg	0.47	0.34	0.39	0.24
Niacin, mg	8.33	9.33	6.8	4.78
Pantothenic acid, mg	1.59	0.723	1.36	0.811
Folic acid, mcg	11	4	11	6
Vitamin C, mg	3.4	1.1	3.4	1.6
Vitamin E, IU	—	—	—	—
Calcium, mg	18	10	13	13
Copper, mg	0.086	0.035	0.069	0.047
Iron, mg	1.57	0.64	1.12	0.93
Magnesium, mg	30	24	25	15
Manganese, mg	0.03	0.016	0.023	0.018
Phosphorus, mg	217	164	177	112
Potassium, mg	285	210	241	142
Selenium, mcg	20	15.7	14.7	12
Sodium, mg	117	60	93	63
Zinc, mg	2.53	0.85	2.18	1.25
Total lipid, g	29.3	1.45	4.7	28.4
Total saturated, g	8.41	0.38	1.2	8.25
Total unsaturated, g	6.4	0.326	1.17	6
Total monounsaturated, g	12	0.34	1.46	12
Cholesterol, mg	130	51	87	79
Tryptophan, g	0.296	0.238	0.256	0.149
Threonine, g	1.09	0.862	0.924	0.564
Isoleucine, g	1.31	1.07	1.15	0.66
Leucine, g	1.93	1.53	1.64	0.985
Lycine, g	2.15	1.73	1.86	1.09
Methionine, g	0.706	0.565	0.606	0.357
Cystine, g	0.358	0.261	0.28	0.192
Phenylalanine, g	1.03	0.81	0.869	0.531
Tyrosine, g	0.85	0.689	0.739	0.43
Valine, g	1.29	1.01	1.08	0.663
Arginine, g	1.68	1.23	1.32	0.9
Histidine, g	0.776	0.634	0.679	0.389
Alanine, g	1.57	1.11	1.19	0.854
Aspartic acid, g	2.38	1.82	1.95	1.24
Glutamic acid, g	3.88	3.05	3.27	2
Glycine, g	1.8	1	1.07	1.08
Proline, g	1.33	0.84	0.9	0.759
Serine, g	0.946	0.702	0.753	0.501

[1]Chicken contains approx. .25 mg vitamin E/100 g; 4.54 mcg biotin/lb.

Chicken[1]

	Breast, bone removed	Drumstick, bone removed	Leg, bone removed	Neck, bone and skin removed	Thigh, bone removed
Measure	½	1	1	1	1
Weight, g	145	73	167	20	94
Calories	250	117	312	31	199
Protein, g	30.2	14	30.3	3.5	16.2
Carbohydrate, g	0	0	0	0	0
Fiber, g	0	0	0	0	0
Vitamin A, IU	121	69	206	29	136
Vitamin B_1, mg	0.091	0.054	0.112	0.011	0.058
Vitamin B_2, mg	0.123	0.13	0.274	0.046	0.144
Vitamin B_6, mg	0.77	0.22	0.48	0.06	0.24
Vitamin B_{12}, mcg	0.5	0.25	0.54	0.06	0.28
Niacin, mg	14.3	3.97	9.07	0.824	5.1
Pantothenic acid, mg	1.16	0.863	1.85	0.218	0.97
Folic acid, mcg	6	6	19	2	7
Vitamin C, mg	1.5	2	4.1	0.5	2.1
Vitamin E, IU	—	0.32	—	—	—
Calcium, mg	16	8	17	5	9
Copper, mg	0.057	0.043	0.097	0.022	0.055
Iron, mg	1.07	0.75	1.68	0.41	0.93
Magnesium, mg	36	16	34	3	19
Manganese, mg	0.026	0.015	0.033	0.007	0.018
Phosphorus, mg	252	113	249	23	136
Potassium, mg	319	151	331	35	181
Selenium, mcg	19.2	10	21	2.7	12
Sodium, mg	91	61	132	16	71
Zinc, mg	1.16	1.46	2.96	0.54	1.5
Total lipid, g	13.4	6.34	20.2	1.76	14.3
Total saturated, g	3.86	1.75	5.7	0.45	4.08
Total unsaturated, g	2.8	1.4	4.4	0.44	3.1
Total monounsaturated, g	5.54	2.46	8.2	0.54	5.9
Cholesterol, mg	92	59	138	17	79
Tryptophan, g	0.344	0.159	0.341	0.041	0.18
Threonine, g	1.26	0.585	1.25	0.148	0.67
Isoleucine, g	1.54	0.715	1.52	0.185	0.807
Leucine, g	2.22	1.03	2.21	0.263	1.17
Lycine, g	2.5	1.16	2.47	0.298	1.31
Methionine, g	0.816	0.379	0.81	0.097	0.431
Cystine, g	0.397	0.185	0.402	0.045	0.217
Phenylalanine, g	1.18	0.55	1.18	0.139	0.630
Tyrosine, g	0.992	0.46	0.982	0.118	0.521
Valine, g	1.48	0.688	1.47	0.174	0.787
Arginine, g	1.87	0.872	1.89	0.212	1.02
Histidine, g	0.906	0.42	0.895	0.109	0.475
Alanine, g	1.72	0.804	1.75	0.191	0.951
Aspartic acid, g	2.7	1.25	2.7	0.313	1.44
Glutamic acid, g	4.46	2.07	4.44	0.525	2.37
Glycine, g	1.78	0.842	1.91	0.172	1.07
Proline, g	1.38	0.65	1.44	0.144	0.796
Serine, g	1.05	0.493	1.06	0.121	0.574

[1] Chicken contains approx. .25 mg vitamin E/100 g; 4.54 mcg biotin/lb.

Chicken[1]

	Wing, bone removed	Gizzard	Heart	Liver	Canned, boned
Measure	1	1	1	1	5 oz
Weight, g	49	37	6.1	32	142
Calories	109	44	9	40	234
Protein, g	8.98	6.73	0.95	5.75	30.9
Carbohydrate, g	0	0.21	0.04	1.09	0
Fiber, g	0	0	0	0	0
Vitamin A, IU	72	80	2	6576	166
Vitamin B_1, mg	0.024	0.013	0.009	0.044	0.021
Vitamin B_2, mg	0.043	0.07	0.044	0.628	0.183
Vitamin B_6, mg	0.17	0.05	0.02	0.24	0.5
Vitamin B_{12}, mcg	0.15	0.78	0.44	7.35	0.42
Niacin, mg	2.9	1.74	0.298	2.96	8.98
Pantothenic acid, mg	0.375	0.278	0.156	1.98	1.2
Folic acid, mcg	2	19	4	236	5.7
Vitamin C, mg	0.3	1.2	0.2	10.8	2.8
Vitamin E, IU	0.22	0.66	—	0.69	0.45
Calcium, mg	6	3	1	3	20
Copper, mg	0.02	0.036	0.021	0.126	0.065
Iron, mg	0.47	1.3	0.36	2.74	2.25
Magnesium, mg	9	6	1	6	17
Manganese, mg	0.009	0.024	0.005	0.083	0.02
Phosphorus, mg	65	50	11	87	158
Potassium, mg	76	87	11	73	196
Selenium, mcg	7.5	20.6	0.26	20	22
Sodium, mg	36	28	5	25	714
Zinc, mg	0.65	1.11	0.4	0.98	—
Total lipid, g	7.82	1.55	0.57	1.23	11.3
Total saturated, g	2.19	0.44	0.16	0.42	3.12
Total unsaturated, g	1.6	0.45	0.165	0.2	2.48
Total monounsaturated, g	3	0.396	0.14	0.3	4.5
Cholesterol, mg	38	48	8	140	88
Tryptophan, g	0.096	0.06	0.012	0.081	0.345
Threonine, g	0.363	0.31	0.043	0.256	1.27
Isoleucine, g	0.421	0.317	0.051	0.305	1.54
Leucine, g	0.632	0.472	0.083	0.519	2.24
Lycine, g	0.698	0.465	0.079	0.435	2.5
Methionine, g	0.228	0.176	0.023	0.136	0.815
Cystine, g	0.125	0.088	0.013	0.077	0.422
Phenylalanine, g	0.341	0.28	0.042	0.286	1.19
Tyrosine, g	0.275	0.205	0.034	0.202	0.993
Valine, g	0.426	0.302	0.054	0.363	1.49
Arginine, g	0.585	0.484	0.061	0.352	1.92
Histidine, g	0.248	0.136	0.025	0.153	0.903
Alanine, g	0.558	0.265	0.06	0.334	1.78
Aspartic acid, g	0.801	0.619	0.092	0.547	2.73
Glutamic acid, g	1.28	1.15	0.141	0.745	4.5
Glycine, g	0.723	0.353	0.053	0.334	1.97
Proline, g	0.502	0.35	0.048	0.285	1.47
Serine, g	0.325	0.302	0.038	0.247	1.08

[1]Chicken contains approx. .25 mg vitamin E/100 g; 4.54 mcg biotin/lb.

	Chicken[1]		Duck		Goose
	Liver paté	Cornish game hen	Domesticated, from a 1-lb bird	Liver	Domesticated, from a 1-lb bird
Measure	1 T	½	10 oz	1	11.2 oz
Weight, g	13	168	287	44	320
Calories	26	336	1159	60	1187
Protein, g	175	29	33	8.24	50.7
Carbohydrate, g	0.85	0	0	1.55	0
Fiber, g	0	0	0	0	0
Vitamin A, IU	94	181	483	17559	176
Vitamin B$_1$, mg	0.007	0.12	0.565	0.247	0.272
Vitamin B$_2$, mg	0.182	0.29	0.603	0.39	0.784
Vitamin B$_6$, mg	0.034	0.5	0.55	0.334	1.24
Vitamin B$_{12}$, mcg	1.1	0.55	0.73	23.7	1.1
Niacin, mg	0.977	9.5	11.3	2.86	11.5
Pantothenic acid, mg	0.34	1	2.73	2.7	1.4
Folic acid, mcg	42	5	37	325	14
Vitamin C, mg	1.3	0.84	8	1.98	13
Vitamin E, IU	0.19	0.74	2.98	5	8.3
Calcium, mg	1	19	30	2.62	38
Copper, mg	0.023	0.08	0.677	13.4	0.864
Iron, mg	1.19	1.3	6.89	—	8
Magnesium, mg	1.7	30	42	10	59
Manganese, mg	0.02	0.027	0.049	0.11	0.06
Phosphorus, mg	23	235	398	118	748
Potassium, mg	12	397	600	101	985
Selenium, mcg	6	19.8	36	30	46
Sodium, mg	50	103	3.91	62	234
Zinc, mg	0.28	1.9	113	1.35	5.5
Total lipid, g	1.7	23.5	37.9	2.04	107
Total saturated, g	0.52	6.5	68.1	0.63	31.3
Total unsaturated, g	0.32	4.65	14.6	0.277	12
Total monounsaturated, g	0.68	10	54	0.312	57
Cholesterol, mg	50	170	218	227	256
Tryptophan, g	0.025	0.32	0.413	0.116	0.66
Threonine, g	0.078	1.18	1.35	0.367	2.26
Isoleucine, g	0.096	1.4	1.54	0.438	2.38
Leucine, g	0.155	2.1	2.58	0.744	4.25
Lycine, g	0.124	2.3	2.61	0.624	4.01
Methionine, g	0.044	0.76	0.835	0.195	1.22
Cystine, g	0.028	0.39	0.517	0.111	0.79
Phenylalanine, g	0.09	1.1	1.31	0.41	2.12
Tyrosine, g	0.064	0.9	1.13	0.29	1.62
Valine, g	0.112	1.4	1.64	0.52	2.48
Arginine, g	0.106	1.8	2.21	0.505	3.15
Histidine, g	0.045	0.84	0.812	0.219	1.41
Alanine, g	0.1	1.7	2.23	0.479	3.12
Aspartic acid, g	0.16	2.56	3.16	0.784	4.56
Glutamic acid, g	0.25	4.2	4.9	1.06	7.54
Glycine, g	0.09	1.9	2.66	0.479	3.21
Proline, g	0.09	1.4	1.97	0.409	2.45
Serine, g	0.089	1	1.4	0.355	2.02

[1]Chicken contains approx. .25 mg vitamin E/100 g; 4.54 mcg biotin/lb.

	Goose	**Turkey**			
	Liver	Light meat, from a 1-lb bird	Dark meat, from a 1-lb bird	Liver	Canned, boned
Measure	1	6.4 oz	5.3 oz	1	5 oz
Weight, g	94	180	152	102	142
Calories	125	286	243	140	231
Protein, g	15.3	39	28.7	20.4	33.6
Carbohydrate, g	5.94	0	0	4.21	0
Fiber, g	0	0	0	0	0
Vitamin A, IU	29138	12	8	18403	0
Vitamin B_1, mg	0.528	0.101	0.111	0.062	0.02
Vitamin B_2, mg	0.838	0.207	0.307	2.21	0.243
Vitamin B_6, mg	0.72	0.86	0.49	0.78	0.47
Vitamin B_{12}, mcg	51	0.37	0.58	64.6	0.4
Niacin, mg	6.11	9.24	4.34	10.35	9.4
Pantothenic acid, mg	5.8	1.1	1.57	7.81	0.97
Folic acid, mcg	694	13	15	752	8.5
Vitamin C, mg	4.2	0	0	4.6	2.8
Vitamin E, IU	—	—	—	—	0.574
Calcium, mg	40	23	26	7	17
Copper, mg	7.07	0.135	0.208	0.512	0.1
Iron, mg	29	2.18	2.57	11	2.64
Magnesium, mg	23	43	31	21	28
Manganese, mg	0	0.032	0.032	0.294	0.024
Phosphorus, mg	245	331	259	319	230
Potassium, mg	216	489	396	303	318
Selenium, mcg	64	40	40	74	0.37
Sodium, mg	132	106	108	98	663
Zinc, mg	2.9	2.82	4.49	2.53	3.4
Total lipid, g	4.03	13.2	13.3	4.05	9.74
Total saturated, g	1.49	3.59	3.92	1.28	2.84
Total unsaturated, g	0.24	3	3.46	0.7	2.5
Total monounsaturated, g	0.76	5	4.56	1	3.2
Cholesterol, mg	484	117	109	475	94
Tryptophan, g	0.216	0.43	0.318	0.288	0.371
Threonine, g	0.684	1.7	1.25	0.908	1.46
Isoleucine, g	0.818	1.95	1.44	1.08	1.68
Leucine, g	1.38	3.02	2.23	1.84	2.6
Lycine, g	1.16	3.54	2.62	1.54	3.04
Methionine, g	0.365	1.09	0.81	0.483	0.939
Cystine, g	0.207	0.428	0.316	0.274	0.378
Phenylalanine, g	0.766	1.52	1.12	1.01	1.3
Tyrosine, g	0.541	1.47	1.09	0.718	1.27
Valine, g	0.97	2.02	1.49	1.28	1.74
Arginine, g	0.943	2.74	2.02	1.25	2.36
Histidine, g	0.409	1.17	0.866	0.543	1
Alanine, g	0.894	2.48	1.83	1.18	2.13
Aspartic acid, g	1.46	3.75	2.77	1.94	3.22
Glutamic acid, g	1.99	6.2	4.59	2.64	5.34
Glycine, g	0.894	2.35	1.71	1.18	2.02
Proline, g	0.763	1.81	1.33	1.01	1.55
Serine, g	0.663	1.71	1.27	0.879	1.47

	Wild Game		**Seafood and Seaweed**	
	Pheasant, from a 1-lb bird	Quail, from a 1-lb bird	Abalone	Agar-agar
Measure	13 oz	14 oz	3 oz	2 T
Weight, g	371	405	85	10
Calories	670	780	89	2.6
Protein, g	84.2	79.4	14.5	0.05
Carbohydrate, g	0	0	5	0.68
Fiber, g	0	0	0	0.05
Vitamin A, IU	655	985	4.25	0
Vitamin B$_1$, mg	0.267	0.988	0.16	t
Vitamin B$_2$, mg	0.531	1.05	0.12	t
Vitamin B$_6$, mg	2.46	2.43	0.128	t
Vitamin B$_{12}$, mcg	2.85	1.7	0.62	0
Niacin, mg	23.8	30.5	1.3	t
Pantothenic acid, mg	3.44	3	2.55	0.03
Folic acid, mcg	22	30	4.3	8.5
Vitamin C, mg	19.6	24.6	1.7	0
Vitamin E, IU	1.64	4	5	0.01
Calcium, mg	46	52	27	5.4
Copper, mg	0.241	2.05	0.167	t
Iron, mg	4.25	16	2.7	0.19
Magnesium, mg	72	93	41	6.7
Manganese, mg	0.063	0.08	0.034	0.04
Phosphorus, mg	794	1112	173	0.5
Potassium, mg	900	874	213	23
Selenium, mcg	58	67	38	0.07
Sodium, mg	150	215	255	0.9
Zinc, mg	3.57	9.8	0.69	0.06
Total lipid, g	34.4	48.8	0.64	0.00
Total saturated, g	10	13.7	0.127	0.001
Total unsaturated, g	4.4	2	0.088	0.001
Total monounsaturated, g	16	17	0.09	0
Cholesterol, mg	263	308	72	0
Tryptophan, g	1.12	1.16	0.163	—
Threonine, g	4.11	3.82	0.626	—
Isoleucine, g	4.55	4.1	0.632	—
Leucine, g	6.93	6.53	1.02	—
Lycine, g	7.47	6.66	1.09	—
Methionine, g	2.38	2.39	0.328	—
Cystine, g	1.13	1.37	0.19	—
Phenylalanine, g	3.25	3.34	0.521	—
Tyrosine, g	2.68	3.43	0.465	—
Valine, g	4.56	4.18	0.635	—
Arginine, g	5.24	5.18	1.06	—
Histidine, g	3.2	2.82	0.279	—
Alanine, g	5.23	5.1	0.879	—
Aspartic acid, g	8.11	6.69	1.4	—
Glutamic acid, g	12.2	10.2	1.97	—
Glycine, g	4.56	6.24	0.91	—
Proline, g	3.48	3.5	0.593	—
Serine, g	3.6	3.79	0.651	—

Seafood and Seaweed

	Anchovy, in oil, drained	Bass, sea	Bluefish
Measure	5	3 oz	3 oz
Weight, g	20	85	85
Calories	42	82	105
Protein, g	5.78	15	17
Carbohydrate, g	0	0	0
Fiber, g	0	0	0
Vitamin A, IU	14	156	338
Vitamin B_1, mg	0.016	0.09	0.049
Vitamin B_2, mg	0.073	0.03	0.068
Vitamin B_6, mg	0.041	0.34	0.342
Vitamin B_{12}, mcg	0.176	3.25	4.58
Niacin, mg	3.98	1.9	5.06
Pantothenic acid, mg	0.18	0.46	0.704
Folic acid, mcg	2.5	4.3	1.4
Vitamin C, mg	0	0	0
Vitamin E, IU	1	0.64	0.63
Calcium, mg	46	8.5	6
Copper, mg	0.068	0.026	0.045
Iron, mg	0.93	0.71	0.41
Magnesium, mg	14	35	28
Manganese, mg	0.02	0.013	0.018
Phosphorus, mg	50	174	193
Potassium, mg	109	232	316
Selenium, mcg	13.6	31	31
Sodium, mg	734	59	51
Zinc, mg	0.49	0.34	0.69
Total lipid, g	1.94	1.98	3.6
Total saturated, g	0.441	0.431	0.778
Total unsaturated, g	0.5	0.63	0.9
Total monounsaturated, g	0.75	0.36	1.5
Cholesterol, mg	17	68	50
Tryptophan, g	0.065	0.169	0.19
Threonine, g	0.253	0.66	0.746
Isoleucine, g	0.266	0.694	0.785
Leucine, g	0.470	1.23	1.39
Lycine, g	0.531	1.38	1.56
Methionine, g	0.171	0.446	0.504
Cystine, g	0.062	0.162	0.183
Phenylalanine, g	0.226	0.588	0.665
Tyrosine, g	0.195	0.509	0.575
Valine, g	0.298	0.777	0.877
Arginine, g	0.346	0.902	1.02
Histidine, g	0.17	0.444	0.502
Alanine, g	0.349	0.911	1.03
Aspartic acid, g	0.592	1.54	1.74
Glutamic acid, g	0.862	2.25	2.54
Glycine, g	0.277	0.723	0.818
Proline, g	0.204	0.533	0.603
Serine, g	0.236	0.615	0.695

Seafood and Seaweed

	Carp	Catfish	Caviar, black and red	Clams	Cod
Measure	3 oz	3 oz	1 T	9 lge	3 oz
Weight, g	85	85	16	180	85
Calories	108	99	40	133	70
Protein, g	15	15.5	3.9	23	15
Carbohydrate, g	0	0	0.64	4.62	0
Fiber, g	0	0	0	0	0
Vitamin A, IU	25	43	299	540	34
Vitamin B$_1$, mg	0.008	0.038	0.03	0.18	0.065
Vitamin B$_2$, mg	0.036	0.09	0.1	0.38	0.055
Vitamin B$_6$, mg	0.162	0.1	0.05	0.14	0.208
Vitamin B$_{12}$, mcg	1.3	0.002	3.2	89	0.772
Niacin, mg	1.34	1.82	0.02	3.17	1.75
Pantothenic acid, mg	0.136	0.424	0.56	0.65	0.13
Folic acid, mcg	13	8.5	8	4.5	5.9
Vitamin C, mg	1.4	0.6	0	23	0.9
Vitamin E, IU	0.8	0.5	1.5	2.68	0.29
Calcium, mg	35	34	42	83	13
Copper, mg	0.048	0.08	0.02	0.619	0.024
Iron, mg	1.05	0.83	1.7	25	0.32
Magnesium, mg	25	21	48	17	27
Manganese, mg	0.036	0.013	t	0.9	0.013
Phosphorus, mg	352	181	54	304	173
Potassium, mg	283	296	27	564	351
Selenium, mcg	10.7	10.7	10.5	43	28
Sodium, mg	42	54	240	100	46
Zinc, mg	1.26	0.61	0.15	2.46	0.38
Total lipid, g	4.76	3.62	2.86	1.75	0.57
Total saturated, g	0.921	0.836	0.65	0.169	0.111
Total unsaturated, g	1.2	1.2	1.18	0.51	0.196
Total monounsaturated, g	1.98	1	0.74	0.14	0.08
Cholesterol, mg	56	49	94	60	37
Tryptophan, g	0.17	0.173	0.052	0.257	0.169
Threonine, g	0.665	0.677	0.202	0.99	0.664
Isoleucine, g	0.699	0.712	0.166	1	0.698
Leucine, g	1.23	1.25	0.341	1.62	1.23
Lycine, g	1.39	1.42	0.293	1.72	1.39
Methionine, g	0.449	0.457	0.103	0.518	0.448
Cystine, g	0.162	0.166	0.072	0.302	0.162
Phenylalanine, g	0.592	0.604	0.171	0.824	0.591
Tyrosine, g	0.512	0.522	0.155	0.736	0.511
Valine, g	0.781	0.796	0.202	1	0.779
Arginine, g	0.907	0.925	0.254	1.68	0.906
Histidine, g	0.446	0.455	0.104	0.441	0.445
Alanine, g	0.916	0.934	0.264	1.4	0.915
Aspartic acid, g	1.55	1.58	0.382	2.22	1.55
Glutamic acid, g	2.26	2.31	0.581	3.13	2.26
Glycine, g	0.728	0.741	0.118	1.44	0.727
Proline, g	0.536	0.547	0.192	0.938	0.536
Serine, g	0.619	0.631	0.304	1.03	0.617

Seafood and Seaweed

	Crab	Eel	Flat fish, flounder and sole species	Haddock	Halibut
Measure	3 oz	3 oz	3 oz	3 oz	3 oz
Weight, g	85	85	85	85	85
Calories	71	156	78	74	93
Protein, g	15.6	15.7	16	16	17.7
Carbohydrate, g	0	0	0	0	0
Fiber, g	0	0	0	0	0
Vitamin A, IU	20	2954	28	47	132
Vitamin B_1, mg	0.037	0.128	0.076	0.03	0.051
Vitamin B_2, mg	0.037	0.034	0.065	0.031	0.064
Vitamin B_6, mg	0.272	0.057	0.177	0.255	0.292
Vitamin B_{12}, mcg	9.08	2.55	1.29	1.02	1
Niacin, mg	0.934	2.98	2.46	3.23	11.97
Pantothenic acid, mg	0.54	0.204	0.428	0.108	0.28
Folic acid, mcg	3.6	12.8	6.8	1	1.8
Vitamin C, mg	1.8	1.3	1.45	0	0
Vitamin E, IU	—	5	2.4	0.49	1
Calcium, mg	39	17	15	28	40
Copper, mg	0.784	0.02	0.027	0.022	0.023
Iron, mg	0.5	0.43	0.3	0.89	0.71
Magnesium, mg	30.8	16.3	27	33	71
Manganese, mg	0.03	0.03	0.014	0.021	0.013
Phosphorus, mg	186	183	156	160	189
Potassium, mg	173	232	307	264	382
Selenium, mcg	31	5.5	30.4	26	31
Sodium, mg	711	43	69	58	46
Zinc, mg	5.05	1.38	0.39	0.32	0.35
Total lipid, g	0.51	9.9	1	0.61	1.95
Total saturated, g	0.076	2	0.241	0.111	0.267
Total unsaturated, g	0.11	0.805	0.28	0.2	0.62
Total monounsaturated, g	0.068	6.1	0.198	0.1	0.64
Cholesterol, mg	35	107	41	49	27
Tryptophan, g	0.217	0.176	0.179	0.18	0.198
Threonine, g	0.63	0.688	0.702	0.705	0.775
Isoleucine, g	0.754	0.723	0.738	0.74	0.815
Leucine, g	1.23	1.27	1.3	1.3	1.44
Lycine, g	1.35	1.44	1.47	1.48	1.62
Methionine, g	0.438	0.464	0.474	0.476	0.524
Cystine, g	0.174	0.168	0.172	0.173	0.19
Phenylalanine, g	0.657	0.612	0.626	0.627	0.691
Tyrosine, g	0.518	0.53	0.541	0.542	0.598
Valine, g	0.732	0.808	0.825	0.828	0.911
Arginine, g	1.36	0.938	0.959	0.961	1.06
Histidine, g	0.316	0.462	0.472	0.473	0.521
Alanine, g	0.881	0.948	0.969	0.972	1.07
Aspartic acid, g	1.6	1.6	1.64	1.65	1.81
Glutamic acid, g	2.65	2.34	2.39	2.4	2.64
Glycine, g	0.938	0.752	0.769	0.772	0.849
Proline, g	0.513	0.554	0.566	0.569	0.626
Serine, g	0.612	0.640	0.654	0.655	0.722

Seafood and Seaweed

	Kelp	Lobster	Mackerel	Oysters	Perch
Measure	2 T	3 oz	3 oz	6 med	3 oz
Weight, g	10	85	85	84	85
Calories	4.3	77	174	58	80
Protein, g	0.168	16	15.8	5.9	15.8
Carbohydrate, g	0.957	0.43	0	3.29	0
Fiber, g	0.13	0	0	0	0
Vitamin A, IU	12	60	140	282	34
Vitamin B$_1$, mg	t	0.368	0.15	0.128	0.08
Vitamin B$_2$, mg	0.015	0.041	0.265	0.139	0.094
Vitamin B$_6$, mg	0	0.05	0.339	0.042	0.2
Vitamin B$_{12}$, mcg	0	0.786	7.4	16	0.85
Niacin, mg	0.047	1.23	7.72	1.1	1.7
Pantothenic acid, mg	18	1.39	0.728	0.155	0.306
Folic acid, mcg	0.3	7.7	1	8.3	7.7
Vitamin C, mg	0.087	0	0.3	3	2.72
Vitamin E, IU	—	1.86	1.9	1.06	1.57
Calcium, mg	17	26	10	38	91
Copper, mg	0.013	1.41	0.062	3.74	0.022
Iron, mg	0.285	0.54	1.38	5.63	0.78
Magnesium, mg	12	15.6	64	46	26
Manganese, mg	0.02	0.047	0.013	0.378	0.013
Phosphorus, mg	42	166	184	117	184
Potassium, mg	8.9	236	267	192	232
Selenium, mcg	0.07	35	37.5	44.4	37
Sodium, mg	429	272	76	94	64
Zinc, mg	0.123	2.57	0.53	76.4	0.41
Total lipid, g	0.056	0.76	11.8	2.08	1.39
Total saturated, g	0.025	0.15	2.77	0.53	0.207
Total unsaturated, g	0.005	0.128	2.85	0.8	0.36
Total monounsaturated, g	0.01	0.22	4.64	0.26	0.53
Cholesterol, mg	0	81	60	46	36
Tryptophan, g	0.005	0.223	0.177	0.066	0.178
Threonine, g	0.006	0.647	0.693	0.255	0.694
Isoleucine, g	0.008	0.774	0.728	0.258	0.729
Leucine, g	0.008	1.29	1.28	0.417	1.29
Lycine, g	0.008	1.4	1.45	0.444	1.45
Methionine, g	0.003	0.45	0.468	0.134	0.468
Cystine, g	0.01	0.179	0.169	0.078	0.17
Phenylalanine, g	0.004	0.675	0.617	0.213	0.618
Tyrosine, g	0.003	0.532	0.534	0.19	0.535
Valine, g	0.007	0.751	0.814	0.259	0.816
Arginine, g	0.007	1.4	0.946	0.433	0.948
Histidine, g	0.002	0.325	0.466	0.114	0.466
Alanine, g	0.012	0.905	0.956	0.359	0.957
Aspartic acid, g	0.013	1.65	1.62	0.572	1.62
Glutamic acid, g	0.027	2.73	2.36	0.807	2.36
Glycine, g	0.01	0.964	0.759	0.371	0.76
Proline, g	0.007	0.527	0.559	0.242	0.56
Serine, g	0.01	0.629	0.645	0.265	0.646

Seafood and Seaweed

	Pike	Pollock	Salmon	Sardines, in oil, drained	Scallops
Measure	3 oz	3 oz	3 oz	2	3 oz
Weight, g	85	85	85	24	85
Calories	75	78	121	50	75
Protein, g	16.4	16.5	16.9	5.9	14.3
Carbohydrate, g	0	0	0	0	2
Fiber, g	0	0	0	0	0
Vitamin A, IU	60	30	34	54	43
Vitamin B_1, mg	0.049	0.04	0.19	0.019	0.01
Vitamin B_2, mg	0.054	0.157	0.32	0.054	0.055
Vitamin B_6, mg	0.099	0.244	0.695	0.04	0.13
Vitamin B_{12}, mcg	1.7	2.7	2.7	2.15	1.3
Niacin, mg	2.16	2.78	6.68	1.26	0.978
Pantothenic acid, mg	0.64	0.3	1.4	0.154	0.122
Folic acid, mcg	13	2.55	1.8	2.8	13.6
Vitamin C, mg	3.2	0	8.2	0	2.55
Vitamin E, IU	0.25	0.29	—	0.1	1.3
Calcium, mg	48	51	10	92	21
Copper, mg	0.043	0.043	0.18	0.045	0.045
Iron, mg	0.47	0.39	0.68	0.7	0.25
Magnesium, mg	27.2	57	26.2	9	48
Manganese, mg	0.018	0.013	0.009	0.026	0.077
Phosphorus, mg	187	188	170	118	186
Potassium, mg	220	302	417	95	274
Selenium, mcg	11	31	31	12.6	19
Sodium, mg	33	73	37	121	137
Zinc, mg	0.57	0.4	0.54	0.31	0.81
Total lipid, g	0.58	0.83	5.39	2.75	0.64
Total saturated, g	0.1	0.115	0.834	0.367	0.067
Total unsaturated, g	0.17	0.41	2.16	1.24	0.22
Total monounsaturated, g	0.133	0.095	1.79	0.93	0.03
Cholesterol, mg	33	60	47	34	28
Tryptophan, g	0.184	0.185	0.189	0.066	0.16
Threonine, g	0.717	0.724	0.74	0.259	0.614
Isoleucine, g	0.754	0.762	0.777	0.272	0.621
Leucine, g	1.33	1.34	1.37	0.48	1
Lycine, g	1.5	1.52	1.55	0.542	1.06
Methionine, g	0.485	0.49	0.499	0.175	0.322
Cystine, g	0.175	0.177	0.181	0.063	0.187
Phenylalanine, g	0.639	0.645	0.659	0.231	0.511
Tyrosine, g	0.553	0.558	0.57	0.199	0.456
Valine, g	0.843	0.852	0.869	0.304	0.623
Arginine, g	0.979	0.989	1	0.354	1.04
Histidine, g	0.482	0.486	0.496	0.174	0.274
Alanine, g	0.99	1	1.02	0.357	0.863
Aspartic acid, g	1.67	1.69	1.72	0.605	1.38
Glutamic acid, g	2.44	2.47	2.52	0.882	1.94
Glycine, g	0.785	0.793	0.81	0.283	0.893
Proline, g	0.579	0.585	0.597	0.209	0.582
Serine, g	0.668	0.674	0.689	0.241	0.639

Seafood and Seaweed

	Shark	Shrimp	Smelt	Snails	Snapper
Measure	3 oz	3 oz	3 oz	3 oz	3 oz
Weight, g	85	85	85	85	85
Calories	111	90	83	117	85
Protein, g	17.8	17.3	15	20	17.4
Carbohydrate, g	0	0.77	0	6.6	0
Fiber, g	0	0	0	0	0
Vitamin A, IU	198	8.26	43	72	85
Vitamin B$_1$, mg	0.036	0.024	t	0.022	0.039
Vitamin B$_2$, mg	0.053	0.029	0.102	0.091	0.003
Vitamin B$_6$, mg	0.3	0.088	0.13	0.291	0.34
Vitamin B$_{12}$, mcg	1.27	0.987	2.92	7.7	2.6
Niacin, mg	2.5	2.17	1.23	0.893	0.241
Pantothenic acid, mg	0.59	0.235	0.542	0.177	0.64
Folic acid, mcg	3	2.6	3.4	5.4	4.3
Vitamin C, mg	0	1.7	0	—	1.4
Vitamin E, IU	1.2	1	0.6	—	0.64
Calcium, mg	29	44	51	48	27
Copper, mg	0.028	0.224	0.118	0.876	0.024
Iron, mg	0.71	2.05	0.77	4.28	0.15
Magnesium, mg	42	31	26	73	27
Manganese, mg	0.013	0.043	0.595	0.38	0.011
Phosphorus, mg	179	175	196	120	169
Potassium, mg	136	157	247	295	355
Selenium, mcg	32	32	31	—	33
Sodium, mg	67	126	51	175	54
Zinc, mg	0.36	0.94	1.4	1.39	0.3
Total lipid, g	3.83	1.47	2.06	0.34	1.14
Total saturated, g	0.786	0.279	0.384	0.026	0.242
Total unsaturated, g	1	0.569	0.75	—	0.39
Total monounsaturated, g	1.5	0.215	0.545	—	0.2
Cholesterol, mg	43	130	60	55	31
Tryptophan, g	0.2	0.241	0.167	0.263	0.196
Threonine, g	0.782	0.699	0.657	0.908	0.764
Isoleucine, g	0.822	0.837	0.69	0.704	0.803
Leucine, g	1.45	1.37	1.22	1.62	1.42
Lycine, g	1.64	1.5	1.38	1.25	1.6
Methionine, g	0.528	0.486	0.444	0.513	0.516
Cystine, g	0.191	0.194	0.161	0.159	0.187
Phenylalanine, g	0.696	0.729	0.585	0.7	0.681
Tyrosine, g	0.602	0.575	0.506	0.645	0.588
Valine, g	0.919	0.813	0.772	0.881	0.898
Arginine, g	1.07	1.51	0.897	2.1	1.04
Histidine, g	0.525	0.351	0.441	0.415	0.513
Alanine, g	1.08	0.978	0.906	1.32	1.05
Aspartic acid, g	1.83	1.78	1.53	2.18	1.79
Glutamic acid, g	2.66	2.95	2.24	3.12	2.6
Glycine, g	0.856	1.04	0.719	1.27	0.836
Proline, g	0.631	0.57	0.53	1	0.616
Serine, g	0.728	0.68	0.611	0.944	0.711

Seafood and Seaweed

	Spirulina	Swordfish	Trout	Tuna, bluefin	Tuna, light, in water
Measure	1 C	3 oz	3 oz	3 oz	1 can
Weight, g	15	85	85	85	165
Calories	44	103	126	123	191
Protein, g	8.6	16.8	17.7	20	42
Carbohydrate, g	3.6	0	0	0	0
Fiber, g	0.54	0	0	0	0
Vitamin A, IU	85.5	101	49	1856	92
Vitamin B_1, mg	0.357	0.031	0.277	0.21	0.05
Vitamin B_2, mg	0.55	0.081	0.261	0.21	0.122
Vitamin B_6, mg	0.055	0.281	1.43	0.387	0.58
Vitamin B_{12}, mcg	0	1.49	6.6	8	4.9
Niacin, mg	1.9	8.23	7.6	7.4	22
Pantothenic acid, mg	0.5	0.35	1.65	0.9	0.35
Folic acid, mcg	15	1.7	11.3	1.6	6.6
Vitamin C, mg	1.5	0.9	0.4	0	0
Vitamin E, IU	1.12	0.6	0.25	1.3	1.3
Calcium, mg	18	4	36	6.8	18
Copper, mg	0.9	0.107	0.16	0.07	0.08
Iron, mg	4.3	0.69	1.27	0.867	2.5
Magnesium, mg	29	23	19	43	45
Manganese, mg	0.285	0.016	0.723	0.013	0.02
Phosphorus, mg	18	224	208	216	268
Potassium, mg	205	245	307	214	391
Selenium, mcg	1.1	41	11	31	133
Sodium, mg	157	76	44	33	558
Zinc, mg	0.3	0.97	0.56	0.5	1.3
Total lipid, g	1.16	3.41	5.62	4.17	1.35
Total saturated, g	0.398	0.932	0.98	1.07	0.386
Total unsaturated, g	0.3	0.78	1.27	1.22	0.556
Total monounsaturated, g	0.1	1.3	2.77	1.36	0.26
Cholesterol, mg	0	33	49	32	50
Tryptophan, g	0.139	0.189	0.198	0.22	0.472
Threonine, g	0.446	0.738	0.774	0.87	1.85
Isoleucine, g	0.48	0.775	0.813	0.9	1.94
Leucine, g	0.74	1.37	1.44	1.6	3.4
Lycine, g	0.45	1.55	1.62	1.8	3.9
Methionine, g	0.17	0.498	0.523	0.59	1.25
Cystine, g	0.1	0.18	0.19	0.2	0.45
Phenylalanine, g	—	0.657	0.689	0.77	1.6
Tyrosine, g	—	0.568	0.596	0.7	1.4
Valine, g	—	0.867	0.91	0.1	2.17
Arginine, g	—	1	1.06	1.2	2.5
Histidine, g	—	0.496	0.519	0.58	1.24
Alanine, g	—	1.02	1.07	1.2	2.55
Aspartic acid, g	—	1.72	1.8	2	4.3
Glutamic acid, g	—	2.51	2.63	2.96	6.3
Glycine, g	—	0.808	0.847	0.95	2
Proline, g	—	0.595	0.624	0.7	1.5
Serine, g	—	0.687	0.72	0.81	1.7

Seafood and Seaweed

	Tuna, white, in water	Wakame	Whitefish
Measure	1 can	2 T	3 oz
Weight, g	172	10	85
Calories	220	0.5	114
Protein, g	41	0.3	16
Carbohydrate, g	0	0.9	0
Fiber, g	0	0.05	0
Vitamin A, IU	33	36	2050
Vitamin B$_1$, mg	0.014	t	0.128
Vitamin B$_2$, mg	0.076	0.023	0.108
Vitamin B$_6$, mg	0.37	0	0.255
Vitamin B$_{12}$, mcg	2	0	0.85
Niacin, mg	9.97	0.16	2.72
Pantothenic acid, mg	0.2	0.07	0.637
Folic acid, mcg	3.4	20	12.8
Vitamin C, mg	0	0.3	0
Vitamin E, IU	4	0.15	0.25
Calcium, mg	24	15	22
Copper, mg	0.067	0.03	0.061
Iron, mg	1.67	0.22	0.31
Magnesium, mg	57	11	28
Manganese, mg	0.03	0.14	0.057
Phosphorus, mg	373	8	230
Potassium, mg	408	5	269
Selenium, mcg	113	0.07	11
Sodium, mg	648	87	43
Zinc, mg	0.826	0.038	0.84
Total lipid, g	5.1	0.06	4.98
Total saturated, g	1.36	0.013	0.77
Total unsaturated, g	1.9	0.022	1.83
Total monounsaturated, g	1.35	0.006	1.7
Cholesterol, mg	72	0	51
Tryptophan, g	0.456	0.004	0.182
Threonine, g	1.78	0.017	0.711
Isoleucine, g	1.87	0.009	0.748
Leucine, g	3.3	0.026	1.32
Lycine, g	3.73	0.011	1.49
Methionine, g	1.2	0.006	0.48
Cystine, g	0.44	0.003	0.174
Phenylalanine, g	1.59	0.011	0.633
Tyrosine, g	1.37	0.005	0.547
Valine, g	2.1	0.021	0.836
Arginine, g	2.43	0.009	0.971
Histidine, g	1.2	0.002	0.478
Alanine, g	2.46	0.014	0.981
Aspartic acid, g	4.2	0.018	1.66
Glutamic acid, g	6.1	0.02	2.42
Glycine, g	1.95	0.01	0.779
Proline, g	1.44	0.009	0.574
Serine, g	1.66	0.008	0.662

Vegetables and Vegetable Juices

	Alfalfa sprouts	Artichoke, globe	Artichoke, Jerusalem	Arugula	Asparagus
Measure	1 C	1 med	1 C	½ C	1 C
Weight, g	33	128	150	10	134
Calories	10	65	114	2.5	30
Protein, g	1.32	3.4	3	0.258	4.1
Carbohydrate, g	1.25	15.3	26	0.365	4.94
Fiber, g	0.83	1.36	1.2	0.16	1.1
Vitamin A, IU	51	237	30	237	1202
Vitamin B_1, mg	0.025	0.1	0.3	T	0.15
Vitamin B_2, mg	0.042	0.077	0.09	T	0.166
Vitamin B_6, mg	0.011	0.143	0.116	T	0.2
Vitamin B_{12}, mcg	0	0	0	0	0
Niacin, mg	0.159	0.973	1.95	0.03	1.5
Pantothenic acid, mg	0.186	0.329	0.6	0.044	0.234
Folic acid, mcg	12.2	94.2	20	9.7	160
Vitamin C, mg	2.7	13.8	6	1.5	44
Vitamin E, IU	0.01	0.36	0.42	0.06	4
Calcium, mg	10	61	21	16	28
Copper, mg	0.052	0.095	0.2	t	0.2
Iron, mg	0.32	2.1	5.1	0.146	0.9
Magnesium, mg	9	60	26	4.7	24
Manganese, mg	0.062	0.426	0.09	0.032	0.286
Phosphorus, mg	23	99	117	5.2	70
Potassium, mg	26	434	644	37	404
Selenium, mcg	0.2	0.256	1.05	0.03	3
Sodium, mg	2	102	6	2.7	2
Zinc, mg	0.3	0.56	0.18	0.047	0.94
Total lipid, g	0.23	0.19	0.02	0.066	0.3
Total saturated, g	0.023	0.045	0	0.009	0.068
Total unsaturated, g	0.135	0.081	0.002	0.032	0.118
Total monounsaturated, g	0.018	0.006	0.006	0.005	0.008
Cholesterol, mg	0	0	0	0	0
Tryptophan, g	—	—	—	—	0.04
Threonine, g	0.044	—	—	—	0.114
Isoleucine, g	0.047	—	—	—	1.5
Leucine, g	0.088	—	—	—	0.178
Lycine, g	0.071	—	—	—	0.194
Methionine, g	—	—	—	—	0.038
Cystine, g	—	—	—	—	0.048
Phenylalanine, g	—	—	—	—	0.096
Tyrosine, g	—	—	—	—	0.064
Valine, g	0.048	—	—	—	0.158
Arginine, g	—	—	—	—	0.192
Histidine, g	—	—	—	—	0.062
Alanine, g	—	—	—	—	0.192
Aspartic acid, g	—	—	—	—	0.476
Glutamic acid, g	—	—	—	—	0.672
Glycine, g	—	—	—	—	0.132
Proline, g	—	—	—	—	0.218
Serine, g	—	—	—	—	0.156

Vegetables and Vegetable Juices

	Beets	Beet greens	Broccoli	Brussels sprouts	Cabbage, common
Measure	1 C	1 C	1 C	1 C	1 C
Weight, g	136	38	88	88	70
Calories	60	0.8	24	38	16
Protein, g	2	0.7	2.6	3.3	0.84
Carbohydrate, g	13.6	1.5	4.6	7.88	2.76
Fiber, g	3.8	1.4	2.6	3.3	1.6
Vitamin A, IU	28	2308	1356	778	88
Vitamin B$_1$, mg	0.068	0.038	0.058	0.12	0.03
Vitamin B$_2$, mg	0.028	0.08	0.1	0.08	0.02
Vitamin B$_6$, mg	0.06	0.04	0.14	0.19	0.066
Vitamin B$_{12}$, mcg	0	0	0	0	0
Niacin, mg	0.54	0.152	0.56	0.65	0.2
Pantothenic acid, mg	0.2	0.096	0.47	0.27	0.098
Folic acid, mcg	126	5.6	62	54	39
Vitamin C, mg	15	11	82	74	33
Vitamin E, IU	0.6	0.85	2	1	0.1
Calcium, mg	22	46	42	36	32
Copper, mg	0.1	0.07	0.04	0.06	0.016
Iron, mg	1.24	1.2	0.78	1.2	0.4
Magnesium, mg	28	28	22	20	10
Manganese, mg	0.47	0.15	0.2	0.29	0.11
Phosphorus, mg	66	16	58	60	16
Potassium, mg	440	208	286	342	172
Selenium, mcg	0.95	0.34	2.6	1.4	0.63
Sodium, mg	98	76	24	22	12
Zinc, mg	0.5	0.14	0.36	0.36	0.12
Total lipid, g	0.2	0.02	0.3	0.26	0.189
Total saturated, g	0.02	0.004	0.048	0.05	0.023
Total unsaturated, g	0.083	0.008	0.147	0.135	0.085
Total monounsaturated, g	0.045	0.005	0.021	0.02	0.013
Cholesterol, mg	0	0	0	0	0
Tryptophan, g	0.024	0.012	0.026	0.03	0.008
Threonine, g	0.06	0.02	0.08	0.1	0.03
Isoleucine, g	0.06	0.014	0.096	0.1	0.04
Leucine, g	0.08	0.03	0.116	0.13	0.044
Lycine, g	0.072	0.02	0.124	0.13	0.04
Methionine, g	0.024	0.006	0.03	0.028	0.008
Cystine, g	0.024	0.006	0.018	0.02	0.008
Phenylalanine, g	0.05	0.018	0.074	0.086	0.028
Tyrosine, g	0.05	0.016	0.056	—	0.014
Valine, g	0.07	0.02	0.112	0.136	0.026
Arginine, g	0.03	0.02	0.128	0.178	0.048
Histidine, g	0.028	0.01	0.044	0.066	0.018
Alanine, g	0.07	0.026	0.104	—	0.03
Aspartic acid, g	0.14	0.04	0.188	—	0.084
Glutamic acid, g	0.74	0.084	0.33	—	0.19
Glycine, g	0.04	0.026	0.084	—	0.018
Proline, g	0.05	0.016	0.1	—	0.166
Serine, g	0.07	0.022	0.088	—	0.05

Vegetables and Vegetable Juices

	Cabbage, Chinese	Carrots	Carrot juice	Cauliflower	Celery
Measure	1 C	1 C	1 C	1 C	1 C
Weight, g	70	110	227	100	120
Calories	9	48	96	24	18
Protein, g	1.05	1	2.47	1.98	0.8
Carbohydrate, g	1.53	11	22	4.9	4.36
Fiber, g	0.7	3	1.9	2.5	2
Vitamin A, IU	2100	30942	24750	16	152
Vitamin B_1, mg	0.028	0.1	0.13	0.076	0.036
Vitamin B_2, mg	0.049	0.064	0.12	0.058	0.036
Vitamin B_6, mg	—	0.16	0.534	0.23	0.036
Vitamin B_{12}, mcg	0	0	0	0	0
Niacin, mg	0.35	1	1.35	0.634	0.36
Pantothenic acid, mg	0.06	0.216	0.54	0.14	0.2
Folic acid, mcg	46	15	9	66	10.6
Vitamin C, mg	31.5	10	20	71	7.6
Vitamin E, IU	0.13	0.75	0.035	0.06	0.64
Calcium, mg	74	30	8.3	28	44
Copper, mg	0.015	0.05	0.11	0.032	0.042
Iron, mg	0.56	0.54	1.5	0.58	0.58
Magnesium, mg	13	16	51	14	14
Manganese, mg	0.11	0.156	0.31	0.2	0.164
Phosphorus, mg	26	48	81	46	32
Potassium, mg	176	356	767	356	340
Selenium, mcg	0.35	2.2	1.4	0.7	1.1
Sodium, mg	45	38	105	14	106
Zinc, mg	0.133	0.22	0.43	0.18	0.2
Total lipid, g	0.14	0.2	0.35	0.18	0.168
Total saturated, g	0.018	0.034	0.066	0.028	0.044
Total unsaturated, g	0.067	0.085	0.192	0.099	0.083
Total monounsaturated, g	0.011	0.009	0.017	0.014	0.032
Cholesterol, mg	0	0	0	0	0
Tryptophan, g	0.011	0.012	—	0.026	0.01
Threonine, g	0.034	0.042	—	0.072	0.022
Isoleucine, g	0.06	0.046	—	0.076	0.024
Leucine, g	0.062	0.048	—	0.116	0.038
Lycine, g	0.062	0.044	—	0.108	0.032
Methionine, g	0.006	0.008	—	0.028	0.006
Cystine, g	0.012	0.008	—	0.024	0.004
Phenylalanine, g	0.031	0.036	—	0.072	0.022
Tyrosine, g	0.02	0.022	—	0.044	0.01
Valine, g	0.046	0.048	—	0.1	0.032
Arginine, g	0.059	0.048	—	0.096	0.024
Histidine, g	0.018	0.018	—	0.04	0.014
Alanine, g	0.06	0.064	—	0.106	0.026
Aspartic acid, g	0.076	0.15	—	0.234	0.136
Glutamic acid, g	0.252	0.222	—	0.266	0.1
Glycine, g	0.03	0.034	—	0.064	0.026
Proline, g	0.022	0.032	—	0.086	0.02
Serine, g	0.034	0.038	—	0.104	0.024

Vegetables and Vegetable Juices

	Celeriac	Chard, Swiss	Chapote	Chicory greens	Chives
Measure	1 C	1 C	1 C	1 C	1 T
Weight, g	156	36	132	180	3
Calories	65	6	25	41	1
Protein, g	2.3	0.64	1.08	3	0.08
Carbohydrate, g	14	1.34	5.9	8.5	0.11
Fiber, g	2.8	0.58	2	7	0.075
Vitamin A, IU	0	1188	74	7200	192
Vitamin B_1, mg	0.078	0.014	0.03	0.11	0.003
Vitamin B_2, mg	0.094	0.032	0.038	0.18	0.005
Vitamin B_6, mg	0.257	0.036	0.1	0.189	0.005
Vitamin B_{12}, mcg	0	0	0	0	0
Niacin, mg	1.1	0.144	0.62	0.9	0.021
Pantothenic acid, mg	0.549	0.062	0.33	2	0.005
Folic acid, mcg	13	5	123	197	3
Vitamin C, mg	—	10.8	10	43	2.4
Vitamin E, IU	0.8	1	0.24	6	0.008
Calcium, mg	67	18	22	180	2
Copper, mg	0.1	0.16	0.16	0.53	0.011
Iron, mg	1.1	0.64	0.45	1.6	0.05
Magnesium, mg	31	30	16	54	2
Manganese, mg	0.25	0.45	0.25	0.77	0.011
Phosphorus, mg	179	16	24	85	2
Potassium, mg	468	136	165	756	8
Selenium, mcg	1.1	0.32	0.26	0.54	0.027
Sodium, mg	156	76	2.6	81	0
Zinc, mg	0.52	0.13	0.98	0.756	0.017
Total lipid, g	0.468	0.08	0.17	0.54	0.02
Total saturated, g	0.123	0.011	0.037	0.13	0.003
Total unsaturated, g	0.23	0.025	0.075	0.236	0.008
Total monounsaturated, g	0.09	0.014	0.013	0.011	0.003
Cholesterol, mg	0	0	0	0	0
Tryptophan, g	—	0.006	0.015	0.056	0.001
Threonine, g	—	0.03	0.053	0.085	0.003
Isoleucine, g	—	0.052	0.058	0.182	0.004
Leucine, g	—	0.046	0.1	0.133	0.005
Lycine, g	—	0.036	0.05	0.12	0.004
Methionine, g	—	0.006	0.001	0.018	0.001
Cystine, g	—	—	—	—	—
Phenylalanine, g	—	0.04	0.06	0.074	0.003
Tyrosine, g	—	—	0.04	—	0.002
Valine, g	—	0.04	0.08	0.14	0.004
Arginine, g	—	0.042	0.05	0.223	0.006
Histidine, g	—	0.012	0.02	0.05	0.001
Alanine, g	—	—	0.067	—	0.004
Aspartic acid, g	—	—	0.121	—	0.008
Glutamic acid, g	—	—	0.165	—	0.017
Glycine, g	—	—	0.054	—	0.004
Proline, g	—	—	0.058	—	0.006
Serine, g	—	—	0.06	—	0.004

Vegetables and Vegetable Juices

	Collards	Corn	Cucumber	Dandelion greens	Eggplant
Measure	1 C	1 C	1 C	1 C	1 C
Weight, g	36	154	104	55	82
Calories	11	132	14	25	22
Protein, g	0.8	4.96	0.56	1.5	0.9
Carbohydrate, g	2	29	3	5	5
Fiber, g	1	4	0.8	1.9	2
Vitamin A, IU	1376	432	46	7700	58
Vitamin B$_1$, mg	0.019	0.208	0.032	0.1	0.074
Vitamin B$_2$, mg	0.047	0.09	0.02	0.14	0.016
Vitamin B$_6$, mg	0.059	0.084	0.054	0.138	0.078
Vitamin B$_{12}$, mcg	0	0	0	0	0
Niacin, mg	0.267	2.6	0.321	0.44	0.492
Pantothenic acid, mg	0.096	1.17	0.26	0.046	0.066
Folic acid, mcg	60	70.6	14.4	15	14.4
Vitamin C, mg	13	10.6	4.8	19	0.14
Vitamin E, IU	1.2	0.2	0.12	2	0.04
Calcium, mg	52	4	14	103	30
Copper, mg	0.014	0.084	0.042	0.09	0.092
Iron, mg	0.068	0.8	0.28	1.7	0.44
Magnesium, mg	3.2	58	12	20	10
Manganese, mg	0.1	0.248	0.064	0.19	0.1
Phosphorus, mg	3.6	138	18	36	26
Potassium, mg	61	416	156	218	180
Selenium, mcg	0.41	0.9	0	0.275	0.246
Sodium, mg	7	23	2	42	2
Zinc, mg	0.047	0.7	0.24	0.225	0.12
Total lipid, g	0.15	1.8	0.14	0.385	0.08
Total saturated, g	0.02	0.28	0.034	0.094	0.016
Total unsaturated, g	0.07	0.86	0.028	0.168	0.06
Total monounsaturated, g	0.01	0.53	0.104	0.008	0.013
Cholesterol, mg	0	0	0	0	0
Tryptophan, g	0.011	0.036	0.004	—	0.008
Threonine, g	0.03	0.102	0.198	—	0.032
Isoleucine, g	0.036	0.198	0.018	—	0.04
Leucine, g	0.05	0.536	0.024	—	0.056
Lycine, g	0.04	0.21	0.022	—	0.042
Methionine, g	0.012	0.1	0.004	—	0.01
Cystine, g	0.009	0.04	0.004	—	0.004
Phenylalanine, g	0.03	0.232	0.016	—	0.038
Tyrosine, g	0.024	0.19	0.01	—	0.024
Valine, g	0.043	0.28	0.018	—	0.046
Arginine, g	0.045	0.2	0.036	—	0.05
Histidine, g	0.017	0.138	0.008	—	0.02
Alanine, g	0.038	0.454	0.018	—	0.046
Aspartic acid, g	0.067	0.366	0.034	—	0.146
Glutamic acid, g	0.073	0.98	0.16	—	0.164
Glycine, g	0.034	0.196	0.02	—	0.036
Proline, g	0.038	0.45	0.012	—	0.038
Serine, g	0.028	0.236	0.016	—	0.036

Vegetables and Vegetable Juices

	Endive	Garlic	Green beans	Jicama	Kale
Measure	1 C	1 clove	1 C	1 C	1 C
Weight, g	50	3	110	120	67
Calories	8	4	34	46	33
Protein, g	0.62	0.2	2	0.86	2.21
Carbohydrate, g	1.68	0.9	7.85	11	6.7
Fiber, g	1.4	0.05	3.7	5.9	1
Vitamin A, IU	1026	0	735	25	5963
Vitamin B_1, mg	0.04	0.006	0.092	0.024	0.074
Vitamin B_2, mg	0.038	t	0.116	0.035	0.087
Vitamin B_6, mg	0.1	0.037	0.081	0.05	0.182
Vitamin B_{12}, mcg	0	0	0	0	0
Niacin, mg	0.2	0.02	0.827	0.24	0.67
Pantothenic acid, mg	0.45	0.02	0.103	0.16	0.061
Folic acid, mcg	71	0.1	40	14	19.6
Vitamin C, mg	3.2	0.9	17.9	24	80.4
Vitamin E, IU	0.3	0	0.67	0.8	0.8
Calcium, mg	26	5	41	14	90
Copper, mg	0.05	0.008	0.076	0.058	0.194
Iron, mg	0.42	0.05	1.14	0.72	1.14
Magnesium, mg	8	1	27	14	23
Manganese, mg	0.21	0.05	0.235	0.07	0.519
Phosphorus, mg	14	6	42	22	38
Potassium, mg	158	16	230	180	299
Selenium, mcg	0.1	0.42	0.66	0.84	0.6
Sodium, mg	12	1	6	4.8	29
Zinc, mg	0.4	0.038	0.26	0.19	0.29
Total lipid, g	0.1	0.015	0.013	0.108	0.47
Total saturated, g	0.024	0.003	0.029	0.025	0.06
Total unsaturated, g	0.04	0.007	0.065	0.052	0.226
Total monounsaturated, g	0.002	0	0.006	0.006	0.035
Cholesterol, mg	0	0	0	0	0
Tryptophan, g	0.002	0.002	0.021	—	0.027
Threonine, g	0.026	0.005	0.087	0.022	0.098
Isoleucine, g	0.036	0.007	0.073	0.02	0.132
Leucine, g	0.05	0.009	0.123	0.03	0.155
Lycine, g	0.032	0.008	0.097	0.03	0.132
Methionine, g	0.008	0.002	0.024	0.008	0.021
Cystine, g	0.006	0.002	0.02	0.007	0.029
Phenylalanine, g	0.026	0.005	0.074	0.02	0.113
Tyrosine, g	0.02	0.002	0.046	0.014	0.078
Valine, g	0.032	0.009	0.099	0.03	0.121
Arginine, g	0.032	0.019	0.08	0.04	0.123
Histidine, g	0.012	0.003	0.037	0.023	0.046
Alanine, g	0.032	0.004	0.092	0.024	0.111
Aspartic acid, g	0.066	0.015	0.281	0.24	0.198
Glutamic acid, g	0.084	0.024	0.206	0.05	0.251
Glycine, g	0.03	0.006	0.072	0.02	0.107
Proline, g	0.03	0.003	0.075	0.03	0.131
Serine, g	0.024	0.006	0.109	0.03	0.093

Vegetables and Vegetable Juices

	Kohlrabi	Leeks	Lettuce, iceberg	Lettuce, Romaine	Mushrooms
Measure	1 C	1 C	1 C	1 C	1 C
Weight, g	140	124	75	56	70
Calories	38	54	10	8	18
Protein, g	2.38	1.3	0.7	0.9	1.46
Carbohydrate, g	8.68	13	2.2	1.3	3
Fiber, g	4.9	1.6	0.77	0.9	0.84
Vitamin A, IU	50	85	250	1456	0
Vitamin B$_1$, mg	0.07	0.05	0.05	0.056	0.072
Vitamin B$_2$, mg	0.028	0.037	0.05	0.056	0.3
Vitamin B$_6$, mg	0.21	0.2	0.028	0.02	0.068
Vitamin B$_{12}$, mcg	0	0	0	0	0
Niacin, mg	0.56	0.496	0.148	0.28	2.88
Pantothenic acid, mg	0.231	0.12	0.1	0.09	1.54
Folic acid, mcg	22	0.015	31	76	8.4
Vitamin C, mg	86.8	14.9	5	13.4	2.4
Vitamin E, IU	0.96	1	0.23	0.37	0.12
Calcium, mg	34	73	15	20	4
Copper, mg	0.21	0.09	0.035	0.02	0.34
Iron, mg	0.56	2.6	0.4	0.62	0.86
Magnesium, mg	27	35	5	4	8
Manganese, mg	0.16	0.43	0.12	0.36	0.078
Phosphorus, mg	64	43	17	26	72
Potassium, mg	490	223	131	162	260
Selenium, mcg	0.95	0.89	0.1	0.1	8.54
Sodium, mg	28	25	7	4	2
Zinc, mg	0.04	0.1	0.1	0.14	0.344
Total lipid, g	0.14	0.267	0.12	0.12	0.3
Total saturated, g	0.018	0.036	0.02	0.007	0.08
Total unsaturated, g	0.065	0.148	0.055	0.06	0.097
Total monounsaturated, g	0.009	0.004	0.004	0.004	0.004
Cholesterol, mg	0	0	0	0	0
Tryptophan, g	0.014	0.015	0.008	0.006	0.032
Threonine, g	0.069	0.078	0.044	0.042	0.066
Isoleucine, g	0.1	0.064	0.06	0.058	0.058
Leucine, g	0.094	0.119	0.056	0.054	0.09
Lycine, g	0.078	0.097	0.06	0.058	0.048
Methionine, g	0.018	0.022	0.012	0.012	0.028
Cystine, g	0.01	0.031	0.012	0.01	0.004
Phenylalanine, g	0.055	0.068	0.04	0.038	0.056
Tyrosine, g	—	0.051	0.024	0.022	0.032
Valine, g	0.07	0.069	0.048	0.048	0.068
Arginine, g	0.147	0.097	0.052	0.05	0.072
Histidine, g	0.027	0.031	0.016	0.016	0.04
Alanine, g	—	0.092	0.04	0.04	0.11
Aspartic acid, g	—	0.174	0.1	0.1	0.134
Glutamic acid, g	—	0.28	0.128	0.128	0.25
Glycine, g	—	0.086	0.04	0.04	0.066
Proline, g	—	0.082	0.036	0.034	0.1
Serine, g	—	0.114	0.028	0.028	0.066

Vegetables and Vegetable Juices

	Mushrooms, enoki	Mushrooms, portobello	Mushrooms, shiitake, dried	Mustard greens	Okra
Measure	1 med.		4	1 C	1 C
Weight, g	3	100	15	56	100
Calories	1	26	44	15	38
Protein, g	0.07	2.5	1.4	1.5	2
Carbohydrate, g	0.2	5	11	2.7	7.6
Fiber, g	0.078	1.5	1.7	1.8	3.2
Vitamin A, IU	0.2	0	0	2968	660
Vitamin B₁, mg	t	0.077	0.045	0.045	0.2
Vitamin B₂, mg	t	0.48	0.19	0.06	0.06
Vitamin B₆, mg	t	0.1	0.145	0.1	0.2
Vitamin B₁₂, mcg	0	0.05	0	0	0
Niacin, mg	0.11	4.5	2	0.448	1
Pantothenic acid, mg	0.028	1.5	3.3	0.12	0.246
Folic acid, mcg	0.9	22	25	105	88
Vitamin C, mg	0.36	0	0.525	39	21
Vitamin E, IU	—	0.19	0.03	1.68	1
Calcium, mg	0.03	8	1.65	58	82
Copper, mg	t	0.4	0.775	0.08	0.94
Iron, mg	0.03	0.6	0.258	0.82	0.8
Magnesium, mg	0.48	11	20	18	56
Manganese, mg	t	0.14	0.176	0.27	0.99
Phosphorus, mg	3.4	130	44	24	64
Potassium, mg	11	484	230	198	302
Selenium, mcg	0.48	11	20	0.5	0.7
Sodium, mg	0.09	6	1.95	14	8
Zinc, mg	0.017	0.6	1.15	0.11	0.6
Total lipid, g	0.012	0.2	0.148	0.112	0.1
Total saturated, g	0.001	0.026	0.037	0.006	0.026
Total unsaturated, g	0.005	0.078	0.02	0.021	0.027
Total monounsaturated, g	0	0.003	0.046	0.052	0.017
Cholesterol, mg	0	0	0	0	0
Tryptophan, g	0.002	0.056	0.005	0.017	0.018
Threonine, g	0.003	0.113	0.075	0.04	0.066
Isoleucine, g	0.001	0.099	0.06	0.055	0.07
Leucine, g	0.004	0.153	0.1	0.046	0.1
Lycine, g	0.005	0.252	0.05	0.069	0.082
Methionine, g	0.001	0.048	0.03	0.014	0.022
Cystine, g	—	0.006	0.03	0.022	0.02
Phenylalanine, g	0.004	0.097	0.07	0.04	0.066
Tyrosine, g	0.003	0.054	0.048	0.08	0.088
Valine, g	0.002	0.115	0.07	0.059	0.092
Arginine, g	0.006	0.123	0.097	0.1	0.084
Histidine, g	0.002	0.067	0.024	0.27	0.032
Alanine, g	0.005	0.187	0.085	—	0.074
Aspartic acid, g	0.008	0.228	0.114	—	0.146
Glutamic acid, g	0.01	0.43	0.387	—	0.272
Glycine, g	0.003	0.11	0.06	—	0.044
Proline, g	0.006	0.176	0.06	—	0.046
Serine, g	0.003	0.13	0.076	—	0.044

Vegetables and Vegetable Juices

	Onions, green	Onions, mature	Parsley	Parsnips	Peppers, sweet
Measure	1 C	1 C	1 C	1 C	1 C
Weight, g	100	160	60	133	93
Calories	26	54	26	102	24
Protein, g	1.7	1.88	2.2	2.3	0.86
Carbohydrate, g	5.5	11.7	5.1	23	5.3
Fiber, g	2.6	2.9	1.98	6.5	1.2
Vitamin A, IU	385	0	3120	0	530
Vitamin B_1, mg	0.07	0.096	0.07	0.11	0.086
Vitamin B_2, mg	0.14	0.016	0.16	0.12	0.05
Vitamin B_6, mg	0.06	0.25	0.098	0.13	0.164
Vitamin B_{12}, mcg	0	0	0	0	0
Niacin, mg	0.2	0.16	0.7	0.2	0.54
Pantothenic acid, mg	0.144	0.2	0.18	0.9	0.036
Folic acid, mcg	64	31.8	91	89	16.8
Vitamin C, mg	18	13.4	80	16	82
Vitamin E, IU	0.19	0.3	1.5	—	0.9
Calcium, mg	60	40	122	50	6
Copper, mg	0.06	0.064	0.293	0.17	0.1
Iron, mg	1.88	0.58	3.7	0.9	1.2
Magnesium, mg	20	16	24.5	40	14
Manganese, mg	0.16	0.2	0.563	0.75	0.14
Phosphorus, mg	32	46	38	96	22
Potassium, mg	256	248	436	587	196
Selenium, mcg	0.6	9.6	0.06	2.4	0.276
Sodium, mg	4	4	27	12	4
Zinc, mg	0.44	0.28	0.44	0.8	0.18
Total lipid, g	0.19	0.25	0.4	0.4	0.175
Total saturated, g	0.032	0.07	0.079	0.067	0.026
Total unsaturated, g	0.074	0.09	0.07	0.06	0.09
Total monounsaturated, g	0.027	0.037	0.177	0.149	0.012
Cholesterol, mg	0	0	0	0	0
Tryptophan, g	0.02	0.028	0.022	—	0.012
Threonine, g	0.068	0.044	—	—	0.03
Isoleucine, g	0.074	0.068	—	—	0.028
Leucine, g	0.1	0.066	—	—	0.044
Lycine, g	0.088	0.09	0.132	—	0.038
Methionine, g	0.02	0.016	0.01	—	0.01
Cystine, g	—	0.34	—	—	0.016
Phenylalanine, g	0.056	0.048	—	—	0.026
Tyrosine, g	0.05	0.046	—	—	0.018
Valine, g	0.078	0.044	—	—	0.036
Arginine, g	0.126	0.262	—	—	0.042
Histidine, g	0.03	0.03	—	—	0.018
Alanine, g	0.078	0.052	—	—	0.036
Aspartic acid, g	0.162	0.1	—	—	0.124
Glutamic acid, g	0.36	0.3	—	—	0.1
Glycine, g	0.086	0.078	—	—	0.032
Proline, g	0.1	0.06	—	—	0.038
Serine, g	0.078	0.056	—	—	0.034

Vegetables and Vegetable Juices

	Peppers, hot	Pickles, dill	Potato	Pumpkin	Purslane
Measure	½ C	1 sm	1 C	1 C	1 C
Weight, g	75	37	150	116	43
Calories	30	6	114	30	7
Protein, g	1.5	0.3	3.2	1.16	0.6
Carbohydrate, g	7	1.5	25.7	7.5	1.48
Fiber, g	1.35	0.4	2.4	0.58	—
Vitamin A, IU	8062	121	0	1856	568
Vitamin B$_1$, mg	0.068	t	0.15	0.058	0.02
Vitamin B$_2$, mg	0.068	0.01	0.06	0.13	0.048
Vitamin B$_6$, mg	0.21	0.005	0.4	0.07	0.03
Vitamin B$_{12}$, mcg	0	0	0	0	0
Niacin, mg	0.713	0.022	2.3	0.7	0.21
Pantothenic acid, mg	0.046	0.02	0.57	0.35	0.015
Folic acid, mcg	17.5	0.37	19.2	19	5
Vitamin C, mg	182	0.7	30	10	9
Vitamin E, IU	0.77	0.09	0.13	1.8	—
Calcium, mg	13	3	11	24	28
Copper, mg	0.13	0.03	0.388	0.147	0.05
Iron, mg	0.9	0.2	0.9	0.93	0.86
Magnesium, mg	19	4	51	14	29
Manganese, mg	0.178	t	0.394	0.145	0.13
Phosphorus, mg	34	8	80	51	19
Potassium, mg	255	43	611	394	212
Selenium, mcg	0.38	0	0.45	0.348	0.39
Sodium, mg	5	474	5	1.2	19
Zinc, mg	0.23	0.05	0.58	0.37	0.07
Total lipid, g	0.15	0.07	0.2	0.015	0.043
Total saturated, g	0.016	0.018	0.04	0.116	—
Total unsaturated, g	0.082	0.028	0.032	0.06	—
Total monounsaturated, g	0.008	0.001	0.002	0.006	—
Cholesterol, mg	0	0	0	0	0
Tryptophan, g	0.02	0.002	0.048	0.014	0.006
Threonine, g	0.056	0.006	0.1	0.034	0.019
Isoleucine, g	0.049	0.007	0.12	0.036	0.02
Leucine, g	0.079	0.01	0.186	0.053	0.034
Lycine, g	0.067	0.01	0.19	0.063	0.025
Methionine, g	0.018	0.002	0.05	0.013	0.005
Cystine, g	0.029	0.001	0.04	0.003	0.004
Phenylalanine, g	0.047	0.006	0.138	0.037	0.02
Tyrosine, g	0.032	0.004	0.1	0.049	0.009
Valine, g	0.063	0.007	0.176	0.04	0.027
Arginine, g	0.072	0.015	0.14	0.06	0.021
Histidine, g	0.031	0.003	0.068	0.02	0.009
Alanine, g	0.062	0.008	0.096	0.032	0.02
Aspartic acid, g	0.215	0.014	0.76	0.12	0.03
Glutamic acid, g	0.198	0.065	0.52	0.213	0.08
Glycine, g	0.056	0.008	0.094	0.03	0.017
Proline, g	0.065	0.005	0.1	0.03	0.03
Serine, g	0.06	0.007	0.136	0.05	0.017

Vegetables and Vegetable Juices

	Radish	Rutabaga	Sauerkraut	Spinach	Squash, summer
Measure	10	1 C	1 C	1 C	1 C
Weight, g	45	140	235	30	130
Calories	7	64	42	6	25
Protein, g	0.27	1.5	2.4	0.86	1.4
Carbohydrate, g	1.6	15.4	9.4	1	5.5
Fiber, g	0.7	3.5	5.9	0.8	2.5
Vitamin A, IU	3	810	120	2014	530
Vitamin B$_1$, mg	0.002	0.1	0.07	0.023	0.07
Vitamin B$_2$, mg	0.02	0.1	0.09	0.057	0.12
Vitamin B$_6$, mg	0.032	0.14	0.31	0.059	0.186
Vitamin B$_{12}$, mcg	0	0	0	0	0
Niacin, mg	0.135	1.5	0.5	0.22	1.3
Pantothenic acid, mg	0.04	0.22	0.22	0.02	0.468
Folic acid, mcg	12.2	29	56	58	30
Vitamin C, mg	10.3	60	33	8	29
Vitamin E. IU	0	0.6	0.35	0.85	—
Calcium, mg	9	92	85	30	36
Copper, mg	0.018	0.11	0.235	0.04	0.22
Iron, mg	0.13	0.6	1.2	0.8	0.5
Magnesium, mg	4	20	31	24	21
Manganese, mg	0.032	0.056	0.356	0.27	0.185
Phosphorus, mg	8	55	42	15	38
Potassium, mg	104	335	329	167	263
Selenium, mcg	0.3	0.98	1.4	0.3	0.26
Sodium, mg	11	7	1755	24	1
Zinc, mg	0.13	0.48	0.448	0.16	0.33
Total lipid, g	0.24	0.28	0.33	0.105	0.28
Total saturated, g	0.014	0.038	0.083	0.017	0.057
Total unsaturated, g	0.02	0.123	0.144	0.044	0.13
Total monounsaturated, g	0.01	0.035	0.031	0.003	0.023
Cholesterol, mg	0	0	0	0	0
Tryptophan, g	0.002	0.018	—	0.012	0.014
Threonine, g	0.013	0.064	—	0.037	0.036
Isoleucine, g	0.014	0.07	—	0.044	0.055
Leucine, g	0.017	0.053	—	0.067	0.09
Lycine, g	0.016	0.055	—	0.05	0.085
Methionine, g	0.003	0.014	—	0.016	0.022
Cystine, g	0.002	0.015	—	0.01	0.016
Phenylalanine, g	0.01	0.043	—	0.04	0.053
Tyrosine, g	0.006	0.032	—	0.03	0.04
Valine, g	0.014	0.067	—	0.05	0.069
Arginine, g	0.018	0.207	—	0.05	0.065
Histidine, g	0.006	0.042	—	0.02	0.033
Alanine, g	0.01	0.046	—	0.043	0.081
Aspartic acid, g	0.022	0.122	—	0.07	0.187
Glutamic acid, g	0.059	0.199	—	0.1	0.164
Glycine, g	0.01	0.038	—	0.04	0.057
Proline, g	0.008	—	—	0.034	0.048
Serine, g	0.009	0.049	—	0.03	0.062

Vegetables and Vegetable Juices

	Squash, winter	Sweet potato	Taro	Tomato, med	Tomato juice
Measure	1 C	1	1 C	1	1 C
Weight, g	205	130	104	123	243
Calories	129	136	116	24	46
Protein, g	3.7	2	1.5	1.1	2.2
Carbohydrate, g	31.6	32	28	5.3	10.4
Fiber, g	2.6	3.9	4	1.35	0.97
Vitamin A, IU	8610	26082	0	766	1351
Vitamin B_1, mg	0.1	0.086	0.1	0.074	0.12
Vitamin B_2, mg	0.27	0.191	0.03	0.062	0.07
Vitamin B_6, mg	0.18	0.334	0.3	0.059	0.366
Vitamin B_{12}, mcg	0	0	0	0	0
Niacin, mg	1.4	0.876	0.6	0.738	1.9
Pantothenic acid, mg	0.56	0.768	0.32	0.304	0.607
Folic acid, mcg	25	18	23	11.5	48
Vitamin C, mg	27	30	4.7	21.6	39
Vitamin E, IU	0.21	0.54	3.7	0.7	3.3
Calcium, mg	57	29	45	8	17
Copper, mg	0.1	0.22	0.18	0.095	0.246
Iron, mg	1.6	0.76	0.57	0.59	2.2
Magnesium, mg	45	14	34	14	20
Manganese, mg	0.2	0.46	0.4	0.15	0.188
Phosphorus, mg	98	37	87	29	44
Potassium, mg	945	265	614	254	552
Selenium, mcg	0.46	0.78	0.73	0.8	1.2
Sodium, mg	2	17	11	10	486
Zinc, mg	0.28	0.36	0.24	0.13	0.1
Total lipid, g	0.26	0.38	0.208	0.4	0.2
Total saturated, g	0.05	0.083	0.043	0.055	0.02
Total unsaturated, g	0.1	0.172	0.086	0.166	0.058
Total monounsaturated, g	0.02	0.014	0.017	0.06	0.02
Cholesterol, mg	0	0	0	0	0
Tryptophan, g	0.041	0.026	0.024	0.009	0.012
Threonine, g	0.082	0.107	0.07	0.027	0.042
Isoleucine, g	0.112	0.107	0.056	0.026	0.036
Leucine, g	0.125	0.157	0.1	0.041	0.052
Lycine, g	0.09	0.105	0.07	0.041	0.054
Methionine, g	0.031	0.053	0.02	0.01	0.01
Cystine, g	0.02	0.017	0.03	0.015	0.01
Phenylalanine, g	0.112	0.129	0.085	0.028	0.04
Tyrosine, g	0.089	0.088	0.057	0.018	0.024
Valine, g	0.122	0.14	0.085	0.028	0.036
Arginine, g	0.158	0.1	0.1	0.027	0.036
Histidine, g	0.041	0.04	0.035	0.016	0.03
Alanine, g	0.121	0.117	0.076	0.031	0.058
Aspartic acid, g	0.302	0.367	0.2	0.151	0.232
Glutamic acid, g	0.522	0.209	0.18	0.402	0.74
Glycine, g	0.1	0.096	0.077	0.027	0.03
Proline, g	0.1	0.094	0.006	0.021	0.042
Serine, g	0.103	0.111	0.096	0.03	0.044

Vegetables and Vegetable Juices

	Tomato paste	Turnips	Turnip greens	Vegetable juice cocktail	Water chestnuts
Measure	1 C	1 C	1 C	1 C	4 avg
Weight, g	262	130	55	242	36
Calories	215	39	15	41	35
Protein, g	8.9	1.3	0.83	2.2	0.5
Carbohydrate, g	48.7	8.6	3	8.7	8.6
Fiber, g	10	2.3	1.7	1.9	1
Vitamin A, IU	8650	0	4180	2831	0
Vitamin B$_1$, mg	0.52	0.05	0.039	0.12	0.04
Vitamin B$_2$, mg	0.31	0.09	0.055	0.07	0.05
Vitamin B$_6$, mg	0.996	0.117	0.145	0.338	0.118
Vitamin B$_{12}$, mcg	0	0	0	0	0
Niacin, mg	8.1	0.8	0.33	1.9	0.2
Pantothenic acid, mg	1.97	0.26	0.21	0.6	0.17
Folic acid, mcg	60	19	107	51	6
Vitamin C, mg	128	27	33	22	1
Vitamin E, IU	16	0.06	0.88	1.15	0.64
Calcium, mg	71	51	105	29	1
Copper, mg	1.4	0.09	0.193	0.484	0.117
Iron, mg	9.2	0.7	0.61	1.2	0.2
Magnesium, mg	50	25	17	26	2.4
Manganese, mg	1.3	0.052	0.256	0.242	0.12
Phosphorus, mg	183	39	23	53	16
Potassium, mg	2237	348	163	535	125
Selenium, mcg	3.6	0.78	0.66	1.2	0.25
Sodium, mg	100	64	22	484	5
Zinc, mg	2	0.35	0.1	0.48	0.18
Total lipid, g	2	0.13	0.17	0.2	0.036
Total saturated, g	0.332	0.014	0.039	0.03	0.009
Total unsaturated, g	0.6	0.069	0.066	0.09	0.015
Total monounsaturated, g	0.2	0.008	0.01	0.034	0.001
Cholesterol, mg	0	0	0	0	0
Tryptophan, g	0.068	0.012	0.014	—	—
Threonine, g	0.226	0.033	0.045	—	—
Isoleucine, g	0.192	0.047	0.043	—	—
Leucine, g	0.276	0.043	0.075	—	—
Lycine, g	0.282	0.047	0.054	—	—
Methionine, g	0.05	0.014	0.019	—	—
Cystine, g	0.058	0.007	0.009	—	—
Phenylalanine, g	0.2	0.022	0.051	—	—
Tyrosine, g	0.134	0.017	0.032	—	—
Valine, g	0.2	0.039	0.056	—	—
Arginine, g	0.2	0.031	0.052	—	—
Histidine, g	0.158	0.018	0.02	—	—
Alanine, g	0.3	0.046	0.057	—	—
Aspartic acid, g	1.24	0.082	0.087	—	—
Glutamic acid, g	3.95	0.169	0.112	—	—
Glycine, g	0.16	0.033	0.05	—	—
Proline, g	0.218	0.034	0.039	—	—
Serine, g	0.236	0.038	0.034	—	—

Vegetables and Vegetable Juices

	Watercress	Yams
Measure	1 C	1 C
Weight, g	35	150
Calories	7	177
Protein, g	0.8	3
Carbohydrate, g	1.1	41
Fiber, g	0.5	6
Vitamin A, IU	1720	0
Vitamin B_1, mg	0.03	0.18
Vitamin B_2, mg	0.06	0.05
Vitamin B_6, mg	0.045	0.51
Vitamin B_{12}, mcg	0	0
Niacin, mg	0.3	1.2
Pantothenic acid, mg	108	0.5
Folic acid, mcg	3	42
Vitamin C, mg	28	18
Vitamin E, IU	0.5	0.36
Calcium, mg	53	8
Copper, mg	0.032	0.44
Iron, mg	0.6	1.2
Magnesium, mg	6.5	62
Manganese, mg	0.189	0.6
Phosphorus, mg	19	100
Potassium, mg	99	1508
Selenium, mcg	0.31	1
Sodium, mg	18	17
Zinc, mg	0.037	0.43
Total lipid, g	0.04	0.255
Total saturated, g	0.01	0.056
Total unsaturated, g	0.012	0.114
Total monounsaturated, g	0.003	0.009
Cholesterol, mg	0	0
Tryptophan, g	0.01	0.018
Threonine, g	0.046	0.081
Isoleucine, g	0.032	0.078
Leucine, g	0.056	0.144
Lycine, g	0.046	0.089
Methionine, g	0.006	0.032
Cystine, g	0.002	0.029
Phenylalanine, g	0.038	0.107
Tyrosine, g	0.022	0.06
Valine, g	0.046	0.093
Arginine, g	0.052	0.191
Histidine, g	0.014	0.051
Alanine, g	0.046	0.095
Aspartic acid, g	0.064	0.233
Glutamic acid, g	0.064	0.272
Glycine, g	0.038	0.08
Proline, g	0.032	0.081
Serine, g	0.02	0.122

Bibliography

Adams, Ruth, and Frank Murray. *Body, Mind, and the B Vitamins.* New York: Larchmont Books, 1972.

———. *Vitamin E: Wonder Worker of the 70's.* New York: Larchmont Books, 1972.

Airola, Paavo, Ph.D. *How to Get Well.* Phoenix, Ariz.: Health Plus Publishers, 1974.

Altschul, A. M. *Proteins: Their Chemistry and Politics.* New York: Basic Books, 1965.

American Journal of Obstetrics and Gynecology, Vol. 61, June 1951.

Ancowitz, Arthur. *Strokes and Their Prevention.* New York: Jove Publications, 1982.

Anderson, Linnea, Marjorie Dibble, Helen S. Mitchell, and Hendrika Fynbergen. *Nutrition in Nursing.* Philadelphia: J. B. Lippincott Co., 1972.

Atkins, Robert C. *Dr. Atkins' Nutrition Breakthrough.* New York: Bantam Books, 1982.

Bailey, Herbert. *Food Facts and Fallacies.* New York: Arco Publishing, 1965.

———. *Vitamin E: Your Key to a Healthy Heart.* New York: Arc Books, 1969.

Baker, Janet. *AIDS: Everything You Must Know About Acquired Immune Deficiency Syndrome.* Saratoga, Calif.: R&E Press, 1983.

Balch, James F., M.D., and Phyllis A. Balch, C.N.C. *Prescription for Nutritional Healing.* New York: Avery Publishing Group, 1990.

Basu, T. K. *About Mothers, Children, and Their Nutrition.* London: Thorsons, 1971.

Bechtel, Stefan. *The Practical Encyclopedia of Sex and Health.* Emmaus, Pa.: Rodale Press, 1993.

Bell, David S., M.D., and Stef Donev. *Curing Fatigue.* Emmaus, Pa.: Rodale Press, 1993.

Bender, A. E. *Dietetic Foods.* New York: Chemical Publishing, 1967.

Benjamin, Harry. *Your Diet—in Health and Disease.* Croyden, Great Britain: Health for All Publishing, 1931.

Bennett, Hal Zina. *Cold Comfort.* New York: Clarkson N. Potter, 1979.

Berkeley, George E. *Cancer: How to Prevent It and How to Help Your Doctor Fight It.* Englewood Cliffs, N.J.: Prentice-Hall, 1978.

Bieler, Henry G. *Food Is Your Best Medicine.* New York: Random House, 1965.

Bland, Jeffrey S., Ph.D. *Clinical Nutrition: A Functional Approach.* Gig Harbor, Wash.: The Institute for Functional Medicine, Inc., 1999.

Bloomfield, Harold H., and Robert K. Cooper. *The Power of 5.* Emmaus, Pa.: Rodale Press, 1995.

Bogert, L. J., George M. Briggs, and Doris H. Calloway. *Nutrition and Physical Fitness,* 9th ed. Philadelphia: W. B. Saunders Co., 1973.

Borsaak, Henry. *Vitamins.* New York: New American Library, 1977.

Bowerman, William J., and W. E. Harris. *Jogging.* New York: Grosset & Dunlap, 1967.

Brand-Miller, Jennie, Ph.D., Kaye Foster-Powell, and Johanna Burani, R.D., C.D.E. *The New Glucose*

Revolution. New York: Marlowe & Company, 2003.

Breggin, Peter R., M.D. *Toxic Psychiatry.* New York: St. Martin's Press, 1991.

Brennan, R. O. *Nutrigenetics.* New York: New American Library, 1977.

Brewster, Dorothy Patricia. *You Can Breastfeed Your Baby.* Emmaus, Pa.: Rodale Press, 1979.

Brody, Jane. *Jane Brody's Nutrition Book.* New York: Bantam Books, 1987.

Brown, Ellen, and Lynne Walker. *Breezing Through the Change.* Berkeley, Calif.: Frog Ltd., 1994.

Brunner, L. W., C. P. Emerson, Jr., L. K. Ferguson, and D. S. Suddarth. *Textbook of Medical-Surgical Nursing,* 2nd ed. Philadelphia: J. B. Lippincott Co., 1970.

Calbom, Cherie, and Maureen Keane. *Juicing for Life.* Garden City, N.Y.: Avery Publishing Group, Inc., 1992.

"Cancer News Journal," *Prevention,* December 1971.

Carey, Ruth L., Irma B. Vyhmeister, and Jennie L. Hudson. *Commonsense Nutrition.* Omaha: Pacific Press, 1971.

Carper, Jean. *Food: Your Miracle Medicine.* New York: HarperCollins, 1993.

———. *The Food Pharmacy.* New York: Bantam Books, 1988.

Castleman, Michael. *The Healing Herbs.* Emmaus, Pa.: Rodale Press, 1991.

Cataldo, Corinne B., Linda K. DeBruyne, and Eleanor N. Whitney. *Nutrition and Diet Therapy,* 3rd ed. St. Paul, Minn.: Marshall, 1992.

Chalker, Rebecca, and Kristene E. Whitmore. *Overcoming Bladder Disorders.* New York: HarperPerennial, 1991.

Challem, Jack. *The Inflammation Syndrome.* New York: John Wiley & Sons, Inc., 2003.

Chaney, Margaret L., and Margaret L. Ross. *Nutrition,* 8th ed. Boston: Houghton Mifflin Co., 1971.

Cheraskin, E., W. M. Ringsdorf, and J. W. Clark. *Diet and Disease.* Emmaus, Pa.: Rodale Books, 1968.

Clark, Linda. *Get Well Naturally.* New York: Devin-Adair Co., 1965.

Clark, Michael. "Vitamin E: The Better Treatment for Angina," *Prevention,* December 1972.

Clayman, Charles B. *Family Medical Guide.* New York: American Medical Association/Random House, 1994.

Collins, Daniel A. *Your Teeth: A Handbook of Dental Care for the Whole Family.* Garden City, N.Y.: Doubleday & Co., 1967.

Complete Book of Vitamins and Minerals. Lincolnwood, Ill.: Editors of Consumer Guide, March 1989.

Cooper, Kenneth H., M.D. *Antioxidant Revolution.* Nashville, Tenn.: Nelson Books, 1997.

Corrigan, A. B. *Living with Arthritis.* New York: Grosset & Dunlap, 1971.

Craig, Grace J. *Human Development,* 6th ed. Englewood Cliffs, N.J.: Prentice-Hall, 1992.

Crain, Lloyd. *Magic Vitamins and Organic Foods.* Los Angeles: Crandrich Studios, 1971.

Crook, William G. *Are You Allergic?* Jackson, Tenn.: Professional Books, 1978.

Darling, Mary. *Natural, Organic, and Health Foods.* USDA Extension Folder No. 280. St. Paul: University of Minnesota, 1973.

Davidson, Stanley, R. Passmore, and J. F. Brack. *Human Nutrition and Dietetics,* 5th ed. Baltimore: Williams and Wilkins Co., 1972.

Davis, Adelle. *Let's Eat Right to Keep Fit.* New York: Harcourt, Brace & World, 1954.

———. *Let's Get Well.* New York: Harcourt Brace & World, 1965.

Davis, Julie. *Young Skin for Life.* Emmaus, Pa.: Rodale Press, 1995.

DeAngelis, Lissa, M.S., and Molly Siple, M.S., R.D. *Recipes for Change.* New York: Penguin Putnam, 1996.

Deutsch, Ronald M. *The Family Guide to Better Food and Better Health.* Des Moines, Iowa: Meredith Corp., 1971.

Dubois, Rene, and Maya Pines. *Health and Disease.* New York: Time-Life Books, 1965.

Ebon, Martin. *The Truth About Vitamin E.* New York: Bantam Books, 1972.

Ehrlich, David, and George Wolf. *The Bowel Book.* New York: Schocken Books, 1981.

Ellis, John M., and James Presley. *Vitamin B$_6$: The Doctor's Report.* New York: Bantam Books, 1972.

Erasmus, Udo. *Fats That Heal, Fats That Kill.* Vancouver: Alive Books, 1993.

Feingold, Ben F. *Why Your Child Is Hyperactive.* New York: Random House, 1975.

Feinstein, Alice. *The Healthy Woman.* Emmaus, Pa.: Rodale Press, 1994.

Feinstein, Alice (ed.). *Training the Body to Cure Itself.* Emmaus, Pa.: Rodale Press, 1992.

Fleck, Henrietta. *Introduction to Nutrition*, 2nd ed. New York: Macmillan Co., 1971.

Fletcher, Anne M., M.S., R.D. *Thin for Life.* Shelburne, Vt.: Chapters Pub. Ltd., 1994.

Fredericks, Carlton. *Eating Right for You.* New York: Grosset & Dunlap, 1972.

———. *Nutrition: Your Key to Good Health.* North Hollywood, Calif.: London Press, 1964.

Furgurson, Hill E., and Halvor L. Harley. *Herpes Sufferers Get H.E.L.P.* Denver: Royal Publications, 1982.

Gaby, Alan R., M.D. *Preventing and Reversing Osteoporosis.* Rocklin, Calif.: Prima Publishing, 1994.

Galton, Lawrence. *The Silent Diseases: Hypertension.* New York: New American Library, 1974.

Garrison, Omar V. *The Dictocrat's Attack on Health Foods and Vitamins.* New York: Arc Books, 1971.

Garrison, Robert H., Jr., M.A., R.Ph. *The Nutrition Desk Reference.* New Canaan, Conn.: Keats Publishing, 1990.

Gershoff, Stanley, Ph.D. *The Tufts University Guide to Total Nutrition.* New York: HarperCollins, 1996.

Goldberg, Philip, and Daniel Kaufman. *Natural Sleep.* Emmaus, Pa.: Rodale Press, 1987.

Gomez, Joan. *A Dictionary of Symptoms.* New York: Bantam Books, 1967.

Gong, Victor, M.D. *AIDS Facts and Issues.* New Brunswick, N.J.: Rutgers University Press, 1986.

Goodhart, Robert S., and Maurice E. Shils. *Modern Nutrition in Health and Disease*, 5th ed. Philadelphia: Lea & Feviger, 1973.

Graham, Judy. *Multiple Sclerosis.* Wellingborough, England: Thorsons, 1982.

Gray, Madeline. *The Changing Years.* New York: Doubleday & Co., 1981.

Guthrie, Helen A. *Introductory Nutrition*, 2nd ed. St. Louis: C.V. Mosby Co., 1971.

Haas, Robert. *Eat Smart, Think Smart.* New York: HarperCollins, 1994.

Hayflick, Leonard, Ph.D. *How and Why We Age.* New York: Ballantine Books, 1994.

Health in the Later Years, rev. ed. New York: New American Library, 1968.

Heinerman, John. *Medical Doctor's Guide to Herbs.* Provo, Utah: Bi-World Publ., 1977.

Heinz Nutritional Data, 6th ed. Pittsburgh: Heinz International Research Center, 1972.

Hendler, Sheldon Saul, M.D., Ph.D. *The Doctor's Vitamin and Mineral Encyclopedia.* New York: Simon & Schuster, 1990.

Herbst, Sharon Tyler. *Food Lover's Companion.* Hauppauge, N.Y.: Barron's Educational Series, Inc., 2001.

Heritage, Ford. *Composition and Facts About Food.* Mokelumne Hill, Calif.: Health Research Center, 1968.

Herting, David C. "Perspective on Vitamin E," *American Journal of Clinical Nutrition*, Vol. 19, 210–216, September 1966.

Hill, Howard E. *Introduction to Lecithin.* Los Angeles: Nash Publ., 1972.

Hoffer, Abram, and Morton Walker. *Nutrients to Age Without Senility.* New Canaan, Conn.: Keats Publishing, 1980.

———. *Orthomolecular Nutrition.* New Canaan, Conn.: Keats Publishing, 1978.

Hoffman, Matthew, et al. *Disease Free.* Emmaus, Pa.: Rodale Press, 1993.

Holvey, David (ed.). *The Merck Manual*, 12th ed. Rahway, N.J.: Merck & Co., 1972.

Hoover, John (ed.). *Remington's Pharmaceutical Sciences*, 14th ed. Easton, Pa.: Mack Publ. Co., 1970.

Howe, Phyllis S. *Basic Nutrition in Health and Disease*, 5th ed. Philadelphia: W. B. Saunders Co., 1971.

Hunter, Beatrice T. *The Natural Foods Primer.* New York: Simon & Schuster, 1972.

Illustrated Medical and Health Encyclopedia. New York: H. S. Stuttman Co., 1959.

Industrial Medicine and Surgery, Vol. 21, June 1952.

Inlander, Charles B., and Cynthia K. Moran. *77 Ways to Beat Colds and Flu.* New York: Walker and Co., 1994.

Jameson, Judy. *Fat-Burning Foods and Other Weight-Loss Secrets.* Ottheimer's Press, 1994.

Jensen, Bernard. *Seeds and Sprouts for Life.* Escondido, Calif.: Jensen's Nutrition & Health Products, undated.

Johnson, Harry J. *Creative Walking for Physical Fitness.* New York: Grosset & Dunlap, 1970.

Jolliffe, Norman (ed.). *Clinical Nutrition,* 2nd ed. New York: Harper & Brothers, 1962.

Joseph, James A., Ph.D., Daniel A. Nadeau, M.D., and Anne Underwood. *The Color Code.* New York: Hyperion, 2002.

Journal of the American Dental Association, August, 1955.

Kaiser, Jon, M.D. *Immune Power.* New York: St. Martin's Press, 1993.

Kalita, Dwight K. (ed.). *A Physician's Handbook on Orthomolecular Medicine.* New Canaan, Conn.: Keats Publishing, 1977.

Kloss, Jethro. *Back to Eden.* New York: Beneficial Books, 1972.

Klotschevar, Lendal H., and Margaret McWilliams. *Understanding Food.* New York: John Wiley & Sons, 1969.

Know Your Nutrition. New Canaan, Conn.: Keats Publishing, 1965.

Kordich, Jay. *The Juiceman's Power of Juicing.* New York: William Morrow & Co., 1992.

Kowalski, Robert E. *8 Steps to a Healthy Heart.* New York: Warner Books, 1992.

———. *8-Week Cholesterol Cure.* New York: Harper & Row, 1989.

Krause, Marie V., and Martha A. Hunscher. *Food, Nutrition and Diet Therapy,* 5th ed. Philadelphia: W. B. Saunders Co., 1972.

Kuhne, Paul. *Home Medical Encyclopedia.* Greenwich, Conn.: Fawcett Publishing, 1960.

Kuntzleman, Charles T. (ed.). *The Physical Fitness Encyclopedia.* Emmaus, Pa.: Rodale Books, 1970.

Lappe, Francis L. *Diet for a Small Planet.* New York: Ballantine Books, 1971.

Lark, Susan M., M.D. *Premenstrual Syndrome Self-Help Book.* Berkeley, Calif.: Celestial Arts Publishing, 1997.

———. *Women's Health Companion: Self-Help Nutrition Guide and Cookbook.* Berkeley, Calif.: Celestial Arts Publishing, 1995.

Lark, Susan M., M.D., and James A. Richards. *The Chemistry of Success.* San Francisco: Bay Books, 2000.

Latavore, Michael (ed.). *Men's Health Advisory.* Emmaus, Pa.: Rodale Press, 1993.

Lehane, Brendan. *The Power of Plants.* Maidenhead, England: McGraw-Hill, 1977.

Lesser, Michael. *Nutrition and Vitamin Therapy.* New York: Grove Press, 1980.

Lewis, Walter. *Medical Botany.* New York: John Wiley & Sons, 1977.

Locke, David M. *Enzymes—the Agents of Life.* New York: Crown Press, 1971.

Lucas, Richard. *Nature's Medicines.* North Hollywood, Calif.: Wilshire Book Co., 1977.

Lust, Benedict, M.D. *About Herbs.* Wellingborough, Northants, England: Weatherby Woolnough, 1961.

Lust, John. *The Herb Book.* New York: Bantam Books, 1974.

Macia, Rafael. *The Natural Foods and Nutrition Handbook.* New York: Harper & Row, 1972.

Mandell, Marshall. *Let's Have Healthy Children.* New York: New American Library, 1979.

Marcus, Norman J. *Freedom from Chronic Pain.* New York: Simon & Schuster, 1994.

Martin, Ethel A. *Nutrition in Action,* 2nd ed. New York: Holt, Rinehart & Winston, 1967.

McDermott, Irene E., Mabel B. Trilling, and Florence W. Nicolas. *Food for Better Living,* 3rd ed. Chicago: J. B. Lippincott Co., 1960.

Medical Economics Data. *Physicians' Desk Reference.* Montvale, N.J.: Medical Economics Data, 1992.

Men's Health Magazine (eds.). *Men's Health Handbook,* Emmaus, Pa.: Rodale Press, 1994.

Meyer, Joseph. *The Herbalist.* Glenwood, Ill.: Meyer Books, 1976.

Michnovicz, Jon J., M.D., Ph.D., and Diane S. Klein. *How to Reduce Your Risk of Breast Cancer.* New York: Warner Books, 1994.

Miller, Fred D. *Healthy Teeth Through Proper Nutrition.* New York: Arco Publ., 1978.

Mindell, Earl. *Earl Mindell's Soy Miracle.* New York: Simon & Schuster, 1995.

Mollen, Art, with Judith Sachs. *Dr. Mollen's Anti-Aging Diet*. New York: Penguin, 1992.

Morales, Betty Lee. *Cancer Control Journal*, March 1973.

Morgan, Lyle W., Ph.D., H.M.D. *Homeopathic Medicine: First Aid and Emergency Care*. Rochester, Vt.: Healing Arts Press, 1989.

Moyer, William C. *Buying Guide for Fresh Fruits, Vegetables, and Nuts*, 4th ed. Fullerton, Calif.: Blue Goose, 1971.

Murray, Frank. *Program Your Heart for Health*. New York: Larchmont Books, 1978.

Murray, Michael T., N.D. *Encyclopedia of Nutritional Supplements*. New York: Three Rivers Press, Random House, 1996.

Murray, Michael T., N.D., and Joseph Pizzorno, N.D. *Encyclopedia of Natural Medicine*. New York: Three Rivers Press, Random House, 1998.

National Academy of Sciences. *Toxicants Occurring Naturally in Foods*. Washington, D.C.: National Academy of Sciences, 1973.

Newbold, H. L. *Dr. Newbold's Revolutionary New Discoveries About Weight Loss*. New York: New American Library, 1979.

———. *Mega Nutrients for Your Nerves*. New York: Berkeley Publishing Group, 1983.

Nixon, Daniel W., with Jane A. Zanca. *The Cancer Recovery Eating Plan*. New York: Times Books, 1994.

Normal and Therapeutic Nutrition, 14th ed. New York: Macmillan Co., 1972.

Nuernberger, Phil. *Freedom from Stress*. Honesdale, Pa.: Himalayan International Institute, 1981.

Null, Gary, and Steve Null. *The Complete Handbook of Nutrition*. New York: Robert Speller & Sons, 1972.

Nutritional Management of Inflammatory Disorders. Gig Harbor, Wash.: The Institute for Functional Medicine, Inc., 1998.

"Nutritive Value of Foods," *USDA Home and Garden Bulletin*, Vol. 72, 1971.

Oakley, Ray, and Charles Ksir. *Drugs, Society, and Human Behavior*. St. Louis: Mosby, 1990.

O'Brien, Edward J. *Cigarettes: Slow Suicide!* New York: Exposition Press, 1968.

Ornish, Dean, M.D. *Eat More, Weigh Less*. New York: HarperCollins, 1993.

Page, M. E., and H. L. Abrams. *Your Body Is Your Best Doctor*. New Canaan, Conn.: Keats Publishing, 1980.

Passwater, Richard A. *Selenium as Food and Medicine*. New Canaan, Conn.: Keats Publishing, 1980.

Pauling, Linus. *Vitamin C and the Common Cold*. New York: Bantam Books, 1971.

Pearson, Durk, and Sandy Shaw. *Life Extension: A Practical Scientific Approach*. New York: Warner Books, 1982.

Pelletier, Kenneth R., M.D. *Sound Mind, Sound Body*. New York: Simon & Schuster, 1994.

Perl, James, Ph.D. *Sleep Right in Five Nights*. New York: William Morrow Co., 1993.

Pfeiffer, Carl C., Ph.D., M.D. *Nutrition and Mental Illness*. Rochester, Vt.: Healing Arts Press, 1987.

Philpott, William H., and Dwight K. Kalita. *Brain Allergies*. New Canaan, Conn.: Keats Publ., 1980.

Pike, Ruth L., and Myrtle L. Brown. *Nutrition: An Integrated Approach*. New York: John Wiley & Sons, 1967.

"Potassium: The Neglected Mineral," *Let's Live*, October 1973.

Prevention Magazine Staff. *The Complete Book of Minerals for Health*. Emmaus, Pa.: Rodale Press, 1981.

———. *Prevention's Best Power Foods*. New York: St. Martin's, 2000.

Price, Joseph M. *Coronaries, Cholesterol, Chlorine*. New York: Pyramid Books, 1969.

"Problem: Lead and What to Do About It," *Prevention*, October 1973.

Reaven, Gerald, M.D., Terry Kristen Strom, M.B.A., and Barry Fox, Ph.D. *Syndrome X: The Silent Killer*. New York: Simon & Schuster, 2000.

Recommended Dietary Allowances, 9th ed. Washington, D.C.: National Academy of Sciences, 1980.

Reiter, Russell J., and J. Robinson. *Melatonin: Breakthrough Discoveries That Can Help You*. New York: Bantam Books, 1995.

Reuben, David, M.D. *The Save Your Life Diet*. New York: Ballantine Books, 1975.

Rodale, J. I. *Age Erasers for Women.* Emmaus, Pa.: Rodale Press/St. Martin's Press, 1994.

———. *Be a Healthy Mother, Have a Healthy Baby.* Emmaus, Pa.: Rodale Books, 1972.

———. *Best Articles from* Prevention. Emmaus, Pa.: Rodale Books, 1967.

———. *Cancer Facts and Fallacies.* Emmaus, Pa.: Rodale Books, 1969.

———. *Complete Book of Minerals for Health.* Emmaus, Pa.: Rodale Books, 1972.

———. *Complete Book of Vitamins.* Emmaus, Pa.: Rodale Books, 1968.

———. *The Encyclopedia of Common Diseases.* Emmaus, Pa.: Rodale Press, 1969, 1982.

———. *The Encyclopedia for Healthful Living.* Emmaus, Pa.: Rodale Press, 1969.

———. *The Health Builder.* Emmaus, Pa.: Rodale Books, 1957.

———. *The Health Seeker.* Emmaus, Pa.: Rodale Books, 1962.

———. *Magnesium: The Nutrient That Could Change Your Life.* New York: Pyramid Books, 1971.

———. *My Own Technique of Eating for Health.* Emmaus, Pa.: Rodale Books, 1969.

———. *No More Headaches.* Emmaus, Pa.: Rodale Press, 1982.

———. *The Prevention Method for Better Health.* Emmaus, Pa.: Rodale Books, 1968.

———. *Rodale Herb Book.* Emmaus, Pa.: Rodale Press, 1976.

———. *Rodale's Illustrated Encyclopedia of Herbs.* Emmaus, Pa.: Rodale Press, 1987.

———. *Symptoms: Their Causes and Cures.* Emmaus, Pa.: Rodale Books, 1994.

———. *Vitamin A: Everyone's Basic Bodyguard.* Emmaus, Pa.: Rodale Press, 1973.

———. *Women's Encyclopedia of Health and Emotional Healing.* Emmaus, Pa.: Rodale Press, 1993.

Rosenberg, Harold, and A. N. Feldzamen. *The Doctor's Book of Vitamin Therapy.* New York: G. P. Putnam's Sons, 1974.

Rosenfeld, Isadore. *Doctor, What Should I Eat?* New York: Random House, 1995.

Sachs, Judith. *The Healing Power of Sex.* Englewood Cliffs, N.J.: Prentice-Hall, 1994.

Samuels, Mike, and Hal Bennett. *The Well Body Book.* New York: Random House, 1973.

Schauss, Alexander. *Diet, Crime, and Delinquency.* Berkeley, Calif.: Parker House Publ., 1981.

Seaman, Barbara, and Gideon Seaman. *Women and the Crisis in Sex Hormones.* New York: Rawson Associates, 1977.

Sheinkin, David, Michael Schachter, and Richard Hutton. *Food, Mind, and Mood.* New York: Warner Books, 1980.

Sherborne House Book of Herbs. Gloucestershire, England: Coombe Springs Press.

Shute, Evan. *The Heart and Vitamin E.* London, Canada: Evan Shute Foundation, 1963.

Shute, Wilfrid E. *Health Preserver: Defining the Versatility of Vitamin E.* Emmaus, Pa.: Rodale Press, 1977.

Simon, Harvey B., M.D. *Conquering Heart Disease.* Little, Brown, & Co., 1994.

Siple, Molly, M.S., R.D. *Low-Cholesterol Cookbook for Dummies.* New York: Wiley Publishing, Inc., 2005.

———. *Healing Foods for Dummies.* Foster City, Calif.: IDG Books Worldwide, Inc., 1999.

Smith, Lendon. *Feed Your Kids Right.* New York: McGraw-Hill, 1979.

"Smoking Depletes Vitamin C," *Prevention*, February 1971.

Smyth, Angela. *The Complete Home Healer.* New York: HarperCollins Publishers, 1994.

Sokoloff, Boris. *Cancer: New Approaches, New Hope.* New York: Devin-Adair, 1952.

Somer, Elizabeth, M.A., R.D. *The Essential Guide to Vitamins and Minerals.* New York: HarperCollins Publishers, 1995.

Stoff, Jesse A., M.D., and Charles R. Pellegrino, Ph.D. *Chronic Fatigue Syndrome.* New York: Harper & Row, 1988.

"Summer Cold; Vitamin C," *Prevention*, July 1970.

Teaff, Nancy Lee, and Kim Wright Wiley. *Perimenopause: Preparing for the Change.* Rocklin, Calif.: Prima Publishing, 1995.

Thomas, William, M.D. *Herbs That Heal.* New York: Charles Scribner's Sons, 1976.

Thompson, Rob, M.D. *The Glycemic Load Diet.* New York: McGraw-Hill, 2006.

Vitamins and Minerals. Springhouse, Pa.: American Family Health Institute/Springhouse Corp., 1986.

Wade, Carlson. *Helping Your Health with Enzymes*. West Nyack, N.Y.: Parker Publishing, 1971.

———. *Magic Minerals*. West Nyack, N.Y.: Parker Publishing, 1967.

Wagman, Richard J., M.D. *The New Complete Medical and Health Encyclopedia*. Chicago: J. G. Ferguson Co., 1989.

Watt, B. K., and A. L. Merrill. "Composition of Foods—Raw, Processed, Prepared," *USDA Handbook* 8, 1963.

Webster, James. *Vitamin C: The Protective Vitamin*. New York: Universal Award House, 1971.

Weil, Andrew. *Spontaneous Healing*. New York: Knopf, 1995.

Weiten, Wayne. *Psychology Themes and Variations*. Pacific Grove, Calif.: Brooks/Cole Pub. Co., 1989.

Wellness Cooking School, University of California at Berkeley (ed.). *The Wellness Low-Fat Cookbook*. New York: Rebus Inc., 1993.

Wheatley, Michael. *About Nutrition*. London: Thorsons, 1971.

White, Philip (ed.). *Let's Talk about Food*, 2nd ed. Chicago: American Medical Association, 1970.

Wildwood, Christine. *The Aromatherapy and Massage Book*. New York: HarperCollins, 1994.

Willett, Walter C., M.D. *Eat, Drink and Be Healthy*. New York: Simon & Schuster, 2001.

Williams, Phyllis S. *Nourishing Your Unborn Child*. New York: Avon Books, 1982.

Williams, Roger J. *Alcoholism—The Nutritional Approach*. Austin: University of Texas Press, 1980.

———. *Nutrition Against Disease*. New York: Pitman Publ., 1971.

Williams, Roger J., and Dwight K. Kalita, eds. *A Physician's Handbook on Orthomolecular Medicine*. New Canaan, Conn.: Keats Publishing, 1977.

Williams, Sue R. *Review of Nutrition and Diet Therapy*. St. Louis: C. V. Mosby Co., 1973.

Wilson, Eva D., Katherine H. Fischer, and Mary E. Fugue. *Principles of Nutrition*, 2nd ed. New York: John Wiley & Sons, 1965.

Winter, Ruth. *Beware of the Food You Eat*, rev. ed. New York: Signet Books, 1971.

———. *Vitamin E: The Miracle Worker*. New York: Arco Publ. Co., 1972.

Wintrobe, M. M. et al. *Harrison's Principles of Internal Medicine*, 6th ed. New York: McGraw-Hill Book Co., 1970.

Yudkin, John. *Sweet and Dangerous*. New York: Peter H. Wyden, 1972.

Index